THE PUBLIC LANDS

The PUBLIC LANDS

STUDIES IN THE HISTORY OF THE PUBLIC DOMAIN

edited by Vernon Carstensen

THE UNIVERSITY OF WISCONSIN PRESS
Madison, Milwaukee, and London, 1968

Published by the University of Wisconsin Press
Madison, Milwaukee, and London
U.S.A.: Box 1379, Madison, Wisconsin 53701
U.K.: 27–29 Whitfield Street, London, W.1

A special Sesquicentennial Edition of this book was published in a limited
edition in 1962 to celebrate the 150th anniversary of the establishment of the
General Land Office.

General edition: First printing (cloth), 1963
Second printing (paper), 1968

Printed in the United States of America
Library of Congress Catalog Card Number 62-21554

EDITOR'S NOTE

To offer an explanation for republishing a group of useful articles on the history of the public domain is perhaps unnecessary. To make such articles easily available stands as sufficient justification for this book. It is not inappropriate, however, to say a word or two about the occasion for this publication and the means employed in selecting the articles.

This volume owes its appearance at this time to the interest of Karl Landstrom, Director of the Bureau of Land Management, in encouraging more research in the public land records, and his concern that the one hundred and fiftieth anniversary of the establishment of the General Land Office, predecessor of the Bureau of Land Management, not pass entirely unnoticed in the rash of centennial observances in 1962. This interest led to the creation of an advisory board consisting of Allan G. Bogue, State University of Iowa; Vernon Carstensen, University of Wisconsin; Marion Clawson, former Director of the Bureau of Land Management and now a member of the staff of Resources of the Future, Inc.; Thomas LeDuc, Oberlin College; Philip M. Raup, University of Minnesota; and three members of the staff of the Bureau of Land Management, Frank Burnett, George Landon, and Charles Plante. The Board agreed that scholarly purpose would be served by selecting and publishing some of the best articles on the history of public land that have appeared in historical and other journals in the past fifty years or so. Such a volume offers a suitable way of commemorating the sesquicentennial of the General Land Office and also emphasizes the friendly interest of the Bureau in encouraging greater research use of the public land records.

The Board selected from an extensive bibliography about sixty of the most promising articles. These articles were photocopied and distributed for further study. At a two-day meeting in March, 1962, the Board agreed that approximately a third of the articles should be included in the book. All the outstanding articles on the public lands could not be included, but the Board believes it has selected a representative group that sheds much light on significant phases of the history of the public lands.

The major periods and topics into which the history of the public lands can be divided are not evenly represented by the articles reprinted here. The acquisition of the public domain, the cession of state claims, by purchase, treaty, and otherwise, is rather lightly represented. More than half of all the articles deal with the disposal of the land and some of its consequences. Nevertheless, many aspects of land disposal are inadequately represented—the mining laws generally, the mineral-leasing laws under which some rights only are disposed of, the selection and disposal of grants to the states, the operation of a number of specialized land acts, such as the Desert Land Act, land disposal in special circumstances, such as Utah under Mormon rule, the South during and after the Confederacy, and others. That part of the story dealing with the reservation of the public domain for permanent federal ownership is completely unrepresented here. Studies of the period of extensive public land management are represented by a few articles, but the period of intensive land management, which began only about 1950, is naturally unrepresented.

But the articles included in this volume, the advisory committee believes, probably represent fairly well those aspects of the history of the public domain that have most interested historians. The disposal of the land was dramatic and important; it varied considerably by regions and by the various applicable laws; practice was often different from expectation when the laws were passed; and data were available to the diligent scholar for work in this field. And a mere listing of the major periods and the relative coverage suggests fields for further research. There are as many gold mines yet undiscovered in those hills as have ever been found.

Thus the articles that follow deal only with some parts of the vast story of the creation, expansion, distribution, and the management of the public lands. The first group, with a short foreword by Philip M. Raup, discuss a few of the many factors that shaped the first public land legislation. The articles in Part II, with an introductory statement by Thomas LeDuc, explore some phases of the distribution of the public lands. The articles in Part III, introduced by Allan G. Bogue, offer a fair sample of what might be called comment, criticism, and analysis of the consequences of public land policy. The last section, with a foreword by Marion Clawson, includes articles that suggest problems of administration and management of the public lands. The appendix reproduces useful materials not easily available elsewhere. It is not assumed that this volume will supplant such older studies of the history of the public domain as Payson Jackson Treat's *The National Land System,* Benjamin Horace Hibbard's *A History of Public Land Policies,* and Roy M. Robbins's *Our Landed Heritage: The Public Domain, 1776–1936,* but it should serve as a useful supplement.

Only a very few changes have been made in text or notes of the articles here reprinted. Some of the articles were first read at learned meetings, and such information has been moved from footnote to headnote, with consequent renumbering of the notes. Where references to the setting of a meeting have been omitted from the text, the deletion has been indicated by ellipsis marks. Typographical errors have been silently corrected. Insertions made by the present editor in the text are given in italics within italic brackets. In the notes, some changes have been made without being indicated: in some cases the style has been altered; occasionally bibliographical information has been added; and where reference has been made to a work in progress, the publication is cited if it has appeared. Except for changes of the kind noted, the articles stand as they were first published.

The Board is indebted to many persons for assistance in preparing this volume. Particular thanks must go to Peter T. Harstad, Edwin D. Karn, and Jack E. Eblen, all of the University of Wisconsin, and Malcolm J. Rohrbough, Princeton University, for their help.

VERNON CARSTENSEN

Madison, Wisconsin
June, 1962

CONTENTS

x · *Contents*

PART V. APPENDIX

INTRODUCTION

VERNON CARSTENSEN

THE vast and intricate story of the creation and expansion of the public domain, the administration, distribution, and management of federal lands, runs from 1776 to the present. But the ideas and values that controlled these matters lay partly in the American colonial past, partly in legal and other institutions imported from England and the Continent. Colonial experience and needs had by the time of the Revolution created different systems for obtaining legal possession of land, and for describing and recording titles in the separate colonies, but in one important respect the differences between the Virginia, Pennsylvania, and Massachusetts systems, for example, were superficial. Men wanted and obtained individual ownership of land, and although they may never have heard of Blackstone, what they did illustrates his declaration that "There is nothing which so generally strikes the imagination and engages the affections of mankind, as the right of property; or that sole and despotic dominion which one man claims and exercises over the external things of the world, to the total exclusion of the right of any other individual in the universe." It was understood and accepted that a "set of words upon parchment" served to "convey dominion on land," or at least that it should.

This view stood in sharp contrast to the Indian attitude toward land, an aspect of which is suggested by the perplexed declaration of the Cayuse Indian chief, Pee-o-pee-o-mox-a-mox, at the Walla Walla treaty council of 1855. He complained that he could not understand the talk by I. I. Stevens and the others there about giving goods for Indian lands. "Goods and the Earth are not equal: goods are for using on the Earth. I do not know where they have given land for goods." Pee-o-pee-o-mox-a-mox's words were probably as unintelligible to the government negotiators as Blackstone would have been to the Indians. The land system spread upon the United States owes much to the values expounded by Blackstone; it owes little more than place names to the Indians.

The process of establishing ownership of land, whether for a sovereign or an individual, rested on the English and European assumption that discovery or settlement gave possession. These rights could be established, if not enforced, by ceremonial acts and loud proclamations. In the empty places of the world Spaniards, Frenchmen, Englishmen, and later Americans, performed the rites of land-taking for king or sovereign. Thus Balboa waded into the Pacific to claim for his sovereign all of it and all it touched; La Salle, near the mouth of the Mississippi, with appropriate ecclesiastical and secular rites, laid claim for Louis XIV to all lands drained by that great river; St. Lusson at Sault Ste Marie claimed all that was "contiguous and ajacent, as well discovered as to be discovered"; Drake, on the coast of California, left "a plate of brass, fast nailed to a great and firm poste" to claim New Albion for Elizabeth; and Bienville carefully buried his lead plates along the Ohio to mark the southern boundary of New France. Captain James Biddle of the United States Navy, directed to take formal possession of the lands at the mouth of the Columbia River after the War of 1812, performed as much of the ceremony of land-taking as he considered proper or could remember— we don't know which. On August 19, according to his own account, he stood off the mouth of the Columbia in the "Ontario." Unable to cross the bar with his ship, he took three boats and more than fifty officers and men, all well armed, and went ashore inside Cape Disappointment. Here, "in the presence of several natives, displaying the flag of the United States, turning up a sod of soil, and giving three cheers, I nailed up against a tree a leaden plate in which were cut the following words: 'Taken possession of in the name and on the behalf of the United States, by Captain James Biddle, Commanding the United States Ship Ontario. Columbia River, August 1818.'" The party then fired another salute, took on wood and water, and departed, no doubt leaving behind some puzzled natives. Just as the act of taking possession of land for a sovereign demanded mystic rites, so too it might be with an individual. The Spanish ceremony, described by Thomas L. Miller in a note in *Agricultural History* in 1954, required the claimant to turn a clod, fire a gun, cut some grass, irrigate, and shout, in the presence of ecclesiastical and secular authorities.

Monuments set upon the land and words pronounced upon the air, written on a piece of paper, or set down in a book of public record, provided the means of establishing and registering title and perpetuating a right to a given piece of land. Vestiges of these ancient rites are still found in the abstract of title to a piece of land. In some states the abstract may recite the establishment and subsequent changes in sovereignty, the appropriate treaty or other arrangement under which Indians yielded possession. In the public land states it also describes the location of the land in terms of base and meridian lines, range, township, and section numbers, and usually records, with Old Testament solemnity, the successive occupiers, each of whom in turn had yielded possession. The title is based on the assumption of the prescriptive right of the first claimant.

The survey and disposal of public land became a matter of concern to the Congress of the United States after Virginia and New York had ceded to the central government their claims to western lands. This area, the Old Northwest, embracing the land west of Pennsylvania and north of the Ohio River, became the first public domain. The initial arrangements under which this land was to be marked out and disposed of were set forth in the Land Ordinance of 1785, the Northwest Ordinance, and the contract with the Ohio Company of 1787. The first of these, the Land Ordinance of 1785, is of primary importance in the history of the public domain. It provided for the rectangular survey of the first seven ranges and in a sense established the six-mile-square township as the basic survey unit.

Private land companies, notably the Ohio Company, and the Virginia Military reservation, prevented the extension of the rectangular surveys immediately to the west of the Seven Ranges. But in 1796 Congress re-established the rectangular survey system and in 1804 provision was made in law for base lines and meridians to control the location of ranges and towns. The different survey systems employed in Ohio under the ordinance of 1785, on the grants of the Ohio and the Symmes companies, the Western Reserve, and the Virginia Military Tract, make Ohio a kind of surveyors' museum.

The arguments against the use of the rectangular six-mile-square township as the basic unit of the public land surveys were formidable, but the justification was also impressive. It provided for a cheap, accurate, and easy way to survey and describe land. The arguments of economy and simplicity prevailed in 1785 and again in 1796. The system has been employed in all of the public land states. When the public domain was enlarged by the Georgia cession in 1802, the Louisiana purchase in 1803, the acquisition of West Florida in 1811, East Florida in 1819, the Oregon settlement in 1846, the Mexican cession of 1848, and the Texas, Gadsden, and Alaska purchases of 1850, 1853, and 1867, all of these areas in turn fell under the rectangular survey system with the six-mile-square townships, the base lines and meridians as shown in the map in Part V, page 483.

The lines of the surveys, as the map shows, move rigidly east and west, north and south, and a grid system has been implacably imposed upon the land. Only impenetrable swamp, as in Florida, or wild, impassable mountain terrain, as in some of the western states, have interrupted the march of the straight survey lines. The patterns of French grants, the lots which the French stretched back from the rivers, and the sprawling but vaguely located Spanish grants have rarely survived, although at Green Bay and Prairie du Chien in Wisconsin a few remnants of the long river lots of the early French settlers can still be found lightly traced in the dominant rectangular pattern, and some light marks of the Spanish grants can be found on the land from the Gulf states west to California.

The rectangular survey—this cheap and simple way of surveying and describing land—was carried into Texas and north into Manitoba and the western Canadian provinces. The system was very useful, particularly in the years after 1850, when land settlement reached vast proportions. Between 1850 and 1900 the number of American farms increased from 1,449,000 to 5,737,000. Had a system of describing land by metes and bounds been employed, with the almost infinite possibility of odd-shaped parcels and hence overlapping and conflicting claims, lawsuits and neighborhood feuds would have been one certain harvest of this vast movement of land-seekers on to new land. Section lines drawn straight and clearly marked, like good New England fences, make good neighbors, or at least neighbors not at law over property boundaries. The rectangular survey had other effects. The straight lines of quarter sections and larger units controlled to some extent the shape and size of fields and hence influenced the tillage. This was something that Washington and other farmers foresaw and complained about in 1785; soil conservationists at a later date lamented the effects. And the patterns imposed on the land by surveys in turn imposed patterns upon the communities that took shape on those lands. This was already clear by the end of the colonial period. The New England town system assured a far different community, even in the rough hill country where economic resources were sparse and scattered, from the kind that came into existence on a basis of the haphazard and dispersed settlement of the southern highlands. The survey township in the public domain provided the basis for a convenient and easily identifiable unit for local government. Roads were laid out, and tax rolls, election districts, and common schools were organized and managed in accord with the township.

More important in the development of the Republic were the decisions about who should get the lands, under what circumstances, and at what price. The Republic, still operating under the Articles of Confederation, faced the task of disposing of the first public domain without the anchors of older societies: it had no king, no established church, no hereditary aristocracy. It was a government new and untried, open on all sides to be influenced by all the forces of society in the distribution of an area of land unmatched in the history of western governments in size, richness, and variety of resources. Moreover, the land was unencumbered by a native population possessed of sufficient enduring strength to compel the newcomers to accommodate to it. Decisions made by the central government, or not made, were profoundly influential in shaping the economic and political structure of the society based upon these new lands. And just as the decisions about the nature of the survey of the Old Northwest provided the basis for a survey system that would be carried across the land, so many of the decisions made by the Congress in 1785 and 1787 concerning the distribution of the land became an enduring part of the laws governing the disposal of the public domain.

The ordinance of 1785 dealt also with the question of how to dispose of the public domain. These decisions were of course based on the experience of the several colonies, and the law reflected a number of compromises. In a general way the ordinance of 1785 established the doctrine, not always adhered to in fact, that the public domain would be handled in an orderly fashion. First, Indian title must be extinguished, then the lands surveyed and offered for sale at auction; and, when they were purchased, a proper deed granting title in fee simple would be issued by the government. A minimum price of $1 an acre plus surveying cost was fixed arbitrarily, if not capriciously. In 1796 the price was increased to $2, and a year's time allowed to complete payment. In 1800 the law was changed to give purchasers four years in which to pay for the land. This credit feature caused much difficulty and in 1820 it was dropped and the minimum price of the land reduced to $1.25. In 1854 the Graduation Act permitted lands that had long been on the market to be sold below the $1.25 minimum. In 1862 the Homestead Act allowed a man to obtain 160 acres for the cost of the filing fee and five years' residence.

The combination of a minimum price and the public auction, it was hoped, would assure a substantial return to the Treasury. This expectation was never realized, nor for that matter did the sale of public land ever provide a reliable means of obtaining funds for the Treasury, simply because sales could not be so arranged as to provide income when needed. In 1880 a Public Land Commission, established by Congress to investigate numerous aspects of the public lands, reported that the public domain had already cost the government a total of $322,049,595.96. Land sales had returned $200,702,849.11 to the Treasury. Thus, as of 1880, Thomas Donaldson could show in *The Public Domain* that the government was $121,346,-746.85 in the red.

But the ordinance of 1785 did not suppose all lands were to be sold. Provision was made to reserve land for the Christian Indians, and the basis was laid to recognize private claims of persons who had established residence in the Old Northwest before 1783. Private claims established in the other territories before the United States obtained possession were subsequently recognized. Since neither the French nor the Spanish government had devised an orderly system of handling land grants, this opened a Pandora's box of legal puzzles and invited hosts of alert schemers to try their hands at obtaining land based on Spanish, French, Mexican, English, and fictitious grants. Some succeeded. Provision was made to give free grants of land to certain classes of settlers in Florida in 1842 and in Oregon, Washington, and New Mexico in 1850–1854. Moreover, from the first it was expected that some of the public lands would be given to war veterans. Hosts of other private grants were made or allowed for one reason or another.

The ordinance of 1785 provided that the land of the Seven Ranges would be offered for sale at the seat of government. Alternate townships would be sold entire; the intervening townships would be offered in lots as small as a section of 640 acres. Thus the government sought to provide for both retail and wholesale disposition of the land. The minimum amount that could be purchased was reduced again and again until, by 1834, 40 acres became the minimum. New Englanders in Congress anticipated that offering whole townships would be attractive to speculators and would encourage whole communities to migrate. There were few buyers for either townships or section lots at the early sales and the failure of the Ohio and the Symmes companies discouraged confidence in large companies. There was much objection from settlers to the inconvenience of holding land sales only in Philadelphia. The act of 1796 provided for land sales at Cincinnati and Pittsburgh as well as Philadelphia, and in the act of 1800 land offices were given a definite form and located in the tracts that were to be offered for sale. Offices were accordingly established at Cincinnati, Chillicothe, Marietta, and Steubenville, each with its own district to serve. In the course of disposing of the public domain, over 380 land offices were established.

In addition to enriching the Treasury and providing bonuses for soldiers, the public domain, many insisted, should be used to support public purposes, principally education and internal improvements. Land grants for schools and colleges were an established method of endowing these enterprises by the time the ordinance of 1785 provided that section 16 in each township in the Seven Ranges be reserved for the benefit of the common schools. This reservation became fixed in later laws and the amount of land was eventually doubled. In 1787 the Northwest Ordinance declared that ". . . Schools and the means of education shall forever be encouraged," but more important, in terms of federal land policy, was the provision in the contract between the Board of Treasury and the Ohio Company under which two townships of land were appropriated "for the purposes of a University." This act would later justify granting two or more townships of land to each new state for the endowment of a university, a provision that opened the way for states west of the Appalachians to attempt to create such institutions early in their political history. Although school and university grants more often than not were carelessly and even dishonestly administered and the proceeds from sale of the lands mishandled and sometimes squandered, the grants were of incalculable importance in establishing common schools and publicly supported universities across the land. Moreover, the mishandling of the lands and funds provided a strong argument to get the state to provide tax support for common schools and universities by way of restitution. In 1862 the adoption of the Morrill Act used public lands for the endowment of the colleges of agriculture and mechanic arts throughout the whole country, not just in the states erected in the public domain.

Demands for land subsidies for support of internal improvements are not reflected in the act of 1785, but thereafter many successful demands were made for land grants to subsidize road building, canal digging, river improvement, and railroad construction. The most substantial grants were made to the railroads—discussion, sometimes acrimonious, about the nature and consequences of such subsidies has run through American history. Grants were also sought and given for the reclamation of both wet lands and arid lands.

Little thought seems to have been given to the handling of mineral lands in the public domain. The ordinance of 1785, no doubt drawing upon the colonial charters, reserved "one third part of all gold, silver, lead and mines to be sold or otherwise disposed of as Congress shall hereafter direct." The act of 1796 made no mention of metals but reserved all salt springs from sale. The existence of lead deposits in Missouri and salt springs in the Northwest Territory led Congress in 1807 to authorize a leasing system in the Missouri district and later in the lead regions of northwestern Illinois, southwestern Wisconsin, and Dubuque, Iowa. The federal government failed to develop adequate administrative machinery to make leasing effective, and vociferous and unyielding local opposition was aroused. In 1829 Congress abandoned the reservation and leasing system in Missouri and directed that the lands be sold. Less than two decades later, a similar law released the remaining lead land for sale. Perhaps these failures played a part in making Congress reluctant to adopt any positive legislation after the California Gold Rush. The gold miners entered the public domain and took and kept whatever gold or other precious metal they could find. They devised their own rules for establishing and holding claims through miners' associations, organizations that owed much in structure and method to the extralegal land-claim associations. Congress acquiesced in the arrangements made by the miners' associations, which, when sanctioned by territorial or state laws, provided a means by which voluntary private associations could in effect alienate public lands without hindrance by public officials.

As settlement pushed west, the various demands for land increased apace and had their effect upon the laws governing the disposal of the public domain. The land laws reflected the strength and skill of numerous and powerful public and private interests, and, as was to be expected, contained conflicting and often contradictory elements. This situation is adumbrated in the remarks of Jacob Collamer, congressman from Vermont, as they were paraphrased in the *Congressional Globe* on May 8, 1848:

He thought a considerable body, upon different sides of this House, composed of very different material, and actuated by very different reasons, were laboring towards the same point, and that point was, *to get rid of the public lands*. That was the purpose. Some were frank enough to own it; others partially owned it; others disguised it even to themselves; and yet this was the common result at which they were aiming. Some were for dispensing wholly with dealings in the land and with revenue from it, under the impression that lands would thereby become cheaper, and be settled more rapidly in their neighborhoods; he charged them with nothing dishonorable. Another said "As to the public land system, I think it a sort of land-jobbing business on the part of the Government, and had better be got rid of any way." Another said he thought it was the tendency of our present system to accumulate large quantities in particular hands, and thereby introduce the system of landlord and tenant in our country, which would be a disgrace to our institutions; and he was in favor of breaking it up for this reason. The reason of another class was, unless they could get the prices reduced to mere nothing, extremely poor people could never settle the lands; they were desirous of aiding them to settle, and if they could succeed, they would throw our public domain open. That was their motive.

But another considerable class, including, he apprehended, a larger part of this House than would at first be supposed, said that you never can have in a government like ours a large quantity of money on hand at the disposal of the government but it is always becoming a corruption fund. It will be at the disposal of Executive power and patronage. It will always be used, therefore, as a means of corruption, for it will stick in the hands of those who have the keeping of it. They contended that the same principle, to a comparatively limited extent, applied to the public lands. How? Why, because it would be considered that the party or candidate who would hold out the largest promises of bribery, by giving away the public lands when they came into power, would be most likely to secure their elevation. He might as well tell the truth. Many and many a man sat in that House who said, "I am disposed to believe the lands have been used in this way, under the idea that the larger the promises gentlemen can hold out to their States and their people, the better their chances for election; and because the possession of our public lands has this tendency to corruption, I am for getting rid of them altogether. I do not care where they go, let them go."

Another motive, which might as well be told while he was about it. There were some men in this nation who said, "If we could get rid of this $2,000,000 or $3,000,000 income from the public lands we would have a protective tariff; and we will vote them away for that reason, and the quicker we get rid of them the better."

These are some few of the many motives which operated on the minds of different gentlemen in voting for these various propositions. There were many more rather more sinister, which perhaps might have weight; but it might be unbecoming a gentleman to suggest that they could be entertained by anybody. . . .

The disposal of the public domain was a matter of large importance throughout the first century of the Republic. Individuals, groups, associations, state, county, and city officials, all sent to Congress a stream of petitions, entreaties, protests, on the disposal of the public lands. The territorial and state legislatures larded the pages of their journals and session laws with their petitions, declarations, and directives on how the public lands should be distributed, and they argued endlessly on how land grants to the states should be used. In 1880 the Public Land Commission, in compiling the laws relating to the public lands, reported that about 3,500 laws dealing with public lands had been adopted by Congress between 1785 and 1880. They might have added that, for every law passed, a number of others had died somewhere along the line toward final passage.

And for each law that was passed, someone, or some group, had to prepare the initial draft, get it introduced into one or both houses of Congress, and then see to it that it got to the proper committee, obtained a hearing or other investigation if need be, got a favorable report from the committee, got to a final favorable vote in both houses, and was signed by the President. Some laws were adopted with little effort on the part of the sponsors; others, such as the Pre-emption and Homestead laws, were before Congress for a decade or more before being passed and were the subject of petitions, entreaties, resolutions, party planks, threats, editorials, sermons, and orations of great length and heat. Sometimes, the mere proposal of a change in land policy set in motion debate that moved far beyond the immediate question. When, for example, Samuel A. Foot, senator from Connecticut, introduced a resolution late in December, 1829, directing that the Committee on Public Lands be instructed to inquire into the expediency of abolishing the office of Surveyor General and of limiting sale of public lands to those already on the market, he provoked a furious debate in the Senate that ran from January to May of 1830. The debate laid bare sectional and partisan jealousies but it also brought into public discussion the leading constitutional questions of the day. And in the course of that debate, in Daniel Webster's second reply to Robert B. Hayne, the young Republic found an eloquent statement of its emerging nationalism. The same speech provided teachers of rhetoric and fledgling politicians with a model of florid nineteenth-century oratory that would resound at the hustings and in rural schoolroom and college chapel well into the twentieth century.

But the passage of a law was only a prelude. The laws directed, required, or permitted something to be done. And bit by bit, policy and a working bureaucracy were created. The law of 1785 had provided for sale of land by the Board of Treasury, and surveys were to be made under direction of the United States Geographer. In 1796, under the Constitution, the first land offices were created but not yet properly manned; a Surveyor General took the place of the Geographer; and procedures for alienating land from the federal government were outlined. Sale of land remained in the Treasury, but Indian negotiations were to be conducted by the War Department, the issuance of titles to land was managed by the State Department, and the President's signature was required to alienate the land. In 1812 the General Land Office was created and a number of functions were consolidated, but not until 1836 was the Surveyor General made responsible to the Commissioner of Public Lands.

The requirement that Indian title be extinguished before the lands be surveyed, that the lands be surveyed before being offered for sale, and, after 1800, that they be offered for sale at land offices established in the districts—these and other regulations required much tedious administrative work. Men had to be appointed, instructed, and supplied if they were to negotiate with the Indians, who must themselves be rounded up, brought to the designated treaty grounds, and cajoled and persuaded to sign the desired treaties. The treaty had then to be approved by the Senate and the President. Thereafter, the Surveyor General in turn had to seek reliable deputy surveyors who would contract the work of surveying to men who, it was hoped, knew enough about surveying to do the actual work. Much of the early surveying was of a kind that led one student to remark that it was much easier to explain than to admire. No sooner did the surveyors take to the field than they began to complain. From Indiana, Jared Mansfield reported in 1804 that prairie fires each year destroyed the wooden corner stakes, and it was doubtful that settlers would want prairie land anyhow, destitute as it was of wood and water. Two years later he reported that near the rivers life was almost impossible for the men because they were pestered by "such miriads of flies and Moschettoes, that neither man nor beast can live there." From Mississippi, Thomas Freeman wrote in 1811 that flooded land made it impossible to get surveying crews into the field until the middle of August or early September and even then "few men can be found hardy enough to stand the poisonous effect of half-dried mud, putrid fish, and vegetable matter—almost impenetrable cane brakes, and swarms of mosketoes—with which these low lands abound after the waters are withdrawn." Lucius Lyon, directed to locate, with the assistance of

John Roundtree, the boundary between Wisconsin and Illinois, which was to provide the base line for Wisconsin surveys, wrote his superior early in December, 1831, that the survey was moving slowly. "It was almost impossible to get Mr. Roundtree to come out at all this season— He is an excellent man, but, having been brought up in the south, he is afraid of winter as a Barn Swallow, and about as hard to keep in a cold climate. In truth, the prospect is not very cheering for the most hardy—Even those who love to skate, ride in sleighs upon the ice, and hunt deer on snow shoes, begin to shiver and gather themselves into the warm places, as cattle are seen to take shelter under the brow of some hill or hay stack in a bleak North-Wester."

The registers and receivers who had charge of the district land offices, like the surveyors in the field, complained about many things and often had reason to complain. Their instructions were obscure, inadequate, sometimes impossible to understand; the pay was too low; the offices they were compelled to use were crowded and uncomfortable; there was too little money for clerk hire; the hours of work were too long; too few people appreciated what they did; and they were frequently subject to personal abuse and denunciation. The receiver at Cahaba, Alabama, in a letter to his superior in 1821, added a new dimension to the complaints. His office, he asserted, was crowded each day from 8:00 A.M. until candlelight. "What has added no little to my embarrassment is the Town of Kahaba has been as well as the country generally unusually sickly and many persons have taken up the idea that a contagious disease prevailed and to prevent their being affected have prepared themselves with some Asafitida-Garlic Onion and all sorts of noxious and strange smelling things. . . ."

It took time for the bureaucracy to learn how to function effectively. The men who carried out the law, the treaters with the Indians, the surveyors, the managers of the land offices, the others, created their own precedents as they worked out the system for disposing of the public domain, and they were always behind in their work. It was an enormous task, one which the Public Land Commission of 1880 thought was on the whole well done despite the numerous cries of incompetence and fraud. Leonard White in *The Jeffersonians*, a study of federal administration, describes the land operation as an immense task that would have been difficult even with the administrative resources of a later age. "That it was accomplished literally by hand, with the compass and chain, quill pen and ink, illuminated by candlelight in rough-hewn prairie offices, was in itself a herculean performance, even though too slow to keep up with the westward migration."

Perhaps no one had a right to expect the task to be done well: the remarkable thing was that it was done at all, that the whole machinery did not collapse.

Historians, to a large extent, have not taken the tolerant view and have properly insisted upon using exacting standards in judging land policies and their execution. Hence they have been quick to see the wide gap that often existed between high intentions and low performance. The history of the public lands has been full of words such as *speculators, land monopolists, rings, corrupt officials, hush money, fraudulent entry, bogus entrymen, land lawyers, land sharks.* No doubt each new community in the public land states, at one time, had its tales of the "innocent deceits" employed to obtain land. The literal-minded eastern lawyer might regard the land-claim association as a conspiracy to prevent open bidding at a land sale, but westerners were inclined to view such associations as a necessary accommodation to inept federal legislation. Few people in the lead country were disturbed by the story of blindfolding a witness and leading him across land. He could then testify at the land office that he had been on the land and had seen no sign of mineral deposits. A boy might stand on the number 21 and answer truthfully, when asked by the land office official, that he was indeed over 21, and an eight- or ten-year-old girl might serve as a wife of record and so give a man right to claim a double portion of land under the Oregon donation law. A bucket of water poured out in a recently ploughed furrow or a shack measured in inches not feet might be used in testimony as evidence of irrigation or habitation. A group of lumbermen in the Puget Sound area was called into court charged with timber theft. They were fined and also sentenced to one day in jail. Their story, told again and again at the annual meetings of the lumbermen's association, was that they paid their fines and then sent the sheriff out for "segars" and potables. When he returned, lumbermen, sheriff, and judge all retired to the jail, the key was turned in the lock, and all hands remained incarcerated for the day. Thus were the demands of the law satisfied.

In 1878 Congress passed the Timber and Stone Act, which provided that surveyed lands in California, Oregon, and Washington, valuable principally for timber and stone and unfit for cultivation, could be purchased in quantities up to 160 acres at a minimum price of $2.50 an acre. The assumption would appear to be that the individual or the family was the appropriate economic unit to harvest timber or quarry stone, just as it was the desirable unit to make and maintain a farm on a quarter-section homestead. The law actually encouraged speculators and lumber companies to obtain timberland illegally through the use of bogus entrymen. Bogus entrymen were advertised for publicly in the Pacific Northwest to make the Timber and Stone Act of 1878 operate "properly," and no one was disturbed, but when a fly-by-night grafter showed up and sought to fleece the bogus entrymen, newspapers expressed shocked surprise that base motives would lead unscrupulous men to plunder plunderers—although that isn't quite the way the editorials put it.

The land grabs, the water grabs, the mineral grabs, the timber grabs, all excite great interest and bring forth lamentations. This represents a melancholy part of the story, but it is not the whole story. The alienation of the public land exhibits much human cunning and avarice, but in many instances what was called fraud represented local accommodation to the rigidities and irrelevance of the laws. The part of the story that involves the vast number of land-seekers who got their land without violating either the spirit or the letter of the law is in one way the least exciting part, but this is the part of the story that provided a lure so strong that it drew millions of people across the Atlantic to the United States in the hope of obtaining land. It was about this aspect that Eugene Davenport, then Dean of the College of Agriculture of Illinois, might have been thinking when in 1915 he discussed briefly the distribution and use of the public domain. Waste and abuse there had been in abundance, "but we have these farms, these cities, these railroads, and this civilization to show for it, and they are worth what they cost."

I

ORIGINS OF THE
PUBLIC LAND SYSTEM

Introduction

PHILIP M. RAUP

THE land system of the new American nation was not evolved overnight. In broad outline, it was put together out of a fertile blend of vision and political expediency in four critical years between the preliminary peace treaty in 1783 and the Northwest Ordinance of 1787. But its roots were deep in the settlement experience of the Thirteen Colonies—an experience that provided pilot models from which the drafters of the ordinances of 1784, 1785, and 1787 drew deeply.

In a paper published over fifty years ago, Payson Jackson Treat traced the gestation of this land policy through the crucial years of the Confederation. The system that emerged was far from perfect. Portions of it remained dead letters from the date of their enactment. Yet the part that survived included the essence of a land-tenure system. The basis was laid for clear title, and the nature of the title was unambiguous. The physical means by which title was related to the land it described was ingenious, simple, and within the capacity of a frontier community to comprehend and to administer.

No one who studies the history of the formative years of the Republic can fail to be impressed with the genius of Jefferson—that original do-it-yourself carpenter of statehood. From him we have inherited a system of land titles in gavelkind—the fee simple that we take for granted instead of the fee tail that was the legacy of

3

feudalism and that still exists in muted form throughout the European world.

But Jefferson sought more order than was to be had in a rumbustious frontier land. He would have kept the military bounty warrants as proxy deeds for land, as Rudolf Freund points out—to be devised and bequeathed but not assigned or sold. He failed, and the resultant salability of land warrants spawned an early discount market in claims on land. The historian's attention usually focuses on the hapless Revolutionary soldier who sold his bounty warrants for pennies on the dollar. Freund's article reminds us that there is another side to this coin. The flexibility injected into the early land system through the military bounty warrants played an important role in attracting to the frontier both the men and the capital needed to set the snowball of westward expansion rolling.

Earl Harrington sketches the nature of the cadastral survey system as it evolved in the nineteenth century and was revised after 1910. Under it, a simple sequence of section, township, and range numbers permit the unique specification of an area of land without recourse to cumbersome metes and bounds descriptions. "Five gores, three surpluses, five strips, one tract, one patent, two grants, and two points"— thus reads a recent inventory of lands in Maine. With few exceptions, this nonsense stopped at Pennsylvania's western border. It is not customary to list the rectangular survey when footing up the wealth of the nation. Without it, the nation unquestionably would have been the poorer.

Throughout the remaining papers of this collection there is recurrent reference to the difficulty of survey ahead of settlement. The New Englanders had visions of an orderly expansion into the West, town by town, but this was not to be. In measuring performance against stated goals, the historian of American land settlement is almost overwhelmed with the evidence of evasion, mismanagement, fraud, deceit, and simple administrative incompetence. The evidence of speculation in land does not require search; it thrusts itself upon the research worker at every turn. But the case is not closed with this documentation.

The relevant comparison is not the defective system as applied with the ideal system as conceived by those who drafted the laws. It is rather with other countries that have struggled with the same problem and have attempted solutions by more "orderly" procedures. The barriers that defective systems of land titles and survey have placed in the path of settlement in Latin America are well documented. There is similar documentation from the Philippines. Admitting all the fraud, mismanagement, delay, and expense, an empire was opened in a hurry. A base was created on which a continent-wide mass-transport system could be constructed, and that in turn could support a mass-market structure—a Common Market no less revolutionary in its day than is the European version today. A land survey and title framework was built that could support a system of land-based credit. And a surprisingly large number of land clearers, settlers, and farmers did end up on the land.

The Maryland Assembly in 1776 equated 100 acres of bounty land with $10 in cash. Here we have a colonial forecast of the postwar price of western lands, which at that time could be had at $3 per hundred. Seven years later, in 1783, the Congress was presented a plan bearing Hamilton's second, in which a commutation price on western land was set at $3.33 per hundred. By 1787, with the first four ranges opened for settlement, the auction price minimum was set at $1 per acre. From $3.00 per hundred in 1776 and $3.33 per hundred in '83 to $100 per hundred in '87—the boom was on. This section gives us some fascinating insights into how it got its start.

Origin of the National Land System under the Confederation

PAYSON JACKSON TREAT

Read before the Pacific Coast Branch of the American Historical Association, in San Francisco, December 1, 1905.

Reprinted from the American Historical Association Report, 1905, *Volume 1, pages 231–239.*

IT seems paradoxical on the face of it that a Congress too poor to own and maintain a capital, too weak to protect itself from the insults of a band of ragged mutineers, should yet be concerned with the disposal of a vast domain of over 220,000 square miles of the richest of virgin soil. And the origin of this national domain discloses a curious compounding of the particularistic feeling which characterized the well-named "critical period" with the growing spirit of nationality which is to mark the succeeding years. For this common land at the disposal of the central government was not considered the result of a successful revolution waged by a united nation, but, rather, its origin can be traced to the successive cessions, on the part of four of the states, of their claims—more or less valid—to the land west of their present limits, while, on the other hand, no acts of the Congress of the Confederation evinced so genuine a national spirit as those by which it exceeded its powers and accepted and prepared to govern and dispose of this splendid common property.

Without stopping to discuss the cessions or the reasons which produced them, let us study the question of the disposal of the soil which confronted Congress in 1784, after the Virginia cession had cleared up the most perplexing of the state claims.[1]

Before the cessions were completed there had been discussions, both in and out of Congress, as to the best means of using these lands. It was of the utmost importance that this vast estate be wisely administered. Of what value would these western lands be if we could not hold them? How long would England or Spain allow that rich Northwest to remain unpeopled? Should not Congress endeavor to encourage the very best form of occupation in that region—the occupation of sturdy pioneers? One thing was certain—the lands would not be carelessly granted or lavished on favorites, for Congress had pledged that they should "be disposed of for the common benefit of the United States," [2] and Virginia, in her deed of cession, had stipulated that they should be "faithfully and bona fide disposed of" for that same purpose.[3] But there were two forms of "bona fide" disposition which merited discussion at such a time. Should the land be used as a source of revenue, or should it be disposed of with especial reference to the proper spread of population? If the former plan was adopted, the land system must provide for the sale of as much land as possible at as high a price as possible. If the idea of settlement was to predominate, then cheap lands or free lands, governmental surveys, and strict provisions for occupation and improvement must be incorporated in the system. Now, the idea of revenue was a very comforting one at this time, when the national credit was all but worthless, when the national paper ceased to circulate, and when interest and principal of the foreign debts were in arrears. And with few exceptions the people who found time to think about the western lands at all considered them a vast fund for meeting the national obligations; but there were others, notably Washington, who believed in providing for the wave of settlements which was already bursting across the mountains. So we must expect to find this idea of revenue kept in mind by any committee which should report a land system, and if they also make some provision for a proper settlement of the region they deserve the more credit.

Congress did not have a perfectly clear field in legislating for the public domain. There were foreign titles to be considered, and Virginia had made reservations in her deed of cession, while more important than all these limitations on the free power of Congress was the fact that the Indians held almost every foot of this soil and until their preemption was extinguished the United States could pass only a very worthless title to prospective purchasers.

But in spite of these difficulties Congress faced the question of disposal. In the spring of 1784 a committee was appointed, consisting of Jefferson; Williamson, of North Carolina; Howell, of Rhode Island; Gerry, of Massachusetts; and Read, of South Carolina, to prepare an ordinance for ascertaining the mode of locating and disposing of lands in the western territory. Before studying this report we should become familiar with the experience upon which they could draw. If there is any one principle which should result from any study of the events of this great period, it is that few things were done *de novo;* that in almost every instance seemingly new legislation is founded on the best of colonial precedents. And so in studying the report of this committee we will not be called upon to praise them for their originality so much as to commend them for their keen discrimination in recommending the best features in the existing systems.

At the outbreak of the Revolution there was no uniform system for the disposal of lands in the American colonies. Each colony had developed its own system and no two of them were exactly alike.[4] In general, we might say that the lands in the royal and proprietary colonies were managed with an eye to revenue, while those in the corporate colonies were more especially looked upon as factors in a proper extension of settlement within their territory.[5] But even such a statement is open to criticism. A safer one would be that in 1776 each state had in operation a system for the disposal of the lands within its limits which had developed as the result of colonial experience. And in the formation of these systems nature herself had played an important rôle, for two systems of disposal represented the extremes of colonial experience—the New England and the southern—and each reflected the natural conditions of the sections.

The New England system provided for settlement by townships.[6] When more land was needed, a township was laid off, generally 6 miles square, and it was settled as a whole, the land surveyed before settlement, and the details of granting left to the town itself. This resulted in a compact spread of settlement, in a colony of townships, in each of which the citizens had small holdings, carefully surveyed before settlement. And there were school and religious reserves in New England; and when Connecticut, in 1737, decided to sell seven townships instead of giving them away to settlers, she ordered that they be sold at auction, with a fixed minimum price, and that the sales be conducted at different towns in the colony, so that all the citizens might have an opportunity to invest in these new lands.[7] But even in this case, as in all preceding cases, strict provisions were made for the improvement and settlement of the tracts purchased. Before this time, forfeiture of the lands was the penalty, but in this case a bond for double the purchase price must be deposited. And in order that the lands might be "properly improved," we find that intruders were ordered out of the lands of the colony and punished for trespass.[8]

Now, the southern system was very different from this in many ways. The physical conditions, which favored the development of the county rather than the town, also caused a corresponding change in the manner of disposal of the land. Instead of small tracts of a few hundred acres at most, the southern planter insisted on holdings well into the thousands. This caused the dispersion of population. But other bad effects followed. Land was taken up by the use of warrants. These could be located on any unappropriated land. But the surveyors, especially the deputies, were poorly trained, and the records were carelessly kept, so that the location of several thousand acres with irregular sides was often made on some former location.[9] And as the bounds were determined largely by natural objects, the fall of a tree or the change of a steam bed might cause a series of lawsuits. These were the great objections to the southern system—indiscriminate locations and the lack of proper surveys and recording.[10] In the older districts, conditions for improvement and settlement were made, but in grants of such extent they were hard to enforce, and after Virginia became a state they were not even insisted upon, which became a source of grievance to settlers beyond the Alleghenies.[11]

With this body of colonial experience to draw upon, the committee prepared its report. Jefferson was the leading member of this committee.[12] Although Gerry and the Carolinians could quote from the experience of their states, Rhode Island had had little opportunity to form a very comprehensive system of disposal for its public lands. This report, however, adopted the leading features of the New England system. There shall be surveys before sales; the grants shall be carefully recorded; the territory shall be divided by rectangular surveys into "hundreds" of 10 square miles, and "lots" of 1 mile square. But the "township planting" of New England was not insisted upon, for although a person might purchase a "lot," the New England system called for the extension of settlements by townships. And there were no reserves for schools or religious purposes, which made the report impossible for any New Englander; nor were conditions of improvement and settlement annexed to the grants. The method of sale was not outlined, nor was a price per acre suggested, while a very impractical feature of the report provided that land sales should follow the complete relinquishment of the Indian title and the laying out of states.[13]

This report, therefore, was a combination of the survey feature of the

New England system with the administrative features of the southern system—the use of warrants, certificates, and caveats.[14] Although it was not acted upon at the time, yet it became the basis of the Land Ordinance of 1785. Of course, with our knowledge of the state experience upon which this committee could draw, there is no excuse for believing that Mr. Jefferson evolved this report from a merely philosophical study of the land question.

Almost a year passed before Congress turned again to the land problem. Then the report of 1784 was twice read and referred to a committee of one member from each state.[15] Jefferson was in Europe, and Virginia was represented on the committee by William Grayson. Rufus King, of Massachusetts, and William Samuel Johnson, of Connecticut, undoubtedly looked after the interests of New England. This committee report, presented on April 14, 1785, was practically a new report, although it retains some of the important principles of the earlier one.[16] Surveys were still to precede sales, but the townships were to be 7 miles square, divided into sections 1 mile square, and the geographical mile was no longer used. In each township two sections were to be reserved —one for schools and the other for religious purposes—while four sections in each township were to be reserved for the future disposition of Congress, as well as one-third part of all gold, silver, and lead mines. The land was to be sold by townships, at auction, and $1 per acre was set as the minimum. Five ranges [17] of townships were to be surveyed, and after the Secretary of War had drawn one-seventh of the whole amount for the use of the Continental Army the balance was to be drawn for sale in the states, the amount to be sold in each state being in proportion to the quotas in the last preceding requisition.

This report adhered more closely to the New England system, the conditions of improvement and settlement being the only provisions lacking.

So much for the report. It now remained for Congress to approve or amend. The southern members were not so easily converted to the benefits of this eastern system. They did not believe in the township system of settlement, and they promptly attacked that feature of the report.[18] Their first effort along this line resulted in a compromise. The land might be sold by sections, but only consecutively, and no second township was to be offered in sections until every section in the preceding one had been sold. Next, the reserve for religion was stricken out. Then the Virginia delegates moved and seconded and succeeded in carrying a motion to reduce the size of the townships from 7 to 6 miles square, hence allowing a smaller number of people to unite to purchase one.[19] They then made repeated attempts to provide for a more general sale of small lots. Believing, as they did, in the propriety of the widest choice in the selection of land, they attempted to free themselves from the compact-settlement idea so stoutly insisted upon by New England. Finally, as the votes of nine states were needed to carry the ordinance, the matter was further compromised, and one-half of the townships were to be sold in sections of 640 acres. An effort on the part of Grayson and Monroe to reduce the lots to 320 acres was lost.[20]

In this form was passed, on May 20, 1785, the first ordinance for the disposal of the public lands of the United States. Like most of the great measures of these early Congresses, it laid down great principles of action which have continued in operation to the present time. As finally adopted, it contained features tending to both revenue and settlement. The land was to be sold at auction, with a rather high minimum; but it was not to be sold until it had been carefully surveyed, so that the titles passed by the United States might be good. The New England system triumphed for the time. The accurate public surveys, the careful recording, the rectangular townships, the school reserves, all were parts of that system. The greatest triumph came when they succeeded in grafting the system of township planting on the public domain. The most the southern members could secure was a provision that in half the townships a person might purchase a section—640 acres —but this section was bounded by the rectangular surveys. The southern custom of indiscriminate location of warrants was not permitted. Yet as this "township planting" was the feature of the ordinance most discussed and objected to, so we will find that it was one of the least permanent features of the system. The same nature which demanded this system of settlement in New England made it unnecessary in the Northwest, and the southern members who opposed it in 1785 lived to see it rejected later.[21] So far as the immediate disposal of the lands went, the ordinance of 1785 had little effect. The surveys were difficult to execute and took time to complete. Before any land had been sold under this system, Congress secured a revenue for its depleted Treasury by means of sales of large tracts to companies—notably the Ohio Company and to John Cleves Symmes. But Congress realized that these were only temporary measures, designed to secure an immediate revenue, and such sales formed no part of the land system of the United States.

In the light of later experience it is easy to criticize the land system devised by the Congress of the Confederation. The economist will tell you that it is a sign of the most crass ignorance to believe that a great revenue can be obtained from waste land. The student of western history will assert that Congress should have devised a scheme for the sale of land in small tracts at a nominal price to actual settlers, with rigid conditions of improvement and settlement, for he believes that the occupation of the west country was of the greatest import to the United States at that time. It certainly would have simplified our relations with England and Spain if our back country had been better peopled. And those who agree with Mr. Wakefield,[22] the English student of colonial questions, would maintain that the terms proposed were too reasonable, that too much land was placed on sale, that our country would have been more prosperous if less inducement had been offered for the dispersion of our then scanty population.

But these would be *ex post facto* criticisms. We must award a liberal meed of praise to the members of the moribund Congress for devising a general system of disposition. The lands were not to be lavished on favorites. No one could obtain an acre except for "value received" or "services rendered." Although large tracts were in two instances sold to companies, yet Congress realized that this was not the best policy and only yielded to force of circumstances. And the best features of the previous colonial experience were incorporated into the national system, so that the present system of township surveys with the good titles which follow is based directly on the ordinance of the Confederation. New conditions have caused modifications in the old system. Township planting was not necessary in the greater West, and one development of the system was along the line of reducing the size of the tracts which might be placed on sale. The credit system was no part of this early plan, and when that was later adopted it proved disastrous. And with the growth and prosperity of the nation came the time when it could afford to give land to the actual settlers. But the one distinctive feature of our present system, the regular system of surveys, dates from the time when a handful of clear-visioned statesmen drew upon the experience of a dozen states to form one national system.

NOTES

1 See *Johns Hopkins University Studies in Historical and Political Science*, H. B. Adams, ed., vol. 3, *Maryland, Virginia, and Washington* (Baltimore, 1885); B. A. Hinsdale, *The Old Northwest* (2d ed., New York, 1899), chaps. xii, xiii; John B. McMaster, *A History of the People of the United States from the Revolution to the Civil War* (8 vols., 1888–1913), 3: chap. xvi.

2 Worthington C. Ford, ed., *Journals of the Continental Congress, 1774–1789* (34 vols., Washington, 1904–1937), 3:535. (Cited hereafter as *Journals.*)

3 *Ibid.*, 4:342–344.

4 James Curtis Ballagh, "Introduction to Southern Economic History—The Land System," in the *Annual Report of the American Historical Association for the year 1897* (Washington, 1898), 107.

5 Herbert L. Osgood, *The American Colonies in the Seventeenth Century* (3 vols., New York, 1904–1907), 1:428; 2:16–17.

6 *Ibid.*, 1: chap. xi.

7 J. H. Trumbull and C. J. Hoadly, eds., *Public Records of the Colony of Connecticut, 1636–1776* (15 vols., Hartford, 1850–1890), 8:134.

8 *Ibid.*, 4:305, 344, 349; 6:127, 355; 9:566; 10:66.

9 W. W. Hening, ed., *The Statutes at Large, Being a Collection of all Laws of Virginia, 1619–1792* (13 vols., Richmond, 1809–1823), 10:50–65, for Virginia act of 1779; N. S. Shaler, *Kentucky: A Pioneer Commonwealth* (Boston, 1884), 49–52; Hinsdale, *The Old Northwest*, 252–253.

10 Theodore Roosevelt, *The Winning of the West* (6 vols., 1889–1896), 3:8.

11 *Ibid.*, 2:398–399. Petition of settlers in counties of Kentucky and Illinois, 1780.

12 Report presented May 7. *Journals*, 4:401.

13 For the report, see *Journals*, 4:416.

14 Compare the report with the Virginia act of 1779.

15 March 4 and 16. *Journals*, 4:477, 482, 500. No member from Delaware given.

16 Report as partially amended, April 26. *Journals*, 4:507–508.

17 Seven ranges, as adopted.

18 For the arguments used by northern men on the committee, see Grayson to Washington, April 15, 1785. George Bancroft, *History of the Formation of the Constitution* (2 vols., New York, 1882), 1:425–428.

19 *Journals*, 4:506. New Hampshire, Massachusetts, Pennsylvania, Delaware, Virginia in favor; Rhode Island, Maryland opposed; New York, North Carolina divided; Connecticut, South Carolina, Georgia not fully represented.

20 *Journals*, 4:520.

21 Reduction in the size of the tracts offered for sale and freedom of location have been notable developments of the system.

22 Edward Gibbon Wakefield, *England and America* (New York, 1834).

Military Bounty Lands and the Origins of the Public Domain

RUDOLF FREUND

This article is a redaction of a paper presented at the joint meeting of the Agricultural History Society with the American Historical Association at Chicago on December 28, 1944.

Reprinted by permission from Agricultural History, *Volume 20* (*1946*), *pages 8–18.*

THE bounty-land policy of the Revolutionary War has often been criticized on two accounts. Historians seem to agree that the measures adopted did not serve their primary purpose of establishing deserving and needy veterans on farms of their own. Almost twenty years of peace went by before the first titles to bounty lands could be conveyed, and during this long delay most of the land warrants had found their way into the hands of speculators and land scouts. Only those veterans who could afford to wait or had pooled their claims were able to reap at least some of the intended benefits. Regarding its second objective, namely an orderly advance of settlement into the new western lands, the military bounty land policy of the United States is held to have failed just as signally. The insistent demands of old veterans and their heirs and assignees forced practically every administration between 1812 and 1862 to relax the stipulations and extend the date lines for the establishment of military claims. The central land office continued to honor these claims up to the end of the nineteenth century in considerable numbers. By that time, between 70 and 100 million acres had been assigned for army warrants of the Revolutionary War and that of 1812 alone, largely on the basis of laws passed as late as 1847 and 1855. If the total of "All Land in Farms" within the four "central" state groups as given in the Census of 1900 is fairly indicative of the farm acreage occupied during the previous hundred years of westward expansion, the military bounty lands alone comprise one-seventh to one-sixth of this acreage.[1] All these lands were acquired, of course, by the bounty claimants without cost.

The incipient stages in the development of this system are said to have had the effect of accustoming the people to "the idea of the government giving away public land."[2] This statement bespeaks the widely held opinion that the westward movement was caused by economic and social forces of overwhelming strength. Consequently, laws and administrative acts are accorded only secondary importance; they must either suit the interests of the pioneer, or be abandoned, or rendered ineffective in some other way. Bounty-land legislation may be viewed as an instance where the original purpose of rewarding the veteran for his services was transformed gradually and unwittingly into a means for helping the people of the frontier to achieve their goal of "free land."

It may be doubted, however, whether this interpretation does not oversimplify the matter. Although the bounty-land policy failed to achieve its intended purposes, nevertheless it contributed to a really remarkable degree toward setting the patterns and erecting the sign-posts for at least the earlier stages of the westward movement. The cession of western lands, the rules governing the administration of the Northwest Territory and its lands, the preferment of the survey principle over indiscriminate location, and last but not least the first settlements on the Ohio River are cases in point. Furthermore, the question may be raised whether the final stages of the westward movement permit a proper perspective concerning legislation which was forged in the crucible of a fateful war and its hardly less fateful aftermath. Are we to believe that the framers of these laws failed to appraise properly the character and the strength of the forces destined to push open the gate to the promised lands of the West? Did they try to impede these forces by virtue of a narrow and "eastern" conception of the future? And can the colorful and fascinating interplay of personalities, ideas, and events which marked the incipient steps of the land policy of the United States be accorded its proper weight when viewed as but an awkward prelude to the grandiose spectacle of the westward movement?

The recent war and victory have made all Americans conscious of the grave problem of the returning veteran. It is easier for us, therefore, than for peacetime generations to understand the anxiety felt by the Founding Fathers and their helpers on this account. But a still more vexing problem which has no present-day counterpart confronted them and called for immediate solution. Independence had thrown into the lap of a none-too-perfect union the vast and unsettled area between the Great Lakes and the Mississippi and Ohio rivers. It was but natural that the deserving and needy soldiers should expect to receive land in this region. But this prospect was by no means the only stake which the veteran hoped to have in the opening of the West. In the newly won territory, a novel type of colonial government and administration was to be established, in which the veterans, and especially the officers, claimed their due share. Some of them, chiefly from New England, held decided opinions as to the principles which they wished to see incorporated in the new western set-up for their own benefit and that of a strong federal union. Their views were certain to be challenged by southerners, though adherence to either camp was not necessarily determined by regional interests and outlooks alone. However, some of the basic issues involved in the future administration and land policies of the new West had been tackled, and in part decided, long before the war ended. An early promise of the Continental Congress to the rank and file of its army brought them to a head.

Curiously enough, land was first promised by Congress, in August, 1776, to Hessians and other foreigners if they would desert from the English army, but nothing much came of it.[3] The story of the military bounty lands really began somewhat later, when Congress decided to offer land to its own nationals as an inducement for enlisting in the new army and for permanent service. The ill-fated summer campaigns of 1776 made it depressingly clear to everybody concerned that the war could not be waged successfully unless the militia was replaced, at least for the purposes of sustained warfare, by an army of regulars who were willing to serve without interruption until victory was won. This was a radical departure from previous practices, and it was clear that substantial rewards had to be offered to achieve the change from temporary to permanent enlistment. Therefore, when Congress decided in September, 1776, to establish eighty-eight regiments on state lines to serve during the war, the former money bounty of $20 was augmented by promises of land, ranging from 100 acres for a private to 500 acres for a colonel. The land was to be provided by the United States, and the expenses connected therewith were to be borne by the states in the same proportion as the other expenses of the war.[4]

These resolutions had been contested hotly in Congress before they were passed, but their execution caused still greater concern. The New

England states believed that the land bonus was not sufficient to overcome the aversion to enlistment; civilians and soldiers complained, it was said, of the long engagement as a contract of servitude. These states wanted, therefore, to raise the money bounty, especially for privates, and passed acts to this effect in their assemblies.[5] Maryland protested that it had no land of its own and thought that it would have to buy land for bounties from other states. Its council of safety proposed to raise the money bounty to the Maryland line by $10 instead of offering land. This caused consternation in the Continental Congress, where it was feared that this precedent might break the back of all North America. Maryland was officially assured that it would not have to make good the bounty grants in its individual capacity, because it was the intention of Congress to provide the bounty lands at the expense of the United States. But Maryland would not recant; and in order to mollify it as well as the New England states, Congress finally permitted enlistment for three years under the money-bounty system and reserved the land bounty to those soldiers and officers who signed up for the full duration of the war or until they were honorably discharged.[6]

Maryland's decided stand against the land bounty was by no means motivated by petty considerations; this state made it abundantly clear that much larger issues were involved. To an earlier suggestion that land might be bought for $3 per hundred, Maryland's delegates had replied "that an Expectation was formed by the People of our State that what was conquered from an Enemy at the joint Expence of Blood and Treasure of the whole should become their joint property but as Claims had been set up opposite to our Ideas of natural Justice it became a wise people rather to prepare for the worst by giving ten Dollars now than trust to the mercy of a few Venders from whom they would be obliged to purchase . . . at any price, the Case of all Monopolies. . . ." And shortly after the compromise of a three-year alternative enlistment had been reached, Maryland urged Congress not to close the door on its request "that the back lands acquired from the Crown of *Great Britain* in the present war, should be a common stock for the benefit of the *United States.* . . ."[7]

Though this motion was not carried, the long struggle over the cession of western lands had commenced. While it lasted, Maryland's and even more so Virginia's moves were largely motivated and conditioned by the bounty-land question. In order to "remove the *ostensible* cause" of Maryland's anxiety to share in the common property of the western lands and its subsequent refusal to join the Confederation, the Virginia Assembly offered in December, 1779, "to furnish lands out of their territory on the north west side of the Ohio river, without purchase money, to the troops on continental establishment of such of the confederated states as had not unappropriated lands for that purpose. . . ." [8] This offer hardly substantiates Maryland's suspicion of the grasping ambition of its big neighbor. Regardless of whether Virginia's generosity or Maryland's insistence can rightly be called the keystone of the Confederation, there is little doubt that the bounty resolutions of Congress in 1776 must be credited with having inaugurated the train of events which eventually led to perpetual union. [9]

Virginia's "Remonstrance" was only the first step toward actual cession. In the long haggling over the terms under which Virginia was to renounce its claims to the territory across the Ohio River, the bounty lands proved one of the main stumbling blocks. Holding immense tracts of unappropriated land, Virginia had very soon adopted the idea suggested by Congress of granting land bounties to its officers and soldiers, both on the state and continental establishment. And being more able to do so, Virginia was more liberal than Congress with grants. By October, 1779, all its officers had been granted ten times, noncoms four times, and privates two times as much land as Congress had stipulated; a year later all bounties were increased by one-third, and new ones were added for generals (following congressional precedent); and in 1782 further increases and bounties for three-year enlistments were granted. George Rogers Clark and his men had been promised lands in the trans-Ohio region that they were to wrest from the English. Finally, a land office created at Richmond in 1779 was charged with the administration and execution of military bounty warrants and of all other claims pertaining to the unappropriated lands of the state. This step had been greatly resented by Maryland and the other landless states because any definite arrangements made by Virginia might render it still more difficult to obtain its consent to the cession of the northwestern territory under reasonable terms. [10]

Most important of all, as early as December, 1778, Virginia had set aside an extensive tract in western Kentucky from which to supply its line officers and soldiers with land. [11] This military reserve became the source of many vexations. When the boundary between Virginia and North Carolina was extended, part of this district fell south of the line. In its final cession offer on January 2, 1781, Virginia stipulated, therefore, that in case the quantity of good lands which it had reserved southeast of the Ohio River proved insufficient, the deficiency should be made up in good lands to be laid off between the Scioto and Little Miami rivers northwest of the Ohio. Even after this clause and the cession had been accepted on March 1, 1784, Congress delayed final action in the matter, until Virginia could prove that its supply of "good land" southeast of the Ohio had really been exhausted. The Senate and the House finally settled the matter by an act of August 10, 1790; the first titles to land in the Military Reserve of Virginia northwest of the Ohio were conveyed in 1791, almost eight years after peace had been declared and more than six years after Virginia had ceded its northwestern territories.[12]

In the protracted struggle over Virginia's claims to bounty lands across the Ohio River, two major issues were involved. The first related to the methods of locating warrants. According to the Land Ordinance of 1785, the lands of the Northwest Territory had to be surveyed and subdivided into rectangular townships and sections before warrants could be located and titles conveyed. An exception was the Virginia Military Reserve,[13] because it was to be settled under Virginia laws which allowed the warrant holder to locate his land himself and to have it surveyed afterward in any shape he and the surveyor thought suitable. Under this practice, good lands, especially the river bottoms, were taken up rapidly. Newcomers pushed farther and farther into the wilderness in search of good lands without bothering about the nearer but second-rate stretches. Thus, new regions quickly became dotted with widely scattered and often unconnected settlements. Determined to give its soldiers the full advantages of "indiscriminate location," Virginia needed large areas in order to satisfy them. This explains why Virginia insisted on making "good land" the measure of its claims to large tracts on both sides of the Ohio and why it grew impatient over the long delay in admitting claimants to its reserve northwest of the river.

In these clashes the ever-present conflict between the North and the South played an important part, though mostly behind the scenes. The Land Ordinance of 1785, just as the famed ordinance of 1787 for the northwestern territory, was widely hailed as a victory for the decided preference of New Englanders for compact settlement and rectangular surveys. Certain groups of New England officers took the lead in the settlement and administration of the new territory, largely through the Ohio Company. These men feared that the Virginians and their ways would prove a disturbing element once they took up lands in the reserve under the laws of their Mother State. The settlers who eventually entered the Virginia Reserve from the south quickly succeeded in taking up the best lands and soon began to play their full and vigorous part in the political life of the territory and the ascendancy of Ohio to statehood.[14] However, the veterans of the Revolutionary War had a comparatively small share in all this because many of them had tired of the long delay and sold their claims to enterprising easterners who in time did a thriving business in locating and selling Ohio lands.

Only a few days after the terms of the preliminary peace had been ratified, a shrewd observer in Congress wrote to an eminent officer: "Our circumstances afford an odd Contrast to those we have heretofore experienced. The Difficulty which heretofore oppres'd us was how to raise an Army. The one which now embarrasses is how to dissolve it." [15] Two months later, mutinous soldiers forced Congress to flee from Philadelphia to Princeton. In this open revolt, the officers had not taken part, but they too were discontented and irritable. They hesitated to resort to desperate means, at least as long as there was hope that Congress would act in their favor. In December, 1782, they had presented the last of a long list of memorials to that body. This petition demanded the prompt settlement of arrearages and the commutation of half pay for life, promised in 1780, into a lump sum of money to be paid on discharge. Congress had sent a committee to investigate, but having no resources of its own it could only recommend speedy action to the states; but they were slow in adopting appropriate measures. Deeply disturbed by rumors of the approaching peace, even the officers' restraint threatened to give way to open rebellion.

Matters came to a head in early March, 1783, at Newburgh. An anonymous officer addressed his comrades in these incendiary terms: ". . . while the swords you wear are necessary for the defence of America, what have you to expect from peace, when your voice shall sink, and your strength dissipate by division? . . . Can you then consent to be the only sufferers by this revolution, and retiring from the field, grow old in poverty, wretchedness and contempt? . . . If you can—go—and carry with you the jest of Tories, and the scorn of Whigs —the ridicule, and what is worse, the pity of the world. Go, starve, and be forgotten!" And then followed a dire threat: ". . . the slightest mark of indignity from Congress now, must operate like the grave, and part you [and Congress] forever: that in any political event, the army has its alternative. If peace, that nothing shall separate you from your arms but death: if war, that . . . you will retire to some unsettled country, smile in your turn, and 'mock when their fear cometh on.'"

Here indeed were the seeds of a serious revolt. The officers were exhorted not to lay down their arms until Congress granted their demands; and if Congress refused, an exodus into the western lands was to be the ultimate answer. No doubt, the addresses made a deep impression upon the officers of the cantonment. But at a meeting of their delegates Washington himself unexpectedly appeared. In a speech which moved some of his hearers to tears he reiterated his belief that Congress, though moving slowly, would eventually do full justice to the wishes of the army. He then solemnly pledged his own support in every way which was consistent with his duty to his country. This appeal dissuaded the officers from their dangerous course and set them once more upon the road to orderly appeal, strongly seconded by their commander in chief.[16]

Congress acted quickly and agreed to commute the promise of half pay for life into a sum in gross amounting to five years' full pay in money or securities such as those given to the other creditors of the United States. By virtue of this last clause, which shows Alexander Hamilton's hand in drawing up the resolutions, the money and pension claims of the army would be treated in exactly the same way as the claims of any other creditor upon the exchequer of the United States. One month later, the proceeds from special imposts on foreign liquors, sugar, etc., a general duty of 5 per cent on imports, and contributions from the states were assigned to the service of the total public debt; it is significant that a proposal to appropriate the 5-per cent duty to the army claims alone was not adopted at the time. Neither were any provisions made to satisfy the land bounties, the obvious reason being that the cessions of western lands had not been completed. Their consummation was urged in order to hasten the extinguishment of the debts.[17]

Indeed, the officers themselves had not asked Congress to attend to the land-bounty matter; they had concentrated on obtaining the commutation of their pensions into hard cash. The seeds of the Newburgh addresses were to ripen in this respect also. The appeal to migrate to the West and begin a new semimilitary life there had not fallen on deaf ears, for this idea had been talked about previously,[18] and its combination with the bounty-land question produced a move which was destined to have far reaching, if slowly maturing, consequences. Soon after the Newburgh incident, two of the main actors on the scene,

Quartermaster Timothy Pickering and Brigadier General Rufus Putnam, together with Brigadier General Jedediah Huntington, were hard at work trying to turn the insidious counsel of the "fellow soldier" into a positive scheme which would utilize the promised bounty lands and other land grants for the establishment of a new state for veterans on the Ohio. By April, 1783, elaborate propositions for the settling of such a commonwealth were drawn up for the benefit of those officers and men who were willing to join an association to be founded for the purpose. These propositions called for concerted action along the following lines: purchase by the United States of a tract corresponding roughly to the present state of Ohio; prompt assignment of the bounty lands promised by Congress during the war; grants of additional and larger tracts but with the same scaling as the bounty lands to actual settlers in the purchased district; payment of the initial expenses of settlement and subsistence for three years from arrearages due to the members of the association; the preparation of a constitution previous to going west which would exclude slavery; and prompt admittance of this state to the Confederation.[19]

This ambitious plan drew from the supposed author of the Newburgh addresses the caustic remark: ". . . this quixotic idea. It originates with men who wish only to amuse and divert the army from the consideration of more important concerns. They ask, what can not be granted. 'Tis absurd." [20] Whatever sentiments John Armstrong harbored, he was right. Pickering and Putnam had simply proposed that the United States should purchase the tract for the new state from the natives, thereby ignoring, probably intentionally, the thorny problem of the cession of Virginia's northwestern claims. For this and perhaps other reasons, the final petition, signed in June, 1783, by almost three hundred officers from New England, merely asked Congress to "assign and mark it out as a Tract or Territory suitable to form a distinct Government (or Colony of the United States) in time to be admitted" to the Confederation and to make provisions for the location and survey of the bounty lands promised.[21]

The petition was sent properly to the commander in chief first, accompanied by a lengthy letter from Putnam. The rugged soldier and pioneer stressed the paramount importance of the Ohio River region as a bastion against England and Spain and the necessity of securing the frontier by a string of forts in order to keep the Indians in check. He then proceeded to voice the expectations of the officers which had been deemed improper to mention in the petition. His comrades, Putnam explained, did not expect to be under any obligation to settle on the bounty lands; if, however, Congress made further and larger grants of land, many were determined to become actual settlers on the Ohio. Putnam went on to emphasize that at least some of the officers held rather decided views as to the manner in which these new lands should be distributed and administered. They were, he declared, much opposed to monopoly and wished to guard against large patents granted to individuals; they hoped, therefore, that no grants would be made except by townships 6 miles square (or multiples), to be subdivided by the proprietor associates themselves and administered after the pattern of a New England town. This township principle was also to apply to private purchasers of land in the region.

Washington forwarded the petition and Putnam's letter to Congress on June 17, 1783, and he himself urged the speedy adoption of the army plan, because its execution would connect the government with the frontier, extend settlements progressively, and plant in the new lands a brave, hardy, and respectable race of people always willing to combat the savages. Despite this endorsement, no action was taken on the proposal by Congress either then or later. During the turbulent days of the insurrection of the Pennsylvania troops, Congress referred the petition to a standing committee, had it read in Congress a week later, and referred back to another special committee which was discharged on October 15, 1783. Upon a pressing inquiry from Putnam, more than a year later, Washington blamed the "want of cession of the land to act upon" as the chief reason for the delay. He was vaguely hopeful that something might be done yet, because the Virginia cession had been accepted, but the plan was never revived in its original form.[22]

Manifestly, it was futile to expect action from Congress in the matter of the bounty lands as long as the squabble over the cessions and their execution lasted. Moreover, Putnam and his comrades had encumbered their plans with political aspirations of pronounced character, the open discussion of which would certainly upset the delicate balance of a none-too-perfect union. However, they did plant the proverbial mustard seed when they urged their fellow officers and land claimants to form a voluntary association with the characteristics of a corporate body. True, the idea of a pioneering land corporation was neither new nor without precedent.[23] But only the critical times of the 1780's had engendered strong enough group sentiments to keep this basic feature of the army plan alive when all other proposals had to be given up. Eight years of war and camp life had rendered many officers unfit for the old ways of life; they were impoverished and despaired of ever again succeeding in living up to the civilian Joneses. On the other hand, the long comradeship in arms had imbued many officers with an *esprit de corps* which persisted and proved of great psychological value in the troubled times of war and peace alike.

Finally, many believed that the western lands were the destined proving ground for the political principles of independence, self-government, and personal liberty for which the war had been fought. Thus, the lands on the Ohio beckoned with the lure of still another Utopia. In these empty expanses would rise a new community from the seeds of a corporation of New England veterans who had forged their swords into plowshares.

These feelings and expectations, though seldom voiced by the tight-lipped backers of the original army plan, prevented the idea of a pioneering land corporation from vanishing. After three years of casting their weights about in various western enterprises, Rufus Putnam and Benjamin Tupper finally launched the Ohio Company of New England, which included officers and men who were destined to play a vital part in the opening of Ohio. In the financial and corporate set-up of the company, military bounty claims again loomed conspicuously, and in the early life of Marietta, the first settlement on the Ohio River, some of the dreams of the army plan of 1783 came true.[24]

The very same routine procedure which buried the army plan in congressional committees obliterated yet another scheme designed to satisfy the soldiers' demands for their bounty lands. Introduced by Theodorick Bland and seconded by Alexander Hamilton, this scheme is of interest here chiefly because it seems to have been a counterproposal to the army plan, though it foreshadows in some respects the system of land sales in Hamilton's famous public credit report of 1790. The plan as presented to Congress in 1783 proposed to merge the army's land claims with the commuted half pay and arrearages, every dollar of which was to be considered equal to a claim for 30 acres of land. The combined land grants were to be assigned within the vacant territory ceded by Great Britain, where districts 2 degrees wide and 3 degrees long, subdivided into townships, were to be laid out. Finally, the United States was to reserve 10,000 acres out of every 100,-000 granted as common and unalienable property, their revenues to be used for military and educational purposes. This plan represented one of the several attempts of the "financiers" to fund at least the army debt *in toto*. It also reflected the fear of the advocates of a strong central government that a new state might upset the delicate balance of the Thirteen Original States, and it combined both political and financial motives in the proposal that the Union keep a permanent interest in the western lands and their future development.[25]

The Bland proposals hinged directly upon the acceptance of the Virginia cession. Indeed, no move in the matter of the promised bounty lands was possible until the United States had acquired clear title to the western lands. As soon as this was accomplished, a gust of fresh air seemed to give new life to this and other questions concerning the future land policy of the United States. The Virginians took the lead, and among them Thomas Jefferson emerged as the leading spirit. True, he did not concern himself much with the bounty-land issue proper; nevertheless, his broad and general approach to the problems of the New West provided a principal solution for this question, albeit one which obliterated most of its political implications. Under his leadership, the legislative framework for the northwestern territory and its administration progressed so far that the lines for future action appeared securely drawn, even though many important changes might occur in carrying out his more detailed plans.

In this respect, one accomplishment stands out clearly before others. Congress agreed (and never deviated from this course) to deal with the problems of the Northwest under two headings: the one relating to the form and powers of government, and the other relating to the disposal of land within the territory. This trend of affairs is clearly shown by the sequence of events after Virginia's deed of cession had been accepted on March 1, 1784. On the very same day, Jefferson laid before Congress his proposals for the "Temporary Government of the Northwestern Territory," which had been under consideration by a committee for some time. They provided for the creation and administration of several western territories of rectangular shape and about equal size, established the procedure for their advancing to full statehood and membership in the Union, stipulated the republican form of government, forbade the admittance of citizens with hereditary titles, and abolished slavery after 1800. With the two last-mentioned provisions stricken out, these proposals became law on April 23, 1784, but they were never put into effect. The unsettled conditions in the West prevented their early application, and in July, 1787, the famous government ordinance for the Northwest Territory was passed which cast Jefferson's ideas, though with important alterations, in a new and permanent form.[26] On April 30, 1784, Jefferson laid before Congress "An Ordinance for ascertaining the mode of locating and disposing of lands in the western territory," the logical sequel and counterpart to the government ordinance just passed. In a measure, the land ordinance shared the fate of its twin; it was assigned to a committee, read in Congress again in the spring of 1785, referred to still another committee, from which it emerged in the new and final dress of the renowned Land Ordinance of May 20, 1785.[27] As a matter of course and propriety, the military bounty lands are dealt with in both Jefferson's draft and the Land Ordinance of 1785. However, there seems reason to believe that the broader and political implications of the land-bounty issue were not entirely absent from Jefferson's mind when he drew up the ordinance of 1784.

The disturbed conditions in the Northwest made it necessary that Congress decide on matters of government first and separately. The Indian claims had to be acquired by Congress, but it seemed impossible that this body should also supervise and enforce the execution of the respective treaties with the Indian tribes. Consequently, the delineation of the territory and its subdivisions, as well as the establishment of proper authorities there, became more pressing. Likewise, the eager settlers could not be allowed to move into a political vacuum, as the troublesome squatters across the Ohio had done. They had to be made responsible for law and order from the very beginning, and this entailed the framing of governmental rules in advance of their coming. In spite of the expediency of framing a government ordinance first and leaving the land law until later, there still remains the possibility, and even the probability, that Jefferson's move was designed to serve his political ideas also. There seems little doubt that the fight against the Society of the Cincinnati raging at the time prompted him to insist on equal male suffrage in the formation of truly democratic governments within the territory and to insert in his ordinance a clause barring citizens with hereditary titles from settling there.[28] In all probability, he was also aware of the fact that the prime movers behind the army plan were all prominent Cincinnati. Was the thunderer against the aristocracy of wealth and privilege unaware of the possible danger that a landed gentry might rise in the West, whose wealth would be based upon bounty lands and additional land grants from Congress and whose privileges would be but a perpetuation of their military merits and insignia? The great civilian among the Founding Fathers was afraid that there would "continue a distinction between the civil & military which it would be for the good of the whole to obliterate as soon as possible. . . ."[29] To attain this goal, he was resolved that the people should be the sole source of democratic government in the East and in the New West. The political realist would know that matters pertaining to landholding might becloud the purity of this principle when included in the same ordinance. Jefferson may have thought it advisable, therefore, to deal with the modes for acquiring land in a separate body of general rules and routine procedures.

That Jefferson was aware of the political implications of the bounty question is shown by a peculiar clause in his land ordinance draft which prescribed that army warrants should pass as lands by descent and device, but not by assignment or by survivorship. The prohibition of assignment had its precedent in a resolution passed by Congress on September 20, 1776. Both this resolution and Jefferson's clause were intended to prevent speculation in land warrants. In cases of landholding, survivorship applied to joint tenancy under a grant and was regarded in Jefferson's time as a survival of feudalism and incompatible with democratic ideas.[30] Of course, this term must have slipped easily from the pen of the author of the laws against entail and primogeniture. The question here is, why just in the case of the bounty lands? True, these alone were grants, whereas all other lands had to be acquired by purchase. But again, why should he be so careful if no possible danger threatened from this direction? However, none of Jefferson's provisions in these matters found a place in the Land Ordinance of 1785. On the contrary this law expressly recognized the right to assign bounty warrants. Nevertheless, his proviso that lands in the new territory should pass in dowry and descent according to gavelkind did become the basis of the first section of the ordinance of 1787, as he had anticipated.

Pertinent features of Jefferson's two ordinances thus appear to reflect his running fight with military and Federalist circles of New England. By no means, however, did he leave this particular battlefield fully victorious. True, the ordinance of 1787 upheld most of his cherished principles of democratic government. But his draft for the land ordinance underwent such drastic changes that it finally resembled the original draft in little more than name. Again, we are concerned with the land-bounty issue, this time wrapped up with the controversy about the proper way of promoting actual settlement in the West.

Jefferson's land ordinance plan combined the regular survey with a modified form of indiscriminate location. He wanted the new territory laid off in hundreds 10 geographical miles square, which in turn, were to be subdivided in lots 1 mile square; the hundreds were to be offered either entire or in lots.[31] However, the actual surveying was not to begin at a definite location but with the hundreds most in demand. This provision, of course, was closely tied up with the modes of acquiring title to land in the territory. Upon paying to the treasurer or loan officer an unspecified purchase price in specie, loan office, or debt certificates or handing over evidences of military rights to lands, the prospective settler would receive a warrant, go out himself to locate it, and describe to the surveyor the particular lot or hundred chosen. The surveyor would then proceed to lay off the land according to these requests and issue certificates of description which finally became the basis of deeds. Jefferson thus favored a rather liberal method of land allotment, albeit within the frame of regular surveys, and accorded no preferential treatment to soldier warrants; it was the idea of first come, first served, applied generally.

In all these respects, the final land ordinance differed widely from Jefferson's scheme. First of all, it authorized the business of surveying and disposing of western lands in a definite and not too extensive area on the upper Ohio River, where seven parallel ranges of townships running due north and south were to be laid off completely before being opened to the location of warrants. The townships were to be 6 miles square and subdivided into lots of 640 acres each. The methods adopted for offering the townships either entire or in lots to prospective settlers, and the procedures prescribed for securing warrant and title were rather complicated. Some of the features, especially those relating to the participation of the states in the scheme, were repealed in July, 1788, without having had much effect. Here it is sufficient to point out the special treatment accorded to the holders of army warrants. As soon as the Seven Ranges were surveyed, the Secretary of War was to withdraw by lot one-seventh of the townships for the use of the late Continental Army; henceforth, military bounty land claims had to be presented to the Secretary of War and be satisfied by him. The remainder of the townships were to be sold by auction at not less than $1 per acre, to be paid in specie or in debt certificates.

In most of these stipulations, the New England viewpoint on the necessity of survey before sale and on more compact settlement and progressive advance into the West had prevailed. In the Seven Ranges it was thought that the United States would acquire a yardstick which would measure and delineate the westward movement in which the veterans would play their due part. In other respects, however, the ordinance clearly represented a compromise between the New England and southern groups in Congress who had waged a hard battle in committees and on the floor before the measure was finally passed.[32]

To the holders of bounty claims and to prospective settlers in general, the results of the ordinance of 1785 were disconcerting. Despite all caution, the Indians remained hostile, the chief geographer fell ill, and after three years not more than four ranges of townships had been laid off. It is not surprising, therefore, that the Secretary of War received incessant inquiries respecting the lands due the late army. In the spring of 1787, he addressed an urgent appeal to Congress. "Too many," he wrote, "have been compelled, by their necessities, to sell the evidences of their public debt, for a small proportion of the nominal sum. These unfortunate men now consider the lands promised them, as their only resource against poverty, in old age, and therefore are extremely solicitous to receive, immediately, their dues in this respect. . . . Assuming the surveys of the last year, as a data, or even supposing double the quantity will be surveyed annually in future, yet a very long period must elapse before the whole quantity due will be delivered. A period, at which very few of those entitled to the land will be living." [33]

Half a year later, when Congress was prodded into high gear by the proposed sale of land to the Ohio Company, an act was passed setting aside 1,000,000 acres north of the Ohio Company lands and west of the Seven Ranges and another tract at the mouth of the Ohio River for the exclusive purpose of satisfying the military bounties of the late army.[34] But only after seven more years and after the Indian war had been terminated by the Treaty of Greenville was Congress able to stipulate the terms and modes under which these lands would be made available for the army, and then three more years elapsed before the first deeds were conveyed.

By an act of June 1, 1796, some of the cumbersome procedures of the Land Ordinance of 1785 were relaxed for the military districts. Townships 5 (instead of 6) miles square were divided into quarters of 4,000 acres each; these were assigned entire and by lot to either a single claimant or to groups of veterans who had pooled their warrants for the purpose, the actual locations of their lands to be left to their own care if they so desired.[35] The effect of these stipulations was that many of the quarter townships were carved up in rather irregular fashion and in about the same way as had been feared from the execution of Jefferson's original plan. On the other hand, the "unmilitary U.S. military district," as it has been called,[36] filled up more quickly than the rectangular sections in the Seven Ranges, thus testifying to the merits of Jefferson's plan as well.

Even this rapid survey shows how slowly and cautiously Congress was compelled to move in the matter of satisfying the land bounties of the Revolution. The first four ranges could not be opened to claimants before 1787, the Virginia Reserve remained closed till 1791, and the United States military districts did not welcome the first veteran settlers before 1800. Secretary of War Knox's dire prophecy that "few of those entitled to the land will be living" to see their expectations fulfilled did not come true literally, but the long delay had induced many of the veterans—soldiers and officers alike—to sell not only their certificates for half pay and arrearages but also their bounty warrants. The assignment of warrants, forbidden during the war, became legal in 1788, and this helped to hasten the sale of warrants by their original, and often destitute, holders. It is not necessary to reiterate here the well-known facts concerning the speculative mania which seized the moneyed parts of the nation after the war and enabled a few persons and firms to reap profits from accumulated certificates and the sales of warrants for western lands. There is, however, need to point to the often forgotten circumstance that the existence of a market in debt certificates and land warrants could and did give to vigorous and enterprising men an opportunity and the means for concerted action of considerable public value and portent, even if they thereby advanced their own fortunes.

NOTES

1 The land-bounty policy of the Revolutionary War is treated in a general way in Payson Jackson Treat, *The National Land System, 1785–1820* (New York, 1910), 232–246, 260–262; Benjamin Horace Hibbard, *A History of the Public Land Policies* (New York, 1924), 117–118, 126–129; and Thomas Donaldson, *The Public Domain* (Washington, 1884), 232–234. The only exhaustive and penetrating study is that of William Thomas Hutchinson, "Military Bounty Lands of the American Revolution in Ohio" (Ph.D. dissertation, University of Chicago, June, 1927). It is deeply to be regretted that this work is not available in print. The author had access to it only after most of his own research was completed.

2 Amelia Clewley Ford, *Colonial Precedents of Our National Land System as It Existed in 1800* (Madison, Wis., 1910), 108.

3 Worthington C. Ford, ed., *Journals of the Continental Congress, 1774–*

1789 (34 vols., Washington, 1904–1937), 5:653–655. (Cited hereafter as *Journals*.) Benjamin Franklin to Thomas McKean, Aug. 24, 1776, and to Horatio Gates, Aug. 28, 1776, in Edmund C. Burnett, ed., *Letters of Members of the Continental Congress* (8 vols., Washington, 1921–1936), 2:59–60, 63. (Cited hereafter as *Letters*).

4 Resolution of Sept. 16, 1776, in *Journals*, 5:762–763. For an appraisal of the military events leading to these steps, see especially the circular letter of the President of Congress (John Hancock) to the New Hampshire Assembly, Sept. 24, 1776, in *Letters*, 2:98–100; and the special plea for the land bounty in the letter of Washington, Sept. 2, 1776, to the President of Congress in Peter Force, ed., *American Archives*, series 5 (3 vols., Washington, 1848–1853), 2:120–121.

5 William Hooper to the President of the North Carolina Convention, Nov. 16, 1776, in *Letters*, 2:154–155. Cf. also the letters of John Adams, William Williams, and Josiah Bartlett, *ibid.*, 57, 61, 85, 89.

6 Resolutions of Congress, Oct. 30 and Nov. 12, 1776 in *Journals*, 6:912–913, 945. New Jersey and Delaware soon fell in line with Maryland for the same reasons. *Letters*, 3:450.

7 See Benjamin Rumsey's letter to James Tilghman, Oct. 24, 1776, in *Letters*, 2:140 n.; Sam'l Chase's letter to the Council of Safety of Maryland, in *American Archives*, series 5, 3:787–788. As to the suggestion that Maryland should buy land, presumably from Virginia, see Jefferson to Edmund Pendleton, Aug. 13, 1776, in *Letters*, 2:48; and the excerpt of a letter from Pendleton to James Madison, in *Journals*, 5:505 n.

8 William Waller Hening, *The Statutes at Large; Being a Collection of All the Laws of Virginia, 1619–1792* (13 vols., Richmond, 1809–1823), 10:559. The word "ostensible" is italicized in the original, the less ostensible causes of Maryland's stand being, in the opinion of the Virginia Assembly, its backing of the land claims of several big land companies. For the part played by the land question in the Virginia Assembly in 1778–1779, see Kate Mason Rowland, *The Life of George Mason, 1725–1792* (2 vols., New York, 1892), 1:320–329, 340–344, 359–367; Thomas Perkins Abernethy, *Western Lands and the American Revolution* (New York, 1937), 242–247; Shaw Livermore, *Early American Land Companies* (New York, 1939), 109–110.

9 Herbert B. Adams, *Maryland's Influence upon Land Cessions to the United States* (Baltimore, 1885), 22–40, where the "ostensible cause" is also discussed. Hutchinson, "Military Bounty Lands of the American Revolution in Ohio," 21, says that the very important consequences of Maryland's stand have often been emphasized but that its inception of the resistance to the Military Bounty Act of 1776 seems to have been overlooked. Treat, *The National Land System*, 234, and Adams, *Maryland's Influence*, 48, hint at this connection without, however, developing its importance.

10 For the bounty laws, see Hening, *Statutes*, 10:24, 27, 160, 331, 375; 11:559–565. On Clark, see Hening, *Statutes*, 10:26, and Rowland, *George Mason*, 1:290, for the first land promise to Clark. On the land

office, see Hening, *Statutes*, 10:50–65; and Abernethy, *Western Lands*, 217–229.

11 Hening, *Statutes*, 10:55 n.; Rowland, *George Mason*, 1:310.

12 For Virginia's offer, see Hening, *Statutes*, 10:564–566. Hening claimed that the term "Virginia troops" included all troops, both on continental and Virginia's own establishment. For Virginia's cession and the opening of Virginia Military Reserve to Virginia's claimants, see Clarence E. Carter, compiler and editor, *The Territorial Papers of the United States* (21 vols. to date, Washington, 1934–   ), 2:6–9, 296–298. (Cited hereafter as *Territorial Papers*.) For the documents relating to the "good land" issue, see *American State Papers: Documents, Legislative and Executive, . . . in Relation to the Public Lands* (5 vols., Washington, 1834), 1:1–3, 12–13, 17.

13 *Territorial Papers*, 2:18.

14 The literature and source material pertaining to the early phases of political life in the Northwest Territory is too extensive to be cited here. For two excellent and comprehensive treatments with copious references, see Beverly W. Bond, Jr., *The Civilization of the Old Northwest* (New York, 1934), and *The Foundations of Ohio* (*The History of the State of Ohio*, ed. by Carl Wittke, vol. 1, Columbus, 1941).

15 Richard Peters to Baron Steuben, Apr. 23, 1783, in *Letters*, 7:150.

16 For the Newburgh addresses, see *Journals*, 24:291–311. See also Louis Clinton Hatch, *The Administration of the American Revolutionary Army* (New York, 1904), 142–181, 198–199. Octavius Pickering, *The Life of Timothy Pickering* (4 vols., Boston, 1867), 1:406–429, contains correspondence concerning John Armstrong's authorship of the addresses. (Cited hereafter as *Pickering*.)

17 *Journals*, 24:257–261.

18 *Pickering*, 1:456–461, 546–549. The merits of the Ohio country as a military refuge had been discussed by Washington and his officers during the war. See William Parker Cutler and Julian Perkins Cutler, *Life, Journals and Correspondence of Rev. Manasseh Cutler* (2 vols., Cincinnati, 1888), 1:141–144. (Cited hereafter as *Manasseh Cutler*.)

19 *Pickering*, 1:546–549; *Manasseh Cutler*, 1:149, 156–159.

20 John Armstrong to Horatio Gates, Apr. 22, 1783, in *Letters*, 7:150 n.

21 *Manasseh Cutler*, 1:159–160. This document has often been regarded as the first step leading to the founding of the New England Ohio Company.

22 Correspondence in *Manasseh Cutler*, 1:167–177. For the action in Congress, see *Journals*, 24:421 n. The Grand Committee mentioned had been appointed on May 30, 1783, "to consider of the best manner of carrying into execution the engagements of the United States for certain allowances of land to the Army at the conclusion of the war." —*Journals*, 24:376.

23 See the introduction by Albert C. Bates in *The Two Putnams, Israel and Rufus . . .* (Hartford, Conn., 1931); Livermore, *Early American Land Companies*, 97–102.

24 For these special aspects of the beginnings of the Ohio Company, see

Manasseh Cutler, 1:178–197; Archer Butler Hulbert, ed., *The Records of the Original Proceedings of the Ohio Company* (Marietta, Ohio, 1917); Joseph Stancliffe Davis, *Essays in the Earlier History of American Corporations* (2 vols., Cambridge, Mass., 1917), 1:130–145; Livermore, *Early American Land Companies*, 134–146.

25 Motion of Theodorick Bland, seconded by Alexander Hamilton, referred to Grand Committee, June 5, 1783, in *Journals*, 24:384–386. *The Bland Papers*, ed. by Charles Campbell (2 vols., Petersburg, Va., 1840–1843), are silent on this subject; see, however, *ibid.*, 2:104–106; and *Letters*, 7:143.

26 On the cession, see *Journals*, 26:112–117. For the government ordinance, see *ibid.*, 118–120, 247–252; and *The Writings of Thomas Jefferson*, ed. by Paul L. Ford (10 vols., New York, 1892–1899), 3:407–410, 429–432, 471. (Cited hereafter as Jefferson, *Writings*.) For the ordinance of 1787, see *Territorial Papers*, 2:39–50.

27 For the draft, see *Journals*, 26:324–330, 27:446–453; Jefferson, *Writings*, 3:475–483. For the Land Ordinance of 1785, see *Territorial Papers*, 2:12–18.

28 Jefferson to Washington, Apr. 16, 1784, to James Madison, Apr. 25, 1784, and Francis Hopkinson, May 3, 1784, in *Letters*, 7:493–495, 499–500, 511–512, and preface, *ibid.*, xxxviii–xli.

29 Jefferson, *Writings*, 4:170–175.

30 Livermore, *Early American Land Companies*, 122 n., 225.

31 See his humorous comments in letter to Hopkinson, May 3, 1784, in *Letters*, 7:511–512.

32 See *Letters*, 8:vii–x, and the letter from Monroe to Jefferson, 90, Grayson to Washington, 95–97, King to Gerry, 104, Howell to Green, 106, Grayson to Madison, 129–130, and others. For the influence of Timothy Pickering, see *Pickering*, 1:504–512; and Gerry to Pickering, King to Pickering, and Grayson to Pickering, in *Letters*, 8:55, 94, 105–106.

33 Secretary of War Henry Knox to President of Congress, Apr. 26, 1787, in *Territorial Papers*, 2:27–28.

34 *Ibid.*, 76.

35 For the act of June 1, 1796, see 1 *U.S. Stat.*, ch. 46. This law supplemented the act of May 18, 1796. *Territorial Papers*, 2:552–557.

36 Hutchinson, "Military Bounty Lands of the American Revolution in Ohio," 136–144, 151.

Cadastral Surveys for the Public Lands of the United States

EARL G. HARRINGTON

Presented at the Eighth Annual Meeting, American Congress on Surveying and Mapping, Washington, D.C., June 21–23, 1948. The author of this article, at that time Assistant Chief Cadastral Engineer, Bureau of Land Management, Department of the Interior, later became Chief, Division of Cadastral Engineering.

Reprinted by permission from Surveying and Mapping, *Volume 9 (1949), pages 82–86.*

A CADASTRAL survey is the act or process of making an official survey or register of lands. The execution of cadastral surveys for the public lands in the United States is the responsibility of the Bureau of Land Management. The Congress established this bureau in the Department of the Interior on July 16, 1946, through consolidation of the General Land Office and the Grazing Service.

Space does not permit detailed presentation of the problems, both technical and legal, involved in executing the public land surveys. It is possible only to acquaint the Congress on Surveying and Mapping with the general procedure and to point out how the surveys and resurveys made by the Bureau of Land Management may be of material value to all government agencies and the public engaged in large-scale mapping projects.

PUBLIC LAND AREAS MONUMENTED FOR MAPPING

At one time the original public domain comprised an area of over 3,000,000 square miles. At its maximum extent this included the Territory of Alaska, the states of Florida, Alabama, and Mississippi, and all states, except Texas, lying north and west of the Ohio and Mississippi rivers. Since the first public land surveys under the rectangular system were executed in the eastern part of Ohio in 1786, the rectangular system has been extended over more than 2,000,000 square miles of public land area. Approximately 92 per cent of the total area of the public land in the continental United States, but less than 1 per cent of the area of the Territory of Alaska, is now *[1948]* covered by the rectangular system.

A vast monumented cadastral net has been created, which may be used for control in connection with general and specific mapping programs. This comprehensive rectangular survey net provides a simple and definite form of land identification and anchors in place the boundaries of the public land.

In conformity with legal requirements the general scheme of survey provides for:

(1) The establishment of governing lines designated as principal meridians and base lines originating at selected points, known as initial points, each to serve as the beginning point for the extension of the surveys in separated localities.

(2) The establishment of guide meridians and correction lines or standard parallels at intervals sufficiently near each other to maintain a practical workable adherence to the legal definition of the primary unit, the township.

(3) The subdivision of the area into townships, each 6 miles square. The townships are numbered to the north or south commencing with number 1 at the base, and with range numbers to the east or west beginning with number 1 at the principal meridian.

(4) The subdivision of the townships into 36 separate units, designated as sections, by running parallel lines through the townships from south to north and from east to west at distances of 1 mile. The sections are numbered from 1 to 36 commencing with number 1 in the northeast section of the township, proceeding west to section 6, south to section 7, east to section 12, and so on, alternately, to number 36 in the southeast section.

The primary purpose of the cadastral surveys executed by the Bureau of Land Management is to mark on the ground the boundaries of the public lands, for disposal and administrative purposes. The original surveys create the boundaries of these lands and provide the basis for their legal description. Mapping is incidental to the cadastral survey, although the important map features are shown on the township plat.

The standard scale for the township plats is 1 inch = ½ mile. At this scale, the 6-mile townships are shown 12 inches to a side on standard-size plat sheets, 19 by 24 inches.

The final survey record consists of field notes describing the details of the survey, including a complete description of the monuments established and how they are marked, and the plat, which is a graphic representation of the survey made in the field. The purpose of the plat is to show the courses and lengths of survey lines between established monuments, the boundaries, description, and area of each tract of land and, as far as practicable, a delineation of the important relief, drainage, and culture. The plat serves as the legal basis for all transactions involving the public lands. The courts hold that when lands are granted according to an official survey, the plat of the survey, with all its notes, lines, descriptions, and landmarks, becomes as much a part of the grant or deed by which lands were conveyed, and controls so far as limits are concerned, as if such descriptive features were written out upon the face of the deed or grant (*Cragin* v. *Powell*, 128 U.S. 691, 696).

The vast monumented net of cadastral surveys consists of monuments established at the four corners of each section, as well as the quarter corners on the boundaries of the sections. These monuments furnish the foundation for the subdivision of the sections as contemplated by law and for the identification of the boundaries of the sections. The monuments—eight to a square mile—also furnish control for practically all types of field work involved in mapping projects.

CADASTRAL SURVEYS BEGUN BY CONTRACT IN 1812

The General Land Office, now the Bureau of Land Management, was organized in 1812 primarily for the purpose of selling the public lands in order to pay the debts of the Revolutionary War. There was a great demand for the western land, and surveys were necessary before the lands could be identified and described. The surveys were made under the contract system. Accurate work, as accuracy is measured today, was not required. The monuments established marked the boundaries of the lands disposed of, regardless of the accuracy required in making the survey in the first instance. It is a principle of law that corners once established, designated, and used to mark land boundaries, cannot be changed if there are existing valid rights based upon said corners.

Unlike scientific surveys of an informative character, which may be amended with changing conditions or because the original surveys were not executed according to the standards now required for accuracy, cadastral surveys made by the Bureau of Land Management cannot be ignored, repudiated, altered, or corrected, if they mark the boundaries of lands patented by the United States. The construction engineer can remove a defective foundation and rebuild; errors appearing in those surveys which supply information for the public can be corrected and new data supplied, but an original cadastral survey which creates boundaries cannot be changed so long as it controls rights vested in the lands affected.

Regardless of the fact that extreme accuracy was not an important factor in executing the early surveys of the public lands and there is considerable difference in some instances between the original record and the actual distances and courses of the lines on the ground connecting the established monuments, the original cadastral surveys are still serving the purpose for which they were made, that is, to mark the boundaries of the public land. The advancement made in accuracy in connection with executing the survey of the public lands is best illustrated by the specifications for that factor contained in the early regulations compared with the present-day standards.

Survey Regulations and Specifications for Increased Accuracy

In the 1855 Manual of Instructions for the survey of the public lands, which was the first general publication issued for the guidance of deputy surveyors, it is stated:

> Every north and south section line, except those terminating in the north boundary of the township, is to be eighty chains in length. The east and west section lines, except those terminating on the west boundary of the township, are to be within one hundred links of eighty chains in length; and the north and south boundaries of any one section except in the extreme western tier, are to be within one hundred links of equal length. The meanders within each fractional section, or between any two meander posts, or of a pond or island in the interior of a section, must close within one chain and fifty links.

The requirements for accuracy at the present time in making cadastral surveys are to a large extent based upon the character of the area being surveyed and its value. Since the established monuments mark the boundaries, and not the reported bearings and distances between those monuments, it would not be good business and it is not necessary to require the same degree of accuracy in rough mountainous areas, valuable for grazing purposes only, as is required in agricultural areas or mineral areas where high values are involved.

1947 Manual of Surveying Instructions

Considering the township as a unit, the 1947 Manual of Surveying Instructions provides that the average closing error shall not exceed 1 : 1,000 for extremely rough mountainous land, covered with dense timber and undergrowth, valued chiefly for grazing and exceptionally difficult to survey; 1 : 1,800 for the average mountainous area valued chiefly for grazing; and 1 : 3,500 for areas containing valuable mineral deposits, improved or cultivated lands, and other areas where this accuracy can be obtained at a reasonable cost. It is believed that the monuments established according to these specifications for accuracy will, in general, be suitable for horizontal control for all types of maps and will provide the necessary control for the actual field work involved in obtaining the map data.

Prior to 1910 the survey of the public land was made by contract. By the act of June 25, 1910, the Congress put an end to this system and inaugurated the "Direct System," under which surveys and resurveys have been executed by a permanent corps of engineers. I have been told by officials of other agencies who have used the monuments established in the survey of the public lands for mapping purposes that the cadastral surveys made since 1910 are without question suitable for control purposes.

Since 1910 when the contract system for executing surveys was abolished, the corners of the public land surveys have been monumented with standard metal posts manufactured from wrought iron or copper-bearing steel pipe filled with a core of concrete. Present specification standards call for posts 30 inches long, 2 inches in diameter, with the planted end split and the two halves spread to form a flange. A brass cap riveted to one end of the post is appropriately marked with steel dies.

All known triangulation stations established by the U.S. Coast and Geodetic Survey and the U.S. Geological Survey are connected to corners of the rectangular system of surveys at the time the field work is executed. Based upon these connections the precise latitude and longitude of each monument in the township can be computed. It is the practice in preparing the plats representing the surveys and resurveys to give the latitude and longitude of the southeast corner of each township. The monumented corners accordingly, when the precise latitude and longitude are known, may be used as the basis for control in any mapping or surveying project.

Use of Aerial Photographs

In areas where aerial photographs are available, copies are secured and furnished the field engineer. While the cadastral survey is in progress, a number of selected points that can be positively identified on the pictures are connected to the established monuments of the survey. Ample control is thus obtained for laying out the section or other lines of the survey on the photographs. When appropriate, the statement, "Aerial photographs, coordinated with ground control obtained during survey have been used in compiling the topography shown on this plat," is placed on the township plat.

Today one of the major problems confronting the cadastral engineering service of the Bureau of Land Management is that involved in the restoration of original corners which have been lost. A lost corner is a monumented point of a survey whose position cannot be determined from remaining evidence of the original marks. In the early surveys the importance of permanent monumentation of corner positions was not realized and many of the corners were marked only by wooden stakes. Time and the elements have destroyed markers of this type, thus making it necessary to resurvey large areas of the public domain for the purpose of ascertaining the original land boundaries. Strict attention must be given to the protection of vested rights in making these resurveys, and the missing corners must be established according to principles laid down by the courts.

Multiple Uses of Solar Transit

The solar transit is the approved instrument for executing the majority of the surveys made by the Bureau of Land Management. Members of the bureau, co-operating with the instrument makers, have designed and developed an instrument which has now reached a high degree of efficiency and simplicity. This instrument is valuable not only for making cadastral surveys but for use in other types of engineering and mapping projects. I do not believe that the majority of map makers and engineers realize the use that can be made of the instrument, especially in the saving in field-party time, which is an important factor in the cost of any project.

The speed and accuracy of instrumental orientation for which it is designed, and is capable of performing, make it an ideal instrument for many classes of surveys, such as the survey of rights of way for all types of construction which constantly intersect property boundaries and where the directions of lines in terms of angular measurement from the true meridian are needed; the running of short control lines for fixing the relation of air photos for scale and orientation; the traversing of the banks of streams, lakes, and other irregular boundaries; the spotting of contours by transit methods; the checking of the azimuth of any line at any given point, and for all preliminary and exploration surveys.

RECORDS OF PUBLIC LAND SURVEYS *[1948]*

Copies of the plats and field notes representing all the public land surveys executed in the United States and Alaska are filed in the Bureau of Land Management, Washington, D.C. Copies of survey records are also filed in the District Offices of the Bureau, located at Phoenix, Arizona; Glendale, California; Denver, Colorado; Boise, Idaho; Helena, Montana; Reno, Nevada; Santa Fe, New Mexico; Salt Lake City, Utah; Cheyenne, Wyoming; and Juneau, Alaska. Each of these offices has the records pertaining to the individual state in which the respective office is located. In the other public land states where the surveys have been completed, the original records, formerly in branch offices of the former General Land Office, have been transferred to those states. The only exception is noted in the case of Oklahoma, where no records have been filed with the state.

The Bureau of Land Management issues a number of publications dealing with the public land surveys and resurveys—the most important and comprehensive of which is the Manual of Instructions for the Survey of the Public Lands of the United States, 1947. The Standard Field Tables and an annual publication of the Ephemeris of the Sun, Polaris and other Selected Stars are also available.

A pamphlet entitled "Restoration of Lost Obliterated Corners and Subdivision of Sections" has been issued for the guidance of county and other local surveyors.

II

Distribution of the Public Lands

Introduction

THOMAS LeDUC

AMONG the many weaknesses of the public land system in the nineteenth century, historians have attacked the appropriation by Congress of land, instead of cash, to support various public policies. Continuing the practice initiated in colonial days and followed by the states and the Confederation, the federal government donated land to military veterans and to settlers in certain frontier areas where it was sought to provide a base from which a militia could be summoned. So far from successful were these policies that historians agree that most of the land thus conveyed was not occupied by the grantees but sold to others. This tendency was so clearly evident in the results of the land bonus voted to soldiers in the War of 1812 that it must be inferred that behind the massive donations of the years from 1847 to 1855 lay the intent to favor speculators as well as veterans.

On an even larger scale, Congress appropriated land to encourage the building of roads, canals, and railroads. Historians have directed most of their study to the railroad grants voted from 1850 to 1871. The theory was that these grants, by encouraging private investment in railroads, would hasten economic development of the interior, carry government traffic at reduced rates, and raise the market value of lands retained by the government. How far these objectives were met has not yet been determined by sufficient study.

Another persistent weakness in the system was the failure of Congress throughout the nineteenth century to provide effective management of government-owned resources. Not only did federal policy contemplate disposal rather than public ownership, but the disposal program was oriented to the sale of lands suitable for tillage. Much of the land, however, was valuable mainly for its timber, grass, minerals, or coal. By neglect, Congress long condemned these resources to depredation or depletion. An early attempt to collect royalties on lead ores was sustained as constitutional but abandoned in the face of passive resistance. Until 1866 no further attempt was made to regulate the mining of metals, and it is estimated that gold and silver to a value of one billion dollars were removed from government land without payment. Attempts to prevent theft of valuable timber were so sporadic as to be negligible; no effort was made to protect the grassland.

Products of the anarchy generated by weak federal administration were the extralegal, and sometimes illegal, private organizations designed to control the use or disposal of public resources. Varying degrees of formality and of secrecy characterized the miners' associations and the claims clubs of settlers on tillable lands, but basically their purpose was to secure for their members economic advantages not allowed by law. The Pre-emption Act of 1841 authorized squatters to purchase at the minimum statutory price as much as 160 acres, provided they paid up before the land was offered for competitive bidding. To extend this valuable privilege, squatters organized to intimidate outside bidders and thus to enable members of the claims club either to postpone payment or to buy, at their pleasure, two, three, or four times as much land as the law permitted. Not at all uncommon was the sale by squatters of undeveloped claims to later settlers. Along with the large-scale absentee speculator, a universal figure on the land frontier was the petty resident speculator.

The Iowa Claim Clubs: Symbol and Substance

ALLAN G. BOGUE

Reprinted by permission from the Mississippi Valley Historical Review, *Volume 45 (1958), pages 231–253.*

THE claim club or squatters' association has long occupied a modest but secure place in western history. The presence of such extralegal organizations on the middle western frontier led students of the federal land system to suggest that the land laws in effect when the Middle West was being settled were ill-adapted to frontier needs.[1] Frederick Jackson Turner and others, going further, saw the claim clubs as a manifestation of the frontiersmen's capacity for democratic action.[2] No social historian, however, has fully explored the possibilities of the frontier claim club as an illustration of social interaction in newly formed frontier groups. Further study of this frontier institution can perhaps illuminate not only our understanding of American democracy but also our knowledge of the federal land disposal system and of pioneer social behavior.

Although claim clubs existed elsewhere in the Middle West, the Iowa variety has occasioned particular comment. When historians have believed citation to be in order, Jesse Macy's early study of institutional beginnings in Iowa, the records of the claim club in Johnson County, Iowa, edited by Benjamin F. Shambaugh, and Shambaugh's article on "Frontier Land Clubs or Claim Associations" have been standard exhibits.[3] To Shambaugh, who built upon Macy's work, the claim club was an organization which the settlers used to protect their claims on the public domain until they could obtain title from the federal government. Squatters organized such clubs, he suggested, so that they might forestall the land speculator and the claim jumper. Although pointing out that the claim club did allow settlers to transfer claims to which they had not received legal title, and that technically the squatters were trespassing, Shambaugh emphasized that these squatters were "honest farmers," establishing homes and improving their claims. Representing "the beginnings of Western local political institutions," the clubs fostered "natural justice, equality, and democracy." [4] Land historians and the authors of widely used western history texts have not deviated to any extent from this general interpretation. One text writer modified Shambaugh somewhat by suggesting that the clubs died out in Iowa because "the Pre-emption Law in 1841 ended the difficulty." [5]

Neither the work of Macy nor that of Shambaugh is heavily documented. Macy discovered the manuscript records of the Johnson County club and printed its by-laws in his essay, as well as the brief regulations of a lead miners' association at Dubuque. Although claiming that there were scores of these associations,[6] he referred specifically to only two. Shambaugh edited the complete record of the Johnson County club and transcribed the minutes of an association at Fort Dodge, drawing upon both of these sources for his article on frontier land clubs. He thought it "safe to say that over 100 of these extra-legal organizations existed in Territorial Iowa." [7] Old settlers who had observed club action still lived when Macy and Shambaugh investigated the claim clubs, and the former at least tapped the memories of some of these. Although they did not cite them, a number of contemporary descriptions and reminiscences substantiating the Macy and Shambaugh interpretation of the role of the squatters' club were also available.[8]

Histories of Iowa counties, most of which were unavailable or were ignored by Macy and Shambaugh, provide additional source material on the claim clubs.[9] They show clearly that Iowa settlers frequently held "claims" in the public domain for varying lengths of time before they tried to obtain title from the federal government. Organized claim clubs, however, definitely existed in only twenty-five counties, if, on the evidence in the county histories, we limit ourselves to those instances where the names of club members are given and to specific descriptions of local club activity. If we accept as authentic a general description of club activity in Cedar County, published in a local newspaper and later copied in two county histories, the number is raised to twenty-six.[10]

A few associations which did not quite conform to type were also described in the county histories. Settlers in Lee County, for example, banded together in opposition to the title of non-resident speculators in the Half Breed Tract during the 1830's and 1840's.[11] Along the Des

Moines River to the north of the Raccoon Fork, settlers on lands claimed by the Des Moines River Navigation and Railroad Company united to fight the title of the eastern grantees of the company in a struggle which continued from the 1860's to the 1890's.[12] In O'Brien and Monona counties, settlers organized to contest the title to lands which railroad corporations claimed as part of their land grants.[13] A number of homesteaders who had falsely certified that they were of legal age banded together in Sioux County to intimidate settlers who might wish to contest their titles.[14] Finally, the local historian of Sac County told of the residents of two townships who packed the land office at Sioux City when their claims were offered at auction to prevent speculators from bidding, because the settlers as yet lacked the means to purchase them.[15]

Of the twenty-six counties in which claim clubs of the usual type existed, nineteen lay contiguous one to the other—outliers running north, south, and east from a solid block of nine counties located in the third and fourth tiers of counties north from the Missouri border and lying in the east central portion of the state. Most of these counties were settled during the 1830's and 1840's, but they were not the only counties settled in that period. In general, also, considerable numbers of settlers of southern stock settled in these counties, although not to the same degree as in the counties in the two southern tiers. Those counties in which the southern stock mingled with Yankee or alien settlers made up the central block of claim club counties.[16] Whether the tensions generated by the mixing of cultural stocks stimulated the formation of organizations designed to deal with the basic problem of control of the land in these frontier settlements can only be conjectured. Very definitely, however, club activity was not linked to the absence of a pre-emption law. In the first place, limited pre-emption laws applied to many of the settlers who moved to Iowa prior to 1841, and secondly the claim clubs in sixteen of the twenty-six counties were active considerably after the passage of the general pre-emption act of 1841.[17]

The county histories contain all or a portion of the club laws in nineteen cases, and in a few instances the original manuscript records are still available.[18] The manuscript records of the Johnson County and the Fort Dodge claim clubs give a much more accurate picture of squatter law in those counties than do the secondary accounts in the published histories of Johnson and Webster counties. The club laws ranged all the way from the general to the specific, depending in part, perhaps, on the degree of pressure to which the organizers believed themselves subject and in part on the predilections of those who drew up the regulations. Granted such local variations, the regulations covered the size of the claims allowed; directions for marking, registering, and transferring claims; and the procedure to be followed when club members contested each other's rights, when members were threatened by claim jumpers, and when the date of the land sale arrived.

In any re-evaluation of the role of the squatters' associations, the responsibilities and the privileges of the members must be carefully considered in order to discover whether they were consistent with the avowed purpose of the clubs. The pioneers justified the organization of claim clubs on a variety of grounds. In some cases formal justification was given as a preamble to the club regulations. Most common was the wording, "Whereas it has become a custom in the western states, as soon as the Indian title to the public lands has been extinguished by the General Government for the citizens of the United States to settle upon and improve said lands, and heretofore the improvement and claim of the settler to the extent of 320 acres, has been respected by both the citizens and laws of Iowa . . ."[19] Other clubs emphasized the need of protection against "reckless claim jumpers and invidious wolves in human form," or the need "for better security against foreign as well as domestic aggression."[20] In a number of cases the acquisition and peaceable possession of land were given in the preamble as objectives of the settlers. Improvement of the claims was usually stated as an obligation of the members. In no case did a preamble specifically mention preservation of the home.

The squatter could expect that his comrades in the club would come to his assistance if claim jumpers threatened his holding and that similarly his friends would intimidate speculators who might seek to outbid him at the land auction. The settlers who organized the Jackson and Mahaska county clubs agreed to protect each other in the enjoyment of their claims for a period of two years, if necessary, after the land sales.[21] The squatters usually placed an upper limit upon the size of the claim to be protected. In ten out of fourteen cases the maximum was set at 320 acres, but in two instances 480 acres was specified, and on one occasion 200 acres. Club members in another county limited themselves to 160 acres, but allowed each other to reserve an additional 160 acres for a non-resident friend. In Poweshiek, Johnson, and Webster counties, where the manuscript claim records were preserved in rather complete form, one did not have to be a resident to enjoy the protection of the club. Nor was it necessary in some clubs for a settler to have attained his majority. In two cases the minimum age of members was set at sixteen years, in one instance at seventeen, and in two others at eighteen. None of the clubs forbade members to sell their claims; indeed the right to make such transfers was specifically guaranteed at times and the purchaser assured of the protection of the club.

If the squatters of a claim club expected to benefit from membership, they also assumed responsibilities. They pledged that they would assist their officers in maintaining club law in their districts should it be challenged. They promised to co-operate with the other members in intimidatory action at the land auction if necessary. In some clubs members paid small sums to the recorder or other club officers for their services. Regulations prescribing the degree to which the member must improve his claim appear in the manuscript records of the Poweshiek, Johnson, and Webster county associations, but not in the selections of the club laws printed in the histories of other counties. The members of the Webster County or Fort Dodge club agreed to expend labor worth $10 on their claims each month after the first month. The members of the Poweshiek Protection Society pledged in their revised by-laws to put in $30 worth of labor on their claims within six months of registration and $30 additional labor for each succeeding six months the claim was held. In the Johnson County club, however, only non-residents were compelled to improve their claims to the extent of $50 worth of labor for each six months held. If the squatters actually envisioned developing their holdings into productive farms and homes, it would seem reasonable to expect more frequent and more stringent improvement requirements in the club laws.

Questions might also be raised concerning the motives of the members in protecting the claims of minors, who were ineligible to purchase land under the pre-emption law. Allowing membership to minors was no doubt justified in the eyes of members on the grounds that the minor might well be of age by the time of the government land sales, but it might also have been used by squatters to acquire additional land through their children. The club laws also reveal that although all clubs regarded the public auction as the main reason for their existence, a number of them pledged themselves to maintain control of the claims beyond the date of the land sales. In addition, most club regulations provided that the squatters could claim an acreage which was much larger than needed for a farm unit in the mid-nineteenth-century Middle West.

Local historians often viewed club activities in the same light as did Shambaugh. Extralegal though its activities might be, the claim club was justified, they said, because it protected the honest squatter against the claim jumper and the land speculator and allowed him to improve his claim and protect his home. As one local historian put it, ". . . the thought was intolerable that speculators, or eleventh-hour newcomers who knew nothing of the burden and heat of the day should enter upon land which actual settlers had staked out and tilled, and upon which they had builded homes." [22] Some writers admitted that inequities perhaps resulted from club action, but they obviously believed that these were trifling in comparison to the beneficial achievements of the clubs. In nine of the twenty-six accounts, however, the authors introduced material which ran counter to the usual interpretation, some apparently not realizing the conflict. For example, a local historian of Cedar County wrote:

Early in the county's history, a ring of mercenary characters, anticipating immigration, claimed all the untaken groves and wooded tracts in the county, and when an actual settler—one who wanted land for a home and immediate occupancy . . . settled on a portion of the land rings' domain, he was immediately set upon by the bloodhounds, and it was demanded of him that he either abandon the claim or pay them for what they maintained was their right. If the settler expressed doubts of their having previously claimed their site, the "ring" always had one or more witnesses at hand to testify to the validity of the interest they asserted. The result was nearly always the same. These settlers, more to avoid difficulties than for any other reason, would purchase their pretended right for forty, fifty or one hundred dollars, more or less, according to value after which the ring was ready for operation in some other locality.[23]

Such activity, continued the writer, led the "settlers who came to find homes" to form mutual protection leagues to resist such bogus land claimants. Undoubtedly, however, the persons in the "ring" defended their behavior on the grounds that they were acting under claim law and as members of a squatters' association.

An incident in Clinton County reveals the possible inequities of claim club activity. David Hess and his family, late-comers to the county, wished to settle near the town of Lyons, where they had discovered former neighbors from the East, but they "found that the 'claim-makers' had ploughed their furrows and set their corner stakes around all the land near the river, leaving their agents to 'sell-out' while they had sought new fields for similar enterprise." [24] The Hesses decided to go elsewhere, but their old neighbors interceded with the other residents of the settlement and they were "informed that they were at liberty to settle upon any lands not occupied by an actual settler, and that the settlers would protect them against all claimants." Here, evidently, the early comers had banded together to sell government land to late-comers on the pretext that it was claimed land, although the claims they were selling had no substantial improvements on them and were not occupied. Daniel H. Pearce, one of the early settlers in Clinton, later wrote:

Some of the chivalry, or gentlemen of elegant leisure, followed the business of making claims and selling them to emigrants as they came through. As soon as a new settler arrived, the above named gentry would ascertain his "pile," by some means best known to themselves. They would then have a claim to suit the newcomer's purpose and purse, and, if he demurred paying anything to them, contending that his right to the public land was as good as theirs, they would very soon convince him of his error. He would be summoned to appear before a justice of the peace as a trespasser, or, as they called it, a "claim jumper." The magistrate issuing the summons belonged to the fraternity, and the poor settler would have to sell out or leave, and, even if he went, would have to go a poorer if not sadder man. [25]

Pearce may have been moved somewhat by resentment, since he admitted having himself contested title to a tract of land with the squatter element, but his account does corroborate the evidence given by Hess.

A similar situation existed in Appanoose County, where a claim club had been organized in 1845. There, the resident friends of a group of newly arrived settlers pointed out to the newcomers good farm locations which were unoccupied but claimed by other settlers. Although the club was called out in force as a result, the local residents who had tried to assist their friends stood fast, maintaining that they would not hesitate to point out surplus lands to inquirers in those instances where the ostensible claimant already held a quarter section plus a reasonable amount of timberland. [26] Some local historians make it clear that claim club action was often precipitated not by a threat to a squatter's occupied claim but rather by the effort of a squatter to defend an unoccupied second tract against the claim of late-comers. The historian of Harrison County tells in language more expressive than precise of a "claim jumper" who "thought that because the claimant held down a good hundred and sixty acre tract, that, having spread himself over this number of acres, that there was not enough left of the said claimant to amount to [as] much as the additional one hundred and sixty acre claim." Within an hour, according to this account, "a score of earnest, angry men," had brought the "claim jumper" before a settler jury. This same historian justified club action because the "'home,' absolute right of all, was invaded." [27]

In his history of Marion County, William M. Donnel pointed out that the spirit of monopoly was not confined to speculators. He wrote: "Many settlers were not content with the amount of land the law entitled them to, but made pretended claims to so large a portion of the territory, that in some instances, it was difficult for a buyer to find an unclaimed lot. Of course such claims were without improvements, but the pretended claimants, by representing themselves as the real owners thereof, would frequently impose upon some unwary buyer, or, by threats extort from him sums, varying in proportion to the supposed value of the claim, or whatever sum could be obtained." [28] Donnel then told of a member of his family who had been forced by the local claim club to reimburse a club member for his rights in land which he had already entered at the land office in the belief that it was unoccupied. Donnel's account incidentally provides an illustration of the way in which the nature of club activities may have been transmuted with the passing of time. Although two subsequent historians of Marion County evidently drew upon Donnel's description of club activities, their narratives, dedicated to the glorification of the pioneer past, omitted the material which failed to show the claim club as the protector of the frontier hearth. [29]

The descriptions of claim club activities in some of the other local histories also show the clubs as protectors of greedy settlers as well as protectors of the home. James W. Merrill, for example, in his history of two townships in Des Moines County, climaxed his account of the claim system with a description of the land sale at Burlington. In general the settlers were not an extremely prosperous group, he said, but "Some sold claims on lands contiguous to their homestead for enough money to make their entry. Others borrowed money for that purpose. Many 'Barretted,'—a word coined to signify allowing a lender to take title till the settler could pay." [30] Here then is one explanation for the large holdings allowed by the claim club to its members. Such holdings represented not only a prospective farm but the means to purchase it, if all went well and a newcomer could be sold an unimproved claim. Many settlers, according to Merrill, did not even take the trouble to purchase the land they claimed from the government. As soon as an opportunity appeared they sold their claims and moved on, leaving the purchasers the problem of establishing their titles.

In writing of Kossuth County, Benjamin F. Reed candidly admitted that "some made considerable easy money by constantly taking claims and then selling their rights to them," although Reed believed that the claim clubs did not countenance such methods.[31] In Madison County, an area which was "singularly free of molestation by land speculation," according to the local historian, a claim club was organized by a small group of settlers. "Half a dozen persons who, in a small and modest manner, were doing something in a legitimate way, at trading in claims to 'accommodate new settlers,' jumped aboard the proposition" to form a club.[32] This squatters' association seems therefore to have been organized as a means of protecting the trade in claims rather than as a device to protect the home from the speculator and the claim jumper. One unusual indication that the clubs were not always considered as desirable institutions appeared in Monroe County, where the members of a local Presbyterian church declared outright defiance of the claim association and ultimately broke it up.[33]

Analysis of the variant accounts in the county histories would seem to cast doubt on the traditional assumption that claim clubs were always a wholesome manifestation of democracy at work on the frontier. Instead, another pattern of club activity seems to emerge, in which the clubs were organized by claim speculators rather than by settlers, and in many instances were actually used against the best interests of the very same settlers who have usually received the credit for creating and operating them. The soundness of this alternative interpretation can perhaps best be tested by a more detailed analysis of the information contained in the manuscript records of the Johnson, Poweshiek, and Fort Dodge clubs.

Professor Shambaugh argued that the Johnson County claim club was "in its organization and administration, one of the most perfect . . . in the West." [34] Actually, the detailed nature and length of the club's published records, which along with the editor's introduction and an index fill 215 pages, suggest the atypical. The size of the club and the activity of its members perhaps stemmed from the fact that the designation of Iowa City as the territorial capital in 1839 made claims more valuable in Johnson County than elsewhere. In all, 325 individuals either signed the compact of the claim club, filed claims, or participated in transactions noted by the recorder between March, 1838, and January, 1843.[35] The members of the group fell into at least nine discernible categories. Ninety-six settlers filed from one to three claims under the auspices of the association. Another seventy-three signed the compact but did not appear in the claim and deed record of the club. In contrast to the members of this group, forty-three individuals appeared in the record four or more times; Samuel Bumgardner, indeed, was a party in twenty-two entries. Although filing no original claims of their own, forty-two settlers purchased from one to three claims. Seventeen pioneers filed claims and also sold claims, not always the same ones. Three groups, each consisting of sixteen individuals, either filed original claims and also purchased claims, or purchased a claim and sold one, or merely sold claims not originally registered in the club records. Finally, a small group of six filed one claim, purchased one claim, and sold one claim.

Further analysis of the Johnson County club membership sheds light on the motivation of these pioneers. The settlers who merely filed claim entries made up only about 30 per cent of the group, although the simple filing of a claim supposedly characterized the Macy-Shambaugh stereotype of a claim club member. The fact that seventy-three names affixed to the club compact do not appear again in the record and that another sixteen club members sold claims which were not on record suggests also that the claim record is not the complete chronicle of membership activity that Shambaugh believed it to be. Some 13 per cent of the association members appeared in four or more entries on the claim record. Although a certain amount of trading in claims might be occasioned by the running of the congressional surveys, there seems little need for the actual settler to have been involved in more than three entries if he simply wished to make, hold, and improve his future home. Close examination of the transactions in which members with multiple entries were involved shows that many of them were dealing in claims—they were, in other words, claim speculators. Six of the first seven men who signed the club compact in Johnson County appeared in four or more entries on the club record, and of the eighteen officers who served the club, thirteen fell into the same category. Although the members might describe their activities as "garding our rights against the speculator," [36] the land dealer and the engrosser were actually in their midst.

Of course the claim dealer's operations were petty in comparison to those of land speculators who purchased large holdings at the land sale or entered considerable acreages at private entry after the auction. But in Johnson County even flagrant land speculators were not excluded from membership in the claim club, despite the worthy resolutions of the squatters. Morgan Reno, who entered one claim on the club record, proved to be anything but an impecunious settler when the land was offered by the federal government. In the townships subject to club law in Johnson County, Reno purchased 2,834 acres, enough land, probably, for thirty farm units. He also purchased land in at least one nearby county. Although it is difficult to be certain, some of his purchases may be illustrations of the time entry system, the practice known among the settlers at the Burlington sales as "Barretting."

Did the claim club insure that the member obtained his claim at the land sale? To this question the abstract of original entries and the deed indexes of Johnson County hold an answer.[37] Of the 325 individuals whose names appear in the club records, 115, or only 35 per cent, actually purchased land from the federal government in the townships where club law was in force. If the claim club in Johnson County was designed to insure that the claim holder purchased his claim, it was manifestly a very imperfect mechanism. What is more, those members who best fit the settlement pattern sketched by Macy and Shambaugh did least well: only twenty-five, or 26 per cent, of those who simply entered claims on the club record purchased land from the federal government at or immediately after the land sales. Conversely, those who most often followed through and purchased land came from the group which comprised the claim speculator element: twenty-two, or 51 per cent, of those individuals purchased federal land.

Not long after the land sales, four squatters in Johnson County obtained deeds to part of their original claims from individuals who had purchased them from the federal government. Since many of the claims filed with the club cannot be identified because the congressional survey descriptions were not given, it is not possible to say how many other settlers may have acquired a portion of their claims in the same way. This was the type of purchase pattern found when settlers resorted to the time entry system. The settler allowed a capitalist to purchase his claim with the understanding that the settler might repurchase all or a portion of it as soon as possible after the government auction. In such an arrangement the capitalist might give a bond for a deed in return for the settler's note. Other squatters in the Johnson County club purchased holdings from land speculators, although they failed to obtain title to their original claims. Perhaps prior agreements between the parties had been reached in these cases as well.

Of the 210 club members who failed to purchase land from the federal government, 68 did obtain land in the community within ten years after the date of the last land sale. Since credit extended under the time entry system was ordinarily short-term in nature, anyone who had resorted to the money-lending speculator at the land sales would undoubtedly have completed his purchase in the ten-year time span. These findings change the picture somewhat: 35 per cent of the squatters purchased government land at the auction, another 21 per cent ultimately obtained land in the community, and 44 per cent did not obtain any holding at all. Perhaps some members of this last group did resort to the speculator but failed to meet their obligations and saw their claims fall into other hands. But among the sixty-eight settlers who ultimately purchased land in Johnson County from vendors other than the federal government, one major sub-category stands out. Thirty-one members of this group obtained title to lots within Iowa City, although often holding other land as well. Were these members squatters intent upon improving their claims and defending their homes, or were they businessmen hoping to profit from the increased value of land in the vicinity of the county seat and territorial capital?

In the case both of squatters who purchased land from the federal government and of those who, failing to do so, subsequently obtained land in the community from other sources, other qualifications must be made. Dealing first with the 115 federal land purchasers, 31 did not appear again in the club records except as signatories to the compact. If they had claims they either did not record them or they purchased them so late in the history of the club that it did not seem worth while to put them on record. The claims of another thirty-five federal land purchasers were described so loosely that it is impossible to locate them accurately, or to determine whether their original claims coincided with their later purchases from the federal government. In twenty-three other cases, however, the squatters bought land other than their own claims. Four squatters who owned several claims did not purchase the claims which they described in terms of the congressional survey, although they may have purchased claims which they had described less precisely. Only 22 of 115 purchasers from the federal government, therefore, ultimately and unquestionably gained possession of their original claims. Similarly, a sizable percentage of the sixty-eight squatters who did not purchase government land but who ultimately obtained land in the community did not acquire their original claims. Of thirty-five persons whose claims could be positively located, only fourteen, by the most generous of interpretations, ultimately obtained title to a portion of their claims, and the land acquired by the remaining twenty-one definitely was not a part of their claims. Where it was possible to check, therefore, fewer than half of the squatters who obtained land in Johnson County actually acquired their original claims—the "homes" which they were defending against the speculator.

Further light is shed upon the role of the Johnson County claim club by a close examination of one of the incidents in which the club exercised its punitive power. Shambaugh gave a detailed account of the incident, drawing upon an unfinished history of Johnson County, which was written by two former members of the association, Cyrus Sanders and Henry Felkner. These writers described the efforts of the club members in 1839 to drive "a man named Crawford" from a claim owned by William Sturgis. When Crawford refused to abandon the claim, even though Sturgis offered to pay for the improvements, some sixty members of the club under the leadership of its marshal tore down Crawford's substantial log and clapboard cabin. Crawford then rebuilt the cabin and moved his family into it. The club members returned to the claim, however, and this time Crawford "adjusted" the matter to the "full satisfaction" of Sturgis.[38]

To both Shambaugh and Roscoe Lokken, the historian of public land disposal in Iowa, the Sturgis-Crawford incident was illustrative of claim club action. Lokken cited it as an illustration of "pioneer justice." [39] The action of the aggrieved squatter Sturgis, however, did not conform to the pattern of squatter democracy sketched by Macy, Shambaugh, and those who have relied upon them. Sturgis apparently had not made any improvements on the claim, for if he had Sanders and Felkner would certainly have mentioned them. Between April 1, 1839, and March 9, 1843, the name of William Sturgis appeared repeatedly on the club record.[40] He filed three claims, purchased five additional claims for an outlay of $270, and sold five claims for sums totaling $400. The amount of the "adjustment" with Crawford does not appear in the claim record. At the land sales, Sturgis purchased 463 acres—much more than any pioneer farmer needed for farming operations. Patently he was no hard-pressed pioneer defending his home; and in the Crawford incident he was playing the role of a claim speculator who used the club for support in extorting tribute from late-comers to the community. That the club membership would twice mobilize to support Sturgis illuminates the sympathies and aspirations of his colleagues in the association.

Records of the Poweshiek County claim club show some patterns of activity similar to that of the Johnson County club. On February 22, 1851, the members of the Poweshiek club revised their claim laws. The reason for the change is not explicitly stated, but a reference to "actual settlers" in the first resolution of the amended rules suggests that the club members may have attempted to exclude claim speculators from the new organization.[41] If that was their aim they did not entirely succeed, as the following analysis of the club records shows.

Ninety-one settlers of Poweshiek County registered claims with the club after the revision of the rules.[42] Of this group, thirty, or 32 per cent, purchased land from the federal government in the sections in which they had reserved claims in the club records.[43] Fourteen of these settlers, however, did not purchase any of their original claim but purchased instead a tract or tracts adjoining. Although the thirty entrymen had originally laid claim to some 5,200 acres, their purchase of government land in the final analysis amounted to only 2,700 acres. Of the sixty-one members who did not purchase federal land, forty-five, or 49 per cent of the total registrants, did obtain title to land in Poweshiek County before the end of 1860. The club recorder preserved a complete description of the claims of all but two of this group of forty-five. Of those whose claims were adequately described on the club roll, sixteen obtained all or, more often, a portion of their claim. But the first deeds of record of twenty-seven, or 60 per cent, of this group embraced lands which had not been part of their claims. The purchasing patterns of three individuals placed them in a separate category. These three settlers bought government land outside the limits of the sections in which their claim was located. In one instance the purchase was considerably removed from the original claim; in the other two cases it lay in an adjacent section. In addition to these purchases from the government, each of these three men acquired tracts of land from private landholders. Of the forty-eight club members who purchased land from holders other than the federal government, fourteen—almost a third—purchased lots in Montezuma, the county seat. We may question, therefore, whether these were genuine pioneer farmers. One further category of claim club members remains to be mentioned. Thirteen, or 15 per cent of the membership, did not purchase land directly from the federal government, nor do they appear on the early deed registers of Poweshiek County as having acquired any landed estate whatsoever.

Evidence in Poweshiek County points to the time entry system more clearly than in Johnson County. In seventeen cases in which a settler subsequently acquired all or a portion of his claim subsequent to its original disposition by the federal government, the grantor could be easily identified as a speculator or land agent. Furthermore, a number of settlers acquired title to tracts lying outside their original claims from members of the speculator group—perhaps by the time entry system.

Although 85 per cent of the members of the reformed Poweshiek club did acquire land in the county, only one-third of them were able to purchase a portion of their claims directly from the government; and their total purchases of government land amounted to only about 50 per cent of the area of their original claims. Quite possibly some of the group sold a portion of their claims before or at the land sale. Almost half of the settlers purchased their land after it had passed through the hands of an intermediary, who in many cases evidently provided a source of credit. For this group the claim club could have been important not because it protected the members from speculator bids but rather because it strengthened the settler's bargaining power when he arranged for the speculator to purchase his claim.

Between July, 1854, and June, 1856, a claim club was active in the district centering at Fort Dodge on the upper Des Moines River, where 255 squatters claimed land which today falls within the boundaries of Webster and Humboldt counties. A few other settlers filed claims to land in other nearby counties, but analysis of the behavior of the settlers in Webster and Humboldt adequately reveals the workings of this association.[44] Sixty-eight of the 255 club members actually purchased all or a portion of their claims from the federal government when the lands were offered for sale at Fort Dodge.[45] Another five settlers purchased land from the government which was not part of their original claims. The seventy-three settlers who thus acquired land directly from the government made up 29 per cent of the total group. These seventy-three purchasers claimed 23,873 acres of land, but they bought only 12,442 acres at the land office. Thirty of the seventy-three were not the original claimants to the tracts which they acquired but had purchased the claims from the squatters who had first filed descriptions.

Another 54 of the 255 claim club members in Webster and Humboldt counties, or 21 per cent, did acquire title to land in these counties before the end of 1866, although they did not purchase their claims from the federal government. In only two cases did the deeds recorded by the members of this group cover a portion of the claims which they had reserved on the club record. If members of this group had conformed to the Macy-Shambaugh stereotype the deeds should uniformly have covered their claims. Actually, thirty-one of the fifty-four members of this group recorded deeds to lots in Fort Dodge or, in two instances, in a nearby townsite.

In Humboldt and Webster counties, 128 of the squatters, or 50 per cent, fell into a third category—those who neither purchased land directly from the federal government nor acquired it from private parties. Seventy-two per cent of the squatters from Humboldt County and 41 per cent of those from Webster County fell into this group.[46] Of the group of 128 squatters who failed to acquire title in the two counties, 20 did transfer their claims to other parties; if the remainder did so, the club records give no clue to the fact.

Although many claims were sold in Webster and Humboldt counties, there seems to have been much less dealing in claims than in Johnson County. Nor can we be certain that the time entry system was at work to any extent in the Fort Dodge area. Ultimately the Fort Dodge club was to be described as a tool of land speculators, but since the charges appeared in a hard-fought political campaign, they should perhaps be discounted.[47]

Comparison of the percentages of entrymen, private land buyers, and non-landholders provides a foundation for generalizations upon the three clubs for which manuscript records exist. Strikingly similar percentages of entrymen were found in each club. About one-third of the members of each club actually purchased land from the federal government. Not all of these purchases by any means, however, represented the purchase of the actual claims recorded with the claim club. In this last respect, however, the Fort Dodge club was exceptional; almost all of the entrymen did obtain a portion of their original claims. Whether their purchases were or were not part of the original claims, the entrymen in each club purchased only about half of the acreage which they had originally reserved on the club record. In both the Johnson and Fort Dodge clubs 21 per cent of the membership failed to buy federal land but did ultimately acquire a holding of some sort from other sources. These percentages contrast sharply with the 49 per cent who fell into this category in Poweshiek. In every case, however, a considerable number of settlers in this group, ranging from slightly less than a third in Poweshiek to more than half in the Fort Dodge area, were very probably town businessmen, since they acquired lots in the county seat. One can question whether such individuals ever seriously contemplated developing their claims as agricultural properties. In Johnson County 44 per cent of the squatters apparently never acquired land in the county, or at least obtained such land so many years after the land sales that the claim club cannot be said to have aided them. The corresponding proportion at Fort Dodge was 50 per cent. In Poweshiek County, however, only 15 per cent of the club members failed to acquire land.

The striking difference in the number of purchasers and non-purchasers in Poweshiek County as compared to that of the other two clubs is puzzling. It is possible that earlier members of the Poweshiek association who had left the community were simply dropped from the rolls when the club reorganized in 1851, and that the claim register of the reorganized club, therefore, did not show all of those who at one time held claims. Possibly, also, more club members in Poweshiek County acquired land because fewer petty speculators were attracted to that area than to Iowa City and Fort Dodge, towns that aspired to become state and regional centers.

These details concerning the behavior of the squatters and the activities of the claim clubs in Johnson, Poweshiek, Webster, and Humboldt counties clearly reveal certain conditions which have not received adequate attention in the standard accounts of claim clubs in Iowa. One of the most striking oversights is the failure to take into account the fact that only a small percentage of the squatters actually purchased their land directly from the federal government. If the claim club was designed to insure that the squatter could purchase his claim from the government, "that practical, inventive turn of mind, quick to find expedients," [48] which Turner saw as a characteristic of frontiersmen, had produced a highly inadequate solution to the problem. The standard accounts have also failed to show that the actual entrymen acquired only about half of the area claimed, and that even such purchases as they made were often not a portion of the original claim. In the light of the evidence that many settlers wanted to sell all or a portion of their claims, these discrepancies between squatters and entrymen and between claim and purchase become more readily understandable. Presumably the squatter might apply the revenue from such sales to the purchase of a clear title to other land—an unsold portion of his claim, perhaps, or unoccupied land elsewhere in the vicinity. This may explain why a large percentage of the Poweshiek entrymen purchased other land close-by instead of their own claims. When the squatter raised funds for buying land by selling his own claim, the club of course had in a way been of assistance to him, since without his fellows at his back he might not have been able to extract anything from the late-coming settler or the speculator.

It was in Johnson County that the sale of claims was most striking. Although many settlers in Webster and Humboldt counties recorded sales or transfers, and some had claims totaling as much as a section and a half, none rivaled the Johnson County club member who participated in more than twenty claim transactions. Holdings in excess of the club rules were common in Johnson County. Ironically, the outstanding illustration of the club militant in Johnson County—the Crawford-Sturgis case—turned out on analysis to be a case of coercion of an actual settler at the behest of a claim dealer.

Neither Shambaugh nor Macy described the time entry system or connected it in any way with claim club activities. When squatters' claims were purchased from the federal government by a land agent or speculator who deeded a portion to the original claimant within a few years, the time entry system was apparently in use. Here the speculator benefited from interest charged on the investment which he made for the squatter, and he might also acquire outright possession of a portion of the claim. Particularly in Poweshiek County, but also in Johnson County, this was the case. The existence of the time entry system shows the hollowness of the squatters' criticism of the speculators. The speculator was a necessity to the squatter who desired to purchase land but who did not have the cash. Had there not been speculators, some settlers would not have been able to acquire title. The claim club could have been of assistance to such a squatter by strengthening his bargaining position.

Thus much of the evidence derived from the records of three Iowa claim clubs and the appropriate county records supports the view of claim club activity given by the dissenting local historians rather than the Macy-Shambaugh interpretation. No doubt squatter associations did protect many an honest settler in the enjoyment of improvements and in the purchase of a home from the federal government, but the clubs also shielded the activities of others whose motives and procedures were far more complex. At times the squatters' association was the vehicle of men who sought simply to capitalize on priority or to meet the financial problem posed by a government minimum price of $1.25 per acre by deriving fictitious values from a cunning mixture of brute force and virgin land. If we are to understand the role of the claim club, therefore, we must not confuse the symbols of agrarian democracy with its substance.

NOTES

1 Benjamin Horace Hibbard, *A History of the Public Land Policies* (New York, 1924), 198–208; Roy M. Robbins, *Our Landed Heritage: The Public Domain, 1776–1936* (Princeton, 1942), 67–68; George M. Stephenson, *The Political History of the Public Lands from 1840 to 1862: From Pre-emption to Homestead* (Boston, 1917), 20–23.

2 Frederick Jackson Turner, *The Frontier in American History* (New York, 1920), 137, 212.

3 Jesse Macy, *Institutional Beginnings in a Western State* (*Johns Hopkins University Studies in Historical and Political Science*, series 2, no. 7, Baltimore, 1884); Benjamin F. Shambaugh, ed., *Constitution and Records of the Claim Association of Johnson County, Iowa* (Iowa City, 1894); and Shambaugh, "Frontier Land Clubs or Claim Associations," American Historical Association, *Annual Report*, 1900 (2 vols., Washington, 1901), 1:67–85.

4 Shambaugh, "Frontier Land Clubs or Claim Associations," 71, 83.

5 Ray A. Billington, *Westward Expansion: A History of the American Frontier* (New York, 1949), 476. See also Robert E. Riegel, *America Moves West* (3d ed., New York, 1956), 410–411; Roscoe L. Lokken, *Iowa Public Land Disposal* (Iowa City, 1942), 69–75; and the general works by Hibbard, Robbins, and Stephenson cited in note 1 above.

6 Macy, *Institutional Beginnings*, 5.

7 Shambaugh, "Frontier Land Clubs or Claim Associations," 72.

8 See Albert M. Lea, *Notes on the Wisconsin Territory; Particularly with Reference to the Iowa District or Black Hawk Purchase* (Philadelphia, 1836), reprinted by the State Historical Society of Iowa as *The Book that Gave Iowa Its Name* (Iowa City, n.d.), 18–21; John B. Newhall, *Sketches of Iowa, or the Emigrant's Guide* (New York, 1841), 54–58; Hawkins Taylor, "Squatters and Speculators at the First Land Sales," *Annals of Iowa* (Iowa City–Des Moines), first series, 8:269–274 (July, 1870); Charles A. White, "The Early Homes and Home-Makers of Iowa," *ibid.*, third series, 4:179–195 (October, 1899).

9 The writer checked all of the Iowa county histories available in the library of the Iowa State Historical Society at Iowa City and in the extensive collection of the library at Iowa State College, Ames. For ninety-eight of the ninety-nine counties in Iowa he found at least one history available, and in some cases as many as four. Such histories are admittedly a treacherous type of source. A number of middle western companies specialized in publishing these bulky catch-alls during the

late nineteenth and early twentieth centuries. Several of the companies accumulated a supply of filler which the editors included in every history, while at the same time supplementing this material county by county with information compiled by anonymous local agents. The reader must take care, therefore, to distinguish between filler and information which bears specifically upon the county under study. The Union Historical Company included a passage of filler on claim clubs in its Iowa county histories, which was supplemented by seemingly authentic local information, when available, or was left to stand by itself at times in apparent but undocumented testimony to the presence of squatters' associations. On the other hand, no publisher could be too cavalier in handling the facts because the major market for the histories lay in the home county and flagrant inaccuracies might cause protest. Nor was the general approach in these histories one that the historian finds conducive to accuracy. Dedicated sometimes to the pioneers in the hope that their "virtues may be emulated and . . . [their] toils and sacrifices duly appreciated," they are unblushingly filiopietistic. No doubt the publishers found this formula to be remunerative, but it could hardly fail to influence both the selection and the interpretation of materials. This being the case, we must give more weight to incidents which show a less flattering side to pioneer behavior than the frequency of their appearance in the county histories might seem to justify.

Since most of the county histories have extremely long titles and since there is little danger of misleading the research study by doing so, shortened titles with ellipses are used in the first citation to each in the references which follow, and the ellipses are omitted in later citations to the same work.

10 Western Historical Company, *The History of Appanoose County, Iowa* . . . (Chicago, 1878), 364–366; Union Historical Company, *The History of Boone County, Iowa* . . . (Des Moines, 1880), 326–331; Western Historical Company, *The History of Cedar County, Iowa* . . . (Chicago, 1878), 325; Western Historical Company, *The History of Clinton County, Iowa* . . . (Chicago, 1879), 444–446; Union Historical Company, *The History of Dallas County, Iowa* . . . (Des Moines, 1879), 324–326; Western Historical Company, *The History of Des Moines County, Iowa* . . . (Chicago, 1879), 377–379; Franklin T. Oldt and Patrick J. Quigley, *History of Dubuque County, Iowa* . . . (Chicago, 1911), 480; Pioneer Publishing Company, *History of Emmet County and Dickinson County, Iowa* . . . (2 vols., Chicago, 1917), 1:256–257; Union Publishing Company, *History of Hardin County, Iowa* . . . (Springfield, Ill., 1883), 967; Joseph H. Smith, *History of Harrison County, Iowa* . . . (Des Moines, 1888), 80–83; Western Historical Company, *The History of Jackson County, Iowa* . . . (Chicago, 1879), 333–335; Western Historical Company, *The History of Jasper County, Iowa* . . . (Chicago, 1888), 350; *History of Johnson County, Iowa* . . . (Iowa City, 1883), 323–331; Union Historical Company, *The History of Keokuk County, Iowa* . . . (Des Moines, 1880), 317–325; Union Historical Company, *History of*

Kossuth, Hancock, and Winnebago Counties, Iowa . . . (Springfield, Ill., 1884), 240; Western Historical Company, *The History of Lee County, Iowa* . . . (Chicago, 1879), 440–443; Herman A. Mueller, *History of Madison County, Iowa* . . . (2 vols., Chicago, 1915), 1:126–137; Union Historical Company, *The History of Mahaska County, Iowa* . . . (Des Moines, 1878), 293–297; William M. Donnel, *Pioneers of Marion County, Consisting of a General History of the County* . . . (Des Moines, 1872), 42–49; Western Historical Company, *The History of Monroe County, Iowa* . . . (Chicago, 1878), 376–377; Johnson Brigham, *Des Moines, The Pioneer of Municipal Progress and Reform of the Middle West, Together with the History of Polk County, Iowa* . . . (2 vols., Chicago, 1911), 1:662–667; Leonard F. Parker, *History of Poweshiek County, Iowa* . . . (2 vols., Chicago, 1911), 1:57–60; Union Historical Company, *The History of Warren County, Iowa* . . . (Des Moines, 1879), 304–305; Harlow M. Pratt, *History of Fort Dodge and Webster County, Iowa* (2 vols., Chicago, 1913), 1:76–78; W. E. Alexander, *History of Winneshiek and Allamakee Counties, Iowa* (Sioux City, 1882), 189–190; A. Warner & Co., *History of the Counties of Woodbury and Plymouth, Iowa* . . . (Chicago, 1890), 70–71.

11 Western Historical Company, *History of Lee County*, 529–531; Charles Mason to D. W. Kilbourne, December 22, 1869, Charles Mason Papers, Iowa State Department of History and Archives, Des Moines, vol. 29.

12 Lokken, *Iowa Public Land Disposal*, 210–235; Nathan E. Goldthwait, ed., *History of Boone County, Iowa* (2 vols., Chicago, 1914), 1:145–151; Webster City *Hamilton Freeman*, February 12 and May 6, 1868; May 11 and 25, 1870.

13 National Publishing Company, *History of Monona County, Iowa* . . . (Chicago, 1890), 202–203; John L. E. Peck, Otto H. Montzheimer, and William J. Miller, *Past and Present of O'Brien and Osceola Counties, Iowa* . . . (2 vols., Indianapolis, 1914), 1:84–107.

14 Charles L. Dyke, *The Story of Sioux County* (Orange City, Iowa, 1942), 99–101.

15 William H. Hart, *History of Sac County, Iowa* . . . (Indianapolis, 1914), 56. This story is not completely plausible, since these lands ordinarily would have become subject to private entry in short order and available, therefore, to any speculator who desired to purchase them at the minimum government price.

16 For an intensive study of the diversity of origins of the population of Iowa between 1850 and 1860, see Morton Rosenberg, "The Democratic Party of Iowa, 1850–1860" (Ph.D. dissertation, State University of Iowa, 1957), 459–501.

17 The pre-emption laws may be found in 4 *U.S. Stat.*, 678 (1845), and 5 *U.S. Stat.*, 251–252, 382, and 453–458 (1845). Lokken, *Iowa Public Land Disposal*, 80, is in error in stating that the Pre-emption Act of 1834 did not apply to Iowa. See, for instance, Records of the General Land Office, Dubuque Land Office Original Entries, nos. 401 and 419, National Archives, Washington.

18 The counties are Boone, Dallas, Des Moines, Dubuque, Dickinson, Jackson, Johnson, Keokuk, Kossuth, Madison, Mahaska, Marion, Monroe, Polk, Poweshiek, Warren, Webster, Winneshiek, and Woodbury. See note 10 above for references to published histories of these counties. A typescript copy of the Poweshiek County revised rules and the deed register is available in the Iowa State Historical Society at Iowa City but the location of the originals is unknown. The Society holds the original manuscript rules and claim register of the Johnson County club and a copy of the Fort Dodge club record. The original of the Fort Dodge record is in the Iowa State Department of History and Archives at Des Moines.

19 Union Historical Company, *History of Mahaska County*, 294–295. John W. Wright and William A. Young, eds., *History of Marion County, Iowa and Its People* (2 vols., Chicago, 1915), 1:61–62; Western Historical Company, *History of Jackson County*, 334.

20 Union Historical Company, *History of Dallas County*, 325–326; Mueller, *History of Madison County*, 1:127; Western Historical Company, *History of Monroe County*, 376–377; Union Historical Company, *History of Warren County*, 305.

21 Western Historical Company, *History of Jackson County*, 334; Union Historical Company, *History of Mahaska County*, 294.

22 Brigham, *Des Moines . . . Together with the History of Polk County*, 1:664.

23 Western Historical Company, *History of Cedar County*, 325.

24 Western Historical Company, *History of Clinton County*, 444–445.

25 Patrick B. Wolfe, *Wolfe's History of Clinton County, Iowa . . .* (2 vols., Indianapolis, 1911), 1:51.

26 Western Historical Company, *History of Appanoose County*, 365–366.

27 Smith, *History of Harrison County*, 82.

28 Donnel, *Pioneers of Marion County*, 49.

29 Union Historical Company, *The History of Marion County, Iowa . . .* (Des Moines, 1881), 325–330; Wright and Young, eds., *History of Marion County*, 59–62.

30 James W. Merrill, *Yellow Spring[s] and Huron: A Local History Containing Sketches of all the People, Institutions, and Events, from the Earliest Settlement to Date of Publication* (Mediapolis, Iowa, 1897), 43. The capitalist whose name became a verb was Richard Barrett of Springfield, Illinois.

31 Benjamin F. Reed, *History of Kossuth County, Iowa . . .* (2 vols., Chicago, 1913), 1:72.

32 Mueller, *History of Madison County*, 1:126.

33 Western Historical Company, *History of Monroe County*, 377.

34 Shambaugh, ed., *Constitution and Records*, xiv.

35 The following analysis of the transactions of the membership is based on a man-by-man study of the club membership, using the claim register and quitclaim deed record of the club.

36 Shambaugh, ed., *Constitution and Records*, 21.

37 Johnson County, Book of Original Entries, and Index of Deeds, 1839–1854, consulted in the County Recorder's Office, Iowa City.

38 Shambaugh, ed., *Constitution and Records*, xv–xvi.

39 Lokken, *Iowa Public Land Disposal*, 73, 75.

40 Shambaugh, ed., *Constitution and Records*, 35, 39, 85, 113, 117, 119, 127, 133, 148, 161, 162, 169, 182.

41 Unfortunately the club recorder did not preserve the original by-laws of the Poweshiek association, and it is not possible to determine what changes were made in preparing the revised regulations.

42 Typewritten copy of the Poweshiek claim records, obtained through the agency of Professor Leonard F. Parker of Grinnell, Iowa, and now held by the Iowa State Historical Society. Parker had himself obtained the record from Joseph Satchell, who discovered the original manuscript while auditor of the county during the early 1880's. Joseph Satchell, Redlands, Calif., to Parker, January 17, 1906, filed with the Historical Society's copy of the claim compact and register.

43 Information concerning original entries and the purchase of land from grantees other than the federal government is based on an analysis of the Poweshiek County Book of Original Entries, and the Index of Deeds, 1849–1860, consulted in the County Recorder's Office, Montezuma, Iowa.

44 The writer used the copy of the Fort Dodge Claim Club records available in the library of the Iowa State Historical Society at Iowa City. The original is in the possession of the Iowa State Department of History and Archives at Des Moines.

45 Information concerning original entries and the purchase of land from grantees other than the federal government is based on an analysis of the Webster County Book of Original Entries, and the Index of Deeds, 1854–1866, consulted in the County Recorder's Office, Fort Dodge, Iowa, and the Humboldt County Book of Original Entries, and the Index of Deeds, 1855–1869, in the County Recorder's Office, Dakota City, Iowa.

46 So high a percentage of those in Humboldt County failed to acquire any title that the writer turned to the federal census records to corroborate his work in the county records. None of the settlers who failed to appear in the abstract of original entries or the deed indexes of Humboldt County greeted the census taker in that county in 1870.

47 Webster City *Hamilton Freeman*, December 10, 1857, and October 5, 1859.

48 Turner, *Frontier in American History*, 37.

The Mineral Land Question in California, 1848–1866

JOSEPH ELLISON

Acknowledgment is due Professor Herbert E. Bolton for advice and suggestions.

Reprinted by permission from the Southwestern Historical Quarterly, *Volume 30 (1926), pages 34–55.*

PLANS FOR THE CONTROL AND DISPOSITION OF THE CALIFORNIA MINES

Mineral Land Policy Prior to 1848

Previous to the discovery of gold in California, the United States government had experience with mining regulations of lands containing only the base metals. The early policy of the government was to reserve the mineral lands, subject to lease by miners. For a few years the miners paid the rent with some regularity, but after 1834 the expense of collecting the rent exceeded the amount collected. Hence in his message to Congress of December 2, 1845, President Polk recommended to abolish the leasing system and to offer the mineral lands for sale. He pointed out that the leasing system had not only proved a burden upon the national treasury, but had led to a wasteful manner of working the mines, and had given rise to much "friction between the United States and individual citizens." [1] By the acts of Congress of July 11, 1846, March 1, 3, 1847, the mineral lands for lead, copper, and other base metals were put on the market for sale. [2]

Attempts to Legislate for the California Mines

When gold was discovered in California [3] the government found itself at a loss for knowledge as to how to act. The plans suggested by the government's agents in California differed greatly. Colonel Mason recommended either to grant licenses to work small tracts of land, of about 100 yards square, at a rent ranging from $100 to $1,000 per annum; or to sell the lands in tracts of 20 or 40 acres, at public auction, to the highest bidder.[4] On the other hand, Thomas Butler King, in his report to the President, strongly opposed the policy of selling the mineral lands. He believed that capitalists, by means of paid secret prospectors, would find out the best lands, overbid the poor miners, and thus monopolize the best mineral lands. The inequality in the distribution of wealth would produce discontent among the poor miners, and it would be doubtful whether any law opposed to the interests of the great masses could be enforced. Even the employment of troops would be ineffectual, for the soldiers would desert, and anarchy would result. His plan was to regard the mineral lands as the common treasure of the American people, and any American citizen, by paying to the commissioner of mines an ounce of gold, or $16, should be entitled to receive a license to dig anywhere in California for one year. The money collected from these gold mines was to be devoted to educational purposes and to the construction of roads and bridges in the mineral districts, and to the discharge of the indemnity to Mexico.[5]

Shortly after Mason's report was received in Washington, President Polk recommended to Congress either to preserve the mineral lands of the Pacific Coast for the use of the United States government; or to sell them in small quantities, at a fixed minimum price which should secure a large return of money to the national treasury, and at the same time "lead to the development of their wealth by individual proprietors and purchasers." [6] In accordance with these recommendations, the Senate Committee on Public Lands reported a bill to divide the mineral lands into lots of about two acres each, to be offered for sale at public auction, at a price not less than $1.25 an acre. Senator Benton was opposed to any plan which aimed to secure revenue from the mineral lands, especially from the placers, which contained only one crop of gold. His own bill provided for agents to grant permits for working the mines without any revenue purposes. His policy, he claimed, would preserve order among the miners, while the plan of the committee would place the miners in opposition to the law.[7] Neither plan was adopted.

Also President Taylor and his Secretary of the Interior, Ewing, took considerable interest in the mineral land question. Secretary Ewing recommended that the quartz mines, which required large capital for their successful working, should be sold, but the placer mines should be leased on favorable terms, so that many industrious citizens could work them and pay the rent out of the proceeds. He did not think that the government would experience difficulties in collecting the rent. In his annual message of December 4, 1849, President Taylor recommended that the gold fields be divided into small tracts "and be disposed of by sale or lease." [8]

In the absence of any legislation, the military officials in California, who had charge of all government property in the territory, adopted the *laissez faire* policy with regard to the gold fields. Colonel Mason believed that the miners ought to pay some rent to the government for the privilege of digging in government lands, but since he had no instructions to that effect, nor sufficient soldiers to enforce such rules in such an extensive territory, he decided not to interfere. General Smith at first intended to expel all the foreigners from the gold fields. He admitted that legally all gold diggers were trespassers, but since Congress always made distinctions in favor of early settlers by granting preemption, he felt justified in allowing American citizens to work in the mines. He wrote to the consul at Panama, asking him to inform the other consuls on the South American coast that the laws of the United States forbidding trespassing on the public lands would be enforced by him in California against all foreigners. [9] Under the color of this proclamation, many American miners undertook to drive out the South American and Mexican miners. But General Riley declared that no persons, neither American citizens nor foreigners, had any right to dig gold in California on government land; but until Congress should legislate in this matter, he would not permit any class of miners to monopolize the gold fields. [10]

Attitude of California to the Mineral Land Question

The question of the regulation of the gold fields attracted great interest in California. The discussion on the subject at the constitutional convention of 1849 indicates that the general sentiment of the delegates, particularly from the mining districts, was in favor either of free mining, or government regulations for the benefit of the state. One resolution requested Congress to allow the free use of the mineral lands to all American citizens. Another resolution recommended that Congress should by legislative enactment throw open the placer mines to all people, at the payment of $5 a month for the permit to dig. The income from this source was to be turned over to the state of California. Some favored the entire relinquishment of the mines to the state. [11]

The first legislature took considerable interest in the mining question. In the assembly two reports were submitted by a select committee, advocating that the privilege of working the mines should be restricted to American citizens, and foreigners who had legally declared their intention to become citizens. The argument was that California had been acquired at the expense of the American nation; hence the benefits from this acquisition should accrue to Americans only. It was also argued that most of the foreign miners were adventurers, peons of low character, who might jeopardize the morals of the young Americans, and in time of war a large foreign population in California would prove a positive danger to the safety of the state. On the question of the disposition of the mineral lands the committee could not agree. The majority was not opposed to leasing or even selling the mineral lands in small tracts. But the minority report opposed the policy of leasing as well as selling, believing that either system would result in the monopolization of all the best placers in the hands of the capitalists. The policy advocated in the minority report was to let the American citizens work the mines freely without a tax other than what might be necessary to secure them some protection.[12] The adoption of the minority report by the assembly indicates that the policy then advocated was commonly favored in California, especially among the mining communities.

Fremont's Bill

Shortly after the California delegation took their seats in Congress, Fremont introduced a bill in the Senate to make temporary provision for the working of the gold mines in California. Its leading principle, in the opinion of its author, was to reject all ideas of making the minerals in California a source of revenue for the federal government; and to prevent any possibility of the lands being monopolized by the capitalists. The bill provided for a number of agents in the mining districts whose duties were to grant permits to American citizens, to visit the mines, and settle disputes. The quantity of land allowed to each miner was to be a 30-foot square lot to be worked by manual labor on a placer, and 210 feet square the size of a lot to be worked by machinery in the rocks. The fee for the permits was to be $1 a month for a placer, and $25 a month for a mine. A certain per cent of the proceeds from the sale of the permits was to go for internal improvements in the state of California. No person could have two permits at the same time; but to encourage prospecting, the first discoverer was to have double the quantity without paying any fee. The agents, together with a jury of six disinterested miners in the neighborhood, were to settle all disputes equitably.

The bill elicited considerable discussion in the committee of the whole. Seward moved to amend the bill, extending the privilege of mining gold to persons who should legally declare their intention of becoming citizens. Such a policy, he said, would induce immigration to California. The California senators agreed to the amendment after it was modified to include only Europeans. The principal objection of Ewing was the absence of any provision in the bill insuring the national government a revenue from the mines, to cover the expenses of the acquisition of the territory. His amendment provided that the miner should deliver weekly the gold collected to the United States district agent and be paid in United States coin at the rate of $16 an ounce, which was the current rate in California. Anyone refusing to comply with this law should forfeit the permit and location. Benton and the California senators opposed the amendment, contending that the government's experiences with the lead mines in Illinois and Missouri were conclusive against any idea of deriving a revenue from the California mineral lands. The amendment was rejected.

Felch, on the other hand, opposed Fremont's bill on the ground that it was a leasing system, which had been found to be impracticable to be carried out in a decentralized government like the United States; and in derogation to the rights of the states, for it withheld from state taxation great quantities of land. His substitute plan provided for the giving of the legislative sanction of the national government to a policy of the freedom of the mines unhindered by any agents and permits. This was the policy that was actually pursued, without legislative provision, up to 1866. It was, however, believed in the Senate that some machinery was needed for the preservation of order in the mines. After being amended, Fremont's bill passed the Senate, but its friends did not succeed in getting it taken up in the House, where it was laid over to the next session.[13]

In an "Address to the People of California," Fremont defended his plan, maintaining that, in view of the novelty and difficulty of the subject, his policy was the most practicable and the most liberal to the miners.[14] But the majority of the people of California were against government regulation of the mineral lands. The bill is odious and impracticable, said the *Picayune*.[15] The *Courier* was opposed to rents or fees, except on the quartz mines.[16] The Sacramento *Transcript* held that on account of distance Congress was not competent to legislate wisely for the gold mines.[17] There is but one method left for the disposal of the California mineral lands, said the *Herald*, and that is the cession of those lands to the state of California, for the state will know better than the federal government how to administer the mines.[18]

California's Opposition to Fillmore's Recommendation

In spite of the determined opposition of California to the policy of selling the gold fields, President Fillmore and his Secretary of the Interior, Stuart, recommended to Congress to divide these lands into small tracts to be sold "under such restrictions, as to quantity and time, as will insure the best price, and guard most effectually against combinations of capitalists to obtain monopolies." They admitted that the leasing system would be more profitable to the government, and would afford the best securities against monopolies, but such a system, they believed, would create feuds between the government and the lessees, making it difficult to collect the rents.[19]

President Fillmore's recommendation was criticized in California as undemocratic and in the interest of the capitalists. The suggestion of President Fillmore, said the *Pacific News*, shows that the authorities in Washington do not understand the situation in California. The adoption of such a policy would inevitably result in monopoly, and in such a case the land would be either kept for speculation and not be mined; or the laboring people would be forced to pay a high price for it. The *Herald* pointed out that the miners had no desire to own the title in fee simple, for as soon as the "lead" gives out they move to another place. The mineral lands, said the *Alta*, are best as they are now, and they can never become a source of revenue for the government.[20] In the assembly a joint resolution was adopted, declaring that the policy of selling the mineral lands would be in conflict with the true interests of the state and nation, for the richest mineral lands would fall into the hands of speculators, resulting in the stoppage of immigration and the retardation of the progress of California. It warned the government that the miners, grown up in a spirit of independence, had become accustomed to consider the mineral lands as a common heritage, and would not brook any interference.[21] The Whig state convention adopted a resolution favoring the retention of the mineral lands by the government, "for the benefit of the miners, to be worked by them, free from any tax or toll whatever." [22] In their messages to the legislature Governors McDougal and Bigler deprecated the policy of leasing or selling the mineral lands.[23]

While the majority of the people of California opposed the leasing or selling the gold fields, there was, however, no unanimity of opinion on any other policy. A convention of miners and settlers was held in Sacramento, but the opinions voiced there were too dissimilar to lead to a well-digested plan for the regulation of the mineral lands. Some held that the rules and regulations adopted by the miners were working satisfactorily; others, however, held that some definite legislation was needed to unify the mining regulations. But the question was who should legislate, Congress or the state legislature. It was contended that for the want of necessary experience Congress could not legislate properly for the mineral lands; hence it should relinquish them to the state.[24]

The determined opposition of California to their former plan convinced President Fillmore and Secretary Stuart that the mineral land question "is a subject surrounded by great difficulties." They now recommended to Congress to leave the gold fields open to the industry of all American citizens "until further experience shall have developed the best policy to be ultimately adopted in regard to them." "It is safer to suffer the inconvenience that now exists, for a short period," said the President, "than by premature legislation to fasten on the country a system founded in error, which may place the whole subject beyond the future control of Congress." [25] The policy of *laissez faire* recommended by President Fillmore was favored in California, especially among the miners.[26]

THE PERIOD OF LAISSEZ FAIRE, 1851–1866

The policy of "non-interference" was practically followed until the passage of the acts of July, 1866, and July, 1870. During this period, however, the mineral land question continued to be a vital issue in state politics. In the first place, there was the feeling of uncertainty and fear that speculators might influence Congress to take up again the proposition to sell the mineral lands. Hence it was deemed necessary at the party convention, and in annual messages of the governors, to reiterate that public opinion in California was opposed to leasing or selling the mineral lands.[27]

Foreign Miners' Tax

Then there was the vexatious question of the foreign miners. The American miners who considered the gold fields as the heritage of the American people looked with jealousy on the continual influx of

Asiatics and Latin Americans into the mines. To check the influx of undesirable foreign miners, and to insure a large revenue to the state, the first legislature passed an act prohibiting non-American citizens from digging gold in California without a foreign miners' license. The license fee was $20 a month.[28]

The foreign miners protested and evaded the law. The American miners and their sympathizers criticized the evading foreign miners as ungrateful people, intruders upon American soil. But the merchants, whose interests suffered by the exodus of a large number of customers, denounced the act as impolitic, unjust, and illegal. The *Picayune* questioned the right of the state to legislate and control property belonging to the United States. It pointed out that the foreign miners' act was in violation of commercial treaties between the United States and Mexico, where it was provided that the citizens of both countries should not be subjected to any other charges or contributions of taxes than such as are paid by the citizens of the states in which they reside. The act, therefore, violated Article 6 of the United States Constitution, which declares that the treaties made by the United States "shall be the Supreme Law of the Land." [29]

In the case of the *People* v. *Naglee*,[30] the California Supreme Court upheld the constitutionality of the law. It held that the state had the power to require the payment by foreigners of a license fee for the privilege of mining within the state; and that the act was not repugnant to the Constitution of the United States, for the power of taxation is one of those powers retained by the state and it cannot be taken away from it by a treaty between the United States and a foreign government.

The opposition to the foreign miners' tax, and the difficulties encountered in collecting the license fee, led to the repeal of the act in 1851.[31] But the American miners held public meetings, protesting against allowing Asiatics and Latin Americans to dig freely in the mines. They petitioned the legislature to enact a law prohibiting the importation of Asiatics, and to prevent those in California from entering the gold fields. The miners threatened to take the law into their own hands.[32]

In 1852 the legislature passed a new foreign miners' bill.[33] Because the license fee was only $3 a month, there was less opposition to the new act. Many protest meetings, however, were held denying the right of the state legislature to pass such laws. Where and when did the federal government authorize California to legislate for the mines?

asked the *Alta*.[34] The French miners felt themselves slighted when they saw how exacting the collectors were with the Latin nations; while the English, Irish, and Germans were seldom required to pay the tax. They protested against the foreign miners' tax and appealed to the French government for protection. The San Francisco *Echo du Pacifique* asserted that the tax on French miners was illegal, because the state had no right to levy a tax on mineral lands which were government property; and also because the act violated a consular convention signed in 1853 by representatives of the American and French governments wherein it was provided that the French people in the United States should not be compelled to pay taxes, except those which were equally imposed on all citizens. The *Echo* advised the French miners to take the case to the Supreme Court of the United States.[35]

Mines and State Taxes

There were also the questions of quartz mining, state taxes, and the settlement of the state. The southern agricultural counties complained that their ranches were taxed to their full market value; while the mining claims, yielding thousands of dollars to their owners, were not paying any taxes. They pointed out that the six southern counties, with a population of 6,367 souls, paid more taxes than the twelve mining counties with a population of 11,917 souls. Yet the mining counties had forty-four representatives in the legislature, while the six southern counties had only twelve representatives. To escape the heavy taxation, the southern counties advocated a revision of the constitution in matters of taxation, or the division of the state.[36] Others complained that the growing quartz mine industry, which required the investment of considerable amounts of capital, was being retarded for the want of titles in fee.[37]

But the great stumbling block in the way of equalization of taxes and the investment of capital in quartz mining was the ownership of the mineral lands by the federal government. Various plans were proposed. The committee on mines and mining interests in the assembly advocated to continue the policy of non-interference in the placer mines, until the time when capital would have to be applied. But it favored granting to the owners of quartz mines a title for a certain period during which time the grantee could "transfer or work *[his]* claim at pleasure." Meanwhile the state should be authorized to levy and collect taxes on the assessed value of the property of the quartz miners. It was also proposed to induce the federal government to grant the mines to the state.[38]

A committee composed of one member from each of the mining counties within the state was appointed in the assembly to report as to the expediency of calling a miners' state convention to consider a policy with reference to the mines. The majority report of the committee, presented March 19, 1853, was opposed to a miners' state convention, fearing that it might result in a recommendation to Congress "for the adoption of some system of which miners would be required to procure a fee simple title to their claims, that they may be subject to additional taxation." The miners contended that the mining occupation was full of hardships, and it would be difficult to assess mining claims fairly; that a fee simple title would not keep the miner a single day longer when he found it impracticable to work his claim.[39] The miner of California, said the Sacramento *Union*, should be as free as the air, and any project of legislating for the mineral lands by the state or federal government would be impracticable and impossible to enforce the law. A fee simple title, said the *State Journal*, would produce confusion and hardship. The policy of the state and nation should be "hands off," said the Placerville *Herald*.[40] Thus an attempt of the agricultural and commercial interests to devise a policy for the taxation of the mines was frustrated by the miners.

State Ownership of the Minerals

There had always prevailed an opinion in California that by right the gold fields belonged to the state and not to the federal government. This doctrine gained considerable popularity when the state Supreme Court held in the case of *Hicks* v. *Bell* that "the mines of gold and silver on the public lands are as much the property of this State, by virtue of her sovereignty, as are similar mines in the hands of private citizens." This principle was reiterated two years later in the case of *Stoakes* v. *Barrett*.[41] The *Placer Times and Transcript* congratulated the people of California upon the "acquisition of so splendid a heritage." Why should we entrust these matters, it said, to those who are removed from us thousands of miles, and who do not possess the necessary knowledge nor sympathy to manage the mines efficiently.[42]

In the Senate, Dosh introduced a bill which assumed for the state, by virtue of its sovereignty, the ownership of all the mines. In his minority report on the bill, Dosh contended that under the Spanish and Mexican law, the minerals in all lands, public and private, were reserved to the sovereignty. The right to the mines in these lands became vested in the "sovereignty which superseded that of Mexico," that is, the state of California. This conclusion was based upon the following argument: For many years previous to the conquest by the United States, the department of California had a "regularly organized government"; this system of laws, with some modifications, continued in force until the time when the state government was put into full operation. *"The first recognition of California by Congress was as an independent sovereignty,"* a state; and by reason of that independent sovereignty, the right of eminent domain "which had been transferred to the government of the United States by the treaty of Guadalupe Hidalgo, by the act admitting California into the Union, passed to the sovereignty of this state." [43]

The majority of the committee reported adversely to the passage of the bill, maintaining that the mineral lands belonged to the federal government. The placer miners feared that the doctrine of state ownership of the mines was fraught with great danger to the mining interest, "that it would not be a great while until those lands would be wrested from the miners and placed in the hands of monopolists." All they asked was *"to be let alone."* They claimed that the federal government, who was the rightful owner of the mines, had "solemnly declared" that these lands should not be surveyed and sold, but should be open to the free use and enjoyment of all American citizens, under the mining laws adopted by the miners themselves. [44]

Miners' Rules and Regulations

These miners' rules and regulations, [45] which seemed to suit the interest of the miners so well, were the outgrowth of necessity and experience, built upon the foundation of the European and Mexican mining laws, and adjusted to the needs of the new environment. By 1860 there grew up a miners' code based on equitable principles, democratic in character. The main object of these rules and regulations was to fix the size, manner of recording, working, and holding the claims. The size varied according to the richness of the placers, ranging from 10 to 150 feet square. In general a reasonable amount of work had to be done in order to establish and hold a claim to a placer mine. The purpose of limiting the size of the claims, and defining the condition of holding them, was to guard the mines from being monopolized. Here we notice the common aversion of the frontier democracy to monopoly. The promulgation of the rules and the settlement of disputes were also handled in a typical frontier democratic fashion. The rules were generally framed and amended at a public mass meeting, conducted in an informal manner. The disputes were settled by an arbitrary board of miners, selected by the disputants from the neighboring mining camps, or by a miners' jury previously appointed at a miners' meeting.

The state legislature, after some consideration, declared by statute that in "actions respecting 'Mining Claims' proof shall be admitted of the customs, usages, or regulations established and in force at the bar, or diggings, embracing such claim; and such customs, usages, or regulations, when not in conflict with the constitution and laws of this state, shall govern the decision of the action." [46] Thus the legislature declared the miners' law to be binding in matters relating to mining claims. The "let alone" policy of the federal government was interpreted by the miners as a tacit approval by the federal government of their mining code.

RENEWED AGITATION AND FINAL SETTLEMENT OF THE MINERAL LAND QUESTION

Awakening of the Mining Question in Washington

Ever since Fillmore's recommendation of 1851, the mining question slept in Congress. In his annual report of 1858, Secretary of the Interior Thompson revived it, pointing out the need of adopting some definite policy with regard to the mineral lands.[47] California immediately protested against "Congressional tinkering" with the mines. Congressman Scott asserted that the government had no right to dispose of the California gold fields, and that it could never enforce such a policy, for California would "resist to the last any such encroachment on the part of the Federal government." The *Alta* and the *Bulletin* warned the government not to attempt to prescribe mining regulations, or expect to realize any revenue from the mines. "A revolution and nothing short of it," they threatened, "would in all probability be the result of any improper interference on the part of the general government, with the rights of that large and deserving class of our population." And if persisted in "would result in the loss of California to the Federal Union." [48]

The California senators now introduced a bill to legalize the existing state of affairs which the government had tacitly sanctioned, and thus remove the technical charge that the miners were trespassers on the public lands. The bill brought forth a long discussion. Senator Latham reminded the Senate that the California Supreme Court had decided that the right to the mines existed in the state. But the opposition contended that such a law would be equivalent to a virtual cession of the mineral lands to the state of California, or to private individuals, without any remuneration to the federal government. The bill was rejected.[49]

Effect of the Civil War on the Mining Question

At the outbreak of the Civil War the mining question was again revived. The costliness of the war and the depleted condition of the national treasury convinced the federal authorities that it would be no more than just to make the valuable gold and silver mines contribute some revenue to the government. Secretary of the Interior Caleb B. Smith and Commissioner of the General Land Office Edmunds called the attention of Congress to the advisability of taxing the mines. "When multiplied demands upon the treasury weigh upon it with unprecedented pressure," argued Commissioner Edmunds, "it could not be deemed unreasonable, after the hundreds of millions of dollars allowed to be taken free of cost, if the government should hereafter subject the product of such mines to a moderate seigniorage." [50]

California immediately protested against the taxing plan, maintaining that it would be a "tax on labor and enterprise"; a policy that would be inexpedient from an economic as well as from a political point of view, for it would discourage the production of the precious metals—the sinews of war. The legislature adopted a resolution opposing the passage of any law taxing the gold and silver mines. In his annual message of January, 1863, Governor Stanford critized the plan to tax the mines. He believed that it would be better to dispose of the land in small tracts, thus enabling the state to tax the mines.[51]

But Commissioner Edmunds and Secretary of the Interior Usher urged the abandonment of the policy of "non-interference." Commissioner Edmunds pointed out that the auriferous regions in British Columbia had been made by proper control and management a source of revenue to the British government, while the mines of the precious metals in the United States had been left open to the people of all nations, without the payment of any tax whatever. Thus during the sixteen years of free mining, $100,000,000 had been extracted from the mines, "without a dollar's revenue to the national exchequer." At a time when the "nation is weighed down with financial obligations," he argued, the mining industry should contribute its share to sustain the government. His plan was to require the placer miner to secure a license to his mine by the payment of a small sum. When found profitable, the claimant could continue to work it by the payment of a reasonable amount per foot, with a certain percentage upon the produce secured.[52]

At the next year, Secretary of the Interior Harlan and Secretary of the Treasury McCulloch urged again the discontinuance of the policy of "non-interference." Secretary McCulloch denounced any system of leasing the mines as impracticable, un-American, and unconstitutional. His advice was to sell the mineral lands and "substitute an absolute title in fee for the indefinite possessory rights or claims now asserted by the miners." Such a system, he held, would give a character of permanency to the mining districts.[53] Commissioner Edmunds, however, maintained that it would be inexpedient to sell the mineral lands. He pointed out that without expensive investigation the government could not fix the minimum price which should bear an equitable ratio between the various locations. And if the explorations should be left to individuals, then the lucky miner who should discover a rich deposit would keep the fact secret until he became the possessor of it. In view of the many difficulties, and the system of mining rights which had grown up in the mining regions, Commissioner Edmunds believed that no wise policy could be devised until the whole question had been more carefully investigated by the government.[54]

There was, however, a prevailing belief in Washington that the time had come to abandon the policy of non-interference. On July 9, 1865, Julian, chairman of the House Committee on Public Lands, reported a bill providing for the sale of the gold and silver mines in small tracts, at the minimum price adjusted according to the size and value of the deposit. It limited the quantity which one individual could buy to 40 acres, and it prohibited combinations among the different bidders. In an elaborate speech Julian denounced the non-interference policy as "financial profligacy," "legislative madness." "How long," he exclaimed, "will the people thus sport with their resources and bear with the public servants who are thus recreant to the public good?" Moreover, the sale of these lands, he argued, would benefit also the mining districts, for under the system of tenancy at will permanent settlements were impossible, and the population was nomadic, dispensing with home life and public life. "It is a conspiracy against the establishment and sacredness of the American home!" he exclaimed. The bill was recommitted.[55] To gain more information on the subject, several members of Congress visited the mineral regions of the Pacific Coast.

Attitude of California

Public opinion in California was divided on the mineral land question. The quartz miners, the agricultural and commercial interests, generally favored a policy which should confer titles in fee to the miners. Such a policy, it was argued, would induce people to settle down and make improvements on their claims, and would result in the equalization of taxation. But the placer miners were opposed to any change, fearing that any system devised by Congress would be inimical to the interests of the miners.[56] "The mining interest of the Pacific States and Territories is destined to receive too much affectionate attention at Washington this winter," said the Sacramento *Union*. The *Union* argued that the nomadic character of the mining population was due not to the want of titles in fee simple but to the very nature of the miners' trade, and no government title could keep the miners after the deposit had become unprofitable.[57]

In an elaborate memorial drawn up at the miners' state convention of January, 1866, and forwarded to Washington, it was pointed out how the policy of selling the mineral lands would revolutionize the whole system of mining under which the mines had been developed to the benefit of the state and the nation. But in view of the existing situation, argued the memorialists, the next wisest policy would be to extend the pre-emption system over the mineral lands; to donate to their possessors the claims which they held under the miners' regulations.[58]

Passage of the Act of 1866

The settlement of the mineral land question came in the first session of the Thirty-ninth Congress. On May 28, 1866, Conness of California, chairman of the Senate Committee on Mines and Mining, reported a bill favorable to the mining interests of the Pacific Coast. After a long discussion the bill passed the Senate. When it came to the House, Julian succeeded in having it referred to his Committee on Public Lands. This meant the defeat of the bill, for Julian insisted on the measure which he had introduced and reported. Finding their plan thwarted in the House, Senators Conness and Stewart called up a

House bill entitled an "Act granting the Right of Way to Ditch and Canal Owners over the Public Lands, and for Other Purposes," and skillfully managed to carry a motion to strike out the whole of the House bill except the enacting clause and insert the mining bill which had been passed in the Senate. In spite of Julian's opposition, the friends of the measure managed to push it through the House, and it became a law.[59]

This great act of July 26, 1866, legalized the miners' rules and regulations which were not in conflict with the laws of the United States, and made it possible to acquire a title in fee simple to the precious-metal–bearing lands. The first section reads:

> The mineral lands of the public domain, both surveyed and unsurveyed, are hereby declared to be free and open to exploration and occupation by all citizens of the United States, and those who have declared their intention to become citizens, subject to such regulations as may be prescribed by law, and subject also to the local customs or rules of miners in the several mining districts, so far as the same may not be in conflict with the laws of the United States.

It also provided to allow miners who had or who would hereafter occupy and improve a mine, according to the local regulations, to receive a patent at the cost of $5 per acre. As a preventive against monopolies it was provided that "no location hereafter made shall exceed two hundred feet in length along the vein for each locator, with an additional claim for discovery to the discoverer of the lode," and no person was to make more than one location on the same lode. The maximum for an association of persons was 3,000 feet.[60]

The new policy was generally well received in California.

> The passage of the bill [said the San Francisco *Bulletin*], whatever defects it may develop when more critically developed and enforced, marks a change in the public land policy equal in importance to the adoption of the pre-emption and homestead system. . . . Eastern and European capital will flow to California and Nevada in large sums under the new system. . . . The new law will furthermore secure equality of taxation. . . . California may well rejoice at its passage.[61]

The *Placer Herald*, a mining paper, hailed the new policy as the dawn of a new era for California. "It is the fairest and most practicable proposition that has yet been considered in Congress," said the *Sacramento Union*. "It is a great stride toward the final adjustment of a dangerous question, and a vast improvement upon the measures broached at Washington at various periods during the past three years." According to the *Bulletin,* not a single newspaper was opposed to the act.[62] In his message of 1866 Governor Low said: "The apprehension of miners in regard to unwise and unfriendly legislation by Congress touching the mineral lands has been allayed by the passage of just and generous laws which guarantee the actual possession to those on whom the prosperity of the state so largely depends." [63]

The act of July 26, 1866, pertained only to vein mines. No provision was made to acquire title to placer mines. The committee in Congress believed that since the placers were becoming exhausted, there was no need to legislate for them. The act of July 9, 1870, provided also for the placer mines, ordering the sale of these mines at $2.50 an acre. It limited the extent of one location by an individual or an association to 160 acres. In other respects the placer locations were to conform to local rules and regulations. The act of May 10, 1872,[64] "to promote the development of the mining resources of the United States," in general reaffirmed the policy outlined in the former two acts, especially with regard to exploration and purchase of the mineral lands.

SUMMARY

The question of the control and disposition of the mineral lands was an agitating subject in the state, and to some extent in Washington, for about eighteen years. During this period the general government made several attempts to legislate for the mines, but it lacked the necessary information and courage to work out a definite policy. As a result the administration floundered from one plan to another: at one time it suggested the system of leasing; at another time, it suggested selling the lands in small parcels; and when California protested against either system, it recommended not to interfere at all with the mines. It was, of course, much easier to follow the policy of "masterly inactivity" than to brave the opposition of California. And thus in spite of some protest against the failure of the government to assert its rights to the mines, the government treasury did not derive any revenue of the hundreds of millions of dollars worth of gold extracted during this period from the Pacific Coast mines by people from all parts of the globe.[65] It was due to the exhaustion of the placer mines, and the heavy cost of the Civil War, that the government finally adopted a policy to derive some revenue from the mines.

The passage of the several mining acts marked the end of the policy of reserving the gold and silver mines to the government. Thus came to a close another chapter in the history of the relations of California with the national government. The controversy about the control and disposition of the gold and silver mines on the Pacific Coast demonstrates the influence and effect of public opinion in a state or particular section of the country upon the policies of the federal government.

NOTES

1   James D. Richardson, ed., *Compilations of the Messages and Papers of the Presidents, 1789–1897* (10 vols., Washington, 1896–1899), 4:410, 454, 504. According to the official records the rent received for the years 1841, 1842, 1843, and 1844 amounted to $6354.74, while the expenses of the system during this period amounted to $26,111.11.

2   9 *U.S. Stat.*, 37, 146–147, 179.

3   Marshall's discovery of gold in Sacramento valley was on January 24, 1848. But long before 1848 gold had been found in California near the Colorado River, near present San Diego County, around Los Angeles, and Monterey. The mineralogist James D. Dana, of the Wilkes expedition in 1841, mentioned in his book on mineralogy that gold had been found in Sacramento valley. In his letter to Secretary Buchanan, Thomas O. Larkin wrote on May 4, 1846, that there was no doubt that gold, silver, and other minerals would be found in California. *Report of Browne upon the Mineral Resources of the States and Territories West of the Rocky Mountains*, November 24, 1866, in House Executive Document no. 29, 39 Congress, 2 session, 13–14 (serial 1289).

4   House Ex. Doc. no. 17, 31 Cong., 1 sess., 532–533 (serial 573).

5   House Ex. Doc. no. 59, 31 Cong., 1 sess. (serial 577).

6   Richardson, *Messages*, 4:643.

7   *Congressional Globe*, 30 Cong., 2 sess., 257–259. Benton held that the gold mines were a curse and not a blessing to a nation, for they demoralize a people.

8   Richardson, *Messages*, 5:20; *Cong. Globe*, 31 Cong., 1 sess., app. 22–23.

9   House Ex. Doc. no. 17, 31 Cong., 1 sess., 704, 707, 708, 710 (serial 573).

10   *Ibid.*, 788–789 (serial 573); Sacramento *Placer Times*, July 9, 1849.

11   John Ross Browne, *Report of the Debates in the Convention of Cali-*

fornia on the Formation of the State Constitution (Washington, 1850), 430–431, 461, 462, 463–464.

12 *California Legislature Journals,* 1850, pp. 802–816.

13 For the bill and debates see *Cong. Globe,* 31 Cong., 1 sess., 1815, 1869, 2018, 2029–2030, app. 2, pp. 1362 *et seq.*

14 The "address" was printed in the San Francisco *Alta,* December 24, 1850, and the San Francisco *Pacific News,* December 24, 1850. ("San Francisco" will not be repeated for the San Francisco newspapers.)

15 San Francisco *Picayune,* November 14, 1850; *Pacific News,* December 6, 1850.

16 San Francisco *Courier,* November 12, 1850; January 31, 1851.

17 Sacramento *Transcript,* December 6, 1850.

18 San Francisco *Herald,* January 30, 1851.

19 House Ex. Doc., 31 Cong., 2 sess., 11, 27–28 (serial 595).

20 *Alta,* March 1, 1851; *Pacific News,* January 28, February 21, February 28, 1851; *Picayune,* September 18, 1851; Sacramento *Transcript,* January 31, 1851; *Herald,* January 5, 25, 30, 1851.

21 *Cal. Legislature Jours.,* 1851, p. 1021. The resolution and long preamble were printed in the *Pacific News,* January 29, 1851.

22 Winfield J. Davis, *History of Political Conventions in California* (Sacramento, 1893), 13.

23 *California Senate Journal,* 1852, pp. 17, 78–79.

24 *Alta,* March 1, August 5, 13, 1851; *Herald,* June 6, 1851; *Picayune,* September 18, October 11, 1851; *Pacific News,* March 6, 1851; Sacramento *Union,* January 26, 1852.

25 Richardson, *Messages,* 5:127; House Ex. Doc. no. 2, 32 Cong., 1 sess., 501 (serial 635).

26 *California Assembly Journal,* 1853, App. Doc. 35, p. 4.

27 *Cal. Sen. Jour.,* 1853, p. 23; 1854, p. 23; 1855, pp. 41–42; Davis, *Political Conventions in California,* 13, 20, 36.

28 *Cal. Legislature Jours.,* 1850, pp. 217, 493–497; *California Statutes,* 1850, pp. 221–223.

29 *Pacific News,* October 10, 1850; *Picayune,* August 14, 1850. Inflammatory bills were posted on the trees in the mines. One of them read: "Note to foreigners: 'It is time to unite, Frenchmen, Chileans, Peruvians, Mexicans, there is the highest necessity for putting an end to the vexations caused by the Americans in California. . . .' "—*Cal. Legislature Jours.,* 1851, p. 660; *Pacific News,* May 28, 1850.

30 *People* v. *Naglee,* 1 Cal., 232–255.

31 *Cal. Statutes,* 1851, p. 424. Instead of a monthly revenue of several hundred thousand dollars, as it had been estimated by the legislature of 1850, the total amount received from this source up to December 15 was only $29,731.16.

32 Meetings were held at Auburn, Horse Shoe Bar, Michigan Flat, and various other places. *Alta,* July 1, 16, 1852; Sacramento *Placer Times and Transcript,* May 9, 1852.

33 *Cal. Statutes,* 1852, pp. 84–87. The fee was raised to four dollars a

month at the next session, and the act was further amended in 1855. *Ibid.*, 1853, pp. 62–65; 1855, pp. 216–217. The receipts for 1854 were $100,557.92, and for 1855, $123,323.28. William C. Fankhauser, *Financial History of California* (Berkeley, 1913), 160.

34 *Alta,* May 12, 1852; June 24, 1853; *Cal. Assembly Jour.,* 1853, App. Doc. 28, pp. 1–21; *Cal. Sen. Jour.,* 1855, App. Doc. 19, pp. 1–13.

35 San Francisco *Bulletin,* June 23, 1860. The reason for the partiality was partly due to the clannishness of the French and their lesser readiness to become citizens. See William M. Malloy, *Treaties, Conventions, International Acts* . . . (2 vols., Washington, 1910), 1:531.

36 *Cal. Assembly Jour.,* 1852, pp. 12–13. Governor McDougal pointed out in his annual message that the six southern counties with a population of 6,367 souls had paid into the state treasury for the fiscal year ending July 1, 1851, the sum of $41,705.26, while the twelve mining counties, with a population of 119,917 souls, had paid during the same period only $21,253.66. The amount of capitation taxes assessed in the twelve mining counties was $51,495.00, and the amount returned as delinquent $47,915.00, while the amount assessed in the agricultural counties was $7,205.00 and the amount returned as deliquent $3,291.50.

37 *Alta,* January 28, December 8, 1852.

38 *Cal. Assembly Jour.,* 1852, pp. 829–835. Also see report of the Senate special committee. (*Cal. Sen. Jour.,* 1852, pp. 584–588.)

39 *Cal. Assembly Jour.,* 1853, App. Doc. 35.

40 For a discussion of the mineral question during this period see *Alta,* March 16, May 20, 1853; Sacramento *State Journal,* February 17, 1853; Sacramento *Union,* January 28, 1856; December 12, 1857; January 22, 1858; February 12, 18, 22, 25, 1859. In the opinion of the *Alta,* the state's taxable property would be increased by $200,000 if the mines were granted to the miners.

41 *Hicks v. Bell,* 3 Cal., 227; *Stoakes v. Barrett,* 5 Cal., 39. But in *Moore v. Smaw,* and *Fremont v. Flower* (17 Cal., 223), the supreme court of California refused to sustain the doctrine advanced in the above cases.

42 San Francisco *Placer Times and Transcript,* August 14, 1853. The *Alta* of August 12, 1853, and the Sacramento *Union* of August 17, 1853, expressed themselves against the doctrine of state ownership of the mines.

43 *Cal. Sen. Jour.,* 1857, pp. 275–281. The same opinion was expressed by J. W. Denver of California in his speech in Congress on the California land claims. *Cong. Globe,* 34 Cong., 1 sess., 1842. There was also considerable controversy between the state and federal authorities with regard to the question whether or not the mineral lands were included in the township grant of 1853. The federal authorities contended that the grant contemplated only such townships that could be legally surveyed and divided into sections. But since the mineral lands were excluded from survey by an act of Congress, there could be no such selections upon them. The California authorities, on the other hand,

maintained that the act of 1853 contained no reservation with regard to the mineral lands, and the mining districts were in need of educational facilities just as well as other districts. See *Cal. Sen. and Assembly Jours.*, 1863, pp. 38–44.

44 *Cal. Sen. Jour.*, 1857, pp. 274–275.

45 Good accounts of the miners' rules and regulations are given in Gregory Yale, *Legal Titles to Mining Claims and Water Rights* (San Francisco, 1867), chaps. vii, viii; Charles H. Shinn, *Mining Camps* (New York, 1885), chaps. ii, x, xiii, xxi, xxiii. See also Browne's *Report* in House Ex. Doc. no. 29, 39 Cong., 2 sess., 226–264 (serial 1289).

46 *Cal. Statutes*, 1851, p. 149.

47 House Ex. Doc. no. 2, 35 Cong., 2 sess., 77 (serial 997).

48 *Cong. Globe*, 35 Cong., 2 sess., 1487; *Alta,* January 14, 1859; *Bulletin,* November 24, 26, 1858.

49 For the bill and debate see *Cong. Globe*, 36 Cong., 1 sess., 1754, 1771, 1777, 1795.

50 Senate Ex. Doc. no. 1, 37 Cong., 2 sess., 445, 489 (serial 1117).

51 *Cal. Sen. Jour.*, 1863, pp. 41–42; *Cal. Statutes*, 1862, p. 601.

52 House Ex. Doc. no. 1, 38 Cong., 2 sess., 5–6, 39–42 (serial 1220).

53 House Ex. Doc. no. 1, 39 Cong., 1 sess., iii–iv (serial 1248); House Ex. Doc. no. 1, 39 Cong., 1 sess., 31–32 (serial 1254).

54 House Ex. Doc. no. 1, 39 Cong., 1 sess., 38–43 (serial 1248).

55 See *Cong. Globe*, 38 Cong., 2 sess., 7, 684–687.

56 *Cal. Assembly Jour.*, 1865–1866, p. 58.

57 Sacramento *Union*, January 6, 1866. Resolutions against selling or taxing the mineral lands were adopted at the state Democratic Convention. Davis, *Political Conventions in California*, 209, 224, 229. But also see *Bulletin*, January 19, June 29, July 6, 31, 1866.

58 The memorial was published in the Sacramento *Union*, January 31, 1866.

59 For the several bills and debates see House Report no. 66, 39 Cong., 1 sess. (serial 1272); *Cong. Globe*, 39 Cong., 1 sess., 1844, 2965; House Rep. no. 105, 39 Cong., 1 sess. (serial 1240); *Cong. Globe,* 39 Cong., 1 sess., 3225–3237, 3451–3454, 3951–3952, 4054. A full account of the history of the passage of the bill was given by a correspondent in Washington, published in the *Alta* on May 17, 1867. A different view of the same subject is given by Julian in his *Political Recollections* (Chicago, 1884), 286–292. "The clumsy and next to incomprehensible bill," he says, "thus became a law, and by legislative methods as indefensible as the measure itself."

60 16 *U.S. Stat.*, 251–252.

61 *Bulletin,* July 31, 1866.

62 Sacramento *Union*, June 23, 1866; *Bulletin*, August 8, 1866.

63 *Cal. Sen. Jour.*, 1867–1868, p. 53.

64 16 *U.S. Stat.*, 217–218; 17 *U.S. Stat.*, 91–96.

65 In his report of 1866, Browne estimated the total production of gold in California up to 1865 at about $900,000,000. The gold exportation

from San Francisco during these years was as follows:

1849	$ 4,921,250
1850	27,676,346
1851	42,582,695
1852	46,588,434
1853	57,330,034
1854	51,328,653
1855	45,182,631
1856	48,880,543
1857	48,976,697
1858	47,548,025
1859	47,649,462
1860	42,203,345
1861	40,639,080
1862	42,561,761
1863	46,071,920
1864	55,707,201
1865	44,984,546
Total	$740,832,623

To this he added $200,000,000, the amount carried away during this sixteen years unmanifested. *Report Upon the Resources of the States and Territories West of the Rocky Mountains* (39 Cong., 2 sess., House Ex. Doc. no. 29, serial 1289), 50.

The Operation of the Land Laws in the Minnesota Iron District

FREMONT P. WIRTH

Reprinted by permission from the Mississippi Valley Historical Review, Volume 13 (1927), pages 438–498.

THE first important discovery of iron ore in Minnesota was made in 1865 by State Geologist Henry H. Eames.[1] Following his report, numerous individuals began exploration for iron in the northeastern part of the state, and great discoveries were reported from time to time in the region known as the Vermilion and the Mesabi ranges.[2] As soon as this district was known to contain iron in merchantable quantities, large areas were acquired by Charlemagne Tower and others associated with him; and on December 1, 1882, the Minnesota Iron Company was organized, with Charlemagne Tower as president.[3] This company became the owner of more than 17,000 acres of iron land which Tower had acquired on the Vermilion range before the company was organized.[4] A railroad was then constructed, connecting the mines opened by this company with Lake Superior, and in 1884, iron ore was for the first time shipped to the lake.[5]

The actual shipment of iron ore was conclusive evidence that the reported discoveries were real, and many other prospectors were attracted to this land of promise. The fact that a railroad had been constructed made the region more attractive. The ore could now be brought to market. Exploration increased, and by the spring of 1887 the Vermilion district was in the grip of a great mining boom. Each day seemed to bring new discoveries of great fields of valuable ore, and the Duluth newspapers lost no time in reporting the facts and advertising this region of "great wealth."

The Duluth *Daily News* in almost every issue wrote of the tremendous wealth that was being uncovered. On March 8, it predicted that "by next summer thousands of acres of mineral lands will have risen from a nominal worth to some such value as that of the Minnesota Iron Company's property." Other similar statements were printed.[6] On April 4, a full page advertisement contained the following optimistic report: "The Most Extraordinary Freak of Nature in All the Continent. A vast Mineral Deposit of Unknown Depth and Thickness Extending from Lake Vermilion Eastward for Seventy-five Miles. The Vermilion Iron Range is the Coming Wonder of the Northwest. A Solid Wall of Mineral." A few days later the inrush of explorers was reported and millions promised for "the hardy pioneers of the range." On April 6, the paper related the result of the great finds as follows: "Iron today is on every tongue, and a tincture to satisfy every speculator and investor. . . . It is the excitement of a people confident in rich returns in a region of endless wealth. Tower, the depot of this great iron region, is alive. Its streets are filled with explorers and land seekers." On May 5, it stated that capitalists were arriving daily and investing in the still comparatively cheap mineral and timber lands.

During all this excitement on the Vermilion, exploration was going on quietly on the Mesabi range, apparently without much success until 1890. The Merritt brothers of Duluth were most active in the exploration of this section.[7] Beginning in 1890, important discoveries were reported in this region, and from 1890 to 1893 great excitement prevailed. Here, as in the Vermilion district following the discoveries of 1887, optimism held sway. Here also enthusiastic reports came with nearly every issue of the newspapers. In fact, the Mesabi boom of 1892 was greater even than the Vermilion boom of 1887. Duluth was the center of exploring operations. A large portion of the people in Duluth were interested in the explorations.[8] The excitement seems to have reached its greatest height in February and March of 1892. From February 1 to March 26, 1892, fifty-one iron companies were incorporated in Minnesota, with a capital stock of $133,700,000.[9] During these months, the Duluth papers again reported stories of "great finds," of the "organization of a stock exchange," of "excursion of capitalists to the ranges," and of "important land purchases." [10]

The discovery and exploration of this section brought to light great wealth in a region in which practically all of the land was still a part of the public domain and could be easily secured under the liberal policy of the federal government. These discoveries, and especially the enthusiastic tales thereof, created a great demand for the lands considered so valuable, and nearly every law by which lands could be alienated from the public domain was used by individuals and corporations to secure mineral deposits of unknown dimensions and untold value.

This desirable mineral land, however, was not subject to the mining laws of the United States, but could be obtained in the same way as ordinary agricultural land. This fact had an important effect on the disposition of these lands and is largely responsible for the abuses that followed. The Mining Act of May 10, 1872, provided for the survey and sale of mineral lands at $2.50 and $5.00 per acre, depending on whether the land contained placer or lode minerals.[11]

Apparently this law was not satisfactory to the mining interests, and on February 18, 1873, an act was passed which provided that in Michigan, Wisconsin, and Minnesota, deposits or mines of iron and coal should be excluded from the operation of the mineral laws in the states named.[12] The bill did not create much discussion in Congress. Senator Casserly objected to it because it would exclude iron and coal from the mineral act in all the states.[13] Senator Chandler of Michigan pointed out that this law was necessary to develop the copper and iron mines of the Lake Superior region. He remarked that it was a purely local measure and would not affect the mines on the Pacific Coast.[14] In the House, there was likewise very little discussion of the bill and it was passed without objection. Representative Waldron of Michigan recommended that the bill pass.[15] In answer to a question why the bill was confined to these states, he said that the intention of the mining law of May 10, 1872, had been to confine it to the precious metals on the Pacific Coast. He declared further that the object of this bill was to protect the copper interests of the Northwest from the provisions of the law of 1872.

This law, therefore, was of great importance and after February 18, 1873, the public domain of Minnesota, whether it contained iron ore or not, was open to entry under the provisions of the homestead and pre-emption laws.

The greatest part of the mineral region is located in the Duluth district. It is, therefore, in the records of the United States General Land Office that an account of the disposition of these ore lands may be found. The Register of Original Homestead Entries [16] shows that few entries were made prior to the discovery of iron ore. In 1880, only 76 were listed; however, the number increased rapidly after mining began. In 1884, the year in which shipment of ore began, 345 entries were listed.[17] In 1887 occurred the great mining boom on the Vermilion, and the excitement it created caused a great increase in the number of people seeking homes in this wilderness, eighty miles from civilization. In that year, 971 made applications, of which more than 500 were made during the months of March and April, at the time when the excitement was at its height.[18] Of these, 97 per cent were on what was then considered the iron range.[19]

A second mining boom came with the great discoveries on the Mesabi range in 1892. This was even greater than the one in 1887, and again the business of the land office increased beyond all reasonable proportions. In this year, 378 of the 1,940 entries were made in March, nearly all on the Mesabi range.[20] During 1892, more homestead entries were filed in the Duluth land district than were made in the same district in the seventeen years from the passage of the Homestead Act in 1862 to 1880, the year iron mining began in Minnesota.[21] It is interesting to note that in fifteen years, 1880 to 1894, more than five times as many homestead entries were made as were made in the seventeen years previous to 1880.[22]

In addition to the homestead law, the pre-emption law, until its repeal in 1891,[23] was used to secure possession of these lands. The pre-emptors were even more careful to select iron lands than were the homesteaders, for a greater proportion of them secured lands on the iron ranges.[24]

The tract books in the General Land Office tell the same story. In some of these townships more than two hundred entries appear.[25] Most of these are homesteads, though some are pre-emptions.

Most of this region, which was so eagerly sought by the home-steaders, was poorly adapted to agricultural uses. A township in which 202 homesteads were made, according to the surveyor's field notes, is very mountainous and broken. The surveyor noted, however, that here were indications of magnetic iron ore. The soil he described as being of poor quality, and he stated that much of the timber had been burned.[26] Township 59 north Range 17 west, in which 255 homestead and pre-emption entries were made, was apparently worthless, according to the surveyor's notes. He stated that the land was of little value, except for the timber, and added that the northern and more level part of the township had been swept by fire and in parts, "even the soil seems to have been burned." The southern portion, he referred to as hilly and in parts rocky and precipitous.[27]

Not all of the timber, however, had been burned and certain parts of this region were first sought by timber-men. Some of the townships were covered with great forests of virgin white pine.[28] The lumbermen came to this region before there was any definite knowledge of iron ore and purchased some of the land for $1.25 an acre. If not permitted to buy it, they often secured it through homesteaders, usually by means of additional homestead rights under the act of 1873.[29]

In 1882 the lumbermen were again active in acquiring lands in this region, this time by public sale rather than by additional homesteads. By proclamation, President Arthur opened government lands in the Duluth district. One hundred and thirty-four townships were offered at a public sale commencing on December 4, 1882. The minimum price to be paid was $1.25 an acre.[30] The average price for the part sold was $1.90 per acre.[31]

By 1882, there were "rumors of iron" in this region, but the main interest of the purchasers was still the timber.[32] At the sale in Duluth in 1882, lumbermen from all over the country were present. Rumors of iron ore added to the interest in the timberland. According to John Stone Pardee, there was considerable rivalry and some feeling. However, truces were made and the price was kept down.[33]

In the eagerness of claimants to get these lands, many conflicting claims were put forth. Numerous contests of ownership resulted. The local land office in Duluth, the General Land Office, the Secretary of the Interior, and even the courts were called upon to decide between the rights of the parties concerned. The most extreme of these contests was that over land located on the Vermilion range, known as "The Section Thirty Case." [34] Several persons asserted claim to this area, and the contest was started with a hearing before the local land office, April 6, 1886.[35] It was not settled until the Supreme Court finally ruled on the matter, January 13, 1902,[36] and closed the case after fifteen years of litigation costing more than a million dollars.[37]

This tract of land seemed so desirable that, following a decision of the Secretary of the Interior by which it was declared open to the first one to file on it, a jam resulted at the land office. Some of those interested arrived at the land office at seven o'clock in the evening and waited all night. The first one to arrive stood holding the door knob in his hand, others crowded in behind, and when the door opened a mob surged into the room. According to reports, some hung on to the side of the door while others were crowded on the tables and on the safe, all anxious to receive this prize, worth millions of dollars, which the government was willing to give away to the first one who should ask for it.[38]

Because of the great value of these lands, the desire to obtain them was exceptionally strong. Not only were the different land laws, which were liberal to begin with, put into use, but they were sub-jected to great abuse. In their eagerness to establish perfect title, the seekers of this great wealth often violated both the spirit and the letter of the law. Violations of the land laws, moreover, were not confined to this region. It seems that during the eighties and nineties there were wholesale frauds throughout the greater part of all the states containing public lands.[39]

During these years when the public conscience did not seriously object to the fraudulent practices in many parts of the country, and while the federal government was trying to suppress them, the Duluth land office was in a deplorable condition. The receiver at that office was in collusion with those who were trying to defraud the govern-ment, and for a consideration permitted the robbery to go on. Special government agents reported that they were satisfied that the charges of fraud made against the receiver were true.[40] The receiver resigned and became a land agent and acknowledged that as an attorney he participated in the unlawful business and that he aided and abetted others in the unlawful entry of these lands. To avoid prosecution he made an agreement with the agents of the government "hereafter wholly and entirely to refrain from every act and deed, direct or indirect, that may in any wise tend to defraud the government by evasion or violation of the pre-emption and homestead laws, and to hold myself aloof from all those who are engaged in such evasion or violation of law." [41]

This policy on the part of the government officials in not prosecuting an offender reflects a lax condition in the administration of the land laws. The government had evidence sufficient to indict and perhaps to convict, but preferred to take a promise of good conduct for the future. But no better conduct was secured as a result of the promise. A year later another special agent wrote: "I have become thoroughly satisfied that he has been acting in bad faith and I am fully convinced that his law office in Duluth is the place where a very large share of the frauds against the government in this Land District are con-cocted. He was dismissed from his office as Receiver for fraud and the reputation he obtained as Receiver has been fully maintained, as a practicing attorney before the United States Land Office." [42]

The demoralized condition of the local land office allowed individuals to take up thousands of acres of valuable timber and iron lands. The government agents reported "pre-emption brokers," who employed gangs of men to go into the pine woods of northern Minnesota to make pre-emption claims, settle on and improve them more or less, prove up on them, and then convey the land to persons interested in acquiring large holdings.[43] These men were paid $150 per claim. Others were employed at $30 per month.[44]

On November 23, 1882, William R. Marshall, special agent of the government, reported forty-seven fraudulent pre-emption entries in Township 59 north Range 18 west. Men were there employed by citizens of Duluth to build pre-emption shanties. Mr. Marshall stated that the improvements on many of these claims were pole pens four poles high, 10 feet square, with no floor, nor roof, and a hole 20 by 30 inches in size for a door.[45] In some cases he found men engaged in building shanties six months after the declaratory statements alleging settlement and the notices of the offering of final proof had been published. In Township 59 north, Range 17 west, nineteen pre-emption entries had been made but no habitable house was found.

On January 29, 1884, another government agent reported twenty-five fraudulent pre-emption entries. He referred to this as one of the worst frauds of its kind on record.[46] With this list he filed an affidavit of a mail carrier between Duluth and Vermilion, who stated that he had signed eight or ten blank land office papers for which he had received $100, and that the receiver of the land office had received $25 for each claim.[47]

On October 28, 1884, a special agent of the government reported to the General Land Office that only a very small portion of the land was adapted to agricultural purposes. However, there had already been 2,361 homestead entries made. He stated that only 273 had proven up on actual homesteads and a very large proportion of these had been old soldiers, who had been compelled to have residence on the land but a short time. There were also 3,280 declaratory statements filed, upon about two-thirds of which final proof had been made. He said: "Thus it will be seen that there have been over 4,300 final entries of this kind made, to say nothing about the cash entries and entries at public sale; and I know that there are less than one hundred actual settlers living upon any of these lands in this land district who make a living by farming, or who are trying to make a living in that way, and although I have made diligent inquiry during my stay of over one year in this place, I have yet to find *one person* who is making a farm or trying to make a farm upon a pre-emption claim. Therefore, I think I am fully warranted in saying that less than one-thirtieth of the claims taken in the Duluth United States land district are taken for actual settlement." [48]

Fraud, or at least bad faith, on the part of the entrymen was seen in the type of people who applied for these lands and in the character of their improvements on them. Most of the applicants followed occupations in which they would have little or no use for a home in this region, and the character of their "improvements" made it evident that they were not intended as a home but rather as a means of securing land, which by the expedient of these bogus "improvements," could be quickly converted into cash.

On October 22, 1903, President Roosevelt appointed a commission to report upon the condition, operation, and effect of the land laws. The investigation showed that 90 per cent of those making commutation [49] entry within the timber and mineral belts were from walks of life other than farming. "Among the commuters within these timber and mineral belts are to be found clerks, mechanics, business men, professional men, schoolteachers, waitresses, woodsmen, cruisers, and city laborers." [50] To this list could be added railroad men,[51] saloon-keepers, and professional gamblers.[52]

The files of the General Land Office contain the records of hundreds of cases of fraud in this section. The acts by which the government meant to give "land to the landless" and provide homes for its citizens were abused and made a means for speculation by which valuable iron lands passed into the hands of a few wealthy corporations without much benefit to those whom the government intended to help. Special Agent Fred W. LeSueur, in a report to the Commissioner of the General Land Office dated October 20, 1894, pointed out that a large part of this region was mineral land on which the timber had no commercial value. He stated that entries made on these lands were speculative and made in the hope that they would develop mineral wealth. On a trip to Ely, Minnesota, he examined a number of claims which had been held for cancellation, all of which had been established for speculation. He reported that all the improvements were of the same general character and that it was perfectly evident that none of the entrymen even intended to make a permanent home on the land. Surrounding these entries which had been held for cancellation, he reported scores of other claims which had passed to patent, none of which had better improvements and none of which were inhabited. In his report he said: "In eight days which I was out on one trip in which I went one hundred and fifty miles, I did not see one man; though I passed many claim shanties, none were occupied." [53]

On November 22, 1894, the same agent wrote again to the General Land Office. This time he reported on the conditions in Cook County, Minnesota. He stated that Cook County comprises sixty towns (townships) with an area of about 2,000 square miles; that only a small portion of it had any timber of merchantable value or size, and that what there was, was of small value from the lack of facilities to market it; that for the most part the county was barren rock and hills which possibly contained mineral wealth; that the actual resident population was less than five hundred men, women, and children, including Indians, and that this population was distributed along the shores of Lake Superior and existed by fishing and trapping. He pointed out that there were but three schools in the whole county, with a total attendance of only forty-five pupils, and but 27 miles of wagon road fit for use. Yet in this county he reported that there were thousands of homestead and pre-emption entries and that more were being made. He remarked that it was self-evident that few ever intended to comply with the law, and that a vast majority of the entries so made were fraudulent. He added that his remarks as to the agricultural possibilities and the adaptability of Cook County to homestead entry applied with equal force to Lake and St. Louis counties.[54] This report is evidence of the character of the speculative entries which defeated the intent of the government by violating the spirit and letter of the settlement laws which were designed to bring benefits to the people in need of land to establish homes.

The character of some of the improvements is told by the Land Commissioners in their report, which stated that it was common knowledge in the city of Duluth that in 1892, 1893, and 1894, persons desiring to commute would take an ordinary dry-goods box and make it resemble a small house with doors, windows, and a shingled roof. This box would be 14 by 16 inches or larger, and would be taken by the entryman to his claim. On date of commutation proof, he would appear at the local office, swear that he had upon his claim a good board house 14 by 16 with shingled roof, doors and windows, etc. This proof was readily accepted by the local office.[55]

Perhaps some of the worst frauds were committed by individuals acquiring lands which later became the property of the Minnesota Iron Company. The tract books of the General Land Office show that in 1880, 1881, and 1882 many homestead and pre-emption entries were made on the Vermilion range.[56] Other records in the Land Office show that these same lands were transferred to the Minnesota Iron Company shortly afterwards.[57] Some of these lands became the object of prolonged litigation, and the testimony brought out the fact that the entries were fraudulent and had been directed by persons interested in the development of iron mines.[58] The testimony shows that a Michigan congressman, an official of the Minnesota Iron Company, had employed a resident of the Duluth district as his agent to pre-empt mineral lands for him. In a letter in which he inclosed a check for $1,500, he told his agent to use it in pre-empting land, but that the money should be used prudently and be made to go as far as possible.[59] This agent then selected pre-emptors who could be trusted to transfer the land after the title had been secured, and paid them $150 each for filling out the required papers and for going to the land and piling up a few logs in an attempt to meet the requirements of the law, which demanded improvement and residence.[60]

On December 1, 1892, the Minnesota Iron Company was incorporated with a capital stock of $10,000,000.[61] It became the owner of more than 17,000 acres [62] of valuable land, including some which had been pre-empted and homesteaded in this fraudulent manner.[63]

The government, by the use of special agents, attempted to check the fraud. In 1892, ninety-five agents were employed, no less than fourteen of whom were operating in the Duluth district.[64] These agents made many investigations and reported on each entry separately. Entries which were suspected were suspended in order that they should not be patented. After suspension the entries were investigated. Much correspondence took place between the special agents and the General Land Office. Volumes VI and VII of the letter books, Division P (Frauds), containing letters to special agents, are almost entirely taken up with the correspondence regarding the Duluth district. Many hearings were held, but often the government lost the cases because of lack of direct evidence.[65]

It was difficult to secure evidence because the people in the community were often in sympathy with the violators of the law, or else they did not consider false testimony, to secure land, a violation of the law. On February 11, 1895, O. W. Stiles, Detailed Clerk of the General Land Office, wrote from Duluth to the General Land Office regarding the entries made in Cook County during the mineral boom and the difficulty of obtaining evidence. "Their attempted frauds are among the most flagrant of which we have knowledge, and public sentiment in this community seems to have been educated to an approval of such transactions, if not an actual belief that they are permissible and that there is no criminality attached to making a false homestead affidavit and final proof." [66]

A similar report came from agent Fred W. LeSueur, who said: "The fact is that in Tower and that locality public sympathy is with the entrymen, and the property and person of one who would testify against his neighbor would be in danger. When brought to the point, they will admit that none make the improvements contemplated by the law—but they seem to argue that custom has made a higher law, and that they have a right to the land, and if they don't get it someone else will." [67] The government was further hampered by the fact that some of the so-called homes were located in almost inaccessible places. At times agents had to walk 20 miles to reach the entry.[68] The problem of securing competent help for the agents was also difficult,[69] and at times blackmail was attempted.[70]

The abuses found in this region were to a large extent due to faulty land laws and to the lax administration of the Duluth office. The three most important laws under which title was acquired were the Cash Purchase Act of 1820, the Pre-emption Act of 1841, and the Homestead Act of 1862. By 1880, the reason for inaugurating the Cash Purchase Act no longer existed. In 1820, the public lands had been looked upon as a valuable source of revenue for a government in need of money. This was no longer the case in 1880. By the enactment of the Homestead Act in 1862, the government had completely changed its policy, and now sought to give the land to its citizens and to aid in the development of the country. In spite of this change of policy, the Cash Purchase Act was continued, although it worked not in the direction of the general development of the country, but rather to allow a few wealthy individuals to obtain control of vast resources of iron and timber. The price of land had originally been placed at a low figure to enable the small purchaser to secure a portion, but in the iron region the law had the opposite effect. It encouraged speculation by allowing individuals to secure vast holdings at a low price, thus defeating the very purpose of the act.

By the Pre-emption Act, also, the government had intended to help the settler. The pre-emption system was established in 1841 when land was abundant. It was a measure to protect actual settlers from land sharks who might buy up their property. As a rule there was then a settler for every claim.[71] By 1880, this had all changed, and the Pre-emption Act became a means by which unscrupulous individuals secured valuable iron lands which were not open to purchase. The pre-emptors were employed by wealthy individuals and corporations and paid to swear falsely and violate the laws and defraud the government. Ignorant and innocent persons were often employed to break the law for the benefit of those who would obtain great wealth.[72]

The Pre-emption Act had outlived its usefulness and been superseded by the Homestead Act of 1862. Its repeal was repeatedly recommended by the Commissioner of the General Land Office.[73] Great benefits had been secured from it before 1882, but now it became a source of corruption. Its repeal was often discussed in Congress and at times at great length. In December, 1883, several bills were introduced in both the Senate and the House.[74] In 1886, the matter was again before Congress and debated at length.[75] A bill repealing the act passed the House [76] but failed in the Senate, and not until 1891 was it finally repealed.[77]

The Homestead Act was likewise abused. This region was not likely to be sought by bona fide homesteaders, yet thousands of homesteads were made. The government had made it easy for the landless to secure land for a home, but as a result the homesteader in this region became a tool for the land shark, and valuable lands passed into the hands of a few individuals, while the ones whom the government meant to protect and benefit did not profit much.

Congress did not remedy the abuses as soon as they appeared. The sentiment in favor of a law which had converted the wilderness into prosperous communities, a law which, since 1841, had served to furnish homes for the settlers and added so much to the country, was difficult to overcome. The Homestead Act continued to operate in Minnesota as elsewhere. Any modifications of the law applying to this state would naturally be suggested by the representatives from the state, and they, apparently, were interested in having it continue unchanged.

NOTES

1 Henry H. Eames, *Report of State Geologist on the Metalliferous Region Bordering on Lake Superior* (St. Paul, 1866), 11.

2 W. G. Swart, Notes of Work Done on the Eastern Mesabi Range by Peter Mitchell, MS in St. Louis County (Minn.) Historical Library. Albert H. Chester, Explorations of the Iron Regions of Northern Minnesota During the Years 1875–80, MS in St. Louis County Historical Library. David T. Adams, MS in private library. Mr. Adams gives the name of persons connected with the exploration.

3 Certified copy of Articles of Incorporation in the United States General Land Office, Division D, File 85/102690.

4 *Ibid.*

5 J. H. Gruber, "Minnesota's First Iron Mine," Duluth *Herald*, Dec. 9, 1911.

6 *Ibid.*, March 7 and 24, 1887.

7 *Hearings Before the Committee of the United States Steel Corporation* (Washington, 1911), 1890. Alfred Merritt, Reminiscences of Early Days at the Head of the Lakes, MS 16 in St. Louis County Historical Library.

8 Walter E. Van Brunt, ed., *History of Duluth and St. Louis County* (3 vols., Chicago, 1920), 1:293.

9 Duluth *Evening Herald*, March 26, 1892. Up to the end of 1890, 284 companies for the purpose of mining and quarrying were incorporated under the laws of Minnesota; 251 of the 284 were incorporated in the decade 1880–90. See N. H. and H. V. Winchell, *Iron Ores of Minnesota* (Minneapolis, 1891), 335–349.

10 Duluth *Daily News*, Feb. 25, 1892; Duluth *Evening Herald*, Feb. 27 and March 5, 1892; *Lake Superior Review*, March 11, 1892.

11 17 *U.S. Stat.*, 91–96.

12 *Ibid.*, 465.

13 *Congressional Globe*, 42 Congress, 3 session, pt. 2, p. 962.

14 *Ibid.*

15 *Ibid.*, 1322.

16 Register of Original Homestead Entries Made at Duluth. Entries are listed according to date of application.

17 *Ibid.*

18 *Ibid.*

19 A study of the Mineral Lease Prospecting Permits, 1–60, MS in the State Auditor's Office in St. Paul, shows that leases were secured over a large area of northeastern Minnesota. Some of the land leased by iron prospectors was 100 miles away from the present ranges.

20 U.S. General Land Office, Register of Original Homestead Entries.

21 Previous to 1880, 1,547 entries were made.

22 From 1880 to 1894, 8,105 homestead entries were made, as compared to 1,547 in the seventeen years previous.

23 26 *U.S. Stat.*, 1097.

24 U.S. General Land Office, Abstract of Declaratory Statements, 1880 to 1889.

25 U.S. General Land Office, Tract Book, Minnesota Townships, 63 N. R. 11 W.; T. 62 N. R. 14 W.; T. 61 N. R. 16 W.; T. 59 N. R. 17 W.

26 Field Notes of the U.S. Deputy Surveyor, 149: 601.

27 *Ibid.*, 140: 260.

28 Chase S. Osborn, *The Iron Hunter* (New York, 1919), 244.

29 In Township 57 north Range 21 west, 106 "additional homesteads" were made on Dec. 10, 1874. See U.S. General Land Office Tract Book, Minnesota, T. 57 N. R. 21 W.; also *ibid.*, T. 56 N. R. 21 W.

30 U.S. General Land Office, Book of Proclamations, Proc. No. 877.

31 Thomas Donaldson, *The Public Domain* (Washington, 1884), 1218.

32 John S. Pardee, In the Treasure Country, MS 5 in private library of Mr. Pardee.

33 *Ibid.*

34 Secretary of the Interior Hoke Smith, in forwarding a decision in this case to the Commissioner of the General Land Office, Dec. 21, 1894, stated that the records of it were probably the most voluminous ever transmitted to the department. See Decisions of the Department of the Interior and General Land Office in Cases Relating to the Public Lands, 19:548.

35 U.S. General Land Office, Letter Book, Division H, to Register and Receiver, 67:466.

36 *U.S. Reports*, 602.

37 Pardee, At the Foot of the Rainbow, MS 5. The Duluth *Daily News*, Feb. 10, 1891, stated that the land was worth $5,000,000, more or less. Again, it said that the land was so valuable that nobody knew what price to put on it. Since the contest closed, it had become less valuable. Mr. Pardee states that three mining companies went bankrupt trying to find the wealth they all knew was there.

38 For an account of this jam, see the Duluth *Daily News*, Aug. 16, 21, 27, 1891.

39 See *Annual Report of the Commissioner of the General Land Office for the Year 1882*, p. 12; also report for 1883, p. 207; for 1884, p. 15; for 1885, pp. 48, 49; for 1886, p. 3.

40 U.S. General Land Office, Division D, File 83/104871.

41 Agreement signed Oct. 11, 1883, *ibid.*

42 *Ibid.*, File 84/76208.

43 *Ibid.*, File 83/91993.

44 *Ibid.*

45 *Ibid.*, File 82/90896.

46 *Ibid.*, File 84/11075.

47 *Ibid.*

48 *General Land Office Report*, 1885, pp. 53 and 54; also *ibid.*, 1886, pp. 80 and 81.

49 March 3, 1891, Congress passed the Commutation Clause of the Homestead Act, which provides that entry under the Free Home-

stead Act may be commuted to cash entry after a period of 14 months' residence and cultivation. See 26 *U.S. Stat.*, 1098.

50 Senate Document no. 189, 58 Cong., 3 sess., 70.
51 U.S. General Land Office, Division D, File 92/56856.
52 *Ibid.*, File 92/90799.
53 *Ibid.*, File 94/110689.
54 *Ibid.*, File 94/121902. On March 19, 1895, LeSueur reported that the fraudulent homesteading had been brought to a standstill, but that the entrymen, encouraged by their attorneys, hoped to see the old system restored. File 95/30819.
55 Senate Doc. no. 189, 58 Cong., 3 sess., 72.
56 U.S. General Land Office, Tract Book, Minnesota, 60:185–192.
57 U.S. General Land Office, File 85/102690.
58 Affidavit of Edward Krelwits, U.S. General Land Office, File 86/64447. Also see U.S. General Land Office, Letter Book Division A to R and R, col. 24, 90–97. Also Files 85/102609 and 85/102813.
59 U.S. General Land Office, File 86/64447.
60 *Ibid.*
61 *Ibid.*, File 85/102690.
62 Duluth *Herald,* Dec. 9, 1911.
63 Deed showing transfer with papers in U.S. General Land Office, File 85/102690.
64 Their names are found in the Letter Books, Division P, 1892. From 1882 to 1902, no less than 40 different agents were assigned to duty in the Duluth district. In 1894, there were 118 districts in the United States. See *General Land Office Report,* 1894, pp. 360–428.
65 U.S. General Land Office, Letter Book, Division P to S.A., 4:117.
66 U.S. General Land Office, File 95/17394.
67 *Ibid.*, File 94/98042.
68 *Ibid.*, File 95/21874.
69 U.S. General Land Office, Letter Book P to S.A., 12:270–271.
70 U.S. General Land Office, File 92/119576.
71 *General Land Office Report,* 1885, p. 68.
72 Commissioner Wm. A. J. Sparks in 1885 reported that in northern Minnesota the pre-emption law served the speculative interests, and that 75 to 90 per cent of the pre-emption entries were fraudulent. *General Land Office Report,* 1885, p. 70.
73 *General Land Office Report,* 1882, p. 8; for 1883, p. 5; for 1884, p. 5; for 1885, p. 70.
74 *Congressional Record,* 48 Cong., 1 sess., 15(1):46, 58, 77, 92.
75 *Ibid.*, 49 Cong., 1 sess., 17(5):5375.
76 *Ibid.*, 5380.
77 26 *U.S. Stat.*, 1095.

The War Veteran and the Public Lands

JERRY A. O'CALLAGHAN

Reprinted by permission from Agricultural History, *Volume 28* (*1954*), *pages 163–168.*

W HEN the thirteen British colonies in North America severed their political connection with Great Britain, it was not at all strange that they should turn to the distribution of their undeveloped lands as a means of making war service more enticing. The vacant lands cried for development; furthermore there was a long historical tradition of granting land to veterans. Herodotus mentions such a practice. The classic example from antiquity is, of course, the Roman custom of rewarding the veterans of its legions with land. The colonies themselves had offered tracts on the frontier to men who would form buffer settlements against Indian forays.[1] The Proclamation of 1763 had provided grants of land to regulars of the British army and navy for service in the French and Indian War.

The colonies had a strong distaste for professional or mercenary forces. In that light, what more appropriate reward could there be for the citizen who had served his country than a portion of the rich, undeveloped land? Although largely unnoticed, the United States is still offering land to its veterans. On the reclamation projects of the Far West, parcels of the public lands are still opened, periodically, to settlement under the Homestead Act and the regulations of the Bureau of Reclamation. Veterans of World War II [were] granted [in 1944] a ninety-day filing preference on land opened for public settlement.[2] In this day of veterans numbering in the millions and arable acres in the thousands, veterans with farm experience (required by the Bureau of Reclamation) are now the only ones who can still acquire a farm under the historic Homestead Act. And even these farms are so limited in number that they are awarded by lottery.

Somewhat ironically, the history of land grants to veterans began in the United States with attempts to woo German mercenaries away from the British armies. On August 14, 1776, the Continental Congress announced a bounty of 50 acres of land to "all such foreigners who shall leave the armies of his Brittanic Majesty in America." [3] Two years later Congress enlarged the grants. In a resolution of April 29, 1778, it offered to "officers and soldiers of the King of Great Britain, not subjects of said King" a land bounty graduated in rank from 800 acres for a captain to 50 acres for a private. [4] From the inconclusive record it is difficult to know whether the response was as enthusiastic as the appeal. It has been determined that there were some 5,000 deserters from a total force of 30,000 German mercenaries. [5] It has not been determined how many subsequently applied for and received land.

A month after the initial appeal to the Hessians, the Continental Congress offered land to its own citizens as an inducement to enter service. Before September, 1776, the military forces of the rebelling colonies consisted of the militia and volunteers of the several colonies. General George Washington was thoroughly dissatisfied with their showing against British regulars. After the defeat at Long Island in the summer of 1776, Washington urged the creation of a continental army and suggested that the "addition of Land might have a considerable Influence on a permanent Inlistment." [6]

Congress acted, on September 16, 1776, by establishing eighty-eight battalions and providing for a land bounty in graduated allotment from 500 acres for a colonel to 100 acres for a private. [7] Congress was thus offering land which it did not have to give. In 1776, all that Congress possessed was the expectation of acquiring the British Crown Lands in America. Maryland at first did not concur in offering land. As the battalions of the Continental Army were raised by the states, Maryland's refusal forced an immediate consideration of the vexatious problem of the future ownership of the Crown Lands. It was a problem not fully settled until 1802 when Georgia, last of seven states with substantial claims, ceded its rights to the central government. [8]

Notwithstanding, Congress, in 1780, extended the land bounty to major generals and brigadier generals in the amount of 1,000 and 800 acres, respectively; and it also granted bounties in the medical department on a scale comparable to those in the line services. [9]

Men came forward to serve, but no effective system was in operation until 1796 to provide their bounty lands. Before Congress could grant any land it had to acquire undisputed title to the western lands. Even after the conclusion of the Revolution this involved not only the claims of seven states but also the problem of Indian title. And last of all, a manner of survey had to be determined. In short, a general land policy had to be outlined.[10] In consequence of all these complications, none subject to quick or easy solution, delay in granting the bounty lands was inevitable.

The famous ordinance of 1785 ". . . for Ascertaining the mode of disposing Lands in the Western Territory" did provide for surveys of bounty lands, but none were conveyed during the life of the Confederation.

In an indirect manner, however, the Confederation did redeem some of the land pledges through the agency of the Ohio Company. The principal promoters of that company were Continental officers eager to use their land bounties in promotion of a land company. The Confederation Congress approved a contract, July 25, 1787, for the sale of public lands to this Ohio Company.[11] It provided that one-seventh of the acreage could be paid in military land warrants. The tract was reserved in Ohio, as was that of John Cleves Symmes, who purchased a tract under a similar arrangement. The sale price in both cases was $1 an acre calculated in the depreciated Continental currency. By these arrangements the government met 238,694 acres of their military land obligations.[12]

An important obstacle to the settlement of the western land problem in general and the bounty-land problem in particular had been overcome on March 1, 1784, when Virginia signed its deed of cession to its western claims.[13] The cession specifically reserved two tracts. A reserve of 150,000 acres, ultimately located near the falls of the Ohio, was assigned to the men of the George Rogers Clark expedition. Another reserve was authorized north of the Ohio River between the Scioto and Miami rivers.[14] The second reserve was established in case there was not enough land south of the Ohio to satisfy the Virginia bounties. The Congress of the new federal government confirmed the reservation in 1790.[15] This reserve is noteworthy. Within its bounds 3,770,000 acres were located.[16] Its administration illustrates how long veteran benefits can command legislative attention. Although the reserve was abolished in 1852 when Virginia, in consideration of a scrip law, ceded the unlocated portions to the United States, Congress passed legislation concerning the Virginia bounties as late as 1871.[17] Between 1790 and 1871 the Congress adopted forty-six acts relating to the Virginia Military District.

In 1796, twenty years after the first bounty enactment, the federal government allotted a tract in Ohio for the location of the Revolutionary bounties.[18] The tract, although not so named in the act, became known as the United States Military District. All land taken as Revolutionary bounty, except that in the Virginia reservation, had to be located here until 1830. Scrip was then issued which could purchase land in Ohio, Indiana, and Illinois.[19] A total of 2,095,220 acres was patented in the district, 70 per cent of it by approximately one hundred men.[20]

Thus the national government delivered 9,549,949 acres of public land to the veterans of the Revolution (or their descendants).[21] The last warrant was issued in 1886, one hundred and ten years after the enactment of the first Revolutionary bounty.[22]

When Congress undertook to organize the military establishment for the War of 1812, it was in a position to act with more assurance, since it now held an indisputable title to the public domain. In increasing the regular army, Congress featured a land bounty as an essential part of the authorization. It offered, in 1811, a 160-acre bounty plus three months' extra pay for the completion of five years of service, or less, if deemed proper by the government.[23] This practice was standard until the very close of the war, when the bounty was doubled.[24] Officers were not given land until 1855, when they received a retroactive bounty. Members of the naval service who had been excluded in this and previous bounties also received land in the 1855 act.

The Congress reserved 6,000,000 acres "fit for cultivation, not otherwise appropriated and to which the Indian title has been extinguished" for the satisfaction of the War of 1812 military warrants.[25] This land was reserved in three tracts of 2,000,000 acres each in Michigan, Illinois, and Louisiana territories between the St. Francis and Arkansas rivers (in the present state of Arkansas). The lands in Michigan were later adjudged unfit for cultivation and new reservations were provided in 1816: one of 1,500,000 acres in Illinois Territory and another of 500,000 acres in Missouri Territory north of the Missouri River.[26] These land awards to old soldiers were not to be seized "by virtue of any process, or suit at law or judgment of court" for debts contracted prior to the issuance of patent. The War of 1812 cost the United States 4,452,760 acres of its public lands.[27]

In the 1830's military land obligations figured prominently in the accelerated speculation in western land. In 1830 Congress authorized the exchange of Virginia warrants for assignable scrip for the purchase of lands open to sale in Ohio, Illinois, and Indiana.[28] There was, however, provision against purchase of more than 200,000 acres by one individual employing such scrip. Two other acts converting military land warrants into scrip were passed in the early 1830's. By these acts Revolutionary and Virginia warrants were converted into scrip for the purchase of public lands.[29] Under the 1832 act, 300,000 acres passed to private ownership; under that of 1833 another 200,000 acres were withdrawn.[30] After 1842, warrants for the Revolution and the War of 1812 were honored for any land open to private entry.[31]

In organizing for the war with Mexico, the public domain was once again used as a means of inducing enlistment. Each soldier who served twelve months was entitled to 160 acres of any land open to public sale.[32] The Congress also gave soldiers the option of land or treasury scrip worth $100 bearing 6 per cent interest. For men who served less than one year, 40 acres or $25 in scrip was offered.

Immediately after the Mexican War the approach to land bounties was radically changed. The land bounty had been an inducement for enlistment. After 1850 land was given to men whose service had not been covered in previous bounty grants. In the first of these inclusive acts, which passed in 1850, land was given to each of the surviving "commissioned and non-commissioned officers, privates, whether of regulars, volunteers, rangers or militia in the War of 1812 or any Indian war since 1790 and to each commissioned officer in the War with Mexico," or their widows or minor children, graduated according to term of service: for nine months, 160 acres; for four months, 80 acres; and for one month, 40 acres.[33]

In 1855 the most important bounty act, in terms of acreage conveyed, granted 160 acres to

. . . commissioned and non-commissioned officers, musicians, privates whether regulars, rangers or militia . . . and every officer, commissioned and non-commissioned, seaman, ordinary seaman, flotilla man, marine clerk or landsman in the navy in any of the wars since 1790, and the survivors of the militia or volunteers, or State troops . . . whose services have been paid by the United States.[34]

Also listed as beneficiaries of the national gratitude were wagon masters and teamsters, volunteers at the Battle of King's Mountain in the Revolution; volunteers at the Battle of Nickojack against "the confederated savages of the south"; volunteers against the British attack on Lewiston, Delaware, in the War of 1812; and the chaplains in all wars. In 1856 the bounty was extended to officers, seamen, and marines in the naval service during the Revolution.[35] To be eligible under the 1855 act, fourteen days' service or participation in one battle was required.

Of the 73,000,000 acres of public land conveyed as bounty for war service, almost one-half (32,000,000) was given under the 1855 grant.[36] This acreage was thrown into the speculative whirl of the 1850's when Congress, in 1852 and 1858, declared land warrants assignable.[37] They were declared such for the ostensible purpose of allowing a veteran who could not take up land himself to realize something on his warrant. For several years during the 1850's the amount of land taken by military warrant was one-third again as much as that sold for cash. The Secretary of the Interior reported in 1851 that in the preceding year 2,454,000 acres had been conveyed by military warrant, while 1,846,847 acres had been sold for cash.[38]

Assignability forestalled placement of freeholding veterans on the land. Warrants and scrip became circulating media, their value noted in newspapers and financial journals. With government land selling at a minimum of $1.25 per acre, there was an automatic ceiling to their value. Prices fell as low as sixty cents per acre. Warrants were purchased in the East, where their number and the distance from available land made them cheap, and sent to the West where they could be sold to the hosts of locators swarming around land offices.[39]

But there was keen opposition in the public land states to this practice of purchasing large blocks of land for speculation. The congressmen from these states were adamant against assignability of scrip. In the 1850's they viewed such bountiful land gratuities as cursed schemes to withhold land from the actual settler. Westerners were particularly stung at the thought of eastern and even foreign capital holding western land *in mortmain.*[40]

To give land and at the same time prevent speculation bordered on the impossible. "I suppose whatever regulation were adopted," one legislator admitted, "unless we adopt the law of primogeniture, and deny to the holders the right of conveying it away [speculation] will follow. . . ." [41] In fact, Thomas Hart Benton, Missouri's famous expansionist senator, advocated such entailment. He wished to entail bounty lands so that they might not be sold. Even if sold, he would have provided that they be made recoverable by widows or other heirs.[42]

Even Congress itself was charged with being a party to speculation in military warrants. One western senator asserted, in 1856, that the House (where he had served in 1852) had a direct stake in assignability because members "had their pockets full of land warrants." [43]

Cash in lieu of land was often suggested as a means of reward, but little attention was given to the proposal. Veterans themselves were more interested in land than in other forms of reward. The 1847 Mexican War bounty gave a choice between land and treasury scrip. In 1850 a report of the Secretary of the Interior indicated an overwhelming preference for land. Land scrip had been allowed for 70,390 men, against 2,992 who wanted Treasury scrip.[44]

The prairie states of the Mississippi Valley were the arena of settlement during the years when the military land warrants were most abundant. It is not surprising, therefore, that Iowa was settled in large measure by application of the military land warrants. In no other state did settlement by military warrant figure so prominently. Over 14,000,000 of Iowa's 36,000,000 fertile acres were conveyed as a reward to veterans, although it is questionable whether the veterans received the real benefits.[45] Illinois and Missouri followed Iowa as second and third states for the location of bounty lands.

The government showed utmost consideration to claimants; at least it would appear so from official records. Its leniency doubtless made it prey to petty frauds, although it denied thousands of fraudulent claims. At the same time, Congress extended itself to make certain that veterans could come into possession of their land warrants. It once went so far as to pass an act accepting verbal evidence as to service.[46] There were numerous acts for re-issuance of lost warrants, and Congress passed numerous acts to extend the time limits for locating bounties.

There was never concerted attack on the principle of granting land to veterans. Robert Toombs, the Georgia statesman, was one of the few outspokenly opposed. Men taking issue during debate were always careful to announce that they were arguing details only.

Echoes of shady dealings and sharp practices sounded in congressional halls. One senator reported that ex-soldiers bothered him for years with letters seeking relief because they had sold their warrants for two, three, or five dollars.[47]

The passage, in 1862, of the long-awaited Homestead Act precluded the granting of Civil War land bounties. Men devoted to the homestead principle realized that the land bounties, if voted, would be a means by which speculators could engross thousands of arable acres to the detriment of home-seeking freeholders. Led by George W. Julian, Indiana Republican and Chairman of the House Public Lands Committee, homestead defenders thwarted repeated bounty efforts.

The original Homestead Act gave minor privileges to Civil War veterans. In 1872, in answer to the demand for a bounty act, veterans were granted the privilege of having their service counted as residence time upon a homestead, except that a minimum residence of one year was required.[48] But even after this concession, proposed by Julian, which certainly made acquisition of land by an interested veteran a simple matter, there was pressure for military bounty land.

Another attempt to vote a land bounty was made in 1873 when an amendment to a bill granting further privileges to veterans under the Homestead Act would have authorized a grant of 160 acres to men who had served more than ninety days in the army or navy during the

TABLE 1

Summary of Land Located under Various Bounty Acts [a]

Warrants	Acreage
Act of 1776	9,549,949
Act of 1812	4,807,520
Act of 1847	12,956,520
Act of 1850	12,864,200
Act of 1852	680,200
Act of 1855	32,627,010
Total	73,485,399

[a] The Revolutionary total is computed from scattered statistics [cf. pp. 111—112]. The remainder are from the U.S. Commissioner of the General Land Office, *Report* [with detailed statement of business by divisions], 1907, p. 195. In 1907 there were 18,730 warrants outstanding, covering 2,138,180 [acres]. In 1951 the Secretary of the Interior refused to accept military warrants filed upon off-shore oil lands in the Gulf of Mexico.

Civil War. This amendment passed in the House but failed in the Senate, possibly because an adverse committee report marshalled a tremendous array of facts against it.[49] Such a grant could conceivably have used all of the remaining arable public lands to satisfy its terms. The Commissioner of the General Land Office practically branded the bill a scheme of land speculators who needed a new issue of military warrants to replenish their "stock in trade." [50]

The blessings of the military land-bounty system were mixed. There are no exact figures, but it is fairly evident that the percentage of veterans receiving land was small. In effect many received a cash bounty to the amount that their warrant would command on the open market. One study has suggested that this was the understanding of both the soldiers and statesmen of the Revolution.[51]

In the interest of orderly disposition of the public lands, an outright cash bounty might have been more to the point, but the veterans themselves were not interested in cash while there was a prospect of obtaining land. And to the West "orderly disposition" would have meant more administration and less land. The cash resources of the federal government left the public domain its one readily available asset to meet the need to reward war veterans. And insofar as the bounty acts promoted "early settlement" and "substantial cultivation," they were justified within the expansive dynamic of nineteenth-century America.

NOTES

1 Amelia C. Ford, *Colonial Precedents of Our National Land System as it Existed in 1800 (Bulletin of the University of Wisconsin,* no. 352, History Series, vol. 2, no. 2, Madison, 1909–1910), 103–107.
2 58 *U.S. Stat.,* 748. The diminishing availability of public land after World War I is reflected in the granting of filing preferences to veterans. 41 *U.S. Stat.,* 434; 42 *U.S. Stat.,* 358; 46 *U.S. Stat.,* 580. For an example of qualifications and procedures see Public Notice No. 43, August 13, 1946, *Federal Register,* 11:8736–8739.
3 Worthington C. Ford, ed., *Journals of the Continental Congress* (34 vols., Washington, 1907–1937), 5:654. (Cited hereafter as *Journals.*)
4 *Ibid.,* 10:405–409.
5 Edward J. Lowell, *Hessians in the Revolution* (New York, 1884), 300.
6 John C. Fitzpatrick, ed., *The Writings of George Washington* (39 vols., Washington, 1931–1944), 6:6.
7 *Journals,* 5:763.

8 See Rudolph Freund, "Military Bounty Lands and the Origins of the Public Domain," *Agricultural History*, 20:8–18 (January, 1946) [*reprinted in this volume, pp. 15–34*].

9 *Journals*, 17:726–727; 18:846.

10 The complications are admirably analyzed in William Thomas Hutchinson, "Military Bounty Lands of the American Revolution in Ohio" (unpublished Ph.D. dissertation, University of Chicago, 1927).

11 *Journals*, 33:400–401.

12 U.S. Congress, *American State Papers: Public Lands* (8 vols., Washington, 1832–1861), 7 Congress, 1 session (1801), 1:119.

13 *Journals*, 26:112–117.

14 *Ibid.*, 115.

15 1 *U.S. Stat.*, 183.

16 Thomas Donaldson, *The Public Domain, Its History with Statistics* (47 Cong., 2 sess., House Misc. Doc. no. 45, serial 2158, Washington, 1884), 233.

17 10 *U.S. Stat.*, 143.

18 1 *U.S. Stat.*, 490–491.

19 4 *U.S. Stat.*, 422–425.

20 Hutchinson, "Military Bounty Lands of the American Revolution in Ohio," 157.

21 This is an approximation based upon the following figures: Ohio Company and Symmes tracts, 238, 700; Virginia Military District, 3,770,000; United States Military District, 2,095,220; scrip (1830–1835), 1,478,293; scrip (1852), 1,041,976; and the act of 1855, 925,760. This total does not include the grants, some of them very generous, made by the various states. See Matthias Nordberg Orfield, *Federal Land Grants to the States with Special Reference to Minnesota* (*University of Minnesota Studies in the Social Sciences*, no. 2, Minneapolis, 1915), 23–25; Allan Nevins, *The American States During and After the Revolution* (New York, 1924), 672.

22 Hutchinson, "Military Bounty Lands of the American Revolution in Ohio," 177.

23 2 *U.S. Stat.*, 669.

24 *Ibid.*, 672; 3 *U.S. Stat.*, 96, 97, 146, 147.

25 2 *U.S. Stat.*, 729–730.

26 3 *U.S. Stat.*, 332. The military lands in Illinois have been studied by Theodore L. Carlson, *The Illinois Military Tract, A Study in Land Occupation, Utilization and Tenure* (*University of Illinois Studies in the Social Sciences*, vol. 32, no. 2, Urbana, 1951). The land passed quickly into the hands of speculators, large and small, at an average $115 per quarter section. The small speculators suffered in the Panic of 1819. The success of large holders was variable, according to the sampling provided by Carlson.

27 Donaldson, *The Public Domain*, 236.

28 4 *U.S. Stat.*, 422–425.

29 *Ibid.*, 578, 665.

30 Donaldson, *The Public Domain*, 236.

31 5 *U.S. Stat.*, 497.
32 9 *U.S. Stat.*, 125–126.
33 *Ibid.*, 520.
34 10 *U.S. Stat.*, 701.
35 11 *U.S. Stat.*, 8.
36 See Table 1.
37 10 *U.S. Stat.*, 3; 11 *U.S. Stat.*, 309.
38 *Congressional Globe*, 32 Cong., 1 sess. (1851), appendix, 9–10.
39 Such transactions are sketched in "Letters of J. W. Denison," *Iowa Journal of History and Politics*, 31:96 (1933).
40 For examples of western feeling, see *Congressional Globe*, 31 Cong., 1 sess., pt. 2(1850), 1275; appendix, 1685–1686.
41 *Ibid.*, appendix, 1686.
42 *Ibid.*, 29 Cong., 2 sess. (1847), 192; 31 Cong., 1 sess. (1850), appendix, 1686.
43 *Ibid.*, 34 Cong., 1 sess. (1856), 928–929.
44 *Ibid.*, 31 Cong., 1 sess. (1850), appendix, 21.
45 Roscoe L. Lokken, *Iowa Public Land Disposal* (Iowa City, 1942), 149.
46 11 *U.S. Stat.*, 8.
47 *Congressional Globe*, 30 Cong., 2 sess. (1849), 265.
48 17 *U.S. Stat.*, 49–50.
49 *Congressional Globe*, 42 Cong., 3 sess. (1872), 167.
50 Senate Report no. 482, 42 Cong., 3 sess., 14 (serial 1550).
51 Hutchinson, "Military Bounty Lands of the American Revolution in Ohio," 7.

The Railroad Land Grant Legend in American History Texts

ROBERT S. HENRY

Mr. Henry wishes to acknowledge the assistance given him in preparing this article by Carlton J. Corliss and L. I. McDougle.

Reprinted by permission from the Mississippi Valley Historical Review, *Volume 32 (1945), pages 171–194.*

I N 1850, the United States government had a public domain of approximately 1,400,000,000 acres, vacant, unoccupied, and, for lack of transportation, largely unusable and unsalable.[1] Between that year and the end of 1871, the government undertook to use a portion of this land to encourage and assist the building of railroads in vacant or sparsely settled sections, in the same way in which previously it had aided the building of wagon roads and canals. The resulting series of transactions came to be known as the federal railroad land grants, a subject frequently mentioned in high school and college texts which are the first, last, and only works on the history of their country read by many, if not most, Americans. This paper is the result of an examination of the treatment of the federal land-grant transactions in thirty-seven representative texts.

Since the treatment of a subject of this sort in such works must be brief, and even, in a sense, incidental, accuracy both as to the essential facts themselves and as to their place and proportion in the whole setting becomes all the more important. This inquiry is directed, therefore, to these facts and the manner of their treatment. It is limited to the federal land grants because those are the grants which, for the most part, are discussed in the works examined, and are the grants about which the most complete information has been compiled, published, and made available.

A balanced story of the federal land-grant transactions requires reasonably correct answers to these questions, at the very least:

How much land was granted to railroads, and what proportion was this of the whole public domain?

What proportion of the railroad mileage of the country received land grants from the government?

What was this land worth?

What were the terms and conditions of the grants? Were they gifts, or did the government get as well as give?

How Much Land?

The first of these questions, purely a matter of recorded fact, deals with the amount of land granted to railroads by the United States government. In the standard general work on the subject, Donaldson's *Public Domain,* published by the government in 1884, the total amount of land that would be necessary to fulfill all the acts granting lands to railroads was estimated at 155,504,994 acres.[2] The amount of land actually patented to railroads, however, fell substantially short of this acreage, for a variety of reasons—non-completion of the lines or other failure to comply with the conditions of the grants, or lack of sufficient acreage within the designated limits to fulfill the terms of the grants. The acreage to which the railroads actually received title appears in the annual reports of the Commissioner of the General Land Office, the latest such report [1943] showing a total of 131,350,534 acres.[3]

Of the thirty-seven American history textbooks examined, twenty-four make specific reference to the area granted to railroads by the federal government. Of these twenty-four, one gives clear and approximately correct figures as to the whole area granted, while one other comes within 10 per cent of the correct figure.[4] Two others which do not state the area as a whole give correct partial figures.[5] In seven works, a substantially correct statement at one place is contradicted elsewhere, either by another larger figure or by a graphic presentation which greatly exaggerates the area granted.[6] Eight others show the area granted, either graphically or in text, or both, as anywhere from nearly one-fifth more than it was, up to about four times the correct area.[7] Five give partial figures only, which either are incorrect or are so presented as to give a misleading impression.[8] Others make neither arithmetical nor graphic presentation of the area granted, but rely entirely on adjectives. In most of the books, in fact, such adjectives as "huge," "vast," "enormous," "staggering," and "breath-taking" are parts of the treatment of the subject of area.

LAND-GRANT MAPS, RIGHT AND WRONG

The most potent source of this exaggerated impression of the size of land grants, and the prevailing confusion of thought and inaccuracies of statement in their measurement, seems to be uncritical acceptance of land-grant maps which are incorrectly understood and described by the text writers.

To understand the official land-grant maps, it is necessary to bear in mind the "checkerboard pattern" in which land was granted to the railroads. First, there were original, or primary, limits within which the grantees were to receive alternate sections, non-mineral in character, or a total of one-half the area within a strip of land of a given width lying on both sides of the track, provided these sections had not previously been granted or otherwise disposed of, or reserved from grant for other public purposes, such as school grants, forest, and other reservations. In lieu of the land which had been previously disposed of or was reserved, the grantee was to be allowed to select a like amount of land from a contiguous zone—the so-called indemnity limits.[9] (It is necessary to bear in mind, also, the fact that the official maps include not only grants to railroads, but also grants for wagon roads, canals, and river improvements.) The four principal patterns followed, with variations, in the several different land-grant acts were:

1. Grants of alternate sections of land in primary strips embracing the area within 6 miles on either side of the proposed railroad, with indemnity limits outside thereof extending 15 or 20 miles from the railroad.

2. Grants of alternate sections of land in primary strips embracing the area within 10 miles on either side of the proposed railroad, some without indemnity limits, others with indemnity limits outside thereof extending 20 or 30 miles from the railroad.

3. Grants of alternate sections of land in primary strips embracing the area within 20 miles on either side of the proposed railroad, some without indemnity limits, others with indemnity limits outside thereof extending 25, 30, or 50 miles from the railroad.

4. Grants of alternate sections of land in primary strips embracing the area within 40 miles on either side of the proposed railroad, with indemnity limits outside thereof extending 50, and in some cases 60, miles from the railroad. This pattern applied to territories only.

Under Pattern 1, for instance, the railroad received the equivalent of six sections of land (three on either side of the railroad) within the primary strips if available; otherwise within the indemnity limits. In no case did the railroad receive more than six sections per mile of road. Thus, where the primary and indemnity limits embraced an area 40 miles in width, the railroad actually received a maximum of only slightly less than one-seventh of that area, or the equivalent of a solid strip 6 miles in width.

Under Pattern 3, the railroad was granted the equivalent of twenty sections of land (ten on either side of the railroad) within the primary strips if available; otherwise within the indemnity limits. Where the indemnity limits extended 50 miles from the railroad, the maximum area that the railroad could receive was one-fifth of the total area embraced by the primary and indemnity strips.

The earliest of the general land-grant maps, apparently, was published by the government in 1878, in connection with a report on arid lands. Revised and brought up to date, it was again published by the government in 1883, and is included in Donaldson's well-known and widely available *Public Domain*. Again brought up to date, the map was republished in 1913 by the United States Department of Commerce and Labor in its report on *The Lumber Industry*.[10]

Each of these maps showed the limits of both the primary and indemnity zones, while the latest of the maps, that of 1913, showed also, by a special hatching, the grants which had been forfeited for non-completion of the roads within the terms of the acts making the grant and under which, therefore, no railroad had received lands. The whole was covered, on this map, by the correctly descriptive caption: "Map of the United States showing the limits within which land grants were made by the Federal Government to aid in the construction of railroads and wagon roads." The map also carried a legend explaining that "the maximum amount of land obtainable was one-half that within the primary limits, the lands granted being in the alternate survey sections. The maximum was often not obtained."

The last sentence refers to the fact that in many of the grants, especially in the older and more settled land-grant states, it was not possible to locate the maximum acreage allowed even within the indemnity limits. The situation is thus outlined on page 222 of the 1913 report referred to:

In this connection the caution is repeated against assuming that the entire area within the limits shown on the map was granted to the railroads. The first set of heavy lines on each side of a road indicates the "primary limits" of the grant . . . within which limits it was to receive each alternate section (or part thereof) not already disposed of or reserved. The possible maximum of a grant, therefore, was half of the land within the primary limits. The second set of heavy lines, seen farther out on each side of the road in many grants, indicates the "indemnity limits" referred to above within which the railroad could select vacant alternate sections (or parts thereof) to make up for lands within the primary limits that had been previously disposed of or reserved. Often so much land had been disposed of or reserved both in the primary and the indemnity limits that a road received considerably less than its possible maximum. In Iowa so much land had already been disposed of at private sale, under warrants and to settlers, that although the State appears practically covered by grants, only a little more than one-eighth its area was received by the railroads. But in regions where there was less of prior purchase and settlement the railroads secured a higher proportion; in some cases the whole of the possible maximum.[11]

The several government publications of the map became the basis of two privately published maps, that of Professors Hart and Bolton in their series of American history maps published in 1919,[12] and that in Paullin's *Atlas of the Historical Geography of the United States*,[13] published in 1932, both of which are careful to give like information, either on the map itself or in accompanying explanatory material.

Even with the most scrupulous explanation, however, it is difficult not to get an exaggerated impression of size from maps which show a shaded area twice as great as the actual grants, as in the case of the Hart map, and approximately four times as great, as in the case of the government publications and the Paullin map. Without such understanding and explanation, the maps become downright wrong. And, unfortunately for popular understanding of the facts of history, it is in this misleading form and with incorrect captions that almost all land-grant maps have been circulated.

The first such use of the map, apparently, was in the presidential year of 1884, when the Democratic party issued a campaign poster featuring what purported to be a map of lands granted to railroads, but was actually a map of the extreme limits of the widest zones within which some lands might have been granted not only to railroads but also to wagon roads and river improvements, under the caption: "How the Public Domain Has Been Squandered—Map showing the 139,403,026 acres of the people's land . . . worth at $2 an acre $278,806,052 given by Republican Congresses to Railroad Corporations. . . ."[14]

Apparently those who compiled the poster overlooked the fact that the shaded area on the featured map represented about four times the number of acres stated in the accompanying text. The figures given in the text, however, are completely overshadowed by the pictorial impression of the map itself—an interesting example of the validity of the Chinese proverb as to the comparative force and effectiveness of words and pictures.

This effective pictorial exaggeration is perpetuated in the maps subsequently appearing in history texts. Nine of the works examined in this study present maps which include wagon road and river improvement grants as well as those for railroads, and which show the full area of the indemnity limits of both completed and non-completed grants, without explanation or distinction as between primary and indemnity zones, and with captions which, in all but two cases, unqualifiedly describe the shaded strips as showing lands granted to railroads.[15]

One work, indeed, enlarges upon its erroneous caption by declaring that "the nation gave the railroad builders a kingdom in land. No such lavish generosity was ever dreamed of before. The map on page 68 tells better than words what vast areas were presented to the railroad companies." [16]

The two books which qualify the statement that the shaded areas of the map show lands granted to railroads point out that they were to receive only alternate sections, or one-half the area shown, but show on their maps not the primary limits but the much more extensive indemnity limits.

Accompanying this article are two maps identified by number. Map No. 1 is typical of the sort published in many of the textbooks examined. In contrast, Map No. 2 is drawn so as to show the approximate location of the grants which were actually completed. The widths of lines are proportioned to show the equivalent of the areas actually certified and patented to the railroads. In many instances, the acreage certified and patented was considerably less than the acreage granted, due to forfeitures, previous transfers, federal reservations, and other causes. The startling contrast between the two maps indicates the extent of the vivid misinformation about railroad land grants which has become all but staple in history texts.

Besides the works which reproduce the erroneous land-grant map (No. 1) itself, others seem to have used it uncritically as the source of information for textual comparisons of area which, of course, reflect

Map No. 1.—This map, originally drawn to show the extreme outer limits of areas within which some land *might be granted* to railroads, is frequently reproduced in American history texts with captions describing it as showing lands *actually granted*—thereby exaggerating by approximately four times the area received by railroads.

Map No. 2.—The federal government granted lands to railroads in alternate sections, retaining the sections between. It is impossible to present this "checkerboard" pattern on so small a map, but the shaded areas show the approximate locations of the land grants, and are in proportion to the amounts actually received by railroads.

the map's own exaggerations and inaccuracies. Thus, according to one work, "more than half of the northern tier of states lying against Canada from Lake Michigan to the Pacific" and "about half of New Mexico, Arizona and California," were included in federal land grants.[17] That would be approximately 272,000,000 acres in only eight states, and yet the same work gives the total area of all the federal railroad grants in twenty-six states as only 155,000,000 acres—which itself is one-sixth more than the railroads actually received.

Table 2 shows, by states, the discrepancy between the approximate acreage of land grants as they appear on Map No. 1 and the actual acreage received by the railroads as reported by the General Land Office.

Of course, the total federal grants, whether the figure be the 155,-000,000 acres which it was originally contemplated might be turned over to the railroads, or the 131,351,000 acres which were finally patented to them, when looked at by themselves, are indeed a great quantity of land. That objection was made in the debate on the bill for the first of the railroad grants, back in 1850. "We are met by the objection," said Senator William R. King, afterwards vice president of the United States, "that this is an immense grant—that it is a great quantity of land. Well, sir, it is a great quantity; but it will be there for five hundred years; and unless some mode of the kind proposed be adopted, it will never command ten cents." The senator was looking at the land involved not as an absolute quantity but as a portion of a domain which, as he said, "can never be of any value . . . unless some direct communication by railroad, or some other way, is made." [18]

That was the way the land-grant transaction was looked upon by the men who urged its adoption in the beginning—the Whigs, Henry Clay and William H. Seward among them, and the Democrats, Stephen A. Douglas, Thomas H. Benton, and Lewis Cass. It was the way in which it was regarded by Abraham Lincoln, in whose administration and with whose approval the policy found its widest use and application. Part of a domain, immense in itself, was to be used to give value to the vastly more immense whole.

This point of comparison, so essential to any proper understanding of the transaction, is almost wholly lost sight of in the works examined. Only three of the twenty-four which discuss the area of the federal land grants, in fact, in any way relate the areas granted to the size of the public domain as a whole, and but one of the three gives the proportion correctly. Of the others, one says that the land grants were

TABLE 2

Federal Land Grants to Railroads [a]

State	Total acreage [b]	Apparent area shown on Map No. 1		Actual area shown on Map No. 2	
		Acres	Per cent of state area	Acres [c]	Per cent of state area
Alabama	33,029,760	14,863,392	45	2,747,479	8.3
Arizona	72,901,760	34,263,827	47	7,695,203	10.6
Arkansas	33,985,280	12,574,554	37	2,586,970	7.6
California	101,563,520	40,625,408	40	11,585,393	11.4
Colorado	66,718,080	6,671,808	10	3,757,673	5.6
Florida	37,478,400	10,868,736	29	2,218,705	5.9
Idaho	53,476,480	8,021,472	15	1,320,591	2.5
Illinois	36,096,000	12,633,600	35	2,595,133	7.2
Indiana	23,226,240	2,322,624 [d]	10	. . . .	. . .
Iowa	36,019,200	32,417,280	90	4,711,328	13.1
Kansas	52,656,640	32,647,117	62	8,234,013	15.6
Louisiana	31,054,720	20,496,115	66	1,375,000	4.4
Michigan	37,258,240	27,943,680	75	3,134,058	8.4
Minnesota	53,803,520	37,662,464	70	9,953,008	18.5
Mississippi	30,538,240	6,718,413	22	1,075,345	3.5
Missouri	44,591,360	12,485,581	28	2,328,674	5.2
Montana	94,168,320	44,259,110	47	14,736,919	15.6
Nebraska	49,431,680	13,840,870	28	7,272,623	14.7
Nevada	70,745,600	8,489,472	12	5,086,283	7.2
New Mexico	77,866,240	26,474,522	34	3,355,179	4.3
North Dakota	45,225,600	22,612,800	50	10,697,490	23.7
Oregon	62,067,840	24,827,136	40	3,655,390	5.9
South Dakota	49,310,080	2,465,504 [e]	5	. . . .	. . .
Utah	54,346,240	4,347,699	8	2,230,085	4.1
Washington	43,642,880	29,240,730	67	9,582,878	22.0
Wisconsin	35,938,560	24,438,221	68	3,666,062	10.2
Wyoming	62,664,960	13,786,291	22	5,749,051	9.2
Total	1,389,805,440	527,998,426	38	131,350,534	9.5

[a] As reported in U.S. General Land Office Information Bulletin, 1939 Series, No. 5, *Transportation.* . . .

[b] Table 1, *Report of Commissioner of General Land Office . . . June 30, 1943.*

[c] *Ibid.,* Tables 76 and 77.

[d] No federal lands in Indiana were granted to railroads.

[e] 443,312 acres of the Winona & St. Peter R. R. extending into Dakota Territory (now part of South Dakota) are included with Minnesota by the General Land Office. No other railroad company received a land grant in South Dakota.

"one-seventh" of the public domain, and another 14 per cent.[19] The actual figure was less than one-tenth.

A fourth work lumps the area of railroad land grants with grants for wagon roads, canals, and river improvements, to arrive at a total of 337,740,000 acres, "equal," the author says, "to one-sixth of the total area of the United States and three times that of France." [20] The acreage given checks with no official report on the subject, but the federal grants to railroads—on which the whole attention of the passage is focused—are much less than half the area mentioned.

How Much Railroad Was Built with the Aid of Land Grants?

The second, and equally simple, question deals with the extent of railroad mileage, the construction of which was aided by the government's land grants. Such grants were made in aid of a total of 18,738 miles of railroad line [21]—less than 8 per cent of the total mileage of railroads built in the United States. The fact that more than 92 per cent of all the railroad mileage in the United States was built without the aid of an acre of federal land grants is nowhere brought out in the texts examined—an omission which tends to throw the land-grant transaction out of all proportion as a factor in the development of the national network of railroads.

The same tendency to exaggerate the government's financial part in railroad building appears in the treatment of the bond aid extended to six of the companies chartered to build the pioneer "Pacific" railroads. The government made a loan of its bonds to these railroads, in the total amount of $64,623,512. The roads were to pay 6 per cent interest on the bonds and to pay them off. During the long period of development and light traffic they were not always able to meet these charges, but in the final settlement in 1898 and 1899 the government collected $63,023,512 of principal plus $104,722,978 in interest—a total repayment of $167,-746,490 on an initial loan of $64,623,512.[22] Professor Hugo R. Meyer of Harvard was well justified in saying that "for the government the whole outcome has been financially not less than brilliant" [23]—but none of this appears in the treatment of the transaction in the texts. Thirty-four of the thirty-seven texts examined mention the bond aid to these Pacific roads. In one-third of the works, it is not made clear whether the financial assistance referred to was a loan or a gift. Three describe the aid definitely as gifts—which they were not.[24] Twenty-one refer to the transactions as loans, but only four [25] mention the fact that the loans were repaid, while three [26] make the positively erroneous statement that the loans were never repaid.[27]

What Were the Land Grants Worth?

One measure of the value of the lands granted—though no one would contend that it is the correct one—would be the cost to the government of acquiring them, which, according to Donaldson, was an average of 23.3 cents an acre.[28] On that basis, the 131,351,000 acres which the railroads received could be said to be worth less than $31,-000,000.

Another possible measure is the standard "minimum" price at which the government offered the public domain for sale in the land-grant period. This price was $1.25 an acre, though the government was never able to realize even this figure as an average selling price. But if the new railroad companies had bought from the government the 131,350,-534 acres actually received, and had paid the full established price, the lands would have cost them $164,188,167.

Still another measure of the value of the lands during the period of the grants is to be found in the Graduation Act, under which the price of lands long on the market and unsold was graduated downward, starting with a price of $1 an acre after ten years, and ending with a price of 12.5 cents an acre for lands unsold after thirty years. Total sales in the years 1854–1862, during which the act was in effect, even under such price arrangements as these, were only 25,696,420 acres.[29]

A more correct measure of value is the one applied in all ordinary transfers between buyer and seller—the worth of the land granted and received at the time of sale. During the period in which the land grants were being made to the railroads, the average sale price of government lands in the land-grant states was less than $1 an acre.[30] Applying that price to the lands granted to the railroads gives a value as of the time of the grants, of less than $130,000,000.

It is sometimes contended that the measure of value in this case should be the amount finally realized by the railroads on their lands, after the roads had been built and after years of colonizing, advertising, sales effort, and development costs had been put upon them.[31] There is no more basis for setting up such a measure of value than there would be for putting it at the 23 cents an acre which it cost the government to acquire the lands in the first place, but because the point is raised in some of the works examined, it may be noted that the average realization of the railroads from their federal land grants, plus the estimated value of the lands remaining unsold, was put at $3.38 an acre according to one government study,[32] while in another report, including both state and federal grants, the average is $2.81 an acre.[33]

Few of the works examined deal in detail with the question of value. An impression of richness is built up with such adjectives as "lavish," "munificent," and "princely," but figures are scarce. One suggests a value of $2 an acre, which is the same figure used in the Democratic campaign document of 1884.[34] Others undertake to measure value by what the railroads realized from the lands when sold. One work states this as an "average price of $4.76 an acre." [35] Another quotes a "careful investigator" to the effect that it "has been under rather than over ten dollars an acre," out of which there had to come the costs of selling, from all of which the author concludes that "the actual financial assistance to the railroads from the land grants has probably been over-estimated." [36]

The real contribution of the federal land grants to the spread of the rails in the West and the newer South was not the cash realized upon them, but the fact that they furnished a basis of credit which got the job started and made it possible to get it done. The land-grant acreage could be certified, patented, and sold only as the railroad itself was completed, in sections, and then could be sold mostly on long-time credit. The selling price had to be low to get it sold at all, and the expense of sale was necessarily high. The net realizations from the sales, particularly during the period of construction, were but a tiny fraction of the cost of building the railroads. Thus, the Auditor of Railroad Accounts of the Department of the Interior reported that up to 1880 the several companies going to make up the five pioneer "Pacific" routes had sold only $36,383,795 worth of land. "The lands have been sold in small tracts, some for cash, but most of them on time," the auditor wrote, in describing the sales of one of the several companies concerned. The cost up to that time of building the several Pacific routes is shown in the same report as having been $465,584,029. This, the auditor thought and so reported, was excessive, or at least much more than similar roads could have been built for when the report was made. Even the lesser figure of $168,045,000, which he estimated as enough to reproduce the roads, however, was considerably more than four times the realizations from land sales up to that date. Looking to the future, the auditor estimated that the value of the railroad lands unsold in 1880 was $78,889,940, making a total estimated value for all lands sold and to be sold of $115,273,735, as against a total estimated cost of the several "Pacific" railroads, to completion, of $634,165,613. The auditor thought that similar railroads could be built for $286,819,-300, but even this figure is more than double the estimated total realizations from the lands granted to the "Pacific's." [37]

The estimated worth of all lands which these and all other land-grant railroads had received, or were to receive, from the federal government was estimated by the Interior Department's auditor as of November 1, 1880, at $391,804,610.[38] By way of comparison, the total investment in railroads in the United States in that year was $4,653,-609,000.[39]

THE NATURE OF THE LAND-GRANT TRANSACTION

The questions dealt with so far—that is, the amount of land granted and its relationship to the whole, the extent of the railroads thus aided and their relationship to the whole, and the value of the aid so extended—are, after all, matters of detail. While these details are more important than the treatment accorded them in so many of the works examined would indicate, they are not of the essence of the land-grant transaction. The main question is, what was the nature of that transaction? Were the federal land grants gifts? Or were they trades by which the government got, as well as gave, direct consideration?

No reference is made here to the immense indirect benefits arising from the early building of the railroads so aided, but only to the direct monetary return which the government of the United States received for the lands which it granted.[40]

Almost without exception, the works examined treat the transactions as "gifts," or "donations," or, as some put it, "free" or "outright" gifts, without in any way referring to the fact that the railroads which received these "gifts" or "donations" were required to haul mail and government freight and passengers at less than their regular charges.[41]

While the conditions of the several grants vary, in the overwhelming majority of cases the acts of Congress making grants to railroads adopted the phraseology of the earlier canal and wagon road grants in requiring that the railroad to be built should "be and remain a public highway for the use of the government of the United States, free from toll or other charge upon the transportation of any property or troops of the United States." The effect of this clause, as finally determined by the Supreme Court, was that the government was entitled to the use of the roadbed without toll, by analogy to the free right of passage for its vehicles or boats over grant-aided wagon roads and canals, but that this did not extend so far as to require the railroad company to provide and operate without charge the engines, cars, and other equipment needed for transportation over the railroads.[42]

Under a formula subsequently worked out by the United States Court of Claims, the deduction from ordinary charges on account of this provision of the land-grant acts was established at 50 per cent.[43] Still later, by a series of acts of Congress, the same percentage of deduction from commercial rates was made applicable to the limited number of land-grant roads whose grants did not contain the "toll-free" provision in this form,[44] while even railroads which received no land grant whatever from the government have long since entered into "equalization agreements" by which they also undertake to handle government traffic at the same rates applying by law on the land-grant lines.[45] Compensation for handling mail on land-grant lines was fixed by act of Congress in 1876 at 80 per cent of the rates applying on other railroads.[46]

In the Transportation Act of 1940, the Congress eliminated these provisions in so far as they applied to mail pay and to rates on the government's civilian passenger and freight traffic. Deductions of 50 per cent were continued, however, on the charges for transportation of military and naval personnel and property moving for military and naval and not for civil uses.[47]

The resulting situation is thus described by a committee of the House of Representatives in the most recent [1945] statement on the subject:

Certain of our railroads, because of lands granted by the Government many years ago to aid in the construction of lines of road now owned by them, are under statutory obligation to transport certain specified classes of Government traffic over such land-grant lines at 50 per cent of their established tariff charges for such transportation. While that statutory requirement applies to only 14,411 miles of railroad, the reduced charges for which it provides have been extended to many times that mileage as the result of so-called equalization agreements entered into with the Government by other railroads to enable them to handle Government traffic.[48]

Thus it is that although less than 10 per cent of railroad mileage received grants of land, either federal or state, the whole railroad system of the nation has paid for them a direct monetary return far exceeding the value of the lands granted.

"It is probable," said the congressional committee report already referred to, "that the railroads have contributed over $900,000,000 in payment of the lands which were transferred to them under the Land Grant Acts. This is double the amount received for the lands sold by the railroads plus the estimated value of such lands still under railroad ownership. Former Commissioner Eastman estimated that the total value of the lands at the time they were granted . . . was not more than $126,000,000." [49]

The total of deductions was not so large when the texts examined were written, of course, but even the fact that deductions are made is completely ignored in all but two of the books examined.

THE MAJOR FACT

The net result of the treatment of the land-grant transaction as a whole is to present to the student a picture of a wastrel Uncle Sam scattering his substance with reckless extravagance, instead of the much more nearly correct picture of a canny landowner using part of his holdings to increase immeasurably the value of the rest, not as a gift but on terms which constituted a bargain shrewder than he realized. As far back as 1859, indeed, Charles Russell Lowell wrote that with the continued movement of troops and military supplies into the West "it may be found that even with the most liberal construction of the grant, the government has not been so 'munificent' as sharp." The same observer noted, about the same time, "that he who buildeth a railroad west of the Mississippi must also find a population and build up business." [50]

The "best and highest interests of the people of the United States in regard to this domain," said William H. Seward in the Senate debate on the passage of the first land-grant bill, "is not to derive from it the highest amount of current revenue" from the sales of lands, "[b]ut it is to bring them into cultivation and settlement in the shortest space of time and under the most favorable auspices." [51]

To that end, the land-grant device was adopted. Its adoption was sought not only by the people of the West and the newer parts of the South, but also by the people of the manufacturing East. [52] In its administration there were errors and abuses, both on the part of government authorities and on the part of railroads, as revealed, for example, in connection with the movement for forfeiture of land grants which reached its height in the 1880's. But the essential thing is that through the use of land grants, the result sought was accomplished. It may not have been the wisest way to achieve these results, though no one even yet has suggested a better way by which a nation long on land and short on cash and credit could have enlisted the driving forces which, in the short space of less than a generation, laced the West with rails. It may not have been the wisest way, but it worked. The job was done.

While the existing monographs on the actual working-out of specific grants confirm this fact, [53] few of the texts examined take note of it.

Two books note the need of some such device for getting railroads built ahead of settlement.[54] Four refer to the value added to the lands retained by the government.[55] Another, although treating the grants as the bestowal of "great gifts of land," recognized that "the transcontinental railroads opened the way for settlers." [56] Two others, while questioning the wisdom of the "gifts" to the railroads, nevertheless recognized the part which the grants played in the earlier development of the country.[57] Although joining in the almost universal description of the land grants as gifts, one book declared that the railroads "earned" what they got, and that it was a "wise use of the public domain." [58]

But for the most part, this essential element in the transaction—its very heart, indeed—is ignored or glossed over in the history texts which form the foundation of the American citizen's idea of the history of his own nation and the forces which have shaped and builded it. From most of these texts, no one could learn that here was a transaction by which lands constituting less than one-tenth of the nation's public domain were granted to railroads constituting less than 8 per cent of the United States mileage, not as gifts but under terms and conditions by which the government received a direct monetary return far greater than the value of the lands granted.

This direct monetary return, however, is by far the smallest part of the gain to the government and the people of the United States from the working out of the land-grant transaction. When the policy was first adopted, nearly two and one-half centuries after the beginnings of permanent settlement on the Atlantic seaboard, the frontier of the United States was but a little way beyond the Mississippi River—still not half way across the continent. And then, within less than a generation, the frontier almost literally leaped across the Great Plains, the mountains, and the vast areas which the old maps showed as the "Great American Desert." Such a difference in the rate of settlement was not due to any one thing, of course, but obviously the most effective cause was the fact of the transportation service of the railroads.

The land grants did not build these railroads, but they furnished a basis of credit which made it possible for them to be built. So doing, they did what never had been done before—provided transportation ahead of settlement. The result is almost beyond measurement. It was to be found in a startling reduction in the cost of transportation, as is abundantly shown in the reports of the Quartermaster General of the Army during that period.[59] And a result "beyond any estimate the

Quartermaster General can make," as W. T. Sherman, then General-in-Chief of the Armies, reported, was to be found in the "opening up to settlement of regions now wild, which would give homes and employ-ment to . . . industrious people." [60] It was to be found in the value added to land and its products. It was to be found in the transforma-tion of non-taxable resources into property which furnishes the princi-pal tax-base for the support of the state and local governments of half a continent.

More important even than these was the contribution of the land-grant railroads to military security and national unity. Indeed, as General Sherman once wrote, at the time of its building the Pacific Railway was "looked upon as a military necessity and as the only thing positively essential to the binding together of the republic." [61]

Almost without exception, however, the history textbooks have failed to develop this major and essential fact that, whatever may have been its shortcomings, the land-grant policy touched off national and indi-vidual energies which in a few short years accomplished the greatest engineering, construction, and colonization project ever undertaken up to that time, a project which transformed the West from a wilder-ness to a civilized community and welded the nation into one.

NOTES

1 On June 30, 1852, the public domain remaining unsold or not used for public purposes amounted to 1,387,534,000 acres. From the opening of the Land Office in 1812 up to that time, the government had sold only 102,113,861 acres. Grants to wagon roads and canals had amounted to 10,007,677 acres. J. D. B. DeBow, Superintendent of the U.S. Census, *Statistical View of the United States . . . Being a Compendium of the Seventh Census* (Washington, 1854), 191.
2 Thomas Donaldson, *The Public Domain* (Washington, 1884), 753.
3 U.S. General Land Office, *Annual Report of the Commissioner,* June 30, 1943, Table 76. Corresponding figures, with slight variations from year to year, appear in this entire series of reports. The report cited is for the latest year available. In addition to federal land grants, it is estimated that railroads received from the states grants totaling 48,883,372 acres. U.S. Federal Coordinator of Transportation, *Public Aids to Transportation* (4 vols., Washington, 1938–1940), 2:32, and Table 13, p. 115, based on federal or state records to June 30, 1933. The state land grants are not dealt with in this discus-sion. For a detailed and careful study of the state grants of Texas, which were by far the most significant, see S. G. Reed, *A History of the Texas Railroads* (Houston, 1941), chap. xxiv. Right-of-way grants, by which the federal government granted to pioneer railroads running

through the public domain strips of land from 80 to 400 feet wide (the most common grants being 200 feet wide) for right-of-way purposes, are mentioned in some of the works examined but are not dealt with in this study. While in the aggregate they amounted to a considerable acreage, the grants were of so little value without railroads, and they were relatively such a minor part of the whole picture, that no separate discussion of them seems necessary. Donaldson, *The Public Domain*, 286–287, 769–771, 940–943, 1262–1263. *Public Aids to Transportation*, 2:48–51.

4 Ralph Volney Harlow, *The Growth of the United States* (2 vols., New York, 1943), 2:15, gives 132,500,000 acres. George M. Stephenson, *American History to 1865* (New York, 1940), 407, compares the grants with states having a total area of 144,224,000 acres.

5 Carl Russell Fish and Howard E. Wilson, *History of the United States* (New York, 1936), 545; John D. Hicks, *The Federal Union: A History of the United States to 1865* (Boston, 1937), 552.

6 Charles H. Coleman and Edgar B. Wesley, *America's Road to Now* (Boston, 1942), 401, 502; Harold U. Faulkner, Tyler Kepner, and Hall Bartlett, *The American Way of Life* (New York, 1941), 296–297; Harold U. Faulkner and Tyler Kepner, *America, Its History and People* (New York, 1942), 388, 455; Willis Mason West and Ruth West, *The American People* (Boston, 1937), map underline facing p. 474, 554–555; Melville Freeman and Eston V. Tubbs, *The Story of Our Republic* (Philadelphia, 1943), Part II, 47, 68; Charles A. and Mary R. Beard, *The Making of American Civilization* (New York, 1942), 552; Edward C. Kirkland, *A History of American Economic Life* (New York, 1941), 379.

7 Asa Earl Martin, *History of the United States* (2 vols., Boston, 1938), 2:122; Charles A. Beard and William C. Bagley, *The History of the American People* (New York, 1943), 501; Rolla M. Tryon, Charles B. Lingley, and Frances Morehouse, *The American Nation Yesterday and Today* (Boston, 1942), 439; Louis M. Hacker and Benjamin B. Kendrick, *The United States Since 1865* (New York, 1943), 160; William A. Hamm, *The American People* (Boston, 1939), 517–518; David Saville Muzzey, *The United States of America* (2 vols., Boston, 1937), 2:27; Samuel Eliot Morison and Henry Steele Commager, *The Growth of the American Republic* (2 vols., New York, 1937), 2:112 and map facing p. 112; George Earl Freeland and James Truslow Adams, *America's Progress in Civilization* (New York, 1942), map facing p. 324.

8 John T. Greenan and Albert B. Meredith, *Everyday Problems of American Democracy* (Boston, 1943), 451; Arthur Meier Schlesinger, *Political and Social Growth of the American People, 1865–1940* (New York, 1943), 47; Gertrude Van Duyn Southworth and John Van Duyn Southworth, *American History, from the Discovery of America to the Present Day* (Syracuse, 1940), 226. In the three works above, the areas granted to the original Pacific railroads are shown as 100 million acres, as against actual grants to these routes of less than three-fourths that amount. Dwight Lowell Dumond, *A History of the United States*

(New York, 1942), 535, states the grants to the first Pacific railroad as 33 million acres, as against an actual grant of slightly more than 18 million acres. Jacob Lewis Stockton, *A Topical Survey of American History* (New York, 1944), 148, takes as an example the grants to the railroad which received almost one-third of all the lands granted by the government to railroads, raises the amount of this grant from its actual figure of 36 million to 47 million acres, and then declares that "other roads were granted proportionate amounts."

9 Donaldson, *The Public Domain*, 261–262, 274–279, 756–763.

10 The original government map and its two revisions and republications are as follows: (1) accompanying an historical article by Willis Drummond on "Land Grants in Aid of Internal Improvements," published in connection with the report of Major J. W. Powell on the "Lands of the Arid Region of the United States," House Executive Document no. 73, 45 Cong., 2 sess., 1878; (2) Donaldson, *The Public Domain*, facing p. 949; and (3) U.S. Department of Commerce and Labor, Bureau of Corporations, *The Lumber Industry: Part I—Standing Timber* (Washington, 1913), 222 and facing.

11 One publication (not included in the present study) which printed the usual land-grant map did so with the caption: "The black bands on the map show the land that the government granted to the railroads. Notice that almost the entire State of Iowa was given to them" —an interesting example of the error against which particular warning is given in the explanation quoted. *Building America: Railroads* (New York, 1940), 5, no. 6, p. 174.

12 Albert Bushnell Hart, assisted by David Maydole Matteson and Herbert Eugene Bolton, *A Teacher's Manual Accompanying the Hart-Bolton American History Maps* (Chicago, 1919), 87–88, and Map A–18: "Western Statehood and Land Grants to Railroads."

13 Charles O. Paullin, *Atlas of the Historical Geography of the United States* (Washington, 1932), 39–40, and plate 56–D.

14 Democratic Party Platform, 1884, *How the Public Domain Has Been Squandered*, broadside, with land-grant map.

15 The seven works which show the whole of the shaded portions of the map as representing lands granted to railroads are Faulkner and Kepner, *America, Its History and People*, 455; Faulkner, Kepner, and Bartlett, *The American Way of Life*, 296; Morison and Commager, *The Growth of the American Republic*, 2, facing p. 112; Hamm, *The American People*, 518; Muzzey, *The United States of America*, 2:27; Freeman and Tubbs, *The Story of Our Republic*, Part II, 68; Freeland and Adams, *America's Progress in Civilization*, facing p. 324. The two works which state that the railroads received only half the area shown are Coleman and Wesley, *America's Road to Now*, 401; West and West, *The American People*, map underline facing p. 474.

16 Freeman and Tubbs, *The Story of Our Republic*, Part II, 47.

17 Beard and Beard, *The Making of American Civilization*, 552.

18 *The Congressional Globe*, 31 Cong., 1 sess., April 29, 1850, pp. 845–846.

19 Coleman and Wesley, *America's Road to Now*, 502, gives correct

figures for the areas of the land grants to railroads and the public domain. The other works referred to are Muzzey, *The United States of America*, 2:27, and West and West, *The American People*, map underline facing p. 474.

20 Beard and Bagley, *The History of the American People*, 501. In a number of the books examined, areas are compared not with the areas of such states as those in which the lands were located, but with foreign countries, as in this case, or with thickly settled eastern states, a favorite selection for that purpose being the six New England states, New York, and Pennsylvania combined. While such comparisons might be arithmetically accurate, they do not present so true a picture as would comparisons with western acreage, such as used in two works: Coleman and Wesley, *America's Road to Now*, 401; Schlesinger, *Political and Social Growth of the American People*, 47.

21 U.S. General Land Office, *Notice of Releases of Land Grant Claims by Railroad Carriers*, May 17, 1941. Similar figures appear in earlier statements and reports of the General Land Office and other governmental departments and agencies concerned. In Lewis Henry Haney, *A Congressional History of Railways in the United States* (2 vols., Madison, Wis., 1910), 2:14, the total mileage is given as 17,724 miles. The total route mileage of railroads on December 31, 1943, in the United States was 227,999 miles. Interstate Commerce Commission, *Statistics of Railways in the United States* (Annual).

22 *Public Aids to Transportation*, 2:59, and Table 19, p. 138.

23 Hugo R. Meyer, "The Settlements with the Pacific Railways," *Quarterly Journal of Economics*, 13:443–444 (July, 1899).

24 Howard C. Hill, *The Life and Work of the Citizen* (Boston, 1942), 392; Jeremiah S. Young and Edwin M. Barton, *Growing in Citizenship* (New York, 1941), 521; Sister of St. Joseph, *American History* (St. Augustine, Fla., 1932), Book II, 116.

25 Repayment is mentioned in Hacker and Kendrick, *The United States Since 1865*, 161; George M. Stephenson, *American History Since 1865* (New York, 1939), 84; Kirkland, *A History of American Economic Life*, 380; Morison and Commager, *The Growth of the American Republic*, 2:113.

26 West and West, *The American People*, 464; Bruce Winton Knight, *Economic Principles in Practice* (New York, 1942), 262; W. E. Woodward, *A New American History* (Garden City, N.Y., 1938), 618.

27 The same sort of disregard of repayment may be observed in the treatment of the government loans made to the railroads at the close of World War I, in connection with the difficult transition from government to private operation at that time. These loans, which totaled $1,080,575,000, are mentioned in three of the books examined. All of this huge sum except $28,698,000 has been repaid, with a total of $220,891,000 in interest (*Annual Report of the Secretary of the Treasury . . . for fiscal year ended June 30, 1944*, p. 173), but the fact is mentioned in none of the texts. The more recent depression loans made by the Reconstruction Finance Corporation and other

federal agencies receive the same type of treatment. Twenty books mention the fact that these loans were made. More than three-fourths of the loans made have been repaid or sold to the public, with a profit to the government in interest. Mention of repayment of any sort is made in only two of the books: Kirkland, *A History of American Economic Life*, 743; Hicks, *The Federal Union*, 2:671.

28 Donaldson, *The Public Domain*, 21 and 524. This figure for cost of acquisition covers not only purchase price and payments to Indian tribes, but also costs of surveying and disposition.

29 Donaldson, *The Public Domain*, 205–206, 291; *Public Aids to Transportation*, 2:35.

30 The latest and most complete calculation of proceeds of federal land sales during the period 1850–1871, when the land grants were made, shows an average sale price of 97.2 cents per acre. This calculation, however, is not restricted to the sale of lands in the land-grant states, but covers also lands sold during this period in the older and more settled states. Eliminating these sales, the average per acre from sales of federal public lands in railroad land-grant states during this period was 94 cents per acre. From report of Federal Coordinator of Transportation, *Public Aids to Transportation*, 2:36.

31 The extent of the effort and expense to which railroads went in marketing and settling their granted lands is indicated in the studies of Paul Wallace Gates, *The Illinois Central Railroad and Its Colonization Work* (Cambridge, Mass., 1934); James B. Hedges, "The Colonization Work of the Northern Pacific Railroad," *Mississippi Valley Historical Review*, 13:311–342 (December, 1926), and "Promotion of Immigration to the Pacific Northwest by the Railroads," *ibid.*, 15:183–203 (September, 1928); Richard C. Overton, *Burlington West: A Colonization History of the Burlington Railroad* (Cambridge, Mass., 1941). The somewhat similar situation in Canada is treated in James B. Hedges, *Building the Canadian West: The Land and Colonization Work of the Canadian Pacific Railway* (New York, 1939).

32 U.S. Board of Investigation and Research, *Report and Comments on H.R. 4184 . . . to the Committee on Interstate and Foreign Commerce of the House of Representatives*, March 9, 1944, p. 28, shows net proceeds of sales of both federal and state land-grant lands to December 31, 1941, of $434,806,671, plus an estimated value of the unsold grant lands of $60,684,032. Of this total of $495,490,703, the sum of $55,090,652 is attributed to state land grants and $440,400,051 to federal land grants.

33 The report of the Federal Coordinator of Transportation, *Public Aids to Transportation*, 2:52, estimated the "aid received from all such grants," that is, state as well as federal, at $516,144,749. This includes both proceeds of sales under federal and state land and right-of-way grants, and also the estimated net value of lands still held by the railroads on December 31, 1927.

34 Hacker and Kendrick, *The United States Since 1865*, 161.

35 Harlow, *The Growth of the United States*, 2:15.

36 Kirkland, *A History of American Economic Life*, 381.

37 Department of Interior, Office of Auditor of Railroad Accounts, *Report on the Quantity and Value of Public Lands Granted by Congress to Aid in the Construction of the Pacific Railroad* (Washington, Jan. 26, 1881); Donaldson, *The Public Domain*, 912–933 (figures on p. 932).

38 *Ibid.*, 753.

39 Interstate Commerce Commission, Bureau of Statistics, *Railway Statistics Before 1890*, Statement No. 32151 (Washington, Dec., 1932), 4.

40 These indirect returns to the government are suggestively outlined in U.S. General Land Office, *Transportation: Information Concerning Land Grants for Roads, Canals, River Improvement and Railroads* (Information Bulletin, 1939 Series, no. 5, Washington, 1940), 1–2. While no figures are available, and the point is developed in none of the reports and studies examined, it is obvious that transfer of lands from federal to private ownership had a substantial effect upon the taxable resources of the states, territories, and local governments. Only in recent years, with the increasing tendency in the other direction, with property passing from private to government ownership, has the importance of this fact begun to be appreciated.

41 This is true of twenty-six of the texts examined. Only two, Stephenson, *American History to 1865*, 407, and Robert I. Adriance, *Using the Wealth of the World* (Boston, 1943), 268, make reference to deductions from railroad rates because of land grants.

42 *Lake Superior and Mississippi Railroad* vs. *United States*, 93 *U.S. Reports*, 442, October term, 1876. Decided Jan. 15, 1877.

43 *Atchison, Topeka & Santa Fe Railway* vs. *United States*, 15 *Court of Claims*, 126, December term, 1879.

44 The first of these acts of Congress was adopted July 16, 1892. 27 *U.S. Stat.*, 174, 180.

45 Since 1914 this agreement has been between the government and the railroads collectively.

46 19 *U.S. Stat.*, 78–82.

47 Transportation Act of 1940, Part II, Section 321 (a), 54 *U.S. Stat.*, 1:954.

48 Committee on Interstate and Foreign Commerce, *House of Representatives, Report No. 393* (79 Cong., 1 sess., March 26, 1945), 1–2.

49 The several authorities for the details of this statement as to the amount of the direct return to the government from the land-grant acts are given in detail, *ibid.*, 4.

50 Overton, *Burlington West*, 156, 159.

51 *Cong. Globe*, 31 Cong., 1 sess., April 29, 1850, p. 851.

52 This may be substantiated by sectional analysis of the vote in Congress on the land-grant acts. See, for example, the 1856 vote on four grants in Iowa. Overton, *Burlington West*, 73–86.

53 See works cited in footnote 31, above.

54 Coleman and Wesley, *America's Road to Now*, 401; Dumond, *A History of the United States*, 535.

55 Kirkland, *A History of American Economic Life*, 378, 380; Stephenson,

American History to 1865, 407; Fish and Wilson, *History of the United States,* 355; Richard J. Purcell, *The American Nation* (Boston, 1937), 529.

56 Roy F. and Jeannette P. Nichols, *A Short History of American Democracy* (New York, 1943), 270, 272.

57 Eugene C. Barker, William E. Dodd, and Henry Steele Commager, *Our Nation's Development* (Evanston, Ill., 1937), 387; Kirkland, *A History of American Economic Life,* 381.

58 Purcell, *The American Nation,* 532.

59 From letter from Quartermaster-General M. C. Meigs to Secretary of War William W. Belknap, Jan. 28, 1873 in House Ex. Doc. no. 169, 42 Cong., 3 sess., vol. 9, relating to savings to the War Department in transportation costs from July 1, 1866, to Jan. 28, 1873, as a result of the building of the Union Pacific Railroad: "The average rates per mile for troops are, on through business, 5⁹⁄₁₀ cents; on local business, 8 cents, being an average of 6⅗ cents per man per mile. The average rates per mile for troops by the Overland Stage Company were, on through business, 12½ cents; on local business, 15 cents, being an average of 12¾ cents per mile per man.

"Assuming that all of these troops would have traveled by stage, in the absence of the railroad (which is by no means probable), the total estimated cost by stage is shown by the following, based on the averaged rates above stated:

Average rate per man per mile: rail .... 6⅗ cents
Average rate per man per mile: stage .... 13¾ cents
Actual cost for troops at railroad rates $1,446,262.25
Estimated cost at stage rates $3,013,046.35

The average rates per 100 pounds per 100 miles charged for freight by the railroad during the period required are, on through business, 19 cents; on local business, 62 cents, being an average of 40½ cents per 100 pounds per 100 miles by railroad.

". . . the estimated cost of the transportation of the freight moved by the Union Pacific Railroad, including express charges as shown above, . . . would be as follows:

Rates per 100 pounds per 100 miles:
  railroad rates .... 40½ cents
Rates per 100 pounds per 100 miles:
  wagon rates .... $ 1.46
Actual cost of freight at railroad rates $1,896,589.57
Estimated cost at wagon rates $6,837,088.32

Showing a total estimated cost for moving the
  troops and supplies by stage and wagon of $9,850,134.67
Total actual cost by railroad $3,342,851.82

Estimated difference . . .
  equivalent to about 66 per cent .... $6,507,282.85"

60 Reports from General W. T. Sherman and the Quartermaster-General transmitted May 12, 1880, by Secretary of War Alexander Ramsey to Hon. R. M. McLane, Chairman, House of Representatives Committee on the Pacific Railroads. Original letters are on file in the Clerk's Office, House of Representatives. General Sherman's letter is reprinted in *Railway World*, May 22, 1880, pp. 492–493, as follows: "I have the honor to acknowledge the receipt, by reference, from you of the resolution of the House committee on Pacific railroads, calling for information as to the probable saving in money to the military authorities by the completion of the Northern Pacific Railroad from Bismarck westward, and its general effect on the military and Indian services in that quarter. . . . In a military sense, the immediate extension of this railroad from Bismarck to the Yellowstone, and up the valley of that river as high as the mouth of the Big Horn, will be beyond any estimate the Quartermaster-General can make, because this railroad will transport men and supplies for ten if not twelve months of the year, while the Missouri river and the Yellowstone are barely navigable by light draft boats for two or at most three months. . . . It is equally important to the military and civil interests of the whole country that Montana should fill up with hardy farmers, and this will be an immediate result of the extension westward of this northern railroad. . . . I am unable to make even an approximate estimate of the saving in cost of transportation of men and military stores by the completion of this railroad, but this bears a small proportion to the great result of opening up to settlement regions now wild, which would give homes and employment to two or three millions of industrious people."

61 Letter from General W. T. Sherman, dated Jan. 16, 1867, to Major-General Grenville M. Dodge, in *How We Built the Union Pacific Railway* (61 Cong., 2 sess., Senate Doc. no. 447), 14.

After "The Railroad Land Grant Legend" by Robert S. Henry, at that time assistant to the president of the Association of American Railroads, appeared in the September, 1945, issue of the Mississippi Valley Historical Review, the editor subsequently published comments by a number of scholars, in support and in opposition. Since Henry presents his position clearly, we have chosen to include only the comment that opposed or went beyond his. Because of the lively interest aroused by the article, a session was arranged by the Lexington Group at the Thirty-ninth Annual Meeting of the Mississippi Valley Historical Association, at which Charles Morgan's paper was read. Professor Gates's statement which appeared nine years later in the Journal of Economic History can properly be considered a fruitful continuation of the discussion.

Comment on
"The Railroad Land Grant Legend in American History Texts"

DAVID MALDWYN ELLIS

Reprinted by permission from the Mississippi Valley Historical Review, Volume 32 (1946), pages 557–563.

A REAPPRAISAL of our land-grant policy is long overdue. Unfortunately Colonel Henry's article if allowed to stand unchallenged would create a new legend. Certainly his findings as to the total acreage involved, the value of the land grants, and the amount of rate reductions are debatable and warrant careful analysis.

Historians will welcome Colonel Henry's pleas for a more critical use of the land-grant map and greater care in the use of statistics. It is good to have underscored the fact that the railroads actually received a total of 131,350,534 acres from the federal government up to 1943.[1] But this figure is far from complete and taken by itself is quite misleading. It merely states the acreage received from the federal government and does not give the total amount of land granted to the railroads.

A comprehensive survey must also include the grants made by the states. Nine states granted 48,883,372 acres to aid railroad construction. These states, with the exception of Maine and Texas, which gave lands from their own public domain, turned over lands (mainly swamp lands) which the federal government had previously transferred to them. To ignore these grants on the ground that the railroads receiving them were not obliged to extend rate concessions would be to subordinate an integral part of our land-grant history to the current [1946] controversy over repeal of land-grant rates.

Furthermore, the amount of land granted by the federal government itself was much greater than the amount of land actually received by the railroads. For example, those lands granted to encourage railroad construction, but subsequently forfeited because of repeated failure to build any railroad mileage, must also be included. These grants to a score of defaulting roads totaled approximately 35,000,000 acres.[2] To be sure, the companies never gained absolute title, but the government offer of free land stood sometimes as long as thirty years.

The Transportation Act of 1940 encouraged many land-grant railroads to give up their claims to unpatented lands still in the process of adjustment. In return for the release of their claims, the carriers were permitted to discontinue preferential reduced rates on government traffic except military or naval property and military personnel when traveling on official duty. With minor exceptions, the railroads hastened to qualify for this privilege. As a result, approximately 8,000,000 acres were restored to the public domain.[3] For more than seventy-five years the railroads enjoyed valid claims to this land. Only the hope of securing greater revenues from the growing non-military traffic of the government induced them to give up their claims.

In short, the railroads were granted lands well in excess of 223,000,-000 acres.

```
Federal grants
    Lands actually received to 1943 ....................131,350,534
    Land claims released to the government under Transpor-
        tation Act of 1940 .............................  8,000,000 (approx.)
    Lands granted but later forfeited ..................  35,000,000 (approx.)
State grants .........................................  48,883,372
                                Total ..............223,233,906 (approx.)
```

These criticisms of Colonel Henry's estimate of land-grant acreage apply with equal force to his newly constructed map. The map question is crucial not only for the average reader who is trained by current publications to grasp statistics by pictorial representation, but also for the scholar who seeks to evaluate the significance of the land-grant policy for the western and southern states. True, the old map has several defects, especially if captions are not clearly written. It exaggerates the amount of land actually received. It gives a distorted picture of land-grant acreage in states such as Iowa where many grants overlapped. It ignores state grants. But the new map likewise tells an incomplete story. Its obvious omissions are the state grants and the forfeited federal grants. Moreover, the new map fails to outline the large tracts whose titles were often in dispute because of the administration of the land-grant policy.

The General Land Office withdrew from public appropriation not only the primary limits as required by law, but also the lands within the indemnity limits. This action was taken after a line was projected and a map of definite location filed in the land office. But the process of adjustment involved endless difficulties: the claims of bona fide settlers along the route; the attempts of speculators to use the Pre-emption Act and other devices to claim part of the land; delays in the land office; constant bickering over each phrase of the loosely-drawn statutes. If the adjustment had been made properly, i.e., if the titles to the land within the primary zone had been ascertained and the amount of indemnity land awarded with dispatch, only a temporary inconvenience would have resulted. Unfortunately several factors in addition to those already mentioned interfered with the smooth operation of the land-grant policy. First, forty out of some eighty-odd subsidized roads did not construct their lines within the time limits (usually ten years) including the extensions.[4] Consequently the railroad and usually the government could not sell the land along the route of the uncompleted road. Furthermore, the railroads frequently failed to patent lands along their constructed lines, either through failure of the government to conduct surveys or because the railroads hoped to avoid local taxes.[5] Most aggravating of all was the uncertain status of land within the indemnity limits. The Secretary of the Interior withdrew the indemnity lands of nearly all the railroads for over thirty years.[6] This action seemed necessary to protect the railroads from losing their rights to lieu lands. But homesteaders and speculators rushed to locate land within the limits and bitterly resisted the efforts of the railroads to select their sections. The railroads sometimes tried to oust genuine homesteaders who had made their selections before the location of the railroad route.[7] The Guilford Miller case dramatized the struggle between railroads and homesteaders, and in 1887 Congress authorized Secretary of the Interior Lamar to adjust the grants as speedily as possible. Lamar revoked the original withdrawals. Approximately 21,323,600 acres were thus restored to public entry.[8] The old map still performs a useful function in outlining the lands in dispute.

A single map representing the significance of the land grants both to the railroads and to western settlement seems impossible to construct. Perhaps a series of maps is necessary, in which the two maps in question should be included. A third map distinguishing between the railroad mileage built within the time limits and that built after the deadline would also be helpful.

How to estimate the value of the land grants is a troublesome question. Representatives of the railroads, water carriers, and trucking associations differ from one another and from the conclusions of the Federal Coordinator of Transportation.[9] Colonel Henry advances the figure of approximately $130,000,000, which he considers was the value of the federal grants at the time of donation.

This approach suffers from several drawbacks. First of all, there seems little question that what the railroads were primarily interested in was the potential value of the grants. In fact, they confidently and as it turned out, correctly, expected to realize a sum far in excess of the current value of backcountry lands. The grants furnished the basis of credit, but the railroads also disposed of much of the land at prices higher than those prevailing during the land-grant era. What the railroads received as public aid must therefore be measured by what they received from the land.

The sounder method is to estimate the amount of public aid which the railroads actually received. This method is the one adopted in the report of the Federal Coordinator of Transportation. More recently the Board of Investigation and Research has revised and brought down to date the statistics of land-grant receipts which the Coordinator's report had compiled. The board estimates that the gross receipts aggregated $602,445,137 up to December 31, 1941. From this sum must be deducted $167,638,466 expended for administration, sale, and taxes connected with the land. The total net proceeds are $434,806,671. The railroads still held some 16,000,000 acres in 1941, worth approximately $60,000,000. The value of the federal grants thus amounted to $440,400,051 and the railroads derived an additional $55,090,652 from the state grants.[10] This total is not complete. It does not include the profits made by subsidiary or affiliated companies which secured valuable coal, mineral, and lumber lands. It takes no account of the numerous rights of way given to the railroads by the federal government. It ignores the 8,000,000 acres of land (admittedly of little value) which the railroads released under the Transportation Act of 1940. Moreover, it disregards the 35,000,000 acres of land granted to the railroads but subsequently forfeited by Congress.

The railroad companies thus acquired over 180,000,000 acres of the estimated 223,000,000 acres originally granted. Eventually the grants netted them well over $500,000,000.

Colonel Henry's discussion of land-grant rate reductions warrants careful analysis. He quotes with approval the figure of $900,000,000 advanced by a House report of March 26, 1945.[11] Probably that estimate is as tenable as any that could be drawn up for that date.

The student must realize quite clearly that this figure includes concessions from a much broader category than the original land-grant roads. The government derives a greater saving in rates from those carriers which received no land grants, but which have signed so-called equalization agreements, than from the land-grant railroads. These railroads have agreed to apply to government shipments moving over their lines the lowest net land-grant charges available to the government via any route between the same points. The pressure to secure traffic has been so compelling for our railroads, burdened as they are with heavy fixed costs and unutilized capacity, that they have eagerly bargained for government traffic even though it might barely cover out-of-pocket costs. As a result practically all railroads carry government freight at reduced rates.

Any attempt to estimate the total savings from rate concessions runs into serious difficulties. The records of both railroads and the government are incomplete and scattered. Furthermore, the government and the railroads are in serious disagreement as to what constitutes "military and naval property" for "military or naval use." Most controversial of all is the basis of computation. Shall the savings derived from equalization agreements be included in the total? Colonel Henry answers affirmatively, presumably arguing that the equalized rate concessions are as real as those received from the land-grant roads themselves.

The fact remains, however, the equalization rates were voluntarily entered into for the sake of profit. The fact that the Great Northern Railroad accepted lower rates in order to share in government traffic did not make the 39,000,000-acre grant to the Northern Pacific less valuable. It does no good to argue that the railroad industry as a whole has necessarily assumed a heavier burden because lower rates have been extended to the government through land-grant and equalization rates. The carriers and the government have never considered these rate concessions as compromising in any way their right to earn a reasonable return on the fair value of their property.

To determine precisely how much of the total savings should be attributed to the land-grant railroads and to those railroads which have voluntarily equalized their rates is an impossible task. Certainly an even division would be more than generous to the land-grant roads.[12] If one-half of the total savings up to April 1 of 1945 is assigned to the original land-grant roads, the figure of $500,000,000 emerges. To this amount there should be added about $10,000,000 a month to September 1, 1945 and perhaps $5,000,000 a month thereafter to October 1, 1946, when the special rate reductions end.[13] Admittedly, these figures on current savings are mere guesswork. Rate savings from land-grant railroads, assuming always that they supplied one-half of the total rate reductions, thus will pass the $600,000,000 mark. This figure compares roughly with the proceeds which the railroads derived from the land.

Few will deny Colonel Henry's closing argument that the real importance of the land grants must be found in their effect upon the construction of the railroad net and the colonization of the West. The work of the Illinois Central, the Burlington, the Santa Fe, and the Northern Pacific bears eloquent testimony to the vital role played by the railroads in promoting immigration to our undeveloped areas. But this writer, even though prepared to admit that the land grants were no more abused than other forms of public aid or more ineptly administered than most of our land laws, is not persuaded that Uncle Sam was a "canny landlord" and not a wastrel of his public domain. The long list of delinquent roads, the delays in adjusting grants, the establishment of large timber holdings, the endless controversies between railroads and homesteaders, bona fide and otherwise, and the unfortunate results of awarding alternate sections in the semi-arid and forest regions certainly counterbalance many of the indirect benefits of the land-grant policy. The inescapable fact remains that the generation which witnessed the operation of the land grants considered that the evils outweighed the benefits. The historian must therefore focus his major attention upon the contemporary effectiveness of land grants in promoting construction and settlement. The financial "bargain," although pertinent and indubitably important, should not be overemphasized.

NOTES

1 U.S. General Land Office, *Annual Report of the Commissioner*, June 30, 1943, Table 76. The report of the Federal Coordinator of Transportation has assembled a wealth of data on land grants. See *Public Aids to Transportation* (4 vols., Washington, 1938–1940), vol. 2. The Transportation Act of 1940 set up the Board of Investigation and Research which was authorized to estimate the extent and effect of public aid. This board has brought down to date the figures of the Coordinator's report. See U.S. Board of Investigation and Research, *Land Grants to Railroads and Related Rates* (A Report submitted to the House Committee on Interstate and Foreign Commerce with Reference to H.R. 4184, Washington, March, 1944). This reply will rely on the figures of these two reports.

2 The General Land Office supplied this figure. U.S. Department of

Commerce and Labor, Bureau of Corporations, *The Lumber Industry: Part I—Standing Timber* (Washington, 1913), 220. During the 1870's Congress forfeited about 650,000 acres; during the 1800's, over 28,250,000 acres; in 1890, 5,627,436 acres. David Maldwyn Ellis, "The Forfeiture of Railroad Land Grants" (Master's thesis, Cornell University, 1939), 25, 60, Appendix, Table B, respectively.

3 David Maldwyn Ellis, "Railroad Land Grant Rates, 1850–1945," *Journal of Land & Public Utility Economics*, 21:218 (August, 1945). I wish to thank the editors of the *Journal of Land & Public Utility Economics* for permission to use material which appeared in this article.

4 *The Lumber Industry: Part I*, 248.

5 U.S. General Land Office, *Annual Report of the Commissioner*, 1885, pp. 45–46.

6 John Bell Sanborn, *Congressional Grants of Land in Aid of Railroads* (Madison, 1899), 339.

7 Roy M. Robbins, *Our Landed Heritage: The Public Domain, 1776–1936* (Princeton, 1942), 255–267.

8 U.S. Department of the Interior, *Annual Report of the Secretary*, 1887, p. 12.

9 A summary of conflicting estimates may be found in *Public Aids to Transportation*, 2:33.

10 These estimates are taken from the Board of Investigation and Research, *Land Grants to Railroads and Related Rates*, 16–28.

11 This writer arrived at a similar figure. For a more detailed discussion of rate reductions, see Ellis, "Railroad Land Grant Rates, 1850–1945," 214–216.

12 Robert E. Webb, Chairman of the Board of Investigation and Research, estimated that equalization agreements brought in far more than one-half. U.S. Congress, *Repeal of Land-Grant Rates on Transportation of Government Traffic*. Hearings before a subcommittee of the Senate Committee on Interstate and Foreign Commerce, 78 Cong., 2 sess., 1944, p. 166.

13 The customary figure for monthly savings throughout 1943 and 1944 has been $20,000,000. Government military traffic continued heavy until the capitulation of Japan in August, and rate concessions continued at a high level. Information is not available as to current [1946] savings, which are tentatively placed at $10,000,000 a month, of which one-half may be assigned to the land-grant roads.

Comment on
"The Railroad Land Grant Legend in American History Texts"

ROBERT E. RIEGEL

Reprinted by permission from the Mississippi Valley Historical Review, Volume 32 (1946), pages 565–566.

PROPAGANDISTS for special causes have long realized, as does Robert S. Henry in his "The Railroad Land Grant Legend in American History Texts," that school texts frequently "are the first, last, and only works on the history of their country read by many, if not most, Americans" [p. 121]. What could be more desirable than having such texts include the points of view favored by the special pleaders? Unfortunately they have been at least partially successful in numerous cases in the past.

Extreme alertness is needed if our history texts are not to deteriorate into vehicles for the propaganda efforts of groups with political power. The improvement of such texts during the past generation has been notable, but if that improvement is to be maintained, all people interested in education must continually be alert to resist pressures that might otherwise be successful.

The Henry article is a good case in point. Without accusing Colonel Henry of any conscious efforts to mislead, the article still tends to create erroneous impressions. The Henry thesis is that the railroad land-grant policy of the United States was not a "reckless extravagance," but that more correctly it should be considered the action "of a canny landowner using part of his holdings to increase immeasurably the value of the rest; not as a gift but on terms which constituted a bargain shrewder than he realized" [p. 135]. This thesis is backed by a four-fold argument:

(1) That at the time of the grants the unsold parts of the public domain were "largely unusable and unsalable" for lack of transportation [p. 121]. This point is clearly overdone. Many of the roads found much of the land of their grants already occupied, while all of them were

anxious to have their grants withdrawn from sale to prevent such claims. Certainly the concept that the lands were unwanted should at least be modified.

(2) That not much land was given. Colonel Henry's figure, upon which he bases his statement, is approximately 131,000,000 acres [p. 122]. In note 3 [see pp. 137–138], he admits that the states gave further grants to make the total about 180,000,000 acres, but at the same time critizes such a text as Hacker and Kendrick [p. 122] for giving a figure larger than the 131,000,000, even though the authors state specifically that state grants are included. Actually, there is a better argument that most texts understate the amount of land given to the railroads than that they overstate it.

(3) That the value of the land received by the railroads was rather small. Colonel Henry gives estimates ranging from $31,000,000 to $392,000,000. While his discussion [pp. 132–133] leaves some doubt as to the figure he approves, it certainly can not be greater than the top figure he gives. The most recent and detailed study of this question, *Public Aids to Transportation* (1940), gives an estimate of about $489,-000,000, but then adds that since many of the original sales were to railroad subsidiaries, the actual return must have been somewhat greater. Colonel Henry does not even mention this estimate.

(4) That the railroads, by their rate concessions and by their mere existence, contributed directly to the government and indirectly to the nation much more than the value of the land they received. Colonel Henry cites with apparent approval [p. 134] a guess of $900,000,000 as the value of the services of the railroads, but does not indicate the basis of the estimate. The figure presented by *Public Aids* is $168,000,000, which Colonel Henry does not mention. As to the indirect effects of railroad construction on total prosperity, any accurate estimate is obviously impossible. Presumably the railroads would in time have been built even without government aid. To what extent the land grants hastened construction, and the value of this earlier construction, are impossible even to guess.

Since Colonel Henry has a thesis to support, he does not mention inconvenient facts. For example, any discussion of government aid should include the contributions of state and local governments, which *Public Aids* estimates at $232,000,000, exclusive of stock and bond subscriptions. Technically, Colonel Henry can find justification for not discussing such assistance, but actually the important point is that such factors would lessen the validity of the thesis that he is supporting.

Looking both at current texts and at the Henry article, the conclusion seems to emerge that while certain slips in the texts are to be regretted, such texts would definitely be worse if they were to take the Henry article at face value.

Comment on
"*The Railroad Land Grant Legend in American History Texts*"

CHESTER McARTHUR DESTLER

Reprinted by permission from the Mississippi Valley Historical Review, Volume 32 (1946), *pages 568–571.*

· · · · · · · · · · · ·

WITH much of Colonel Henry's thesis few historians will quarrel. The gist of it, in fact, was stated by Richard C. Overton in Harold F. Williamson's *Growth of American Economy* (pp. 366–68). Certainly a policy of subsidy through land grants or direct financial assistance was a legitimate method of building trunk lines in advance of settlement as a means of binding the Far West to the Union or of opening up inaccessible lands. In terms of end results the West and South did benefit from the development of a trunk-line network, the Union was bound together by steel bands, and the federal government received rate reductions on its mails, personnel, and freights. Mr. Overton anticipated Colonel Henry in fixing the total of congressional land grants, although he puts the subsidized mileage constructed some 2,000 miles above the latter's figure, with emphasis upon the large additional mileage subsidized by Texas land grants. Mr. Overton observes, furthermore, that in the sixties and seventies the federally aided lines were a much larger proportion of western railway mileage than they are today after extensive, later construction.

Over and above Overton's thesis, which the article in question reproduces with more or less accuracy, Colonel Henry has rendered a service in calling the attention of textbook writers to specific errors of fact in their discussion of federal aid to railways and particularly to the mistaken visual impression made by some of the land-grant maps in the textbooks. Another contribution is the pointed reminder that in its final settlement of the bond subsidy with the Union and Central Pacific railroads, the federal government came off very well indeed. Of course all students of the period after the Civil War know that the building of the western railroads, subsidized or not, had the effect of accelerating tremendously the pace of western settlement.

The omission of a number of pertinent considerations gives this article, however, something of the character of a special plea. Historians must look to contemporary as well as to long-range results of such an important policy. They must count the social, economic, and larger political costs of what was not originally and cannot now be regarded as a simple business transaction. Nor can they be content to let the case rest after a partial presentation of the evidence.

Any definitive total of land grants to railroads must include the rights of way with larger areas around stations which promoters developed into speculative town sites. It must include the Indian lands turned over to railroad builders through the agency of the Department of the Interior, or through state governments out of lands released to them by the federal government. Independently made state, county, and city land grants must be included. Only then will it be possible for the historian to compare the total and its estimated value with the available domain, with the area of the states where the railroads were built, and with the cost of building the railroads.

Historians alert to the main issues of the Reconstruction Era will wish to examine the effect that adoption of the land-grant policy had upon opening the doors of government on all levels to the corrupt activities of railroad promoters. They will examine the relation of the inevitable building of railroads far beyond immediate transportation requirements to the swift development of rebating, pooling, and other practices that undermined the free enterprise system in older and newly settled areas alike. They will wish to know the effect that railroad administration of the land grants had upon types of land tenure and the incidence of taxation in new areas. Was tax avoidance, through deliberate delay in patenting grants long after construction, related to the continued political activity of the railroads in the counties and states that they traversed? To what extent was the long prostitution of representative government to the railroads attributable to the land-grant policy? Was a portion of this due to the thirty-year attempt of the pioneer "Pacific" railroads to evade payment of interest on their federal bond subsidies through investment of substantial sums in corrupting Congress?

The casual reader may consult *The Railway Problem* (St. Paul, 1891), by A. B. Stickney, a railroad man and president successively of two railroads operating between Chicago and St. Paul. He may also examine the notorious Collis P. Huntington letters that were published in the San Francisco *Chronicle* in 1883, or study the political activities of Jay Gould and Tom Scott in the late seventies. And what gyrations in judicial precedents, set by state and federal supreme courts between 1865 and 1905, may be attributable to the influence of the railroads that came into easy possession of great domains which they wished to exempt from taxation?

Enough has been written by a series of noted historians, including Robert E. Riegel and John D. Hicks, to indicate that these are pertinent questions that no student of the land-grant policy can avoid. They relate directly to the recurring attempts of a determined democracy to reform its land policy, to purge representative government of corruption and restore it to the service of the public at large, and to hold railroads to their common-law obligations. The successful termination of the land-grant policy in 1871 and the subsequent movement to reclaim all that could be legitimately recovered of unredeemed grants were but part of this story.

Finally, why does Colonel Henry not tell his readers the character of the rates charged by the railroads today on the federal government's military and naval freight? Are these the high-class rates? Or do the railroads charge the government the low-commodity rates, less the percentage reduction which Colonel Henry alleges that they give? This matter should be clarified . . . Is it possible that the rate reductions which his article describes, and the consequent savings accruing to the federal government by virtue of the land-grant policy, are more substantial in argument than they are in fact?

Comment on
"The Railroad Land Grant Legend
in American History Texts"

FRED A. SHANNON

Reprinted by permission from the Mississippi Valley Historical Review, Volume 32 (1946), pages 572–574.

As a piece of special pleading for the current [1946] lobby of railroad interests to secure the repeal of clauses in the land-grant acts of 1850–1871 for rate concessions on the carrying of government traffic, Robert S. Henry's article in the September, 1945, issue of the *Review* is totally unconvincing. He underestimates both the amount and the value of the land contributed, and he overrates the returns made by the carriers to the government.

Though in note 3 [see pp. 137–138] he admits that 48,883,372 acres were granted by the states, thereafter he omits this huge area from all of his calculations, and nowhere does he explain that this was in fact an indirect federal grant. Furthermore, he omits the 4,000,000 or possibly 8,000,000 acres yet to be received by the railroads, though the figures are quite plain in one of his sources (*Public Aids to Transportation,* Vol. II, p. 33). Thus, his entire argument is vitiated. Instead of his 131,350,534 acres, he should figure on approximately 188,234,000 acres. His failure to do this makes a mockery of his criticism of the land-grant map against which he levels his major attack.

That map, by the way, is far more accurate than he admits, and it is nearer to the truth than his own map. The main fault of the old text-book map is that it is not adequately labeled and shaded. Call it "Land Grant Zones" instead of "Land Grants"; print it in crosshatch instead of solid, so as to indicate the alternate section idea; then *widen* the strips by 50 per cent so as to show the indemnity zones—and then the map will be accurate enough for all ordinary purposes. It must not be forgotten that until 1887 settlement was excluded from government sections within the extreme limits of the land-grant zones and from 50 per cent of their width clear beyond the zones proper unless the railroads had earlier secured title to all their claims. Thus, the 40 square miles to the mile of right of way of the Northern Pacific became a third of a 120-mile strip across North Dakota, Montana, Idaho, and Washington. Unless the pioneer chose to buy at the railroad's terms, he had to settle at least 60 miles from a shipping point.

Here was one of the greatest evils of the whole system. Consequently, in showing the injustice to settlers, Colonel Henry's map is far less useful than the one he condemns. The textbook map shows two-thirds of the evil, Colonel Henry's only one-third—and it looks like even less than a third. Remember too that the original grants as promised were even larger than the 188,000,000 acres listed above, and for years free settlement was denied within an area three times greater than the promised acreage. *Public Aids*, Vol. II, p. 33, says: "The estimated total of the grants represents 286,230 square miles, or approximately 7.65 per cent more than the area of Texas and 9.46 per cent of the area of continental United States." But the writer of these words reduced his estimate by 6,250 square miles before he made this calculation. Obviously, then, the railroads got just about one-tenth of the United States and for years restricted settlement in three-tenths of the United States. The ratio is much higher in the West, where most of the grants lay.

And what about the value of this tenth of the United States which became railroad property? Colonel Henry, ignoring nearly a third of the acreage (and, since it was in the states, the more valuable third) and taking the lowest available estimate of the value of the reduced acreage at the time of the grants, says that it was "worth less than $31,000,000" [p. 131]. Now this estimate is far from a candid one. The question is: What profit did the railroads get from the lands? The answer in *Public Aids*, Vol. II, p. 40, is that to December 31, 1930, and after all deductions for cost of handling and of railroad services to the United States, the profit was $489,337,199. But the statement follows that this amount does "not reflect large but incalculable profits accruing to some railroads as a result of sales of lands by subsidiaries or affiliates." Obviously the railroads made well over half a billion dollars out of the transactions.

Colonel Henry is equally lacking in candor in his estimates as to what the railroads have paid back to the government in reduced transportation charges. Space here is limited, but David Maldwyn Ellis gives a far more reasonable estimate in *The Journal of Land & Public Utility Economics* for August, 1945.

Here is another point that might be considered. In one way or another, and including only items that can be determined with some accuracy, public aids to all railroads down to the end of 1930 amounted to $1,443,000,000 (*Public Aids*, Vol. II, p. 101), and the incalculable aids would no doubt expand this amount to at least two billion dollars. But, to return to the subject, the half-billion dollars in land alone to the land-grant railroads was worth more than the railroads were when they were built. Credit from the possession of this land made possible their building and expansion. All additions to the value of the railroads since their building have come from profits obtained from government munificence. If any lobbying is justifiable today it should be from a people's lobby. It should demand that after three-quarters of a century (in some cases almost a century) of private profit from public gifts, it is now time for the people to take back the property without further recompense, so that in the future the benefits shall be reaped by the people who paid. Any reimbursement to the people made by the land-grant railroads, to the present, has just been a little interest on the original obligation.

Comment on
"The Railroad Land Grant Legend in American History Texts"

EDWARD C. KIRKLAND

Reprinted by permission from the Mississippi Valley Historical Review, *Volume 32* (1946), *pages 574–576.*

. . . ROBERT S. Henry's "The Railroad Land Grant Legend in American History Texts" . . . criticizes a number of texts because, among other things, they failed to appreciate how shrewd a bargain the government made in its land grants to western railroads.

It was written by the assistant to the president of the Association of American Railroads and published at the precise time when the railroads were seeking from Congress legislation doing away with the lowered rates upon government property shipped over the land-grant lines. Whatever it is, such an article cannot be scholarship, say [its] accusers.

Their case seems built upon several premises, not always concretely formulated or sharply delineated from one another. Conceivably some doubt the scholarly competence of any investigator or writer employed in the business world. I cannot agree. When training in the techniques of scholarship has been dowered upon thousands, it is difficult to believe that academicians have a monopoly of scholarship or that technical competence does not exist outside their charmed circle. Perhaps others feel that writers in the pay of business cannot intellectually divest themselves of the loyalties and interests of their occupation. I fail to see, however, why it should be inherently more difficult for businessmen to transcend such limitations than for professors to rise above theirs. We tend to forget, for instance, that most professors, since they have neither riches nor the hope of riches, are prone to question the values of an area ruled by the acquisitive instinct. Loyalties and interests are limitations upon researchers and writers, whether or not they are in academe.

There still remains a more critical question: Does an employee of a business organization have the freedom to discover and publish facts painful to his employer? Has he the freedom to be objective? In other words, if Colonel Henry's quest for fact had led honestly to the opposite conclusion—that, in fact, the land grants to railroads had injured the nation—would it have occurred to him to publish this conclusion? If he had, could he have kept his job? I cannot answer for Colonel Henry or the Association of American Railroads, but until employees of business groups testify more frequently to the hurt of their employers, their articles must be approached with more initial caution than those by investigators and teachers in universities and colleges blessed with the tradition of "let the chips fall where they may." Since, however, it is still possible for a man testifying in his own interest to speak the truth, that testimony should have a hearing. If the world of scholarship has not enough insight, self-confidence, and sophistication to evaluate such testimony, it might as well surrender. A blanket proscription of articles by businessmen may protect the innocence of the learned; it is hardly a tribute to their brains.

As a writer of one of the "thirty-seven representative texts" put through the wringer by Colonel Henry, I have no intention of entering a defense of my own. Exchanges between reviewers and reviewed have usually seemed to me dull and about as unfruitful as some of today's stenographic reports of the collective bargaining process. I should, however, like to make a brief comment upon Colonel Henry's procedure. Since he must have a measuring rod, he formulates four questions to which "a balanced story of the federal land-grant transactions requires reasonably correct answers." In my estimation one of these questions—"what proportion of the railroad mileage of the country received land grants from the government?"—is unimportant; and he, in turn, omits questions—notably an evaluation of the effect of land-grant policy upon railroad financing—which are of fundamental significance. Both his praise and blame derive from too limited a standard. Furthermore, his colorful summary of the undoubted advantages bestowed by the construction of the land-grant railroads, proceeds throughout on the unproven assumption that they would not, perhaps could not, have been built without such assistance. The advantages of the results are used to consecrate the means. "It may not have been the wisest way, but it worked." Other historians can certainly be forgiven their assumptions that the wisest way can be the best policy and that it is the function of writers upon policy to weigh its wisdom by more inclusive standards than those of Colonel Henry. It is impossible not to sympathize, however, with his surprise that textbooks can be factually so inaccurate. Unhappily, textbook writers, like teachers of courses, have not the time to resort to sources for all their data. They have to depend upon secondary material; sometimes, regrettably, they copy from each other. Colonel Henry's more intensive research on a phase of their material will, therefore, prove highly useful to our hard-driven brotherhood.

Problems in the Appraisal of the Railroad Land Grants

CHARLES S. MORGAN

This paper was read before the Lexington Group at the Thirty-ninth Annual Meeting of the Mississippi Valley Historical Association in Bloomington, April, 1946.

Reprinted by permission from the Mississippi Valley Historical Review, *Volume 33 (1946), pages 443–454.*

I AM glad to join in this discussion of Colonel Henry's interesting paper. I do so in a purely personal capacity and by reason of work done on the subject of land grants for the former Federal Coordinator of Transportation.[1]

In my opinion, as a layman, Mr. Henry has demonstrated that the treatment given the railroad land grants in history textbooks generally has been inadequate and often has been misleading.[2] It is doubtful, however, that the injury done the railroads has been as great as he implies.

On this point we have the results of a survey made in 1944 for the Association of American Railroads by the Opinion Research Corporation of Princeton, New Jersey.[3] According to this survey, as reported in *Railway Age*, 48 per cent of the persons interviewed had never heard of the land grants; of the remaining 52 per cent, approximately 40 per cent thought the railroads had repaid the government for this assistance, less than a fourth felt otherwise, and over a third (which is not surprising) had no opinion on this necessarily technical question. If one accepts the results of surveys of this kind, and it appears that the railroads find them valuable, it follows that about one person in eight had the "wrong answer." Without excusing the texts, it appears they have done the railroads little harm.

The same survey, however, indicated that only 17 per cent of the persons who had an answer had what the railroads considered the "correct" answer to the question: Which form of transportation has received the least assistance from the public treasury? It is not clear whether reference was to the least aggregate amount of aid or the least in relation to the size of the several branches of transportation. The answers, however, were as follows: Trucks and busses, 44 per cent; river and canal transportation, 27 per cent; railroads, 17 per cent; and airlines, 12 per cent. These answers, whatever their merits, are mentioned here because of the part which the land grants play in the thinking of the railroads and their competitors on the public aids problem in general. The railroads for years have waged and are now waging a battle on this problem. This battle breaks out in the form of intermittent skirmishes, attacks and counterattacks, with rarely a retreat or admission of weakness on any side. Only one who watches these skirmishes closely can see when the ammunition has run out or that "playing dead" is a weapon successfully used by some of the contestants. One weapon, the land grants, which its users appear to regard as heavy artillery, always is aimed at the railroads.[4] The desire of the railroads to put the land-grant episode in its proper setting in order that it may not continue to plague them unduly is understandable. The great importance of giving sound consideration to where the public interest lies in proposals for further large public expenditures on the nation's transportation plant makes it, in fact, not inappropriate to have this controversial question cleared up so far as may be possible.

There is substantial agreement as to the net acreage received under the grants, the value of this land at the time of the grants, the net proceeds of sale, and the miles of grant-aided road constructed; there also is general recognition that these lands were an important factor in financing the construction of these early railroads. There is less agreement as to the amount the government has saved in transportation charges. The differences lie mainly, however, in the interpretation of accepted facts and in the determination of what constitutes a fair over-all statement of the public aid the railroads received through the land grants.

Before turning to the questions still in dispute, let me say that I agree with Dr. Ellis [David Maldwyn Ellis] that the state grants most definitely should be discussed along with the federal grants in future texts. Also, I see no objection to his suggestion that the total acreage made available—the total grants—be set out, provided it is made entirely clear that for various reasons, some beyond their control, the railroads did not realize on certain of the grants. Mr. Henry appears to concur in this point. There also should be mention in at least a general way of the many other kinds of public aid the railroads received. While the railroad land grants naturally inspire an interest on the part of the historian which he scarcely can feel toward aids to other forms of transportation, fairness to the railroads seems to require that adequate space be given to the public aids received by other forms of transportation both in the past and in more recent years. Thus, the antecedent land grants for wagon roads and river improvements most certainly should be mentioned, as may the likelihood that these grants would have been very large had the railroads not entered the picture.[5] If the historian enters this broader field he must realize, however, that he will have to run the gauntlet of conflicting opinions and interests, and recognize that compression into a limited space entails serious dangers.

A first question of interpretation is whether it is wrong, as Mr. Henry states, to describe the federal grants as "huge," "vast," "enormous," "staggering," and "breath-taking."[6] It would seem that the receipt of 210,000 square miles of federal grants, equivalent to 1 square mile in 14 in continental United States, justifies adjectives of the order indicated, though "breath-taking" and "staggering" seem scarcely appropriate and suggest a limited vocabulary.

A second question is the significance of the land grants in the building of the railroads. A pamphlet distributed by the Association of American Railroads in April, 1944, refers to the federal land grants as "made to a small mileage of pioneer railroads more than three-quarters of a century ago."[7] This statement is not untrue as a matter of cold fact and has merit in current discussions of public aid, but it necessarily overlooks the historical importance of the land grants. The 18,000 miles of pioneer railroad built with federal land-grant aid constituted about 40 per cent of the mileage built from 1850 to 1870, the period of the grants.[8] The net proceeds of federal and state land grants, not including the realization by certain affiliated and subsidiary interests, represented about one-third of the recorded cost of construction to 1882 of land-grant railroad mileage west of the Mississippi River.[9]

It is somewhat difficult to add anything new to the discussion of the next and more important question of interpretation: How is the land-grant aid to be measured? The report of the Federal Coordinator of Transportation, the foreword of the late Commissioner Joseph B. Eastman, and the subsequent report of the Board of Investigation and

Research,[10] written after further presentation of the railroad viewpoint, all found that the aid can be measured properly only by consideration of the net proceeds, with appropriate allowance for the land-grant deductions; the railroads adhere steadily to the view that the value of the lands at the time of the grants is determinative. It was conceded in the Coordinator's report that, "from a strictly legal standpoint, assuming the existence of an issue requiring the determination of property rights, the aid received could be measured by the market value of the lands at the time of the grants. . . ."[11] Let us see where this line of reasoning leads.

A "legal" approach presupposes the existence of something of a contractual relationship. Mr. Henry says Uncle Sam, a "canny landowner," drove a shrewd "bargain" by exchanging lands, of which the government had a surplus, for reductions in rates and fares to it. A "bargain" presupposes a meeting of minds and that both Congress and the railroads, at the time of the "bargain," weighed what each party was giving against what each was getting and individually concluded that there was sufficient agreement in the number of dollars involved to "make it a deal." The insistence of some railroads on receiving more acreage than Congress at first was disposed to grant is of interest in this connection.

This line of reasoning, essential to the position of the railroads, is all out of perspective. Congress in 1850 was exercising a basic developmental and defense function of government when it made the railroad grants. It was not exchanging dollars of land value for dollars of reduced rates, but land for the development and security of the country. No one can turn these objectives into dollars. That, as Mr. Henry adds, Congress hoped the remaining government lands would rise in value has no bearing, as the government's objective at this time was to secure the settlement of these lands; the increased return from sale of other government lands was incidental, though it doubtless helped in selling the legislation to Congress.

The view that Uncle Sam was a shrewd bargainer could be demonstrated only if it could be proved that the majority in both the House and Senate foresaw that there would be the volume of government traffic that subsequently developed and which reached a torrent stage during World War II. Rather, Congress was accused at the time of "giving away" lands and of being anything but a shrewd trader. It could have foreseen a volume of government traffic which was a mere trickle, even in relation to the small total volume of business the railroads did in the years immediately following the building of the land-grant railroads. The size of our armed forces is some indication of the amount of the land-grant deductions in various periods. It is true that some leaders in Congress foresaw the coming of the War between the States. Union forces, including naval forces, reached a peak of about 1,118,000 men in that war; the relatively small land-grant mileage available and in northern hands at that time was put, however, to substantial use. In 1878, the regular army numbered less than 20,000 men. In the Spanish-American War the peak size of our armed forces was in the neighborhood of 225,000 men, but again a reduction occurred. In World War I, during most of which, however, the railroads were operated by the government, the maximum was about four million; in World War II it was twelve million. There had been no blossoming of the so-called economic functions of the government in 1850, and none occurred for decades thereafter. We can say no more than that Congress may have foreseen a rise in government traffic over the years, but that its boldest thinkers could not have foreseen the volume of government business that would develop. Neither, for that matter, could the railroads.

If, then, it were to be granted that a "bargain" was made, it would be necessary to consider both sides of the bargain in terms of the benefits each party hoped at the time to get. In this view, the $900,000,000 of saving in rates we now hear discussed is so far out of line with the hopes of 1850 to 1870 as to be without historical or legal significance. As late as 1937, when the deductions, despite rising government traffic, did not exceed $7,000,000 a year,[12] anyone who predicted they shortly would reach $24,000,000 or more a month would have been considered rash, to say the least. If the railroads insist on having the value of the lands they received stated in terms of the value they had prior to the building of the railroads, they must cut down the savings to the government to an amount reasonably predictable at that time, which would be a hardly recognizable fraction of the $900,000,000 or more now discussed.

Also, if the land grants constituted a "deal" or contract, what position do the railroads find themselves in after the successive reductions in the obligations they incurred? Considering the presently immeasurable volume of traffic which in the long future will involve no land-grant deductions, their competitors will find much more to hurl at them than they could if they discarded the idea of a *quid pro quo* and its implications and rested their case, as was done to some extent in the recent *[1944]* hearings on the Boren bill (H.R. 4184), on the un-anticipated and large benefits the government has received. The public in the period of the grants and afterward grew increasingly critical of what the railroads were doing with these lands, as Dr. Ellis points out, but time has blurred these incidents and has left the informed public with a belief that the land grants fully justified themselves and that, as a nation, we owe an enormous debt to the railroads for making possible the extraordinarily fast and secure development of the country and its resources. The balance on the land grants now appears to stand in their favor, whatever the basis on which the aid is computed. A narrow legal approach to this question, lacking historical justification, can do the railroads no good. Mr. Henry refers to this issue as "a matter of detail." It is scarcely that, but his view may furnish reason to hope that the issue will be seen in its true perspective by railroads generally.

There are other considerations, however, which should not be overlooked. It sometimes is said that the railroads could have bought at ninety-seven cents or less an acre all of the lands they were given. Such was definitely not the case. They lacked the financial means, the government would not have sold the lands to them in this block fashion, and the price would have gone up if the railroads had made the attempt. It also is erroneous to assume, as is common in some quarters, that the lands never would have risen in value had the land grants not been given. In some cases the grants held back the development of railroads.[13] More important are the facts, first, that other pioneer railroads were built without land grants and, second, that, on the average, railroads would have been extended through the undeveloped sections within ten or at the most fifteen years from the time they were built, had there been no land-grant aid.[14] That the land grants contributed to speculative overbuilding also needs to be noted.

The following, from our report on *Public Aids*, sums up the situation as well as is possible:

The view that the railroads and the Government struck a bargain does not, however, signify that the current value of the lands which passed to the railroads was the consideration which induced them to undertake the building of lines. Aside from use of the lands as a basis of financing, it was obviously the increment in value which the railroads sought, whether only that to be realized immediately upon construction of the lines or the larger increment which would develop over a period of years. From any other viewpoint, the railroads would have been a mere fiscal agent of the Government, turning back to it the "profits" on land operations. The railroads realized substantially more than the pre-railroad value of the lands, secured credit on the basis of the added value which the lands shortly had, and, where the lands were sold immediately, indirectly participated in the increment in value through the attraction it held out to settlers and others who produced traffic for them to carry.[15]

I come now to a final question suggested by Mr. Henry's paper, viz., the amount and significance of the land-grant deductions. The figure of $900,000,000, subject to additional accruals, has been mentioned above. How accurate is it? It derives largely from estimates assembled by the staff of the former Board of Investigation and Research and prior estimates in the Coordinator's report. Whatever the final estimate may prove to be, well over three-fourths of it must be attributed to World War II. It necessarily is subject to the effects of future adjudication of charges on government traffic during the war. Thus, there are outstanding issues as to what constituted "military" traffic subject to land-grant deductions; whether adjudication of these issues will increase or decrease the present figure of land-grant deductions cannot be stated. Also, there is the possibility that some efforts will be made to secure downward adjustments in rates paid by the government during the war. As in the past, the majority of the government's traffic moved during World War II under regular tariff rates. The assumption is involved that these rates were reasonable for all classes of government traffic and for purposes of computing land-grant deductions. Such may not always have been the case. A committee of experts appointed by the Bureau of the Budget reported last December [1945] to Senator Burton Wheeler that, while the majority of these rates were not excessive, "many of the rates, ratings, and charges studied and evaluated by it have been and/or are excessive." [16] There are other considerations, such as the net effect of the special reduced rates quoted under Section 22 of the Interstate Commerce Act, which there is not time to mention here. The committee, however, gave the railroads credit for important reductions in charges to the War Department.

These points are mentioned here to make it clear that there is need for careful evaluation of all angles of the matter of land-grant deductions before complete acceptance may be given savings to the government which currently are said to approach a billion dollars. Not to be overlooked, however, is the fact that railroads paid heavy taxes on their profits during the war.

It scarcely needs saying that the figure cited reflects all land-grant deductions, whether by reason of statutory requirement or under the so-called equalization agreements. These agreements were made voluntarily for the purpose of profit by carriers (or lines) which did not receive land-grant aid. They have not lessened the amount of that aid; if the deductions were a burden to the land-grant railroads, the burden has been shared by other railroads.[17] In fact, their competitors have been eager to share it. Further, if the idea of a "bargain" were to prevail, the land-grant railroads could scarcely reason, with logic, that what other railroads have contributed was a part of their bargain. Allowance may be made, however, for the fact that equalizations also have been made by railroads which received land grants. In the *Public Aids* report the statutory deductions were taken at about 55 per cent of the total deductions. This per cent definitely is high; a more accurate estimate should be developed. If, however, this percentage were applied to the aforementioned total, the picture would be quite different from the one that is painted.

It is of interest to mention another viewpoint on this matter. The report of the staff of the Board of Investigation and Research states:

> Since most of the aggregate rate concessions have accumulated very recently, whereas most of the net proceeds were received much earlier, it is to be doubted that the railroads *collectively* have made much more than adequate compensation.[18] (Italics supplied)

It was noted, however, that the deductions "are continuing to accumulate on a substantial scale. . . ."

An evaluation of the land grants also requires consideration of how far the reductions in rates on government traffic have come out of the railroads' pockets. It was concluded, in our staff report on *Public Aids,* that the early construction aids confer substantially no benefit on present railroads or their owners and that the land-grant deductions cause their owners no disadvantage.[19] This conclusion was based on the "buying for value" concept and on the many changes in the ownership of the railroads. On this basis, substantially all of the early railroad aids were "wiped out" in setting up the aids to all forms of transportation on a comparative current basis. The railroads appear to have made no use of this conclusion, possibly because it conflicted with their statements that the land-grant deductions meant revenue losses to them. Let us see how far such has been the case.

In adjusting particular rates the commission obviously has not considered the fact that land-grant deductions will be made,[20] as to do so would defeat the purpose of Congress. On the other hand, in so-called revenue or general level rate cases the commission has had to consider the past and prospective earnings of the railroads and their revenue needs. To the extent that the earnings on government traffic have been and will be less on account of the land-grant deductions, other traffic has tended to bear higher rates.[21] This process is far less simple than this statement indicates. When the deductions were only a few millions a year, they could easily be lost sight of. When, however, they reached such an order of magnitude as they did during the last war, they constituted a substantial consideration. However, this matter is more one of trends than of definite proof.[22]

Passage of the Boren bill really stands largely to the credit of the National Industrial Traffic League and other representatives of shippers. Discriminations between shippers with and shippers without land-grant rates available and uncertainties incident to the use of land-grant rates made shippers almost unanimous in urging passage of this legislation.

A final observation: Aside from the several problems of land policy of interest to the economic historian, to which Dr. Ellis has referred, there are highly technical questions involved in an evaluation of what is now substantially a closed chapter in railroad history. The railroads and the public deserve to have this episode definitively appraised and placed in its relation to public aids in general. May it not be possible a little later, when some of the existing uncertainties have been cleared up, for a group of men of all the callings involved—historians, economists, rate experts, and others—to bring their data and views to a common meeting ground and there thresh out their differences? This procedure will require months of patient endeavor. It will not result in agreement on all points, but it will make the areas of agreement clear to the future historian and show him, for his appraisal, the reasoning behind the still divergent views. I merely raise the question; I feel no assurance that the results will be all that might be desired.

NOTES

1 *[Charles S. Morgan was]* formerly Director, Section of Research, Federal Coordinator of Transportation; later Chief Carrier Research Analyst, Bureau of Transport Economics and Statistics, Interstate Commerce Commission. The views expressed are the personal views of the author and are not intended to indicate what might be the views of the Interstate Commerce Commission.

2 It may be noted that none of the more advanced texts on the economic

history of the United States was examined in Colonel Henry's paper.

3 "Railroads Popular, Their Ills Ignored," *Railway Age,* 127:888–889 (December 9, 1944). The survey reported in this article is indicated to be the fourth such survey for the Association.

4 A recent example is the interchange between A. J. Tobin, Executive Director of the Port of New York Authority, and an editor of the *Railway Age.* Mr. Tobin, in response to a criticism of proposed expenditures on a public terminal for use by trucking companies, said that the railroads have received "about $650,000,000 of land." The reply was made that the correct figure was about $178,000,000. This figure was credited to the report on *Public Aids to Transportation,* released by the Federal Coordinator of Transportation. While this figure appears in that report, it definitely was rejected in the finding of public aid. *Railway Age,* 120:609 (March 23, 1946). The same error is found in Henry, "The Railroad Land Grant Legend in American History Texts," 189. *[See above, p. 134.]*

5 U.S. Federal Coordinator of Transportation, *Public Aids to Transportation* (4 vols., Washington, 1938–1940), 2:10.

6 Henry, "The Railroad Land Grant Legend in American History Texts," 174. *[See above, p. 123.]*

7 Association of American Railroads, *Land Grants—What Land Grants Were—What Land Grant Deductions Are—How They Work in Practice TODAY—and Why They Should Be Terminated NOW,* April, 1944.

8 Miles operated, 1850, 9021; 1870, 52,927. In 1880, the total had risen to 93,263 miles. Interstate Commerce Commission, Bureau of Statistics, *Railway Statistics Before 1890,* Statement No. 32151 (December, 1942).

9 *Public Aids to Transportation,* 1:42–43.

10 Board of Investigation and Research, *Public Aids to Domestic Transportation* (79 Cong., 1 sess., House Doc. no. 159).

11 *Public Aids to Transportation,* 2:34.

12 Report of Commissioners Splawn, Eastman, and Mahaffie in the President's message on . . . *Intermediate Relief for the Railroads* (75 Cong., 3 sess., House Misc. Doc. no. 583, vol. 2), 19.

13 Frederick A. Cleveland and Fred W. Powell, *Railroad Promotion and Capitalization in the United States* (New York, 1909), 253.

14 *Public Aids to Transportation,* 1:43.

15 *Ibid.,* 2:34.

16 *Congressional Record,* 79 Cong., 2 sess., 697. Thus far, the entire report has not been made public.

17 *Public Aids to Transportation,* 2:47.

18 *Public Aids to Domestic Transportation,* 134.

19 *Public Aids to Transportation,* 1:39–40, 41.

20 See, for example, *United States* vs. *Southern Pacific Co.,* 25 *Interstate Commerce Commission,* 255–258; *Monolith Portland Cement Co.* vs. *Atchison, Topeka & Santa Fe Railway Co.,* 169 *Interstate Commerce Commission,* 689, 694.

21 "The railroads have got to maintain themselves in a good financial condition in order to serve the public efficiently and they also have the right under the Constitution to a fair return upon their property values, and that need and that right persist notwithstanding the land-grant reductions, and if they cannot get the necessary income out of the Government traffic, then they have got to get it somewhere else."—Commissioner Joseph B. Eastman, House Hearings on H.R. 6156, *Repeal of Land-Grant Rates on Transportation of Government Traffic,* 77 Cong., 2 sess., 10. See also *Immediate Relief for the Railroads,* 32; and see testimony of Commissioner Mahaffie in Senate Hearings on H.R. 4184, *Repeal of Land-Grant Rates on Transportation of Government Traffic,* 78 Cong., 2 sess., 10. The latter said, in answer to a question: "Speaking generally and over the long term, that [the public has made up in increased rates what the railroads have lost by reason of land-grant deductions] is true. Shippers who pay the rates must support the railroad system. Some shippers getting their service at a reduction would mean that others have to pay that much more to support the railroads."

22 "The most that can be said, from the railroad point of view, is that the concessions undoubtedly decreased the revenue which would otherwise have been received from the Government, and that it cannot be known that more revenue was exacted from other patrons because of this fact."
—*Public Aids to Transportation,* 2:47.

The Railroad Land-Grant Legend

PAUL WALLACE GATES

Reprinted by permission from the Journal of Economic History,
Volume 14, Number 2 (Spring, 1954), pages 143–146.

IN a recent review of L. L. Waters' *Steel Trails to Santa Fe*, Joseph T. Lambie challenged the claim long maintained by persons who deem it proper to defend railroad land grants on the grounds that the government lost nothing by donating one half the public land in broad strips 12 to 80 miles wide, since it doubled the price it charged for the reserved sections within the same strip.[1] Mr. Lambie refers to D. Philip Locklin, *Economics of Transportation*,[2] for the fallacy in the argument. Unfortunately, Mr. Locklin's treatment is theoretical and he confuses rather than clarifies the issue. That Mr. Waters should have entertained at this late date such a quaint notion, for which no substantial evidence was ever offered other than loose statements based simply on the fact that the government did double the price of the reserved lands, shows how long misconceptions can last and how difficult it is to have well-documented corrections commonly accepted.

The claim has validity only if, of the following assumptions, combinations of (1), (2), (4), and (5), or of (3), (4), and (5) are correct. The assumptions are: (1) that within the primary grant there would be as many reserved sections as granted sections; (2) that in areas previously surveyed and opened to pre-emption little or none of the reserved land had been disposed of at the time the grants were made; (3) that the double minimum price extended to the alternate sections outside the primary grant in the "lieu" area; (4) that the reserved land was sold; (5) that it sold for $2.50 or more an acre.

Assumption 1 is theoretically correct only for a small group of railroads having land grants, including the Illinois Central, Mobile and

Ohio, Cairo and Fulton, Pacific of Missouri (two branches), Hannibal and St. Joseph, and two other lines in Arkansas and Mississippi. In a series of acts in 1850, 1852, and 1853, alternate *even* sections within a strip of land extending 6 miles on each side of the proposed railroads were given to Illinois, Missouri, Arkansas, Mississippi, and Alabama, which in turn gave them to these companies to aid in building their lines. Since section 16 in each township in these states had earlier been given for common schools, the railroads could take land in lieu thereof in the "indemnity" or "lieu" area between 6 and 15 miles farther from the lines. Theoretically the railroads would get on each side of their lines seventeen sections within a township in the primary area and one lieu section in the indemnity area for every 6 miles of road, and the government would reserve eighteen sections within the primary area on each side to be sold at the double minimum price. Assumption 1 applies theoretically to grants containing 7,276,000 acres or 5.5 per cent of the total acreage contained in the railroad land grants, but it does not apply to 94.5 per cent of the acreage contained in the grants.

Beginning in 1856 all land grants with the exception of a small one to Mississippi provided for the donation of *odd* sections in place of the *even* sections previously donated.[3] By this change the school sections would come out of the double minimum tracts reserved to the government. In Michigan, Wisconsin, Iowa, Florida, and Louisiana, the land-grant railroads would theoretically receive one more section in each township than the government would reserve at the double minimum price. In Minnesota and Kansas and other states in which the Pacific railroads were located, the beneficiary lines would theoretically receive two more sections in each township than the government would retain. To put it differently, the government gave the Santa Fe, Union Pacific, Northern Pacific, and all other land-grant railroads west of the Missouri 12.5 per cent more land than it reserved to itself within the primary area.[4]

Assumption 2 is easily discarded as having no basis in fact. Before the grants were voted, settlers and speculators anticipated the railroads by making many selections of land that otherwise might have fallen to the railroads. For example, the Illinois Central along great stretches of its line could find no land to select either within the primary or lieu areas and in consequence took all the even sections in other areas where settlers had previously shown no interest. Within the primary grant area there were only 1,223,921 acres in the reserved odd sections that were priced by the government at $2.50, whereas the railroad had received 2,595,053 acres.[5]

In eastern Kansas the amount of land taken up by settlers and speculators or reserved for Indians was so great that the Kansas and Neosho Railroad, later the Missouri River, Fort Scott and Gulf, received only 21,341 acres of a grant that at its theoretical maximum would have been 1,024,000 acres. Representatives of this railroad later found the obligations accompanying the grant far heavier than the lands were worth and successfully urged its forfeiture as an act of relief.[6] For a distance of 105 miles in eastern Kansas, the Leavenworth, Pawnee and Western, now the Kansas branch of the Union Pacific, received practically no land.[7] The Leavenworth, Lawrence, and Galveston Railroad for its line from Lawrence to the southern border of Kansas was entitled to over a million acres, but actually acquired title to only 62,510 acres.[8] None of these lines were to get compensation in lieu areas elsewhere, but three other Kansas railroads were in a different and more favorable position.

The land grants to the Missouri, Kansas and Texas (Katy), the Atchison, Topeka, and Santa Fe, and the St. Joseph and Denver railroads included the odd sections within 10 miles on each side of their lines and the right to select lieu lands in the indemnity area 10 miles beyond on each side. Similar privileges to the eastern Kansas railroads had not been very helpful, for neither within the primary nor the indemnity areas were there lands for selection. The Katy, the Santa Fe, and the St. Joseph and Denver being extended into central Kansas, where lands had not been picked over, were able there to get compensation in whole or in part in the lieu area for the odd sections they were denied in the more eastern portion of the state. Since the experience of the Santa Fe best illustrates this point, emphasis is placed on it.

For a distance of 112 miles from Atchison westward, the Santa Fe picked up only a few tracts of the 716,800 acres to which it was entitled. Beyond Cottonwood Falls (Strong on the railroad) for a distance of 180 miles, the Santa Fe secured in the lieu area compensation for all the land it failed to get in the eastern portion and for such odd sections within the primary area beyond Cottonwood Falls as had been entered by settlers before its grant was made in 1863. In its advertising literature the Santa Fe showed its grant as being 40 miles wide including alternate sections within both the primary and lieu areas from Cottonwood Falls to Kinsley and 20 miles wide from Kinsley to the Colorado border.[9]

This concentration of selections within the lieu area which resulted from the loss of lands in the primary area farther east is significant because the government derived no compensating advantage from double minimum price land in the lieu area. Assumption 3 is false; the double minimum applied only to the primary area of the grants. Since all the early grants were in partly developed territory where the sections that might have brought the double minimum had already been taken up, there was no prospect that the return from sales would compensate for the donations. Though the grants to the Union Pacific, the Kansas Pacific, and the Central Pacific did not provide for lieu lands, they did provide for odd sections which, because of the education donations, assured that the reserved sections would never equal the granted sections.

Assumption 4 that the reserved sections bearing the double minimum price were sold pays scant attention to the free grant policy embodied in the Homestead Act of 1862 and to the statistics of land sales. True, until 1879 homesteads of only 80 acres could be located within the primary grants (Civil War veterans were allowed to homestead full quarter sections by the act of July 15, 1870),[10] and settlers wishing to round out a quarter had either to pre-empt another 80-acre tract at $2.50 an acre or buy from railroads at higher prices. In 1879 the unit of homestead entry on the double minimum was increased to 160 acres for all.[11] Speculators, farm-makers wishing to get title in order to borrow on it, town planners, cattlemen, and lumbermen continued to buy land after 1862, but not in such quantity within the primary grants as to return to the government from the double minimum anything more than a small fraction of the value of the lands given to the railroads.

Kansas may be neither a typical nor representative state in the consideration of public land questions, but a glance at the statistics of land sales in it will serve to show how little there is to the legend under examination. The total of federal grants to railroads in Kansas, whether made directly or through the state, is 8,346,603 acres. To have come out even on the grants, the government would have had to sell an equal number of acres within the primary area at the $2.50 price. No such amount of land was sold, but instead in all of Kansas both within and outside the primary areas only 4,323,779 acres were sold between 1863 and 1890, when sales ended except for scattered tracts, and these brought not $2.50 but a mere $1.39 an acre.[12] Instead of the $20,866,507 the government needed to recoup its loss from the donations, it received only $6,140,630, and much of this came from acreage sold outside the primary area and was in no way the result of the land grants or the double minimum.

In summary: Assumption 1 is only applicable to 5.5 per cent of the area granted to railroads; assumption 2 applies to none of the early grants that are included in the area just mentioned; assumption 3 is completely wrong; assumptions 4 and 5 apply to such a limited amount of land as to make them untenable. The railroad land-grant legend should henceforth appear in no other form than as a legend originally offered as an argument in support of donations to railroads and later used to defend past policy.[13]

NOTES

1   *Journal of Economic History,* 12:299–300 (Summer 1952).

2   (Chicago: Business Publications, Inc., 1938), 69.

3   *U.S. Stat.,* vols. 9–14.

4   In Arizona and New Mexico four *even*-numbered sections were reserved for common schools, hence the Santa Fe (Atlantic and Pacific) received 25 per cent more land in these states than the government retained at the double minimum price.

5   I have developed this point in my *Illinois Central Railroad and Its Colonization Work* (Cambridge, Mass., 1934), 105 ff.

6   David M. Ellis, "The Forfeiture of Railroad Land Grants" (Master's thesis, Cornell University, 1939); and the same author's "The Forfeiture of Railroad Land Grants, 1867–1894," *Mississippi Valley Historical Review,* 33:27 ff. (June, 1946).

7   *Emigrants' Guide to the Kansas Pacific Railway Lands* (Lawrence, 1871), 3.

8   A larger amount was patented to the Leavenworth, Lawrence, and Galveston in the Osage reserve, but the Supreme Court later ordered the return of 186,936 acres. (92 *U.S. Reports,* 733 ff.)

9   *Description of the Atchinson, Topeka and Santa Fe Railroad Company Lands in South Central and South West Kansas* (*ca.* 1881), a folded brochure.

10   16 *U.S. Stat.,* 321 (1870).

11   Act of March 3, 1879, 20 *U.S. Stat.,* 472 (1879).

12   Computed from Annual Reports (Commissioner of the General Land Office, 1863–1890, 1932).

13   For other corrections of the treatment by historians of railroad land grants, see Robert S. Henry, "The Railroad Land Grant Legend in American History Texts," *Mississippi Valley Historical Review,* 32:171–194 (September, 1945) *[reprinted in this volume, pp. 121–144],* and the numerous replies to Colonel Henry's criticisms in the same journal, 32:557–576 (March, 1946) *[reprinted in this volume, pp. 145–161].*

Some Crucial Years
of the General
Land Office, 1875–1890

HAROLD H. DUNHAM

Reprinted by permission from Agricultural History, *Volume 11* (1937), *pages 117–141.*

No account of America's "robber barons" is complete without a description of the activities of the General Land Office of the Department of the Interior during the years 1875 to 1890. At the beginning of this period the bureau had supervision of nearly one billion acres of public land, or approximately one-half of the United States. These lands contained immensely valuable natural resources and drew the attention of land-grant railroads, timber and irrigation companies, stock raisers, and other groups eager to exploit them. These groups promoted the rapid development of the West which, according to Lord Bryce, was inimical to its welfare. Yet in so doing they were only following the practices of their eastern business contemporaries who were finding concentration so advantageous.

Although Henry George noted that concentration was the trend of the times as early as 1871, he believed that it was possible to delay land monopoly with consequent benefit to the country.[1] His opinion is borne out by the nexus which developed between the government and western predatory interests. A contemporary, Judge David Davis, later described the relationship as follows:

The great corporations and other monopolies have for many years been stretching out their strong and unscrupulous arms over the public lands remaining for enterprising and honest settlers. Millions of acres of this domain have been seized and stolen, and I have to say this robbery could not have succeeded without the collusion and cooperation of agents employed to protect the interests of the people. . . . Immense combinations have been formed, including the ties of political and social life, for a common object—to break down all attempts at Washington to crush out a venal system which has flourished by departmental indifference or favor.[2]

The questions naturally arise as to how millions of acres of public land could be stolen, why the General Land Office was indifferent to the robbery, and in what way it co-operated with the thieves. The answers can be found in the history of the bureau from 1875 to 1890. During these crucial years the federal government had the opportunity to provide a comprehensive plan for land disposal under a department of public lands. Instead of adopting a suitable policy, Congress permitted reckless absorption through inadequate and faulty administration.

The generation that preceded the closing of the frontier lines witnessed a constant increase in the land business. The government enacted a host of new land laws from 1862 to 1878, including the Homestead, the Timber Culture, Desert Land, and Mineral acts, and railroad and educational grants. The work of the General Land Office was augmented because of the remarkable increase in the absorption of lands which resulted from these laws. In 1877 the government disposed of 4,850,000 acres, and in 1884 the amount was 27,530,000 acres.[3] For the years 1884 to 1890, the annual average was about 20,000,000 acres.

While the duties and responsibilities of the General Land Office were thus expanding, its machinery for handling them remained inefficient, antiquated, and inadequate.[4] Created in 1812, it had been reorganized only once, and that was back in 1836. It had been placed under the Interior Department in 1849, and no legislative changes had been made thereafter. With a long list of bureaus with diverse interests and objectives demanding his attention, the Secretary of the Interior was unable properly to supervise the Office. In addition to Cabinet duties and political responsibilities, he was supposed to administer the bureaus dealing with the public lands, Indian affairs, patents, pensions, the census, railways and wagon roads, education, and sundry local works and institutions in the federal capital. Cases on appeal and requests for instructions formed his principal contact with the Land Office, unless perchance he had a personal interest in a particular matter. Many of the appealed cases were handled by the law officers of the department and received only his formal attention. If his personal interest was involved, the Secretary could direct the Commissioner of Public Lands to submit the particular case for review, and the law officers could be called on for the necessary precedents.

Cases of real doubt might be referred to the Attorney General's office.[5]

The Secretaries felt no obligation to establish consistent policies in land rulings. Evidence on this point is found in an amusing incident referred to in *Copp's Land Owner*, the foremost land paper of the time. On November 15, 1885, it congratulated a retiring law officer on his services to the government, remarking that he had furnished "valuable precedents on all sides of nearly every question of importance . . . during the past fifteen years." This two-edged compliment must have brought a protest from the official, for the following issue of the paper explained that it had meant no insult. It recognized that "no subordinate in the land service can be held responsible for the decisions of his superior officers." [6] The *Land Owner's* unintended indictment called attention to a situation which it repeatedly emphasized.

The manifold duties of the Secretary placed most of the responsibility for supervising the General Land Office on its directing head, the Commissioner of Public Lands. This division of authority hampered efficiency and yet left greater duties on the Commissioner than one man could properly discharge. Abram S. Hewitt of New York asserted in Congress that the Commissioner was "a most overburdened official," and by way of emphasizing the need for a reorganization of the Office, pointed out that he was also "the most important law officer of the Government if measured by the money involved in his decisions." [7] Until 1884 when provision was made for an Assistant Commissioner, the Commissioner often spent several hours a day merely signing his name to documents. The reorganization of 1836 had established the survey, private land claims, and public lands divisions, and the railroad, swamp land, recording, draughting, accounting, pre-emption, and mineral divisions had been created from time to time by the Commissioner as responsibilities accumulated due to new land laws. The result was a difference in rank and pay between heads of divisions; for instance, the railroad chief with his greater responsibilities did not equal the chief of survey.[8]

Every report of the Land Office for the score of years preceding 1890 included a convincing plea for a larger and better paid staff of clerks and additional office space. Support for these requests appear in numerous congressional committee reports,[9] the Public Lands Commission Report of 1880, and the annual reports of the Secretary of the Interior. In 1876 a 25 per cent cut in the staff left only 145 clerks, or less than the office had in 1855.[10] It needed everyone who had been dismissed, but Congress was slow in making replacements.

In 1883 the Commissioner lamented that the "increase in working force and appropriations has been doled out in pittances, and seemingly more to accommodate the Department than to meet the demands of the service." To reveal the needs he stated, "If but one-half of these claims should be perfected into title it would take the present force employed upon this work three years to complete the adjustments, leaving the whole volume of business that might come up within that period unprovided for." [11] He estimated that the Office required two hundred extra clerks, some to be kept permanently to clear up work in arrears. That conditions were not greatly improved by 1888 is indicated by the testimony of Secretary William F. Vilas. "My attention has been drawn to no branch of governmental administration which appeals so cogently, in every respect of wisdom and justice, for intelligent, thorough and effective Congressional action for its relief as the Land Office." [12] Although the Office staff had increased two and one-half times between 1876 and 1887, the amount of land absorbed had risen five-fold.[13] The insufficiency of the staff in 1887 stands out clearly in comparison with the number employed in 1931 when there were five-sixths the number of clerks to do one-fifth the current work and practically no arrears.[14]

The employees of the Land Office were also underpaid. Comparison with the Patent Office in 1876 revealed that there were over twenty high-ranking clerks in each bureau. The annual salary for those in the Patent Office was $2,250, but for the Land Office it was only $1,600.[15] Subsequently there was some improvement for the latter, but a sizable discrepancy still existed in 1888.[16] A Senate investigating committee reported that the Land Office clerks showed more ability than would be expected from men whose salary enabled them to "eke out a bare subsistence" and seemed to find a certain smug satisfaction in declaring that it was greatly to the credit of the clerks that so little was alleged against their honor, since they frequently decided cases covering more than a million dollars in value.[17]

The Public Lands Commission in 1880 recommended improvement in the Land Office force by an increase in the number of higher-paid clerks and a decrease in those with lower pay. The commission demonstrated that such a step would not only result in higher efficiency, but in a saving to the government.[18] Congress refused to authorize the improvement, however, apparently not desiring efficiency even at a saving, and even refused to allow the Office to retain the $8,000 a year that it earned by copying records for interested parties.[19] The time consumed by such work detracted from regular business, and this amount would have enabled the Office to hire eight lower-grade clerks to handle the arrears of business.

There were always applicants for Land Office positions, but the low pay resulted in the constant loss of the ablest men. New clerks readily learned the government routine and then sought transfer to positions of similar rank but higher pay in other bureaus. Many acquired an adequate knowledge of land laws and Land Office procedure and then resigned for private practice before the department. Land corporations enticed a large number of trained men by offering good salaries. The New York *World* noted especially the number that gravitated to railroads, insinuating, with plausible evidence, that railroad employment was frequently given for favors received in land decisions while the clerk was serving in the Office.[20] Among a list of about twenty former employees the paper included the names of two successive Commissioners, Burdett and Williamson, who became associated with railroads after leaving office.

Besides the constant turnover of clerks, overcrowded office rooms seriously handicapped efficiency in the Land Office. In 1880 the Public Lands Commission stated that the "room allotted to the General Land Office is not quite the worst that it could be, nor is it wholly inadequate, but it approximates both." The commission felt that the cramped quarters caused a waste of one-fourth of all the money appropriated for the clerical force.[21] Two years later a Senate committee found that insufficient space, light, and ventilation was damaging the health of the employees and declared that the Land Office needed a new building more than any other bureau or department. The lack of room also exposed valuable papers to damage by fire and theft. There had been a serious fire in 1877 and both before and after that time other papers were destroyed by mold and decay or the ravages of insects and vermin.[22] In 1888 Secretary Vilas observed: "When one reflects upon the almost incalculable value of the records and documents of the Land Office, . . . the cost of providing safe and commodious quarters, in which it will be possible to efficiently reorganize the Bureau so as at least to approximate the objects of its existence, becomes so insignificant as only to intensify the reproach justly due the neglect of such action." [23]

The establishment of a law library was one of the major improvements in the Land Office during the period 1875–1890. The library in 1876 consisted of a few law textbooks and broken sets of Supreme Court reports but no state law reports. Of the books on hand there was frequently only one copy for the simultaneous use of several clerks. The land laws had not been codified, and no one was authorized to print the decisions, orders, and circulars for the bureau.[24] The library was ultimately supplied, and the Public Lands Commission of 1879 codified local, temporary, and national laws and decisions. The records were periodically revised thereafter.

The unremedied handicaps of the General Land Office—crowded quarters, inadequate personnel, overburdened officials, low pay, and rapid turnover of clerks—contributed to unbusinesslike methods and the need for land lawyers. The inefficiency of the methods is revealed by the litigation over the undelivered patent of Thomas McBride of Utah.[25] The case was taken to the Supreme Court and for the second time in history a mandamus was served on a Cabinet officer.[26] McBride had filed an entry for a homestead in Utah in 1869. Five years later he proved up, paid his fees, and secured his certificate from the local land office. But for three years the General Land Office at Washington did not have time to issue his patent. Meanwhile, papers were filed for the incorporation of Grantsville, Utah, as a town, and declaration was made on February 24, 1877, that McBride's homestead entry embraced land rightly within the town and that his entry should therefore be disallowed. The resulting legal contest does not seem to have been recorded in the Land Office, however, either because the clerical work was at fault or the filing system inaccurate. In any case a patent was issued to McBride on September 26, 1877, seven months after the inception of the contest, and sent to Salt Lake City, but before the patent was delivered the Land Office discovered its error and recalled it. McBride went to Washington and demanded his patent. When the department refused to present it to him, he filed a petition for a writ of mandamus against Secretary Carl Schurz in the Supreme Court of the District of Columbia. McBride received a hearing from the United States Supreme Court and won his right to the patent. In its decision the Court expressed regret that Schurz was obliged to pay the expenses of the proceedings. Greater efficiency in the Land Office would have prevented the trouble and the Secretary's monetary loss.[27]

Additional evidence of inefficiency is found in Commissioner N. C. McFarland's reply to a congressional inquiry on the status of railroad grants. He explained that it had taken all of his available clerks forty days to prepare the material requested. This delay, he added, "has been caused almost entirely by the failure on the part of this office in the past . . . to adopt and perfect a comprehensive system of procuring and keeping in a concise and convenient form all matters of information relative to each particular grant." Former Commissioners had used the staff to handle current work only.[28] Another report of the Commissioner to Congress stated that his answer must only be taken as approximate, as it was impossible for him to obtain accurate data on the railroads under discussion.[29]

The work of land lawyers grew steadily as a result of the situation in the Land Office. In 1888 Secretary Vilas said: ". . . few cases can safely proceed now without counsel." He found the judicial functions of the Commissioner and the Secretary bearing "a strong semblance of the court of chancery, with much of the machinery, methods and peculiarities, *mutatis mutandis,* of that venerable tribunal; . . . the ingenuity of seekers for the landed wealth of the Government and their counsel provokes a seemingly limitless enlargement." [30] If, however, cases were not appealed to the higher authorities, the "company" lawyer had several advantages for his client. When the government or a settler had an adverse interest in a case there was apt to be no opposing counsel. In addition, the lawyer had direct access to the clerk handling his case,[31] and underpaid and inexperienced clerks naturally welcomed assistance from experienced persons. Although these contacts probably did not result in corruption in most cases, they did open the door to undue or biased influence.

This access of the lawyers to the clerks resulted in what was called a "patent steal" in 1890.[32] A patent to valuable mineral land in the Duluth, Minnesota, region was being held up in the Office because an affidavit charging fraud in the process of acquisition had been filed. The pertinent papers were secured by the attorneys for the claimants, and the affidavit and the order to investigate removed. Then, in the absence of the clerk who had been handling the case, another clerk was prevailed on to rush the patent through.

Lawyers developed the practice of having a case marked "Special," thereby insuring its being handled out of turn. This procedure aided clients who did not want to wait two or three years, and they were charged a fee of $50 or more for this service.[33] Why the Office permitted the privilege is not quite clear. One of the major objections to Comissioner Sparks developed from his efforts to check the free access of the lawyers to clerks handling their cases and from his drastic limitation on "Special" cases after 1885. The relapse after he had left office brought comments which reveal the extent of previous abuses. In suggesting that the reforms should be permanent, *Copp's Land Owner* stated flatly: "The day should be forever past when a few attorneys stalked through the General Land Office, leading the Commissioner by the nose, bulldozing clerks, ordering their cases made special and dictating the decisions therein." [34] This statement is a convincing indictment of the lawyers' methods and of Land Office procedure.

"Bulldozing" was not the only method used in securing co-operation. Influence, friendship, and even family ties were used. The New York *World* quoted a Washington lawyer as saying: " 'Almost the first question every client asks is, "Have you special influence in the Land Office?" If the reply is in the negative the client generally retires and seeks some one else.' " The same newspaper declared that the outstanding success of the firm Britton and Grey, both former employees of the Land Office, was traceable to two brothers-in-law in the Office. One of these relations was chief clerk and the other was assistant chief of the railroad division.[35]

The unscrupulousness of many land attorneys in handling cases before the Office and in defrauding their clients became notorious. Beginning with Secretary Chandler in 1875, the department periodically refused attorneys with unsavory practices the right to appear before it. In 1878 Secretary Schurz proscribed 127,[36] and later lists of eight to sixteen were published in the *Land Owner*. After Schurz retired, one debarred attorney, charged with trying to bribe a Land Office clerk, attempted to sue him for ruining an alleged $40,000-a-year practice.[37]

The land service was also burdened by antiquated machinery, inefficient work, and occasional corrupt practices of the district land offices. There were ninety-eight district offices in 1876, each presided over by a register and a receiver.[38] Because the salaries of these officials were small they were allowed fees on all contested cases, until a certain maximum had been reached. Necessity induced many of them to create contests so that their pay would be adequate. Cases which might otherwise have been handled in the district offices were forwarded to Washington, too often without sufficient testimony for a proper decision. In defense of the district offices, however, it should be observed that frequently the practice of forwarding cases was necessary because of the inconsistent decisions of the central office. Evidence on this point again comes from *Copp's Land Owner*. In June, 1885, that paper stated, "On our visit to Dakota last year, the land rulings were continually assailed with protests, profanity and ridicule. Local officers, from sheer despair, were compelled to rely on their own judgment without reference to the instructions they received, and attorneys, on a given statement of facts, never pretended to forecast a decision." [39]

The Public Lands Commission suggested a consolidation of the register and receiver offices and the payment of an adequate salary, without fees, to the new office.[40] Congress did not see fit to make this improvement in behalf of efficiency, perhaps because it would have reduced the number of political plums. Another suggestion frequently made regarding the district offices was to give registers and receivers authority to summon witnesses when they suspected fraud.[41] The need and justice of such power was obvious, but after years of delay a Senate committee sententiously reported that the expediency and constitutionality of this authority was questioned, and so it was not provided. Witnesses usually refused to testify voluntarily since fraud was frequently backed up by violence or threat of violence.[42]

Irrespective of the need for this power, some of the most notorious cases of land fraud passed through the local land offices without a hitch. The registers and the receivers appeared to be the only persons in the community who were unaware of the fraud. An outstanding example is found in the acquisition of coal lands in Colorado. In 1873 sixty-one pre-emption entries were filed for about 10,000 acres of supposed agricultural land near Trinidad, Colorado.[43] All of the entries and the witnesses to them were fictitious, but the entries were allowed to be completed by the local office. It seems practically impossible that the register and receiver were ignorant of the fraud. Payment was made for the land chiefly in scrip and certificates were issued to one man, A. C. Hunt.[44] The entries were forwarded to the General Land Office for patent. At the same time, the Office received a warning from an outsider that the agricultural lands were known to cover coal and that the entrants were fictitious. The Land Office either did not consider the warning valid, had no time to investigate, or there was someone in collusion with the defrauders, for the patents were issued. Later, other officials discovered the fraud and endeavored to correct it by bringing a suit to set the patents aside. Hunt had transferred his title to others, and the land had come into the possession of the Colorado Coal and Iron Company. The suit for annulment was therefore brought against this company. The case worked its way to the Supreme Court, which held in 1887 that the titles had passed to the entrants although the latter were fictitious and that, since the Colorado Company was an innocent purchaser of the titles, it was therefore permitted to keep the lands.[45] The decision presents some interesting angles, but the most serious aspect of the case is the reflection which it casts on the integrity of the local land office officials as well as on the General Land Office.

In the absence of direct evidence it is difficult to select the primary reason for congressional neglect of the Land Office. Undoubtedly indifference, apathy, and concern for other problems existed. Yet is seems certain that if the regions most affected had been dissatisfied there would have been protest and change. As the Public Lands Commission pointed out in 1880, it was still easy to acquire land, so actual settlers had no cause to complain. The system worked for them, but it also worked for the corporate predatory interests. In 1879 Representative Charles Foster of Ohio defended the need of improvement in the Land Office. He observed, "Why western members upon this floor have not made for years past and do not now make a point upon this matter, I cannot understand."[46] He would not have been so puzzled if he had understood the railroad, timber, cattle, mining, and surveying interests that backed some of the senators and representatives from California, Colorado, Kansas, and other states.

The West could protest vehemently whenever Congress attempted to repeal obnoxious laws or when administrative reforms checked wholesale fraud. For instance, Commissioner Sparks suspended entries under certain abused laws in anticipation of their speedy repeal.[47] Immediately, vocal elements of the West protested and caused Congress to adopt a resolution asking the department by what authority the action had been taken. Not only did the West exert pressure on minor phases of land administration, but it prevented the repeal which the Commissioner had anticipated. Donaldson described a similar defeat for an earlier attempt at repeal.

Perhaps the outstanding example of the western position is found in Representative Laird's attack on Commissioner Sparks for the latter's "vendetta against the best interests of all the territory beyond the Missouri River." Actually the Commissioner was attempting to reform the violation of land laws and the representative's brother had participated in high-handed and fraudulent action in acquiring land for a cattle ranch.[48]

Powerful landed groups often manifested their concern for land administration in a subtle manner. Aside from the instances noted elsewhere in this paper, there are several notorious cases which should be listed. They include the removal of special agents sent to investigate timber frauds in Humboldt County, California; [49] the dismissal of Special Agent Conrad at the request of the California and Nevada senators after he was prepared to aid in the prosecution of survey frauds; [50] the payment of sums for fraudulent surveys by the Treasury Department despite the rejection of those surveys in the Land Office where control existed; [51] and the close connection between officials and groups seeking advantages in Indian land openings.

It can be inferred that similar influences secured a drastic cut in appropriations for resurveys in districts where fraudulent or inefficient work had been performed.[52] This cut accompanied insufficient appropriations to pay the legal salaries of the surveyors general. Economy could not have been the basis for the slash, as there was a large and troublesome surplus in the Treasury.[53] Apparently it was an attempt to embarrass an honest administration and render it unpopular.

The control of congressional appropriations was long in the hands of Samuel J. Randall, a Democrat from Philadelphia.[54] The Republican-controlled legislature refused to gerrymander the district from his control, probably because he was a "protectionist" Democrat. But the Republican party of the Keystone State was influenced by the Pennsylvania Railroad as well as protectionist industries. Some of the leading railroad men had extensive interests in western lands, particularly in Mexican grants, and it is known that Randall performed minor favors for several of these leaders. His "favors" do not imply corruption, for Randall died a poor man, but it is possible that they extended to obligingly crippling the land service; the facts may be known if and when Randall's papers are made public.[55]

All of the Secretaries of the Interior and the Commissioners endeavored to improve the land service, although some were more conspicuously zealous than others. Generally speaking, the Secretaries tended to dominate the policies of the service. They were chiefly western men and their former connections usually included landed groups of one kind or another. The Secretaries and Commissioners were sympathetic to western or corporate interests while in office. The word "sympathetic" is used advisedly and does not imply corruption. Instances of collusion will be noted, however, for public-land robbery obviously was not the result of inadequate equipment alone.

President Grant selected the Radical Republican ex-Senator Zachariah Chandler of Michigan to succeed the incapable Columbus Delano of Ohio as Secretary of the Interior.[56] Taking office in October, 1875, Chandler overhauled the malodorous Indian and Patent bureaus and built up the morale of the entire department. He stopped one glaring fraud in the Land Office and conspicuously refused a bribe in a case on appeal which was given publicity at a time when charges of fraud and bribery were hanging over the Republicans in the election of 1876.[57] The party was thus aided by having its chairman of the national campaign committee posed as a model of rectitude. His attention to party affairs during the summer of 1876 detracted from his duties at the department. The Commissioners who served under Chandler were Samuel S. Burdett of Missouri, whose ill-health soon forced him to resign, and General James A. Williamson of Iowa. Both made notable efforts to build up the Land Office.

Carl Schurz of Missouri had become noted as a Liberal Republican and reformer and President Hayes brought him into the Cabinet in 1877.[58] After making a number of cautious changes in the personnel of the department,[59] Schurz devoted considerable attention to the proper method of handling public timberlands and is credited with inaugurating a movement for conservation.[60] Instrumental in securing the Public Lands Commission in 1879, he supported its recommendations, particularly those for improving administration. After leaving office, his policies regarding land-grant railroads were roundly attacked, but he was able to make a creditable defense of his actions, especially with reference to disputes between settlers and railroads.[61]

The lengthy service of Commissioner Williamson included definite efforts to improve the Office. He served as a member of the Public Lands Commission, though his official duties held him in Washington and did not permit his accompanying the body on its western tour. He is credited with starting the movement for codification. On the other hand, some of his actions are open to serious question. In 1869, seven years before his appointment, he had staked out a settlement claim in Utah,[62] but, according to the Land Office, he did not fulfill the requirements necessary for patent at the time of his application and the case was left open for further proof of settlement and cultivation. No further developments occurred until 1876, when he became Commissioner. During that year, Acting Commissioner Baxter went over the papers connected with the case and decided that the proof formerly rejected was adequate, and a patent was issued to his superior, Commissioner Williamson. In effect, the Commissioner reversed a predecessor's ruling for his own benefit.

Williamson's handling of the Maxwell Land Grant case as it passed to patent is an even darker stain on his name. This famous case warrants extended treatment as an illustration of how "great corporations" stretched "their strong and unscrupulous arms over the public lands." The grant dated from the time of Mexico's nominal control over New Mexico. It came into the hands of the famous frontiersman Lucien B. Maxwell, who sold it to a syndicate called the Maxwell Land Grant and Railway Company, later reorganized as the Maxwell Land Grant Company.[63] Over twenty years after the United States came into the possession of New Mexico, the Maxwell Company sought patent for about 2,000,000 acres, as the amount covered by the grant. Secretary of the Interior Jacob D. Cox ruled that the company was entitled to only 97,000 acres, which was the maximum amount that could have been granted under Mexican law.[64] The company refused this restriction on its claim and waited for a change of Secretaries.

In 1871, after Columbus Delano replaced Cox, the company made a new appeal for the 2,000,000 acres. Delano, however, refused to reverse his predecessor's decision, thus denying the claim a second time.[65] Checked but not defeated, the company's lawyers sought a new basis for appeal.[66] A case involving another Mexican grant, somewhat similar to the Maxwell grant, was then being prosecuted in the Colorado courts. The Maxwell Company lawyers aided in bringing this case, *Tameling* vs. *U.S. Freehold and Immigration Company*, before the Supreme Court. Its decision was suitable as a precedent for Interior Department rulings on Mexican grants.[67] However, the lawyers of the company did not make a new appeal to the department for the Maxwell grant. Instead the initiative was taken by Commissioner Williamson when he wrote to the Secretary calling attention to the Supreme Court ruling in the Tameling case. Noting that it appeared to conflict with the departmental decision in the Maxwell case, the Commissioner asked for instructions in deciding future cases. Secretary Schurz replied that "hereafter" the principles of the Court should be followed,[68] and the Commissioner appears to have used this letter of general authority for the future in re-opening the Maxwell case and ordered a survey of most of the land which the company had claimed. This survey covered over 1,700,000 acres of rich coal, gold, timber, and pasture lands. After it had been returned to the Land Office, the Commissioner further compromised himself by replying to inquiries with the statement that the returns had not yet been received.[69]

The Land Office found that the survey contained several discrepancies when checked with the records of the Office. The Commissioner prepared a letter to the surveyor general of New Mexico, pointing out the errors and demanding their correction. This letter was not sent, however. On its margin is a note saying that the Commissioner had decided to issue patent,[70] and thus, after years of litigation and effort, the Maxwell Company succeeded in acquiring the land it claimed. The rôle played by Williamson in the case appears rather dubious. What prompted him to re-open the case which a Secretary had refused to consider, why did he prevaricate over the returns of the survey, and what caused him to ignore his duties regarding correct surveys in his haste to issue patent, are questions that remain unanswered. His actions indicate undue influence from, or improper connection with, the Maxwell Company.

In 1880, the year following the issuance of the Maxwell patent, Williamson visited New Mexico. A signed newspaper report of the time stated that the Commissioner had a large interest in land grants of the Territory, and his visit was said to be for the purpose of looking "after his shares." [71] The report continued: "It is now, and was while he was here, openly alleged that he became interested so largely for pushing through, completing and issuing patents to many of the grants." This statement must be taken for what it is worth; it does not refer directly to the Maxwell Grant nor is it proof of corruption, but it adds further doubt to suspicious evidence. The Maxwell case gained notoriety at a later date when the government brought suit to set the patent aside on the ground that Secretary Cox's decision had rightly interpreted the law. The Supreme Court upheld the validity of the patent though it recognized that there had been dubious transactions connected with it.[72] When Williamson left office he became connected with a southwestern railroad, the Atlantic and Pacific, and he was later made its president.

Secretary Schurz was succeeded by the former railway president and Civil War governor of Iowa, Samuel J. Kirkwood. Upon President Garfield's death, Kirkwood resigned, though he remained in office until April, 1882. His term was brief and "was not marked by any notable constructive activity." [73] President Arthur appointed the reluctant Henry M. Teller, senator from Colorado, to succeed Kirkwood.[74] Senator Teller had been interested in western cattle companies and had also been a lawyer for the western railroads of Jay Gould.[75] These interests influenced his actions while Secretary. He leased Indian lands at low rates to cattlemen, contrary to treaty rights.[76] His ruling interpreting a railroad right of way as anywhere within 50 miles of the line was preposterous. It was a legal dodge to allow the railroads enormous timber resources. His efforts to rush the questionable "Backbone" railroad patents through the Land Office at the eleventh hour were highly suspicious. Jay Gould had an interest in the "Backbone" grant, and the Secretary worked the Office staff evenings and Sunday in order to have the patents completed before President Arthur's administration expired.[77]

Since the policies of the Secretary dominated the Land Office, his Commissioner, Noah C. McFarland of Kansas, was chiefly concerned with the onerous duties imposed by an increasing amount of land absorption. The accompanying fraud in this absorption became so serious that the Office secured the aid of the President in submitting a special message to Congress.[78] The department requested either the repeal of the more abused settlement laws or additional assistance in its effort to protect the public domain. The Commissioner asserted that, "This office has never been furnished with facilities or means to secure a compliance with the requirements of the public land laws." Congress responded to the request by providing special agents to investigate cases of alleged irregularity, but it did not repeal or revise the land laws which were so grossly violated. The special agents could not effectually stop the rampant fraud on the public domain because of inadequate numbers, vastness of territory to be covered, lack of reform in the land system itself, temptations of bribery, and removal for thwarting powerful interests.

When President Cleveland led the Democratic party into power in 1885, he selected ex-Senator Lucius Q. C. Lamar of Mississippi as Secretary of the Interior. As a member of a reform administration, Lamar labored to improve the land service, as shown by his lengthy annual reports and his support of Commissioner William Sparks of Illinois. Lamar dismissed some office workers to make way for deserving Democrats, though removal was by no means wholesale.[79] His easygoing nature permitted the zealous Commissioner to take the initiative in many land reforms, but he could be firm when necessary and he did curb unwise action. After serving for three years, Lamar was promoted to the Supreme Court. Before leaving he forced a quarrel with his Commissioner which brought about the latter's resignation.[80] This step was at the instigation of the incoming Secretary, William F. Vilas of Wisconsin, who disliked Sparks.[81] The disputed question involved an interpretation of railroad-land indemnity wherein the Secretary had been more favorable to the roads than the Commissioner.[82]

During his three years in office Commissioner Sparks established a record practically unique in Land Office history. He attempted with considerable vigor to improve the methods, practices, and conditions of the Office, and he made it, for practical purposes, an almost independent department. At times he blundered, but there is no question of his honesty. His reports are a mine of information on reprehensible land practices. He worked with the hope that he could secure congressional assistance, but Congress only confronted him with additional handicaps.

Among Sparks's constructive efforts is the famous April 3, 1885, order suspending final action on patents in certain classes of cases.[83] He intended to secure a check-up in regions where fraud was most glaring. The order was followed by the creation of a special board of review to pass on all cases going to patent.[84] Commissioner McFarland had declared in 1883 that the Office had "been compelled for years past to treat doubtful claims as valid, and to pass over to claimants the title of the United States because it could not investigate the facts." [85] The board was to make careful investigation in doubtful cases, and despite charges to the contrary, it did not slow down the machinery for issuing patents.

President Cleveland probably hoped that Secretary Vilas would be able to establish the same efficiency in the Interior Department that he had created for the Post Office Department.[86] However, after Vilas assumed the office in 1887, he found that there were handicaps to proper reorganization inherent in the system because of congressional neglect. His remarks on the condition of the Office have already been quoted. It should be noted that Vilas was not a "squeamish" reformer, unmindful of the "needs" of the West. When he took office, newspapers referred to his former connection with groups interested in government timberlands, and one paper suggested that his opposition to Commissioner Sparks had developed from the latter's suspicions regarding the timberland entries of the Secretary's brother.[87] The fact, therefore, that the Secretary had been interested in timberlands and had served land-grant companies lends weight to his requests for an improved service. He must have had businesslike procedure rather than nebulous reform in mind when he sought congressional co-operation.

Denied the assistance desired, Vilas made a number of administrative changes to speed up the work of the Land Office, though several of them were at the expense of proper protection of government land. He took personal charge of land decisions from his assistant and liberalized the rules of procedure in the Office so that 3,633 patents were issued within a week, one-third as many as the number for the previous three and one-half months.[88]

The Commissioner who served under Vilas was S. M. Stockslager of Indiana, a boyhood friend of his predecessor, Sparks. Stockslager sent letters to government land-agents and officers, asking them if they had noted any improvement in the land service over former years.[89] His purpose was to secure the reaction of the field force to the efforts of the former Commissioner. Forty-six of the fifty-seven replies noted "marked improvement." If there had been advancement under the former administration, there was evidence that the service was already losing its gains. *Copp's Land Owner* issued a warning that the department should take "no steps backward. The improvements and reforms of the last two years should not be lightly set aside."[90] The warning was ignored, however, and greater laxity followed under President Harrison.

John W. Noble of Missouri, who succeeded the short term of Vilas, had formerly served as United States District Attorney in St. Louis until his resignation in 1870 for private practice. Some of his principal clients were the large corporate and railroad interests of the Southwest. Noble had also invested in mining operations, so that he was acquainted with some of the major economic activities of the West.[91] Like his predecessor he tended to dominate the policies of the Land Office. He surpassed Vilas in "liberalizing" the rules of the Office in an effort to clear up the arrears of work. He particularly speeded up timber cases that had been waiting inspection. They were ground out at the rate of five hundred a day, making careful inspection impossible, but the Office was thus able to dispose of the seventeen to eighteen thousand cases pending before the board of review.[92] If Noble was guilty of practically throwing away the public domain to dishonest entrymen for transfer to corporations, he was equally guilty of the inexcusable discharge of Special Agent Conrad on the grounds that he was "too suspicious."[93] On the other hand, Secretary

Noble gave valuable assistance to the efforts to preserve timberland. His sympathetic co-operation with the men of the American Forestry Association made possible the Twenty-fourth Section of the Forest Reserve Act of 1891. By this section the President of the United States was authorized to establish forest reserves by proclamation. It was one of the bright spots in land legislation during the latter part of the nineteenth century, though its adoption was almost accidental.[94]

Lewis A. Groff of Nebraska served as Commissioner under Secretary Noble until ill-health brought his resignation in favor of Thomas A. Carter of Montana.[95] Groff is noted for the partisanship shown in his annual reports. He attempted to discredit the efforts of Commissioner Sparks and to point with pride to the Republican Homestead Act.[96] In attempting to discredit the Democrats he had to minimize the fraud which both Republicans and Democrats had exposed.

While Congress passed the Land Act of 1891 to remove some of the more grossly abused laws, it failed to improve the means of administration. Rigorous control had to await the conservation movement. Canada had adopted a comprehensive plan of administration in 1879, but the Americans had allowed their opportunity of 1880 to slip quietly away. New issues of a dynamic industrialism and frenzied finance came to demand public attention. The American frontier lines were disappearing and with them the possibility of establishing a department of public lands.

Undoubtedly the creation of such a department would have checked many of the unfortunate developments. Its supervision would have brought centralization under an official who could devote full time to land needs; equipment and personnel would have been improved; and there would have been greater publicity on policies. During the 1870's labor groups had demanded the establishment of such a department,[97] and in the next decade a Senate committee, after examining the the decrepit condition of the Land Office, was forced to the conclusion that the need for it was "so patent that it needs no discussion." [98] Perhaps the committee failed to recognize that Congress seldom acts without discussion, but in any case constructive action in behalf of the land service was singularly lacking throughout the period.

It is perhaps important to recall that the principle of *laissez faire*, implying a hands-off policy on the part of the government in the economic activities of its citizens, was not abridged until the passage of the Interstate Commerce Act of 1887. Yet there is nothing in that theory which emphasizes the necessity for fraud. The unwarranted connections of economically minded citizens with the government in land administration made *laissez faire* impossible. They also left problems, economic, political, and social, which continue to plague the nation. Judge Davis's indictment, illustrated from the record, describes a development of which no honest citizen can be proud. The public lands were absorbed and concentrated in far larger quantities than the laws intended because greedy interests could work through the amenable and inadequate General Land Office.

NOTES

1 Henry George, "Our Land and Land Policy," in *Writings of Henry George* . . . (Memorial ed., 10 vols., New York, 1901), 9:97–99.
2 *Congressional Record*, 17:6245 (June 28, 1886).
3 U.S. General Land Office, *Annual Report*, 1877, p. 1, and 1884, p. 4. Hereafter cited as *General Land Office Report*.
4 Milton Conover, *The General Land Office; Its History, Activities and Organization* (Baltimore, 1923).
5 New York *Sun*, Jan. 1, 1883.
6 *Copp's Land Owner*, 12:213, 225 (Nov. 15, Dec. 1, 1885).
7 *Congressional Record*, 8:1205–1206 (Feb. 11, 1879).
8 Conover, *General Land Office*.
9 Senate Report no. 362, 47 Congress, 1 session, v–vi.
10 *General Land Office Report*, 1876, pp. 14–15.
11 *Ibid.*, 1883, pp. 31–32.
12 Dept. of Interior, *Annual Report*, 1888, 1:viii.
13 *General Land Office Report*, 1887, p. 5.
14 *Ibid.*, 1931, pp. 1, 40.
15 *Ibid.*, 1876, pp. 14–15.
16 25 *U.S. Stat.*, 285–287 (1888).
17 Senate Report no. 362, 47 Cong., 1 sess., vi–vii.
18 U.S. Public Lands Commission, *Report of the Public Lands Commission, Created by the Act of March 3, 1879, Relating to Public Lands in the Western Portion of the United States and to the Operation of Existing Land Laws* (46 Cong., 2 sess., House Executive Document no. 46), xii–xiv.
19 *General Land Office Report*, 1883, pp. 26–27.
20 New York *World*, May 23, 1885.
21 U.S. Public Lands Commission *Report*, xiv.
22 Senate Report no. 362, 47 Cong., 1 sess., i.
23 Dept. of Interior, *Annual Report*, 1888, 1:viii.
24 *General Land Office Report*, 1877, pp. 3–4.
25 Senate Executive Document no. 181, 46 Cong., 2 sess.
26 "The McBride Case," in *Copp's Land Owner*, 7:146 (January, 1881).
27 102 U.S. 378.
28 Thomas Donaldson, *The Public Domain* (Washington, 1884), 811,

quoting House Executive Document no. 144, 47 Cong., 1 sess., 32.

29 Donaldson, *Public Domain*, 908, citing House Executive Document no. 223, 47 Cong., 1 sess.

30 Dept. of Interior, *Annual Report*, 1888, 1:ix.

31 *New York Times*, Jan. 11, 1886.

32 New York *Tribune*, Jan. 16, 1890.

33 *General Land Office Report*, 1886, p. 48.

34 *Copp's Land Owner*, 14:221 (Jan. 1, 1888).

35 T. C. Crawford, "The Great Land Steals," in New York *World*, May 23, 1885, pp. 1–2.

36 "Disbarred Attorneys," in *Copp's Land Owner*, 5:90–91 (September, 1878).

37 *New York Times*, Mar. 11, 1881.

38 U.S. Public Lands Commission, *Report*, xviii; *General Land Office Report*, 1877, pp. 30–31.

39 *Copp's Land Owner*, 12:65 (June 1, 1885).

40 U.S. Public Lands Commission, *Report*, xviii.

41 *General Land Office Report*, 1877, p. 32.

42 R. S. Yard, *Our Federal Lands* (New York, 1928), 100.

43 *New York Times*, Nov. 10, 1883.

44 *Ibid.*, Nov. 27, 1887. Hunt was governor of Colorado, 1867–1869.

45 123 U.S. 307.

46 *Congressional Record*, 8:1175 (Feb. 10, 1879).

47 Author's interview with Judge Samuel V. Proudfit, former Interior Department employee.

48 *Congressional Record*, 17:5734–5735 (June 15, 1886); *New York Times*, June 21, 1886.

49 *General Land Office Report*, 1886, p. 94.

50 New York *World*, Oct. 25, 1889.

51 Dept. of Interior, *Annual Report*, 1889, 1:xxxiv.

52 *General Land Office Report*, 1887, pp. 94–95.

53 J. F. Rhodes, *History of the United States from Hayes to McKinley, 1877–1896* (New York, 1919), 305–306.

54 *New York Times*, Apr. 7, 1888; *Dictionary of American Biography*, 15:350–351.

55 S. J. Pomerantz, "S. J. Randall" (M.A. thesis, Columbia University, 1932). Pomerantz found that the Randall family refuse to open Randall's papers to the public.

56 *Dictionary of American Biography*, 3:618. Detroit Post and Tribune, *Zachariah Chandler: An Outline Sketch of His Life and Public Services* (Detroit, 1880), 340–348.

57 *New York Times*, Jan. 8, 1876, Feb. 13, 1877; New York *Tribune*, Nov. 25, 1875.

58 C. M. Fuess, *Carl Schurz* (New York, 1932), 237–251.

59 Carl Schurz, *Reminiscences of Carl Schurz* (3 vols., New York, 1908), 3:380–381.

60 Fuess, *Carl Schurz*, 267–268.

61 G. W. Julian, "Railway Influence in the Land Office," *North American*

Review, 136:237–256 (March, 1883); Carl Schurz, *Speeches, Correspondence and Political Papers of Carl Schurz*, selected and edited by Frederic Bancroft . . . (6 vols., New York, 1913), 4:168–181.

62   Senate Ex. Doc. no. 181, 46 Cong., 2 sess.
63   R. E. Twitchell, *The History of the Military Occupation of the Territory of New Mexico from 1846 to 1851 by the Government of the United States* . . . (Denver, 1909), 267–269.
64   *General Land Office Report*, 1885, pp. 127–129.
65   *Ibid.*, 129.
66   New York *Tribune*, June 30, 1885.
67   93 U.S. 644.
68   *General Land Office Report*, 1885, p. 130.
69   Transcript of Record, U.S. Supreme Court, October term, 1886, vol. 27, no. 974.
70   General Land Office files under "Maxwell Private Land Claim."
71   New Orleans *Times*, Oct. 9, 1881 (Columbia University Clipping Bureau).
72   121 U.S. 325.
73   D. E. Clark, *Samuel Jordan Kirkwood* (Iowa City, 1917), 363.
74   *New York Times*, Apr. 7, 1882.
75   *Ibid.*, Mar. 29, 1882, quoting the Denver (Colo.) *Tribune*, Mar. 24, 1882.
76   G. F. Howe, *Chester A. Arthur* (New York, 1934), 212–213.
77   *Congressional Record*, 17:7–13 (Mar. 9, 1885); Senate Ex. Doc. no. 31, 48 Cong., 1 sess.
78   Senate Ex. Doc. no. 61, 47 Cong., 2 sess.
79   Edward Mayes, *Lucius Q. C. Lamar* (Nashville, Tenn., 1896), 469–505.
80   New York *Tribune*, Nov. 12, 1887; *New York Times*, Nov. 16, 1887.
81   Judge Proudfit interview, and *New York Times*, Nov. 13, 1887.
82   *General Land Office Report*, 1887, pp. 303–315.
83   *Ibid.*, 1886, p. 43.
84   *Ibid.*, 49.
85   Senate Ex. Doc. no. 61, 47 Cong., 2 sess., 5.
86   *National Cyclopaedia of American Biography*, 2:409–410.
87   *New York Times*, Dec. 7, 9, 1887.
88   Washington *Critic*, Jan. 20, 23, 1888.
89   *General Land Office Report*, 1888, p. 56.
90   *Copp's Land Owner*, 14:221 (Jan. 1, 1888).
91   *Dictionary of American Biography*, 13:539–540.
92   *Ibid.*; *General Land Office Report*, 1889, p. 8.
93   New York *World*, Oct. 25, 1889.
94   John Ise, *United States Forest Policy* (New Haven, 1924), 115–118.
95   *New York Times*, Mar. 16, 1891.
96   *General Land Office Report*, 1889.
97   D. S. Muzzey, *The United States of America* (2 vols., Boston, 1933), 2:96.
98   Senate Report no. 362, 47 Cong., 1 sess., viii.

III

COMMENT, CRITICISM, AND
CONCERN WITH CONSEQUENCES

Introduction

ALLAN G. BOGUE

THE very magnitude of the federal government's task in managing and disposing of the public lands would have been enough of itself to attract the attention of historians concerned with the administrative problems of government. But clearly the significance of the public lands goes far deeper than this. Frederick Jackson Turner called the tune when he suggested that the "continuous recession" of "an area of free land," and "the advance of American settlement westward, explain American development," and more specifically, "So long as free land exists, the opportunity for a competency exists, and economic power secures political power." Without necessarily accepting Turner's *dicta,* scholars have tried to enrich their understanding of the American democratic experience and the economic development of the country through study of the public land system. The returns are not all in, but some of the results are interesting.

The articles presented in Part III vary in focus from some that are almost purely economic in emphasis to others in which concern with American democracy or the effectiveness of democracy's government is paramount. Harry L. Coles files a dissent to the usually accepted position that the administrative system of survey and patent issue worked uniformly well during the first half of the nineteenth century. In Louisiana he discovered that the terrain and the federal surveys were hard to reconcile and that prior French and Spanish titles complicated the task of issuing patents. In Arthur H. Cole's article we offer a pioneering effort to link land policies to the behavior of the American economy. Two of the authors evaluate the "safety valve" corollary to the Turner hypothesis which held that the public lands offered a direct alternative for the labor of eastern industrial workers. Clarence H. Danhof meticulously calculates the farm-making costs of the middle western pioneer of the 1850's and concludes that the number of industrial workers who could have moved to the public lands was extremely limited. Fred A. Shannon argues that the Homestead Act little affected the lot of the eastern laboring man. The most productive of American historians of the public domain, Paul Wallace Gates, points out in his first article that the Homestead Law did not end the sale-for-revenue principle in American land policy and that for thirty years the democratic objectives of the act were subverted. In his second offering Professor Gates discusses the role of the land speculator who, he obviously believes, should have had little place in a democratic system of land disposal. The Bogues set more limited objectives for themselves in suggesting the economic functions of the speculator, outlining a method for the calculation of speculator profits, and presenting some representative returns on midwestern lands held for speculation. In his study of the way in which the state governments disposed of their agricultural college land scrip, Thomas LeDuc questions the effectiveness with which state governments used the grants which the federal government bestowed upon them. Sanford A. Mosk raises the same question concerning the state-held lands of eleven western states during the twentieth century.

Historians still have good reason to consider the consequences of the American land system. We can regard few of the answers given in Part III as final. Capital accumulation from landholding and the exploitation of minerals and timber in the communities of the public land states still need study, as do the political and social results of the process. The effects of the land disposal system on long-run tenure and land-use patterns will reward further investigation. There may be less relationship than some historians and economists have asserted. The place of land policy in the broader picture of American economic development is still incompletely understood. Since land policy represents only one of many economic factors involved in economic growth, we should not make the mistake of studying it in isolation. Despite much study, land policies as political issues require continued attention. There is still work ahead for the historian of the American public domain.

Applicability of the Public Land System to Louisiana

HARRY L. COLES, JR.

Reprinted by permission from the Mississippi Valley Historical Review, *Volume 43 (1957), pages 39–58.*

During the period of the Confederation and the early Republic the federal government adopted four basic policies with regard to the disposal of the public domain: a rectangular system of surveys to be made prior to legal entry, public auctions for the raising of a revenue, the issuance of patents by the federal government as evidence of title, and the reservation of school lands. Of these policies, the one pertaining to revenue has had its critics, while the others have generally been hailed as wise and foresighted. The Founding Fathers have been praised for their wisdom in adopting a system of land disposal that was scientifically correct, internally consistent, and capable of adaptation. Historians customarily point out that the rectangular system of surveys made possible definite boundaries, and that the system of patenting lands made for simplicity and reduced litigation over titles and boundaries. There have been few studies, however, of the manner in which the policies were actually carried out as a matter of administrative operation. For example, although the rectangular survey is usually praised as a great improvement over the indiscriminate system, the general histories of the public domain say little about the actual handling of the surveys and the problems encountered in adapting or extending them to newly acquired territories. Still another topic that goes practically unmentioned in the general histories is the nature of the problems which arose from the conflict between the

United States land system and the systems that preceded it. Preoccupation with the formulation of land policy has led historians all too often to end their treatment of the national land system prematurely.[1]

The basic policies of the national land system were drawn up of course to be applied to the original public domain—the area north of the Ohio and east of the Mississippi—and the first opportunity to test their applicability outside that region came with the purchase of Louisiana by the United States in 1803. A study of some of the problems involved in applying the system in this newly acquired public domain, with special reference to that portion which was first organized as Orleans Territory and then became the state of Louisiana, should throw light on the difficulties which arose in trying to adapt general land legislation to a particular region. In Louisiana the chief problems centered about extension of the system of land survey and settlement of private land claims. In that state, both prior to its admission to the Union in 1812 and for at least a half-century afterwards, efforts to fit federal land legislation to the peculiar conditions of the region brought a mass of administrative entanglements which required remedial legislation and resort to the courts for settlement of numerous title disputes. Actually, a study of the administration of the public domain in Louisiana, as will be pointed out, has broader implications and points to the need for similar studies in other regions.

In formulating the system to be applied to the Old Northwest, the federal government proceeded largely on the assumption that it was beginning with a clean slate and would not need to bother with previous or conflicting systems of land disposal. But as the federal land policies were put into operation in the area, titles were encountered which had an origin under governments earlier than that of the United States. Such titles came to be known as private land claims and makeshift provisions were made for handling them.[2] With the purchase of the Louisiana territory the government was faced with the problem of private land claims on a much larger scale, for on the lower Mississippi there was a widespread settlement of people of French and Spanish origins and a land system that had been in operation for over a hundred years.[3] Furthermore, the topography of the alluvial area of the southern part of the territory was unusual, and thus it raised problems, particularly with regard to land surveys, which were essentially different from those encountered in the old public domain. These facts were not wholly unknown to officialdom in

Washington, but apparently no thought whatever was given to any radical departure from the policies already in operation.

In formulating its land policies for this new domain, Congress was influenced by three conditions or considerations: the scanty knowledge of the territory and its land system, an outburst of fraud and speculation that followed the cession, and widespread disaffection among residents of the territory. So little was known in Washington that President Jefferson adopted the device of sending long questionnaires to prominent men in the territory.[4] The information collected from these and other sources was not encouraging, for the Spanish land system had been amorphous and haphazard, at least from the American point of view. Few landowners held complete titles and some claims were based only on the written permission of a commandant. Even more questionably, the majority of claims were derived from the verbal permission of the commandant or from mere occupancy. The Spanish government apparently had not insisted that its settlers perfect their land titles; indeed, imperfect titles had been passed on from generation to generation. If private records of ownership were inadequate, the official ones were hardly better. The registry of titles was incomplete and many of the returns of surveys were destroyed in fires that had occurred in New Orleans.[5] The sorry state of the existing titles was aggravated by the advent of eager American speculators who moved into Louisiana following its transfer to the United States.[6] The speculators, with the co-operation of former Spanish officials who were willing to forge the necessary evidence of land ownership,[7] acquired at least claims to title and further complicated the handling of the land problem by Congress.

Hampered by inadequate information about the older land systems, and confronted with reports of fraud, Congress at first adopted policies aimed more at preventing fraud than confirming titles to private property. In 1804 all grants made by Spanish authorities subsequent to the treaty of San Ildefonso (October 1, 1800) were declared null and void.[8] In the following year provision was made for the registration of land titles by the establishment of two land offices in the eastern and western districts of the Orleans Territory.[9] The register of each land office and two other appointees in each district were to constitute a board of commissioners to collect evidence and to decide all matters respecting claims. The Secretary of the Treasury was to appoint an agent whose duty it would be to work with each of the boards and to protect the interests of the government against fraud and deception. The same legislation which set up the boards also extended the powers of the previously created office of "Surveyor General of the Public Lands of the United States South of the State of Tennessee" over all lands within the Orleans Territory, and instructed him to execute the surveys, as nearly as the nature of the country would permit, in the same manner as provided by law for the public lands north of the Ohio. In extending the system of surveys without significant modification and in setting up boards of commissioners whose consideration of private land claims was bound by strict rules, Congress laid the basis for a century of administrative difficulties.

The problems of private land claims and the surveys were closely related, but it may be well to consider first the question of the surveys.[10] In accordance with the legislation of 1805 the Secretary of the Treasury authorized Isaac Briggs, surveyor general for the department south of Tennessee, to carry out three types of operations in Orleans Territory: (1) the survey of private claims; (2) the laying out of 160-acre tracts in the alluvial country; and (3) the survey of several ranges of townships in the usual rectangular fashion in the western part of the territory.[11] Briggs tried to get the surveys under way, but he soon reported that his efforts were being frustrated by certain malcontents who were trying to convince the old inhabitants that Louisiana would soon be turned back to Spain.[12] The government, concerned about the unstable conditions reported by Briggs and others, took steps to strengthen its position by hastening the surveys and encouraging the migration of native American citizens to the frontiers. Briggs was authorized to appoint a principal deputy for each of the two land districts in the Orleans Territory and was instructed particularly to expedite a survey in the western district of the territory.[13] Since Briggs, whose office was at Washington, Mississippi, had an extensive jurisdiction reaching over the entire lower South, the purpose of the new system was to relieve him of some of the details of the far-flung operations of his district, to decentralize the organization, and to hasten the surveys to the west. His new deputies were told that it was his intention to give only general instructions, leaving room for the exercise of individual judgment as to details.[14] In creating the system of principal deputies for Orleans Territory, Congress was adopting an unusual—and, as it turned out, an entirely unsatisfactory—administrative organization in an attempt to meet a particular need.

One of the first steps in extending the surveys into new areas was to establish a principal meridian and a base line from which townships could be laid off and numbered. Accordingly Briggs instructed the principal deputy of the western district to run a base line on the thirty-first degree of north latitude (approximately through the center of the present state of Louisiana) from the Mississippi west to the Sabine River. A meridian was then to be established extending from the Red River to the sea and running sufficiently west of the Mississippi to avoid its inundations. The original base line was laid out by John Cook, who completed his work in 1807. In stressing the need for haste, Secretary of the Treasury Albert Gallatin had told Briggs that it might be necessary to sacrifice the correctness that would otherwise be desirable to the dispatch that was absolutely necessary to be ready for the expected entry of large numbers of Anglo-Americans. As it turned out, not only scientific correctness but even the ordinary rules were sacrificed to accomplish a field survey so defective that an accurate representation of the country on the township maps was delayed for many years. In fact, it was eventually necessary to resurvey the base line. In addition, the survey of the Louisiana meridian was also found to be defective. The inaccuracy in establishing the location of the principal lines was symptomatic of the early surveys in Louisiana.[15]

One reason why so little was accomplished in surveying, as in the handling of other undertakings in the early years, was that basic policies were ill-adapted to local conditions. It was apparent almost from the beginning that the usual methods of surveying would not be suitable to the physical character of the region. There was a considerable quantity of valuable land lying in narrow strips along the margins of rivers and bayous but surrounded by extensive tracts of unsalable inundated land. The low lands were covered with a luxuriant vegetation and an almost impenetrable undergrowth. They were interspersed, too, with soft and boggy quagmires, or cut up with deep and turbid bayous whose waters were filled with venomous reptiles. Despite unusually difficult terrain in many parts of the territory, the surveyor general was not allowed to increase the compensation for surveying beyond the maximum allowed by law of $4 per mile.[16] Furthermore, neither Briggs nor Seth Pease, who succeeded Briggs in 1807, considered himself at liberty to adopt a different mode of surveying, since it was at least theoretically possible even in this part of the country to lay out regular townships and sections. The survey therefore was conducted according to customary modes, although it was attended with the useless expense of dividing an unsalable swamp into sections.[17] To remedy this situation, Congress in 1811 enacted legislation that permitted a variation in the mode of surveying.[18]

Another partial compromise was also made with the peculiarities of the antecedent land system and local conditions. Under the Spanish regime, grantees along the Mississippi were permitted to take a single concession by which they acquired land to a depth of 40 acres from the river, or a double concession by which they acquired all the lands between the river and the lakes or morasses that approached its borders on either side. A few of the early grantees had accepted double concessions, but a majority had contented themselves with single concessions, knowing that the additional land would be granted when wanted. The single concessionists now asked Congress to grant them the back lands in accordance with Spanish custom.[19] Congress proceeded to do this in 1811 by allowing to persons who, by virtue of a French or Spanish grant, owned a tract of land bordering on any river or watercourse, a preference in purchasing any vacant land, not exceeding 40 arpents in depth, behind the front tract.[20]

Though the good intentions of Congress may be applauded, the granting of back pre-emptions created further difficulties in the land system as it was applied to Orleans Territory—which, by congressional act in 1812, became the state of Louisiana. The survey of both private land claims and the pre-emptions became complicated almost beyond hope of solution. Under the legislation of 1811 the surveys of back tracts were to be made only on application of owners of front tracts, who had three years in which to file and who were later granted two extensions of time. Such being the case, applications for surveys were slow in being presented. At the same time, before issuing a patent on a confirmed private claim, the General Land Office insisted that the tracts be connected with township lines to permit giving them their proper section numbers. Areas where private land claims were situated, therefore, could not be surveyed because one or two pre-emption claims might change the numbering of all sections in a whole township. Not until 1823 was the surveyor general authorized to survey all the lands that might be claimed as back tracts.[21]

Obviously many difficulties could be laid to inefficient policy formulation in Washington, but there were other obstacles hindering the administration of the national land system that the most prescient government could hardly have avoided. For example, a survey of the coast, with which the surveyor general hoped to integrate the inland surveys, was never carried out because of the interference of pirates.

In 1813 and 1814, floods, sickness, desertion of deputies, and the War of 1812 retarded the surveys; and as late as 1815 several of the deputy surveyors were still engaged in military duty.[22] After the war the surveys gradually got under way again and in 1819 the surveyor general for the department south of Tennessee was authorized to appoint a principal deputy for two land districts lying east and west of the Pearl River. This principal deputy had jurisdiction over lands lying in two states, the district east of the Pearl being in Mississippi and the district west of the Pearl being in Louisiana.[23] There was thus an overlapping with one of the older districts and a total of three deputies with conflicting assignments.

In addition to ill-conceived laws and a cumbersome administrative organization, the surveys in Louisiana also suffered from a series of incompetent officials. After Thomas Freeman died in November, 1821, the office of surveyor general for the department south of Tennessee remained unfilled until January, 1822, when Levin Wailes took over. A few months after he took office, the congressional delegations from Mississippi and Louisiana began to complain of delay; the Commissioner of the General Land Office repeatedly asked for reports and information, but Wailes would not even furnish an estimate of the funds needed for his department. Finally, on June 1, 1824, he was removed from office, and George Davis was appointed to succeed him.[24] If Wailes wrote too little, Davis wrote too much. Apparently his entire time was consumed in badgering Washington for detailed instructions and arguing both with his superiors and with his subordinates. His correspondence with the General Land Office, consisting of over three thousand pages, is bound in four large volumes in the National Archives. And yet this utterly incompetent official held office for four years. In other words, during the years 1822 to 1828, under Wailes and Davis, the surveys in Louisiana slowed down and then came to a standstill.

James P. Turner, who succeeded Davis, was an able administrator, but even the most competent officials were staggered by the lack of adaptability of the system under which they were working.[25] The completion of the survey of private claims proved so difficult that Turner at last decided to organize a task force to invade the bayou country. He selected ten of his best surveyors and proposed to launch a drive the first week in October, 1829. Just at this time, however, he was removed from office, apparently for political reasons.[26] Joseph Dunbar, who was appointed in December, accepted the post with diffidence. "Conscious that I am deficient in some of the material qualifications for that office," he said, "I should have declined it, had I been consulted previously on the subject—as it is, I feel it my duty to accept it for a short time at least." [27] As might be expected, little was accomplished by an official with such lukewarm resolution.

By 1830 the weaknesses in the administrative organization of the surveying department in the South had become thoroughly manifest. Elijah Hayward, Commissioner of the General Land Office, wrote the chairman of the Committee on Public Lands of the Senate that the duties and responsibilities of the surveyor general for the department south of Tennessee and his three principal deputies had become so divided and confused that the whole system should be reorganized and simplified by the abolition of the office of principal deputy surveyor and the creation of a separate department for Louisiana. [28] In accordance with Hayward's suggestions, Congress enacted legislation in March, 1831, that abolished the system of principal deputies and established the office of surveyor general for Louisiana. Horé Browse Trist, the first appointee to this position, was instructed to afford the surveyor general of the department south of Tennessee all possible aid in sorting and arranging the documents and papers of the office at Washington, Mississippi, preliminary to their transfer to Donaldsonville, Louisiana. The General Land Office sent Samuel D. King as special agent to expedite the transfer of the proper records. [29]

Trist arrived at the Washington office during August, 1831, and reported that he found King in a "mighty maze of confusion." [30] Relatively speaking, the Louisiana department was in a better condition than the one in Mississippi, but there was nothing resembling order in either. Trist and King worked at the task of separating the papers for two months, and in October Trist reported that he had deposited the papers relating to Louisiana at Donaldsonville. He had also been to Baton Rouge to take possession of the papers pertaining to the district west of Pearl River; and the condition of that office he described as follows:

A great majority of the township plats have nothing to give them authenticity, no evidence of approval, nothing upon them showing by whom surveyed, nor when, and dirty, blotted, and pencil marked. . . . The field notes are of all shapes and sizes, and their ill looking outsides are ominous of the sorry condition within. . . . An old trunk without hinge or lock forms a very appropriate receptacle for these lame and impotent materials. [31]

Thus ended what must be one of the most dismal chapters in federal administrative history. The reorganization of 1831 brought improvement, but it did not prove to be a cure-all. The process of settling old accounts, the setting up of a new office, and inadequate appropriations for both office and field work brought further delays.[32] One surveyor general informed the General Land Office that labor, both intellectual and physical, commanded a higher price in Louisiana than elsewhere, and "if scientific attainments are required as is the case in question, they are not usually to be met with on the spot, and assurance of considerable pecuniary profit must be held out to induce those who possess them to move to a country, the climate of which is reputed to be very inimical to life."[33] After considerable pressure was brought, Congress finally made extra appropriations for clerk hire, and in 1837 it raised the compensation for surveying from $4 to $8 per mile in certain areas.[34] During the next few years there was an increased demand for lands, and generous sums were annually appropriated for surveying. By 1841 the surveyor general of Louisiana was able to report that almost all the original surveying had been completed and that the principal work remaining would consist of corrections, mainly in the Greensburg district in eastern Louisiana, and in certain erroneously located private claims.[35]

The errors in the Greensburg district, which comprised all that portion of Louisiana east of the Mississippi and west of the Pearl, were of long standing. They had their origin in a multitude of incorrect or fraudulent surveys, field notes, diagrams, and plats. In 1837 the Commissioner of the General Land Office ordered an investigation and the task of examining errors continued for five years, during which time the General Land Office refused either to order a resurvey or to issue patents on the basis of the old.[36] Finally, in 1842, Congress authorized a resurvey and appropriated money for the refunding of the purchase price where patents could not be issued.[37] Beginning in 1844 the resurvey of the Greensburg district was prosecuted vigorously by the surveyors general of Louisiana and was brought substantially to a conclusion by 1853. Although the resurvey of about one hundred and fifty townships took nearly ten years and was very expensive, it was thoroughly and efficiently done.[38]

In addition to the resurvey of the Greensburg district there were also extensive resurveys and corrections made in the other three land districts in Louisiana. In 1843, the surveyor general of Louisiana reported that there were records of fraudulent returns for sixteen townships in the district north of Red River, for twenty-five townships in the southeastern, and for forty-six in the southwestern district. During the next few years several suits were instituted against deputies and their sureties to recover losses arising from fraudulent surveys. But the correction, or rather actual execution, of the surveys could not await the outcome of lawsuits. In 1845 Congress appropriated $20,000 for the correction of fraudulent or faulty surveys in the land districts exclusive of the Greensburg district. Similar appropriations were made for several years.[39]

Fraud and speculation seemed to be rife in Louisiana during the 1840's. In June, 1845, Pierre T. Landry succeeded F. D. Newcomb as surveyor general. He soon discovered that certain documents relating to financial matters were missing from the files of his office. When copies of vouchers were forwarded from the General Land Office, "a system of fraud and forgeries of the deepest magnitude" was discovered. Newcomb was arrested in Texas and brought to New Orleans for trial.[40] Surveyor General Landry was plagued not only by the misdeeds of his predecessor but also by collusion with the speculators by members of his own office force. A few months after taking office he learned that a speculating company composed of a "capitalist, a lawyer, and a surveyor" had been formed in Donaldsonville. The surveyor involved was Landry's chief clerk, Andrew Jackson Powell, who had obtained lands for the benefit of speculators. Powell was fired, of course, as were others found guilty of misconduct, but the prospect of being dismissed from an office of such trifling emoluments exerted slight restraint on the conduct of the incumbents.[41]

In spite of dishonest employees and the floods, plagues, and epidemics that hindered the surveys from time to time, most of the original work was completed in Louisiana by the late 1850's.[42] It was estimated that the remaining field operations, which consisted of selections under the swamp-land grants, the survey of detached parcels of reclaimed lands, and the location of private claims, could be completed by 1861, and that the office of the surveyor general might be closed soon thereafter. Developments on the political scene, however, soon made the question largely academic. On February 6, 1861, following the secession of Louisiana from the Union, the surveyor general closed his office and informed the Commissioner of the General Land Office of his intention of delivering the records to the state government.[43]

The foregoing discussion has centered about the difficulties posed by the execution of the surveys. Other major complications existed because of a problem in administrative adjudication that had to be met simultaneously with the execution of the surveys. This was the problem of determining the validity of private land claims. Congress, it will be recalled, had decided to deal with claims coming down from the Spanish and French regimes as a legislative rather than a judicial matter, and in 1805 it had set up boards of commissioners to administer the regulations. Although the exact number of claims was not known at the time, it was revealed later that there were nearly ten thousand in Louisiana, covering perhaps 4,500,000 acres,[44] and including some of the most valuable land in the state. It is not possible to discuss here all the laws, rules, and regulations that were passed from time to time in regard to private land claims, but in general it can be said that Congress at first passed ill-considered laws that had to be completely revised.[45] The tendency was to extend the deadlines within which notices and evidence could be filed and to liberalize requirements. For example, the harsh provisions originally promulgated were relaxed somewhat by legislation in 1807, which provided for the confirmation of tracts not in excess of 2,000 acres if the claimants were in possession on December 20, 1803, and for ten consecutive years preceding. The commissioners were given full powers to decide, according to the laws and established customs of the French and Spanish governments, upon all claims to lands within their respective districts, provided the claimant had been an inhabitant of Louisiana on December 20, 1803, and if the claim was for a tract not exceeding a league square (5,760 acres).[46]

The actual workings of the boards were slow and cumbersome because of a general lack of information, the scattered location of many settlements, and the long distances over which it was necessary to travel in order to register claims. The members of the boards were often ignorant of the principles under which they were supposed to be deciding claims and they were given little guidance from Washington. The work of the boards was further impeded by neglect and absenteeism on the part of some of the commissioners.[47]

As the investigations of the boards continued over the years it became evident that much more land was claimed under foreign titles than the government had originally expected. A great deal of land that had been surveyed as public was later found to be covered by private claims, many of which not only conflicted with each other but also interfered with the public lands, thus giving rise to dissatisfaction, disputes, and disorder. The surveyor general reported that in the southern part of the state the records of not one in ten of the townships containing private claims would stand the test of the most superficial office examination.[48]

After laboring for some five years, the boards of the eastern and western districts finally reported on some 6,500 claims, about one-fourth of which they rejected because of lack of evidence or suspicion of fraud.[49] If the various lists of claimants are examined, it soon becomes evident that many of the original owners of claims gave up the struggle for confirmation and sold their rights to speculators. To cite but one example, Daniel Clark was granted confirmation on at least fifteen claims totaling over 7,000 acres scattered throughout both land districts. The report for the land district east of the Mississippi and west of the Pearl River (created in 1812) reveals the same situation of a few individuals buying up small claims from the original owners. An examination of some of the rejected titles discloses that the speculators were willing to take a chance on practically any shade of title, provided only the price was right. Brown and McDonough, for example, bought up claims to 120,000 arpents for four cents per arpent.[50] Their claim was rejected because the Spanish patent bore the embarrassing date of March, 1804.

In view of the fact that so many private land claims had fallen into the hands of speculators it seems more than probable that this group was mainly responsible for pressures that were brought to liberalize requirements and to keep the land offices open to the reception of claims. As late as 1835 a law was passed to provide for "the final adjustment of claims to lands in the State of Louisiana." By this measure the land offices were kept open two more years for the reception of claims recognized as valid by former laws. Only some three hundred claims were submitted under this act and Congress recognized less than half of them as valid.[51]

By 1837 the vast majority of private land claims had been settled by means of administrative adjudication. There still remained, however, a few large claims involving complicated principles of law. Feeling that it would be unwise and impracticable to dispose of these cases through legislative methods, Congress decided to turn the matter over to the courts. In 1844, therefore, jurisdiction over all land claims originating with the Spanish, French, or British authorities was given to the United States district courts for five years.[52] Under the provisions of this legislation some of the most extensive claims in Louisiana and a number of neighboring states were settled.[53]

By turning the matter over to the courts, Congress achieved a short respite from the consideration of a perennially vexing problem. However, as soon as the provisions for judicial settlement expired in 1849, applications for special legislation again began to pour in on Congress. Representatives from Louisiana complained that an inordinate amount of their time was consumed in correspondence concerning private land claims, and in 1860 Senator Judah P. Benjamin succeeded in getting the land offices opened again for the presentation of claims.[54] This put the government in about the same position it had occupied fifty years previously.

Benjamin's bill had hardly gone into effect when the Civil War broke out and brought a total suspension of the federal system in Louisiana. Following the war, the land offices in the state were slow in getting back into business, but when operations were finally resumed one of the main administrative difficulties, as before the war, was that of private land claims. One problem centered around some 288 claims covering about 80,000 acres which were generally designated as "located but unconfirmed." By this expression the land offices meant that the claims had been placed on the maps during the execution of the surveys, not in recognition of their validity but to show their boundaries for the information of the General Land Office. Among the owners of such claims were some of the most prominent and influential citizens of the state. After repeated but unavailing attempts to get some decision, the surveyor general of Louisiana recommended in 1874 that an act be passed specifically enumerating such tracts and relinquishing all claim of title to them by the United States. The legislation which Congress finally enacted in 1897, relinquishing title to the lands in question, was an acknowledgment that the efforts of a century had failed to work out an adequate administrative settlement of the public land problem involved.[55]

Another administrative problem that was encountered in the postwar years was the issuance of various types of scrip. It sometimes happened that Congress confirmed private claims that either had no specific location or, for some other reason, could not be located in place. To compensate the confirmees in such cases, an act passed in 1858 authorized the surveyors general to issue a certificate for the whole or any part of an unsatisfied claim.[56] The certificates, or "surveyor general's scrip," as they were commonly called, were issued very slowly because of the vast amount of checking, copying, and other clerical work involved. By the time the surveyor general's office was closed in 1909, however, certificates had been issued for some 600,000 acres.[57] In this, as in so many other cases, it was the speculators rather than original claimants who were the principal beneficiaries. The intent of Congress had been to make the act remedial only, but through probate proceedings in the parish courts, speculators were able to obtain recognition as the legal representatives of deceased confirmees, and thus to procure the scrip for a nominal sum, usually simply the amount of the court costs.[58]

In addition to the surveyor general's scrip there was another type of certificates, known as Supreme Court scrip, which was authorized by the act of June 22, 1860, the measure sponsored by Senator Benjamin to obtain a "final" adjustment of land claims. This act not only opened the land offices to claims but also made it possible for claimants to bring their cases before the federal courts. If the Supreme Court should finally decide in favor of the claimants and if the lands so confirmed had already been sold, scrip was to be issued. Since such scrip was made assignable, it is probable that most of it, like the surveyor general's scrip, fell into the hands of speculators.[59]

Obviously, the pattern of the whole administration of the public land system in Louisiana was the continuing search for ways in which to make general legislation workable for a region which it did not neatly fit. The inadequacies of the system became apparent early in the proceedings. The execution of the surveys was a difficult enough problem in itself but the situation was further complicated by an intricate problem in administrative adjudication—the determination of the validity of private land claims—which had to be conducted simultaneously. It can be said on the credit side of the ledger that Congress guarded against the worst frauds, especially in the early years. Also, Congress was generous with actual settlers: practically all the acts confirmed claims based on actual settlement and cultivation. On the debit side, it may be said that this generosity often worked to the advantage of speculators.

Aside from benefiting speculators, the long delay in the settlement of private land claims was also partly, but only partly, responsible for the early failures in the surveying department. The government was attempting to impose a new type of land system on an old, even though the former was thoroughly incompatible with the latter; it was attempting to extend its scientific system of survey and its exact method of patenting lands without significant adjustment to a new situation. In practically all the general studies of public land history the system of rectangular surveys receives unstinted praise and is held up as a model of good planning. Yet a close study of the actual administration of the policy in this region discloses that it did not necessarily work well at all times and in all places.[60] In attempting to apply the system to the lower Mississippi Valley, inadequate attention was given to modifications made desirable by the informality of the early surveys, the great distances and poor communications of the time, and the special nature of the agricultural interests of the region. Difficult terrain, inadequate compensation for office and field work, and a defective organization hindered the execution of the original surveys and made numerous corrections and resurveys necessary. As a result of the slow and inept deliberations of the private land claims boards and the retarded and inaccurate surveys, the entire federal land system in Louisiana was characterized by a century of bungling and maladministration.

Although no sweeping conclusions can be drawn from this study, it should at least indicate the need for similar studies on the administration of the surveys, private land claims, school lands, and related problems in other regions. The general histories dealing with the public domain obviously could not be expected to provide such detail concerning actual operations. The subject is so vast and the sources are so numerous and complex that any attempt to cover a considerable chronological period almost inevitably stops with a description of conditions leading to the adoption of certain laws and to subsequent changes and amendments. Only through monographic studies would time or space be available for an examination of how any given policy was worked out in practice.

But the monographic literature of United States land history, although extensive, deals not at all or only incidentally with the types of problems that have been discussed here with relation to Louisiana. The general picture that emerges, both from broad surveys and from monographic studies, is that for nearly a hundred years the land system as it operated east of the Mississippi was internally consistent and reasonably well adapted to the areas where it was applied; that it was only in the latter half of the nineteenth century, when an attempt was made to apply the system to the trans-Mississippi area, that weaknesses and inadequacies appeared.[61] From the facts developed in this study it is apparent that there was a wide gap between theory and practice: it was one thing to formulate policies in Washington and quite another to execute them in the field operations. It may be concluded that the public land system was perhaps as inadequate in the lower Mississippi Valley as Paul W. Gates and others have shown it to have been in the prairie-plains region, or as Walter P. Webb has demonstrated for the cattle country and the semi-arid Southwest.[62]

NOTES

1 The general histories include Benjamin Horace Hibbard, *A History of the Public Land Policies* (New York, 1924); Roy M. Robbins, *Our Landed Heritage: The Public Domain, 1776–1936* (Princeton, 1942); Payson Jackson Treat, *The National Land System, 1785–1820* (New York, 1910). Typical of the studies emphasizing political aspects of land problems for particular periods are George M. Stephenson, *The Political History of the Public Lands from 1840 to 1862* (Boston, 1926), and Raynor G. Wellington, *The Political and Sectional Influence of the Public Lands, 1828–1842* (Cambridge, Mass., 1914). Another period study is E. Louise Peffer, *The Closing of the Public Domain: Disposal and Reservation Policies, 1900–1950* (Stanford, 1951).

2 Treat, *The National Land System*, 198–229, gives an account of the private land claims. See also Beverley W. Bond, Jr., *The Civilization of the Old Northwest: A Study of Political, Social, and Economic Development, 1788–1812* (New York, 1934), 278–315.

3 The Spanish system of land grants has been described by Francis P. Burns, "The Spanish Land Laws of Louisiana," *Louisiana Historical Quarterly*, 11:557–581 (October, 1928), and Louis Pelzer, "The Spanish Land Grants of Upper Louisiana," *Iowa Journal of History and Politics*, 11:3–37 (January, 1913). Both of these studies are based primarily on Joseph M. White, *A New Collection of Laws, Charters, and Local Ordinances of the Governments of Great Britain, France, and Spain Relating to the Concessions in their Respective Colonies, etc.* (Philadelphia, 1839), and the documents that appear in the *American State Papers: Public Lands* (8 vols., Washington, 1832–1861), 5:631–774.

4 Thomas Jefferson to Governor William C. C. Claiborne, July 17, 1803, in Clarence E. Carter, ed., *The Territorial Papers of the United States* (21 vols. to date, Washington, 1934–   ), 9 (1940), *The Territory of Orleans*, 3–4.

5 *American State Papers: Miscellaneous* (2 vols., Washington, 1834), 1:344–356.

6 Isaac Briggs to Secretary of the Treasury, October 8, 1803, Letters Received from the Surveyors General. (Unless otherwise noted, all

manuscript citations in this article are to the Records of the General Land Office, National Archives, Washington. Several letters to the surveyor general of the department south of Tennessee are printed in *General Public Acts of Congress, Respecting the Sale and Disposition of the Public Lands with Instructions Issued from Time to Time . . .* [2 vols., Washington, 1838], and in Carter, ed., *Territorial Papers.* Since both of these compilations are selective, only the manuscript documents will be cited.)

7 John W. Monette described the activities of the speculators in a bitter vein in *DeBow's Review* (New Orleans), 8:409 ff. (May, 1850). See also Charles E. A. Gayarré, *History of Louisiana* (4 vols., New York, 1866), 4:68–69.

8 2 *U.S. Stat.*, 283–289 (1799–1813). In any study of legislation dealing with land titles in Louisiana the following dates are important: (1) October 1, 1800, the date of the treaty of San Ildefonso, whereby Louisiana was re-ceded by Spain to France; (2) April 30, 1803, the date of the treaty for the cession of Louisiana by France to the United States; and (3) December 20, 1803, the date on which the United States took formal possession.

9 2 *U.S. Stat.*, 324–329 (1799–1813).

10 There is no satisfactory general history of the public land surveys. Useful data may be found in Jerome S. Higgins, *Subdivisions of the Public Lands* (St. Louis, 1894); Edmund R. Kiely, *Surveying Instruments: Their History and Classroom Use* (New York, 1947); and Lowell O. Stewart, *Public Land Surveys* (Ames, Iowa, 1935).

11 Secretary of the Treasury to Briggs, May 27 and July 2, 1805, Record Copies of Letters Sent to the Surveyors General.

12 Briggs to Secretary of the Treasury, March 3 and April 7, 1806, Letters Received from the Surveyors General.

13 2 *U.S. Stat.*, 391–395 (1799–1813); Secretary of the Treasury to Briggs, May 8, 1806, Letters Sent to the Surveyors General.

14 Briggs to Gideon Fitz, September 23, 1806, copy inclosed with Briggs to Secretary of the Treasury, September 27, 1806, Letters Received from the Surveyors General. No satisfactory history of the General Land Office is available. The only published account, Milton Conover, *The General Land Office: Its History, Activities, and Organization* (Baltimore, 1923), is merely a brief summary.

15 *Annual Report of the Surveyor General of Louisiana,* August 30, 1873 (43 Congress, 1 session, House Executive Document no. 1), 51–58.

16 Briggs to Secretary of the Treasury, December 31, 1804, and August 31, 1805; Thomas Freeman to Secretary of the Treasury, October 20, December 30, 1811; January 25, February 27, 1812, Letters Received from the Surveyors General.

17 *American State Papers: Public Lands,* 1:587–588.

18 Lands adjacent to rivers, lakes, or bayous could be surveyed into tracts of 58 poles in front and 465 poles in depth, of such shape and bounded by such lines as the nature of the country might render

practicable. By a later act, May 24, 1824, the President was authorized, whenever in his opinion it would promote the public interest, to direct that land on any river, lake, bayou, or watercourse be surveyed in tracts of 2 acres in width and 40 acres in depth. 2 *U.S. Stat.*, 662–666 (1799–1813); 4 *U.S. Stat.*, 34 (1829–1835).

19 *American State Papers: Public Lands,* 1:250–251.
20 2 *U.S. Stat.*, 662–666 (1799–1813).
21 Freeman to Secretary of the Treasury, October 20 and December 30, 1811; January 25, February 27, 1812; January 21, 1813, Letters Received from the Surveyors General; Commissioner of General Land Office to Levin Wailes, July 27, 1823, Letters Sent to the Surveyors General.
22 Freeman to Commissioner of General Land Office, January 21, July 10, September 3, 1813; January 16, March 17, November 14, 1814; October 7, 1815, Letters Received from the Surveyors General.
23 3 *U.S. Stat.*, 528–532 (1813–1823); Commissioner of General Land Office to Freeman, March 20, 1819, Letters Sent to the Surveyors General.
24 Commissioner of General Land Office to Wailes, July 27, December 31, 1823; January 12, March 4, April 1, and June 1, 1824, Letters Sent to the Surveyors General.
25 James P. Turner to Commissioner of General Land Office, February 14, June 12, June 30, July 11, July 14, July 15, and July 29, 1828, Letters Received from the Surveyors General.
26 Turner to Commissioner of General Land Office, May 22, September 4, October 19, 1829, Letters Received from the Surveyors General.
27 Joseph Dunbar to Commissioner of General Land Office, January 22, 1830, Letters Received from the Surveyors General.
28 *American State Papers: Public Lands,* 6:267.
29 Commissioner of General Land Office to Horé B. Trist, June 20, 1831; Same to Gideon Fitz, June 30, 1831, Letters Sent to the Surveyors General.
30 Trist to Commissioner of General Land Office, August 28, 1831, Letters Received from the Surveyors General.
31 Trist to Commissioner of General Land Office, October 1, 1831, Letters Received from the Surveyors General.
32 *American State Papers: Public Lands,* 6:513–515.
33 Trist to Commissioner of General Land Office, July 6, 1831, Letters Received from the Surveyors General.
34 Commissioner of General Land Office to H. T. Williams, March 27, 1837, Letters Sent to the Surveyors General.
35 *Annual Report of the Surveyor General of Louisiana,* 1841 (27 Cong., 2 sess., House Ex. Doc. no. 24), 66–85.
36 Commissioner of General Land Office to Williams, November 23, 1837, Letters Sent to the Surveyors General.
37 5 *U.S. Stat.*, 540 (1836–1845).
38 *Annual Report of the Surveyors General of Louisiana,* August 30, 1873 (43 Cong., 1 sess., House Ex. Doc. no. 1), 71.

39 Annual Report of the Surveyor General of Louisiana, 1843 (28 Cong., 1 sess., Senate Ex. Doc. no. 15), 99–105; Commissioner of General Land Office to Pierre T. Landry, February 28, 1846, Letters Sent to the Surveyors General.

40 *Annual Report of the Surveyor General of Louisiana,* 1846 (29 Cong., 2 sess., House Ex. Doc. no. 9), 87–91; Landry to Commissioner of General Land Office, March 5, April 27, December 31, 1846, Letters Received from the Surveyors General.

41 Landry to Commissioner of General Land Office, November 18, 1845, Letters Received from the Surveyors General.

42 William J. McCulloh to Commissioner of General Land Office, July 12, 1860, Letters Received from the Surveyors General; Commissioner of General Land Office to McCulloh, June 30, August 22, October 13, 1860, Letters Sent to the Surveyors General.

43 *Annual Report of the Commissioner of the General Land Office,* 1862 (37 Cong., 3 sess., House Ex. Doc. no. 1), 40.

44 Senate Ex. Doc. no. 189, 58 Cong., 3 sess., 140.

45 The following consideration of the problems arising in connection with the private land claims is largely a condensation of the more extensive treatment of the subject in my article, "The Confirmation of Foreign Land Titles in Louisiana," *Louisiana Historical Quarterly,* 38 (4): 1–22 (October, 1955).

46 2 *U.S. Stat.,* 440–442 (1799–1813). Just what was intended by the phrase "according to the laws and established usages and customs of the French and Spanish governments" no one seemed to know exactly. Secretary Gallatin pointed out that the words could be construed to mean that all the former laws of Congress on the subject were repealed. He endeavored to get the phrase stricken from the bill but was unsuccessful. Before sending out instructions to the land officers the Secretary attempted, apparently without success, to get some guidance from the President. He finally transmitted copies of the law to the registers without interpretations or instructions as to its meaning. Joseph M. White, in making a compilation of French and Spanish land laws, stated that he had examined all the reports of the various boards of commissioners from their organization down to 1829, but he found very few references to the French or Spanish laws or customs. Seldom could any uniform rules be found, but the few adopted consisted of common law principles rather than French or Spanish laws or customs. *American State Papers: Public Lands,* 5:631.

47 John W. Gurley to Secretary of the Treasury, November 3, 1807; Benedict Van Pradelles to Secretary of the Treasury, March 8 and June 11, 1808; Philip Grymes to Secretary of the Treasury, May 22, 1809, Letters Received from the Registers and Receivers.

48 *Annual Report of the Surveyor General of Louisiana,* 1846 (29 Cong., 2 sess., House Ex. Doc. no. 9).

49 *American State Papers: Public Lands,* 2:258–439, 745–841; 3:77–269.

50 *Ibid.,* 3:6–76. See also Coles, "Confirmation of Foreign Land Titles in Louisiana," 9–12.

51   4 *U.S. Stat.*, 749–750 (1824–1835); 5 *U.S. Stat.*, 491–493 (1836–1845).

52   See John Perkins, "The Public Lands and Land System of the United States," *DeBow's Review*, 17:140–173 (August, 1854); 5 *U.S. Stat.*, 676 (1836–1845).

53   See Coles, "Confirmation of Foreign Land Titles in Louisiana," 16–17.

54   *Congressional Globe*, 35 Cong., 1 sess., 2045–2047; 36 Cong., 1 sess., 1478–1480; 12 *U.S. Stat.*, 85–88 (1859–1863).

55   *Annual Reports of the General Land Office*, 1870–1874, and 1897.

56   11 *U.S. Stat.*, 294–295 (1855–1859). Louisiana was only one of eighteen public land states to which the legislation applied.

57   *Annual Reports of the General Land Office*, 1880–1910; Senate Ex. Doc. no. 189, 58 Cong., 3 sess., 158.

58   *Annual Report of the General Land Office*, 1887; Senate Ex. Doc. no. 67, 49 Cong., 2 sess.

59   Senate Ex. Doc. no. 189, 58 Cong., 3 sess., 159. The certificates could be located in legal subdivisions on any public land subject to sale at private entry at $1.25 per acre, or, under the act of January 28, 1879, could be received from actual settlers in payment of pre-emption claims or in commutation of homestead claims, even where the lands were subject to entry at the double minimum of $2.50 per acre. Thomas Donaldson, *The Public Domain* (Washington, 1884), 950–958. My colleague, Mary E. Young, who has made an extensive but unpublished study of the operation of the act of June 22, 1860, informs me that most of the Supreme Court scrip was issued on the basis of claims originating in the West Florida parishes of Louisiana.

60   Earl Pomeroy, "Toward a Reorientation of Western History: Continuity and Environment," *Mississippi Valley Historical Review*, 41:583–584 (March, 1955), has pointed out that the ordinance of 1787 has been examined more from the point of view of origins and establishment than from the evolution of political life under it. Along the same line, the present article represents an attempt to suggest that the ordinance of 1785 and the various land policies flowing from it should be examined from the point of view of actual operation.

61   If one excludes the early pioneering works, the writers on the public domain may be roughly divided into two groups: the frontier historians and the economic historians, though obviously some have, or had, a foot in both camps. Delving into local and regional problems, the frontier historians have generally advanced the thesis that environmental conditions peculiar to various parts of the West rendered some of the old land policies obsolete. A good list of references, too numerous to include here, can be found in Ray A. Billington, *Westward Expansion* (New York, 1949), 779–780, 797–798. The economic historians seem to have concerned themselves primarily with what might be called economic democracy. They have judged land policies primarily on the basis of their leveling effects: those policies that tended to give land to the landless were good, those that made the rich richer were bad. Earle D. Ross, "Squandering Our Public Land," *American Scholar*, 2:77–86 (January,

1933), mentions most of the points developed by the economic historians. See also Paul W. Gates, "Research in the History of American Land Tenure: A Review Article," *Agricultural History*, 28:121–126 (July, 1954), and Thomas LeDuc, "The Disposal of the Public Domain on the Trans-Mississippi Plains: Some Opportunities for Investigation," *ibid.*, 24:199–204 (October, 1950).

62 Walter P. Webb, *The Great Plains* (Boston, 1931), 398–399, maintains that not a single land law passed by Congress was suitable to conditions on the Great Plains. Basing his detailed research primarily on the prairies of the Middle West, Paul W. Gates has produced some sharp strictures against land policies that favored speculation or tended to increase tenantry. Among Gates's principal works are: "The Disposal of the Public Domain in Illinois, 1848–1856," *Journal of Economic and Business History*, 3:216–240 (February, 1931); "Land Policy and Tenancy in the Prairie Counties of Indiana," *Indiana Magazine of History*, 25:1–26 (March, 1939); "The Role of the Land Speculator in Western Development," *Pennsylvania Magazine of History and Biography*, 46:314–333 (July, 1942 [reprinted in this volume, pp. 349–367]; *Frontier Landlords and Pioneer Tenants* (Ithaca, 1945); *Fifty Million Acres: Conflicts over Kansas Land Policy, 1854–1890* (Ithaca, 1954).

Cyclical and Sectional Variations in the Sale of Public Lands, 1816–1860

ARTHUR H. COLE

The collection of the statistical material upon which this study is based was made possible by an appropriation from the Milton Fund for Research, Harvard University, and by the courteous assistance of Mr. C. L. Bullion, Chief Accountant of the Public Land Office, Washington, D.C.

Reprinted by permission of the publishers from The Review of Economics and Statistics, *Volume 9, pages 41–53, Cambridge, Mass.: Harvard University Press, 1927.*

STUDIES that have been made of land sales by the national government in the pre-Civil War period—among others those of Donaldson, Treat, and most recently Hibbard—have presented the general course of the movement. Such statistics as these writers have advanced indicate that there were three occasions when the volume of sales reached particularly great heights. These occasions were the years preceding the crises of 1819, 1837, and 1857. At these several times, speculation was rampant and the rush of purchasers to the local governmental agencies was so great that feverish activity of any sort came thereafter to be commonly described as "doing a land-office business." But these accounts of land sales fail in several respects to give as full a picture of this important phenomenon as could be wished. Based on annual data, they do not show the timing of the speculative movements with a closeness desirable for the study of business cycles. As the course of commodity prices and other statistical series has been exhibited, or will shortly be exhibited, upon a monthly basis, there is reason for wishing the course of this speculative series of land sales to be available upon at least a quarterly basis.[1] Secondly, since previous studies have presented data only for the country as a whole, little is definitely known as to the course of sales in the several sections of the country, especially as to the particular areas in the nation most affected at the different periods of speculative buying.

Fortunately there exists in the records of the General Land Office material which makes possible a thorough study. The books of this Office give data by quarterly periods of the moneys received and deposited in the Treasury by the numerous local land offices, as shown by accounts submitted by such periods to the General Land Office in Washington. These data extend as far back as 1801, but before 1816 they are not full enough for our purpose—except for particular areas—since the reports do not become regular by quarters until this later date. However, covering the forty-five-year interval 1816–60, they embrace the occasions of the chief speculative activities, as far as land sales are concerned, and, indeed, the important periods of general speculative activity in the decades before the Civil War. Moreover, these financial items can be supplemented and tested by statistics of the quantity of land sold appearing in the annual reports of the Commissioner. These data also apply to the several land offices and are presented first—1820 to 1845—as single annual data, but later—after 1845—by half-yearly periods. By means of these two sets of figures, one can ascertain not only the significance in money terms of total land sales by the relatively short periods of quarter-years, but also receipts by each land office for similarly brief periods and the acreage sold office by office each year or half-year. For the interpretation of cyclical movements in the sale of public lands and for the determination of the sectional variation in these sales, such detailed statistics are invaluable.

In the analysis here made of the new data, some simplification of the material has been thought advantageous, and this has been accomplished by grouping together the statistics relating to the land offices located in each of the several states, and by employing only the summations of moneys received or acreage sold in each group of offices for the various time periods. Since the boundaries of land districts (over each of which a single land office had control) usually did not extend over state lines, this method of operation serves merely to divide the country into conveniently sized areas for descriptive purposes, i.e., states. Moreover, chief reliance has been placed upon the data of moneys taken in, and for two reasons: these figures are available by quarterly periods, whereas those of acreage sold appear only for annual or at best semi-annual intervals; and, secondly, they extend back in time somewhat further than do the statistics of acreage. For most of the period under consideration, the decades preceding 1860, it is, to be sure, a matter of indifference which set of data is used. Public land was sold under regulations of certain minimum prices per acre; the minimum prices (as we know) usually formed the actual purchase price; and so the two quantities move together. Indeed, if the annual receipts from the sale of public land for the country as a whole be plotted on a logarithmic scale with the other feature, the acreage annually disposed of, no significant variation between the curves will be found to appear before the very last years of the period are reached. In 1854, Congress passed the graduation scheme, as it was called, under the terms of which land which had been on the market for a given period was to be lowered in price according to a specified gradation. Substantial areas of land were taken up under this act, and so a disparity occurs in the course of the value and acreage curves. The acreage figures achieve in 1854-55 a somewhat higher peak relative to the preceding low point (1852) and the declination from that peak through 1860 not only proceeds more slowly but does not reach as low a point. If we use this low point of 1852 as a base (100), the movement of the two elements in the subsequent years may be indicated by the index numbers now presented:

(Items for 1852 = 100)

	1853	1854	1855	1856	1857	1858	1859	1860
Receipts	363	827	812	342	220	129	134	108
Acreage	423	1544	1366	586	471	409	448	284

Still the general configuration of the curves is similar, and our conclusions, whether concerned with the sudden upswing of sales after 1852 or with the timing of the movement, are practically the same if we utilize either set of data. At most, the course of land sales viewed as the transition of land from public to private hands, would for this particular, brief period be thrown into somewhat higher relief if it were convenient to employ acreage figures for the decade of the fifties.[2]

I

Let us first confine our attention to these latter figures of receipts by quarter-years from land sales, employing at the start statistics for the country as a whole. Inspection of these total figures indicates that there were three major periods of land speculation, with at least two less important periods. (These data converted to the annual basis are presented as the heavy line on Charts 2–5. The figures themselves are given in Table 3.) The peaks reached in 1818, 1836, and 1854–55 stand out with marked prominence, but the smaller peak in 1824, the secondary bulge of sales in 1838–39, and the lower, more regular movement between 1842 and 1850 are also noteworthy.[3]

Such peculiarities of movement call for explanation. A steady volume of sales, or even a volume increased somewhat in size as the years went by, would be attributable simply to the westward trend of population. But how shall one explain the rather violent swings that sales actually do exhibit? At least three forces must be taken into account. The first is the influence of the movement of immigration into the United States. This movement we know was not regular. Perhaps its variations synchronized with those of land sales. To test this hypothesis, I compared the annual movement of immigration—annual figures alone being available—with the annual figures of land sales, from the time when immigration statistics first began to be collected (1820) to the close of the period under consideration. It became apparent from this comparison that in the years preceding 1839 there was some correlation, especially if one allows a lag of a year or two of sales behind the flow of immigrants—and such a lag would not be incompatible with the circumstances of the problem.[4] Moreover, it was notable that the break in the volume of land sales in the fifties came at a time when for a few years the inflow of foreigners had hesitated and ceased to advance in any marked degree. But it was equally obvious that other relations between the two movements were not so close. Land sales reached a peak in 1836 not fairly warranted by the course of immigration; the fall thereafter was more precipitous than the decline of immigration; all during the forties little correlation seems to exist; and the extraordinary rise of land sales between 1852 and 1854 is inexplicable from a consideration of the immigrant movement alone. Even allowance for changing constituents in the immigration flood, such as the rôle played in the forties and early fifties by the town-loving Irish, does not explain

TABLE 3

Receipts from Public Land Sales by the United States Quarterly, 1815–1860 [a]

(Unit: $1,000)

Year	First Quarter	Second Quarter	Third Quarter	Fourth Quarter	Total
1815	...	...	...	...	2410 [b]
1816	721	601	821	1497	3640
1817	748	1189	1957	1189	5083
1818	3970	1292	3389	4967	13619
1819	3707	3234	1514	525	8980
1820	1088	173	166	309	1736
1821	220	205	526	328	1279
1822	241	244	241	291	1017
1823	142	135	118	412	807
1824	159	315	726	300	1500
1825	376	356	198	363	1292
1826	330	205	227	368	1130
1827	383	315	304	403	1405
1828	207	191	248	574	1219
1829	311	309	873	669	2163
1830	479	351	520	1059	2409
1831	406	1029	1029	902	3366
1832	597	524	630	1052	2803
1833	608	799	768	1998	4173
1834	1054	982	955	3073	6064
1835	1990	3144	4083	6949	16165
1836	5847	8423	5859	4805	24934
1837	3479	1834	699	928	6941
1838	548	524	700	2239	4011
1839	1823	1672	1282	1710	6487
1840	950	794	468	536	2747
1841	416	313	367	416	1512
1842	253	591	263	345	1453
1843	551	388	473	638	2050
1844	497	489	525	729	2241
1845	447	531	690	794	2462
1846	630	955	665	631	2881
1847	537	860	943	931	3272
1848	729	770	506	529	2533
1849	380	381	409	573	1743
1850	451	301	341	697	1790
1851	800	517	595	680	2592
1852	502	188	428	275	1392
1853	493	608	1784	2164	5049
1854	1894	3193	2514	3901	11502
1855	1556	3390	2388	3948	11282
1856	1260	1808	786	902	4756
1857	528	1257	762	519	3066
1858	415	465	452	461	1793
1859	509	354	503	503	1869
1860	470	353	279	406	1507

[a] Compiled from records in the Public Land Office in Washington, D.C.

[b] In a small degree estimated.

TABLE 4

Receipts from Public Land Sales by States: Annually, 1814–1860

(Unit: $1,000)

Year	Ohio	Illinois	Indiana	Michigan	Arkansas	Missouri	Iowa	Wisconsin	Alabama	Mississippi	Louisiana	Florida
1814	1620 [a]	168	...	...	...	...	...	...	87	14	...	...
1815	1656 [a]	53	369	...	...	...	...	...	157	175	...	...
1816	1332	207	1202	...	...	...	...	...	398	501	...	...
1817	1416	572	1080	...	...	...	...	...	1718	298	...	...
1818	881	1491	1272	119	...	793	...	...	8676	387	...	...
1819	958	611	458	52	...	2461	...	...	4148	293	...	...
1820	142	87	272	11	...	128	...	...	1067	29	...	...
1821	155	64	363	9	4	123	...	...	378	42	140	...
1822	236	35	326	26	30	40	...	...	202	13	108	...
1823	158	76	203	38	2	105	...	...	181	41	4	...
1824	243	58	724	94	1	98	...	...	169	113	...	...
1825	194	82	223	136	10	108	...	...	318	115	5	91
1826	169	110	250	75	17	73	...	...	230	106	33	66
1827	215	81	263	55	5	200	...	...	163	90	143	189
1828	208	121	315	33	5	185	...	...	215	87	5	45
1829	277	282	490	90	3	192	...	...	597	127	35	68
1830	199	402	604	185	3	268	...	...	447	136	85	79
1831	442	420	713	403	17	372	...	...	842	49	72	36
1832	544	261	685	323	13	314	...	...	519	42	91	12
1833	695	381	692	563	52	297	...	...	565	801	111	15
1834	599	440	843	623	213	281	...	21	1444	1473	106	20
1835	828	2688	2078	2272	700	824	...	317	1986	3836	572	65

Year	Ohio	Illinois	Indiana	Michigan	Arkansas	Missouri	Iowa	Wisconsin	Alabama	Mississippi	Louisiana	Florida
1836	1665	4003	4063	5242	1205	2072	...	720	2378	2532	944	111
1837	590	1271	1571	969	354	820	...	153	478	321	289	126
1838	305	983	756	122	231	645	344	40	210	69	220	87
1839	316	1421	778	175	193	1307	373	822	159	25	848	72
1840	41	492	150	33	141	713	661	161	74	27	222	33
1841	64	440	120	28	70	339	93	128	70	31	120	8
1842	54	544	73	36	32	201	64	165	152	59	65	7
1843	19	520	64	17	60	555	179	214	226	46	139	10
1844	48	616	137	29	69	570	139	333	115	39	126	19
1845	289	611	99	34	46	315	264	551	98	36	94	25
1846	151	600	146	36	71	238	330	885	98	145	135	47
1847	195	615	348	67	126	303	344	800	187	113	140	35
1848	115	374	708	94	120	257	195	345	119	37	146	23
1849	77	319	277	63	78	209	123	260	181	44	92	18
1850	53	313	135	93	83	292	141	97	369	54	125	33
1851	81	421	150	193	194	610	250	92	361	44	133	44
1852	58	492	49	49	77	304	42	37	144	44	65	27
1853	106	1218	104	331	217	803	1015	393	352	212	182	69
1854	95	1562	78	668	212	1234	4605	1529	573	286	166	126
1855	14	897	6	410	137	1539	4310	2039	369	157	171	93
1856	3	473	18	160	257	1304	735	760	228	72	92	36
1857	2	155	11	45	547	973	588	121	62	82	95	22
1858	2	12	1	24	417	567	97	62	68	72	277	28
1859	5	12	1	37	492	325	18	52	176	198	266	32
1860	2	...	31	46	450	117	11	41	178	136	298	27

* In a small degree estimated.

satisfactorily the divergencies in the two curves. In short, while the influence of the demand for land on the part of new arrivals from Europe cannot be ignored, this factor cannot serve by itself as a sufficient cause of the peculiar movements in land sales.[5]

A second element to be taken into account is the progress of "internal improvements." While, since the landing of the Pilgrims, there has been no time when the means of transportation were not under betterment, the advance along this line has not been without periods of boom and times when particularly significant developments came suddenly to fruition. Possibly, then, the course of improvement in roads, canals, and railways has something to contribute in explanation

TABLE 5

Receipts from Public Land Sales by States
Annually, 1855–1860
(Unit: $1,000)

Year	Minnesota [a]	Oregon	Kansas	Nebraska	California	Washington
1855	1121	17	..	..	..	1
1856	603	17	..	..	..	..
1857	147	21	86	98	10	3
1858	29	12	74	24	27	1
1859	12	4	62	35	140	3
1860	85	2	25	14	45	2

[a] Receipts from public land sales in Minnesota for 1849–54 were, respectively, 3, 5, 18, 5, 47, and 366 thousand dollars.

of the movement of land sales. And upon reflection such, indeed, seems to have been the case. For example, the years preceding 1818 were years of conspicuous activity in the improvement of transportation facilities, in part engendered by the military difficulties experienced by the country in the War of 1812. Particularly important from our point of view was the gradual extension of the Cumberland Road westward until in this same year 1818 it was opened to traffic as far as Wheeling on the Ohio River, and, again, the invention of the steamboat. The former gave a direct through route to the West, affording to prospective settlers an easy access into southern Ohio and southern Indiana. The steamboat, soon introduced upon the Great Lakes and the Mississippi, similarly offered to would-be settlers of the West a better means of maintaining contact with the outside world than that area had previously possessed.

In the years preceding 1836, the extension of "internal improvements" was even more notable than it had been twenty years earlier. General communication with the West had been established with the completion of the Erie Canal in 1825. Then, in the next decade, the construction of the canal and the portage-railway between Philadelphia and Pittsburg, and the digging of canals in the Northwest states gave added inducements to those who contemplated moving into Ohio, Indiana, and Illinois. Improvement of steamboat service during this period upon the Mississippi and Ohio rivers and on the Great Lakes might also be taken into consideration as affecting the movement of immigrants into other parts of the West.

Finally, the rapid expansion of land sales in the early fifties is perhaps not unconnected with the completion of the East-and-West railroad communication and with the building of railway lines within the West itself. The Erie Railroad reached the lake for which it was named in 1851; the Baltimore and Ohio was pushed through to Wheeling in 1853; while in the same year the Pennsylvania Railroad extended its connections beyond the Ohio River to such growing towns as Indianapolis, Lafayette, and Terre Haute, Indiana. Meanwhile, further west the Illinois Central, started in 1851, was penetrating the central counties of that state; the Rock Island had three years later reached the Mississippi River opposite Iowa; and railroad construction was beginning to open up the interiors of Michigan, Wisconsin, and Missouri. As far as the West was concerned, obviously these years were of peculiar significance as the culmination of a movement begun with the launching of the Baltimore and Ohio in 1828. Thus large sections of the West were made readily available for settlement, whereas ten or even five years before, when the lines were uncompleted, serious difficulties still confronted the west-bound traveler. Now, as it were, the gates were swung open and a pent-up flood of settlers sought western lands.

Obviously, a fairly strong case may be built up as to the influence of transportation development upon the course of land sales. And yet to me it is not convincing. Not only was the continuity of improvement above noted the predominant feature despite some irregularities of movement, but the influence of each betterment would continue to be felt after it was put through. Accordingly, while the improvement of the means of communication was undoubtedly a stimulus to land sales, there seems to be little in this factor alone which would explain the sharp declines in sales that always followed a boom period. On the basis solely of changes in transportation facilities, one would rather expect a continually mounting volume of land sales, though such increase would not proceed at a regular rate. Again, the factor of "internal improvements" would not explain adequately such a brief expansion of land sales as occurred in 1838–39, nor would it account for the particular timing of the breaking points in the upward trends of sales before 1818, 1836, and 1854–55. Perhaps then, we may view this element as a prerequisite to the characteristic movement in the disposition of public lands, but no more than immigration a sufficient cause for the intensity of that movement. We must look to a third factor for this.

The third force, speculation, is suggested by the mere enumeration of the several high points in the volume of land transfers. These peaks occur in periods of marked business activity for the country as a whole, and the height of the several booms in land distribution corresponds generally with the intensity of speculative movement at the several times as otherwise measured. Thus, the upswings of business which preceded the crises of 1819, 1837, and 1857 unquestionably were the years of most intense and broadest speculative activity in the history of the country before 1860, and the occasions of greatest land speculation are closely connected therewith. On the other hand, cyclical movements in general business were very moderate in character during the twenties and forties, and so were the contemporary fluctuations in land sales.

Again, while it appears that the course of land distribution is closely associated with the general cyclical movements of these periods, there is some evidence showing that the course of land sales was usually associated therewith in a very special way: the peak in the sale of public lands preceded the breaks of the several crises, at least as the latter is indicated by the movement of commodity prices, and frequently recovery in the volume of land sales preceded that in general business. To be sure, the issuance of the famous Specie Circular in July, 1836, may be held accountable in large part for the break of land sales in that year. But the phenomenon is to be seen also in the attainment of a high point in 1824, preceding the minor crisis of the succeeding year; in the occurrence of the peak at the end of 1838, whereas commodity prices continued to move upward until March of 1839; and in the maintenance of large land sales through the fourth quarter of 1855, although the approaching crisis did not break until the early fall of 1857. (Chart 1 gives a comparison of relatives to the base 1834–42 = 100, for land sales and for commodity prices, the latter being my index number above noted for 1825–45.) Less consistent with this generalization are the movements in land sales culminating in 1818 and 1846. At the earlier period, the decline in such sales and the break in commodity prices seem to have occurred at about the same time.[6] Yet it is to be observed that in the older public land states, such as Ohio and Indiana, the volume of sales tended downwards from the end of 1817. The high level of sales in 1818–19 is to be attributed almost wholly to the course of activity in the newer

CHART 1

Receipts from Public Land Sales by the United States
Compared with General Commodity Prices
Quarterly, 1825–1845
(Average 1834–1842 = 100 per cent)

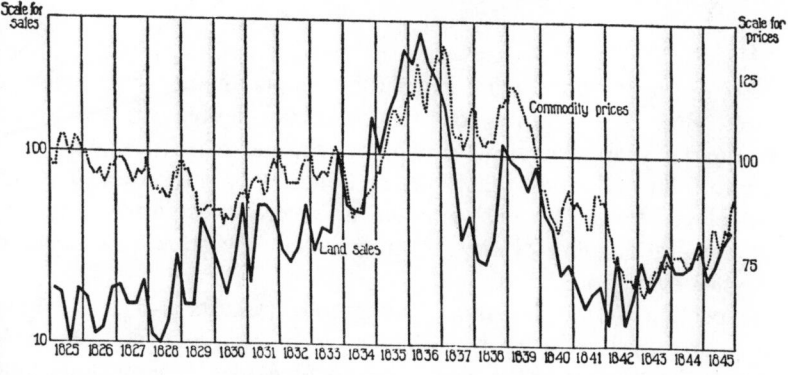

areas, especially in Alabama, where sales mounted in such fashion as to countervail and conceal the movement in the other regions.[7] In the forties, the peak of sales did in fact occur before commodity prices had fully run their course or at least no later than the maximum of the commodity price movement; but the sales, after a slump in the latter part of 1846, rose to a height in the second half of 1847 almost as great as that reached in the spring of the preceding year. Then, too—as a later inspection of individual state figures will show—at this period there is no appreciable similarity of movement among the several states. On the other hand, the commencement of an upward movement after a period of depression seems to have come first in land sales: note, e.g., the lift in sales in 1828, 1838, and 1842 (Chart 1). On the whole, then, there seems reason to conclude that the course of land sales in this forty-five-year period was one which in timing preceded that of commodity prices. And this, it may be added, is consonant with the feature already pointed out, the importance of the speculative element in the distribution of public lands; for recent investigations have shown that there are certain highly speculative activities, such as that of the stock market, the movement of which customarily anticipates that of general business conditions.[8]

In brief, then, consideration of the general course of land sales indicates that the speculative fever so widely prevalent in the United States during these decades [9] was chiefly responsible for variations in the movement of sales. Less significant, but surely not without some influence in the matter, were the factors of immigration and the improvement of transportation. Together these elements go far to explain the broad swings in the transference of public lands from the control of the government to that of individuals.

II

Let us turn to an examination of the receipts divided by the several states. Here it is advantageous to use annual figures, since those on the quarter-year basis display such irregular movements as to be difficult to follow. Besides, what we are now chiefly interested in is the part played by the various states in the several speculative activities, not the exact timing of the movements state by state with relation to other events of the period.

Inspection of the accompanying graphs (Charts 2–5), in which the course of land sales by calendar years in the several states is compared with that of the country as a whole, yields many significant facts. Particularly it shows that the degree in which the states shared in the boom movements varied markedly one state from another, and that not infrequently there were special movements for individual states which do not fit in with the analysis of speculative activity above presented for the country as a whole.

As to the first point, one may note the following:

(*a*) In the speculative movement which culminated in 1818, Alabama was affected in a particularly large measure, and only in somewhat smaller degree, Illinois and Mississippi. On the other hand, the volume of sales in Ohio does not appear to have followed the general course. While, to be sure, sales fell sharply with those of other states, they seem to have been proceeding for some time upon a high level. Missouri, too, presents an exception. Presumably on account of the

CHART 2

Receipts from Public Land Sales by the United States as a Whole
and by Ohio, Illinois, and Indiana
Annually, 1814–1860
(Unit: $1,000)

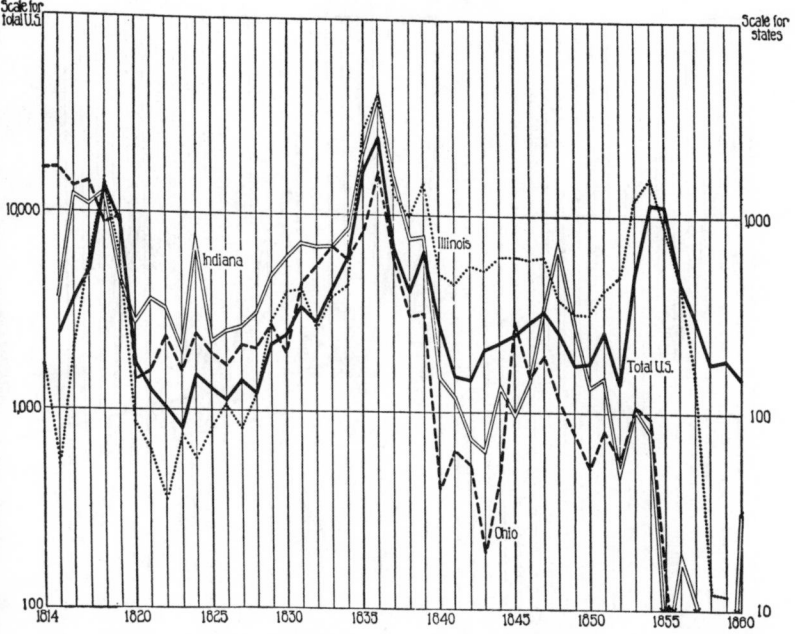

recent opening of a land office in that area, the quantity of sales did
not reach its peak until 1819.

(*b*) The special activity in land sales culminating in 1824 was
much less general than the above. Indiana shows an upward thrust
for the single year 1824; Mississippi exhibits a rising volume of sales
in the years immediately preceding, but no considerable downward
trend thereafter; and Michigan alone reveals a pronounced rise and
fall around that date.[10] Ohio, Illinois, Alabama, and Missouri are little
affected, if indeed they show any effect at all.

(*c*) The breadth of speculative movement was particularly great
in the years preceding 1836. All states were drawn in upon a greater
or lesser scale. The intensity of the movement, however, differed
appreciably among the several states. In some cases, e.g., Ohio or
Alabama, there was a gradual enhancement of sales extending over six

CHART 3

Receipts from Public Land Sales by the United States as a Whole
and by Michigan, Wisconsin, Minnesota, and Iowa
Annually, 1816–1860
(Unit: $1,000)

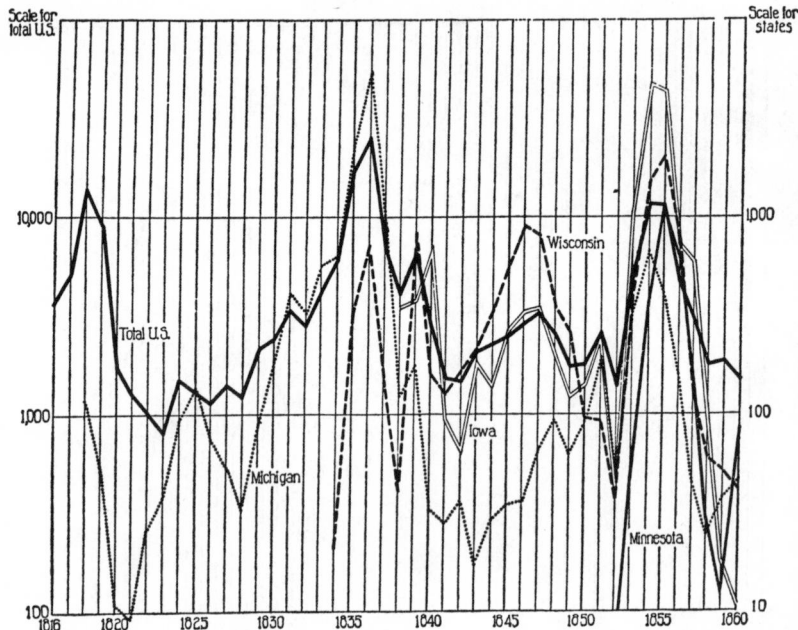

or eight years. For Illinois, indeed, the volume swells with only minor recessions over the whole period 1822–36. On the other hand, the rise and fall are peculiarly rapid and extreme in the cases of Michigan, Mississippi, and Arkansas. In those newer areas, speculation seems to have played particular havoc.[11]

(*d*) Various states manifest in a minor way the secondary movement which culminated for the country as a whole in 1839—for example, Ohio and Michigan; but those especially concerned are Louisiana, Wisconsin, and Missouri.

(*e*) The period of the forties presents exceptional diversity of movement among the several states. Scarcely any two lines move together. Apparently the connection of land sales with the crises of 1846, tenuous at best, breaks down under this closer investigation. Nothing of a broad and general course can be established.

CHART 4

Receipts from Public Land Sales by the United States as a Whole
and by Missouri, Arkansas, and Louisiana
Annually, 1816–1860
(Unit: $1,000)

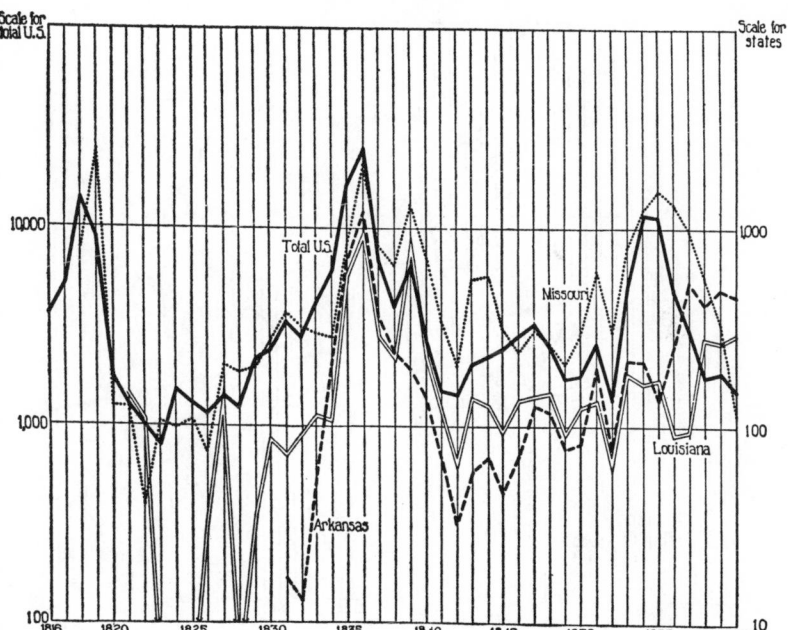

(*f*) In the period of the middle fifties, however, strong forces of a general character again seem to be operating. As in the movement that reached its peak in 1836, nearly all the states were more or less affected at this time. In some, e.g., Ohio and Indiana, there was no appreciable upswing, but the decline in 1855 in both these cases is too precipitous to be attributed to particular causes. In other cases, notably Wisconsin, Minnesota, and Iowa, the boom was exceptionally pronounced. Again the new areas were those especially affected.

The second feature above mentioned, the special movements in the cases of individual states, is apparent at a casual inspection of the charts. Those of the forties are particularly numerous, but they occur elsewhere. The high point reached in Louisiana in 1827 and the course of transactions in Arkansas during the latter fifties are cases in point. Sometimes such odd movements are due to the fact that land offices

CHART 5

Receipts from Public Land Sales by the United States as a Whole
and by Alabama, Mississippi, and Florida
Annually, 1814–1860

(Unit: $1,000)

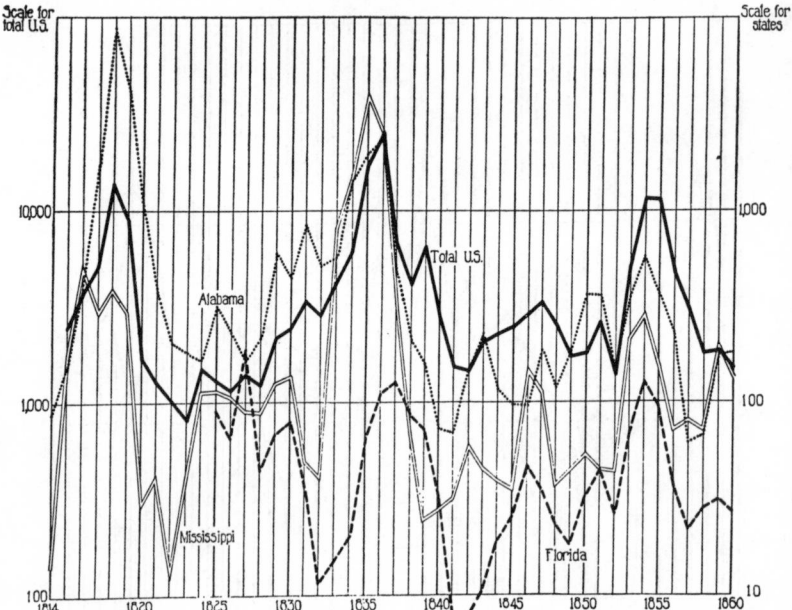

in a particular area had been recently opened up. In those circumstances people who had already come into the region and who had been occupying public lands as "squatters" rushed to the new office and purchased the land that they had staked out for themselves. At other times, changes in transportation facilities or the like seem to have occasioned the particular events. Then only a single section of a state would be appreciably affected. Two instances of this sort may be found in the exceptional rise of sales in Indiana during the years 1845 to 1852, and in Mississippi during 1845 to 1848. In the former case, only the Indianapolis, Fort Wayne, and Winamac land districts were much concerned—districts which lay generally in the northern and northeastern portions of the state. The full reasons for this particular phenomenon are not wholly clear, but there seems reason to give much emphasis to the influence of the Wabash and Erie Canal. This waterway was opened on July 4, 1843, from Toledo on the

Lakes to Lafayette on the Wabash, traversing the area under consideration. Entrance of settlers into the region and the export of products from it were easier than ever before.[12] In the second instance—that of Mississippi in 1845–48—the increase of sales was confined almost wholly to the districts of Columbus and Grenada. These districts covered a broad area running across the north-central section of the state. And here the explanation for the brisk but short-lived increase of sales during 1846–47 seems to be the incidental effects of a land boom still farther north. The area at the very top of the state had in 1832 been ceded by the Chickasaw Indians to the United States with the understanding that the land should be sold to settlers and the proceeds turned back to them. This territory was first opened for sale in 1836 and yet by 1848 nine-tenths of the area was sold. There is evidence, too, that the rush of purchasers suggested by this rapid turnover of land reached particularly great proportions in the middle forties. Thus, in his inaugural address of 1846, the governor of the state made special mention of the "advances in population and in agriculture" in the Chickasaw purchase during the preceding decade.[13]

In yet another connection, the historian might look to the new data upon land sales for help—to secure a closer picture of the settlement in the various sections of the country than is given by the decennial censuses of population. Here are annual figures of the purchases of public lands divided not merely by states but by land districts; and the maps that are available of land districts period by period indicate the particular areas of each state to which the divers figures pertain.

To test the value of the land-sales statistics for this purpose, graphs were prepared upon a logarithmic scale, in which the course of these sales on an annual basis for the two states of Michigan and Missouri, respectively, were compared with the movement of population in each as indicated by the federal censuses.[14] It was at once obvious that a certain amount of correlation exists between the two movements. The periods of greatest growth in population in these states, such as the decade of the thirties, were periods of marked activity in land sales, and contrariwise the intervals covering slumps in land distribution, e.g., the forties, were also times when population stood still or increased with peculiar slowness. The rate of increase, too, over certain portions of the whole forty-five-year period was somewhat similar in the two movements, at least if one should measure the rate of growth for the land sales by a straight line fitted to the data over corresponding time-intervals. There, however, the correlation stops.

By reason of the speculative character of the land sales, above suggested, it seems sure that year-by-year movements of such sales cannot be taken to mirror changes in population at correspondingly short intervals. The land was bound in some measure to pass into the hands of men who did not intend to settle in the particular district under observation, i.e., into the hands of "speculators" in the simplest sense—and we know otherwise that such individuals did exist in pre-Civil War days and did play some part in connection with public land distribution.[15] But such objections would not attach to somewhat longer periods, for example, half-decades. Purchase of land by "speculators" for retention over any lengthy interval appears not to have been quantitatively an important factor in the public land sales of this era; and one is probably justified, therefore, in giving a presumption in favor of correlative movements in land sales and increase of population for anything like five-year periods. Thus, in the cases specifically examined, the peculiarly heavy sales in Michigan in the years 1830–35, followed soon by a marked slump, is presumably indicative of a more rapid real settlement of that state during the first half than during the latter half of the decade; and the large volume of sales in Missouri during the middle fifties likewise probably indicates those years as the period when increase of population was marked. In short, we have here evidence of much value to the political and social historian, which, if used with care, will assist him materially in filling in the picture of the country's development.[16]

CONCLUSIONS

The analysis of the new data with respect to public land sales in the period before 1860 leads to certain broad conclusions, while further study of the figures in connection with more specific and detailed problems will, it is hoped, throw additional light upon the course of American settlement in these decades.[17] The broader results may be summarized as follows:

The transference of public lands into the possession of private individuals was dominated throughout the period 1816–60 by the element of speculation. Three outstanding episodes appear in the data, the booms culminating in 1818, 1836, 1854–55, though at other times the influence of the speculative fever is evident. Purchase came chiefly in waves, not in any orderly and methodical advance. The receipts turned into the Treasury during the speculative movements— 1816–20, 1830–39, and 1853–56—exceeded by 190 per cent those accumulated during the other years of this period.

As with other statistical series in which speculation plays a large part, the movements in the sale of public lands usually preceded the movements in general business, at least in so far as the latter are reflected in the course of commodity prices. The volume of sales began to pick up, after a period of depression, before commodity prices began their upward trend, and the peak of land sales usually antici- pated the peak of the commodity-price movement. For the pre-Civil War era, then, this statistical series should be taken into account as one forecasting the general course of business, just as the action of the stock market has proved in more recent times a good indicator of the future movement of general business.

Less significant factors in this general movement of land sales, but factors not wholly to be neglected, are the influences of immigration and of "internal improvements." Sometimes supporting the effect of the broad speculative tendencies, and sometimes offering a suggestion for the explanation of special features in the course of sales, the influence of immigration must be given appropriate consideration; but the absence of any marked correlation between the two move- ments over the period 1820–60 viewed as a whole leads one to place only minor emphasis upon this factor. Incidentally, it may be noted that the lack of this correlation between the two movements is not without import to the student of immigration or of the westward trend of American settlement. Where did the immigrants settle who came over in the forties and early fifties, if their coming had so small an effect upon the sale of public lands? On the other hand, the influence of transportation development upon land sales is clearer. The periods of largest land sales were also periods of conspicuous advance in internal improvements, and undoubtedly the latter may be looked upon as giving support to the former. The development of more adequate transportation facilities, however, simply does not go far enough in explanation of the variations in land sales, especially in accounting for the intensity of the up-and-down swings to which public land sales were subject. For the more adequate explanation, one must turn to the above-mentioned factor of speculative activity.

When one looks at the data in greater detail, it becomes evident that the several public land states were all more or less affected in the more prominent speculative episodes, but at the successive periods the areas most powerfully affected were the newer states. In the years around 1818, Illinois, Alabama, and Mississippi suffered more extremes of movement than the other states; by the middle thirties, Michigan, Arkansas, and again Mississippi displayed the most violent variations in activity; while in 1854–55 the center of wildest speculation had moved out to Wisconsin, Minnesota, and Iowa. Here as in other aspects of American life, there was a westward movement in passing decades.

Beyond the general changes, there are special cases of rapid but short-lived expansion in sales, limited usually to the land offices of a single state. These are in the nature of local booms, produced apparently by changes in local conditions. Such movements are particularly notable in the decades of the forties, when no broad speculative forces swept the whole country. Typical of these movements are the events in Indiana during 1845–52 and in Mississippi during 1846–48, when the construction of a canal and a sudden interest in Indian lands were the most obvious causes of the phenomena. Instances of this sort, however, frequent as they are, form in substance only a small part of the story. The dominant note in the sale of public lands still remains the broad speculative movements which put the land by millions of acres into the hands of private individuals and ultimately into those of actual settlers.

Finally, one may call attention to the value of these new data upon land sales as supplementary to the census figures upon population in tracing the increase of settlement in specific areas within decennial periods. There is a sufficient similarity of general movement by census dates between the course of such sales and the increase of population, at least in the case of individual states, so that one is inclined to confidence in the picture which the land-sales figures give of the intradecennial intervals. Handled with circumspection, these figures should enable the political and social historian to secure a closer view than has heretofore been possible of the movement of settlement by local areas. As such, they should prove a highly useful addition to our stock of historical data.

NOTES

1 Investigation into the course of business in the pre-Civil War decades—as shown by commodity prices and other phenomena—is under way in various quarters. Professor Walter B. Smith of Wellesley College is studying the period before 1825; and I am attempting to bring together material upon the decades that lie beyond that date. See my study of prices 1825–45 in the *Review of Economic Statistics*, 8:69–84 (April, 1926).

2 To be sure, the results as far as individual states or land-office areas are concerned might well be affected, if one rather than the other basis were employed: the graduation scheme would not affect all states or land-office areas alike. But this is a refinement of analysis into which I do not care to go. For our purposes it is sufficient to note that the older public land states would undoubtedly be the ones most affected, and, as suggested in the text, the results as far as actual distribution of public land is concerned would be merely somewhat exaggerated if we could employ acreage figures in these latter years.

3 Also worthy of remark are the facts that the secular trend during this 45-year period is not sufficiently great to interfere with immediate use of the original data in the study of cyclical movements (a straight line fitted to the annual figures giving an annual decrement equal to .507 per cent of the first ordinate and .648 per cent of the final ordinate), and that there is no seasonal movement of consequence during the larger part of the interval under consideration.

The relative importance of the several peaks spoken of above may be seen in the following figures of the receipts at the maximum quarters in these movements:

4th quarter of 1818	$4,967,000
3rd quarter of 1824	726,000
2nd quarter of 1836	8,423,000
4th quarter of 1838	2,239,000
2nd quarter of 1846	955,000
{ 4th quarter of 1854	3,901,000
{ 4th quarter of 1855	3,948,000

4 To be sure, the lag in land sales is not consistent, sometimes being one year and sometimes two or three years.

5 Something of the relationship between the movements of immigration and of land sales is apparent in the following tabulation of relatives based on the first low points in the two curves after 1820, i.e., 1823. With the exception of 1836, I have used regular five-year intervals after this last date. I have employed the acreage figures as far as land sales are concerned, as here the feature of land settlement is particularly important, not the financial element.

	1828	1833	1836	1838	1843	1848	1853	1858
Immigration	430	923	1200	612	1100	3565	5800	1880
Land sales	148	590	3070	522	246	288	579	560

6 In the matter of commodity-price movement, I am relying on the pre-liminary results of the above-mentioned investigation into the course of commodity prices during these years now being carried on by Professor Walter B. Smith of Wellesley College. I am indebted to him for permission to use his figures.

7 The amounts of purchase money turned in by the land offices in Alabama during the years 1816–1820 were as follows:

1816	$ 398,000
1817	1,718,000
1818	8,676,000
1819	4,148,000
1820	1,067,000

8 See various publications of the Harvard Committee on Economic Research.

9 For example, see my "Agricultural Crazes," *American Economic Review*, 16:622–639 (December, 1926).

10 In fact, the culminating point for Michigan lies in 1825, not 1824, the movement being prolonged perhaps by peculiar local factors.

11 Sales in Florida seem to have followed a largely independent course, especially in so far as they reach a peak later than the sales in the other states.

12 Considerable activity along the canal, with the beginnings of an export trade in local produce, is spoken of during the middle forties. "Docks, warehouses, and elevators were springing up over night at Logansport, Attica, Peru, . . . (etc.). All kinds of craft swarmed on the canal."— Logan Esarey, *History of Indiana* (New York, 1922), 386.

13 *Report of the Commissioner of the Public Land Office*, 1848, p. 19; *Speeches, Messages, and Other Writings of the Hon. Albert G. Brown*, (Philadelphia, 1859), 90.

14 The states were selected more or less at random, avoidance only of states such as Alabama or Mississippi with a predominant Negro population being exercised. It was thought that if the picture was satisfactory with respect to areas of predominantly white population, comparison could be extended to these other sections.

15 See Benjamin Horace Hibbard, *A History of the Public Land Policies* (New York, 1924), chap. xii, *passim;* and selections brought together by E. L. Bogart and C. M. Thompson, in their *Readings in the Economic History of the United States* (New York, 1916), 458–464.

16 In view of the rather broad character of the treatment here given the new data on land sales, and also of the really limited conclusions which analysis of the state figures permits, I have not carried further, e.g., to

land-office areas, the inquiry as to possible correlation of land-sale and population statistics. Such a study, too, would entail much labor. The particular arrangement of land districts in any given state, as they existed from time to time, would have to be matched to the areas of the then-existing counties—the census figures of population being presented on the basis of these small local divisions. Analysis of this sort would appear more suitable to local studies of settlement, population movement, and the like.

17 A complete file of the statistics of receipts from land sales distributed both by individual land offices and by quarter-year intervals, and of the statistics of the acres disposed of by annual or semi-annual periods at the several land offices—figures much too voluminous for full presentation in this article—has been deposited with the Harvard University Library; and a similar set has been presented to the office of the Chief Accountant at the General Land Office, Washington, D.C.

In addition to the above statistical data, I have deposited with the Harvard University Library a set of photostatic copies of maps showing the areas of the land districts in the several public land states as they existed from time to time in the period before 1860. The originals—unofficial data—may be found in the office of the Chief Surveyor, General Land Office, Washington, D.C.

Farm-Making Costs and the "Safety Valve": 1850–1860

CLARENCE H. DANHOF

Reprinted by permission from the Journal of Political Economy, *published by the University of Chicago Press, Volume 49 (1941), pages 317–359.*

THE fundamental importance to American economic development of the settlement of the federal landed domain is among the axiomatic propositions of economic history. The recognition of this relationship of land to the economic development of the United States has encouraged widespread acceptance of the more specific dictum that the opportunities provided by the easily available western lands strongly influenced, if they did not actually determine, the course of development of the American wage-earning classes. The theory has been widely accepted that the western lands drew off eastern labor whenever eastern industrial conditions were unsatisfactory, and in this way western lands performed the function of a safety valve for socio-economic conflict. Recent debate indicates that this interpretation remains an unproved hypothesis.[1] Particular importance attaches to this view because the disappearance of this alleged safety valve, as a result of the settlement of the public domain, is often considered a turning point in the industrial history of the United States and is occasionally used to buttress arguments favoring the adoption of economic reforms.

The assumptions upon which the safety-valve theory rests are few and simple. It is assumed, in the first place, that under certain conditions, such as those of depression and unemployment, onerous working conditions, and unsatisfactory wages, labor found it desirable to take advantage of the opportunities afforded by the cheap western lands; in the second place, that wage labor could if it so wished participate with little difficulty in the exploitation of this land; and, third, that labor acted upon this opportunity in significant numbers. The present study proposes to examine the validity of the second of these assumptions by an examination of the costs of farm-making as well as of the ability of wage labor to meet such costs. Our study is confined to the conditions existing in the decade 1850–60—a decade in which agriculture, particularly in the northern states, under the impact of a spreading network of railroad communications and the rapid introduction of new agricultural implements, emerged entirely from its earlier self-sufficiency into a maturely capitalistic, profit-seeking, and market-focused system.[2]

I

At the outset we must appreciate that the economic aspects of pioneering and its relations to the larger economic life of the nation are not to be understood without adequate analysis of the costs which the farmer and farm-maker faced. The editor of the *New England Cultivator* in 1852 succinctly indicated a factor in the agriculture of his period that the economic historian may not safely overlook: "No error is more universal than for Tyros in farming operations to suppose that the business of farming may be pursued without means and that first crops may be obtained from the soil without additions."[3] Farm-making in the 1850's, whether carried out on the prairie or in forested areas, in the North or in the South, at the frontier of settlement or in well-settled regions, involved a variety of costs which were definite and inescapable. To a degree these costs might be met by the labor and sacrifice of the farm-maker and his family, but this was less possible in the fifties than it had been in the preceding decades. The would-be farm-maker had to acquire land and then prepare it for cultivation, which involved fencing and clearing or breaking; he had to possess draft animals and livestock, seed, and implements with which to conduct farming operations; he had to procure transportation to the West; and he had to build a shelter for his family and to support them through the waiting period until the first crops were harvested. Certain if not all of these were costs which had to be met with money outlays, and any would-be farm-maker consequently found the possession of some capital essential.

The fact that capital was required as a preliminary condition for undertaking agriculture is reiterated continuously in the agricultural literature of the period.[4] Condemnation of the futility of acquiring land without the possession of capital adequate to work it constantly recurs.[5]

Though a distinction was commonly made between "farming" and "making farms," the necessity for capital was fully recognized in either case. The sums considered necessary to carry on farming operations were surprisingly large.[6] Similarly, though the numerous writers describing the opportunities of the West generally addressed their observations to the "poor man," examination of their meaning reveals that their remarks were clearly not directed at the impoverished; they wrote in terms of persons of limited or moderate means,[7] and their discussions invariably took for granted the possession of some capital.[8] Large sums of capital actually did accompany immigrants to the farm-making frontiers.[9] Individuals who lacked what these writers considered adequate funds were singled out for special attention. It was pointed out to them that the West offered opportunities for employment and savings which might eventually lead to the ownership of a farm. Foreign immigrants in particular were told that agricultural wage employment in the West provided them an opportunity for learning American methods as well as for accumulating funds. It was suggested to farmers that they could rent improved farm lands on shares and, after four or five years, proceed to purchase their own lands with their savings.[10] They might alternatively contract to improve, on a share arrangement, wild lands owned by someone else [11] or might bid for the lease of state-owned lands.[12] In any case they could accept agricultural employment for wages.[13] Wage employment in the rapidly growing western towns and cities was frequently pictured to eastern mechanics as providing excellent opportunities to share in the growth of the West, since labor was in demand and wages were high.[14] Even schoolteaching was suggested as a method by which the propertyless person might gain a foothold in the West.[15]

Considerable information regarding the amount of capital which was considered necessary to the undertaking of western farm-making is to be had from contemporary sources. Nathan Parker, an Iowa land agent and author of a series of western guidebooks, quotes with approval an estimate that a capital of at least $1,000 was necessary to equip an 80-acre western farm, exclusive of the land.[16] Another observer wrote with reference to Illinois that "any man who wants to commence farming on the prairies must be possessed of means and energy, and not expect to make a fortune too easy. A section of land requires about $5,000 cash to commence profitably, while it will require all of the half of that sum to farm a quarter section as it should be done." [17] Fred Gerhard cites a number of instances of 80-acre

Illinois farms which required investments of from $785 to $2,127 to produce first crops.[18] It was asserted with reference to Texas that "any man with $500 can become an independent farmer . . . ,"[19] though such a capital was certainly a minimum figure; and Frederick Law Olmsted wrote, in contrast, that "a labouring man, who has not one thousand dollars at command will probably find his account in first accumulating that sum by working for others."[20] Elsewhere it was pointed out, also with reference to Texas, that "for success as a cattle raiser the emigrant needs from six to ten thousand dollars."[21] The editor of the *Country Gentleman,* in reply to an inquiry, advised several young mechanics who possessed capitals of from $700 to $1,400 each against buying new lands to farm.[22]

Among foreign travelers reporting on this matter, Stirling suggested to his English countrymen that £200 would secure a start in Iowa; more might permit settlement in Illinois or possibly in Ohio.[23] Cunynghame advised a capital of £300 for transportation to and establishment on an 80-acre farm in the Des Moines valley of Iowa.[24] It was estimated by still another writer that $955 would buy a 200-acre farm, break and fence 60 acres, and build a log cabin and other small buildings.[25] Regan considered the sum of $550 an absolute minimum for an English immigrant designing to settle in the West.[26] An English traveler whose interest was specifically in American lands wrote that "an intelligent, prudent man, with five hundred pounds in his pocket, may rely on finding that sum sufficient to start him successfully on 320 acres of prairie land, if he avails himself of this credit system," land purchase not being provided for in this sum. He goes on to note that "a man with his wife and four children could not transport himself and them from this country to Illinois and place himself comfortably even on a forty acre farm for less than £100."[27] The estimates here quoted as well as others are itemized in Table 6.[28]

The estimates included in Table 6 indicate clearly that substantial amounts of capital were considered necessary to farm-making by contemporary observers. The conditions assumed in these calculations vary widely, however, and the computations likewise differ in their content and inclusiveness. The costs noted, moreover, are at variance in their requirements for liquid capital. Certain items could sometimes be met through the use of credit, others could be provided by labor or sacrifice, and money outlays could sometimes be avoided if the needed property were held. We may profitably consider in detail the individual items in the farm-maker's cost prospect and the possibilities of escaping capital investment in each case.

II

Land acquisition was the basic factor in the farm-maker's problem, and we may begin with an examination of the land market. This market was a complex one; the situation is not described by reference to federal lands at $1.25 per acre, despite the fact that the federal government was the original owner of most of the available lands.[29] From the point of view of the farm-maker there were actually five major sources from which lands could be obtained: the federal government; the state governments; land-grant corporations; private speculators; and private holders of partially improved lands.

The principal method of land sale employed by the federal government was that of auction. Lands offered at auction were held for a minimum price of $1.25 per acre, that price applying also to lands sold to pre-emptors and lands sold privately after having failed to sell at auction. The federal government also sold to private individuals after 1854, at reduced, graduated prices, certain lands which had been on the market for various periods of years. Transfers of land by the federal government to individuals totaled almost 50,000,000 acres during the decade. Of this total, 43 per cent was sold at prices below $1.25 per acre.[30] Only 24 per cent of the total land area alienated by the federal government during this decade was disposed of by sale, and only 13 per cent was sold at or above the $1.25 minimum price. As important as land sales were the federal government's grants of lands to individuals. Under the military land-grant acts of 1847 and subsequent years, the government presented, to more than half a million individuals, tracts of lands varying from 40 to 160 acres each and totaling more than 57,000,000 acres.[31] These lands came on the market after the warrants granting them were made assignable in 1852, and an active market was conducted in them with prices substantially below the federal minimum.[32]

The federal government assigned to individuals by these two methods—sale and grant—about 57 per cent of its total land transfers made during the decade. The remaining land conveyances were made as grants to the states, in the form of school, university, internal improvement, and swampland grants, and to canal and railroad corporations. In making these grants the federal government established new sources from which the farm-maker could purchase his land. In most cases the government exercised no regulation as to the price or the method of disposition of these lands. There was no uniformity of policy on the part of the various states with regard to their lands, but the

TABLE 6

Estimated Costs of Farm-making: 1850–1860

(Contemporary Observers)

Location	Total Cost	Size Acres	Land Cost	Breaking	Fencing	Seeding	Harvesting	Livestock	Provisions	Buildings	Other
California [a]	$ 2,000	640	$ 800	$ †	$ 600	$ †	$ †	$ 500	$100	$ °	$ †
California [b]	3,000	40	400	†	1,400	200	†	700	†	†	30(
Illinois [c]	550	40	50	†	100	20	†	140	50	20	17(
Illinois [d]	785	80	100	130	320	40	195	†	†	†	†
Illinois [e]	896	34	170	87	100	468	71	†	†	†	†
Illinois [f]	920	200	320	†	173	†	†	†	†	100	2
Illinois [g]	930	45	500	†	†	20	†	140	50	†	22(
Illinois [h]	1,411	80	360	150	400	145	456	†	†	†	†
Illinois [i]	2,100	160	1,000	400	400	†	†	†	†	300	†
Illinois [j]	2,127	80	1,200	175	320	236	196	†	†	†	†
Illinois [k]	2,290	320	240	1,500	†	°	°	†	†	°	55(
Illinois [l]	2,750	160	1,600	225	400	†	†	†	†	500	2
Illinois [m]	2,800	100	1,000	1,250	°	°	°	†	†	†	55(
Illinois [n]	12,200	640	6,400	1,300	1,200	800	2,500	†	†	†	†
Iowa [o]	440	40	50	80	160	†	†	†	†	†	15(
Iowa [p]	850	160	200	320	320	†	†	†	†	†	†
Iowa [q]	1,034	80	†	†	†	†	†	310	†	450	37(
Iowa [r]	1,500	80	250	75	75	75	†	200	100	100	55(
Iowa [s]	2,650	160	200	600	600	150	200	†	†	650	25(
Iowa [t]	3,000	400	1,400	180	300	†	†	305	†	150	66(
Michigan [u]	277	40	†	220	40	17	†	†	†	†	†
Michigan [v]	2,475	160	225	1,012	°	°	338	†	†	900	†
Minnesota [w]	705	160	200	†	†	†	†	315	73	†	11(
Texas [x]	500	100	200	†	50	†	†	50	100	50	(
Texas [y]	715	50	150	†	60	150	†	260	25	65	†
Texas [z]	1,000	160	400	†	†	†	†	150	150	150	1(
Texas [aa]	7,800	160	400	°	600	†	†	4,450	†	750	1,6(
Texas [bb]	9,000	1,000	2,500	°	500	†	†	5,250	†	750	
Wisconsin [cc]	1,690	200	250	480	400	160	400	†	†	†	†
Wisconsin [dd]	2,000	640	800	100	200	†	†	350	150	°	4(
Wisconsin [ee]	2,500	100	1,600	°	°	†	†	560	100	°	2(

An asterisk (°) indicates that the item is included in the first preceding figure; a dagger (†) indicates that the item is not included in the estimate.

[Notes to Table 6 on following page]

258

Notes to Table 6

[a] Ernest Seyd, *California and Its Resources* (London, 1858), 141. The estimate assumes that 90 cres are fenced. Seed is included with provisions, implements with livestock, and buildings with ncing.

[b] Franklin Langworthy, *Scenery of the Plains, Mountains and Mines* (Ogdensburg, N.Y., 1855), 95–196. The "Other" item includes $100 for implements.

[c] John Regan, *The Emigrant's Guide to the Western States of America* (Edinburgh, 1852), 353. Other" includes $50 for furniture and $120 for implements.

[d] Fred Gerhard, *Illinois as It Is* (Chicago, 1857), 294.

[e] *Prairie Farmer*, 15:344 (1855).

[f] Josiah T. Marshall, *The Farmer's and Emigrant's Hand-Book* (Utica, N.Y., 1852), 402–403. The timate includes 160 acres of land at $1.25 per acre and 40 acres of timberland at $5.00 per acre. Other" includes $15 for a well. The estimate applies to prairie lands in general and not to Illinois ecifically. A very similar estimate by an English writer appears in *Working Farmer*, 2:270 (1850).

[g] Regan, *The Emigrant's Guide*, 356–357. The estimate includes the purchase of 40 acres of proved land—fenced, broken, and including buildings; also of 5 acres of timbered land at $20 per re. "Other" includes $100 for furniture and $120 for implements.

[h] Gerhard, *Illinois as It Is*, 294.

[i] *Country Gentleman*, 5:141 (1855). Provisions for a year are specified in addition.

[j] Gerhard, *Illinois as It Is*, 295.

[k] James Caird, *Prairie Farming in America* (New York, 1859), 91. Includes 100 acres broken, nced, sown, and harvested; also buildings. "Other" includes horses, implements, and harness.

[l] Gerhard, *Illinois as It Is*, 299.

[m] Caird, *Prairie Farming in America*, 89. The item of $1,250 is for breaking, fencing, and harvesting e first crop, as well as for buildings. The "Other" item is for hired labor.

[n] *Ibid.*, 55. Original figures in sterling. Includes entire area fenced and cultivated.

[o] *Connecticut Valley Farmer and Mechanic*, 1:153 (1854).

[p] *Northern Farmer*, 1:290–291 (1854).

[q] Nathan Parker, *Iowa Handbook for 1856* (Boston and New York, 1856), 159–160.

[r] Arthur Cunynghame, *A Glimpse at the Great Western Republic* (London, 1851), 103–106 and 8. "Other" includes $350 for passage from Great Britain to Iowa and $200 for miscellaneous and rplus. Implements included with seed. Original figures in sterling.

[s] *Iowa Farmer and Horticulturist*, 5:102 (1857).

[t] *Rural New Yorker*, 5:222 (1854). Includes the breaking and cultivation of 80 acres only.

[u] *Michigan Farmer*, 8:265 (1850). This is an estimate of capital required for undertaking farm-king on a share basis, the land being owned by a second party with whom the produce is equally vided. Half the required seed is included.

[v] Sidney Smith, *The Settler's New Home* (London, 1850), 91 (citing William Ferguson).

[w] *New Hampshire Journal of Agriculture*, April 14, 1859. Includes $90 for transportation from w England.

[x] *DeBow's Commercial Review*, 10:640–641 (1851). Includes $50 for transportation.

[y] *Southern Cultivator*, 13:125 (1855).

[z] Frederick Law Olmsted, *Journey through Texas* (New York, 1860), 460. The "Other" item in-des wages, tools, and working cattle.

[aa] Jacob De Cordova, *Texas, Her Resources and Her Public Men* (Philadelphia, 1858), 55. The ther" item includes $900 for wages for agricultural labor and $700 interest on capital for the first r.

[bb] Olmsted, *Journey through Texas*, 205. The estimate is for a stock farm in western Texas. Fifty es are assumed fenced and broken. The stock includes 200 head of cattle and 650 sheep. Olmsted es another estimate involving the same total for a cotton plantation in the same area which in-des 70 acres broken, $800 for livestock and implements, and $6,400 for slaves (p. 206).

[cc] *Working Farmer*, 2:270 (1850).

[dd] Seyd, *California and Its Resources*, 139. Assumes 20 acres cleared. Costs of log house included fencing. "Other" item of $400 is for implements.

[ee] *Wisconsin Farmer*, 8:440–441 (1856). Specifies 50 acres broken. Includes $150 for implements. one's means are moderate, one-half of that sum can be made to answer every purpose, by going to newer portions of the State, and purchasing as good but cheaper land—by substituting two yoke oxen for the horses and harness, and starting with three cows instead of five. . . ."

eventual result was in most cases that the lands were thrown on the market for quick sale. Lands not thus sold were then placed open to private sale, often at much lower prices. The prices realized by the states from such sales varied greatly, ranging from as little as ten cents per acre to as much as $10.

The guidebooks describing the western states and addressed to the prospective immigrant rarely failed to warn him that he must not expect to buy desirable lands at $1.25 per acre. "The immigrant must not come here, as many do, expecting to find first rate land, with timber and water, all spread out before him, very near to some city or town for $1.25 an acre; it is not to be had." [33] Complaints that good lands were not available at government price to the settler were numerous; in order to obtain lands at $1.25 per acre, location had to be made far on the outskirts of settlement if not beyond, or else on poor lands in undesirable locations where communications were difficult and markets distant.

The enthusiasm of the authors of these guidebooks focused upon the "secondhand" lands—virgin lands no longer owned by state or federal government but held by railroad and canal corporations and by private speculators. Such lands were available in large acreages in every state in which farms were being made, at prices two to ten times the federal minimum. These lands generally included, wherever settlement was under way, the remaining choice, fertile, and well-located sites. It was frequently pointed out that the differences in prices of these lands as compared with their desirability made them better values than federal minimum-price lands.[34] The most important of the corporation lands on the market during the fifties were those of the Illinois Central Railroad. The prices obtained for these lands ranged substantially above those realized from government sales.[35] More significant were the holdings of virgin lands in the hands of private speculators. Of the importance of the speculator in the land markets of the 1850's, particularly in the northern states, there can be no doubt.[36] In the case of Iowa, which was the most popular immigrant state of the decade, the state census for 1862 reported that some 15,000,000 acres, more than half the privately owned lands in the state, were owned by non-residents, and commented: "Most of these lands are doubtless held, where they are located very eligibly for speculation." [37] Lands held by speculators were usually priced at upward of $3 per acre.

The fifth land market to be considered was that in improved lands—lands on which some breaking, some fencing and building, and possibly some cropping had been done. The supply of such lands came to a large degree from a distinct and well-defined type of farm-maker or speculator who carried out the preliminary tasks of farm-making on purchased or pre-empted lands and who was satisfied to sell out after a few years, taking as his reward the increase in the price of the land which his labor and the increase in surrounding population had produced.[38] These specialists in farm-making were replaced by a more permanent population which itself had been, and indeed continued to be, subject to the similar temptation to sell—to convert the increments in the value of their lands into a cash profit.[39] The supply of such cleared and semicleared farms was contributed to by the California, Pikes Peak, and Oregon migrations.[40] Such lands were sometimes sold as low as $3 per acre but were generally valued at from $7 to $10 and frequently higher.[41] Advice to immigrants regarding such lands was conflicting. Some observers pointed out the profitability of buying such farms, which were ready to farm. They argued that improvements could frequently be purchased cheaper than they could be made and that such lands possessed the advantages of civilization, such as neighbors and schools, and were frequently located where markets were cheaply accessible.[42] Others argued that such lands might be seriously injured by crude and careless cultivation and might for that reason be unwise purchases.[43]

The wide choice of sellers which the prospective farm-maker found available was paralleled by the variety of the terms of sale. The federal government sold its lands only for cash or federal land warrants. State lands, however, were frequently sold on credit terms,[44] and credit was usually given by the landed corporations and by private speculators. The period over which credit was given was rarely long, ranging from a year or two to the six years offered by the Illinois Central Railroad. On the other hand, full title to lands might be obtained without investment in certain areas. The states of Maine and Arkansas offered lands to actual settlers, the purchase price to be paid in land scrip which was issued to the settlers as payment for labor performed in road-making and drainage.[45] Arkansas and Michigan gave outright donations of certain lands to actual settlers,[46] and Texas, after 1853, gave homesteads to settlers upon payment of office fees and surveying costs.[47]

An important form of land credit was the common practice of laying claim to federal lands beyond the area proclaimed for sale, such lands being put to use without investment of any kind. Such "squatters" or pre-emptors enjoyed the opportunity to improve their claims, with the hope that they could make sufficient from the cultivation of the land to pay for it when it was proclaimed for sale. If unfortunate in that respect, they were protected in the value of their improvements by claim associations which guaranteed that, should others desire their claims, they would receive compensation for their improvements.[48] In any case, the squatter could with little effort at agriculture or improvement hope for a speculative profit in selling desirable claims to later settlers.[49] The squatter was not, however, the typical farm-maker. He was rather a distinct and well-defined type who undertook a limited number of the operations of farm-making without possessing adequate capital. The great migrations which converted the wild forests and prairies into farms were not composed of squatters; that class had preceded it. The great migrations occurred after federal survey and proclamation of its lands. The typical settler came looking for fertile agricultural land, well located, with a little timber if it were prairie land, close to markets and neighbors.[50]

III

Land was the raw material from which farms were made, but it was nevertheless only one of the factors involved. James Caird, an English observer, pointed out that the "price of land is the least consideration that a British emigrant need take into his calculations" [51]—a caution that was frequently repeated and applicable to the native farm-maker as well as to the foreign immigrant.[52] Following the purchase of the land, began a process which was expensive of labor, capital, and time. The initial task was that of preparing the soil for the seeding of the first crop. In the case of forested lands the timber had to be cleared away; in the case of prairie, the sod had to be broken and rotted. In each case it was possible for the farm-maker to carry out the task by his own labor, but the differences between the two tasks and also the differing character of the period in which forest-clearing predominated from that in which prairie-breaking was typical revealed themselves in the fact that forest-clearing was most generally done by the farm-maker himself, while prairie-breaking was very frequently performed by professional breakers on contract.

The cost of clearing timbered land varied from $5 to $20 and upward per acre.[53] What was considered one of the cheapest and, frequently, also the best method of clearing forest land required that the trees be girdled and then permitted to stand from four to six years, cattle being fed on the land during this period to keep down the underbrush. At the end of the period the timber would be thoroughly dried and could be easily cut and burned. This method was estimated to cost from $5 to $8 per acre.[54] Though crops might be sown among the dead trees, falling limbs and trunks were a cause of considerable damage.

It was, of course, desirable to hasten the process; this could be done only at increased labor and cost and frequently involved delay in total area cleared and also resulted in a poorer quality of clearing.[55] One of the most common methods of forest-clearing involved the cutting of timber and brush into windrows during the winter, after which the timber lay about two years, and then those parts suitable for rails were removed and the remainder burned. This method was estimated to cost about $10 per acre.[56] The quickest method consisted of chopping the timber in the spring, preferably after the trees had been girdled the previous fall, the logs being burned during the first dry weather; then the ground was harrowed and sown to some crop such as corn or potatoes, which was followed by wheat in the fall.[57] The costs of this method were estimated at $14 or $15 an acre,[58] and the results were less satisfactory than other more time-consuming methods, since the land remained incumbered for many years with green stumps which continued to sprout, defying removal and remaining obstacles to plowing for some years longer than did the roots of girdled trees.[59] Oak openings and brushlands were special problems, since they had both to be cleared and broken. The tough roots present in the soils of such areas made breaking a particularly difficult task. After the timber had been removed from the oak openings of Michigan, a difficult task in itself, the contract cost of breaking the soil, ranging from $3.50 to $5.00 per acre, remained to be met.[60] Brushland was very general along the timbered edges of the prairies and was commonly grubbed at a cost of $10 to $12 per acre, although it was also sometimes merely plowed roughly and seeded, the shrubs, saplings, and roots being destroyed by burning.[61]

The task of preparing the open prairie lands for cultivation was quite different. Once the sod was turned under, little further labor was required and immediate seeding of a crop was possible. A period of waiting for the sod to decay ensued, but the period required was measured in months and not in years. In any case the task was far lighter than that of clearing forested lands, but it was a task unfamiliar to the immigrant from the East, and it involved difficulties and required special tools and skills. The plow used was commonly a heavy, specialized, prairie-breaker, pulled by three to eight yoke of oxen.[62] The skill derived of experience in breaking was a valuable asset, particularly since a poorly broken field in which part of the sod escaped uninjured was a serious handicap for many subsequent years, much as a "bad burn" handicapped the forest-clearer.[63] Timing was also important, the best period for breaking being a short one of about two months in the spring after the sod had sprung up and before it had ceased its early rapid growth.[64] If broken earlier, the grass was liable to reappear, while if broken after this period, the sod would not rot well and might interfere with the production of a satisfactory crop the following year. It was possible to produce a crop of sod corn on the earliest breaking, but it was very common for the farm-maker to spend an entire summer in breaking, with little or no effort made to get in a crop until wheat was sown in the fall or until the following spring.[65]

Despite these considerations the task of breaking was within the abilities of the average prairie farm-maker.[66] Yet, and in contrast to the custom in forest-clearing, the practice of contracting out the breaking of prairie sod to specialists for a money payment was a very common one.[67] The costs of breaking the sod by contract varied somewhat with the region and the character of the work. A commonly quoted price was $2.50 per acre, prices ranging from $1.50 to more than $5.00.[68] The general practice of breaking by contract was based upon important considerations aside from those of skill and specialized implements suggested above. The whole tempo of farm-making as conducted on the prairies was far more rapid than had been the case earlier when the forest had been the farm-maker's problem. Instead of attempting to clear a 40-acre tract in ten or fifteen years, the prairie farm-maker usually thought in terms of clearing his 80 or 160 acres in two to four years.[69] The amount of land which could be placed in crops was limited by no serious problems of decay but only by the area broken. The availability of profitable markets made it desirable to get as much land into crops as possible. Furthermore, no individual could break enough land in the short period available each year and at the same time carry out the many other tasks facing him. Obviously the farm-maker with capital was able to get his land into production far more rapidly than the settler who was forced to do his own breaking. No one could afford to forgo breaking services if they were within his means, particularly as the possibility existed that the first crop would return the entire investment.[70]

Fencing was, next to breaking, the most important farm-making task and was an essential part of the first farm-making operations.[71] The wild, uncultivated lands were the free range of livestock which were always a threat to growing crops. No farmer could afford the risk of even a partial loss of crops from the depredations of such animals. Adequate fences were required under the laws of most of the states in case reimbursement was to be sought for damages inflicted by animals belonging to another. In very sparsely settled areas broken fields were sometimes seeded before they could be fenced.[72] This practice was recognized as bad management, and numerous reports occur of crops lost for this reason.[73] Though it was possible to postpone until farm profits provided the capital all or part of the investment in fencing by vigilance in turning cattle away from cultivated fields or by local agreement to inclose the animals,[74] common practice seems to have regarded fencing as the earliest task of the farm-maker, equal in importance with breaking, and to be completed at the first opportunity. The fact that the area under fence in Iowa in 1862 exceeded the area under cultivation is evidence of the importance attached to fencing in the farm-making process.[75] Throughout the nation, and not only in the farm-making regions, fencing was looked upon as a serious problem and a heavy financial burden, and a solution was eagerly sought in hedging and in wire fencing.[76] It was pointed out that "fences are to a prairie farm one-third its value." [77] It was certainly a rare farm-maker who had not to invest more capital—or its equivalent in labor in the case of forested areas—in his fence than in land.[78] Where timber was to be had for the taking, the Virginia rail fence was the easiest and cheapest to build. The labor cost involved was estimated at from thirty-five to seventy cents a rod, which meant that the 320 rods required to fence a 40-acre field involved a cost of from $112 to twice that sum. A 160-acre field requires 640 rods of fence, and thus its cost of fencing was twice that of the 40-acre area. In any case the costs were heavy. Where timber was scarce, as on the prairies, liquid capital was necessary with which to purchase local or imported timber or a nearby woodland.[79] Since economy of timber was required under such conditions, the post and rail fence was standard in these areas. Its cost was, however, substantially higher than that of the Virginia rail fence —from $1 a rod up, depending upon the value of lumber. A fence around a 40-acre field cost at least $320; a farm of 160 acres broken into four fields required an investment considerably in excess of $1,000 for fences alone.[80]

IV

Clearing and fencing prepared the soil for the farming operations which were to follow. Capital was again required for implements, seed, and livestock. It was no doubt possible for a farm-maker to be possessed of no implements other than a cheap shovel plow, hoe, scythe, spade, harness, and wagon, but such a list represented an investment of perhaps $100. In the South the investment in implements per worker was much smaller, but this list of implements was very inadequate for the West. There the plows used could not be confined to a single type of cast iron but were of numerous varieties and made preferably of the more expensive steel.[81] If corn was cultivated in Iowa in the fifties it was generally done with the horse-drawn cultivator and not with the hoe. The use of the seed drill was beginning to be considered desirable, though its use in the fifties was largely confined to the regions east of the Mississippi.[82] It was the wheat crop which called for the heaviest investment in agricultural implements. The tasks of reaping and harvesting far exceeded the capacity of the western labor supply, and the purchase or hire of both machines was essential to maximize returns from the land.[83] Though thrashing was commonly done on contract, the reaper was usually purchased; and though it was possible to buy 100 acres of land at government price for approximately the price of a mower or reaper, the land had little but speculative value without the machine to make possible its profitable cultivation.

The reaper and drill were not essential implements to the farm-maker, though the advantages to be obtained from their use were so great as to require their acquisition at the earliest opportunity. Excluding these instruments, the common 100-acre wheat-corn farm required an investment of at least $100 in implements and tools. An estimate for a 100-acre Wisconsin farm allocated $150 for plow, drag, cultivator, and small tools to start with.[84] The new machines, however, were frequently considered indispensable.[85] Parker gives a breaking plow, a common plow, a reaper, and a thrasher as a very minimum of implements, representing an investment of at least $375, without mentioning small tools, cultivators, harrows, rollers, or drills.[86] A 160-acre farm in Illinois was estimated to require among other equipment a breaking plow, two common plows, two cultivators, harness for four horses, a reaper, and a thrashing machine, which would require more than $700.[87] Certainly a minimum of $100 had to be set aside for implements. The value of the implements of the farms of the western states as revealed by the census of 1860 averaged $156 per each 100 acres in farms, compared with a national average of $150 and an average for the farms of New England of $134.[88]

Since the possessors of capital invested much more readily in lands than in animals, livestock was relatively scarce on the farm-making frontiers, though the desirability of animals to take advantage of the pasturage freely afforded on the prairies was well recognized.[89] Draft animals were, nevertheless, essential in farming operations, and hogs were indispensable as a source of food, as well as providing a marketable crop which matured quickly and required little capital. The draft animals might be a team of horses, themselves as expensive as a quarter section of government land; less likely a yoke of cheaper oxen.[90] A minimum investment in draft animals, a few hogs, and some poultry involved from $150 to $200.[91] A well-stocked farm included a small herd of cattle which might well increase the investment required to, or above, $500.[92] Sheep were uncommon in farm-making areas.[93] Capital was also required for the purchase of seed. In the North where wheat was the common initial cash crop, the necessity for $1 to $2 per acre for seed was a significant capital requirement.[94] Corn required a smaller investment, while cotton seed was virtually without value in the South.

Farm-making involved an interval of waiting after the initial investment had been made for the first returns to come in—a period of from six to eighteen months or more.[95] During this interval the maintenance of the family had to be provided for from the farm-maker's capital or credit resources. The period between the beginnings of production and its reward might be reduced to six months if corn and hogs were produced in sufficient quantity the first year to give adequate support.[96] This could be done, however, only if the farm-maker arrived at his new homestead very early in the spring, which was obviously difficult in partially or entirely unsettled country lacking adequate roads. In such case, prairie-breaking almost certainly had to be contracted out or, if not, the farm-maker had to content himself with a very limited area planted in crops. Arrival in the late summer and early fall in time to build adequate housing and to collect wild hay to winter the animals involved the longer waiting period but was common and was considered the most desirable.[97] Though the period in which family maintenance had to be supplied from capital was thereby lengthened, arrival at such a time permitted the work of housing and fencing to be completed by spring so that the problem of breaking and seeding could be given uninterrupted attention.

With good fortune the farm-maker could raise within the first year or year and a half enough corn, potatoes, and pork to feed his family. Capital to maintain the family for at least a year was highly desirable. The sod corn was at best an uncertain crop, under any conditions yielding only moderately and frequently producing nothing but cattle fodder.[98] Moreover, it was considered by some to be desirable to permit the breaking to lie without a crop of any kind, since the sod decayed more thoroughly.[99] The wheat sown on land broken the previous summer as well as on land bearing the sod-corn crop provided the first important marketable crop the following spring.[100] Clearly, the advantages were all in favor of the longer waiting period. The sum of $100 was estimated as the cost of the first year's maintenance for a family.[101] That there actually did exist a considerable degree of dependence on the part of new farm-makers upon the purchase of food supplies is indicated by the fact that the earliest settlers in an area ordinarily considered the later arrivals as excellent markets for the produce.[102]

Little generalization is possible regarding travel costs. Emigrants from areas bordering on the farm-making frontier probably traveled with their stock and equipment, and to them the chief costs were time and subsistence. Emigrants from the east coast could travel by water to New Orleans, by canal, lake, and railroad, or entirely by rail, to the Mississippi. The railroad fare from Boston to St. Louis in 1855 was about $29 first class, $13 emigrant class.[103] The expenses of travel are not to be dismissed as trivial, as they were a large item to the eastern immigrant.[104]

Housing was still another necessity which called for some capital in the hands of the farm-maker. In forested areas, house, barns, and outbuildings did not present acute problems, since lumber was cheap and log houses could always be temporarily utilized if better could not be afforded. The board shanty or cottage was, however, more easily erected and more desirable than the log house and was built whenever possible. In prairie areas board houses were standard, though substitutes such as log cabins, sod houses, and even tents were used. The costs of housing varied widely of course. Log cabins were estimated to cost from $25 to $100.[105] The cost of a four-room cottage, which was perhaps the most common form, varied from $245 to $450.[106] The materials for a small two-room house could be obtained for as little as $150 on the Illinois prairies, while larger houses cost as much as $1,000. Barns and similar buildings appear in few estimates; they were scarce in any area where farms were still in the making and were among the last items into which capital was placed.

V

No doubt farm-making was frequently undertaken by individuals possessing capital of less than $1,000. In view of the facts presented, however, that sum must be considered as the minimum required for western prairie farm-making under the conditions as they existed in the 1850's. Such a sum permitted the breaking and fencing of 40 acres of land, but not of its purchase, and would supply the minimum required of implements, livestock, and subsistence.[107] This figure was particularly applicable to the prairie areas from Texas to Minnesota—those regions upon which were focused the migrations of the decade. Elsewhere, in forested areas and at the fringes of settlement, somewhat smaller capital might have sufficed. In any case the farm-maker's wealth could not fall much short of $1,000; to the degree that it did, the farm-maker was inevitably forced to undertake farm-making in some roundabout fashion, perhaps working part of his time for wages (which implies the possession of capital on the part of the employing farmer) and taking a longer period to develop his farm than the individual who did possess the suggested sum. He would, moreover, suffer correspondingly greater risks and discomforts, the added burden of borrowing capital at the high rates of the West, and probably had to accept smaller and less certain returns.[108]

It is altogether clear that the West of the 1850's cannot be regarded as offering great agricultural opportunities for the poor and poverty-stricken. Cheap land there was in abundance, to be sure, but it was raw land, not capable of furnishing an immediate livelihood. It was but the bare surface, requiring much labor and capital before its fertility could be elicited.[109] In contrast we cannot doubt that the possession of a moderate capital such as has been suggested opened the opportunity to develop in a very short time valuable and profitable farm properties.

The sources of the farm-maker's capital were either cash savings or the proceeds from the sale of property. The liquidation of property was, of course, the common method of eastern farmers of raising cash capital for westward removal; such property was purchased by others, and thus, ultimately, the capital taken West came from savings. Such savings were sums brought from abroad by foreign immigrants, or they were accumulations derived from wages, profits, or property incomes. It is doubtful if immigrants from abroad brought any large sums into the United States,[110] and it seems certain that far the larger part of the capital that was invested in western farm-making had its origin in the savings of agriculturists or of wage- and salary-earners in the East. Ultimately, it was thus the profitability of eastern agriculture[111] and the ability of a rapidly growing and profitable eastern industry to pay high wages that made possible the movement of capital to the West.

It is not to be implied that the necessary capitals were easily come by. Common wages for ordinary labor in the fifties did not reach $1 per day.[112] Agricultural labor, the class certainly most directly concerned with western opportunities, generally received about $150 per year, besides board and room.[113] From such wages it is unreasonable to expect that savings could greatly exceed $50 a year.[114] The accumulation of a fund adequate for western migration was thus no mean undertaking for the individual and was made doubly difficult, no doubt, by the unsatisfactory banking structure. Certainly the notion that a dissatisfied wage-earner could, within a year or two of his decision to go west to undertake the making of a farm, pack up and do so is completely fallacious. Equally certain is it that the West offered no desirable escape at a time of financial crisis or depression, when accumulated savings might be lost or difficult to liquidate, when credit was difficult or impossible to secure, and when the attractiveness of western agricultural profits had vanished along with the profits of industry and the security of an industrial wage.

Given a class of men who moved west with adequate capital, it was possible for others lacking such capital to emigrate also. Western development was not exclusively agricultural; it included the development of towns and cities as well as of trade, transportation, and local industries; in fact, all the varied parts of a complex economic structure.[115] Those who wished to emigrate but lacked capital for agricultural enterprise or who had no wish to undertake farming would go west, nevertheless, as laborers on the railroads, in lumber camps, and elsewhere, as tradesmen, and as skilled mechanics, finding economic opportunity in those towns and cities the growth of which paralleled that of agriculture. Wages were higher in the West than in the East, since the supply of labor, particularly of skilled mechanical labor, was smaller, relative to the opportunities for their employment. Cheap land exercised in this way an indirect influence, marked though immeasurable, upon the status and wage of the eastern laborer.

The relationship of the farm-making frontier to eastern economic society was, of course, not simple. The scarcity of capital in the East was at all times a serious deterrent to eastern industrial development, and any movement of capital westward must have accentuated this scarcity and thus must have had a detrimental effect upon the demand for labor and hence upon wages. On the other hand, the western farm-making frontier unquestionably favorably influenced the position of the eastern wage-earner. Even though eastern mechanics themselves participated in the migration only on a small scale,[116] they were nevertheless favorably affected if population were drawn west which might alternatively have been drawn into industry and thus increased the eastern labor supply. The movement of native population out of eastern agriculture in the 1850's was in fact not into surrounding industry but rather largely to the West.[117] To the extent, moreover, that foreign immigrants moved westward or replaced emigrating eastern agricultural population, the effect of foreign immigration upon the eastern wage-earner was less serious than might otherwise have been the case. The development of the West expanded the largest market open to the industrial East and thus stimulated the demand for the products of eastern wage labor. The fact that the West exported agricultural staples abroad was likewise a favorable factor, since the capital supply open to the East was thus increased.

In view of the costs of farm-making in the West, it is clearly an error to consider western farm-making opportunities as directly determinate of the status of eastern wage labor. To the degree that the eastern wage-earner actually entered western migration, this was possible only as a result of the high wages being paid in the East. The agricultural population moving westward did so also in large part because of the possibility of selling its eastern property and transferring the necessary capital to the West. Without a prosperous development of industry, the East could not have settled the West (the cotton South excepted) with anything approaching the rapidity actually achieved. The ability of that young eastern industrial economy to continue to develop rapidly in the face of the transfer of large sums of wealth to the new agricultural West testified to the fact that fundamentally the productivity and profitability of eastern industry made high wages possible. Rapid growth guaranteed that such wages would actually be paid, since industry was under the necessity of attracting sufficient numbers of new wage-earners for its expanding needs. Such new wage-earners came from eastern agricultural populations and foreign immigrants as well as from the natural increase of the wage-labor populations. No doubt the western frontier might have functioned to prevent serious exploitation had such exploitation been at all possible, and doubtless on occasion eastern industry faced competition from the West for labor, since the wages received by labor in some cases at least permitted the wage-earner to accumulate funds for emigration. Such influences were, however, certainly and distinctly secondary.

NOTES

1 Notably, on the one hand, Carter Goodrich and Sol Davison, "The Wage-Earner in the Westward Movement," *Political Science Quarterly*, 50:161–185 (1935); 51:61–116 (1936); and, on the other, Joseph Schafer, "Concerning the Frontier as Safety Valve," *ibid.*, 52:407–420 (1937). See also Joseph Schafer, "Some Facts Bearing on the Safety-Valve Theory," *Wisconsin Magazine of History*, 20:216–232 (1936); Murray Kane, "Some Considerations of the Safety-Valve Doctrine," *Mississippi Valley Historical Review*, 23:169–188 (1936); and "Some Considerations on the Frontier Concept of Frederick Jackson Turner," *ibid.*, 27:379–400 (1940); Rufus S. Tucker, "The Frontier as an Outlet for Surplus Labor," *Southern Economic Journal*, 7:158–186 (1940); Fred A. Shannon, "The Homestead Act and the Labor Surplus," *American Historical Review*, 41:637–651 (1936) *[reprinted in this volume, pp. 297–313]*. For a general bibliography on the safety-valve doctrine see E. E. Edwards, *References on the Significance of the Frontier in American History* (U.S. Department of Agriculture, Library, Bibliographical Contributions, no. 25, 1935).

2 Horatio Seymour in an address before the New York State Agricultural Society distinguished between the "old" self-sufficient agriculture and the "new" agriculture of the 1850's, focused upon profits and markets. *Transactions of the New York State Agricultural Society*, 12:26–30 (1852).

3 *New England Cultivator*, 1:201 (1852).

4 "No error is more common than to suppose that the farmer does not require Capital."—*Working Farmer*, 11:148 (1859). "To be something before-handed in worldly goods is essential before settling upon a farm; a little ready cash, besides paying for land and stock of cattle is absolutely indispensable if we should farm it ready and have farming pleasant and successful."—*Homestead*, 5:310 (1860). "A certain amount of capital is necessary and indispensable to success in farming."—*Rural New Yorker*, 5:261 (1854). "The want of capital is a serious obstacle in the way of most young men, which induces them to

go into other business in preference to farming. The farmer is under the necessity, about here, of possessing a few thousands of capital to be able to work his farm to advantage."—*New England Farmer,* 4:478 (1852); 9:148 (1857).

5 "A farmer with five or ten thousand dollars is much more likely to invest the whole of it in acres, than in the materials to work his acres with profitably. Unused acres do not pay the taxes on them, and yet they would think it the straight road to ruin to sell an acre."—*Connecticut Valley Farmer and Mechanic,* 2:98 (1854). "They almost invariably purchase or hire too much land, and thereby exhaust their resources at once, leaving nothing but their manual labor and a precarious credit to turn the use of this land to good account."—*American Agriculturist,* 15:127 (1856). "They forget that the ownership of this very unimproved land will be sure to prevent their ever having the means to improve it. They don't reflect that the interest upon the value of this unimproved land and the taxes upon it, would buy the land twice over at the end of ten years."—*Iowa Farmer and Horticulturist,* 1:3 (1853). "We will suppose a man to come in possession of a farm of fifty acres of land, with the necessary buildings for farming purposes and one thousand dollars in cash. Now do I not state a fact when I say that instead of keeping the $1000 as a capital to conduct the business of the farm with profit and success, seven men out of the nine would seek at once to buy more land, investing the $1000 in this way and perhaps even buying so much more land as to run in debt $1000. . . ."—*Albany Cultivator,* cited in *Colman's Rural World or Valley Farmer,* 2:254 (1850). Cf. *American Agriculturist,* 9:256 (1851); 10:92 (1852); 12:387 (1854); 15:65 (1856); *American Farmer,* n. s., 13:86–87 (1857); *Carolina Cultivator,* 2:205 (1856); *Colman's Rural World,* 2:109 (1850); 3:58 (1851); *Connecticut Valley Farmer and Mechanic,* 1:7 (1853); *Genesee Farmer,* 18:193 (1857); *Homestead,* 1:753, 786 (1855); 3:673 (1858); 4:138, 171 (1859); 5:51, 310 (1860); *Iowa Farmer and Horticulturist,* 4:3, 130–131 (1856); *Journal of Agriculture,* 2:361 (1852); *Northern Farmer,* 2:266 (1855); *Plough, Loom and Anvil,* 4:723 (1852); *Rural New Yorker,* 5:364 (1854); *Western Agriculturist,* 1:55 (1852); *Working Farmer,* 8:220 (1856); Massachusetts Board of Agriculture, *Annual Report of the Secretary,* 9:107 (1861); Ohio Board of Agriculture, *Annual Report,* 4:55 (1849); U.S. Patent Office, *Annual Report: Agriculture,* 1852, p. 134; James Caird, *Prairie Farming in America* (New York, 1859), 52–54; John Gregory, *Industrial Resources of Wisconsin* (Milwaukee, 1855), 61–62.

6 A detailed estimate of the equipment required on a farm of 100 improved acres in New York is presented in the *Illustrated Register of Rural Affairs* (1855), 323–325 (also in *Country Gentleman,* 5:213, cf. p. 278 [1855]). The items included had an estimated value of $2,009.50, of which $1,010 was allocated to stock, $75 for seed for the first year, $400 for animal food until the first harvest, $350 for hired help, and $424.50 for implements. The latter item did not include seed

drills, mower, reaper, thrasher, or horsepower, all of which could be rented. Costs of land and the support of the family during the first year are not included in the total.

Another estimate for a farm of similar size in the same state provided $870 for stock, $437 for implements, $63 for seed, $320 for labor, and $142 for maintenance of animals, a total of $1,832 (quoted with approval by Edwin F. Freedley, in *Practical Treatise on Business* [Philadelphia, 1852], 65–71, from a New York State Agricultural Society Premium Essay on Farm Management). For similar lists see *Genesee Farmer*, 19:213 (1858); *Rural Affairs and Cultivator Almanac* (1858), 131; *New England Farmer*, 5:568 (1853).

The question raised as to the use of $1,000 on a 200-acre Pennsylvania farm led to the conclusion that such a capital was inadequate and that at least $2,000 was required on a farm of that size. Pennsylvania Agricultural Society, *Annual Report*, 5:277 (1859). The editor of the *Soil of the South* in reply to the query, "Can I, with a capital of $1,000, purchase and work a small farm and make a comfortable living out of it . . . ," says: "From such an investment for farming purposes, a *support*, may be very certainly expected but not very large gains." He suggested a very modest farm of 30–50 acres, a horse, a cow, a sow, and crops such as roots, fruits, and vegetables. *Soil of the South*, 6:11 (1856).

7 Some of the phrases used in referring to those who were evidently considered desirable prospects included: "man of moderate means"— *Rural New Yorker*, 6:202 (1855); "man of slender means"—*ibid.*, 302; "a small capital"—*ibid.*, 14; "small means"—*ibid.*, 7:69–70 (1856); "A young man with steady, frugal, industrious habits, with $200 or $300 (more is not objectionable)"—*ibid.*, 9:198 (1858); "young men, and women, too, of limited means"—*ibid.*, 5:317 (1854); "The immigrants are principally men of small means"—*American Agriculturist*, 12:128 (1854); "limited means"—*Cultivator*, n. s., 8:355 (1851); "The good, honest, upright settlers . . . who with their industry and their capital will make the natural prairie look like an old farm in one year's time"—*Rural New Yorker*, 5:286 (1854); "those who have only a small or moderate capital"—*Genesee Farmer*, 16:27 (1855); "A man with small means"—Fred Gerhard, *Illinois as It Is* (Chicago, 1857), 289–290, 445. A writer who states that "the west is the refuge of the poor and those of very limited means" carried on his discussion in terms of $1,000 and more as the capital required. *Ohio Cultivator*, 8:258–259 (1852).

8 "For a man to take a family there with barely money enough to defray expenses of the journey, it is worse than foolishness; better work here for $120 a year or even $100."—*New Hampshire Journal of Agriculture*, December 1, 1860. The writer was referring to Minnesota and considered $1,000 as a minimum capital for a man with a family. "You cannot build a house, fence and break your 160 acres, and cultivate it all with $2,000, and I advise you not to attempt it. But despite all I have written you can build a small house, fence and break 40 acres to

begin with and live comfortable and make a little money perhaps."—
Rural Register, 2:356 (1860). "It is questionable policy for a man who
has reached middle life to cut himself loose from old ties and go to new
places in search of fortune. But to the young man of robust constitution and some capital, the younger States undoubtedly afford more
abundant opportunities for the profitable use of his energy and capital,
than the older states, and to the man of capital, they offer inducements
that are exceedingly attractive."—Freedley, *Practical Treatise on Business*, 257.

The secretary of the New England Emigrant Aid Company wrote:
"As already suggested the Company *advises no one, entirely destitute
of means, to go out, at this early period;* individuals who can command
the requisite funds, (which indeed are but small,) to sustain them the
first year, in other words until a crop is raised, or employment is sure,
can go in perfect safety, and unquestionably *should* better their condition by going; others *may* find sufficient work to supply means, but it
is premature for a very large number of such to go although thus far
the supply of laborers has not kept pace with the demand; . . ."—
Thomas H. Webb, *Information for Kansas Immigrants* (Boston, 1855),
16.

Cf. J. Richard Beste, *The Wabash or Adventures of an English Gentleman's Family in the Interior of America* (2 vols., London, 1856),
1:281–283; vol. 2, chap. xi; Horace Greeley, *An Overland Journey
from New York to San Francisco in the Summer of 1859* (New York
and San Francisco, 1860), 67–68; Nathan Parker, *Missouri Handbook* (St. Louis, 1865), 44; *North-Western Review*, 1(6):2 (1857);
Wisconsin and Iowa Farmer, 7:10–11 (1855); 8:54 (1856).

9   "Inasmuch as every immigrant comes provided with the means for entering land and defraying expenses till he can make a crop, money has
been in freer circulation here than in any other part of the country."—
Nathan Parker, *Iowa as It Is in 1855* (Chicago, 1855), 57. "From one
town in New Hampshire, two hundred Mechanics have gone West
this Spring, carrying with them at least $100,000."—*Western Farm
Journal*, 2:221 (1857). "Every emigrant must take some three hundred dollars with him and thus the State is drained not only of muscle
but money."—*Maine Farmer*, February 12, 1852. Another writer in
similar vein states that the three hundred thousand men who, it was
estimated, would emigrate in 1857 would take $20,000,000 with them.
Western Farm Journal, 2:197 (1857). "The exodus from New England in population and wealth will be equivalent to the removal of the
whole city of Boston, men, women and children."—*Working Farmer*,
9:142 (1858), citing the *Chemung County Republican;* cf. *Ohio
Farmer*, 8:409 (1859).

In an address on the state of New Hampshire farming, the comment
is made: "Thousands of our young and most energetic men, whom we
were least able to spare, have left our borders. Nor have these gone
empty handed. It were vain to attempt an estimate of the value of the
intelligence and industry in this manner lost to us; but consider for a

moment, the pecuniary capital thus abstracted. Many have been persons of wealth. Nearly all have had something. This although of uncertain amount, has left us and gone to swell the inventories of other states."—*New Hampshire Journal of Agriculture,* November 10, 1859.

10 A Wisconsin correspondent of the *Rural New Yorker* wrote in reply to a query regarding the attractiveness of the terms of renting farms in the West: "Although he applies his inquiries only to Illinois and Iowa, they are applied by others to Wisconsin. The renting of farms is much more common in the Southern part of the State than in either of the others named. The customary terms are as follows: The land alone draws one-third, the renter furnishing his own team, tools, house, etc. Where the owner finds team, tools, house-rent, fire-wood, etc., and half the seed, he receives one-half in the half-bushel. This gives the man who has no capital as good a chance as he can ask. . . . Surely such a prospect offers strong inducements to a poor man; for, if he is industrious and economical, in a short time he can purchase a farm of his own."—*Rural New Yorker,* 6:230 (1855). Cf. Caird, *Prairie Farming in America,* 50 and 93; Gerhard, *Illinois as It Is,* 404; *New England Farmer,* 12:258 (1852); *Working Farmer,* 2:270 (1850); *Farmer and Mechanic,* n. s., 5:46 (1850). Tenancy in the West was by no means uncommon. Cf. Paul Wallace Gates, "Large-Scale Farming in Illinois," *Agricultural History,* 6:20–21 (1932), and the descriptions of the methods of large landowners such as Jacob Strawn in Indiana and Illinois (*Genesee Farmer,* 20:173–174 and 205 [1859]; *Illinois Farmer,* 3:213 [1858]; 5:117 [1860]; *Farmer and Mechanic,* n. s., 5:46 [1851]; *Pennsylvania Farm Journal,* 5:292 [1855]).

Farming on shares did not entirely eliminate the need for capital, as the citation given above indicates. Funds were required for the purchase of family provisions until the first crops were harvested and in many cases for the purchase of seed, implements, and animals. Credit for such items was frequently available, but interest rates were high. For a pessimistic description of tenancy see *Ohio Cultivator,* 13:164–165 (1857).

11 "Many of our citizens have wild lands that they will lease for improvements. A man with a family may go on such land, clear and fence it, and have the use of it for five years, for the labor of clearing and fencing it, and during that time make money enough to buy a farm of his own."—*Western Agriculturist,* 1:121 (1851). See also Caird, *Prairie Farming in America,* 93; Gerhard, *Illinois as It Is,* 404; Parker, *Iowa as It Is in 1855,* 67; *Country Gentleman,* 11:33 (1858).

12 State-owned school lands were leased to the highest bidders in Illinois, Indiana, Minnesota, and Texas. Cf. G. W. Knight, "History and Management of Land Grants for Education in the Northwest Territory," *American Historical Association Papers,* 1(3):44–49, 64, 80–81 (1895).

13 "If they have not the required capital to take a farm at once, three or four years will probably place him in funds to commence his career as a proprietor of the soil."—George T. Borrett, *Out West: A Series*

of Letters from Canada and the United States (London, 1866), 129. "Very few of the original settlers brought any property with them; consequently, it has been very general for a man disposed to locate himself to begin by working out for a season, to enable him to provision himself for the first year and buy a team; these are by far the most successful."—*Plough, Loom and Anvil,* 4:687–688 (1852). "The laboring man in Ohio can, with suitable economy in one or two years, save enough for a farm to support himself and family, during life and have a home of his own."—*Western Agriculturist,* 1:121 (1852). "Many a poor Eastern boy, who has gone West with but a small balance of funds in his pocket, has hired out to work the first year on the farm. The proceeds of this enables him to work a farm on shares the second and third years, and by the end of the fourth year would enable him to purchase a farm of his own."—"Commencing on the Prairies," *Rural American,* 1:130 (1856). It was pointed out that the immigrant who stops in a city as a day laborer will always be that, but "he who hastens to the country and hires out upon a farm will in a few years be able to purchase and stock a farm in the west, with skill to work it profitably. . . ."—*Colman's Rural World or Valley Farmer,* 2:274–275 (1850). Cf. *Rural New Yorker,* 6:126 (1855); *Farmer's Journal,* 3:204 (Raleigh, 1854); James S. Ritchie, *Wisconsin and Its Resources* (Philadelphia, 1857), 168; Ernest Seyd, *California and Its Resources* (London, 1858), 146 and 156 ff.; Sidney Smith, *The Settler's New Home* (London, 1850), 43–44. Jacob Strawn commonly employed two to three hundred men in cultivating his farms in Indiana and Illinois. *Colman's Rural World or Valley Farmer,* 11:145 (1859).

14 "I have said that Kanzas was not suited to the poor man; I only intended to refer to those who design to till the ground. But to the poor mechanic it offers great inducements. To all carpenters especially and to stone and brick masons it will give constant employment and high wages. The rudest beginner receives $1.50 per day; good workmen, as journeymen receive in regular employment from $2.00 to $3.00 per day. Their expenses are light, the cost of living being low" (quoted in Webb, *Information for Kansas Immigrants,* 19; also in C. W. Dana, *The Great West* [Boston, 1858], 215; and *Northern Farmer,* 3:168 [1856]). Cf. C. C. Andrews, *Minnesota and Dacotah* (Washington, 1857), 130–131; Samuel Freeman, *The Emigrant's Hand Book and Guide to Wisconsin* (Milwaukee, 1851), 95; Gerhard, *Illinois as It Is,* 446; Parker, *Iowa as It Is in 1855,* 190; Parker, *Iowa Handbook for 1856* (Boston and New York, 1856), 154–155; John Regan, *The Emigrant's Guide to the Western States of America* (Edinburgh, 1852), 351–352.

15 Gerhard, *Illinois as It Is,* 450; *New Hampshire Journal of Agriculture,* December 1, 1860.

16 Parker, *Iowa Handbook for 1856,* 158–160.

17 *American Agriculturist,* 16:252 (1857).

18 *Illinois as It Is,* 292–307 and 409–412.

19 J. D. B. DeBow, *DeBow's Commercial Review*, 10:640–641 (1851).

20 *Journey through Texas* (New York, 1860), 460.

21 "Otherwise he must go to the extreme frontier and shift his stock from place to place, as settlements crowd upon him. He has to depend for protection against the Indians upon his rifle and revolver, and leads a life of constant danger and hardship, without neighbors, and debarred the necessaries and comforts enjoyed by the negro on one of our poorest Southern plantations."—Correspondent of *New York Evening Post*, cited in *New England Farmer*, 12:554 (1860). Cf. Olmsted, *Journey through Texas*, 205.

22 "Our opinion is, that most of those accustomed to regular mechanical employment only, with a capital of only about one thousand dollars, would find it difficult to buy a farm with buildings, stock it with animals, furnish wagons, carts, and implements generally, and food until a return is made in crops. We would never advise such persons to buy *new* lands but whether they settle west or east, to procure a place even if quite small already under cultivation and with at least some buildings.

"It will be some time before the *most skillful* will receive an amount equal to *two* dollars a day; and we would therefore advise all mechanics, not already well versed in the practical operations of farming, to endeavor to retain for themselves, at some wages, mechanical employment during the most leisure portion of the year—to begin in a small way, to avoid running into debt, and to *feel their way* before engaging in any considerable expenditures."—*Country Gentleman*, 5:8 (1855).

23 James Stirling, *Letters from the Slave States* (London, 1857), 19–20.

24 Arthur Cunynghame, *A Glimpse at the Great Western Republic* (London, 1851), 103–106.

25 *Working Farmer*, 2:270 (1850).

26 *The Emigrant's Guide*, 353. "Thus for $550 or about £110 sterling, may a man make a promising beginning, and not for less. Those who cannot command this small capital must not think of commencing to operate with land, except indeed it be as renters, in which case a man who has been accustomed to farming may make a beginning on almost nothing; and even with the aforesaid capital, a man must have some ingenuity to carry him through the difficulties of a beginning. I have repeatedly seen in guide books the sum of £100 set down as sufficient to establish a man on 80 acres either in Illinois, Iowa or Wisconsin. This might do were the settler to begin with oxen and fence but a few acres at first. Mr. Newhall, who is considered no mean authority, says, indeed, that the cost of a house, implements, stock and eighty acres of land may be set down at £80! An estimate in which I am unable to concur because I would rather not incur the responsibility of misleading any one."—*Ibid.*, 353–354. The reference to Newhall is to J. B. Newhall, *The British Emigrant's Handbook and Guide to the Western States of America* (London, 1844), 61–63. Regan also points out that the frequently cited estimate of Solon Robinson of $200

for prairie farm-making assumes that the farm-maker rents a farm for two or more years and that he possesses in addition to his $200 capital the necessary livestock, implements, and food (*The Emigrant's Guide*, 360–365).

27 Caird, *Prairie Farming in America*, 91, 93. "I cannot, therefore, advise men who are unable to scrape more together than will merely pay their traveling expenses to go to Illinois. And far less can I advise them to go farther west. Suppose they could obtain land in Iowa or Minnesota, 400 miles farther away, at only half the price, the saving of 1s. 6d. an acre in their deposit, would never compensate even the cost of travel for the additional distance, while every article which they require to purchase must bear an enhanced price from the same cause" (p. 93).

28 All the estimates cited refer to the period 1850–1860. Similar estimates are available for earlier dates: e.g., Anon., *Illinois in 1837: A Sketch* (1837), 14 and 70; Robert Baird, *View of the Valley of the Mississippi or the Emigrant's and Traveller's Guide to the West* (Philadelphia, 1834), 231–232; W. J. A. Bradford, *Notes on the Northwest* (New York, 1846), 146–147; S. H. Collins, *The Emigrant's Guide to the United States of America* (Hull, 1829), 101; Henry W. Ellsworth, *Valley of the Upper Wabash* (New York, 1838), 49–60 and 65–68; James Hall, *Statistics of the West at the Close of the Year 1836* (Cincinnati, 1836), 203–204; A. D. Jones, *Illinois and the West* (Boston, 1838), 140–164; Patrick Shirreff, *A Tour through North America* (Edinburgh, 1835). See also Theodore C. Blegen, "Ole Rynning's True Account of America," *Minnesota History Bulletin*, 1:248–255 and 260–262 (1917–1918); William Cobbett, *The Emigrant's Guide in Ten Letters* (London, 1830), 46; Joseph Pickering, *Inquiries of an Emigrant* (London, 1832).

29 The exceptions were the state-owned lands of Texas and Maine, which were never ceded to the federal government. These lands were on the market in the 1850's.

30 During the calendar years 1850–1859, 207,000,000 acres of federal lands were alienated. Of this total, 50,000,000 acres were sold; 52,-000,000 acres were granted to individuals; 76,000,000 acres were granted to states; and 28,000,000 acres were granted to corporations. Of the lands sold from 1854 to 1860, 22,000,000 acres went at graduated prices.

Since much attention will be paid in this study to farm-making conditions in Iowa, it should be pointed out that Iowa was by far the most popular state in the Union for land purchases. During the decade more than 12,000,000 acres were sold in that state, all at or above the $1.25 minimum, though much of this was purchased with land warrants. This acreage was about 34 per cent of the state's area. Next largest sales were made in Missouri, where 7,500,000 acres were sold, and in Alabama, where 4,750,000 acres were transferred. In both these states the large sales were stimulated by the low prices under the Graduation Act. More than half the 2,500,000 acres sold in Mississippi were sold at these lowered prices. Almost 15 per cent of the area of Arkansas was sold, two-thirds of it at graduated prices. Sales were relatively small in Louisiana and Florida. Among the northern states, aside from Iowa, more than 2,000,000 acres were sold in Michigan and only slightly smaller quantities in Illinois and Minnesota. Data compiled from United States Commissioner of the Land Office, *Annual Reports*, 1850–1860.

31 Under the Military Bounty Land Grants of 1847, 1850, 1852, and 1855, 530,479 warrants were issued, involving 57,781,570 acres of land. Up to September 30, 1860, a total of 49,584,990 acres had been located. United States Commissioner of the Land Office, *Annual Report*, 1860, p. 47.

32 The warrants "could be secured from brokerage houses in New York and Washington in unlimited quantities," at prices of from 50 cents to $1.15 per acre, the larger acreages bringing the lower prices. *New York Tribune*, February 5, 1852. Cf. *ibid.*, March 11, 1852. Prices of warrants were frequently quoted in the *New York Journal of Commerce*. See also *Hunt's Merchants' Magazine*, 39:65 (1858); 42:427 (1860); *Rural New Yorker*, 3:159 (1852); 4:51 (1853); *Ohio Cultivator*, 8:175 (1852); *North-western Review*, 1(3):13 (1857); *Michigan Farmer*, 12:96 (1854); *Rural Register*, 2:176 (1860).

33 Parker, *Iowa as It Is in 1855*, 68. "Strangers coming to Wisconsin are not to be deceived by supposing that they can get land in any part they please at government price."—Gregory, *Industrial Resources of Wisconsin*, 310. "Let me correct an erroneous idea, which many of our Eastern friends entertain in regard to the prices of land here at the West. Let no one think that good land can be procured for a trifling sum. All the unimproved lands in the older counties have been taken up by speculators who demand a higher price for them in proportion to their value, than that of improved farms."—*Northern Farmer*, 3:171 (1856). (The reference is to Wisconsin.) Cf. *Rural New Yorker*, 5:366 (1854); *New England Farmer*, 7:140 (1855); Robert Baird, *Impressions and Experiences of the West Indies and North America* (Philadelphia, 1850), 336.

34 The emigrant "must be especially careful not to tempt himself too far from the market, by a cheap bargain, and never to forget that in an inverse ratio from what it is at home, here the first price of the land is by no means the weightiest part of the investment."—Cunynghame, *Glimpse at the Great Western Republic*, 102. Cf. Parker, *Iowa Handbook for 1856*, 102; *Northwestern Farmer*, 2:127 (1858); *Rural New Yorker*, 7:118 (1856); *Genesee Farmer*, 17:116 (1856).

35 The lands of the Illinois Central came on the market in 1854, and, by 1860, 1,279,382 acres had been sold at an average price of $11.50 per acre on terms of up to six years' credit. Paul Wallace Gates, *The Illinois Central Railroad and Its Colonization Work* (Cambridge, Mass., 1934), 159 and 260–262. The Hannibal & St. Joseph Rail Road placed some of its lands on the market in 1858, priced at from $5.00 to $20.00 per acre, with nine years' credit. Hannibal & St. Joseph

Rail Road, *Farms and Homes in Northern Missouri* (1857), 17. Lands of the Illinois and Michigan Canal were sold in small quantities during the decade at prices of from $4.50 to $12.50 per acre. Gates, *Illinois Central Railroad,* 156; *Hunt's Merchants' Magazine,* 28:277–279 (1853); *Rural New Yorker,* 4:170 (1853). Lands of the Des Moines Navigation Company were also offered. *Iowa Farmer,* 4:187 (1856).

36 The federal land office asserted that speculative purchasing was relatively unimportant. The 1857 *Annual Report* estimated that three-quarters of the land located and sold was taken for actual settlement. Commissioner of the Land Office, *Annual Report,* 1857, p. 80. The 1859 *Report* said, "We have the fact that our whole operations, sale and locations, have generally been for actual settlement and cultivation, and not for speculation."—*Ibid.,* 1859, p. 171. President Buchanan in his *Annual Message* in 1857 expressed a contrary opinion. "Speculation has of late years prevailed to a great extent in the public lands. The consequence has been that large portions of them have become the property of individuals and companies, and thus the price is greatly enhanced to those who desire to purchase for actual settlement."—*Annual Message of the President* (35 Cong., 1 sess.), 31.

The land-office claim no doubt possessed some truth as applied to the sales of land at graduated prices, but with regard to other sales all the evidence available confirms President Buchanan's opinion. From the Des Moines Land Office came the report of "men entering land by wholesale, without ever going to see it, staking a quarter section here and another there, shrewdly guessing that genuine hard working men will come after and pick up the vacant lots and soon want *their* lots at $5 to $10 per acre."—*Country Gentleman,* 4:45 (1854). Similar conditions were reported from the Dubuque and Decorah offices. *Iowa Farmer,* 3:178 (1855). In southwestern Michigan there remained much unoccupied land, "mostly owned by Eastern speculators, and held at from $3 to $5 per acre."—*Farmer's Companion and Horticultural Gazette,* 3:184 (1854). An Illinois observer wrote that "there are such shoals of 'land sharks' (so-called here) or speculators that they absorb *all* the best claims as soon as the lands are offered for sale, that a large proportion of actual settlers have to buy their lands of dealers, at double and many times, more than double, the usual cost at government price."—*Genesee Farmer,* 17:116 (1856). The Janesville *Free Press* opposed the issuance of land warrants for military service on the ground that nine-tenths would be in the hands of speculators who got the best lands, increased prices, prevented men with small capitals from coming in, or placed them at the mercy of eastern capitalists (cited in *Colman's Rural World or Valley Farmer,* 5:177 [1853]). In Minnesota, speculators were said to have located a great many land warrants as well as having purchased much of the best land—"a great curse to a new country" and a disadvantage to the actual settler (Andrews, *Minnesota and Dacotah,* 129–130). Emigrants were reported returning from Kansas in 1856 because "all the locations on which there is timber or water are in the hands of claimants or speculators."—*Wisconsin and Iowa Farmer*, 7:186 (1856). Speculation was not absent in the South. *Southern Cultivator*, 11:276 (1853). Such speculation could not fail to make itself felt in the East. "In 1857, it is probable that upwards of eight hundred millions of dollars were invested in idle Western lands, and lots in proposed cities, which had been paid for to the extent of one-fourth, the remainder continually being paid in installments."—D. W. Mitchell, *Ten Years in the United States* (London, 1862), 328. "In all parts of the East, and here in New York as well as elsewhere there prevails a great inclination to emigrate westward. There is also a continuous stream of money, issuing from those who remain behind, that goes westward to be invested in new lands. The country banks here, which usually hold large deposits of money belonging to the rich agricultural community around, all complain of their deposits being completely drawn away." —*Ohio Valley Farmer*, 2:74 (1857). "We are told that a certain bank, in a certain dairy county in the centre of this State had on deposit, in the spring of 1856, the sum of $455,000, money of the farmers. Week before last its deposit account footed up only some $25,000, and the farmers of that county were borrowing money for their spring's operations. The deposits in the bank had been drawn down for investment in the far West. A portion went directly into lands to be held for a rise. The residue and the larger part was transmitted to be loaned at three, four, five, and six percent a month, on real estate security and legal assurance of unlimited usury laws. We have also been informed that the surplus moneys of very many counties of this State have gone the same way as the deposited earnings of the dairy district mentioned."—*Albany Evening Journal*, cited in *Western Farm Journal*, 1:148 (1856); *Maine Farmer*, May 28, 1857.

It is of interest to note that speculation was not confined to the West. There was during the fifties, for example, much speculation in lands around New York City. Cincinnati mechanics were reported as having invested in lots in villages around that city. *American Agriculturist*, 12:322 (1854). Cf. *American Agriculturist*, 12:128 (1854); 10:63 (1856); *Iowa Farmer*, 5:98 (1857); *Maine Farmer*, April 30, 1857; *Northwestern Farmer*, 4:277 (1859); *Ohio Cultivator*, 8:334 (1852); *Prairie Farmer*, 14:217 (1854); *Rural New Yorker*, 7:242 and 358 (1856); *Wisconsin Farmer*, 8:487 (1856); Gates, *Illinois Central Railroad*, chap. vi; Benjamin Horace Hibbard, *A History of the Public Land Policies* (New York, 1924), 220–225; Addison E. Sheldon, *Land System and Land Policies in Nebraska* (*Publications of the Nebraska State Historical Society*, vol. 22, Lincoln, 1936), 39–46.

37 The census reported 28,336,345 acres assessed for tax purposes of which 4,170,496 acres were improved and 4,784,886 acres were attached to farms but unimproved. *Census Returns of the Different Counties of the State of Iowa for the Year 1862*, 1863, pp. 61–64. With regard to these figures, W. D. Wilson (*Description of Iowa and*

Its Resources [Des Moines, 1865], 82) says: "Of the taxable lands, it is very probable that not less than 15,000,000 acres are owned by non-residents." And further: "Yet the most of them can be obtained for from $2.50 to $5.00 per acre, even in the older settled counties, and from five to ten miles from railroads in, or soon to be in operation." Paul Wallace Gates estimated that 9,000,000 acres in Illinois were in the hands of speculators in 1856 ("The Disposal of the Public Domain in Illinois, 1848–1856," *Journal of Economic and Business History*, 3:321 [1931]).

38   Speaking of farms being established in the West, one observer commented: "Of the whole number thus commenced, the owners of about *one-half* remain on these new places as permanent residents. The other half consists of a normal class, that is wandering, but never satisfied in any one place. They either enter Government land, or buy from some railroad or other company at a moderate price, commence farming operations by putting up a shanty and a few rods of fence, and breaking from ten to forty acres of land. They raise a sod crop of corn and sometimes a wheat crop and then a fit of restlessness takes possession of them, and thinking they are making money when they are able to get $5 per acre more for their land than what they gave for it, they sell out, and make a new purchase either in the same State or farther West."—*American Agriculturist*, 16:277 (1857). Another wrote: "They are a class by themselves. They never have a home for ten years in a place. They 'settle' as they call it—on the outskirts of civilization—remain a few years in clearing up and 'bringing to' a patch of land. Sometimes they own it and sometimes not. As soon as society begins to thicken inconveniently around them, they get discontented, pull up stakes, and hie off to another wild, unsettled region. A better class comes in, buys out their investments for a trifle and settle themselves permanently on their squattings."—*Ibid.*, 15:224 (1856). Cf. *American Farmer's Magazine*, 8:212 (1858); *Indiana Farmer*, 4:146 (1854–1855); *Plough, Loom and Anvil*, 6:594 (1854); *Prairie Farmer*, 12:378 (1852); *Rural New Yorker*, 7:122 (1856); New York State Agricultural Society, *Annual Report*, 21:682–683 (1852); Andrews, *Minnesota and Dacotah*, 115; Smith, *The Settler's New Home*, 101.

39   "For the last ten years there has been a vast migration to Illinois, Iowa, Minnesota and Nebraska. This has uniformly been the case with all the states where lands come to $30 or $50 per acre and is caused simply by the fact that it then becomes a speculation for farmers to sell out and commence new farms at government prices."—New York *Journal of Commerce*, February 11, 1857, quoting the *Cincinnati Gazette*. The prominence of Ohioans among westward migrants was explained thus: "Here soil is too rich and dear to retain a dense population. A poor man can earn enough from a three years' lease on his neighbor's farm to move West, buy a quarter or half section and set up free-holder for himself. A farmer with a few acres of land can sell it to his richer neighbor, go West, and purchase a large farm."

"The temptation is too powerful to be resisted. Thus the large farms are becoming larger and the small free holds are becoming absorbed in them."—*Iowa Farmer*, 2:87–88 (1854). A similar analysis is applied to emigration from Illinois: "Many of the land owners of this region are the worthy pioneers who settled it when it belonged to the United States, and have since purchased it. As soon as the Nebraska bill passed many of them thought earnestly of emigrating thither. They saw that land was rising so much above $1.25 per acre, that with their limited means they should not be able to give each of their children 160 acres of prairie and 40 of timber as they always hoped to do and had for their older children. Now that this unprecedented drought has come upon us, many of them are determined to emigrate soon. They are determined to sell their farms at some price."—*Prairie Farmer*, 14:346 (1854).

40 "For the benefit of those preferring improved lands, I would say that the Oregon and California fevers are continually seizing our oldest pioneer settlers and often others, and they consider it quite a treat to be 'bought out.' These improved lands sell for $8 to $15, and sometimes $20 per acre; are not much injured by culture, and are very desirable spots for the exact farmer, who can bear to have his farm bounded by other cultivated lands instead of the open wilds; in other words, for those who can bear the restraints of civilization." The reference is to Illinois. *Prairie Farmer*, 12:378 (1852). Cf. *Rural New Yorker*, 7:58, 122 (1856); *Farmer's Companion and Horticultural Gazette*, 3:184 (1853); *Iowa Farmer*, 1:216 (1853).

41 In western Missouri: "Choice tracts of wild land are now selling for from $3 to $5 per acre. Improved lands from $4 to $8. The improvements consist of log houses, and stables, and more or less land plowed and fenced, with now and then a peach orchard."—*North-western Review*, 1(7):35 (1857), cited in *Rural New Yorker*, 8:382 (1857). In Illinois "a fair average for unimproved farms would be from three to eight dollars per acre, for improved farms from five to twenty-five dollars, depending upon the location with reference to a village and the value of the improvements upon them."—G. W. Hawes, *Illinois State Gazetteer and Business Directory, 1858–1859*, (Chicago, 1858), xxxiii. Prices are very commonly quoted. See *Illinois Farmer*, 2:184–185 (1857); *New England Farmer*, 8:260–261 (1856); *Northern Farmer*, 3:209 (1856); *Ohio Cultivator*, 11:170 (1855); *Prairie Farmer*, 14:217, 241, 346 (1854); *Rural New Yorker*, 5:294 (1854); Gerhard, *Illinois as It Is*, 401–405.

42 "This, usually, is the better way for emigrants from old farms because they thus procure farms where improvements are begun and some land is already prepared for crops, and it has a habitable tenement for their families, until they have time to prepare a better one. We believe the very best bargains, and many of the best locations for permanent homes are made in buying out these pioneers."—*American Agriculturist*, 15:224 (1856). "There is here a great deal of government land not taken up in the Northwestern counties [the reference

is to Iowa], but there are thousands of farms for sale, now in first or second hands, from $2 to $10 an acre, that are cheaper in the end than to purchase government lands at $1.25. We mean by this, that as a man has but one lease of life, if he can command a few hundred dollars, he had better pay $5 an acre for his farm where it is already settled than $1.25 for that where it is a desolate wilderness."—*Northern Farmer*, 3:395 (1856). "You can buy an improved farm cheaper than you can buy wild land and improve it."—*Iowa Farmer*, 1:192–193 (1853). Cf. William and Robert Chambers, *The Emigrant's Manual* (Edinburgh, 1851), 119–121; Freeman, *The Emigrant's Handbook*, 95; Regan, *The Emigrant's Guide*, 353 and 356; Smith, *The Settler's New Home*, 81, 85, 105.

There were also arguments against the purchase of "second-hand" land. "The emigrant who has only a small capital to start with, will naturally seek the cheapest method of getting a home, and among the many farms offered for sale, and the rich prairies inviting the farmer to labor, he will be in doubt as to what he should buy. A careful comparison of the cost of making the usual improvements on a western farm, with the cost of wild prairie, convinces us that the latter is decidedly the cheapest. A man who has not calculated the difference will pay $15 an acre for an improved farm—as it is called—when he could get the same quality of unimproved land close to hand for $5 an acre. A house ready to go into with his family and fields already enclosed are tempting baits to the weary emigrants, but a simple calculation will convince him that the improvements have cost him twice as much as they are worth. Often in their purchase the emigrant must take from one to two hundred acres of unimproved land with the farm, and for which he pays the full price of improved lands. . . ." —*North-western Review*, 1(6):4–5 (1857). Cf. *Illinois Farmer*, 1:26 (1856); *New England Farmer*, 7:554 (1855); Gregory, *Industrial Resources of Wisconsin*, 310.

43 *Cultivator*, n. s., 9:67 (1852); *Ohio Cultivator*, 9:338–339 (1853); Thomas Mooney, *Nine Years in America* (Dublin, 1850), 20–21.

44 Knight, "History and Management of Land Grants," 80–81.

45 Maine: Maine State Land Office, *Circular from the Land Office Descriptive of the Public Lands of Maine*, 1858, p. 4; Maine Land Agent, *Annual Report*, 1853, pp. 6–7; Maine, *Governor's Annual Message*, 1860, pp. 10–11; Maine Board of Agriculture, *Annual Report*, 4:180 (1859); *Maine Farmer*, September 26, 1850; April 21, 1853; August 11, 1853; August 3, 1854; March 5, 1859; August 25, 1859; October 5, 1859.

Arkansas: Arkansas, *Report of the Swamp Land Secretary Made to the Governor for 1859–1860*, 1860; *Scientific American*, 3:389 (1860).

46 *American Agriculturist*, 18:271 and 315 (1859); James M. Lewis, Arkansas Commissioner of Immigration and State Land: *Natural Resources of the State of Arkansas*, 1869.

47 Alden S. Lang, *Financial History of the Public Lands of Texas* (*Baylor*

University Bulletin, vol. 35, 1932), 46–48; Reuben McKitrick, *The Public Land System of Texas* (*University of Wisconsin Bulletin, Economics and Political Science Series*, vol. 9, 1918), 49–52.

48 E. W. Farnham, *Life In Prairie Land* (New York, 1846), 328–329; Mooney, *Nine Years in America*, 19; Nathan Parker, *Kansas and Nebraska Handbook* (Boston, 1857), 66–68; Jacob Ferris, *The States and Territories of the Great West* (New York, 1856), 319; *Maine Farmer*, May 26, 1853; B. O. Shambaugh, "Frontier Land Clubs or Claim Associations," *American Historical Association Reports*, 1901, 1:69–84; C. J. Ritchey, "Claim Associations and Pioneer Democracy in Early Minnesota," *Minnesota History*, 9:89–95 (1928).

49 Horace Greeley wrote: "I am confident there is not at this hour any kind of a house or other sign of improvement on one-fourth of the quarter-sections throughout Kansas which have been secured by pre-emption. The squatter who thus establishes a 'claim' sells it out, so soon as practicable, to some speculator, who follows in his wake, getting from $50 to $300 for that which the future bona-fide settler will be required to pay $250 to $1,500 for. . . . To see a man squatted on a quarter-section in a cabin which would make a fair hog-pen, but is unfit for a human habitation, and there living from hand to mouth by a little of this and a little of that, with hardly an acre of prairie broken (sometimes without a fence up), with no garden, no fruit-trees, 'no nothing'—waiting for some one to come along and buy out his Claim and let him move on to repeat the operation somewhere else—this is enough to give a cheerful man the horrors."—*An Overland Journey from New York to San Francisco*, 65, 70.

50 The farm-making frontiers of the 1850's were not confined to the frontier of settlement but were rather very broad. They included parts of Maine, Georgia, Florida, New York, Pennsylvania, western Virginia, besides the major belt: Michigan west into Minnesota, Indiana into Nebraska, Missouri, and Kansas, Alabama into western Texas.

51 *Prairie Farming in America*, 92.

52 The comment of the Maine State Land Office directed at western lands that "cheapness ends with the price of land" was universally applicable (*Circular from the Land Office Descriptive of the Public Lands of Maine*, 13).

53 Lands in Aroostook County, Maine, which could be purchased for 50 cents per acre required $15 per acre for clearing. *Maine Farmer*, August 3, 1854; Maine Board of Agriculture, *Annual Report*, 5:205 (1860); New York State Agricultural Society, *Annual Report*, 11:681 (1851). The cost of clearing Michigan woodlands was estimated at $10 per acre (E. H. Thomson, *Emigrant's Guide to the State of Michigan* [1849], 11), and the cost of clearing and fencing Minnesota timbered lands was given as from $18 to $30 per acre. Nathan Parker, *Minnesota Handbook for 1856–57* (Boston, 1857), 131; cf. Parker, *Missouri Handbook*, 131; *Transactions of the Wisconsin State Agricultural Society*, 1:243–246 (1851).

54 *Michigan Farmer*, 8:275 (1850); 9:70–71 (1851); *Ohio Cultivator,*

15:36 and 119 (1859); *Southern Cultivator*, 11:209 (1854). In the South the "almost universal practice" was to girdle the trees and let them stand to rot in the moist climate four or five years. *American Agriculturist*, 19:32 (1860).

55 *Ohio Cultivator*, 15:2–3 (1859).

56 *Michigan Farmer*, 9:70–71 (1851); 8:265 and 374 (1850); 13:365 (1855); *New Jersey Farmer*, 3:216 (1857).

57 *Michigan Farmer*, 8:11 (1850); 12:231–232 (1854); *Northern Farmer*, 1:261 (1854); *Ohio Cultivator*, 15:54 (1859).

58 *Michigan Farmer*, 9:70–71 (1851); 8:275 (1850); 12:297 (1854); *Rural New Yorker*, 10:262 (1859); Josiah T. Marshall, *The Farmer's and Emigrant's Hand-Book* (Utica, N.Y., 1852), 18, 21.

59 *Michigan Farmer*, 9:71 (1851); 13:365–366 (1855); 8:374 (1850); *Southern Cultivator*, 11:209 (1854).

60 *Michigan Farmer*, 8:265 (1850).

61 *Northwestern Farmer and Horticultural Journal*, 2:216 (1857); *Cultivator*, n. s., 9:67 (1852); *Prairie Farmer*, 11:151 (1851).

62 *Illinois Farmer*, 5:150 (1860); *Plough, Loom and Anvil*, 6:519–520 (1854); Parker, *Iowa as It Is in 1855*, 72; Franklin Langworthy, *Scenery of the Plains, Mountains and Mines* (Ogdensburg, N.Y., 1855), 273.

63 "If there is anything that should be well done on a farm, it is this breaking up of virgin sod."—*Prairie Farmer*, n. s., 3:339 (1859). A poorly broken field might require to be entirely broken again and, in any case, would cause serious difficulties in working the soil. *Rural New Yorker*, 10:204 (1859).

64 This period is stated as from May 1 to June 30 in Illinois (*Rural New Yorker*, 3:358 [1852]; *Prairie Farmer*, n. s., 3:339 [1859], Gerhard, *Illinois as It Is*, 311); May 10 to July 10 in Wisconsin (*Wisconsin Cultivator*, 8:277–278 [1851]); May 15 to July 15 in Minnesota (*Northwestern Farmer and Horticultural Journal*, 5:352–353 [1860]); May 1 to July 15 in Kansas (Dana, *The Great West*, 214); May 1 to August 1 in Iowa (*Genesee Farmer*, 18:141 [1857]). Cf. Marshall, *Farmer's Hand-Book*, 399–402.

65 "In Kansas where we have much land to spare, the sod is generally turned under during the summer and allowed to decay till the next spring, and then when plowed over again, yields enormously."—*New England Farmer*, 12:250–251 (1860). Cf. *Prairie Farmer*, n. s., 2:312 (1858); *Cultivator*, n. s., 7:277–278 (1850); Dana, *The Great West*, 214.

66 *Illinois Farmer*, 2:151 (1857); *Prairie Farmer*, 14:361–362 (1854).

67 "It is a very common practice throughout the entire western prairie country to get the sod broken by contract at a given price per acre, which ranges from $1.50 to $2.50 according to contract, according to the character of the work and the local influences governing the value of labor."—*Cultivator*, n. s., 9:67 (1852). "Many thousands of acres are thus broken up."—*American Agriculturist*, 16:252 (1857). "The cost of breaking prairie is from two to three dollars an acre; it is prin-

cipally done by men who keep teams for the purpose and do their work by the job. A three horse team will break two acres per day, and a heavy ox team with a 36 inch plough will break three acres per day." —Gerhard, *Illinois as It Is*, 311. Cf. Ferris, *The Great West*, 210; Parker, *Kansas and Nebraska Handbook*, 36: Stirling, *Letters from the Slave States*, 18–19; *Genesee Farmer*, 17:84–85 (1856); *Northwestern Farmer*, 1:128 (1856); *Plough, Loom and Anvil*, 5:519–520 (1853).

68 Costs of breaking by contract are very frequently quoted—e.g., Illinois: $2.00 (*Ohio Cultivator*, 9:338–339 [1853]); $2.50 and board (*Genesee Farmer*, 17:84–85 [1856]); $2.00–$2.50 (*Northwestern Farmer*, 1:128 [1856]; $1.50–$2.50 (Gerhard, *Illinois as It Is*, 294–300 and 412); $2.50–$3.00 (*American Agriculturist*, 16:252 [1857]). Iowa: $3.00 (*Prairie Farmer*, 15:159 [1855]); $1.50–$2.50 (*Cultivator*, n. s., 9:67 [1852]); $2.25–$2.50 (Parker, *Iowa Handbook for 1855*, 67, 72). Kansas: $3.00 (*Maine Farmer*, September 2, 1858); $3.50–$5.00 (*New England Farmer*, 12:89 [1860]); $2.50–$4.00 (Parker, *Kansas and Nebraska Handbook*, 36); $3.00 (Dana, *The Great West*, 214). Minnesota: $8.00–$12.00 (Rodney C. Loehr, *Minnesota Farmer's Diaries* [St. Paul, 1939], 15); $4.50–$7.00 (Parker, *Minnesota Handbook*, 131). Missouri: $2.50–$3.00 (*Northwestern Review*, 1[7]:35 [1857]). Wisconsin: $1.75–$2.00 (*Cultivator*, n. s., 7:277–278 [1850]); $3.00 (*Transactions of the Wisconsin State Agricultural Society*, 1:243–246 [1851]).

69 "The first summer is usually spent in breaking, the fall in building, and the winter in getting out fence. . . . In subsequent years, the proceedings are much the same as in older countries, except that in many cases the fence is incomplete the second year." The reference is to Minnesota (*Plough, Loom and Anvil*, 4:687–688 [1852]). Cf. Parker, *Iowa as It Is in 1855*, 73 and 80.

70 *Ohio Cultivator*, 9:338–339 (1853); *Northern Farmer*, 1:290–291 (1854); *Plough, Loom and Anvil*, 6:519–520 (1854); *Prairie Farmer*, 15:344 (1855); *Working Farmer*, 8:35 (1856); Gerhard, *Illinois as It Is*, 293–307, 412.

71 "In order to farm successfully, even on the fertile prairies of the 'Great West' the first consideration, after all, is to be able to fence. . . ."— *Prairie Farmer*, 14:146 (1856). "Our fence is the heaviest matter we have to attend to, but one that cannot be neglected."—*Colman's Rural World and Valley Farmer*, 2:74 (1850). In Minnesota "the first winter is usually spent in getting out rails and fencing stuff to enclose the ground he purposes to cultivate the next season."—*American Agriculturist*, 12:128 (1854). Cf. *Cultivator*, n. s., 7:277–278 (1854); *Carolina Cultivator*, 1:163–164 (1856); *Farmer's Journal*, 3:204 (Raleigh, N.C., 1854); *Genesee Farmer*, 17:84–85 (1856); *Plough, Loom and Anvil*, 4:687–688 (1852); *Rural American*, 1:130 (1856); *Michigan Farmer*, 14:68–69 (1856); *U.S. Economist*, 2:24 (1853); *Tippecanoe Farmer*, 1:6 (1854–1855); Loehr, *Minnesota Farmer's Diaries*, 15.

72 "A large proportion of the prairie farms are cultivated without a fence

to protect the first year's crops."—*Rural American*, 1:130 (1856). "It is several years, usually, before the whole farm gets enclosed."—*American Agriculturist*, 12:128 (1854). "But few farms are well fenced."—*Plough, Loom and Anvil*, 6:328–329 (1854). Cf. *American Agriculturist*, 15:74 (1856); *Michigan Farmer*, 14:68–69 (1856); *New Hampshire Journal of Agriculture*, October 20, 1860, referring to Illinois; *Plough, Loom and Anvil*, 4:687–688 (1854); 8:212 (1858); *Rural New Yorker*, 8:269 (1857), referring to Illinois; *Rural Register*, 2:356 (1860); Beste, *The Wabash*, 1:165; Caird, *Prairie Farming in America*, 50; Regan, *The Emigrant's Guide*, 349.

73 *Prairie Farmer*, 11:164 (1851); *Carolina Cultivator*, 1:226 (1855); *Country Gentleman*, 6:368 (1855); *Colman's Rural World or Valley Farmer*, 2:125 (1850); U.S. Patent Office, *Report: Agriculture*, 1851, p. 390.

74 *Prairie Farmer*, 12:199–200 (1852).

75 According to the census, the area under cultivation was 4,170,496 acres, that under fence 4,784,886 acres, and that attached to farms but unimproved 4,135,613 acres. Wilson, *Description of Iowa*, 82.

76 Few subjects received more attention in the agricultural press than did that of fencing; scarcely a number of any of the journals failed to discuss the costs of fencing or the desirability of securing some substitute for the wood fence. See *Rural New Yorker*, 6:221 ff. (1855); *Indiana Farmer*, 5:344, 361–362 (1856).

77 *American Agriculturist*, 16:278 (1852); American Institute of the City of New York, *Reports*, 1859–1860, pp. 151–153.

78 It was estimated that the amount expended in building fencing in the largely forested state of Wisconsin exceeded the original cost of all the enclosed land in the state. *Prairie Farmer*, 14:324 (1854). The costs of fencing were particularly heavy in Texas and California. In Texas, "the expense of fencing a farm is two or three times greater than the first cost of the farm itself."—*Plough, Loom and Anvil*, 7:417 (1855). Langworthy thought that it would cost $1,400 to fence a 40-acre field in California (*Scenery of the Plains, Mountains and Mines*, 195). Other estimates place the cost of fencing in California at from $300 to $600 per mile (J. S. Hittel, *The Resources of California* [San Francisco, 1863], 165; *Rural New Yorker*, 9:110 [1858]). The costs of the fences were said to exceed the selling value of many New England farms. *American Farmer*, n. s., 1:52 (1861). Cf. Freedley, *Practical Treatise on Business*, 74.

79 Large areas in Illinois were reported fenced with timber from northern Wisconsin and Minnesota. Indiana State Board of Agriculture, *Annual Report*, 1854–1855, p. 231. One of the benefits expected of the building of the Illinois Central Railroad was that it would furnish the prairies with cheap lumber. Ferris, *The Great West*, 209.

80 The editor of the *Indiana Farmer* wrote with reference to his state: "The man who owns a farm of 80 acres and has two-thirds of it enclosed, and divided into fields of convenient size, has about 1200 rods of fencing. This at a fair estimate is worth about 75 cents per rod, mak-

ing a total of $900 as the prime cost of his fences, which is equal to nearly $17.00 per acre for all the land enclosed."—*Indiana Farmer,* 5:344 (1856). Each 120 acres in farms in Wisconsin was estimated to represent an investment of $1,000 for fencing. *Wisconsin Farmer and Northwestern Cultivator,* 9:116 (1857). Estimates for 40-acre fields fenced with post and board are given as $506 by Gerhard for Illinois (*Illinois as It Is,* 312); and as high as $620 for Minnesota (*Western Journal and Civilian,* 3:339 [1850]). Cf. *American Agriculturist,* 18:175 (1859); *Colman's Rural World or Valley Farmer,* 1:31 (1849); *Prairie Farmer,* 4:67 (1854); Gerhard, *Illinois as It Is,* 294–299 and 412; Dana, *The Great West,* 217.

These cost estimates compare closely with those of the older states. The cost of fencing was estimated to average $250 per mile throughout Ohio. Ohio Board of Agriculture, *Annual Report,* 10:18 and 275 (1855); 9:192 (1854). The average costs of fencing per farm in Maine, Pennsylvania, and Massachusetts where the average farm included less than 100 acres was estimated at $700, and in New York and New Jersey at $900. American Institute, *Transactions* (1851), 186–187. Cf. Massachusetts Board of Agriculture, *Annual Report,* 9:89–90 (1861); *Pennsylvania Farm Journal,* 2:359 (1852–1853); Solon Robinson, *Facts for Farmers* (New York, 1864), 861.

81 Of the plows recommended by the *Valley Farmer,* as good for the West, the Peoria and Moline Steel plows varied in price according to size from $8 to $28. In contrast, the Phoenix, Jewett, and Eagle plows which were cast iron varied in price from $3 to $20, with the more common sizes priced at about $6.00 to $7.50. *Colman's Rural World or Valley Farmer,* 4:266 (1854); Ohio State Board of Agriculture, *Annual Report,* 10:528–529 (1855). The steel plow was standard in the West by the middle of the decade, though its relatively high cost prevented it from entirely displacing the cast-iron implement. Gerhard, *Illinois as It Is,* 317. The Deere plow works at Moline produced 1,600 plows in 1850 and ten years later had reached an annual output of 10,000. Robert L. Ardrey, *American Agricultural Implements* (Chicago, 1894), 176.

82 Broadcast sowing of wheat remained the most common method throughout Iowa during the decade. Iowa State Agricultural Society, *Annual Report,* 6:323–324, 376, 378, 402 (1859); 7:390 and 433 (1860). Drills seem to have been introduced first in 1851 in Lee County (U.S. Patent Office, *Annual Report: Agriculture,* 1851, p. 450), but the editor of the *Iowa Farmer* knew of only one in Burlington County up to 1853 (*Iowa Farmer,* 1:4 [1853]). By 1857 both Pennock's and Moore's drills were being manufactured in the state (*ibid.,* 5:44 and 125 [1855]), and their use was spreading. U.S. Patent Office, *Annual Report: Agriculture,* 1857, pp. 195, 229, 236, 243, 257, 331, 359; *ibid.,* 4:88 (1856). Drills were in use in Missouri in 1853, and their manufacture was begun in St. Louis in the following year. U.S. Patent Office, *Annual Report: Agriculture,* 1853, p. 136; *Valley Farmer,* 9:121 and 147 (1857); 8:101 (1856). In 1865 they

remained, however, little known. Missouri State Board of Agriculture, *Annual Report*, 1865, p. 101.

83 "All grain is here cut by machine. Cradles are out of the question. . . . If grain be too badly lodged to be so gathered, it is quietly left alone." And, "You observe that this work done by machinery is not very much cheaper than it could be done by hand—but the great question is—where are the hands to come from?" The reference is to Illinois. *Iowa Farmer*, 5:139 (1857). "We must purchase or hire a reaper; if we purchase one of McCormick's the price is $130.00 cost and freight; if we hire the price is from fifty to seventy-five cents per acre which is about half the cost of harvesting. In thrashing we must do the same way—purchase or hire, which will cost five cents per bushel for wheat, and three for oats."—U.S. Patent Office, *Annual Report: Agriculture*, 1852, p. 396.

84 *Wisconsin Farmer and Northwestern Cultivator*, 8:440–441 (1856). Marshall (*Farmer's Hand-Book*, 16), suggests $254 as necessary on timbered land.

85 The rate of adoption of the reaper during the fifties would seem to indicate that it was. In 1849 there were 2,800 McCormick's, 180 Easterley headers, and "say 100" of all other machines combined in the hands of users, mostly located in the East. *Prairie Farmer*, cited in *Genesee Farmer*, 10:255 (1849). McCormick estimated that 73,000 reapers were in operation in the West (west of the Alleghanies) by 1859 (*Country Gentleman*, 13:259–260 [1859], cited by Leo Rogin, *The Introduction of Farm Machinery in Its Relation to the Productivity of Labor in Agriculture during the Nineteenth Century* [*University of California Publications in Economics*," vol. 9, Berkeley, 1931], 78); and Flint considered that the two-horse reapers in operation by 1861 performed the work of a million men (Charles L. Flint, *A Hundred Year's Progress* [U.S. Department of Agriculture, *Report*, 1872], 286).

86 Parker, *Iowa Handbook for 1856*, 159–160.

87 *Rural American*, 1:114 (1856).

88 *Eighth Census of the United States*, 1860, "Agriculture," x. The southern states averaged $148 per each 100 acres in farms; the middle states, $207.

89 It was for lack of capital and not because of greater profits that wheat-farming was typical of farm-making areas in the North. "Today the production of grain for export is the most precarious and worst paid direction which the farmer of Illinois or Iowa can give to his labor. The same amount of effort devoted to the production of Horses, Cattle, Hogs or Sheep, will pay twice as well. But the poor cannot await slow returns and the labor invested in growing Spring wheat or planting Corn can be turned into Cash in the course of six months, while the stock grower must wait three or four years for his reward; so Grain will be grown and shipped, at least until the farmers of the Northwest shall be less generally harassed by debt."—*Working Farmer*, 11:39 (1859). Cf. *American Agriculturist*, 10:117 (1852); *Iowa Farmer*,

1:254 (1853); *Prairie Farmer*, 10:299 (1850); *Rural New Yorker*, 2:403 (1851); *Wisconsin and Iowa Farmer*, 2:254 (1850); *Wisconsin and Iowa Farmer and Northwestern Cultivator*, 4:58–59 (1852).

90 Farm horses were valued at from $100 to $150 each in the northern farm-making regions; oxen at $80 to $100 per yoke; mules $100–$200. Parker, *Kansas and Nebraska Handbook*, 36.

91 In Minnesota, an investment of $315 was suggested to include a yoke of oxen, two cows, one horse, swine, and young stock. *New Hampshire Journal of Agriculture*, April 14, 1859. Gerhard thought that "a pair of good horses, a wagon, one cow, a couple of pigs, several domestic fowls . . . are all that is necessary for a beginning" (*Illinois as It Is*, 446), the group requiring probably about $300. In Texas, where livestock was very cheap, two yoke of oxen, a cart, one hoe, five cows, calves, and a supply of hogs and poultry were estimated to require $260. *Southern Cultivator*, 13:125 (1856). Cf. *Rural New Yorker*, 5:222 (1854).

92 "An investment of $560 was suggested to include a "good substantial low-priced horse team, wagon and harness, five cows, pigs and poultry."—*Wisconsin Farmer and Northwestern Cultivator*, 8:440–441 (1856).

93 "If we only had the money to buy them with"—*New Hampshire Journal of Agriculture*, June 2, 1860. Cf. *Prairie Farmer*, 14:165–166 (1854).

94 Gerhard, *Illinois as It Is*, 204–303; Parker, *Kansas and Nebraska Handbook*, 37.

95 "It will be seen that the cost of 'breaking' must be advanced about fifteen months before any returns can be obtained from the land. There are very many who cannot make the advance. It is, in fact, a serious impediment to the advancement of all farmers, even after they have obtained a fair beginning."—*Wisconsin Farmer and Northwestern Cultivator*, 9:122 (1857). Cf. *Plough, Loom and Anvil*, 7:493 (1855); Loehr, *Minnesota Farmer's Diaries*, 15; n. 63 above.

96 "Any farmer of ordinary capacity having his team and tools, and being on the ground by the first of April, will be able to raise enough food to keep his family through the winter till another harvest."—Parker, *Kansas and Nebraska Handbook*, 24.

97 *Northern Farmer*, 1:440 (1854); *New Hampshire Journal of Agriculture*, April 14, 1859; Smith, *The Settler's New Home*, 103.

98 "Half a crop"—*Cultivator*, 7:277–278 (1850). "I have raised partial crops of 'sod corn,' on my earliest breaking . . . but of course, only partial crops."—*Rural New Yorker*, 6:358 (1855). "Indian corn is frequently sown as the first grain on newly broken lands; but as there is no reliance to be placed upon sod-corn many farmers prefer to leave the broken land lying fallow, until September, when it is sown with wheat."—Gerhard, *Illinois as It Is*, 323. "Of course, every farmer knows that newly-plowed ground never yields a great crop the first season."—*New England Farmer*, 12:250–251 (1860). Cf. *American Agriculturist*, 12:128 (1850); *DeBow's Commercial Review*, 21:96–97

(1856); *Genesee Farmer*, 17:84–85 (1856); 18:141 (1857); *Plough, Loom and Anvil*, 6:519–520 (1854).

99 *Rural New Yorker*, 10:204 (1859).

100 *Indiana Farmer*, 3:292 (1853).

101 Cunynghame, *Glimpse at the Great Western Republic*, 103–106; *De-Bow's Commercial Review*, 10:640–641 (1851); 21:96–97 (1856); *Rural Register*, 1:9 (1859); *Wisconsin Farmer*, 8:440–441 (1856); Smith, *The Settler's New Home*, 106.

102 "The emigration itself furnishes him a local market and by the time that fails, railways will secure him a more permanent though perhaps less profitable market."—Stirling, *Letters from the Slave States*, 18–19. "The immigrant for the first year is a purchaser and consumer, and of course creates a temporary home demand for our produce."—Iowa State Agricultural Society, *Annual Report*, 2:38 (1854). "Already with thousands of emigrants coming into our territory who necessarily have to be sustained for at least twelve months before their labors aid in swelling the common fund, and with other thousands passing through bound for the Pacific coast with their herds and flocks, consuming as they go vast quantities of grain, the amount of produce shipped from our river towns is very great."—*Iowa Farmer*, 1:33 (1853). The references are to Iowa. A resident of Wisconsin wrote: "Corn we raise in large quantities, but consume it principally at home. . . . Small quantities only have been hitherto exported; as besides the uses first mentioned, we have had a large influx of hungry Germans and other emigrants to feed, who have consumed no small amount of our marketable grain, while they were preparing the means to live themselves and afford the staff of life to others."—*American Agriculturist*, 9:15 (1851). The rapid growth of Minnesota was ascribed to the "ready market which is found in the limits of the territory for everything which can be raised from a generous soil. . . . This arises from extensive emigration."—Israel D. Andrews, *Report . . . on the Trade and Commerce of the British North American Colonies and upon the Trade of the Great Lakes and Rivers . . .* (Washington, 1853), 171. "Multitudes have rushed from the farm to the building of railroads, from cultivating the soil to speculating in land, from homes in the East where on a harder soil, they were producing a little more than they consumed, to homes in the more fertile West, where, of course, they produce for a year or two, at first, less than they consume."—*American Farmer's Magazine*, 10:193–194 (1858). "The probability is that we shall have food enough for our needs, which has not been the case previously since the settlement of this territory." —*American Agriculturist*, 19:15 (1860), referring to Nebraska. A similar comment is made with reference to Sheboygan County, Wisconsin, concluding that enough will be produced to support its permanent and transient population, "something that the best counties in the state cannot boast of."—*Wisconsin and Iowa Farmer and Northwest Cultivator*, 3:145 (1851). Cf. *Colman's Rural World or Valley Farmer*, 9:335 (1857); *American Agriculturist*, 12:128 (1854); *Ohio*

Farmer, 8:386, 409 (1859); *Wisconsin and Iowa Farmer*, 7:41 (1854).

103 Dana, *The Great West*, 394. The cost of the trip from New York to Nebraska by rail or rail and water was about $45. James M. Woolworth, *Nebraska in 1857* (Omaha, 1857), 9. Cf. F. W. Bogen, *The German in America* (Boston, 1851), 49; Joseph H. Colton, *The Emigrant's Handbook* (New York, 1848), 134; Regan, *The Emigrant's Guide*, 403–404.

104 "Land in the far West at only $1.25 per acre is sometimes practically almost as remote and inaccessible to citizens of the United States as to the good people of Amsterdam and Harlem themselves. . . ."— U.S. Patent Office, *Reports: Agriculture*, 1855, p. 128. "The fertile farms of Iowa and Minnesota, the rich plains of Kansas and Nebraska, the gold and silver of Montana, Colorado and California, are all his— if he can only get to them. It is only to 'go West.' But a poor man with a family finds it as difficult to get from his one room tenement house in New York to a farm beyond the Mississippi as a Londoner in Bethnal Green would to transport himself to Australia."—T. L. Nichols, *Forty Years of American Life* (New York, 1937 ed.), 414.

105 *Country Gentleman*, 4:157 (1854); *Northern Farmer*, 1:440 (1854); *Southern Cultivator*, 13:125 (1856); C. B. Boynton and T. B. Mason, *Journey through Kansas: With Sketches of Nebraska* (Cincinnati, 1855), 68–69; Parker, *Kansas and Nebraska Handbook*, 37; Dana, *The Great West*, 213; Webb, *Information for Kansas Immigrants*, 17; Regan, *The Emigrant's Guide*, 189 and 401.

106 In Illinois, though the figure is applicable to the prairie regions in general. *Rural American*, 1:114 (1856). A two-room house, 14 by 26 feet, was quoted at $225–$250; a five-room house, 16 by 28 feet, one and a half floors, at $400–$425. Caird estimates the cost of a three-room house, 18 by 24 feet, at $200 (*Prairie Farming in America*, 50). Parker quotes with approval the observation that a four-room house, 24 by 24 feet, could be built for $300–$350; a five-room, 20 by 28, one and a half stories, for $450–$500 (*Iowa Handbook for 1856*, 159–160). The Illinois Central Railroad advertised its willingness to supply purchasers of its land with the materials for houses ready to set up at a cost of $150 for a two-room house, $400 for a four-room house, and $500 for five rooms. *Northwestern Farmer, and Horticultural Journal*, 1:128 (1856). Cf. *American Agriculturist*, 16:252 (1857); Dana, *The Great West*, 213–214; Marshall, *Farmer's Hand-Book*, chap. iv; Regan, *The Emigrant's Guide*, 300 ff.; Smith, *The Settler's New Home*, 17, 43, 79.

107 The items include the breaking of 40 acres of prairie on contract at $2.50 per acre, or $100; fencing this 40 acres, $320; seed and implements, $100, which is a low figure; livestock, $250; maintenance, $100; housing, $250. This total of $1,120 includes no provision for land or for travel expenses. The land was obtainable on credit or by squatting on the federal domain; its purchase required from $100 to $1,000 more. Though the figure for fencing may be considered some-

what high, it cannot reasonably be reduced, nor can any of the other items be cut to bring the capital required below $1,000, though credit might be obtained for part.

108 In defense of the safety-valve doctrine, descriptions of farm-making involving less capital than we have suggested may easily be obtained. Such accounts commonly ignore various elements of the farm-making process and are generally stamped with the extreme optimism characteristic of the speculative atmosphere of the frontier. The following is an illustration:

"We will suppose a blacksmith, a carpenter or some one who has been supporting a family and saving a very little by his daily labor in the eastern and middle states, makes up his mind in April or May to come to the state of Illinois. He can count when he gets here, all told, say $150, perhaps twice as much, or at most four times that amount. He locates or to use the classical language of the country, 'squats' near a grove on the border of some fine prairie. Not an acre is 'fenced in' for miles around. In a week or two . . . he has a log cabin built and his wife and their children . . . are safely housed. . . . He has taken care, after he makes his location, to find who owns the land he is on. If it belongs to the government, he takes out a preemption, or enters it at $1.25 per acre; if it belongs to some individual, he has got a bond for a deed, at from three to five dollars per acre, payable 'one quarter down,' the balance in one, two and three years, or longer. A few days finds half an acre fenced in and the garden seeds are all planted. Twenty acres are at once plowed, the corn is planted. Then hurrah for the fence while it is coming up. Drive the cattle off on the prairie for a week or two, if the fence don't get done in time, and as for the venerable, matronly old porker, with her numerous family, she must be kept in the yard till the corn is ripe. Fall finds him with six or eight hundred bushels of corn, potatoes and pork enough for his family for the winter, and three or four fine hogs to spare, hay enough for his cattle, cut wherever he pleased on the prairies, and his corn ground sown with winter wheat."—Hawes, *Illinois State Gazetteer,* xxxiii. Cf. n. 26.

109 "In the business of squatting on the public lands, there is a deal of delusion. The settlers are too apt to think that, having got a claim to a hundred and sixty acres of land, they have got a farm; whereas all they have got is a part of the raw material out of which, with labor and expense, patient waiting, and the investment of capital a farm may be made."—*Maine Farmer,* May 5, 1859.

110 The census of 1860 estimated that the 4,000,000 foreign-born enumerated in 1860 had brought not less than $400,000,000 into the country. A record kept of third-class passengers (immigrants) arriving at Castle Garden, the immigrant depot of New York City, by the Commissioners of Immigration of the State of New York, revealed an average of $65 brought in per passenger. Other estimates ranged from $60 to $180 per passenger. *U.S. Eighth Census,* 1860, "Population," xxiv. William Hayes Lord wrote: "I have known hundreds of German families who have taken out with them from 10,000 to 40,000 florins each

family—from $5,000 to $20,000. It may be admitted as a fact that out of twenty German emigrants, nineteen take out with them the means to establish themselves in the inland states."—*A Tract for the Times* (1855), 25. On the other hand, it was believed that "nearly three-fourths of the whole expense of emigration from Ireland is being defrayed by remittances made by previous emigrants."—Baird, *Impressions and Experiences . . . of North America*, 340. The U.S. Census of 1860 reported that from 1850 to 1860 some $50,000,000 was remitted by private individuals from the United States to Great Britain through large banking and mercantile firms ("Population," xxiv; cf. *Rural New Yorker*, 4:18 [1853]). The best study of this problem is that of Marcus Lee Hansen, *The Atlantic Migration, 1607–1860* (Cambridge, Mass., 1940), 243 ff.

111 High land prices in the East were observed to stimulate agricultural emigration to the West. *Rural New Yorker*, 5:317 (1854). The English agriculturist, Johnston, pointed out that "speaking generally, every farm from Eastport in Maine to Buffalo on Lake Erie, is for sale. The owner has already fixed a price in his mind for which he would be willing, and even hopes to sell, believing that, with the same money, he could do better for himself and his family by going still farther West."—James F. W. Johnston, *Notes on North America: Agricultural, Economic and Social* (2 vols., Boston, 1851), 1:162–163.

112 Edward Young, *Labor in Europe and America* (Washington, 1876), 743. Skilled labor received from $1.50 to $2.00 per day (*ibid.*, 745).

113 *Ibid.*, 739–742.

114 "If a young man saves $52 a year he is doing well."—*New Hampshire Journal of Agriculture*, December 17, 1859. The observation was made of New England farm operators that they "do not average saving one hundred dollars yearly, each" (*Homestead*, 3:221 [1858]). "Is not a farmer who saves this amount [$100] doing well?"—*New Hampshire Journal of Agriculture*, December 24, 1859. Cf. *New England Farmer*, 7:454 (1855).

115 Emigrants were urged to form groups in the East which would include all the necessary trades in the desirable proportions. *The West as It Is: The Chicago Magazine*, 1:341–344 (1857). The suggested occupational distribution of such a group is given in Daniel S. Curtiss, *Western Portraiture, and Emigrant's Guide* (New York, 1852), 292–293.

116 There is no doubt that some mechanics emigrated, but there is considerable question as to how many. This is the issue between Goodrich and Davison, on the one hand, and Schafer, on the other. See n. 1 above.

117 Tucker, "The Frontier as an Outlet for Surplus Labor," 176.

The Homestead Act and the Labor Surplus

FRED A. SHANNON

This paper was first read at a meeting of the Mississippi Valley Historical Association at Cincinnati, on April 26, 1935.

Reprinted by permission from the American Historical Review, *Volume 41 (1936), pages 637–651.*

EVERY American historian and all students of western history are well acquainted with the declaration of the Superintendent of the Eleventh Census of the United States that by 1890 "the unsettled area [of the United States] has been so broken into by isolated bodies of settlement that there can hardly be said to be a frontier line." [1] The reader of these words need not become prematurely alarmed—it is not the purpose of this paper either to amplify or attack the Turner hypothesis. [2] Only some of the later perversions of the frontier philosophy will be considered. The Superintendent of the Census was very cautious in the phraseology of his statement, and Professor Turner, in his original essay, did not attempt to read more into the sentence than its literal meaning conveyed. But long repetition, without frequent reference to the original text, plays tricks with the memory. Within a few years students were being told that by 1890 the frontier was gone, next that by 1890 the West was filled up with settlers, and finally that by 1890 all the free land in the West had been homesteaded. Since 1920 a fair proportion of the college textbooks in American history have contained such exaggerated statements as these in one form or another. Three out of five picked off the same shelf repeated the dogma in varying style. The pronouncements are so readily found that there is no need to make any embarrassing commitments concerning the authors or titles of the books examined.

Easy as it is to record such misinformation, culminating in the absurdity that the Homestead Act of 1862 wrought this miracle in the West, a half-hour spent with the Land Office reports or the Public Lands Commission report of 1905 will reveal the error. By June 30, 1890, only 372,659 homestead entries had been perfected, granting 48,225,736 acres to supposed settlers—an area less than that of the state of Nebraska and equal only to 3.5 per cent of the total territory west of the Mississippi River.[3] By that date more than four times as much land had been given to the railroad companies. Furthermore, four times as many acres of homestead land have been deeded by the federal government since 1890 as before that date. For that matter, more has been taken up since 1910 than in all the earlier forty-eight years.[4] To the contention that only inferior lands were left for free distribution after 1890, the answer is that most of the choice land in the country (land suited for general agriculture, and having sufficient rainfall to ensure crops) had been picked over before the Homestead Act was passed; and that, in the semi-arid regions where most of the free land was to be found, the first comers were far from always being the best choosers.

A more valid objection is that the number of homesteads was only a minor fraction of the total number of farms in the homestead states. But even this does not demonstrate that the West was filled up by 1890, or that the opportunity to go west and grow up with the country was past. A little comparison will illustrate this point better than a mass of figures. In 1890 little Delaware, with, as John J. Ingalls said, three counties at low tide and two at high, had half again as many farms as Idaho or Montana, three times as many as Wyoming, seven times as many as Arizona, or eight times as many as Nevada. Maryland had more farms than any of the eleven far western states or territories except California, and was not far behind her. Mississippi had as many farms as the whole eleven combined, though the latter contained two-fifths of the land area of the nation, and Ohio had nearly twice as many. But perhaps western farms were larger than eastern. Very well —Ohio had about half as many acres in farms as the entire Far West, and a larger percentage of Ohio's land was improved. Delaware equaled the average of Arizona, Idaho, New Mexico, and Utah, and was only a little under Wyoming, Montana, or Nevada.[5]

No further demonstration is necessary to show that the filling up of the West had merely begun by 1890. There is an old saying that figures do not lie, but liars will figure. This is no more true than that armchair philosophers still continue to spin hypotheses out of thin air. Oftentimes their formulas, evolved sheerly by guesswork, become more firmly established in the student's mind than any solidly grounded historical fact. A writer, proceeding from the old assumption that free land was gone by 1890, next conjures up the fiction that as long as abundant free land remained it furnished relief from economic pressure in the industrial centers; that it drained off the dissatisfied and restless elements from the eastern cities; that it gave to the underdog, wherever located in the country, the opportunity to start life on a new and higher level in the West; that free or cheap land had always been a safety valve for economic and social discontent.[6] It would almost seem, from such logic, that if there was any social discontent, any underdog, any labor trouble or unemployment before 1890, it was due purely to the shiftlessness of a portion of the population which would not even accept the heaven-sent boon of fertile farms when it was offered them. The next conclusion is that all the labor troubles since 1890 were the consequence of the drying-up of the national fount of every blessing in the West. The hypotheses and conclusions here mentioned were gleaned from books which college students by the thousands have been required to read within the last decade. The writers selected were from the foremost and best in their field, in order to show the more clearly how strong a hold the idea of limitless opportunity, furnished by a boundless frontier, has had on the popular mind. Certain facts, not difficult to demonstrate, call for a re-examination of this thesis, but the argument must be more prolonged than that of the preceding paragraphs.

The notion of an American Utopia, to be procured through free land in limited quantities to actual settlers, dates back a century or more, but found its most profound expression in the pious hopes of the land reformers of the 1840's. George Henry Evans and his fellow agrarians, writing for the columns of the *Working Man's Advocate,* the *True Workingman,* the New York *Daily Tribune,* and other labor or general newspapers, harped incessantly on the issues of widespread misery, poverty, and unemployment as a consequence of capitalism and land monopolies. All this they confidently expected to be remedied by a homestead policy which would give land to all who could use it. Eighty thousand persons in the city of New York alone, or a fifth of its population in 1845, it was asserted, were "receiving pauper relief or charity." [7] Newly arrived immigrants were adding to the congested eastern slums because, all the land within easy reach being monopolized, they were left with no prospect of relief except to "move off into the desert, and trust . . . [themselves] to the mercy of the wild Indian far beyond the aid of civilized man." The laborer, when he had a job at all, was pictured dragging out his weary existence and leaving to his family the heritage of poverty—the privilege of continued exploitation at the hands of capitalists and land monopolists. Break down the "hoary iniquities of Norman land pirates" and "Capital could no longer grasp the largest share of the laborer's earnings, as a reward for not doing him all the injury the laws of feudal aristocracy authorize . . . ." Give the people their right to the soil and "tens of thousands, who are now languishing in hopeless poverty, will find a certain and speedy independence. The labor market will thus be eased of the present distressing competition; and those who remain, as well as those who emigrate, will have the opportunity of realizing a comfortable living." [8]

These agrarians were not timid about accusing the abolitionists of callous disregard concerning the fate of northern wage slaves, both white and black, whose plight, they said, made that of the southern slave seem idyllic by comparison. Gerrit Smith was accused of condemning 50,000 laborers to "a worse state of ignorance, degradation, misery, and vice, than any fifty thousand you could pick out in a Southern State," because of his withholding from them vast New York estates—an indictment which helped induce him to give away about 200,000 acres to the poor of both races.[9] Further arguments contained the prophecy that the steam engine, existing power machinery on the farm, and machines yet to come in all lines of industry would virtually replace human labor everywhere.[10] All this debate, and much more to the same point, took place after the adoption of the general Preemption Act—when all the oppressed laborer had to do was to move out to the public domain, start farming, and accumulate the minimum price of $100 for 80 acres before the surveyor and land office moved in. But where was this semipauper to secure the cost of transportation for the journey of several hundred miles; who would buy him a team and farming equipment when he arrived, who extend him credit during the two or three years' grubbing of stumps before a decent living could be secured? Who would take the trouble even to teach him the elements of frontier farming? Having once been caught in the toils of poverty and hired labor, free will was at an end. Farmers might sell their eastern acres and move west, and so they did in order to provide farms for each of their sons, but the promise of cheap western land to the common laborer was as futile as a signboard pointing to the end of a rainbow.

But possibly these agrarian agitators imagined most of the poverty and unemployment of the 1840's. If you think so, then read the debates in Congress over the Homestead Bill of 1852. Representatives from the South and Northwest alike demanded that the homeless, destitute, and downtrodden, whether in eastern cities or on tenant farms in the South, be given the opportunity to start life anew on the public domain. Andrew Johnson of Tennessee pleaded for the poverty-stricken people of the South, while Representative Fayette McMullin of Virginia gloated over the prospect of the landed proprietors of his state being compelled to "go to work themselves" should the poor tenants be drawn away to the West. The latter denounced the eastern manufacturing interests who were blocking the Homestead Bill, declaring that they "fear that the laborers . . . will leave the manufacturing districts and go to the West, and that, in consequence of the diminution of laborers, the wages of labor will advance among them." Representative Albert G. Brown of Mississippi deplored the fate of thousands of homeless people who "look out upon your vast domains, and see them tenanted only by wild beasts . . . ." These persons, he said, "will ask, is my poverty so great a crime that my Government prefers these beasts to me? Am I to be kept in penury and in want, and leave to my children no inheritance but poverty, whilst my Government guards . . . this mighty wilderness, which God in his providence has created for man, and not for beasts?" He realized that the prospective free territories would get the first advantage of settlement, but, having been a squatter himself in his early days, he felt that the release of human misery in the South was worth the political advantage of the North. Representative William R. Smith of Alabama affirmed it to be "the duty of Congress to help the cities to disgorge their cellars and their garrets of a starving, haggard, and useless population." But he cherished the vain hope that capitalists would advance the money to enable poor men to move to the free land. They would be glad to get rid of undesirable neighbors. Without this safety valve, the "rapid *increase of labor-saving machinery*," which was gradually driving the mechanic from the workshop, would create intolerable conditions.[11]

The statements thus far are all from southerners—those persons who are supposed to have been most bitter against homestead legislation. If an aside is permissible, it is worth the effort to state that it was a division of votes between the Altantic Coast states and the West, rather than between the slave and free states, which defeated the Homestead bills of 1852–1853. In the House vote of May 12, 1852, thirty-six slave state representatives (thirty-one being from the West) voted for the bill, as compared with thirty-three against (twenty-eight of them from the Atlantic states). Seventeen of the twenty-three negative votes of the North were from the Atlantic states, five from Ohio, which industrially was becoming an eastern state, and one from Michigan.[12] Had the thirty-six homestead advocates of the South reversed their position and joined with the twenty-two opposition votes from the industrial states, the bill would not even have passed the House of Representatives, despite the large northern majority in that body. The decisive vote did not come in the Senate till February 21, 1853, when a motion to take up the bill was made with the express intention of showing who was for it and who against. This motion was defeated by a vote of 23 to 33.[13] An analysis of the vote shows that eight of the twenty-three favoring the measure were from the Lower South, but only four were from the North Atlantic division. As to party support, nineteen were Democrats and four were Whigs. Of the thirty-three opponents, twenty were from the slave states and eleven from the North Atlantic region. The party division showed fifteen Democrats and eighteen Whigs. But consider the vote again as an issue between the Atlantic Coast states and the West—leaving North and South, slavery and freedom, out of the question—and what is the result? The East gave five yeas and twenty-four nays; the West eighteen yeas and nine nays. Most clearly, the issue in 1852–1853 was drawn between western Democratic homestead advocates and eastern Whig capitalists. These were the days when Hannibal Hamlin, later the running mate of Abraham Lincoln, and Gerrit Smith, the abolitionist, free-soil capitalist, were voting to restrain the westward migration of wage slaves,[14] while a good proportion of earnest southerners were ready to give the North an advantage in western colonization in order to relieve poverty in both sections. It was only when the Republican party became militant over the free-soil question that the South consolidated its ranks against the homestead policy.[15]

If it be supposed that the southern arguments of 1852 were merely to save the face of slavery men, by depicting conditions in the North, then read the declarations of free-state men of the same period. Representative Charles Skelton of New Jersey said that the Homestead Bill "relieves the older States of the redundancy of labor which contributes to depress and paralyze the arm of industry in those States." The plight of landless and jobless free Negroes in the North is depicted in the words of Representative Samuel W. Parker of Indiana. "Go into the streets of our cities," he said, "through the lanes and highways, the filthy hovels, damp cellars, and dirty sculleries of our own free land, and we will find that poor, forlorn, outcast, downtrodden, disfranchised people still enslaved, and in a desperate thraldom, that would freeze our pure Christian blood, I fear, could we only extract some of the motes from our eyes." [16]

Through nearly all these orations and prophecies there runs the confident expectation that free land in the West would of itself alone furnish release from the oppression of poor laborers, tenants, and the unemployed. This is the theme, later blindly accepted as an accomplished fact, that is found in so many of the accounts of the consequences of the Homestead Act of 1862. A more reasonable point of view is reflected in the speech of Representative Orlando B. Ficklin of Illinois, April 24, 1852. Though he favored the Homestead Bill, he argued that there would be no sudden or excessive rush to the public lands. Those persons able to buy would prefer to remain closer to the old home and the greater conveniences of a developed country. Another class, he said, "are too poor to find means to pay the expense of emigrating from the older to the new States, and of settling on these lands; therefore those persons can not go." The actual settlers "will be generally of the middle, or rather not of the very poorest class, and . . . the number will not be so large by a great deal as is anticipated by some gentlemen." [17] Here is the sanest prophecy of the whole crop of the 1840's and 1850's.

The trouble with the Homestead Act in operation, as with the Preemption Act, was that Congress merely adopted the law and then did absolutely nothing in the way of helping the needy persons out to the land or extending them credit and guidance in the first heartbreaking years of occupancy. Perhaps these functions were outside the scope of federal authority, at least as then conceived, but without them the Homestead Act could benefit only monopolists or persons of fairly ample means.[18] The Graduation Act of 1854, disposing of hitherto unsalable land in the older states at prices as low as twelve and one-half cents an acre, had helped nobody but neighboring farmers and speculators.[19] Now that free land was provided, the results were not widely different. If the families of all persons making good on homesteads before 1890 had averaged five each, a population of considerably less than 2,000,000 would have been provided for. But so many families spread out over several homesteads that it would be injudicious to assume so large an average family for each farm. A population increase of 30,000,000 in thirty years failed to be benefited in any way by free land.

The bulk of these persons was added to the urban population, to be absorbed by industry or swell the ranks of the unemployed and destitute. Most of them were not even within yearning distance of the public domain. Of the twenty-nine states ultimately to exist in the regions where the public land lay in 1862, only eight were east of the Mississippi River, and three of these (Ohio, Indiana, and Illinois) were able to provide only 208 farms in forty-two years. Three others were Gulf states, which did not attract settlers from the industrial centers.[20] Michigan and Wisconsin were, therefore, the only states east of the Mississippi which could entice farmers and laborers from the congested regions. Before the industrial worker could even consider applying for a homestead he had to figure where, if possible, he was to raise the money to transport himself, and probably a family, from 500 to 1,000 miles to the new Canaan. This in itself might be the equivalent of six months' wages; and many times as much more was necessary if he made a success of his venture as a frontier farmer. Even the land-owner who sold out in the East and transplanted himself on a home-stead was more likely than not to find himself wandering forty years in the wilderness before reaching Canaan. Hardly more than a third of the homesteaders in the years before 1890 remained long enough to perfect their claims.[21] It was hard enough for an experienced farmer to make a success of the venture. To the industrial laborer of the second generation it was virtually an impossibility.

Down to 1860, even when the illegal squatter dominated the frontier, it was the unusual thing, rather than the customary, for the pioneer to make his ultimate home farther than one state removed from that of his birth. Even the California Gold Rush, the Oregon Trail, and the mining stampedes of the late 1850's do not invalidate this statement. "In thirty States out of thirty-four," said the Superintendent of the Census in 1860, "it will be perceived that *the native emigrants have chiefly preferred to locate in a State immediately adjacent to that of their birth;* and in the four cases of exception, the persons removing have proceeded from Maine to Massachusetts, from Maryland to Ohio, from Mississippi to Texas, and from Missouri to California. The second preference, in a majority of cases, has been to another adjoining State."

The population of Kansas, with all due deference to the Emigrant Aid societies, came chiefly from Missouri, Illinois, and Iowa.[22] The trend was not greatly different during the next twenty years. Half of the final homestead entries to 1890 were in Minnesota, Kansas, and Nebraska. Wisconsin, Michigan, Arkansas, Missouri, Iowa, California, and Dakota Territory accounted for three-fourths of the rest.[23] Again, it was the territory closest to the older states which received the emigrants. And from what regions and walks of life did the pioneers come? According to the United States Industrial Commission, investigating the situation at the close of the century, they were generally native Americans from the eastern and southern states, "who have sold their small farms in order to buy large ones in a new section," so that the parents could "leave a farm to each child." [24] The movement was from the farm to the farm, or, as will be shown later, from the farm to the city. Rarely was it from the city to the farm—from the laborer's hut to the homestead.

Professor Gates shows *["The Homestead Law in an Incongruous Land System" and "The Role of the Land Speculator in Western Development"]* how easily speculators acquired great tracts of land in the period since 1862.[25] The evidence of their activities in monopolizing the public domain is abundant. The Public Land Commission reported that, "The land laws, decisions, and practices have become so complicated that the settler is at a marked disadvantage in comparison with the shrewd business man who aims to acquire large properties." A premium was put on perjury. ". . . In very many localities, and perhaps in general, a larger proportion of the public land is passing into the hands of speculators and corporations than into those of actual settlers who are making homes." And again comes the statement: "Nearly everywhere the large landowner has succeeded in monopolizing the best tracts, whether of timber or agricultural land." Some objections were being raised, but there was no general outcry. The influential persons whose complaints might have been heard were among the beneficiaries. The result was that a tenant or hired-labor system was taking the place of freehold farmers.[26] The usual practice in North Dakota, said the Industrial Commission, was for settlers to mortgage their farms to the limit and then let the loan companies take them. This may be regarded as typical of the West in general. The speculators formed syndicates to induce easterners to take up western land. But the alien element of the urban centers was avoided.

"The surplus population of Eastern cities is considered to be lazy and generally not fit for colonization purposes after they have once had a taste of city life." [27]

This practice was made worse by the amendment of 1891 which permitted settlers to commute their claims by a money payment after fourteen months of nominal or eight months of actual residence. [28] Between 1882 and 1904 nearly 139,000 settlers commuted homesteads comprising 20,000,000 acres. In some years nearly two-thirds of the deeds were secured by commutation, and one-third of all the final entries from 1882 to 1890 were completed by this method. [29] This abuse was particularly noted in timberland, where people got quick possession and then sold out. In some counties nine-tenths of the tracts were disposed of within three months after the titles were secured. Meanwhile, the settlers had made a living and some profit by selling timber. The commuters were often Canadians or other aliens who returned to their old homes after their profitable ventures. A large proportion were women—schoolteachers and the like—who used this method of supplementing their salaries during the vacation months. In consequence of this monopolistic tendency, large areas of proved-up homesteads had neither habitation nor "evidence of genuine occupation" as homes. [30]

Oftentimes the speculation took the form of bonanza farming. Many thousands of acres would be amassed by hook or by crook, and the whole would be operated on a basis somewhat of a mixture between a feudal barony and a modern factory. Tenants and wage laborers worked with laborsaving machines of the latest design and highest efficiency. An investigator in the early 1880's traveled westward and southwestward from St. Paul and found numerous farms of from 20,000 to 40,000 acres. He also mentioned holdings in Kansas of from 10,000 to 100,000 acres, and some in Texas of from 50,000 to 350,000 acres. In the latter case he probably confused some cattle-range rights with actual ownership. In the twenty years following 1860 the number of United States farms of from 500 to 1,000 acres had increased from 20,000 to 76,000, while the number above 1,000 acres had grown from less than 6,000 to nearly 29,000. [31]

Abuses in application of the Timber Culture Act of 1873, the Desert Land Act of 1877, and the Timber and Stone Act of 1878 were comparable to those under the Homestead Act, when not worse. Little advantage was taken of the Timber Culture Act. Till 1890 only about 9,000 entries were proved up, [32] and the measure was repealed in the following year.[33] But persons having filed claims were allowed to continue under their contracts, and by 1904 over 65,000 entries had been perfected. By that date the annual number of final entries had dwindled to small proportions.[34] The Desert Land Act likewise failed to attract settlers, but it also was flagrantly abused. Of 37,000 original filings only 11,000 claims were proved up in the twenty-three years to 1900.[35] Most of these tracts had been absorbed by the big cattlemen and speculators. Two or three persons would get a half section each, and then form a corporation which was entitled to another 320 acres. Then they would form another corporation for the same purpose, and so on indefinitely. The speculator would buy stock in an irrigation ditch which connected with no reservoir, or would put up a pump where there was no water, and claim that he had qualified under the law for final title.[36]

Equally as certain as that railroad companies, private speculators, and loan companies profited most from the government's land policy, is the fact that the labor surplus became a constantly increasing factor in the national life after 1864. Between 1860 and 1890, while the total population of the country was doubling, the number of persons engaged in manufactures was multiplied by three and one-fourth. In the two decades following 1870, as the population increased 63.5 per cent, manufacturing labor more than doubled in number, while the total engaged in agriculture grew by only 45 per cent.[37] The same years undoubtedly showed a growth in mining, transportation, clerical, and commercial labor commensurate with that of the manufacturing industries. But to the ranks of wage laborers there ought to be added also the hired workmen on the land and, as far as independence is concerned, the tenant farmers as well. The Industrial Commission accounted for 8,395,634 persons engaged in agriculture in 1890, of whom 3,004,061 were hired laborers. In addition, there were no less than 1,500,000 tenant workmen.[38] This leaves less than 4,000,000 persons tilling land of their own, including all the mortgaged farms. Only three-eighths of the families of the United States were cultivating the soil "as owners, tenants, or laborers," and the ratio was declining constantly.[39] Over half of these were on an economic basis scarcely if any better than that of the city laborer.[40]

Even though farm help was scarce before 1900, the agricultural depression and low wages prevented recruiting from the unemployed in the cities. In fact, the scarcity was said to be "greatest in the vicinity of manufacturing establishments . . . and in sections where railroads or other public works are being constructed." Farmers in Vermont were making use of the immigration offices, and in California the Chinese-labor bureaus were patronized. Not only was the working-man unable to take advantage of free land in the West, he could see no prospect of gain in changing from factory to farm employment even in the East. Farm population increased "faster than its opportunities for rural employment"; [41] then the surplus moved to the towns or cities, and, once caught in the industrial toils, seldom returned. The farm added its toll to the unemployed of the industrial centers, but the city, like a devouring Moloch, failed to give back its victims. The years of agricultural distress in the 1870's and 1880's were accompanied by an ever-increasing roll of unemployed in the cities. Even the pioneers on the homesteads, baffled by fortune and beaten by nature, edged their way back, more often than not, to the ancestral farms and from there to the factory and, too frequently, to the bread line.

Henry George, writing a full fifteen years before "Coin" Harvey achieved fame, spoke of the "harder times, the lower wages, the increasing poverty perceptible in the United States." From every civilized country he heard "complaints of industrial depression; of labor condemned to involuntary idleness; of capital massed and wasting; of pecuniary distress among business men; of want and suffering and anxiety among the working classes." His rallying tocsin was that "amid the greatest accumulations of wealth, men die of starvation, and puny infants suckle dry breasts. . . ." [42] Ah yes! but why listen to Henry George? He was just a single-tax "crank." Or why hearken to the vaporings of that Utopian dreamer Edward Bellamy? Perhaps also Henry Demarest Lloyd should be waved aside as being possessed of a single-track mind, or, better yet, for having a mind at all. But still other witnesses raise their heads—men who gained the ear of the respectable classes who would listen neither to radicals nor "high brows." One of these was Godwin Moody, who published testimonials from David Davis, George W. Curtis, and George F. Hoar as to the soundness of his thinking. Davis accepted without question the statement that a third of the whole population of the country was "prostrated by want of employment and of reasonable reward for their toil." Hoar assumed as part of his own thinking that laborers must get higher wages and fewer hours as "their share of the increased production caused by the invention and perfection of machinery." Moody himself saw, as the principal changes of a half-century before 1880, the rise of bonanza and tenant farming side by side, the growth of congested slums, the development of armies of compulsorily unemployed—half of the people overworked and the other half idle.[43]

But Moody was inclined to exaggerate. Of 17,000,000 belonging to the productive classes, he could find that 7,000,000 were idle or working so little of the time as to be dependent. Also, after all, he must have been a radical, for he proposed a six-hour day at increased wages as the only solution for unemployment.[44] The historian, therefore, must return to the established authorities. No person has denied that there were a million men unemployed in the North alone in 1865, and none has demonstrated that the number ever became perceptibly or permanently smaller. Most textbooks will recount the wage-cutting orgies of the 1870's and the suppression of labor revolt by armies of hired retainers or by military force. They will tell also of the railroad, steel, and mining strikes in the great upheaval of the 1880's, when the coldest of official and judicial brutality toward the hunger-driven jobless could be hailed as the sublimation of social justice. Where then was the siren call of the free lands? Carroll D. Wright, and he is a conservative enough authority, after the most careful of deductions, listed the number of unemployed in all fields except those of professional and personal service in 1885 at 998,839. But he admits that, taking all kinds of unemployment, the number was above 1,300,000.[45] However, he is best in his last report as labor commissioner in Massachusetts. Of 816,470 total employable persons in that state in 1884–1885, he accounted for 241,589, or 29.59 per cent of the total, idle or employed only a few months in the year.[46]

Before the establishment of the Massachusetts Bureau of Statistics of Labor, in 1869, there were hardly any reliable calculations of unemployment. But a fairly trustworthy source listed 20,000 idle in the city of New York in 1868.[47] Some reports credited Massachusetts with as many as 300,000 unemployed mechanics during the dismal years following 1873, but Wright would cut the number to a tenth as many. On this basis he would also reduce the estimated 3,000,000 for the United States in the same proportion.[48] But his own liberal estimate for 1885 might tend to show that he was unduly conservative in his earlier calculations. The difference between mechanics and all employable persons is a wide one, and it is difficult to believe that the depression of the middle eighties was so much worse than the Panic of 1873.

But, whatever the basis of calculation, it cannot be denied that unemployment was a major economic ailment in every decade from 1865 to the close of the century, and it is equally certain that free land did not solve the problem. No doubt there was once a time in American history when underpaid, unemployed, or dissatisfied laborers could take their choice between continuing as intermittent wage employees or becoming freehold farmers; that wages of industrial labor were higher for that undefined period than they otherwise would have been; and that industrial strife, in consequence, was kept at a minimum. A more certain fact is that such conditions have not existed since the coming of the factory system. In other words, the much-vaunted cheap or free public lands of the country, whatever may have been their effect in other regards, since the rise of a class-conscious labor group have not been of measurable consequence as an alleviator of labor conditions.

NOTES

1 This statement, as repeated by Frederick Jackson Turner, has been printed in various places, but can most conveniently be found in his *Frontier in American History* (New York, 1920), 1.

2 Since April, 1935 *[when this paper was first read]*, Professor Carter Goodrich and Mr. Sol Davison have published two articles on "The Wage-Earner in the Westward Movement," in the *Political Science Quarterly*, 50:161–185 (June, 1935); 51:61–116 (March, 1936), in which substantially the same conclusions were reached as are set forth here. These studies—theirs and my own—having been made independently, but based upon different evidence and following different procedures, tend rather to corroborate than to duplicate each other. Another article entitled "A Critical Analysis of the Safety Valve Idea in American History with Particular Reference to the Period Centering around the Depression of 1837," written by Murray Kane and as yet unpublished, shows the weakness of the theory at a very early period of American industrialism.

3 *Report of the Public Lands Commission,* 1905 (58 Congress, 3 session, Senate Document no. 189), 175. Proved-up homesteads equaled 75,353 square miles as compared with 2,145,313 in the trans-Mississippi West or 77,520 in Nebraska.

4 To 1910 inclusive, 118,922,354 acres had been deeded to settlers. By 1933 the figure had grown to 237,099,586, and, though the rate was falling off, nearly a million acres were patented in the latter year. The largest number of acres patented in any one year was 10,009,285 in 1912–1913. *Statistical Abstract of the United States,* 1934, no. 56, p. 126.

5 *Eleventh Census*, 1890, "Statistics of Agriculture," 84, 92, 100.
6 There is more than a suspicion of this sort of reasoning in some of Turner's own later writings. In 1903, ten years after his original essay, he wrote: "Men would not accept inferior wages and a permanent position of social subordination when this promised land of freedom and equality was theirs for the taking. . . . In a word, then, free lands meant free opportunities."—*Frontier in American History*, 259–260. Again, in 1910, while discussing the subject of class stratification, he asserted that "the sanative influences of the free spaces of the West were destined to ameliorate labor's condition . . . and to postpone the problem."—*Ibid.*, 275.
7 John R. Commons and others, eds., *Documentary History of American Industrial Society* (11 vols., Cleveland, 1910–1911), 8:32 ff.
8 *Ibid.*, 7:299, 301, 302, 306–307.
9 *Ibid.*, 354. See also 352–362, *passim*, and 8:24. For Smith's land donations, see Octavius Brooks Frothingham, *Gerrit Smith* (New York, 1878), 102–112.
10 Commons, *American Industrial Society*, 7:302–304.
11 *Congressional Globe*, 32 Cong., 1 sess., app., 511, 512, 514–516 (italics in original), 519, 530.
12 *Ibid.*, pt. 2, p. 1351, for the House vote. The total was 107 yeas and 56 nays. Fifty of the negative votes were from the Atlantic Coast states and industrial Ohio. The affirmative vote of the North showed 37 from the East and 34 from the West (Ohio's rural vote included).
13 *Ibid.*, 32 Cong., 2 sess., 739–747. Vote on p. 747.
14 For Hamlin's vote in 1853, see *ibid.*, 747. His thorough denunciation of the Homestead Bill is in the Appendix, 33 Cong., 1 sess., 1103. For Gerrit Smith's vote in 1854, see *ibid.*, pt. 1, p. 549.
15 Some of the later significant votes on homestead bills may be found in the *Cong. Globe*, 33 Cong., 1 sess., pt. 1, p. 549, for House vote of March 6, 1854 (see p. 2 for state and party affiliations of members); *ibid.*, pt. 3, p. 1844, for Senate vote to substitute the Graduation Bill for the Homestead Bill; *ibid.*, 35 Cong., 1 sess., pt. 3, p. 2426, for Senate vote on May 27, 1858, to postpone action on a homestead bill (Andrew Johnson voting "yea" in order to secure reconsideration; see also *ibid.*, 35 Cong., 2 sess., pt. 2, p. 1074, for explanation of the significance of this vote); *ibid.*, 1075, 1076, for Senate votes of Feb. 17, 1859. The legislative history of the bill in 1860–1862 is common knowledge.
16 *Cong. Globe*, 32 Cong., 1 sess., app., 380, 509.
17 *Ibid.*, 523; also in pt. 2, p. 1183.
18 See Robert Tudor Hill, *The Public Domain and Democracy* (*Columbia University Studies in History, Economics and Public Law*, vol. 38, no. 1, New York, 1910), 45 ff.
19 See United States General Land Office, *Report*, 1860, pp. 32, 48; Thomas Donaldson, *The Public Domain* (Washington, 1884), 291.
20 These were Mississippi, Alabama, and Florida. *General Land Office Report*, 1860, p. 9; Senate Doc. no. 189, 58 Cong., 3 sess., 175. The small

portions of Louisiana and Minnesota lying east of the Mississippi River are scarcely enough to include those states in the list.

21 By 1880 there were 162,237 final entries as compared with 469,782 original filings. Donaldson, *The Public Domain*, 355. The figures for 1883 are given as 213,486 and 608,677 in Frederic L. Paxson, *History of the American Frontier* (Boston, 1924), 549.

22 *Eighth Census*, "Population," xxxiv, xxxv. The italics are in the original.

23 Donaldson, *The Public Domain*, 355.

24 *Report*, 19:120.

25 Various other related matters which are merely alluded to or ignored entirely here are discussed in detail by Professor Gates. No attempt has been made to eliminate the occasional small items of duplication of subject matter.

26 Senate Doc. no. 189, 58 Cong., 3 sess., xxiii–xxiv.

27 *Industrial Commission Report*, 10:789; 19:109, 110.

28 Senate Doc. no. 189, 58 Cong., 3 sess., 65–66. Commutation had been allowed by the act of 1862. *United States Revised Statutes*, sec. 2301.

29 Compare *ibid.*, 175 and 180.

30 *Ibid.*, viii, xvii–xviii, 69–78.

31 Wm. Godwin Moody, *Land and Labor* (New York, 1883), 33–61, 75.

32 Senate Doc. no. 189, 58 Cong., 3 sess., 183.

33 26 *U.S. Stat.*, 1095–1103. The repeal act of March 3, 1891, is also mentioned in *Public Land Statutes of the United States*, Daniel M. Greene, compiler (Washington, 1931), 711. This volume, besides listing the acts in force at date of publication, also serves as an excellent index for land acts in general. The heading to paragraph 5116 in *U.S. Compiled Statutes*, 1918, John A. Mallory, compiler (St. Paul, 1918), lists the dates of the various amendments to the Timber Culture Act prior to its final repeal.

34 Senate Doc. no. 189, 58 Cong., 3 sess., 183. Persons inclined to jeer at the idea of successful forestry projects on the western Plains might well travel through Nebraska and the Dakotas and view for themselves the flourishing results of experiments started half a century ago under the "Tree Claim" Act.

35 *Industrial Commission Report*, 19:113.

36 Senate Doc. no. 189, 58 Cong., 3 sess., xix–xx.

37 *Statistical Abstract*, 1913, no. 36, pp. 660, 666. This number was used instead of an older one merely because it was the earliest easily available and as good as any for the purpose. Agricultural labor for 1870 is listed at 5,922,471 and in 1890 at 8,565,926 (the latter figure is slightly more than the one given by the Industrial Commission, see text and next note). For the corresponding dates, manufacturing labor stood at 2,053,996 and 4,251,535.

38 *Industrial Commission Report*, 11:77; the *Statistical Abstract*, 1931, no. 53, p. 647, shows 1,294,913 tenants in 1890 but, counting the work of the families, the number of laborers must have been considerably more.

39 George K. Holmes, "The Supply of Farm Labor," American Academy of Political and Social Science, *Annals*, 33:362 (January–June, 1909).

40 The average wages of farm labor from 1879 to 1899 ranged from $10.43 to $14.07 a month, with board. *Industrial Commission Report*, 11:139.

41 *Ibid.*, 10:xix; 19:121.

42 Henry George, *Progress and Poverty* (New York, 1879), 5, 8, 354.

43 Moody, *Land and Labor*, see testimonials in back, pp. 286–288.

44 *Ibid.*, 252–275, 310.

45 United States Commissioner of Labor, *First Annual Report: Industrial Depressions* (1886), 65.

46 Massachusetts Bureau of Statistics of Labor, *Eighteenth Annual Report* (Boston, 1887), 277.

47 Cited in John R. Commons and others, *History of Labour in the United States* (4 vols., New York, 1918–1935), 2:123.

48 United States Commissioner of Labor, *First Annual Report: Industrial Depressions*, 64.

The Homestead Law in an Incongruous Land System

PAUL WALLACE GATES

The material for this article was gathered in part while the writer was Fellow of the Social Science Research Council in 1933 and 1934. Grateful acknowledgments are due to the Council and especially to Donald Young of its staff for many kindnesses. The article was completed while the writer was engaged in a study of Recent Land Policies of the United States for the Land Policy Section of the Agricultural Adjustment Administration, later the Resettlement Administration.

Reprinted by permission from the American Historical Review, Volume 41 (1936), pages 652–681.

THE Homestead Act of 1862 is one of the most important laws which have been enacted in the history of this country, but its significance has been distorted and grossly misinterpreted. An important misconception concerning the Homestead Act is that its adoption marked a more or less complete break with the past, in that the lands which previously had been considered as a source of revenue were now to be given free to settlers. As part of this interpretation it is held that direct land sales virtually ceased except for transactions under the Pre-emption Law, the commutation clause of the Homestead Act, the Timber and Stone Act, and the Desert Land Act. Each of the first three of these acts permitted the purchase by individuals of 160 acres and the Desert Land Act permitted the purchase of an additional 640 acres, making a total which could be acquired under them of 1,120 acres. Aside from this maximum which was open to purchasers, the accepted view is that speculators[1] in lands were barred from direct transactions at the land offices and that, to secure large tracts, they were forced to operate through dummy entrymen or buy from states and railroads.

To state this view differently, it is held that after 1862 the chief way in which settlers and speculators alike acquired land from the government was through the Pre-emption and Homestead laws and their subsequent modifications. Indeed, some writers have maintained that the region beyond the Mississippi was largely settled by homesteaders taking up free land under the act of 1862. Congressman Harvey B. Ferguson stated in 1914, "It was great statesmanship that created the homestead laws under which such a State as Iowa developed." [2] Another writer made an even broader statement, as follows: "Under the homestead law were taken up the rich agricultural alluvial lands of the central Mississippi basin. . . ." [3] Even Professor Hibbard, the authority on American land policies, misunderstood the developments in land matters after 1862. He states that land sales made after 1862 were "only in connection with preemption and miscellaneous parcels of land, the preemptions covering by far the larger part of the operations." He also states that a congressional resolution, expressing opposition to the further sale of agricultural lands, which passed the House in 1868 but failed of adoption in the Senate, was virtually "tantamount to a law." [4] As these views have been widely accepted, it is essential to examine briefly their source and then to test their accuracy.

The principle of free homesteads for settlers had long been the goal for which the West had struggled, and as each succeeding land law, more liberal than its predecessor, was passed, that goal came constantly nearer until, in 1862, it was attained. So generous seemed this policy in contrast with the earlier one of regarding the lands as a source of revenue, and so significant did it appear prospectively, that it became the subject of eulogy at the outset. Furthermore, the measure had been sponsored by the Republican party and when this party was later accused of representing the interests of large capitalistic combines and of neglecting the farmers, its leaders pointed to the Homestead Act as a refutation of the accusation. [5] Consequently there was built up around the law a halo of political and economic significance which has greatly magnified the importance to be attributed to it and which has misled practically every historian and economist who has dealt with land policies. The Homestead Law has been considered the capstone of an increasingly liberal land policy, and to it has been ascribed the rapid settlement of the West and the large percentage of farmer-owners in the United States. It has also been regarded as providing an outlet for the discontented and surplus labor of the East, with the result that, as compared with European countries, high wage rates have prevailed in that section. The influence of free land has been blithely discussed by writers who have never taken the time to examine the facts with which they dealt so lightly.[6]

The source of most of these ideas concerning the Homestead Law is, of course, the *Congressional Globe,* later the *Record,* upon which so many writers completely depend. A careful reading of the congressional debates should, however, lead one to question the general conception above outlined. Professor Hibbard bases his generalizations upon even more untrustworthy evidence. He quotes from the *Report* of the Commissioner of the General Land Office for 1863, wherein it is stated that it is not the design of Congress "to look to the public lands as a source of direct revenue,"[7] and, from the exceedingly small amount of sales reported in the first year that the Homestead Law was in operation, draws the inference that cash sales were thenceforth of no importance. Professor Hibbard may also have been depending upon a statement made by that great compiler of land statistics, Thomas Donaldson, in his book, *The Public Domain,* originally published in 1880, in which it is stated that lands available for cash entry are few and isolated, except for those in the five southern states of Alabama, Louisiana, Florida, Arkansas, and Mississippi. The statement was correct in general in 1880, insofar as it applied to the lands ordinarily described as "public domain,"[8] but there were many million acres of rich agricultural lands which at that time were rapidly being brought into the market for cash sale by the federal government.[9] It would not apply at all to the period prior to 1880 when large areas of the best agricultural lands in the country were subject to sale.

It is the purpose of this paper to show that the Homestead Law did not completely change our land system, that its adoption merely superimposed upon the old land system a principle out of harmony with it, and that until 1890 the old and the new constantly clashed. In presenting this view, it will appear that the Homestead Law did not end the auction system or cash sales, as is generally assumed, that speculation and land monopolization continued after its adoption as widely perhaps as before, and within as well as without the law, that actual homesteading was generally confined to the less desirable lands distant from railroad lines, and that farm tenancy developed in frontier communities in many instances as a result of the monopolization of the land. The efforts to abolish cash sales will also be outlined briefly.

The moderate land reformers of the mid-nineteenth century believed that the enactment of a homestead measure would retard if not end speculation in public lands.[10] They argued that, once free homesteads were available to settlers, speculators would no longer have a market for their lands and all inducements to purchase in advance of settlement would be ended. Parenthetically, similar arguments have been advanced by certain historians to prove that there was little or no profit in land speculation.[11] The land reformers reckoned too lightly, however, with the astuteness of the speculators who in the past had either succeeded in emasculating laws inimical to their interests or had actually flouted such laws in the very faces of the officials appointed to administer them.

From the outset the cards were stacked against the efficient and successful operation of the Homestead Law. Other acts in existence in 1862 greatly limited its application, and new laws further restricting it were subsequently enacted. The administration of the law, both in Washington and in the field, was frequently in the hands of persons unsympathetic to its principle,[12] and western interests, though lauding the act, were ever ready to subvert it. The existence of the Pre-emption Law and its later variations, the Desert Land Act, the Timber Culture Act, the Timber and Stone Act, the land grants to railroads and states, the cash sale system, the Indian land policy, the acts granting land warrants to ex-soldiers or their heirs, and the Agricultural College Act of 1862, which granted millions of acres of land scrip to eastern states, tended to make it practically as easy for speculators to engross huge areas of land after 1862 as before.

The retention of the Pre-emption Law and the commutation clause of the Homestead Law made it possible for timber dealers,[13] cattle graziers, mining interests, and speculators to continue to acquire lands through the use of dummy entrymen, false swearing, and, often, the connivance of local land officers. That this was done on a large scale is evident by the frequent and sometimes pathetic admissions of the apparently helpless Land Commissioners. The Desert Land Act, the Timber Culture Act, and the Timber and Stone Act provided even greater opportunities for dummy entrymen to enter lands and assign them to hidden land engrossers.[14] The palpable frauds committed and the large areas transferred under these acts and their interference with the homestead principle lead one to suspect that their enactment and retention were the results of political pressure by interested groups.

It was not entirely necessary, however, for speculators to resort to these illegal and fraudulent methods of acquiring land, since Congress proceeded to aid their schemes by enacting a series of laws which went far toward vitiating the principle of land for the landless. By continuing after 1862 the policy of granting lands to railroads to encourage their construction, Congress from the outset struck a severe blow at the principle of free homesteads. In the eight years after the passage of the Homestead Law, five times as much land was granted to railroads as had been given in the twelve preceding years; 127,628,-000 acres were granted between 1862 and 1871 to aid in the extension of the railroad net and 2,000,000 acres were granted for wagon roads and canals. Such imperial generosity was at the expense of future homesteaders who must purchase the land.[15] As it was necessary to withdraw all lands from entry in the regions through which such roads were projected to prevent speculators from anticipating the railroads in making selections of land, and as the routes were rarely definitely established when the grants were made, more than double this amount of land was withdrawn from entry and remained unavailable to settlement for a long period of years.[16]

The railroads were, of course, built through undeveloped regions and, other things being equal, routes were selected which would ensure to the companies the largest amount of what was then considered to be the best agricultural land. When the alternate government sections were finally restored to market, settlers were frequently outbid for them by speculators.[17] Moreover, the provision in the Homestead Law which confined the homesteader to 80 acres within the limits of a railroad grant [18] was sufficient to send many homeseekers farther afield. On the railroad sections, of course, no free homesteading was permitted and thus the prospective settler found it necessary to go far from transportation facilities in order to take advantage of the government's bounty. In numerous instances the land policies of the railroads encouraged speculative and large-scale purchases, with the result that millions of acres were turned into bonanza farms, such as those found in Dakota Territory, or were rented or leased to incoming settlers who had expected to find free land available to them.[19]

These grants to railroads after 1862 were a limitation on the homestead principle and indicate cynical indifference to the idealistic expressions constantly voiced concerning the principle. That some doubt existed among members of Congress as to the propriety of continuing to make grants for railroads is revealed by a resolution adopted by the House in 1870 which stated:

That in the judgement of this House the policy of granting subsidies in public lands to railroad and other corporations ought to be discontinued; and that every consideration of public policy and equal justice to the whole people requires that the public lands of the United States should be held for the exclusive purpose of securing homesteads to actual settlers under the homestead and preëmption laws, subject to reasonable appropriations of such lands for the purposes of education.[20]

Although adopted without any debate, the resolution was just a bluff, for within the next twelve months Congress made one of the largest and most indefensible of the railroad grants which, together with a number of smaller ones, totaled nearly 20,000,000 acres.[21] The antirailroad feeling which swept over the West in the early seventies finally brought these grants to an end. After 1871 no more grants were made,[22] although various interests were at the time seeking additional grants which, if made, would have required practically all the valuable lands remaining to the government.

The continuation of the policy of granting to the states federal lands within their borders was likewise contrary to the homestead principle. With the exception of the swamp-land grants, the purpose of these donations was to provide the states with a valuable commodity, the sale of which would produce revenue or endowment for educational and other state institutions. Over 72,000,000 acres were granted to states which came into the Union after 1862, while other states had their grants increased subsequent to the enactment of the Homestead Law.[23] It is safe to say that over 140,000,000 acres of land were in the hands of the states for disposition after 1862.[24] The philosophy behind the grants, and frequently the conditions embedded in the donations, required their sale at the highest market price. The states were prevented, therefore, from giving homesteads to settlers, and the prices asked for their lands, with the exception of the swamp lands, which were generally sold at low prices or granted to railroads, made them the prey of speculators. It is true that limitations were sometimes placed on the amount of land which individuals could purchase, but dummy entrymen were usually employed to circumvent such restrictions.[25] The states, like the railroads, naturally endeavored to secure the best possible lands in order to ensure large returns therefrom. Table 7, showing the land sales of and the prices received by representative states, reveals clearly that persons seeking cheap or free lands found little encouragement from state officials.

The maintenance of the cash sale system after the Homestead Law went into operation did even greater violence to the principle of free lands. It is not generally appreciated that there were available in 1862 for cash sale 83,919,649 acres of land.[26] Contrary to the views of

Hibbard and others, this figure was later increased to well over 100,000,000 acres by the opening up of new lands to the auction and cash sale system.[27] Throughout the sixties and seventies and, indeed, until 1888, the government continued to offer land at auction in Oregon, Washington, California, Kansas, Nebraska, Colorado, New Mexico, and in practically all of the states in the Lakes region and in the Mississippi Valley where it still had land. It is true that after 1870 most of the land so offered was timbered, but by then a goodly portion of the arable lands had been surveyed and opened to sale. The richest and most fertile sections of Kansas, Nebraska, Missouri, California,

TABLE 7

Land Sales of Various States and Prices Received [a]

State	Net amount of land sold to [1935]	Average price per acre
Idaho [b]	838,140	$16.90
Kansas	3,064,547	3.22
Minnesota	2,306,600	6.53
Montana	1,587,488	15.50
North Dakota	1,686,436	16.73
South Dakota	873,960	35.22
Utah	3,448,876	2.44

[a] Computed from reports of the land offices of the respective states.
[b] To 1918.

Washington, and Oregon were thus open to the cash purchaser after the enactment of the Homestead Law and, as will be seen later, great landed estates were acquired through outright purchase in these states.

Little attention has been devoted by historians to the Indian lands and yet there is a story involved in their disposition totally at variance with the conventional account of the era of free land. At the time the Homestead Law was passed, the government was following the policy of concentrating the Indians on reservations where they would be in less conflict with white settlers. The rights of the Indians in lands claimed by them were recognized and, when they were persuaded to leave a hunting area over which they claimed ownership to dwell in a reservation, they were generally compensated for their lands either by the federal government or by a purchaser acting with the consent of the government. Some of the lands were ceded outright to the government for a consideration; others were ceded in trust, the lands to be sold for the benefit of the Indians; the disposition of still others to railroads was authorized in a number of treaties. As these Indian lands were frequently the very choicest and contained some improvements, they were much desired by speculators. No uniform policy concerning their final disposition was worked out—both legislative and administrative regulations as to their disposal varying widely—and consequently speculators were able to get their grasp on them more easily than if the lands had been subject to a clearly defined policy. The only consistent rule concerning them was that they must be sold for a consideration, which, of course, denied to the homesteader the right to enter them free. The obligation of the government to compensate the Indian for his land did not necessitate a policy of sale to settlers, but the revenue complex with reference to the public lands was still prevalent in spite of the Homestead Law, and the Indian lands were reserved for cash sale.

The amount of land in Indian reservations or claimed by the Indians in 1862 was probably 175,000,000 acres.[28] The land was scattered throughout the western states, but large amounts were concentrated in the states of Kansas and Nebraska and the Dakota and Indian territories into which settlers were eagerly pressing in the sixties, seventies, and eighties, or where they looked longingly for lands. At the outset, these lands were sold in large blocks to groups of capitalists and railroads, as is seen below, without being offered in small lots. Slightly later they were appraised, generally at high valuations, offered at auction and sold to the highest bidders. Still later, some of the Indian lands were sold in small tracts to settlers, a slight concession to the homeseekers.[29]

The Indian Allotment Act of 1887, as modified by the Burke Act of 1906 [30] and subsequent measures, was undoubtedly in part the result of western pressure to have the lands of the Indians made available to white settlement. These acts provided for the allotment of Indian lands and eventually for their sale. The Dawes Act continued the policy whereby the government purchased the surplus lands from the Indians and subsequently resold them, but it provided that lands so acquired in the future should be reserved for actual settlers in tracts of 160 acres. This provision did not apply to ceded lands transferred before 1887 nor did it open the ceded lands to free homesteading. Congress has been consistent at least in requiring payment for Indian land. Between 100,000,000 and 125,000,000 acres of Indian land have been sold since 1862, practically one-half as much as the total acreage which has been entered under the Homestead Law.[31]

With over 125,000,000 acres of railroad lands,[32] 140,000,000 acres of state lands, 100,000,000 acres of Indian lands, and 100,000,000 acres of federal lands for sale in large or small blocks, and with the opportunities for evasion of the Homestead and Pre-emption laws and their variations outlined above, it is obvious that there were few obstacles in the way of speculation and land monopolization after 1862. As before, it was still possible for foresighted speculators to precede settlers into the frontier, purchase the best lands, and hold them for the anticipated increase in value which the succeeding wave of settlers would give to them. It has heretofore been maintained that the existence of free land after 1862 greatly diminished the speculators' chances of profit and consequently limited their activities. This view will not bear careful scrutiny. Except for the squatters' claims, the speculators were generally able to secure the most desirable lands, that is, those easily brought under cultivation, fertile and close to timber, water, markets, and lines of communication. The subsequent settler had the choice of buying at the speculators' prices, from the land-grant railroads which held their alternate tracts at equally high prices, from the states whose land policies were less generous than those of the federal government, or of going farther afield to exercise his homestead privilege where facilities for social and economic intercourse were limited. The fact that their lands were more advantageously situated was effectively advertised by the land companies. Thus the American Emigrant Company, in advertising its Iowa lands in the sixties, summed up under the caption "Better than a Free Homestead" all the disadvantages of free land:

> Under the homestead law the settler must, in order to get a good location, go far out into the wild and unsettled districts, and for many years be deprived of school privileges, churches, mills, bridges, and in fact of all the advantages of society.[33]

Settlers arriving in Kansas—to consider a typical state—between 1868 and 1872 were greeted with advertisements announcing that the choicest lands in the state had been selected by the State Agricultural College, which was now offering 90,000 acres for sale on long-term credits. The Central Branch of the Union Pacific Railroad offered 1,200,000 acres for prices ranging from $1 to $15 per acre; the Kansas Pacific Railroad offered 5,000,000 acres for $1 to $6 per acre; the Kansas and Neosho Valley Railroad offered 1,500,000 acres for sale at $2 to $8 per acre; the Capital Land Agency of Topeka offered 1,000,000 acres of Kansas land for sale; [34] Van Doren and Havens offered 200,000 acres for $3 to $10 per acre; T. H. Walker offered 10,000 (or 100,000) acres [35] for $5 to $10 per acre; Hendry and Noyes offered 50,000 acres, and even the United States government was advertising for bids for approximately 6,000 acres of Sac and Fox Indian lands.[36] That virgin lands in Kansas were selling for substantial prices in this period is shown by Tables 8 and 9.

TABLE 8

Sales of State Lands in Kansas [a]

Lands	Years	Acres	Average price per acre
Common School	1865–1882	450,764	$4.00
Agricultural College	1868–1882	48,465	4.78
University	1878–1882	6,224	2.88
Normal School	1876–1882	4,966	4.72

[a] *Biennial Report*, Auditor of State, Kansas, 1882, pp. 359–360.

TABLE 9

Land Sales of Atchison, Topeka, and Santa Fe Railroad: [a]

Total Sales from March 1, 1871, to Dec. 31, 1879

Year	Acres	Principal	Average price per acre
1871	71,801.51	$ 425,013.75	$5.91
1872	45,328.81	269,627.66	5.94
1873	133,507.30	748,977.25	5.61
1874	200,459.96	900,973.30	4.49
1875	75,415.33	416,409.85	5.52
1876	122,201.17	665,455.17	5.44½
1877	85,047.78	423,477.49	4.98
1878	267,122.47	1,206,527.64	4.52
1879	104,744.41	494,353.73	4.72
Total	1,105,628.74	$5,550,815.84	$5.02

[a] Compiled from *Annual Reports* of the Atchison, Topeka, and Santa Fe Railroad, 1873–1880.

Such sales—and many others might be cited—are evidence that free homesteads on the most desirable land were not available in this state to incoming settlers.

A strong impulse to speculation was provided by the existence of large amounts of land warrants, chiefly those of the act of March 3, 1855,[37] which were to be had in the market at prices of a dollar an acre or less.[38] They could be used to locate solid blocks of land wherever the surveyed area of the public domain was open to cash entry. In addition, it is startling to find a provision in the Agricultural College Act of July 2, 1862, whereby 7,672,800 acres in land scrip,[39] which likewise could be used to locate surveyed lands open to cash entry, were thrown on the market. Within a comparatively short time this scrip depreciated greatly in value. Some states sold their scrip for an average price of less than fifty cents an acre and such prices tempted many individuals to purchase and locate large areas in the Western states.[40] Probably no other scrip or warrant act was used so extensively by speculators to build up large holdings as was this Agricultural College Act. Other special acts were passed after 1862 creating smaller amounts of Indian land scrip and other compensatory scrip, part of which possessed the special privilege of being subject to location on any part of the public domain, whether or not it was surveyed or had been offered for sale.[41]

The existence of large areas of rich lands open to speculative entries and the availability of warrants and scrip at depreciated prices made possible large-scale engrossment after the Homestead Law was passed. Some of the richest and most fertile sections of Iowa, Kansas, Nebraska, Missouri, California, Washington, and Oregon were thus open to cash or warrant entry, and after the adoption of the Homestead Law they were quickly engrossed by speculators.

Some of the land entries [42] made after 1862 are interesting to note. Senator John Sherman, who, like most politicians of his day, was not averse to speculating in lands, located with Agricultural College scrip 2,560 acres in Missouri in 1868; Robert Mears with the same kind of scrip located 29,280 acres in the Boonville district of Missouri; Amos Lawrence, prominent among the promoters of the Emigrant Aid Company at an earlier date, located 58,360 acres in Kansas in 1866 with Agricultural College scrip; Charles and Henry Stebbins and Henry M. Porter entered 53,760 acres in Kansas and Nebraska in 1866, 1867, and 1868 with the same kind of scrip; John C. Work and Rufus Hatch of New York, John J. Blair of New Jersey, and James C. Cusey of Sioux City, Iowa, entered in western Iowa in 1869 and 1870, 12,200, 28,671, 20,970, and 9,280 acres respectively; John P. Crothers, of Berks County, Pennsylvania, later of Clark County, Ohio, entered with scrip and cash 44,140 acres in Nebraska; William Scully, one of the greatest landed proprietors in the United States, whose relations with his tenants have been the subject of much hostile comment and legislation,[43] purchased for cash in a single land district in Nebraska in 1870, 41,421 acres; Ira Davenport of Steuben County, New York, whose land operations extended throughout most of the northwestern states, entered with cash and land warrants 16,949 acres in the Dakota City district of Nebraska. Perhaps the largest purchasers of land in Nebraska were a group of Providence, Rhode Island, speculators, consisting of Robert H. Ives, John Carter Brown, Charlotte R. and Moses B. I. Goddard. Ives alone had previously purchased 82,431 acres in Illinois, 50,000 acres in Iowa, and smaller amounts in Minnesota and Missouri, while Brown had acquired over 30,000 acres in Iowa and Illinois. These four individuals entered with cash over 96,000 acres in the Dakota City district. Between 1862 and 1873, twenty-seven other persons entered a combined area of 250,000 acres in Nebraska. Numerous other illustrations could be cited to indicate that speculation in agricultural lands in the Great Plains area did not cease with the passage of the Homestead Law.

Not only were the best agricultural lands being snapped up by speculators but the richest timberlands remaining in the possession of the United States were being rapidly entered by large dealers during the post-Civil War period. There were three areas in which vast amounts of timberland were still owned by the federal government, the Lake states, the Gulf states with Arkansas, and the Pacific Coast states. In each of these three regions millions of acres of pine, spruce, hemlock, and fir were available for cash entry and in the Pacific area lands covered with the rich redwood and other trees peculiar to that region had been, or were just being, brought into the market. In the timberlands of these three sections some of the largest purchases by speculators or lumbermen took place. Many thousands of acres in Wisconsin and Michigan were located by Isaac Stephenson, Philetus Sawyer, and Russell A. Alger, influential lumber dealers, who were subsequently to become members of the Senate of the United States. Ezra Cornell located 385,780 acres in the Eau Claire, Wisconsin, land district, 76,180 acres in the Bayfield district, 29,200 in the Stevens Point district, 12,480 acres in Minnesota, and 4,000 acres in Kansas, all with Agricultural College scrip of New York. A group of New York magnates, Thomas F. Mason, George B. Satterlee, and William E. Dodge, entered 232,799 acres in the Marquette, Michigan, district,

10,850 acres elsewhere in that state, and 10,359 acres in Wausau, Wisconsin. Francis Palms purchased in Wisconsin and Michigan 286,208 acres, and with Frederick E. Driggs entered in the eighties about 200,000 acres more in the Marquette district. Three Ithaca, New York, lumber dealers, Henry W. Sage,[44] John McGraw, and Jeremiah W. Dwight, like Ezra Cornell benefactors of Cornell University, entered 277,000 acres in Michigan, Wisconsin, and Minnesota, and 75,000 acres in Mississippi, Alabama, and Arkansas. Other large timberland entrymen in the Northwest were Calvin F. Howe of New York, who acquired 105,000 acres in Minnesota, Thomas B. Walker,[45] who alone and with others acquired 166,000 acres in the St. Cloud, Minnesota, district, George M. Wakefield, who accumulated 110,000 acres in the Marquette district, and Jesse Spaulding and H. H. Porter of Chicago, who purchased 113,000 acres in the same district. Fifty-six other persons purchased a total of 1,514,000 acres in Michigan, mostly in the Marquette district.

The same concentration of ownership of timberlands developed in the South after 1877. Some of the large purchases in this section were Daniel F. Sullivan's purchase of 147,000 acres in the Montgomery, Alabama, district in 1880–1882; Jabez B. Watkins's purchase of 145,000 acres in the New Orleans district; Delos A. Blodgett's purchase of 136,000 acres in the Jackson, Mississippi, district in 1885 to 1888; Lutcher and Moore's purchase of 108,000 acres in Louisiana in the eighties; and Franklin Head's and Nathan B. Bradley's purchases of 110,000 and 111,200 acres respectively in the New Orleans district. Sixty-eight other persons entered 2,110,000 acres in the southern districts. Altogether, over 5,500,000 acres of land were sold in the five southern states between 1880 and 1888, exclusive of pre-emption sales. Practically all of this area went to large land and lumber dealers. These lands comprised some of the very choicest timbered areas in the South and within less than a generation were selling at prices which brought enormous profits to the owners. It is worthy of note that many of the large timber dealers in Wisconsin, Michigan, and Minnesota made great acquisitions in the South.

The engrossment of timber and agricultural lands on the Pacific Coast proceeded at an even more rapid rate than in other sections of the country. Here in the years immediately following the Civil War a relatively small group of speculators sought to monopolize the best timber and agricultural lands. A group of eastern speculators consisting of W. W. Corcoran of Washington, ex-Senator Bright of Indiana, and

Elisha and Lawrason Riggs, whose land acquisitions in the Middle West had been very profitable, purchased over 7,000 acres in Washington and Oregon in the early seventies; another group of San Francisco speculators purchased 59,000 acres in the Olympia, Washington, district; J. W. Sprague of Minnesota purchased 24,000 acres in the same district, and five other persons acquired 42,000 acres. More spectacular were the huge entries in California.

Land monopolization in California dates back to the Spanish and Mexican periods, when large grants were made to favored individuals. After investigation by an American commission, 588 of these claims amounting to 8,850,143 acres, or an average of 15,051 acres each, were confirmed.[46] Following 1848 there came a rapid influx of settlers which, together with the large profits realized from the grazing industry in the interior valleys, created a land boom and led to extensive purchases. With great areas of land in the San Joaquin and Sacramento valleys open to cash purchase, the opportunity for speculative profits was unparalleled elsewhere; nor was the opportunity neglected. From 1862 to 1880 land sales and warrant and scrip entries in California were on an enormous scale, surpassing all other states for the period and in some years comprising well over half of the sales for the entire country. In the single year, ending June 30, 1869, 1,726,794 acres were sold in this state by the federal government, and for the entire period from 1862 to 1880 well over 7,000,000 [47] acres were entered with cash, warrants, or scrip. It should also be remembered that the state of California, which received 8,426,380 [48] acres from the federal government, was disposing of its most valuable holdings at this time.

Greatest of all the speculators operating in California was William S. Chapman, whose political influence stretched from Sacramento to St. Paul, Minnesota, and Washington, D.C. Of him it was said, with apparent justice, that land officers, judges, local legislators, officials in the Department of the Interior, and even higher dignitaries were ready and anxious to do him favors, frequently of no mean significance. Between 1868 and 1871 Chapman entered at the federal land offices approximately 650,000 acres of land in California and Nevada with cash, scrip, and warrants. At the same time he entered additional land through dummy entrymen, purchased many thousands of acres of "swamp" lands from the state of California, and otherwise added to his possessions till they totaled over 1,000,000 acres. Fraud, bribery, false swearing, forgery, and other crimes were charged against him, but he passed them off with little trouble.[49] The most remarkable feature about his vast acquisitions is that when plotted on a land-use map today they appear to be among the choicest of the lands. Chapman was not able to retain this vast empire for long. He became deeply involved in a grand canal project and eventually lost his lands, many of them going to a more constructive but equally spectacular land plunger, Henry Miller.[50]

Miller, unlike Chapman, bought lands for his cattle business, which was his main interest. As the activities of his firm—Miller and Lux, of which he was the chief promoter—expanded, he pushed its land acquisitions until they mounted to over a million acres. One hundred and eighty-one thousand acres of this amount were acquired directly from the federal government, with cash, Agricultural College scrip, and military warrants; large amounts were purchased from Chapman and other big land speculators and from the state of California. Miller's lands were slowly irrigated, parts were disposed of to small farmers, and upon them today exists a veritable agricultural empire.[51]

Other large purchasers of land in California were Isaac Friedlander, E. H. Miller, and John W. Mitchell, who acquired 214,000, 105,000, and 78,000 acres respectively. The total amount purchased from the federal government by Chapman, Miller and Lux, Friedlander, E. H. Miller, and Mitchell was 1,250,000 acres. Forty-three other large purchasers acquired 905,000 acres of land in the sixties in California. Buying in advance of settlement, these men were virtually thwarting the Homestead Law in California, where, because of the enormous monopolization above outlined, homesteaders later were able to find little good land.

Further details concerning the widespread speculative activity in public lands—both agricultural and timbered—after the passage of the Homestead Act are unnecessary; it is clear that speculation and land engrossment were not retarded by the act. Homeseekers in the West, being unwilling to go far afield from means of transportation or to settle upon the inferior lands remaining open to homestead, and lacking capital with which to purchase farms and to provide equipment for them, were frequently forced to become tenants on the lands of speculators. Thus farm tenancy developed in the frontier stage at least a generation before it would have appeared had the homestead system worked properly. In the states of Kansas and Nebraska, in which large-scale land monopolization has been revealed, 16 and 18 per cent respectively of the farms were operated by tenants in 1880, the first year for which figures are available, and in 1890, 28 and 24 per cent respectively were operated by tenants.[52] This continued monopolization of the best lands and the resulting growth of farm tenancy led reformers and others who feared the establishment of a landed aristocracy similar to that existing in many European countries to advocate the ending of the cash sales system entirely. Their demands were expressed in petitions to Congress, agitation in the press, and union of effort with other antimonopoly groups which were coming into prominence in the last third of the nineteenth century. Their agitation and the growing seriousness of the monopoly movement led to a series of halting steps toward the abandonment of cash sales, which frequently were offset by movements in the opposite direction.

The first step in the direction of abolishing the cash sale system was taken in June, 1866, when Congress provided that all public lands in the five southern states of Alabama, Arkansas, Florida, Louisiana, and Mississippi should be reserved from sale and subject only to entry under the Homestead Law.[53] The avowed purpose of this apparent discrimination against land speculation in the South while it was permitted to flourish elsewhere was to prevent speculators from monopolizing the land when it was restored to market—all land transactions had of course ceased in these states during the Civil War—and to encourage the growth of small holdings among the freedmen. By the South, the act was regarded, perhaps rightly, as a punitive measure. Certain it is that much of the 46,398,544 acres [54] thus reserved from cash entry was unsuited to small-scale farming and the freedmen showed no great desire to take advantage of the homestead privilege thus safeguarded. Nevertheless, the act was the first attack on the cash sale system.

Two backward steps were tried the same year, however. In the same month that the law was passed restricting southern public lands to homestead entry, an apparently innocuous measure slipped through Congress without much debate or opposition, giving to the New York and Montana Iron Mining and Manufacturing Company the right to purchase at $1.25 per acre twenty sections—12,800 acres—of unsurveyed and unopened lands in the territory of Montana, three sections of which might contain iron ore or coal and the remaining sections would presumably be timberlands. This measure was put through by Benjamin Wade of Ohio and Thaddeus Stevens of Pennsylvania, of whom it cannot be said that the interests of the homesteaders were nearest to their hearts.[55] It gave a gross extension of privilege to a group of speculators or land monopolists. Never had such a *carte blanche* grant been made before, though frequently petitioned for, and it aroused the indignation of President Johnson, who, in a ringing veto message, declared that the privileges conferred by the act "are in direct conflict with every principle heretofore observed in respect to the disposal of the public lands." [56] If the measure had been signed, the principle of granting lands free or for the minimum price to mining companies and other industrial organizations might have been established and the remaining portion of the public domain might have been divided among such capitalistic groups, just as millions of acres were being parceled out among the railroads. In placing himself squarely against the law, President Johnson aided in preserving the lands from speculators.

President Johnson's opposition to the granting of such special privileges to private business groups did not end the matter, however, for a similar measure passed the Senate in 1870. This second measure would have authorized the Sierra Iron Company of California to purchase 640 acres of land containing iron ore in the vicinity of Gold Lake, California, and 3,200 acres of timberlands for $2.50 per acre. As originally proposed by Senator Cole of California it would have permitted the purchase of 10,000 acres of timberlands at $1.25 per acre but was amended as above. The measure was rushed through the Senate at a night session when there was a very small attendance, but was later reconsidered, amended to provide further safeguards, and sent to the House, where the opponents of land monopoly succeeded in preventing its adoption. [57] Eternal vigilance on the part of true friends of the homesteaders was essential to prevent such laws being slipped through without adequate consideration.

The second backward step was a series of Indian treaties and administrative measures by which substantial areas of land in the Great Plains were sold to railroad companies and other speculative groups. When railroads were projected through Kansas and Nebraska, it was found that they must run through Indian reservations. Congressional land grants did not apply to such lands and the railroad officials therefore sought to purchase the lands which they could not receive as a gift. Instead of asking for alternate sections, however, as in the grants, they sought to purchase solid areas which would enable them to secure the entire benefits resulting from the construction of the railroads. As the Granger period had not yet arrived, railroads were still popular throughout most sections of the country. Furthermore, they possessed great influence at the seat of power and it was not difficult for them to prevail upon the proper officials to make treaties for the cession or sale of Indian lands. The Senate at this time was far more friendly to the railroads than to the homeseekers, as shown by its generous land grants and financial subsidies to the former and its refusal to place restrictions upon speculative purchases of land. Apparently it saw little difference between making donations of alternate sections of the public domain to the railroads and selling solid blocks of Indian lands to them for a low price. It therefore ratified such treaties with little hesitation.

In the years immediately following the enactment of the Homestead Law, a number of such treaties and subsequent sales contracts were ratified, providing for the sale of several million acres in Kansas to railroad companies.[58] That which aroused the greatest local opposition was the sale of some 800,000 acres of Cherokee Indian lands in southeastern Kansas. A treaty was negotiated with the Cherokees which permitted the sale of 800,000 acres to a single individual or corporation for $1 per acre, and which completely disregarded the white settlers already on the lands. Before ratification, the treaty was amended to permit the sale of tracts of 160 acres to the squatters.[59] In the meantime, the Secretary of the Interior had sold this great tract to the American Emigrant Company. This company was organized to operate under the nefarious contract-labor law of 1864 but quickly saw that larger profits were to be realized in land speculation and it began to deal in lands. Its record of land deals is obscure but is accompanied by sufficient evidence to indicate that the transactions were not always legitimate.[60] The purchase of 800,000 acres of Cherokee lands at $1 per acre on long credit was the result of secret negotiations; the lands were not offered at public sale, and the settlers were given no opportunity to purchase the tracts upon which they were squatting. The sale was, then, an outrageous violation of the principle of land for the landless and was immediately attacked as a gross fraud upon the public. Subsequent investigations revealed much that could not be satisfactorily explained and the Attorney General held that it was not in conformity with the treaty with the Cherokees.

Meantime, the Cherokee tract, through widely circulated rumors as to its fertility and desirability for settlement, was attracting the attention of many interested people. Following 1866, settlers flocked to the area in large numbers so that by 1867 there were reported to be 10,000 or 12,000 people there [61] and the number was shortly increased to 20,000. The settlers expected from the government the same lenient attitude toward their intrusions upon land not open to settlement as was being rendered to other people in similar circumstances elsewhere. Unfortunately for them, the value of the tract was appreciated by a number of railroad groups which desired to secure ownership of the entire area as a means of financing the construction of their lines. Concrete proposals for the purchase of the tract were made by three railroads—the Tebo and Neosho Railroad Company of Missouri,[62] the Atlantic and Pacific Railroad, and the Kansas City, Fort Scott, and Gulf Railroad. Prominent Missouri and Kansas politicians John C. Fremont and James F. Joy—"The Railroad King"—were interested in these lines and each sought to secure the much-coveted lands for his company. Although not the highest bidder, the sale was finally awarded to James F. Joy, who purchased the land for the Kansas City, Fort Scott, and Gulf Railroad. After the sale was made and the rival proposals turned down, the lenient officials of the Department of the Interior permitted Joy to surrender his contract and to substitute the original but less exacting contract with the American Emigrant Company, which was now assigned to him. This necessitated a supplementary treaty with the Cherokees to validate a contract previously held to be illegal. The contract was modified, however, to permit settlers who resided upon the land in 1866 to purchase their tracts at the appraised value.[63] Joy was required to pay but $1.00 an acre and generous credit was allowed him, while the settlers were asked to pay an average of $1.92 per acre in cash.[64]

The second sale was an equally great violation of the principle of free homesteads, and, it should be noted, was ratified by the Senate the same year that the House resolution frowning upon the further sale of agricultural land was passed. Secretary Browning, who, as Harlan's successor, had negotiated the sale, came in for as bitter accusations as had his predecessor and, it must be admitted, with some justification. The sale was made to his brother-in-law, Joy; his partner was at the time employed by Joy to negotiate the transaction; Browning himself had earlier represented Joy, and the following year was again retained by him in a series of important cases.[65] Furthermore, as was pointed out in a joint resolution adopted by the House on July 13, 1868,[66] the sale failed to consider the rights of a large number of people who had settled upon the tract between 1866 and 1868 and who were subsequently forced to purchase their lands from the railroad. Petitions from settlers upon the Cherokee tract demanding the abrogation of the sale poured in upon the Interior Department; [67]

the governor of Kansas denounced the sale as "a cheat and a fraud in every particular, and should have been encircled with hell's blackest marks," a "gigantic swindle"; [68] and in 1868 both the Republican and Democratic state conventions condemned the policy of disposing of Indian lands to "speculators and foreign corporations." [69] The campaign to have the second sale annulled was unsuccessful but, combined with the opposition to similar sales of Indian lands, it was eventually to end the policy.

Equally inconsiderate of the rights of settlers were the sales of the lands of the Delaware, Pottawatomie, Kickapoo, and Sac and Fox of the Mississippi Indians in Kansas. Treaties authorizing the sale of the surplus Delaware and Pottawatomie lands to the Leavenworth, Pawnee, and Western Railroad for $1.25 per acre were proclaimed on August 22, 1860, and April 19, 1862, respectively. [70] This railroad was unable to carry through the purchase of the Pottawatomie lands but did succeed in negotiating a sufficiently liberal contract for the Delaware lands whereby it acquired title to 223,966 acres of rich farming lands in Leavenworth, Atchison, and Jefferson counties for $286,742 paid in its own bonds, instead of cash as originally required. [71] In 1866, the Delaware Indians, having decided to abandon their diminished reserve in Kansas, which had been allotted in severalty, accepted a second treaty, which provided for the sale of the 92,598 acres contained in the reserve to the Missouri River Railroad for $2.50 per acre, exclusive of improvements, which were to be appraised and sold at a fair valuation. [72]

The Pottawatomie lands were subsequently sold, in 1868, to the Atchison, Topeka, and Santa Fe Railroad. This sale called for the payment of $1.00 per acre, not $1.25 as the earlier treaty provided, and five years' time was given during which no payments were required except advance interest of 6 per cent annually upon the purchase sum. The government thus not only denied to settlers the right to acquire the land directly but gave the railroad company the use of 340,180 acres of rich agricultural lands for annual payments of $20,410 for five years. At the end of this time a payment of $340,180 was required, which could be paid in greenbacks. [73] The policy of making land sales to settlers on credit had been abandoned in 1820 and Congress had resisted all efforts to restore the credit system, but credit was extended to railroads in the sixties. The Atchison, Topeka, and Santa Fe Railroad proceeded to sell the lands at prices well over double their cost, and charged 7 per cent interest on delayed payments. By 1873 it had received in cash and notes $646,784 and valued the remaining lands at $507,366,[74] no small profit for the times. A substantial part of the amount due the government in 1873 was paid from cash sales. The mortgage bonds based on these lands, obtained for only $20,410 down, enabled the railroad to begin construction without the promoters' having to supply any capital of their own worth mentioning.

A treaty similar to that with the Pottawatomie Indians was concluded with the Kickapoo Indians, under the terms of which 123,832 acres were sold in 1865 to the Atchison and Pike's Peak Railroad for $1.25 per acre, on generous credit.[75] This treaty was negotiated with a railroad whose president, Samuel C. Pomeroy, was not only senator from Kansas and thus in a position to support its adoption, but was also very close to the administration of the Indian Office and the Department of the Interior. Pomeroy represented the attitude of his state in demanding the speedy removal of the Indians and the disposal of their lands, but he went against popular opinion in supporting the sale of the Cherokee, Delaware, Pottawatomie, Kickapoo, and Osage lands to railroads.

The sale of the Sac and Fox Indian lands differs somewhat from those previously mentioned. These lands, comprising 272,200 acres, were advertised for sale to the highest bidders but, unlike the public land auctions, the bids were to be submitted by letter. This of course had the effect of preventing settlers upon the lands from combining into a claims association and preventing outsiders from bidding, as was done at the public auctions. As a result, most of the land was acquired at low prices by speculators, among whom the largest buyers were John McManus,[76] William B. McKean, Fuller and McDonald, Robert S. Stevens, and the Hon. Hugh McCulloch, who acquired respectively 142,915, 29,677, 39,058, 51,689, and 7,014 acres.[77]

The treaty providing for the largest sale of Indian lands was negotiated in 1868 between the Osage Indians of Kansas and representatives of the Department of the Interior, according to which 8,000,000 acres of land were to be sold to the Leavenworth, Lawrence, and Galveston Railroad for $1,600,000.[78] This was at the rate of twenty cents an acre for lands to which settlers were eagerly looking for homes. Characterized by Governor Crawford as "one of the most infamous outrages ever before committed in this country," it was indeed a most disgraceful and unjustified action. If adopted, it would have deprived the state of Kansas of 500,000 acres of school lands, robbed the Indians of a fair price for their lands, and would have killed a number of rival railroads, including the Atchison, Topeka, and Santa Fe. Worst of all, the treaty ignored the rights of settlers already on the lands. Furthermore, it was stated that a substantially higher bid had been turned down in order to accept that of the Leavenworth, Lawrence, and Galveston Railroad. The hand of James F. Joy was again seen, for the latter road had already come under his control as part of the great transportation system he was constructing. The Osage treaty brought to a climax the utter disregard shown by the officials of the Department of the Interior for the rights of settlers and aroused a storm of criticism, both in Kansas and in Washington.[79]

Representative George W. Julian, than whom no one had the interests of the homesteader more at heart, saw the iniquity in these Indian treaties and subsequent land sales to railroads and others. He introduced a resolution into the House of Representatives to the effect that these sales were a usurpation of power by the Senate which was endangering the entire land system and urged upon the Senate the advisability of ratifying no more such treaties. He pointed out that by using the treaty-making power in this way it was possible for the Senate to transfer all the public lands to the Indians and then by other treaties to arrange for their sale to railroads or other speculative groups, thus completely frustrating the Homestead Law and subverting the land system. Julian succeeded in winning the support of the House for his view and the resolution was adopted.[80] The enactment of this resolution and the storm of criticism which rained upon the Senate apparently had some effect, for the treaty with the Osage Indians, although urgently supported by the Commissioner of Indian Affairs, was not ratified, and Congress later provided for the sale of the Osage lands to actual settlers.

One may plainly see from events in Congress during 1867 and 1868 how insincere that body was in rendering lip service to the homestead principle. In this year Representative Julian introduced two measures into the House, the action on which throws a flood of light on the question. The first was a resolution that:

> In order to carry into full and complete effect the spirit and policy of the preëmption and homestead laws of the United States, the further sale of the agricultural public lands ought to be prohibited by law and that all proposed grants of land to aid in construction of railroads, or for other special objects, should be carefully scrutinized and rigidly subordinated to the paramount purpose of securing homes for the landless poor, the actual settlement and tillage of the public domain, and the consequent increase of the national wealth.[81]

The second was a bill to prevent any further sale of the public lands except as provided for in the Pre-emption and Homestead laws.[82] In support of these measures Julian made a number of strong speeches in which he described the evils resulting from speculation in lands, showed that, except for the southern states, free homesteading was restricted to the least attractive lands, and denounced the land monopoly which was rapidly being created by the lavish grants to the railroads. Julian was followed by two congressmen from Michigan districts in which lumbering was the chief industry. They favored large grants to railroads and no restrictions on land sales, and argued that Julian's bill, if passed, would ruin the lumber industry, increase speculation and fraudulent entries, and thus frustrate its own purpose.[83] Although unanimously reported by the Committee on Public Lands, nothing further was heard from the bill to end cash sales. The resolution, on the other hand, which had no binding effect but which favored exactly the same policy toward cash sales as the bill, passed the House without any important opposition.[84] Congress was far from ready in 1868 to end cash sales, and the passage of the resolution was certainly not "tantamount to a law." [85]

Between the enactment of this resolution in 1868 and 1876, the forces interested in opening up the public domain to large-scale purchases were fighting the advocates of the homestead principle on two grounds; they struggled to repeal the act of 1866 which placed restrictions on cash sales in the South, and they tried to prevent further limitations on land engrossment in the West.

The discriminatory character of the restrictions upon cash sales in the South and its obviously punitive features rankled with the southern congressmen who sought to repeal the act of 1866. They were vigorously supported by representatives from other sections who were either interested in the lumber industry themselves or whose constituents looked with longing eyes upon the rich pine lands of the South. In the early seventies the movement for repeal gained headway. Its leaders harped on the discriminatory features of the act of 1866, its retarding effects upon immigration and the lumber industry, and argued that it led to the public lands being stripped of their only valuable commodity—timber. In 1875 the Commissioner of the General Land Office came to the support of the repealists. Indeed, the Land Commissioners in their reports of 1875, 1876, and 1877 favored opening up all public lands to cash sale.[86] Strong opposition was voiced against the repeal measure by the northern Radicals for political purposes and by land reformers who foresaw the effects of such a backward step, but the combination of southern resentment and northern economic interests was too strong, and the measure became a law on July 4, 1876, without the approval of President Grant.[87] Southern lands were again made subject to cash entry, the unfortunate results of which have already been seen in the large-scale monopolization by lumber interests, mostly from the northern states.

Although defeated in the South, the land reformers, under the leadership of Senator Harlan of Iowa and Representative Julian of Indiana, continued the fight to limit or end cash sales to large purchasers. In the House three measures were passed in 1870, one to end cash sales in California, another to end cash sales in Dakota Territory, and the third to prevent cash sales in Nebraska, Nevada, California, Arkansas, and Utah.[88] Similar measures were introduced in the Senate but were uniformly unsuccessful, because here the interests of lumber men, mining groups, and large speculators were well represented. In 1872 a congressman from California proposed an amendment to the Constitution which would have prohibited the further disposal of the public lands except to actual settlers, but it made no progress.[89]

From the date of the repeal of the restrictions on cash entry in the South until 1889, there was not a session of Congress in which the question of reserving all the public lands for homestead entry was not fiercely debated. Continued efforts were made to end the cash sale system. Following 1880, the Pre-emption, Timber and Stone, Timber Culture, and Desert Land acts came in for much criticism, since it was apparent that, like the commutation clause of the Homestead Law, they lent themselves to abuse and fraud. In the eighties the movement was given a great impetus by the discovery of enormous frauds in which foreign corporations and titled noblemen were engaged for the purpose of building up vast estates. The fact that most of this alien ownership was English [90] was used effectively by the Anglophobes and, added to the antimonopoly movement which was rapidly gaining in strength, it made easy the conversion of many politicians to the cause of land reform.

President Cleveland's Land Commissioner, William A. J. Sparks, dramatically brought the issue to the front by revealing with overwhelming evidence that "the public domain was being made the prey of unscrupulous speculation and the worst forms of land monopoly through systematic frauds carried on and consummated under the public land laws." [91] In cold, biting language, he accused the administration of the General Land Office of being either extraordinarily inept in its management or directly involved in the great frauds which he unearthed. So general were the illegal or fraudulent entries that within a month after his accession to office he suspended all final entries under the Timber and Stone Act and the Desert Land Act, and in Colorado, Dakota, Idaho, Utah, Washington, New Mexico, Montana, Wyoming, Nevada, and parts of Minnesota, Kansas, and Nebraska suspended all entries except those made with cash and scrip. The evidence of fraud continued to come in, and, as the demand for complete suspension of all non-homestead entries stimulated speculators and monopolists to feverish activity, Sparks in desperation, in 1886, ordered the land officers to accept no further applications for entries under the Pre-emption, Timber Culture, and Desert Land acts.[92] This precipitate action stirred up a veritable hornets' nest of opposition and the order was rescinded, but its effect remained.

The onslaught of the antimonopolists had the effect of stimulating the speculators, cattlemen, lumber and mining companies to prompt action before the public domain should be closed to them. Land sales and entries under the Pre-emption, Timber Culture, Timber and Stone, and Desert Land acts and the cash sales system shot up to a high point in 1888, exceeding those of any year since 1856 and being surpassed only four times in our entire history.

This enormous speculation, added to the widespread frauds which were being uncovered, produced a demand for reform which swelled to a tremendous volume. Hundreds of petitions with innumerable signatures flooded Congress, urging changes in land policy and administration. They made it plain that public opinion had been aroused and could no longer be ignored.

Measure after measure providing for repeal of the objectionable laws passed the House in the eighties only to be defeated in the Senate. Finally, under the stimulus of Sparks's dramatic gesture, repeal measures passed both houses in 1886 and again in 1887, but were defeated through failure to harmonize conflicting views. These were to be the last defeats, however, because Congress was rapidly being forced into a position where it had to take action. In May and July, 1888, two measures were passed by which land sales in the five southern states were temporarily suspended, and the act of 1876 was reversed. This was followed, on March 2, 1889, by an act ending all cash sales of public lands except in Missouri, where the remaining lands were mostly mineral in character or scattered fragments of little value for agriculture. In 1890 a rider was attached to an appropriation act by which it was stipulated that henceforth no person should acquire title to more than 320 acres in the aggregate under all of the land laws.[93] Finally, in 1891 a combination of antimonopoly land reformers and conservationists placed upon the statute books a law which was as far reaching, as important, perhaps, as the Homestead Act of 1862. This law [94] repealed the Pre-emption and Timber Culture acts and placed additional safeguards in the Desert Land Act and the commutation clause of the Homestead Act. Except for Indian lands and small isolated tracts, the speculators could no longer purchase whole counties for the minimum price, and land engrossment by fraudulent means was at least made more difficult. Unfortunately these land reforms were not enacted until the best of the area suitable for farming without irrigation had passed into private ownership.

The most important section of the act of 1891 was that which authorized the creation of forest reservations on the public lands. Here was the first fundamental break with the underlying philosophy of our land system—the desire to dispose of the lands and hasten their settlement. The conservationists had now convinced the country that a part of our natural resources must be retained in public ownership and preserved for the future. Unfortunately, conservation, when first adopted, was embedded in an outworn *laissez faire* land system of a previous age, just as the free homestead plan had been superimposed upon a land system designed to produce revenue. In both cases the old and the new clashed with disastrous effects.

NOTES

1 The word "speculator," as used in this article, refers to large-scale land operators, and does not include many farmers who speculated in a small way.

2 "Grazing Homesteads and the Regulation of Grazing on the Public Lands," *Hearing before the Committee on the Public Lands,* House of Representatives, 63 Congress, 2 session, pt. 1, p. 358.

3 Leifur Magnusson, *Disposition of the Public Lands of the United States with Particular Reference to Wage-Earning Labor* (Washington, 1919), 29. See also Arthur C. Cole, *The Irrepressible Conflict, 1850–1865* (New York, 1934), 119, 357; John Ise, *The United States Forest Policy* (New Haven, 1920), 56.

4 Benjamin Horace Hibbard, *A History of the Public Land Policies* (New York, 1924), 111, 112.

5 The shallowness of this contention was pointed out by George W. Julian in 1884 (*Political Recollections, 1840 to 1872* [Chicago, 1884], 218).

Speaking of the continuation of cash sales, railroad grants, and disposal of the Indian lands as fatal to the homestead principle, he said that they furnished "a remarkable commentary upon the boasted friendship of the Republican party for the landless poor."

6 In contrast, Herbert Heaton ventures the view that the importance of free land in drawing immigrants to America has been overestimated, while the influence of high wages has been underestimated. "Migration and Cheap Land—the End of Two Chapters," *The Sociological Review,* 26:237 (July, 1934).

7 *Report,* 1863, p. 7. See also *Report,* Secretary of the Interior, 1862, p. 4.

8 1884 edition, pp. 25, 415. It is worth noting that a total of 4,851,296 acres was entered in Michigan, Wisconsin, and Minnesota in the eighties with cash, scrip, and warrants. This is exclusive of pre-emption, homestead, and other limited entries.

9 These lands, which were being ceded by the Indians, are neglected by both Donaldson and Hibbard.

10 The more advanced reformers demanded that all sales should be discontinued, grants to railroads and other special interests ended, and all the public lands reserved for actual settlers under the provisions of the homestead measure. The differences between what may be called the moderate and the radical land reformers is apparent in the congressional debates. See also George M. Stephenson, *The Political History of the Public Lands from 1840 to 1862* (Boston, 1917), 166 and elsewhere; Roy M. Robbins, "Horace Greeley: Land Reform and Unemployment, 1837–1862," *Agricultural History,* 7:26, *passim* (January, 1933); St. George L. Sioussat, "Andrew Johnson and the Early Phases of the Homestead Bill," *Mississippi Valley Historical Review,* 5:253, *passim* (December, 1918); Hibbard, *History of the Public Land Policies,* 347, *passim;* John Bell Sanborn, "Some Political Aspects of Homestead Legislation," *American Historical Review,* 6:19, *passim* (October, 1900).

11 Speaking of the period from 1836 to 1876, Professor Joseph Schafer writes: "It was, in this period, a rare thing for an outside speculator in wild lands to make any profit on his speculation." *Wisconsin Magazine of History,* 13:428 (June, 1930). See also his *The Wisconsin Lead Region* (*Wisconsin Domesday Book: General Studies,* vol. 3, Madison, 1932), 153; *Wisconsin Domesday Book: Town Studies,* vol. 1 (Madison, 1924), 10.

12 Wm. A. J. Sparks, Commissioner of the General Land Office, in his *Report* for 1885 (pp. 3–4), writes as follows concerning the land laws: "I found that the magnificent estate of the nation in its public lands had been to a wide extent wasted under defective and improvident laws and through a laxity of public administration astonishing in a business sense if not culpable in recklessness of official responsibility.

"The widespread belief of the people of this country that the land department has been very largely conducted to the advantage of speculation and monopoly, private and corporate, rather than in the public interest, I have found supported by developments in every branch of the service. It seems that the prevailing idea running through this office and those subordinate to it was that the government had no distinctive rights to be considered and no special interests to protect; hence, as between the government and spoilers of the public domain, the government usually had the worst of it. I am satisfied that thousands of claims without foundation in law or equity, involving millions of acres of public land, have been annually passed to patent upon the single proposition that nobody but the government had any *adverse* interest.

"The vast machinery of the land department appears to have been devoted to the chief result of conveying the title of the United States to public lands upon fraudulent entries under strained constructions of imperfect public land laws and upon illegal claims under public and private grants."

13 Ise, *The United States Forest Policy, passim*, has drawn together and summarized the published information concerning the vast frauds committed by the lumber interests in their efforts to acquire great areas of timberlands. See also Jenks Cameron, *The Development of Governmental Forest Control in the United States* (Baltimore, 1928), *passim*.

14 The Commissioners of the General Land Office from 1875 onward recommended annually the repeal of the Pre-emption Law; in 1883 the Commissioner recommended the repeal of the commutation clause of the Homestead Law and the Timber Culture Act (*Report*, 1883, pp. 6–7); in 1884 the Commissioner suggested the repeal of these laws and the Desert Land Act and the Timber and Stone Act. *Ibid.*, 1883, pp. 6–8. (These documents are cited hereafter as *General Land Office Report*.)

15 Computed from Donaldson, *The Public Domain*, 258–273. The best criticism by a contemporary of the railroad land-grant policy, is found in Henry George, *Our Land and Land Policy, National and State* (San Francisco, 1871). See also George W. Julian, "Railway Influence in the Land Office," *North American Review*, 136:237–256 (March, 1883), and his "Our Land-Grant Railways in Congress," *International Review*, 14:198–212 (February–March, 1883). For more recent treatments see Robert S. Henry, "The Railroad Land Grant Legend in American History Texts," *Mississippi Valley Historical Review*, 32:171–194 (September, 1945) *[reprinted in this volume pp. 121–144];* comments on "The Railroad Land Grant Legend in American History Texts," *Mississippi Valley Historical Review*, 32:557–576 (March, 1946) *[reprinted in this volume, pp. 145–161];* Paul Wallace Gates, "The Railroad Land-Grant Legend," *Journal of Economic History*, 14:143–146 (Spring, 1954) *[reprinted in this volume, pp. 175–179],* and comment on the same in *Journal of Economic History,* 15(1):112 (1955).

16 *General Land Office Report*, 1885, p. 26, *passim*. As late as 1883, twelve years after the last land grant was made to railroads, it was estimated that more than 100,000,000 acres were withdrawn from settlement pending selection of the railroad sections. Julian, "Railway Influence in the Land Office," 252.

17 For large speculative purchases within the limits of the Illinois Central Railroad grant, see Paul Wallace Gates, *The Illinois Central Railroad and Its Colonization Work* (Cambridge, Mass., 1934), 107, 123 ff.

18 This provision was practically repealed by the acts of March 3, 1879 (20 *U.S. Stat.*, 472), July 1, 1879 (21 *U.S. Stat.*, 46), and June 15, 1880 (*ibid.*, 238).

19 James B. Hedges, "The Colonization Work of the Northern Pacific Railroad," *Mississsippi Valley Historical Review*, 13:327 (December, 1926); Harold E. Briggs, "Early Bonanza Farming in the Red River Valley of the North," *Agricultural History*, 6:26, *passim* (January, 1932); Alva H. Benton, "Large Land Holdings in North Dakota," *Journal of Land and Public Utility Economics*, 1:405–413 (October, 1925); Paul Wallace Gates, "Frontier Landlords and Pioneer Tenants," *Journal of the Illinois State Historical Society*, 38:143–206 (June, 1945).

20 *Congressional Globe*, 41 Cong., 2 sess., 2095.

21 Donaldson, *The Public Domain*, 272.

22 Lewis H. Haney, *A Congressional History of Railways in the United States* (2 vols., Madison, 1910), 2:20–22; Stephenson, *Political History of the Public Lands, 1840–1862*, 122, n.

23 Computed from *General Land Office Report*, 1932, pp. 45–50.

24 A total of 230,088,219 acres have been patented to the states, of which 38,206,487 acres were given for railroads, 3,359,188 acres for wagon roads, and 6,842,921 acres for canals. Most of these special grants were quickly transferred to construction companies or disposed of by the states. The total also includes 7,672,800 acres in land scrip which was granted to the states in which there were no remaining public lands for the endowment of agricultural colleges. The scrip could not be located by the states and had to be sold promptly. Of the remaining lands granted, or which were subsequently granted to the states, it seems safe to say that at least 140,000,000 acres were still unsold to 1862.

25 U.S. Department of Commerce and Labor, Bureau of Corporations, *The Lumber Industry: Part I* (1913), 252.

26 *General Land Office Report*, 1862, p. 8.

27 Volumes of Proclamations for Public Land Sales, General Land Office; *General Land Office Reports*, 1862 and following. It is true that 46,-000,000 acres in the South were withdrawn from cash entry under the act of June 21, 1866, but these lands were restored to sale in 1876 and during the interval the amount of land disposed of was small, amounting to only 2,000,000 acres by 1871. Computed from *General Land Office Report*, 1871, p. 343.

28 Indian reservations and claims were not sharply defined in 1862, much of the area not having been surveyed. In 1875 the Commission of Indian Affairs (*Report*, 1875, p. 142) gave the acreage in Indian reservations as 165,729,714 acres. The amount of Indian lands sold directly to individuals and corporations and that sold through the General Land Office during the years 1862–1875 would bring this figure to 175,000,000 acres for 1862.

29 The most important published source on the Indian lands and their management and sale is the *Annual Reports* of the Commissioners of Indian Affairs during the years after 1865.

30 24 *U.S. Stat.*, 388; 34 *U.S. Stat.*, 182.

31 Recent addresses by John Collier, Commissioner of Indian Affairs, and

Senator William H. King have called attention to the alienation of Indian lands since the Allotment Act of 1887, but they have not been concerned with the previous crowding of the Indians on the reservations and the forced cession or sale of their surplus lands which antedated that act. See the speech of Senator King on "Condition of Indians in the United States," Senate Document no. 214, 72 Cong., 2 sess. It is difficult to estimate the total amount of Indian land which was sold prior to 1887 and after 1862, but it would certainly bring the total Indian land sales since 1862 to over 100,000,000 acres.

32 The railroads have received 132,425,574 acres of land directly from the federal government or from grants originally given to the states for railroad construction. *Report*, Secretary of the Interior, 1934, p. 73. This amount would be greatly augmented by grants made by the state of Texas from its public lands and by other states from the swamp lands received from the federal government, and also by the lands purchased by railroads from the Indians. As used here, only the 132,425,574 acres are considered. Only a small part of this vast area was sold prior to 1862. Not all of it was available for sale even by 1871, but this total represents all the land which the railroads received from congressional land grants.

33 Pamphlet: *Two Thousand Families Wanted for Iowa*, n.d., n.p.

34 Letterhead of letter of W. C. Fitzsimmons, a member of the firm, July 15, 1871, to E. S. Parker, Commissioner of Indian Affairs, file of material on Indian land sales, Indian Office.

35 In June, 1870, Walker was advertising 10,000 acres of Kansas land for sale (Leavenworth *Bulletin*, June 13, 1870), while in February, 1871, he was advertising 100,000 acres for sale (*ibid.*, Feb. 7, 1871). Thaddeus H. Walker of Topeka, Kansas, formerly of Washington County, New York, had entered in 1855 to 1859 in the Kickapoo, Kansas, Land District 16,000 acres, 46,000 acres in the Lecompton, Kansas, Land District, 14,000 acres in the Junction City, Kansas, Land District, and 4,600 acres in the Decorah, Iowa, Land District. The lands were entered mostly with military land warrants. See the abstract and entry books of the above-mentioned land districts in the General Land Office.

36 The advertisements appeared in the *Kansas Farmer*, the Leavenworth *Bulletin*, the Lawrence *Republican Daily Journal*, the *Cultivator and Country Gentleman*, and the *American Agriculturist*.

37 10 *U.S. Stat.*, 701–702. It should be pointed out that prior to the adoption of the prospective pre-emption principle, public lands were not subject to disposal until they had been surveyed and offered at public auction. Lands then remaining unsold were subject to private entry for cash, scrip, or warrants. After prospective pre-emption was adopted, settlers could make claims upon surveyed but unoffered lands, thus preceding the speculators. When the homestead idea was being debated, its advocates argued that its effects would be largely mitigated unless all lands were withdrawn from speculative entry upon its passage. Such a radical proposal was too much for many homestead advocates and it failed of serious consideration. Nevertheless, it was expected

by many people that no additional lands would be offered at auction after 1862 and therefore the area open to private entry would become progressively smaller as time passed. Unfortunately, additional land was put up at auction in the sixties, seventies, and eighties, thus increasing the areas open to speculative and large-scale entries. At the same time, land was being opened to homestead and pre-emption entry which was not offered at auction and therefore not subject to private entry for cash, scrip, or warrants.

38 *General Land Office Report*, 1862, p. 9. In 1862 there were 7,123,380 acres of military warrants outstanding.

39 12 *U.S. Stat.*, 503–505; *Report of the Public Lands Commission*, 1905 (58 Cong., 3 sess., Senate Doc. no. 189), 361. For detail concerning the management of the land scrip of Rhode Island, Illinois, and New York, see Paul Wallace Gates, *The Wisconsin Pine Lands of Cornell University* (Ithaca, 1943), *passim*.

40 Of course the southern states did not receive their scrip until after the Civil War but it took some time for the Land Office to handle the details involved in issuing it and consequently most of it was located between 1864 and 1868. The price which each state received for the sale of its scrip is given in *History of the Agricultural College Land Grant of July 2, 1862, together with a Statement of the Conditions of the Fund derived therefrom as it now exists in each State of the Union* (Ithaca, 1890), xvi, xvii.

41 *General Land Office Report*, 1875, p. 69; *Public Land Statutes of the United States*, Daniel M. Greene, compiler (Washington, 1931), 637–639.

42 These land entries were compiled from hundreds of volumes of abstracts in the General Land Office, Department of the Interior, Washington, the listing of which would be almost impossible and equally futile. Following are the chief types of entry books: Abstracts of Lands Entered (for cash), Military Warrant Abstracts, Agricultural College Scrip Abstracts, Indian and other miscellaneous scrip abstracts, and Registers of Receipts.

43 See C. F. Taylor, ed., *The Land Question from Various Points of View* (Philadelphia, 1898), 44, *passim*.

44 The land empire of Henry W. Sage alone is said by a local historian to have included over 500,000 acres. John H. Selkreg, ed., *Landmarks of Tompkins County, New York* (Syracuse, 1894), pt. 2, p. 4.

45 Walker acquired 700,000 acres of valuable sugar pine and western pine timberland in California, chiefly through the use of dummy entrymen. Bureau of Corporations, *The Lumber Industry: Part II* (1914), 91.

46 *Report of the Public Lands Commission*, 1905, p. 140; Paul Wallace Gates, "Adjudication of Spanish-Mexican Land Claims in California," *The Huntington Library Quarterly*, 21:213–236 (May, 1958).

47 *General Land Office Reports*, 1862–1880.

48 *General Land Office Report*, 1932, p. 46.

49 There is a mass of testimony offered to prove these charges in *Reports of the Joint Committees on Swamp and Overflowed Lands, and Land*

Monopoly, presented at the Twentieth Session of the Legislature of California (Sacramento, 1874). There is additional information on Chapman's land business in California in my "California's Agricultural College Lands," *Pacific Historical Review,* 30:103–122 (May, 1961). For a different view of Chapman see Gerald D. Nash, "Henry George Reexamined: William S. Chapman's Views on Land Speculation in Nineteenth-Century California," *Agricultural History,* 33:133–137 (July, 1959).

50 Edward F. Treadwell, *The Cattle King* (New York, 1931), 73.

51 The story of Henry Miller is interestingly told in Treadwell, *The Cattle King.* A more detailed and objective study of the land and cattle business of Miller and Lux would shed much light on the history of the Far West.

52 *Eleventh Census,* 1890, "Statistics of Agriculture," 4. There is some detail on the relation of land policy and farm tenancy in an article by the present writer on "Recent Land Policies of the Federal Government" . . . in Part 7 of the Supplementary Report of the Land Planning Committee to the National Resources Board, entitled "Certain Aspects of Land Problems and Governmental Land Policies."

53 Act of June 21, 1866, 14 *U.S. Stat.,* 66–67. See Paul Wallace Gates, "Federal Land Policy in the South," *Journal of Southern History,* 6:303–330 (August, 1940).

54 *Cong. Globe,* 39 Cong., 1 sess., 715 ff.; 2736.

55 *Ibid.,* 2193, 2218, 2219, 2303, 2965, 2966.

56 Message of June 15, 1866, *Senate Journal,* 39 Cong., 1 sess., 532.

57 *Ibid.,* 41 Cong., 2 sess., 3659–3670, 4543–4546.

58 These treaties are included in *United States Statutes-at-Large,* vols. 12, 13, 14. They are analyzed and the areas conveyed by them are pictured on maps in Charles C. Royce, *Indian Land Sessions in the United States* (*Eighteenth Annual Report of the Bureau of American Ethnology to the Secretary of the Smithsonian Institution, 1896–1897*), pt. 2. I have dealt with the management and sale of the Kansas Indian reserves in my *Fifty Million Acres: Conflicts over Kansas Land Policy* (Ithaca, 1954), *passim.*

59 14 *U.S. Stat.,* 799–809.

60 The sale of 18,000 acres of "swamp lands" in Wright County, Iowa, to the American Emigrant Company for $1,500 and the subsequent recovery of a portion of the land is described by W. J. Covil in the Webster City *Freeman-Tribune,* July 13, 1904, republished in *Annals of Iowa,* 3d ser., 7:360 (1905).

61 Governor S. J. Crawford, Topeka, Kansas, Aug. 19, 1867, to Secretary Browning, file of material on Indian land sales, Indian Office.

62 P. A. Ladue, St. Louis, Missouri, Jan. 19, 1867, to L. C. Bogy, Commissioner of Indian Affairs, *ibid.*

63 The sale of the Cherokee lands is discussed in a letter of Charles Mix, Acting Commissioner of Indian Affairs, Apr. 21, 1869, to J. D. Cox, Secretary of the Interior, Cherokee File, Indian Office. Secretary Harlan's interpretation of the sale may be read in *Cong. Globe,* 40 Cong.,

3 sess., 409 ff., and 41 Cong., 1 sess., 21–23; also in Johnson Brigham, *James Harlan* (Iowa City, 1913), 235 ff. See also Eugene F. Ware, "The Neutral Lands," *Transactions of the Kansas State Historical Society*, 6:147–169 (1900).

64 *Report,* Commissioner of Indian Affairs, 1869, p. 502.

65 Theodore Calvin Pease and James G. Randall, eds., *Diary of Orville Hickman Browning* (*Illinois State Historical Library Collections*, vols. 20, 22, Springfield, 1925–1933), 1:645–646; 2:219, 239, 257, 276, *passim*.

66 *Cong. Globe,* 40 Cong., 2 sess., 4000–4001.

67 These petitions are filed in the Indian Office, Cherokee File.

68 Samuel J. Crawford, *Kansas in the Sixties* (Chicago, 1911), 310. Crawford, as governor, took an active part in the campaign to end the sale of large tracts of Indian lands to railroads and other speculative groups. Aside from his interest in the settlers who were being deprived of the right of buying their holdings directly from the government, he opposed the Indian land policy on the ground that it deprived the state of the 16th and 32d sections which it would otherwise get for its public schools.

69 D. W. Wilder, *Annals of Kansas* (Topeka, 1886), 481, *passim*. In this book are found a number of items indicating the emotions which were aroused in the settlers of the Cherokee tract by the arbitrary sale of the lands.

70 12 *U.S. Stat.,* 1129, 1193. This railroad later became the Union Pacific Railway Company, Eastern Division, and still later the Kansas Pacific Railroad.

71 *Ibid.,* 1177.

72 14 *U.S. Stat.,* 793–794; O. H. Browning, Secretary of the Interior, Oct. 21, 1867, to C. E. Mix, Commissioner of Indian Affairs, Delaware Files, Indian Office.

73 15 *U.S. Stat.,* 535–536; *Report,* Commissioner of Indian Affairs, 1869, p. 504.

74 *Report,* Atchison, Topeka, and Santa Fe Railroad, 1873, p. 10. It is true that in later reports the meager data given indicate the estimate of return contained in the *Report* for 1873 as somewhat optimistic.

75 13 *U.S. Stat.,* 623 ff.; *Cong. Globe,* 40 Cong., 2 sess., 1715; Royce, *Indian Land Sessions, passim*.

76 John McManus, of Reading, Pennsylvania, was a director of the Kansas Pacific Railway Company, which had the largest land grant in Kansas. *Report,* Kansas Pacific Railway Co., 1870.

77 *Report,* Commissioner of Indian Affairs, 1865, p. 549 ff. See also speech of Representative Julian in *Cong. Globe,* 40 Cong., 2 sess., 1715.

78 *Report,* Commissioner of Indian Affairs, 1868, p. 5.

79 *Crawford, Kansas in the Sixties,* 299 ff.

80 *Cong. Globe,* 40 Cong., 2 sess., 2753, 2814, 3278–3279.

81 *Ibid.,* 97.

82 *Ibid.,* 371.

83 *Ibid.,* 1712–1715, 2380–2387.

84 *Ibid.*, 1861.
85 See p. 316 of this article.
86 *Cong. Globe*, 41 Cong., 3 sess., 539–540; *Cong. Record*, 43 Cong., 1 sess., 4633, *passim;* 44 Cong., 1 sess., 815 ff., 1090, 3655; *General Land Office Report*, 1875, pp. 8–9, 17–19; 1876, p. 7; 1877, p. 34.
87 *Cong. Record*, 44 Cong., 1 sess., 4469; 19 *U.S. Stat.*, 73–74. The debates on the repeal measure are discussed in Ise, *The United States Forest Policy*, 49–53.
88 *Cong. Globe*, 41 Cong., 2 sess., 738–739, 5129.
89 *Cong. Globe*, 42 Cong., 3 sess., 84.
90 In 1884 the Senate called for an investigation of the foreign landholdings and the resulting report contains some interesting information on the practices and holdings of a number of well-financed British land and cattle companies. See Senate Doc. no. 181, 48 Cong., 1 sess.
91 *General Land Office Report*, 1885, p. 48.
92 *Report*, 1886, pp. 43, 135.
93 25 *U.S. Stat.*, 622, 626, 854–855; 26 *U.S. Stat.*, 371, 391.
94 26 *U.S. Stat.*, 1095–1103.

The Role of the Land Speculator in Western Development

PAUL WALLACE GATES

This paper is, in part, a synthesis of a number of articles previously published, as follows: "The Homestead Law in an Incongruous Land System," *American Historical Review*, 41 (1936), 652–681; "Land Policy and Tenancy in the Prairie Counties of Indiana," *Indiana Magazine of History*, 35 (1939), 1–26; "Land Policy and Tenancy in the Prairie States," *Journal of Economic History*, 1 (1941), 60–82. The data concerning land entries was compiled from the abstracts of land entries in the General Land Office, now in the National Archives. Acknowledgment is made to the Social Science Research Council and Cornell University for financial assistance which made possible the research embodied in this article.

Reprinted by permission from the Pennsylvania Magazine of History and Biography, *Volume 66 (1942), pages 314–333.*

THE land-use pattern of the twenty-nine public land states of the South, the Middle West, and the Far West is the result of a long process of development and adaptation in which such factors as speculation, absentee ownership, credit, usury, farm mechanization, transportation, and government controls have played important roles. Only recently has the United States come to realize the monstrous errors it permitted to develop in this land-use pattern. Likewise, only recently has it become apparent that this pattern is the product in part of mistaken land policies which were once thought to be establishing a democratic system of landownership. Wishful thinking, unwillingness to face the facts, and political oratory combined to obscure the appearance of ominous signs that a democratic pattern of ownership was not being achieved. A few notable spokesmen protested against policies which permitted concentration of landownership; but Americans, big and little, were too much concerned with the accumulation of wealth through land speculation to listen to their Cassandra-like predictions.

From the seventeenth to the nineteenth centuries European immigrants, many of them from classes to which actual landownership was denied, brought with them to America a craving for land. Land for a home and a competence was first desired; then land to assure wealth and social position was wanted. This craving for land explains much in American history and is one of its central themes. It was the motivating force which sent hordes of settlers into the expanding frontier, and it drew forth large sums of money for investment in America's unsettled areas. Until the modern corporation came to be the dominant factor in American economic life the principal opportunity for investment was in real estate. All persons seeking land for investment rather than for a farm home have been called land speculators, and the term, loose as it may be, has an important position in our terminology.

The term "land speculator" meant different things to different people and different sections. To a frontiersman it meant an eastern capitalist who bought large quantities of newly offered land in anticipation of settlers to come; or it meant a railroad or canal construction company to which had been given alternate sections of land in a strip 10 or 20 miles wide paralleling the line of the improvement; or it meant a pine-land baron who acquired 5,000, 10,000 or 50,000 acres of rich timberland. The frontiersman distinguished between resident and absentee speculators. Only non-resident owners of land who were not contributing to the development of the West by making improvements upon their lands were regarded by him as speculators and were the object of his resentment. Land grants for internal improvements were strongly favored by the frontier, which thirsted for connections with the outside world, but the frontiersman expected these lands to be sold promptly and on the pre-emption system.

To an urban worker, the term "speculator" meant someone who laid out towns or additions to them, donated lots for churches and schools, attracted industries or state institutions to the new communities and peddled out building lots at high prices to newcomers. To Horace Greeley the term meant, in addition, the thousands of persons settling the West who sought a stake in the land greater than they could expect to use personally. Greeley also applied it scornfully to those westerners of means who purchased wild lands as an investment, as did their eastern associates. All were speculators; all contributed their share to the pattern of ownership which exists today.

Although frontiersmen, as a rule, possessed little or no capital, they were anxious to own as much land as possible. The first wave of settlers who followed the fur trader squatted upon choice locations, made rude improvements, and, when new arrivals came in, sold their claims and moved on to a new frontier before the government auction took place. These squatters were in a sense speculators. They sought to engross a half section or more and established claim associations to protect their rights. Henceforth these quasi-legal claims were bought and sold just like patent titles.

The second wave of settlers remained on the land until the auction sale, on which occasion they borrowed to the hilt to buy as much land as possible. The more successful, who had brought considerable money with them, or who had accumulated something from land and barter exchanges on the frontier, might have sufficient credit at the western banks to enable them to purchase 320, 480, or 640 acres. Loose banking policies made credit easy to secure, and everyone attempted to borrow for land speculation. Rosy dreams of profits to be made distracted the attention of frontiersmen from the business of making farms in the wilderness. An English observer shrewdly remarked: "Speculation in real estate . . . has been the ruling idea and occupation of the Western mind. Clerks, labourers, farmers, storekeepers, merely followed their callings for a living, while they were speculating for their fortunes. . . . The people of the West became dealers in land, rather than its cultivators." [1] Calvin Fletcher, an Indianapolis banker and large landlord, deplored the granting of credit for speculative purchases of land. "The consequence is," he said in 1838, "that for the last 4 years say 6 years there has scarcely been the extension of a farm. No new fields opened & at the same time an enormous increase of consumers—What Son will go to work or what farmer will draw out the energies of his family where they can dress them, clothe them & feed them on the glorious anticipations of a years accidents which may or may not pay the debt without an effort." [2]

On every frontier the settler-speculator was present. He rarely learned from experience. By claiming 320 acres instead of 160, he separated himself that much more from his neighbor. He had to bear a heavier proportion of the cost of road construction and maintenance;

his school costs were increased or the establishment of schools was delayed and his children were denied educational opportunities; the expense of county and state government, in a period when the land tax was the principal source of government income, was burdensome. Other social institutions like churches, granges, and libraries came more slowly because the population was so dispersed. Furthermore, railroads, which all settlers wanted in their vicinity, could not be pushed into sparsely settled areas without large subsidies. State and county subsidies required special assessments upon the already overburdened taxpaying farmers, and land grants, whether by federal or state governments, created a near land-monopoly. Careful observers like Greeley saw many of these results and urged settlers to be content with smaller tracts which they could conveniently cultivate.

The chance of making a fortune in wild lands or town lots in the rapidly expanding communities of the West was an allurement difficult to resist. Fantastic stories of the profits others had won were printed in the newspapers and retold in letters from the West. Here, in 1818–1819, 1835–1837, or 1850–1857, was the lodestone to quick wealth. Touched by the fever of land speculation, excited people throughout the country borrowed to the extent of their credit for such investments. Men from all walks of life permitted their dreams to overcome their better judgment. Politicians, bankers, writers, ministers, planters, and poets, everyone, it seemed, who had any resources at all undertook to invest in western lands. Levi Beardsley, a prominent New Yorker who went west in 1836 to invest some $20,000 in wild land has left an interesting description of the speculative excitement of that year:

Every one was imbued with a reckless spirit of speculation. The mania, such it undoubtedly was, did not confine itself to one particular class, but extended to all. Even the reverend clergy doffed their sacerdotals, and eagerly entered into competition with mammon's votaries, for the acquisition of this world's goods, and tested their sagacity against the shrewdness and more practiced skill of the professed sharper.[3]

The existence of a class of professional land agents facilitated land purchases by absentee capitalists. Eastern papers with a wide circulation among the wealthy contained numerous advertisements of these land agents during the years from 1830 to 1857. In every enterprising community on the frontier were found agents who were prepared to buy or enter land for others with cash or warrants.[4] For a commission of 5 per cent or a share in the transaction, generally from a third to a quarter, they would select land, sometimes by personal investigation, sometimes by a superficial search of the entry books, and make purchases for their principals.

Some of the more important of these land agents were Henry W. Ellsworth of Lafayette, Indiana; Cook and Sargent of Davenport, Iowa; and Henry C. Putnam of Eau Claire, Wisconsin. Ellsworth published a booklet, *Valley of the Upper Wabash*,[5] to attract attention to western Indiana and eastern Illinois, and he and his father, Henry L. Ellsworth, Federal Commissioner of Patents, were able to induce hundreds of easterners, mostly New Englanders, to invest in the West. Cook and Sargent maintained offices in each of the eight land-office towns in Iowa, where they entered nearly 200,000 acres.[6] Putnam's entries in Wisconsin exceeded a half million acres.[7]

These western land agents rank with the registers and receivers of the land offices as among the most important people on the frontier. They dealt in land warrants and scrip, ran a local note-shaving business, purchased exchange, sometimes operated a bank of issue with funds provided by eastern capitalists, loaned eastern funds to squatters at frontier rates ranging from 20 to 60 per cent, bought and sold land, paid taxes for absentee owners and undertook to protect their lands against depredations. At a later date, they arranged for renting land, made collections, and sold produce received in payment of rent. Small investors in the East were obliged to work through these agents, to submit to their exactions, and to suffer from their inefficiency, and could not effectually protest against their obvious neglect. The agent could take his commission from rents or sales before any money was remitted to the owner, could sell his own land to prospective purchasers, rather than that of the owners he represented, could neglect tax payments and get the title involved, or could pay taxes on the wrong land. In numerous cases western agents took advantage of their clients, used the prestige which their contacts provided for personal interests, and constantly minimized the value of the land they represented in order to increase sales and thereby commissions. In this way, absentee investors whose eastern responsibilities did not permit them to give personal attention to their possessions in the West were imposed upon and victimized.

A case in point is that of Senator Henry H. Hubbard of New Hampshire, who, in association with Daniel Webster and other Yankees, invested well over $50,000 in western lands. Hubbard sent Moses M. Strong of Vermont to Wisconsin Territory in 1836 to invest a part of this money. Land was acquired and some sales were made by Strong before the crash of 1837 put a stop to the business. Thereafter the investment went from bad to worse. Strong's charges for the slight services he rendered after the actual purchase were so heavy that Hubbard was forced to sell part of the land at distress prices. When sales declined, Strong neglected the business for politics, and Hubbard was obliged to supplant him.[8]

An analogous case is that of Cyrus Woodman, who represented a group of New England capitalists organized as the Boston and Western Land Company. This company invested $100,000 in 60,000 acres of wild land and in numerous embryo towns in Illinois, Wisconsin, and Missouri in 1835 and 1836. The crash of 1837 broke the market; lands could scarcely be sold at any price, and interest, taxes, and agents' costs further discouraged the Boston promoters. Woodman, who was sent to the West to retrieve something from the wreck of the company's once-ambitious scheme, made no effort to put the investment in its best light but, from the first, filled his letters with pessimistic forebodings of ever greater contraction in prices accompanied by rising taxes. It is small wonder then that the owners became discouraged and sold their property to Woodman for a fraction of its cost. The land was that good prairie and timberland which in the fifties was to bring prices that almost justified the optimistic hopes of the thirties; but the original purchasers were not to share in the prosperity.[9]

One of the most successful agent-speculator relationships was that of William A. Woodward and Henry C. Putnam, who were natives of New York State. Both were shrewd judges of land values, and both knew thoroughly the techniques of the land business. Putnam went to Wisconsin in the fifties, where he invested funds of Woodward and other New Yorkers in short-term loans to settlers and in timber and prairie land. The fees Putnam received for the numerous services performed for his eastern principals made him a leading businessman in the rising town of Eau Claire. He aided in selecting the university, school, and swamp land, became land agent for a land-grant railroad, was elected register of deeds and county surveyor, and appointed deputy United States assessor, and with others founded the leading bank in Eau Claire. When Ezra Cornell was looking for someone to help him locate the million acres in land scrip which New York State had received under the Agricultural College Act, Woodward and Putnam persuaded him to let them make the selections in the Chippewa Valley, where, Cornell was assured, Putnam virtually controlled all land entries by means of his position in the United States land office at Eau Claire. Cornell gave them the agency, and from it they both made substantial profits.[10]

A great impetus was given to land speculation in the mid-thirties by federal and state banking policies. The failure to recharter the Second Bank of the United States removed the curbs on state bank policy, while the lure of federal deposits led to a scramble for such easy funds and to a mushroom-like growth of new banks in the South and West. Loans on real estate at inflated valuations were easily secured. Rising land values and easy credit attracted unprecedented quantities of capital from the East for investment in wild lands and corner lots. The federal surplus produced by increased land sales was distributed among the states, thereby providing funds for elaborate schemes of internal improvements. Canals, railroads, highways, were projected throughout the newer states, regardless of their feasibility. This combination of an easy banking policy with large government expenditures on public works came at a time when emigration to the western country was greatly accelerated. The total purchases of the hordes of immigrants and the speculators who were attempting to anticipate settlers' needs made the public land sales of these years the largest in American history.

Between 1835 and 1837, 38,000,000 acres of public lands were sold, 29,000,000 of which were acquired for speculation. A minimum speculative investment of $36,000,000—exclusive of agents' costs, interest, and taxes—was thus tied up in unimproved lands. To this figure should be added perhaps as large an amount for investments in town and city lots.

Much of this land purchasing was done by banks or bankers. For example, Isaac Bronson and his sons Frederick and Arthur, prominent bankers of New York, together with Charles Butler, brother of the Attorney General of the United States, and a group of New York capitalists, used funds of the New York Life Insurance & Trust Company and other banks with which they had connections to buy a third of a million acres in eight states and territories. The prominence of the promoters and the fact that some of them were closely identified with an administration which favored land reform and denounced land speculators gave the Whigs an opportunity of showing how hollow were the pretensions of some Jacksonians.[11]

Another group whose purchases of land were made with credit of banks it controlled consisted of such well-known Massachusetts financiers as John Tillson, Jr., John Shaw Hayward, Charles Holmes, Jr., Winthrop Gilman, and Griggs, Weld & Company. These men controlled the state bank of Illinois, from which they were able to borrow for their extensive land speculations. When the bank itself undertook to loan funds to squatters and to buy large quantities of land, it came to be regarded as the great financial octopus of Illinois and Iowa, against which numerous antimonopoly tirades were directed.[12]

A group whose operations in banks, land, and railroads was scarcely to be matched consisted of Alvah Buckingham and Solomon Sturges of Zanesville, Ohio, and their numerous children. They acquired or established banks of issue in Ohio, Indiana, and Illinois, some of which received federal deposits. The banks made it possible for them to pyramid their land purchases until they ultimately reached 275,000 acres, or the equivalent of 1,760 quarter-section farms. Railroads, grain elevators, and lumber yards were added to this princely estate. Neither the Panic of 1837 nor that of 1857 destroyed the economic power of Buckingham and Sturges, and for a generation their names were widely known from Ohio to Nebraska.[13]

Throughout the East and, indeed, to a somewhat less degree in the Old South, other banks, directors, and customers of banks were using the credit to buy public lands. For years thereafter, these banks or their receivers were engaged in disposing of quantities of wild land they had bought directly or acquired through mortgage foreclosures.

Squatters upon the public lands did not benefit from the easy banking policies of the thirties. Since they had no property to mortgage, credit was available to them only on the most usurious terms.

When newly surveyed lands were first announced for sale, the squatters had to arrange for the purchase of their lands—made valuable by their improvements—before the opening of the auction, or run the risk of losing them to speculators. Claim clubs and special preemption laws gave them protection against speculators only to the date of the sale. Squatters were inclined to put their meager capital into stock, housing, fencing, and clearing, which seemed the most essential for the moment, and to hope that the land sale would be postponed until they could accumulate money with which to purchase their claims. The sale, although announced in advance by advertisement, seemed always to catch the settlers unprepared and obliged them to borrow from the "loan shark."

These moneylenders were the representatives of western banks and eastern capitalists. Their charges were 5 per cent for arranging loans and from 2.5 to 5 per cent for making collections. Such eminent westerners as William B. Ogden,[14] James W. Grimes, and Lucius Lyon,[15] later to become respectively president of the Chicago and Northwestern Railroad, and United States senators from Iowa and Michigan, made their start by lending eastern funds on such a basis.

Loan sharks were present at every public land auction, and their agents were stationed in every land-office town, prepared to buy claims for squatters. The 10 or 12 per cent allowed by the usury laws did not satisfy these moneylenders, who found it possible to evade such restrictions. They would buy claims on which squatters had their improvements, according to previous agreements, and would then re-sell the land to them for an advance of $30 above cost on a quarter section. The squatter would agree to pay at the end of one or two years the maximum interest allowed by law. If the legal interest was 12 per cent and the debt was paid in one year, the lender would net 28 per cent upon his investment. The loan agents always denied that they were violating the usury laws, but they were exceedingly loath to have cases involving their transactions taken into the courts. Thousands of desperate squatters throughout the West snatched at the aid offered by the moneylenders who personally or through land agents invested many millions of dollars in this lucrative business. When later the squatters had difficulty in meeting their obligations, they turned against their creditors and raised the cry of usury.

Jackson's specie circular of 1836 struck squarely at the rapidly ex-panding volume of land purchases. It showed that the Chief Executive, unlike many of his followers, such as Butler, Kendall, Walker, and Ellsworth, did not approve of the operations of land speculators and moneylenders. The President's purpose in issuing the circular was to "repress alleged frauds, and to withhold any coun-tenance or facilities in the power of the Government from the mo-nopoly of the public lands in the hands of speculators and capitalists, to the injury of the actual settlers in the new States, and of emi-grants in search of new homes. . . ." Jackson further explained his purpose in his annual message of December, 1836, wherein he said the circular was intended to "save the new States from a nonresident proprietorship, one of the greatest obstacles to the advancement of a new country and the prosperity of an old one." [16] Except for Jefferson, Jackson was the only American President who seriously deplored that feature of public land policy which permitted speculators to buy land in unlimited amounts.

The specie circular required that only gold or silver be accepted from purchasers of land, except actual settlers, who were permitted to use bank notes for the remainder of the year. The order brought down the whole bloated structure which had been erected by unsound banking practices, the deposit of federal funds in the state banks, and the elaborate programs of internal improvements undertaken by the states. Land purchases by speculators stopped immediately; only the business of lending money to squatters remained.

The federal government's need of revenue caused the moneylending business to thrive for a time after the crash of 1837. Quantities of land were ordered into the market when it was clear that squatters could raise the purchase price of their claims only with the greatest difficulty. Despite pleas for postponement, the sales were held. Western banks were now closed, only gold or silver was accepted at the sales, and only eastern bankers could furnish it. In 1838 and 1839 Ogden found it possible to loan eastern funds to squatters to net 30 per cent a year before the deduction of commissions. Such usurious interest rates continued into the forties and, indeed, were increased in the fifties when it was possible for brokers to use in place of cash the military land warrants then in wide circulation at prices ranging downward to fifty cents an acre. By this means returns of 40, 50, and even 60 per cent could be secured from squatters.

Ogden, Grimes, and Lyon had assured their principals that there was no risk in lending money to squatters to buy their claims, since their improvements had already raised the value of the land above the government minimum price and since they would make every possible effort to pay their debts and secure title to land on which they had expended years of toil. These men did not foresee the deplorable situation into which the West was plunged after 1837. Squatters, now attempting to meet their payments under the most trying circumstances, fought a losing battle. Payments were delayed and then completely suspended. Many settlers became discouraged and moved on to another frontier to try once more to gain ownership of a piece of land.

Moneylenders, land speculators, and gamblers in town lots now found themselves loaded with financial burdens which they could not carry. Their land was unsalable, yet their taxes continued to mount, as did also the interest on the money they had borrowed. Having invested everything in property not easily liquidated, they now were forced to surrender much of their land to the banks when these institutions began to call in their loans. The abstracts of conveyances for the years following the Panic of 1837 show a tremendous volume of mortgage foreclosures of large estates.[17]

These foreclosures, the suspension of most of the wildcat banks and the bankruptcy of many financial institutions in the East all combined to keep land titles in the West in a state of chaos. Taxes were paid tardily, if at all, tax titles of a dubious nature were annually issued, and the difficulties of an already complex situation were thereby increased. During the period of stress, settlers accumulated grievances against the absentee owners which seemed to justify stealing their timber, despoiling their fences and buildings, and using their land for pasture. New settlers moved on the absentee-owned land, sometimes bought a tax title and set up a claim of ownership by right of possession and the tax deed. Absentee owners were powerless to deal with such a problem unless their property investment was sufficiently large to enable them to maintain a local agent employed on a full-time basis to watch over their interests.

During the bleak years of the early forties, the equity of absentees was gradually eaten up by tax titles, agents' costs, interest, and depredations. Ultimately the burden became too great, and many sold their holdings for less than the original cost, disregarding interest, fees, and taxes. It was this situation that induced Dr. Joseph Schafer, for years a careful student of land problems and policies, to conclude that land speculation was on the whole an unprofitable business.[18]

The career of Calvin Fletcher, a cautious Hoosier from New England and reared in an atmosphere of conservative finance, sheds much light on this era of unbridled land speculation. The craze for speculation overcame Fletcher's better judgment and with Nicholas Mc-Carty, likewise a Hoosier, he engaged in a joint speculation with $40,000 borrowed from the state bank of Indiana, of which Fletcher was a director. The mental torture Fletcher went through during the following years as a result of this "hazardous" investment is recorded in his diary. Unlike the majority of settler-speculators, who lost their land when the depression years set in, Fletcher was able to carry his investment until it began to produce returns. In 1846, when the banks had foreclosed many mortgages and thousands of farmers, having lost their homes, had either gone elsewhere to make another attempt at securing ownership of land or had sunk to the position of tenants upon their old claims, Fletcher stated that one-third of the voters of Indiana were then "tenants or day laborers or young men who have acquired no property."[19]

On the frontier the fog of depression is quickly dissipated by rising commodity prices, quickened immigration, and a new influx of capital. In the middle forties these factors were again at work and there followed a new era of land speculation, in which old residents and new settlers participated equally. The curve of land purchases shot upward as people in all occupations once more neglected their routine work to buy raw prairie land or corner lots in newly platted cities. Eastern capitalists again established banks of issue in the West and South under the lax systems still prevailing there and used the funds to purchase land. Land agents, professional locators, loan sharks, townsite promoters, flourished. Few seemed to have learned from experience.

The peak years of speculative purchasing were 1854 to 1858, when a total of 65,000,000 acres of public domain were disposed of to purchasers or holders of land warrants. To this figure should be added an equal or greater amount of land which was granted to the states for canals, railroads, swamp drainage, and education, and by them sold, mostly to speculators, large and small. A comparison of the census figures of land in farms with the land-office figures of land sold shows a tremendous concentration of speculator-owned land in all public land states, especially in the newer states like Iowa, Wisconsin, Illinois, Missouri, and Arkansas.

The speculators' contributions to the present-day pattern of land-ownership and land use are most important. For a generation, agricultural economists have said that tenancy was an inevitable result of the commercialization of farming and rising land values. This is true, but tenancy got its start in the Middle West as a result of the activities of land speculators and moneylenders. Squatters who could not meet their usurious demands had their contracts canceled and their equity confiscated. They might, however, remain on their old claims as tenants and pay rent for the land, or they might make a new contract for the land but at a higher valuation. In either case, the farmer found ownership difficult to attain. Elsewhere speculators dismayed at the cost of carrying their projects sought relief by inducing land-seekers to settle on their holdings, the sole condition being that they must pay taxes. If land was scarce it was not difficult to persuade immigrants to settle upon speculators' tracts, perhaps with the understanding that they might be able to buy later. The farmers' improvements raised the value of the property but did not bring in immediate cash income sufficient to enable them to make payments upon the land. As the value went up, the owners' price increased;

ownership proved unattainable to many. Tenancy thus had come to stay in the first generation of settlement in Illinois, Indiana, Iowa, Kansas, and Nebraska. Furthermore, owners of small farms had borrowed heavily to secure title, and from their debts many were never to be free. Some were ultimately depressed to the state of tenancy.

Speculator ownership and tenancy did not always result in the best use of the land. It has already been seen that speculator ownership forced widespread dispersion of population and placed heavy tax burdens upon farmers, whose improved lands could be more heavily assessed than the speculators' unimproved land. Furthermore, speculators were slow to pay taxes. They resisted increased levies, secured injunctions against expenditures for buildings and roads, and sometimes simply refused to pay taxes. Heavy interest penalties and tax titles did not trouble them particularly, since they knew they could later make a compromise settlement with the hard-pressed county boards, or could have the tax titles set aside by the courts. All of this meant that the tillers of the soil, if they were to enjoy the benefits of schools, roads, and local railroads, had to dig down into their own jeans more deeply because the speculators were not carrying their share of the burden. Taxes continued to climb and rarely or never declined, even in a period of depression. They are one of the rigid costs which trouble the farmers deeply when their own income is sharply declining. Heavy tax burdens forced farm practices which depleted the soil, produced erosion, and diminished land values.

Speculators left their mark on the West in other ways than in landownership. The nationalizing influence of their investments in western lands should not be neglected. Speculators were naturally inclined to favor internal improvements in the vicinity of their land. The Wabash Canal, the Illinois and Michigan Canal, the Des Moines River Navigation and Improvement Company, and the Fox and Wisconsin Canal were all the work of speculators who sought to increase the value of their holdings by bringing transportation facilities to them at government expense. The investments of Daniel Webster of Massachusetts and John Rockwell of Connecticut in central Illinois made them keenly aware of the need for internal improvements in the prairie state and led them to support the movement for railroad land grants for that area.[20]

The land and town-lot speculators were also influential in securing state, county, and municipal subsidies for local railroads. Many railroad enterprises were in themselves as much land speculations as transportation developments. The pinery railroads of northern Wisconsin promised few or no profits from operations, but the land grants included valuable stands of white pine from which large returns might be secured. Some of the other railroads for which there now seems little justification were doubtless chartered for the sake of the land grant.

Land and town-lot speculators had much to do with railroad strategy in the West. During the territorial period of Kansas and in the first decade of statehood, the struggle between the supporters of rival routes for land grants for their railroad enterprises is one of the chief issues, transcending in importance the slavery and union issues. Out of the melee certain groups emerged triumphant, such as that which revolved around one of the most notorious corruptionists in American history, Samuel C. Pomeroy. Two railroads of which he was an officer and stockholder received land grants, one was permitted to buy a valuable ceded Indian reservation for less than its current value, and three were required to converge on his own town of Atchison. The struggle over the location of the eastern terminus of the Union Pacific Railroad, the efforts of Cairo, Illinois, promoters to require the Illinois Central to locate its southern terminus at that point, the desire of the Northern Pacific to build up its own town on Puget Sound, are illustrations of how speculators, whether operating within or without the railroad companies, have influenced the location of railroad routes and their terminal points. Another factor which tended to prevent railroads from selecting the shortest line between two points was the desire of their promoters to secure the largest possible land grants.

The petty fights over the location of county seats, territorial and state capitals, land offices, state universities, agricultural colleges and normal schools, and institutions for the insane, the blind, and the criminal comprise no small part of the political controversies of the time. That some of these institutions were located in remote, inaccessible places wholly unsuited to the functions they were to perform may be blamed upon speculators who succeeded in having them established in the vicinity of their lands.

Westerners were united in their demand that the federal government should donate to the states the land within their boundaries. This demand was never attained in full, but it was achieved in part through a piecemeal system of securing special grants for education, canals, river improvements, and the drainage of swamp lands. As successive states entered the union, they were given larger proportions of their land, the proportion running as high as one-third in the case of Arkansas, Louisiana, Michigan, and Minnesota, to two-thirds in the case of Florida. The states were expected to sell these lands for the best possible price, and the proceeds, if derived from education grants, were to provide endowments. Speculator influence in the state capitals and county seats tended to break down the effective utilization of these grants.

Numerous scandals marked the sale of state lands and indicate that state and local governments were even more subject to speculator influence than was Congress and the General Land Office. The two-township grant for state universities brought in little return, the common school sections were in many cases wastefully administered, the agricultural college lands or their scrip equivalent were sold for a pittance by Rhode Island, Massachusetts, Indiana, Ohio, and other states, and the river improvement grants were wasted away. Worst managed of all were the swamp lands, of which 64,000,000 acres were patented to the states. Some were sold for as low as ten cents an acre; others were given to railroad companies to aid in construction; still others were granted to drainage companies for the improvements they contracted to make. Little or no security was ever required by the local officials for the performance of the contracts and in few cases were the improvements actually made. One prairie county of Illinois permitted its judge to contract 47,000 acres to a Utica, New York, resident on the understanding that he would drain the lands. The latter were conveyed but no improvements were made; later it was found that the judge had an interest in the business.[21]

Indian lands were fair game for speculators who used both legal and illegal means to secure them. Traders and speculators devised a method by which treaties of cession would include 640-acre allotments of the choicer lands to chiefs and half-breeds. They could easily be induced to sign away their allotments for an extra potion of whisky. By this means most of the desirable land along the upper Wabash Valley in Indiana and other valuable tracts in Illinois, Mississippi, Alabama and Wisconsin passed into the hands of speculators, including the great trading firm of W. G. & G. W. Ewing of Fort Wayne, Senator John Tipton of Indiana, and Simon Cameron of Pennsylvania.[22]

In Kansas speculator influence carried this method of land acquisition even further. Here Indian tribes such as the Pottawatomie (whose members had already been victimized by the Wabash traders), the Kickapoo, the Delawares, the Cherokees, and the Osage were induced to cede over 9,000,000 acres of land in trust, to be sold for their benefit. Such lands were not to become part of the public domain and were, therefore, not subject to the general land laws. Until Congress woke up to what was going on, these tracts were being rapidly conveyed to groups and individuals close to the Indian Office for distinctly less than their actual market value at the time.

Speculators pressed for the general allotment system which was adopted in 1887. They also co-operated with the lumbermen of Wisconsin and Minnesota in securing the opening of reservations containing valuable stands of white pine.

To gain their objectives, the speculators were forced to enter politics. Whether from the East or West, they opposed a free homestead policy which, they feared, would reduce the value of their holdings. They favored grants for railroads and measures to make easier land-accumulation. They were influential in local and state governments, which they warped to suit their interests. Thus one sees Wisconsin in the seventies and eighties controlled by a tight little group of lumbermen-speculators, including Cadwallader Washburn, Jim Thorp, Nelson Luddington, Philetus Sawyer, William Price, and Isaac Stephenson. Elsewhere the story is the same. These men opposed land reform, fought other agrarian legislation, championed protective tariff duties, and condemned monetary heresies. They represented the creditor, the large property owners, the railroads, and the rising industrialists. Not until 1888 and 1889, by which time the best of the public land was gone, were they ready to abandon their long struggle to prevent the public domain from being reserved for actual settlers only, a recommendation long since made by Jefferson and Jackson.

The successful land dealer of one generation became the banker, the local political oracle and office-holder, or the country squire of the next. Scarcely a city or country town in the West but had its first family whose fortune had been made by shrewd selection of lands and their subsequent sale or rental to later comers. Wealth which had come easily to them through their speculations had become a vested interest which they sought to protect against the demagogues who demanded the ten-hour day in the sawmills, or the imposition of an income tax, or the regulation of railroads.

The influence of the speculator may also be noted in the cultural field. The owners of western lands were not only responsible for a flood of pamphlets, booklets, guidebooks, and emigrant gazettes advertising their projects, but also for many travel books published for the same purpose. It is well known that Samuel Augustus Mitchell's *Illinois in 1837* was published to aid the sale of the 124,000 acres of land purchased in 1836 and 1837 by John Grigg, Mitchell, and other Philadelphians. Similarly, none can doubt that Henry W. Ellsworth's *Valley of the Upper Wabash* is a real estate advertisement and not a careful appraisal of the Grand Prairie of Indiana and Illinois. William Ferguson, J. G. Kohl, and Richard Cobden also wrote accounts primarily to aid the sale of lands in Illinois. James Caird, an English agricultural journalist, on the other hand, disguised his land promotion propaganda so effectively that reputable historians have continued to borrow from his *Prairie Farming in America*, little realizing how prejudiced and distorted it is. Even Charles Dickens, whose investment in Cairo real estate proved disastrous to him, was attracted to America, in part, out of curiosity to see the investment which had repaid him so poorly.[23] The productions of numerous other writers who were interested in western lands were widely read at the time of their publication and for years were drawn upon by subsequent travelers and compilers of guide books.

For better or for worse, the speculator, whether absentee or resident, squatter or banker, local politician or eastern senator, was present on every frontier. He affected every phase of western development and left in all places his indelible mark. His motives and his deeds one may deplore, but so characteristically American was he, so dynamic a part did he play in shaping land and cultural patterns, that it is difficult to imagine an American frontier without him.

NOTES

1 D. W. Mitchell, *Ten Years in the United States: Being an Englishman's Views of Men and Things in the North and South* (London, 1862), 325–328.

2 Entry of August 22, 1838, manuscript diary of Calvin Fletcher, Indiana Historical Society, Indiana State Library.

3 Levi Beardsley, *Reminiscences: Personal and other Incidents . . .* (New York, 1852), 252.

4 A writer in Janesville, Wisconsin, in 1855, speaks of the "hundreds of land agents and dealers watching to show some new comer . . . and all manner of tricks to gull the unsuspicious." *Rutland* (Vermont) *Herald,* Nov. 16, 1855.

5 New York, 1838.

6 For advertisements of Cook and Sargent, see the Davenport *Iowa Sun*, May 16, 1840; *Davenport Democratic Banner*, Feb. 10, May 5, 1854; *Davenport Democrat and News*, Nov. 2, 1859. Circulars of Cook and Sargent dated October 15, 1847, October 15, 1850, are in the Corcoran and Riggs papers, Library of Congress.

7 The Woodward-Putnam letters are in the Regional History Collection, Cornell University. Putnam's land business and his complicated relations with Woodward, Ezra Cornell, Henry W. Sage, and Frederick Weyerhaeuser are described in my *Wisconsin Pine Lands of Cornell University: A Study in Land Policy and Absentee Ownership* (Ithaca, 1943).

8 The papers of Moses Strong in the Wisconsin Historical Society Library contain the story of the Hubbard-Strong land business. Joseph Schafer used them in the preparation of an article entitled "A Yankee Land Speculator in Wisconsin," *Wisconsin Magazine of History*, 8:377–392 (June, 1925).

9 Cyrus Woodman was a methodical businessman who kept his papers, including impression copies of letters he wrote. They are now in the Wisconsin Historical Society Library and comprise one of the most valuable extant collections on the land business.

10 See note 7.

11 Aside from the publications and advertisements of the American Land Company and the numerous attacks upon it, which may be found in the *United States Telegraph*, quoted in the Indianapolis *Indiana Journal*, July 23, 1836; New York *Havanna Republican*, July 31, Nov. 27, 1839; and *Chicago American*, Aug. 12, 1839, the William B. Ogden papers in the Chicago Historical Society Library, and the Butler papers in the Library of Congress are important.

12 Dubuque *Iowa News*, May 18, Sept. 7, 14, Nov. 23, 1839; *Iowa Territorial Gazette and Burlington Advertiser*, Nov. 21, 1838, Jan. 26, Feb. 2, May 4, 1839; *Burlington Hawkeye and Iowa Patriot*, Aug. 12, 1841.

13 *Prairie Farmer*, May 20, 1858; *History of Muskingum County, Ohio* (Columbus, 1882), two pages and photograph inserted after p. 72.

14 Ogden Manuscripts, Chicago Historical Society Library.

15 There are many Lyon letters in the Ogden collection; others are published in Michigan Pioneer and Historical Society, *Historical Collections*, 27:414–604 (Lansing, 1897).

16 *American State Papers, Public Lands* (8 vols., Washington, 1832–1861), 8:910; James D. Richardson, ed., *Compilation of the Messages and Papers of the Presidents, 1789–1902* (10 vols., New York, 1903), 3:249–250.

17 The conveyance records of the following counties have been used: Vermillion, Champaign, Iroquois, McLean, Logan, Sangamon, and Christian, Illinois; Benton, Newton, White, and Carroll, Indiana; and Iowa, LaFayette, and Sauk, Wisconsin.

18 Joseph Schafer, *Wisconsin Domesday Book: Town Studies*, vol. 1 (Madison, 1924), 10 and note; Schafer, *The Wisconsin Lead Region*

(*Wisconsin Domesday Book: General Studies,* vol. 3, Madison 1932), 153.

19 Diary of Calvin Fletcher, entry of March 23, 1846.

20 Webster and Rockwell were both warm supporters of the measure to grant land for the aid of the Illinois Central Railroad. Rockwell is said to have received for his share in securing the land grant 2.5 per cent of the land or its equivalent. Fitz Henry Warner, Washington, D.C., December 1, 1852, to Charles Mason, Burlington, Iowa, Mason MSS, Iowa State Department of History and Archives, Des Moines.

21 H. H. Beckwith, *History of Iroquois County* . . . (Chicago, 1880), 375 *passim;* Iroquois County Deeds, 27:37.

22 I have described this method of land disposal in the Introduction to *The John Tipton Papers,* edited by Nellie Armstrong Robertson and Dorothy Riker (*Indiana Historical Collections,* vols. 24–26, Indianapolis, 1942) 1:3 ff.

23 For Ferguson, Cobden, Caird and Dickens, see Paul Wallace Gates, *Illinois Central Railroad and Its Colonization Work* (Cambridge, Mass., 1934), *passim.*

"Profits" and the Frontier Land Speculator

ALLAN G. BOGUE
MARGARET BEATTIE BOGUE

Reprinted by permission from the Journal of Economic History, *Volume 17, Number 1 (March, 1957), pages 1–24.*

FROM the days of the confederation through the nineteenth century, the frontier land speculator was a familiar figure in the United States.[1] Perambulating foreigners recorded the activities of this gentleman, and land speculation was discussed in both Congress and in the editorial columns of western newspapers. Many twentieth-century students of America's political and economic development have dealt in one way or another with frontier land speculation. They have depicted the land speculator at times as a sinister figure, corroding the morals of national or state legislators as the lawmakers endeavored to formulate land policy. Writers have sketched the antagonism between speculator and "actual settler." Nor have they ignored the effect which the speculator had upon the social and economic development of the region in which he operated. Such commentators have contributed to a literature that has its share of colorful characters and even displays the occasional symbol: star-crossed Robert Morris entering debtors' prison;[2] the desperate debtors of the Holland Land Company advancing upon the Batavia land office;[3] the little spade that William Scully lashed to his saddle as he set out to transplant Irish tenancy to the Illinois prairies.[4]

There are, however, a number of overlapping and interdependent questions concerning frontier land speculation to which the answers are as yet far from complete. How and to what extent, for example, did land speculators affect the economic development of the United States?[5] To what degree did western land speculation contribute to the concentration of capital in America during the nineteenth century?[6] How, if at all, did this alternative avenue of investment affect the policy decisions of the American businessman? Did the land speculator actually get something for nothing, as some writers seem to suggest?[7] What rate of return did speculators in the raw lands of the frontier actually derive from their capital?[8] The answers to the first four questions obviously are closely related to the one given to the fifth; this article will be primarily concerned with the answer to the last question.

Land speculation was a recurrent theme in Joseph Schafer's careful analysis of the settlement process in Wisconsin. In two volumes of the Wisconsin Domesday series, Schafer considered the profits of specific land speculators, and he generalized his findings to some extent in *The Social History of American Agriculture*.[9] He concluded that the state lands in Wisconsin provided better speculations than did federal government land and that pine-bearing federal land was more remunerative than farm land. When speculators bought land shortly before settlers arrived "they of course made money fast." But in "their expectations of profit from holding farm lands speculators were often disappointed. For in numerous instances the holding period was long, and when the lands came to be wanted by farmers it was difficult to sell, in competition with land-office sales of Congress land, at prices that would recoup the speculators for both principal and interest, to say nothing of such taxes as they had to pay in the interim."[10]

Schafer based his conclusions on the cost and sale data of a number of speculators, but in several instances he did little more than compare sale and cost figures in impressionistic fashion without resorting to careful calculation. When he did present a more elaborate analysis of the returns obtained from 20,000 acres purchased on behalf of Sir Charles A. Murray during the 1830's,[11] he was to be criticized for mishandling the item of sales commissions and for neglecting the possibility that the speculator might have received some returns from rent prior to sale.[12] More serious, however, were the defects in his method of calculating returns. In brief, Schafer compounded interest at an arbitrary 5 per cent on Murray's costs until 1880 when the last tract was sold. Similarly he compounded interest at 5 per cent against the receipts from sales to the same year and then compared the two totals at his terminal date, concluding that Murray had met a small loss because the accumulated costs of $266,000 outweighed the compounded receipts by $6,000. But much of Murray's land was actually sold during the 1850's and 1860's, and it was highly misleading to continue compounding interest against the investment in land which was sold long prior to the terminal date. Similarly it was confusing to compound the receipts, since such returns actually signified that the speculation from which they were derived was closed.

During the early 1940's two graduate students at the University of Mississippi, Mattie Russell and Edwin W. Chapman, undertook intensive study of speculation in two Mississippi counties between 1836 and 1861, with the express purpose of determining whether or not investors in wild land realized profits. Subsequently their graduate director summarized their findings in *The Journal of Southern History*.[13] Both Russell and Chapman defined "speculators" as all land companies, individuals, and partnerships purchasing 2,000 acres or more, "unless a large amount of the land was held by an individual at the time of his death."[14] Using this yardstick, the researchers compiled lists of large owners from the deed records and abstracted all their individual purchases and sales. Then the authors calculated both total and average purchase and sale prices for the entire acreage purchased by each speculator. They presented the difference between these purchase and sale figures as profit. If an investor's transactions covered a span of fifteen years, then total profit divided by 15 was taken as the yearly profit on the investment. Both students concluded that speculators as a group did not realize "large returns" on their investments.[15] Their method of calculating profit, however, hardly inspires confidence. They made no effort to compound interest; they did not consider costs of ownership other than the original purchase price of the land; and they failed to take into consideration the fact that speculators usually liquidated their investment at an uneven rate.

In the writings of Paul W. Gates may be found a more optimistic evaluation of the profitability of land speculation for at least some investors. He has referred to the commonplace of "first families" in middle western communities whose financial strength grew from "shrewd dealings in real estate."[16] In the *Wisconsin Pine Lands of Cornell University* this author went beyond such generalizations and presented an analysis of expenditures and income arising from Cornell's speculation in some 512,400 acres of land in Wisconsin, Minnesota, and Kansas. Subtracting from all income the items of expense incurred by ownership of the land including taxes, interest, location fees, legal expenses, salaries, commissions, and the cost of land scrip, he found that the venture returned a net profit of approximately $5,000,-000 to the university. All expenses totaled $1,728,596. Gates concluded: "The Cornell land business was one of the outstandingly successful land speculations in American history. . . ." [17] The preservation of university records relating to the land business made possible so concrete an answer to the question of whether this speculation was or was not profitable, but Professor Gates did not consider it feasible to reduce his net profit to a per cent per annum basis.[18]

Several other students of land history have ventured conclusions on the profits to be derived from frontier land speculation, after somewhat less elaborate analysis of their sources. In 1941 Robert Diller concluded that the speculators on the whole fared poorly in an eastern Nebraska community which was settled during the 1860's and 1870's. Most of the speculators unloaded their lands in the depression of the 1870's. Only a few persevered in their speculations and benefited from the rising land prices of the 1880's. "These few tenacious speculators, or investors, may at least have realized modest gains; the rest of the speculators would have been better off if they had kept their money at home," he argued.[19] Diller did not explain his methods of calculation other than to write that he took into consideration "the amount originally invested, taxes and expenses, and normal income during the period of ten to fifteen years in which the land, while patented, remained unsettled and unproductive prairie." [20]

More recently Theodore L. Carlson probed the complexities of speculative investments in the Illinois Military Tract in his book on that area. After studying the transfer of about 1,400,000 acres of speculative holdings between 1827 and 1833, he apparently concluded that the majority of owners "were forced to take a loss." [21] Speaking of speculators whose investment experience extended beyond the 1827–1833 period, Carlson, after comparing purchase and sale prices in many individual cases, concluded that "the profits made by the greater number of land speculators in the tract were not enormous." In some individual cases "the land was held for many years, so that in time, with the gradual increase of land values, a profit was sure to accrue." [22] To support this last statement he cited a $15 per share dividend which the Munn Illinois Land Company paid to its shareholders in 1851, but he failed to mention either the current value of the shares, or their original cost, or whether a dividend of this size was exceptional, customary, or extraordinary. Carlson seems to have defined profit as the difference between the purchase price of land plus taxes and the eventual sale price.

At the close of his excellent study of the Holland Land Company holdings in New York and Pennsylvania published in 1924, Paul Evans estimated that "the original investment was retrieved with interest of 5 to 6 per cent." [23] The accounts of the company, however, were not opened to him and he did not explain how he arrived at this figure. In her study of the Pulteney Purchase, Helen Cowan concluded that the Pulteney investment by 1812 showed "a real profit on its books." [24] But Miss Cowan failed to present any precise measure of this profit or to reveal the route by which she reached her conclusion.

The historians who have discussed the profits of frontier land speculators on the basis of their own research have pursued a variety of approaches, of necessity using different types of records, and presenting conclusions ranging from the very general to specific figures or percentages. Few have explained their methods of calculation. Most have thought too little about calculation techniques and the costs involved in landownership. At the same time the authors of a variety of general surveys and history texts have ventured opinions on this subject as well. [25] Some have used the materials analyzed in the preceding paragraphs, but others have relied entirely upon the judgment of contemporaries, sometimes without questioning their bias or attempting to check the accuracy of their statements. A few have simply presented unsupported generalizations. A number of historians in both major categories have used the word "profits" in unsophisticated fashion and have failed to make a distinction between interest on invested capital and profit.

Although there are notable exceptions to this point of view, one can hardly study the body of literature bearing on speculator profits without concluding that speculation in western lands was usually a losing business. James Silver reflected this prevailing point of view in his summary of the work of Russell and Chapman when he wrote, "An occasional bonanza proved to be the exception to the rule," and claimed that the work of his students added "confirmatory evidence that many buoyant hopes and expectations of speculators in frontier farm lands faded into disillusionment under the harsh light of reality." [26] If historians accept such generalizations they are forced by logic to a rather unflattering evaluation of the perspicacity of American businessmen during the nineteenth century. Many of them were gamblers indeed who persisted in buying land on speculation, although the returns were consistently low and although, to borrow Professor Silver's phrasing, "greater success with much less risk could have been secured in commercial enterprises in the more settled Eastern communities." [27] Or perhaps we should conclude that there was an obtuse element among American capitalists whose members stubbornly diverted capital from more remunerative uses into frontier land speculation although its wide and continuing prevalence must have demonstrated that the "bonanza" was exceptional. Actually the evidence is so scattered and so unsatisfactory that historians are hardly justified in generalizing upon the losses and gains of the frontier speculator.

Because the evidence bearing upon the profits from frontier land speculation is inadequate at this point, we have ventured to work up and present relevant material which we accumulated in the course of other research. We have calculated the returns obtained by land speculators from the purchase and sale of some three townships of agricultural land in the Middle West between 1835 and 1904. Stated differently, these figures picture the returns obtained from 77,529 acres of land divided into 946 tracts which were held for periods of time varying from but a few months to some thirty-five years.

These data can be summarized most easily by presenting them in two parts; one section is devoted to five speculative ventures in the Grand Prairie of Illinois and a second describes the operations of the Davenport brothers of Bath, New York, in eastern Nebraska. Both groups obtained and sold greater acreages than are treated here. In order to be certain, however, that the calculations involved only land which had not been improved at the owner's expense prior to resale, considerable acreage was discarded. In the case of the Davenports another major criterion of selection was applied as well; since it was wished to have one portion of the study stand as a clear-cut illustration of the speculative opportunities presented by federal land policy, land which the brothers purchased from grantors other than the federal government, the state government, or the land-grant railroads was discarded. The cost, sale, and tax figures for the Illinois lands were derived from the federal land-entry books, county records, and a collection of business papers belonging to one of the speculators. The land account book and business correspondence of the Davenports provided the basic data for the Nebraska study. In neither case, as shall be pointed out in greater detail later, were the sources completely free from defects.

The method of calculating returns on the investments of the speculators was not complicated. For each parcel of land that was sold as a unit, a schedule was prepared showing the initial investment and yearly taxes. Some of the Davenport schedules were more complicated than others because the brothers paid for some of their land in installments, and revenue was obtained prior to sale from rents and abortive sales. For each tract of land the rate of interest was found which, when compounded against the original investment and subsequent costs, gave a total investment at the date of sale equal to the sale price.[28] This was called the rate of return on invested capital. When rents or the occasional down payment from a canceled sale were obtained from a tract of land, such income was subtracted from the total investment in the tract at the date when it was received. This procedure, of course, raised the rate of return. The various rates of return on tracts sold in the same year were combined into weighted means, showing the average rate of return per dollar invested.[29] Second, the total investment and the average rate of return per dollar invested at five-year intervals for both the Illinois and the Nebraska lands have been shown. It has been assumed in this last calculation that each tract returned year by year the rate which its ultimate sale price revealed. Knowledge of these rates was, of course, denied to the speculators themselves, prior to the sale of any given tract.

The Illinois lands totaled 34,300 acres, located in the Grand Prairie region of east-central Illinois. Scattered through Champaign, Iroquois, McLean, Piatt, Livingston, and Vermilion counties, these tracts were predominantly prairie. This acreage included portions of the holdings of Matthew T. Scott and Associates, Robert B. M. Wilson, James McReynolds, Ramsey McHenry, and Arnold Naudain and Associates.

The son of a well-to-do banker of Lexington, Kentucky, Matthew T. Scott completed his college education in 1846 and spent a year or two managing family farm lands in Ohio. Becoming interested in the possibilities for investment in the unsettled prairies of east-central Illinois, he induced a number of friends and relatives to join him in entering thousands of acres of federal land at the Danville and Vandalia land offices.[30] Between 1848 and 1859 they purchased 45,070 acres, scattered over the two land districts. Their cash investment amounted to some $51,220. Almost 41,000 acres of the total were entered with land warrants purchased at an average cost of $1.10 per acre. Cash purchases made up the balance.[31] In addition, Scott and his group bought more than 9,000 acres in McLean and Livingston counties from private parties and the Illinois Central Railroad.[32] These 9,000 acres are of minor importance in the statistics that follow, for with the exception of one 80-acre tract all the lands used in this study were acquired from the United States. Scott moved to McLean County in 1855 to direct the development of his farm lands. For the next thirty-five years he continued in the role of large landlord, improving, renting, and selling farms. His investments gradually spread into many phases of business. In the late 1860's Scott channeled some of his funds into the McLean County Coal Company at Bloomington. Later he invested in Kansas lead and zinc land, western gold and silver mining stock, a toll road, a Texas ranch, and finally, in the late 1880's, in Tennessee timber and mineral land. For a time he owned the Bloomington *Bulletin*.[33]

The second investor in the Illinois group, Robert B. M. Wilson, like Scott, was more than a "speculator" in the usual sense of the word, for he, too, developed portions of his real estate. Wilson, an Irishman by birth, established a medical practice in Washington, Illinois, in 1848. Ten years later he was mixing in local politics and by the 1860's was buying real estate.[34] With borrowed funds he acquired 27,000 acres of unimproved Iroquois County land in 1864 and 1867, at an average cost of $2.45 per acre.[35] These holdings were originally part of the county's swamp-land grant. Wilson quickly sold much of the land and turned several thousand acres into tenant-operated grain and livestock farms.[36]

The careers of the remaining three investors are much more obscure. None of them developed any prairie real estate. All acquired their land much earlier than Scott and Wilson, during the great land boom of the 1830's. James McReynolds has been described as "an influential citizen of Kaskaskia," although he probably lived in Macon County during the 1830's. There he and a business associate platted an addition to Decatur in 1837.[37] His venture in wild, unimproved federal land totaled 1,360 acres, located principally in Champaign County and purchased for $1.25 per acre.[38] Little has been discovered about Ramsey McHenry other than the fact that in 1836, when he purchased 15,000 acres of federal land in the Danville, Illinois, and Crawfordsville, Indiana, districts for $1.25 per acre, he was a resident of Baltimore.[39] Arnold Naudain, the principal figure in a series of investments made in 1836 and 1837 in partnership with Edward Tatnall, Merrit Canby, and John Macoboy, was a Delaware politician.[40] This group of investors purchased 28,000 acres of federal land in the Danville and Crawfordsville districts at the cash minimum price.[41]

The following statistics that show the rate of return per dollar invested in land at the year of sale and at five-year intervals represent combined returns from the unimproved holdings of the five speculators lying in the six counties mentioned above. We may be reasonably certain that they were not rented prior to sale. Of the total, 13,607 acres were Scott lands; 13,905 acres belonged to Wilson; 1,109 to James McReynolds; 3,988 acres to McHenry; and 1,526 to Naudain and Associates. The calculations were based upon purchase and sale prices compiled from federal land-entry books and county deed records and upon the outlay which the owners made for taxes. The tax data were gleaned from a substantial collection of tax receipts found in Matthew T. Scott's personal papers showing the payments that Scott made on his Illinois holdings between 1854 and 1885. From these data a schedule of average rates paid per acre on unimproved land in each year in each county was prepared. In the absence of figures showing the exact taxes paid by investors other than Scott, these averages were used as an estimated tax upon their lands. Tax data for the period preceding 1854 were necessary for the three investors who purchased their lands during the 1830's. These were estimated at one cent per acre per year. The figure was the amount paid on unimproved land in 1854 in the counties where the tracts involved were located, and this rate apparently had not varied to any extent over the two previous decades, if scattered contemporary comments can be trusted. In addition to taxes these five investors undoubtedly paid agent fees; some of them had to pay interest on the money borrowed to make land purchases; and some became involved in minor litigation over their holdings. No allowance has been made for such costs in calculating rates of return.

The first set of figures showing the combined average returns from the real estate at the time of sale (Table 10) illustrates how varied the earnings from investments with different histories could be. The figures for the years 1840 through 1855 represent the earnings of lands owned by two investors of the 1830's, Ramsey McHenry and James McReynolds. In comparison with the percentages that follow for 1856 through 1872, the earlier figures are low, for both men purchased their lands when the Grand Prairie was yet very sparsely settled, and

TABLE 10

Average Returns on the Illinois Lands Studied, by Year of Sale
1840–1885

Year sold	Acreage	Sale price	Per cent return
1840	80	$ 123	4.0
1844	80	292	11.0
1845	109	431	14.3
1846	40	116	7.0
1848	160	480	7.0
1850	195	580	6.0
1851	193	666	6.4
1852	120	698	9.1
1853	2,720	6,886	10.3
1854	2,340	10,183	7.1
1855	220	1,077	7.4
1856	440	1,800	17.5
1859	40	440	46.0
1860	160	1,110	17.1
1861	440	2,090	15.0
1862	80	840	30.6
1863	1,784	16,478	19.2
1864	2,522	23,392	16.7
1865	1,152	10,671	18.1
1866	3,634	41,686	20.5
1867	1,292	14,850	21.5
1868	4,656	35,820	125.3
1869	1,598	14,694	41.5
1870	1,093	10,300	19.1
1871	3,493	32,340	24.1
1872	1,600	14,480	17.9
1873	160	2,600	12.0
1874	1,540	9,697	12.1
1875	333	3,334	14.0
1877	640	3,000	4.0
1882	800	8,000	8.0
1883	700	6,900	7.4
1885	160	800	−.4

held the real estate for many years before any appreciable increase in land values occurred. The 14 per cent return from 109 acres sold by McReynolds in 1845 is the highest received by any of the investors on land purchased during the 1830's. The returns from the Naudain lands, also purchased in the 1830's, are obscured in this set of figures, for these lands were sold in the 1860's during the same years that

Scott and Wilson were disposing of their lands. Naudain and Associates realized a rate of return from their holdings very similar to that obtained by McHenry and McReynolds.

The higher figures for the years 1856 through 1872 reflect the good fortune of Matthew T. Scott and Robert B. M. Wilson. Scott purchased and sold his unimproved real estate, almost exclusively prairie land, at a much more advantageous time than had the investors of the 1830's. During the early 1860's the wartime need for agricultural produce, the demand by settlers for farm lands, and the successful use of improved farm machinery combined to boost land values rapidly. For the remainder of the century they continued to climb. Scott's 13,600 acres, purchased almost entirely between 1851 and 1855 at an average cost of about $1.14 per acre, brought, on the average, $9.50 per acre after being held for an average of thirteen years. While his tax burden was greater than that of the investors of the 1830's, the rapid rise in land values brought him earnings twice as great as theirs. The Wilson investments are primarily responsible for an average return on the lands sold in 1868 of 125 per cent. Wilson's land business was even more successful than was that of Scott, for Wilson did not have to wait a full year in many cases for the real estate which he had purchased at a few dollars per acre to attract buyers at $4 to $10 per acre. He retained his 13,900 acres for an average of only four years and sold them at an average of slightly more than $8 per acre. Returns from scattered Scott and Wilson sales between 1877 and 1885 were much less satisfactory. There was, for instance, no return from the investment in a quarter section of Wilson land purchased in 1867 at $2.94 per acre and sold in 1885 for $5.00 per acre, rather .4 per cent per annum loss.

Turning to Table 11, which shows the total investment in these Illinois lands and the rate of return per dollar invested at five-year intervals, we note that the rate falls from 8.5 per cent in 1835 to 6.4 per cent five years later; climbs to 18.9 per cent in 1870; declines in 1875 to 6.4 per cent, and swings up to 9.4 per cent in 1880. The 1835 figures reflect the returns obtained by James McReynolds from 670 acres of land. Of the three who purchased land during the 1830's, McReynolds held his real estate the shortest length of time and, perhaps because a good portion of it was timberland, found buyers at prices yielding a higher return than those received by either McHenry or Naudain and Associates. He held his lands for an average of fifteen and one-half years and sold them at an average price of about $5 per acre. The 1840, 1845, and 1850 figures are somewhat below the level of

1835, for they represent the combined earnings of the Naudain, McHenry, and McReynolds lands. The McHenry and Naudain holdings were predominantly prairie. McHenry held his real estate seventeen years after purchase on the average and sold it for approximately $3.50 per acre. The Naudain group realized slightly more than $8.50 per acre, but held its land much longer than did the other two investors—for twenty-seven years on the average. The higher averages of 1855 and subsequent years stem from the Scott and Wilson investments. Wilson lands were primarily responsible for

TABLE 11

Per Cent Return on the Illinois Land Studied, at Five-Year Intervals, 1835–1880

Year	Investment on December 31	Per cent return
1835	$ 910	8.5
1840	11,179	6.4
1845	14,824	6.4
1850	19,186	6.8
1855	29,589	13.8
1860	58,983	16.1
1865	75,599	17.9
1870	63,347	18.9
1875	11,591	6.4
1880	13,799	9.4

the returns of 17.9 and 18.9 per cent in 1865 and 1870. The 1875 and 1880 figures decline markedly from the 1870 level, for they represent the investments of Scott and Wilson in lands held over a considerable period of years and sold in less prosperous times than were their other holdings.

Considerable mention has been made in the preceding discussion of variations in the returns obtained by the five investors. Perhaps it would be well to summarize briefly the experience of the speculators individually after considering them in the composite. As might be expected, the three holdings acquired during the 1830's made the poorest showing. The McReynolds investment brought a return of 8 per cent; the McHenry lands, 6 per cent; the Naudain holdings, 7 per cent. The Scott and Wilson lands brought average returns to these speculators of 16 and 22 per cent.

In closing the discussion of the Illinois group, attention might be called to those factors which were apparently most important in determining the rates of return which the members obtained. The time of purchase in relation to the phase of the business cycle was important, as were the business conditions at the date of sale. The speed with which settlers entered an area was largely controlled by business conditions, and the rapidity of settlement, of course, strongly influenced the frontier land market. These elements, plus the preconceptions of the speculators concerning the value of their holdings, undoubtedly governed the length of time which land was held to a considerable extent. Apparently the longer land was held, the less likely was the speculator to make a spectacular killing. Differences in the type and quality of the land—timber or prairie, wet land or dry land—made for variations in return. Although evidence on these points is scanty, undoubtedly the adequacy of transportation facilities and the success of local farmers in adapting to the peculiarities of their district also were important in explaining variations in returns.[42]

John and Ira Davenport of Bath, New York, were able to weigh the merits of a number of types of investment during the last thirty-five years of the nineteenth century. In the years after 1815 their father, Ira Davenport, Sr., accumulated capital in the mercantile business of central New York and soon turned his attention as well to the possibilities for investment that lay in the West. By the 1850's he was lending money to farmers in Michigan and Illinois, speculating in middle western lands, and also dabbling in the tax title business. At the date of his death in 1868 Ira Davenport, Sr., was a millionaire. In his will he named John and Ira as his executors and divided most of his fortune among four living children and the minor heirs of a deceased daughter. The two sons, therefore, had the task not only of managing their own shares of the estate, but for almost twenty years they supervised the investment of trust funds destined for their young relatives as well.[43]

John and Ira Davenport kept the trust funds invested in western farm mortgages which were negotiated on lands in Michigan, Illinois, Iowa, Kansas, and Nebraska, while handling a portion of their own funds similarly. All told, the brothers channeled some $5,500,000 into farm mortgages between 1868 and 1904.[44] But in managing their personal investments the brothers were attracted by the possibilities in land speculation. Although some of the land was inherited or acquired in the loan business, they held at one time or another title to more than

75,000 acres of agricultural land in Nebraska, Iowa, Illinois, and Kansas, as well as timberland holdings in Michigan. A western agent might warn them of the "develtree there," but the offerings of Wall Street were not neglected either, and Ira, particularly, invested in railroads, public utilities, and state bonds, although this part of the Davenports' financial history is unfortunately much less clear than is the story of their western business. Trained in the idiosyncrasies of frontier investments by their astute father, while at the same time living within convenient distance of the financial capital of the country, the Davemport brothers were in a position both by training and location to turn the funds under their control into a wide range of investments. Significantly they invested heavily in the raw lands of the frontier.

Chosen for study here are some 43,229 acres of raw land which John and Ira Davenport acquired in six counties, located in the rolling prairie of eastern Nebraska, during the years 1870, 1871, and 1880, and sold during their lifetimes. The brothers purchased this acreage in part directly from the federal government and in part obtained it from major land-distribution agencies which had acquired the land from the federal government. Neither speculator nor hopeful farmer had intervened in the chain of title prior to the Davenports. Nor did the brothers endeavor to enhance the value of this land in any way by adding improvements at their own expense.

Of this acreage, the New Yorkers purchased 16,521 acres in Dodge County from the Union Pacific Railroad Company during 1870 and 1871, at prices ranging from $4 to $7 per acre. In making this purchase the brothers took advantage of the five-year credit plan offered by the railroad and cut their outlay by tendering in payment the company's land-grant bonds which they could buy at a considerable discount during the early 1870's. Both of these circumstances have been taken into consideration in calculating the return of the Dodge County lands. In 1880 John and Ira Davenport acquired another 4,817 acres of railroad lands in the Nebraska grant of the Burlington line. These holdings lay in Madison County and cost on the average $2.40 per acre.

From those lands given by the federal government to finance the construction of a state penitentiary in Nebraska, the New Yorkers purchased 5,285 acres in Lancaster and Seward counties during 1871. The price of individual tracts in this purchase varied from $3.50 to $5.00 per acre. During the same year the Davenport brothers located 16,606 acres of government land by private entry in Wayne and Pierce counties, using military bounty warrants which they had acquired at a cost of approximately $1.15 per acre through brokers in New York and Chicago. Land-office fees, purchase of settler locations, and the services of an agent at Omaha combined to raise the initial cost of these lands to an estimated $1.25 per acre.

L. D. Richards of the firm of Richards, Keene and Company, located at Fremont, Nebraska, supervised the administration and sale of all the Davenport land in the six counties, although he selected local representatives in several counties with whom he split commissions. These amounted to approximately 3.5 per cent of the sale price. Consistently the Davenports urged that their lands be sold to actual farmers on adjacent lands, and that the sale price be fully equal to the actual use value of the land so that speculators would not be attracted. Detailed study of individuals who purchased the Dodge County lands showed that Richards heeded these admonitions in that county at least. For some 22,500 acres of Davenport land almost complete tax lists could be prepared. For the remainder, specific information was generally available for more than half the years. The gaps in the tax series were filled in with estimates which were placed at as high a figure as seemed credible in the light of the yearly payments of which definite record was found. Undoubtedly there were additional petty expenses chargeable to land account which were not discovered but they could not have been very important. The Davenports began to offer their Dodge County lands in 1877, and over the next ten years also opened the lands in the other five counties to sale. Between 1878 and the death of the surviving brother, Ira, in 1904, the brothers sold land from their Nebraska holdings every year.

When the average returns on these Nebraska lands by year of sale are considered, it is found that they ranged from 9 to 12 per cent over the first four years of sales.[45] Then followed a number of years in which the rate of return did not fall below 11 per cent per annum and in one year stood slightly above 19 per cent. With 1887 the returns dropped back to nearly the level of the first years, holding fairly steady between 10 and 12 per cent. The year 1893 marked a sharp break and thereafter returns held between 6.9 and 9 per cent until 1901, when 2,803 acres of land yielded an average return of 5.7 per cent on the investment. In the following three years the returns held at 6 and 7 per cent with the exception of one 40-acre tract in Dodge County which had been rented since the early 1880's and on which rental payments raised the rate of return up to 12 per cent.

When the calculation of the total investment of the Davenports in their Nebraska land at five-year intervals along with the average return per dollar invested was made, the results appeared less striking than the year-by-year analysis. Returns on the investment fund dropped steadily from just under 11 per cent on the $267,974 in-

TABLE 12

Average Returns on the Nebraska Lands Studied,
by Year of Sale, 1877–1904

Year sold	Acreage	Sale price [a]	Per cent return
1877	40	$ 386	12.0
1878	1,521	15,643	11.0
1879	359	4,130	8.9
1880	4,592	52,014	9.2
1881	430	6,481	16.0
1882	7,050	74,778	19.2
1883	4,308	73,964	11.9
1884	1,432	22,742	14.0
1885	727	14,465	11.3
1886	160	2,007	16.0
1887	80	926	13.0
1888	320	4,632	10.0
1889	800	12,313	11.9
1890	1,880	27,205	9.6
1891	2,684	52,025	10.2
1892	640	9,187	12.2
1893	1,982	35,126	8.3
1894	200	4,574	7.3
1895	160	4,178	7.2
1896	200	6,118	7.7
1897	84	1,563	6.9
1898	640	14,919	8.6
1899	2,720	52,932	8.0
1900	5,326	108,312	7.1
1901	2,803	55,529	5.7
1902	859	23,063	6.9
1903	473	8,499	6.0
1904	40	2,895	12.0

[a] Sale commission has been deducted. Income from rent is not included in this column.

vested in 1880 down to 6.5 per cent on the $93,946 invested in the year 1900.

Some of the variations in return become more understandable when the county averages that underlie the aggregate averages are discussed. The relatively high returns of the early 1880's (Table 12) reflect a real estate killing which John and Ira Davenport made on the lands purchased from the Burlington Railroad in Madison County. The brothers bought these lands in 1880 and sold them in short order on a rising land market. Although the return on individual tracts ran still higher, of course, some 4,000 acres of these lands averaged 39.5 per

TABLE 13

Per Cent Return on the Nebraska Land Studied,
at Five-Year Intervals, 1875–1900

Year	Investment on December 31	Per cent return
1875	$193,962	9.4
1880	267,974	10.9
1885	194,360	8.1
1890	239,442	7.9
1895	207,050	6.9
1900	93,946	6.5

cent on the investment when sold in 1882. By 1885 the stimulating effect of the Madison lands had disappeared from the averages. In general through the 1880's the yearly rate of return on the Union Pacific land and on the acreage obtained by locating land warrants held between 10 and 12 per cent, but the returns on penitentiary land pulled the over-all average downward. When western real estate prices fell generally in 1893, and returns on the Davenport lands fell across the board, the penitentiary lands still stood as the least remunerative among these investments. On 800 acres of Lancaster land that were sold in 1901, the Davenport brothers realized but 3 per cent on the funds invested.

Contrary to the case in Illinois, the survey reports describing Nebraska soils are sufficiently detailed that discussion of the relation between speculator returns and soil productivity is possible.[46] We must remember, however, that most of the Davenport lands were located and sold before the characteristics of eastern Nebraska soils were known in more than a general way. Nor were the pioneer farmers fully aware of the variations in rainfall which, along with topography, are important in determining the productivity of agricultural land in eastern Nebraska. The Davenport lands comprised a percentage of the choicer soil types that equaled or was greater than the equivalent county percentage with the exception only of the holdings in Lancaster County. There soil types now considered unsuitable for cropping made up 32 per cent of the Davenport lands, while the county as a whole contained but 6 per cent of the same soils. Taking soils, rainfall, and topography into consideration, the most desirable Davenport lands lay in Dodge, Wayne, and Madison counties, and it is significant that the brothers realized their highest returns in those counties. Despite the fact, however, that the farmer works under more favorable conditions in Dodge and Wayne counties, the lands in Madison County produced the highest rate of return to the speculator. Obviously productivity was not the only factor affecting proceeds.

The initial cost of the Davenport land varied from county to county, as did the tax rate. So did the length of time which the land was held, but, as was explained in the discussion of the Illinois lands, such variation is most properly considered a reflection of other factors. In Madison County, productive land, a relatively low purchase price, a low tax rate, and fast turnover on a buoyant market produced a high rate of return even though the sale prices, ranging usually between $5.50 and $8.00, were little greater than those which the Davenports paid for their Union Pacific and penitentiary lands. Much of the penitentiary land in Lancaster County, on the other hand, was held for more than twenty years. When the tax rate in Madison County was but five cents per acre, it stood at more than twenty cents per acre in Lancaster County, and there the quality of much of the Davenport land was inferior. Undoubtedly the Davenports misjudged the future in Lancaster County, but their mistake is not difficult to understand. The capital was located in this county, and a seat of government, speculators generally assumed, was a guarantee of rising land values. In this case it seems rather to have guaranteed a high tax rate. Parcels of Lancaster land commanded prices ranging from $20 to $30 per acre during the 1890's, but the per cent return was disappointing.

The initial cost per acre of the Union Pacific lands in Dodge County was on the average higher than that of the other types of land purchased by the New Yorkers, but these lands proved to be a satisfactory investment. The tax rate was moderate and most of the Dodge lands were sold prior to the depression of 1893. Reflecting the fact that Dodge was to emerge as one of the state's most productive counties, land values were checked in their upward surge only briefly during the 1890's. In one sale after 1900 in this county the purchaser paid $75 per acre to Ira Davenport, a price, however, which would have represented only 8 per cent per annum on the investment had not the land brought in revenue in rent. Much of the land located with military bounty warrants during 1871 was held into the 1890's. But the initial cost of this land was low and the rate of return on the Wayne holdings was slightly more satisfactory than that derived from the railroad land in Dodge County, although few tracts brought more than $25 per acre. The sandy soils of Pierce County no doubt largely account for returns in that county, which were significantly lower than those obtained in adjacent Wayne County.

In conclusion it should be emphasized that the tables undoubtedly do not exactly mirror the returns obtained by the speculators whose operations were studied. In the process of analysis sins of omission and estimation were committed. Yet the work was based on the actual cost and sale figures of the Illinois and Nebraska lands, and it is believed that the estimates are close to actual fact. Neither the amount of the location fees paid by the Illinois speculators nor the rate of commission which they paid to real estate agents for selling their lands was known. In the case of the Davenports these costs were known, but the rates of return would not have been significantly higher had they been ignored. Such charges were of little moment in comparison to the cost price of the land, the accumulation of interest, and to a lesser extent the tax payments, although it was discovered that a year more or less of taxes seldom made much difference in the rate of return. Had interest been compounded semi-annually the rates of return would have been lowered slightly. The rate of return, of course, does not stand as a synonym for profit. Some, perhaps, would prefer to substitute the term "yield" for "rate of return" and to this there is no great objection, although it should be obvious that yield in its usual sense does not involve our type of calculations. If the reader desires a figure which he can call profit, he must allocate an interest rate to the invested capital and subtract this from the rate of return. To go one step further and subtract an allowance for the time spent by the speculators in supervision of their holdings, thereby isolating a figure which could be called net profit, would involve estimation of a factor—administration cost—which undoubtedly varied widely among speculators.

It is reasonable to say that a well-informed resident of east-central Illinois could have purchased unimproved land in his neighborhood with his own funds, given the land his personal supervision, and earned something from his investment. If he bought during the mid-1830's and sold the land twenty to thirty years later, the money might have earned 6 to 8 per cent. Had he purchased land from the United States for about $1.10 per acre in the early 1850's, he might have realized 16 per cent upon his investment if he sold the land during the 1860's and 1870's. Or real estate bought during the mid-1860's at low figures and sold rapidly between 1867 and 1870 might have returned very large earnings.

Were residents of Illinois well advised to divert their funds into land speculation in preference to other uses? If the earnings from every alternative opportunity were known, a more meaningful answer could be given. The rates of return obtained by our Illinois speculators can be compared with the rate realized by moneylenders on real estate mortgages in the same region. The usual rate on such loans down to the mid-1870's was at least 10 per cent. Those who put their money into unimproved land in the 1830's might have done better, therefore, had they financed the land purchases of others. Having lent their money, however, they quite possibly would have found themselves owners of unimproved land by foreclosure. Those who paid cash for tracts of raw prairie in the 1850's and 1860's and later sold them perhaps fared better than the moneylender. Each alternative presented elements of risk. Yet none could predict the future with complete accuracy, and the optimism of boom times in the 1830's and 1850's tinged the judgment of the most clairvoyant.

From their Nebraska lands the Davenport brothers received handsome returns on a sizable investment. As it happened, they were also lending funds on the security of farm real estate in the same region.[47] Although the mortgage rate stood at more than 12 per cent during the early 1870's, it had dropped by the end of the decade to the vicinity of 8 per cent, while the average rate of return per dollar invested in the Nebraska lands at the close of 1880 stood at 10.9 per cent. Although the gap had been closed considerably by 1890, the rate of return on real estate stayed above the mortgage rate until the death of Ira Davenport. Had the brothers turned their funds during the early 1870's into railroad bonds,[48] or had they enjoyed the "average experience" of those investing in common stocks between 1871 and 1904,[49] they would have done less well than they did by turning to the trans-Missouri prairies.

In this article we have endeavored to make some contribution to the literature bearing on the returns derived from frontier land speculation, as well as to stimulate historians toward a greater precision of method in calculating such returns. There were, evidently, a considerable number of factors which, interacting over time, might bring either losses or munificent returns to the land speculator; particular attention has been called to some of these in recounting the experiences and in calculating the returns of half-a-dozen individuals or groups who hazarded funds on the assumption that the raw lands of Illinois and Nebraska would rise sufficiently in value after purchase that a lucrative return might be won by resale. Their experience does not prove either that frontier land speculation in the United States during the nineteenth century was generally well rewarded or generally unremunerative. Despite the assumptions of a number of historians, perhaps neither alternative is correct, and the speculative losses of some real estate plungers were canceled by the speculative gains of others. When careful studies of the returns from frontier land speculation on an area basis are available, historians will be in a better position to suggest answers to all of the questions posed in the introductory remarks and at the same time will have a much clearer understanding of the economic development of our frontier regions.

NOTES

1 Exact definition of the word "speculator" is difficult. Later in this article the word is used as it was in the newspapers of the Middle West during the mid- and late nineteenth century, where generally it denoted an individual who purchased large acreages of unimproved land, intending to sell after land values had risen sufficiently to make their sale remunerative and who was not interested in working the land as a personal enterprise or in building up a long-term tenant estate. Motivation becomes crucial, therefore, in identifying the speculator. But the student cannot always discover this. He is reduced to classifying as speculators those landholders whose motives he can discover to have been speculative and those who in all or in part of their land operations behaved in the same way as the members of the first group. Thus William Scully and Matthew Scott (pp. 369–380) sold part of their original purchases in an unimproved condition; a portion is still owned by their

descendants and farmed in tenancy. As far as we are concerned, the land which was sold represented speculation. The Davenports (see p. 374) revealed in their correspondence that their intentions in Nebraska were purely speculative; yet they were willing to rent land as a means of defraying the cost of taxes and a way of enhancing the value of the land through the breaking which the tenants performed. The fact that they rented land for a time prior to its sale made them no less speculators. Local use of the term "speculator" during the nineteenth century was colored somewhat by whether or not the large landholder was resident in the community where his land lay. Historians have pointed out that the settler who held but a quarter section or less might be just as speculative in intent as the large holder; on the other hand, some would classify the land-grant railroads as land speculators. Both the settler speculators and the railroads are excluded from consideration by this definition. It will be obvious from the text of the article that the speculator is considered to be a type of investor.

2   W. G. Sumner, *Robert Morris* (New York, 1892), 137–169; E. P. Oberholtzer, *Robert Morris: Patriot and Financier* (New York, 1903), 335–357; Ruth L. Higgins, *Expansion in New York with Special Reference to the Eighteenth Century* (Columbus, 1931), 116–133.

3   Paul Demund Evans, *The Holland Land Company* (*Buffalo Historical Society Publications*, vol. 28, Buffalo, 1924), 397–427.

4   Scully's spade is mentioned by both Paul Wallace Gates, *Frontier Landlords and Pioneer Tenants* (Ithaca, 1945), 36, and Homer E. Socolofsky, "The Scully Land System in Marion County," *Kansas Historical Quarterly*, 18:337–375 (see p. 338) (November, 1950).

5   In *The Age of Enterprise: A Social History of Industrial America* (New York, 1942), 4, 11, 39, 84, 107–108, 214, Thomas C. Cochran and William Miller gave some attention to this problem. Economists concerned with the problems of economic development have given little consideration to the effect which speculation in natural resources may have in conditioning economic growth.

6   A clue to the importance of land speculation in contributing to the concentration of capital in America during the nineteenth century is found in the list of 4,047 Americans, who were "reputed to be worth a million or more," published by the New York *Tribune* in 1892. Of this group, 271 allegedly owed their fortunes to investment in some type of real estate and another 1,100 had derived their wealth in part from the same source; 34 per cent in all. Sydney Ratner, *New Light on the History of Great American Fortunes: American Millionaires of 1892 and 1902* (New York, 1953). The figures given here are based on the writer's analysis of the 1892 list, rather than on the recapitulation found on p. 90.

7   See Fritz Redlich, *History of American Business Leaders: A Series of Studies*, vol. 1 (Ann Arbor, 1940), 21–22; Joseph Dorfman, *Thorstein Veblen and His America* (New York, 1935), 350; Thorstein Veblen, *Imperial Germany and the Industrial Revolution* (New York, 1939 ed.), 334. The negative quality of the land speculator's role is so often stressed that it is well to remember that he did make a positive con-

tribution at times. After Congress struck the credit provisions from the land laws in the revision act of 1820, the impecunious settler could still purchase land on time from the speculator. Although they often carried it with poor grace, the speculators in the Middle West bore a substantial share of the tax burden as new communities developed. Particularly was this the case within the limits of those railroad land grants in which the alternate sections were settled by homesteaders enjoying immunity from taxation until they fulfilled the residence requirement of the homestead laws. When the speculator purchased from the land-grant railroads he sometimes helped these corporations to realize a return from their grants more quickly than otherwise would have been the case, thereby assisting in the construction of transportation facilities. The returns obtained by the land speculator may be regarded to an extent, therefore, as a reward for services rendered. An incidental dividend from speculation may well have stemmed from the fact that actual settlers frequently could not afford to purchase farms large enough to make economic units in the commercial agriculture of the nineteenth century. Where speculators held land nearby, such farmers could build up their holdings without squeezing neighbors off the land. Specific instances to the contrary, of course, can be presented in contradiction of these generalizations.

8 Strangely enough there has been little effort made to study regional land values on a historical basis, although such work would be highly useful. In his *One Hundred Years of Land Values in Chicago* (Chicago, 1933) Homer Hoyt blazed a good many interesting trails for the student who follows this approach.

9 Joseph Schafer, *Wisconsin Domesday Book: Town Studies*, vol. 1 (Madison, 1924); *Wisconsin Lead Region* (*Wisconsin Domesday Book: General Studies*, vol. 3, Madison, 1932); "A Yankee Land Speculator in Wisconsin," *Wisconsin Magazine of History*, 8:377–392, (June, 1925); *The Social History of American Agriculture* (New York, 1936), 23–26.

10 Schafer, *Wisconsin Domesday Book: Town Studies*, 1:10, including n. 5.

11 Schafer, *Wisconsin Lead Region*, 148–154.

12 Paul Wallace Gates, *The Wisconsin Pine Lands of Cornell University: A Study in Land Policy and Absentee Ownership* (Ithaca, 1943), 85, n. 48.

13 Mattie Russell, "Land Speculation in Tippah County 1836–1861" (Master's thesis, University of Mississippi, 1940); Edwin W. Chapman, "Land Speculation in Tate County 1836–1861" (Master's thesis, University of Mississippi, 1942). James W. Silver summarized these studies in "Land Speculation Profits in the Chickasaw Cession," *The Journal of Southern History*, 10:84–92 (February, 1944).

14 Russell, "Land Speculation in Tippah County," iv; Chapman, "Land Speculation in Tate County," ii.

15 Russell, "Land Speculation in Tippah County," 72. The quoted phrase is on p. 73. See also Chapman, "Land Speculation in Tate County," 65–66.

16 Paul Wallace Gates, "The Role of the Land Speculator in Western Development," *The Pennsylvania Magazine of History and Biography,* 66:314–333, especially p. 332 (July, 1942) *[see p. 364 in this volume];* Gates, *Frontier Landlords and Pioneer Tenants,* 2–3.

17 Gates, *The Wisconsin Pine Lands of Cornell University,* 243.

18 Paul Wallace Gates to Margaret Bogue, June 24, 1955.

19 Robert Diller, *Farm Ownership, Tenancy, and Land Use in a Nebraska Community* (Chicago, 1941), 20.

20 *Ibid.*

21 Theodore L. Carlson, *The Illinois Military Tract: A Study of Land Occupation,Utilization and Tenure* (*University of Illinois Studies in the Social Sciences,* vol. 32, no. 2, Urbana, 1951), 41.

22 Carlson, *The Illinois Military Tract,* 57 and supporting n. 63.

23 Evans, *The Holland Land Company,* 435.

24 Helen I. Cowan, *Charles Williamson, Genesee Promoter: Friend of Anglo-American Rapprochement* (*Rochester Historical Society Publications,* vol. 19, Rochester, 1941), 293.

25 Theodore Roosevelt, *The Winning of the West* (4 vols., Homeward Bound Edition, New York, 1910), 4:220; Frederick Jackson Turner, *The United States, 1830–1850: The Nation and Its Sections* (New York, 1935), 292–293; Carl Russell Fish, *The Rise of the Common Man: A History of American Life,* vol. 6 (New York, 1946 print.), 130; Edward C. Kirkland, *A History of American Economic Life* (3rd ed., New York, 1951), 137; Charles Abrams, *Revolution in Land* (New York, 1939), 14; Louis M. Hacker, *The Triumph of American Capitalism: The Development of Forces in American History to the End of the Nineteenth Century* (New York, 1940), 210–214, 323, 327, 329; A. M. Sakolski, *The Great American Land Bubble: The Amazing Story of Land-Grabbing, Speculations, and Booms from Colonial Days to the Present Time* (New York, 1932); Addison E. Sheldon, *Land Systems and Land Policies in Nebraska* (*Publications of the Nebraska State Historical Society,* vol. 22, Lincoln, 1936); Shaw Livermore, *Early American Land Companies, Their Influence on Corporate Development* (*Publications of the Foundation for Research in Legal History,* Columbia School of Law, Julius Goebel, Jr., ed., New York, 1939).

26 Silver, "Land Speculation Profits," 92.

27 *Ibid.*

28 The student interested in calculating such returns is reminded that compound interest tables do exist, that a formula for calculating compound interest is available, and that, depending upon the nature of the data, calculus may yield short cuts. The work, however, was complicated by the fact that many of the returns ranged beyond the limit of conventional tables. Also, it was hoped to present the results in part as in Tables 11 and 13, which necessitated calculating the investment in a particular tract of land at the end of a number of years prior to the eventual sale. Income prior to the date of sale further complicated computation. Because of these considerations and the fact that the same cost figures and tax rate often applied to a sizable number of tracts it

was found most convenient, if rather cumbersome, to construct tables year by year. A number of rates were applied to the cost data and then the sale price was checked against these tables in the appropriate year to find the rate which gave a sum (purchase price, plus taxes, interest, and other costs minus income) equal to the sale price. One of the several accountants and statisticians consulted characterized this method as composed of equal parts of brute strength and ignorance, but agreed that it would give accurate results. At least two refinements in method would have produced more elegant figures. In the first place, interest rates could have been compounded semi-annually rather than annually, which would have had the effect of lowering the rates slightly. Second, the rate of return on individual tracts could have been worked past the decimal point (figures beyond the decimal point in the four tables presented here were derived in the process of averaging the returns from individual tracts). It was decided that the extra calculations involved would not improve the results sufficiently to repay the time taken to make them. Others working in this same area may decide differently.

29 These means were obtained by multiplying the sale prices by the rate of interest which they returned and dividing the sum of the products by the sum of the sale prices.

30 Biographical sketches of Matthew T. Scott, Jr., are found in George B. Pickett, *A Short Sketch of the Life and Character of Matthew Thompson Scott of Bloomington, Illinois* (Bloomington, 1891); Newton Bateman and Paul Selby, eds., *Historical Encyclopedia of Illinois and History of Christian County* (Chicago, 1918), 1:472; *Transactions of the McLean County Historical Society*, 2:664–667 (Bloomington, 1903).

31 Compiled from the federal cash and military bounty warrant entry books, Danville and Vandalia, Illinois Land Districts, National Archives, Washington, D.C.

32 Compiled from the Deed Records, McLean and Livingston counties, and from the deeds in the Matthew T. Scott Collection, Collection of Regional History, Cornell University, Ithaca, New York.

33 For a detailed discussion of the Matthew T. Scott land business during the nineteenth century, see Margaret Beattie Bogue, "Patterns from the Sod: Land Use and Tenure in the Grand Prairie, 1850–1900" (Ph.D. dissertation, Cornell University, 1955), 154–199.

34 *History of Tazewell County, Illinois* . . . (Chicago, 1879), 703.

35 Compiled from the Deed Records, Iroquois County, Illinois.

36 For a discussion of the Wilson land and cattle business see Margaret Beattie Bogue, "Patterns from the Sod," 82–83, 122–123.

37 Newton Bateman and Paul Selby, eds., *Historical Encyclopedia of Illinois and History of Champaign County* (Chicago, 1905), 2:675; Mable E. Richmond, *Centennial History of Decatur and Macon County* (Decatur, 1930), 272–273.

38 Compiled from the federal cash entry books, Danville, Illinois, Land District, National Archives, Washington, D.C.

39 Compiled from the federal cash entry books.

40 *The National Cyclopedia of American Biography* . . . , 11:504.
41 Compiled from the federal cash entry books.
42 For a more detailed discussion of the factors that influenced the size of speculative returns in Illinois see Margaret Beattie Bogue, "Patterns from the Sod," 200–277.
43 A considerable collection of correspondence and business records relating to the Davenports' business ventures is available in the Collection of Regional History, Cornell University. The basic record, in so far as the Nebraska land investments are concerned, is an account book, labeled "Fannie Davenport Ledger," and referred to in other records and correspondence as "the land book."
44 Allan G. Bogue has discussed the mortgage investments of the brothers in *Money at Interest: The Farm Mortgage on the Middle Border* (Ithaca, 1955), 7–75.
45 Mr. C. Ashley Ellefson assisted in the computation of the data that are summarized in Tables 12 and 13.
46 The soil surveys of Seward, Dodge, Wayne, and Madison counties are to be found in the *Field Operations of the Bureau of Soils*, 1914, pp. 2253–2288; 1916, pp. 2071–2119; 1917, pp. 1957–2002; 1920, pp. 201–248, published by the United States Department of Agriculture, the Nebraska Soil Survey co-operating. Those of Pierce and Lancaster counties appeared under the same auspices as *Soil Survey Reports*, series 1928, no. 9, and series 1938, no. 15. See also L. F. Garey, *Factors Determining Type-of-Farming Areas in Nebraska* (University of Nebraska College of Agriculture Experiment Station, Bulletin 299, Lincoln, 1936), and *Systems of Farming and Possible Alternates in Nebraska* (*ibid.*, Bulletin 309, Lincoln, 1937).
47 Allan G. Bogue, *Money at Interest*, 61, Table 4.
48 Frederick R. Macaulay, *Some Theoretical Problems Suggested by the Movement of Interest Rates, Bond Yields and Stock Prices in the United States Since 1856* (*Publications of the National Bureau of Economic Research*, no. 33, New York, 1938), Table 3, p. 33 *et seq.*, and Table 4, p. A. 108 *et seq.*
49 Alfred Cowles 3rd *et al.*, *Common Stock Indexes, 1871–1937* (Bloomington, 1938), Series Ya, 372 *et seq.*, and Series R, 404 *et seq.*

State Disposal of the Agricultural College Land Scrip

THOMAS LeDUC

Reprinted by permission from Agricultural History, *Volume 28* (*1954*), *pages 99–107.*

PUBLISHED histories of state colleges of agriculture contain only brief and usually inadequate references to the disposal of the endowments of land or of land scrip granted by Congress. Some writers, indeed, seem unaware that most of the "land-grant" colleges received not land but scrip which could be used as currency in the purchase of certain categories of public land.[1]

Under the act of July 2, 1862, the federal government donated to the states land or scrip to the amount of 30,000 acres for each senator and congressman.[2] States in which there lay a sufficient supply of public land open to private entry at $1.25 an acre were given the right to select their entitlements within their own borders from that class of land.[3] Under this provision eleven states selected 1,769,440 acres.[4] Public land states later admitted to the Union received similar grants.[5]

The federal government issued scrip to states in which public land open to private entry at $1.25 an acre was non-existent or insufficient. The scrip could be used by assignees of the beneficiary states to purchase public land open to this class of entry in other states or territories.[6] Twenty-seven states eventually received scrip instead of land and almost 8,000,000 scrip-acres were so issued.[7]

How did the states convert this grant of scrip into an income producing endowment for the land grant colleges? How well did they perform their trust in administering the federal grant? What were the conditions under which the scrip came on the market? It is to these and associated questions that this paper is devoted.

Most important of the restrictions on the use of college scrip imposed by Congress was that prohibiting the states from entering, i.e., acquiring land themselves. Their assignees might enter land but the states themselves might not. Whether the colleges constituted independent assignees or were to be construed as agencies of their respective states was a question never adjudicated. Most of the states seem to have assumed that the colleges were barred from entering land and thus either sold the scrip or conveyed it to colleges that sold it. Brown University, to which Rhode Island assigned its scrip, did succeed in entering some land after successfully challenging an adverse ruling of the General Land Office, and the University of Illinois used about 5 per cent of its scrip for the acquisition of investment land.[8]

The law providing for the grant prohibited the use of scrip for entering land before July 2, 1863. Even by that date the General Land Office, chronically behind in its work, had not yet issued the scrip to the states.[9] Most of the state legislatures were equally slow in providing for the disposal of the scrip, and marketing extended over a nine-year period from March, 1864, to April, 1873.

Delays of the state governments may be explained in a number of ways. Preoccupation with Civil War problems was not insignificant, but in some states there was massive indifference and even hostility to the establishment of state-supported colleges of agriculture and engineering. Almost everywhere opposing groups contended for the allotment of the federal subsidy to existing institutions. Everywhere there was ignorance as to the probable value of the grant. Public land paper was a currency unfamiliar in the East to all but a handful of dealers and investors. Most of the scrip fell to states distant from the public lands.[10] How best to liquidate it was a new problem in state administration. Many of the legislators and administrators tended to overvalue the scrip in terms of actual market factors. Inexperienced in converting land paper to land, many seem to have believed that its value should approximate the price of the land that could be acquired with it. Actually, of course, the General Land Office was selling little public land at the $1.25 price in the years 1862–1866.[11] Furthermore, land paper had always sold at a discount because of the cost of "locating," or finding attractive public land to enter with it. Investors in land had accumulated a body of experience in using veterans' land warrants in the years 1847–1862. Cyrus Woodman, an old hand at the business, wrote in 1867 that men getting ten dollars a day to locate land with warrants were "worthless" and offered to pay a reliable agent one-fourth of the land he secured.[12] Insured transportation and interest on the investment in idle paper were but two of several items in the cost of using land paper.

Finally, supply and demand factors were operating to diminish the value of college scrip. Most of the veterans' land warrants had come on the market in the years before June 30, 1860, when there was a high rate of demand from both settlers and investors. It is probable that during the 1850's land entry had outrun settlement and development of new land, and much attractive and accessible land in private hands was still unexploited.[13] Lands available to entry were correspondingly remote. On top of this backlog of excessive entry came the Civil War and the adoption of the Homestead Act. The Civil War diverted an undetermined number of prospective entrymen from the public land. The Homestead Act disturbed the market in two ways. It not only took prospective settlers out of the market for land paper, but threatened that much land open to private entry would be claimed by homesteaders.

With this background we may trace and interpret the disposal of the scrip by the states. The process was generally one of disappointment; the irony is that the southern states, where opposition to the defeated land-grant bill of 1857–1859 was most pronounced, were the ones to realize the best proceeds from the scrip. When they finally got their scrip after the war it was sold on better terms than the northern states generally secured and the quantity was increased by the termination of the old three-fifths rule governing representation in Congress.

The few northern states that moved promptly in 1864 did better than those that delayed until 1866 or 1867. In March and April, 1864, Vermont sold 150,000 acres at an average of 81.8 cents.[14] Veterans' warrants, eligible for use on both offered and unoffered land, were then selling in New York for around 90 cents.[15] Most of the Vermont scrip was taken by two experienced New York dealers. George Woodman reported that he had purchased 60,000 acres and that John Thompson had taken a major part of the rest.[16] Both of these men were typical Wall Street dealers in bank notes, government bonds, land warrants, and other negotiable paper. Thompson, publisher of the familiar *Bank Note Reporter*, had, like George Woodman, good connections in the West.[17]

Connecticut, in selling 180,000 acres of scrip at 75 cents, in May, 1864, was almost equally fortunate in view of the condition of the market.[18] At retail the scrip would bring not more than 85 cents, and the state of New York sold only 76,000 acres in small lots at that price.[19] Other states had similar experiences of trying to sell scrip in retail lots to small purchasers. Administrative expenses on such sales were high and, in terms of prevailing interest rates, inventory costs on unliquidated scrip were substantial. Eventually the states learned that a higher net could be realized by prompt sale to a dealer.

The Massachusetts record is obscure. In June, 1864, George Woodman was approached to make a corrupt deal with the state executives under which they would turn over the scrip on favorable terms in exchange for a kickback. Woodman was dubious about the prospects of profit in case other states should throw their scrip on the market, and rejected the offer.[20] The state seems thereafter to have attempted to sell the scrip at retail. Prior to 1866 about 140,000 acres had been sold at an average price of 81 cents.[21]

By December, 1864, the market for college scrip had broken. New Jersey started selling at 70 cents but, after placing 36,000 acres at that price, unloaded the remaining 173,920 acres at 50 cents to Hiram Slocum and Francis Howland of New York in late October, 1865.[22] By that time the prospect of an abundance of offerings had led to collapse. Congress had not yet passed a relief act and the states were under mandate to establish their colleges by July 2, 1867.[23]

In December, 1865, the commissioners appointed to sell the Ohio scrip at the statutory minimum of 80 cents reported that they had sold only 11,040 acres, or about 8 per cent of the state's grant. They asserted that in response to their invitation to other states, an agreement had been reached to set a price of 80 cents but that some states had chiseled on the fixed price and that the market had broken in consequence.[24]

In March, 1866, Maine found that it could place small quantities at relatively high prices but that in order to sell most of its 210,000 acres it was necessary to accept wholesale bids at a little over 53 cents. David Preston of Detroit bid for varying quantities at different prices and finally took 96,000 acres at 53⅛ cents. Cyrus and George Woodman, perhaps through the collusion of state officers, were permitted to take 60,000 at the lowest price of 52½ cents.[25] In April of the same year West Virginia sold 80,000 acres to J. H. Atkinson and 60,000 acres to T. K. McCann at 52 cents. The remaining 9,920 acres had been sold earlier at somewhat higher prices to give the state an average return of about 52½ cents an acre.[26]

It was at this stage, in the summer of 1866, that another dealer, Gleason F. Lewis of Cleveland, Ohio, came into the market. Eventually he was to secure a monopoly of agricultural college scrip and to buy most of what was thereafter offered. Between July, 1866, and April, 1873, he bought almost 5,000,000 acres of scrip, or 67.7 per cent of all that was issued and marketed. His transactions in land paper were strictly those of a dealer. He bought and sold scrip and veterans' warrants on a small spread but never acquired an acre of public land. His achievements were to secure control of the supply of college scrip and to develop a wide market for its sale. In both fields he was more astute than other dealers like George Woodman, John Thompson, or Lunt, Preston, and Kean of Chicago and Detroit.[27] From an early date, Woodman recognized the scale of operations necessary to effect a monopoly and generally took so pessimistic a view of the retail market that he was never a major figure in the business.[28] After his purchases from Vermont and Maine he never again succeeded in bidding sufficiently high to get any more from the states, although he may have occasionally stocked his shelves from the supply held by other dealers.[29] Thompson's only sizable purchase after 1864 was of 180,000 acres from South Carolina in October, 1870.[30] Preston occasionally bid but, apart from his Maine purchase, seems to have secured only 16,000 acres which he took from Pennsylvania in 1866, and 48,000 acres from the same source in 1867.[31]

Lewis got his start in the land-paper business in the mid-1850's when supply and demand both rose sharply.[32] Between 1847 and 1855 Congress voted to military veterans land-grant bounties on the basis of which claims to 61,000,000 acres were established by half a million beneficiaries. Until 1852 only the veterans or their heirs could use the warrants in land entry. Most of them had no desire to do so and their bounties consequently went unclaimed. Congress eventually made the warrants negotiable and a regular market for them developed at a time when purchase of public land reached its all-time peak.[33]

To reach both sellers and buyers of land paper, Lewis published the *Old Soldiers Advocate* at Cleveland, Ohio, from 1859 to 1878.[34] This monthly newspaper, purportedly devoted to veterans' interests, was mainly an advertising medium for Lewis's business activities. It was as much designed to reach the mass sales market as to establish contact with sources of warrants. The extent of this market has not been accurately determined by systematic analysis of Land Office records, but it is clear that the market was much broader than scholars have sometimes thought. It is true that the use of college scrip was less diffuse than that of military warrants and that it was used in California and in the Lake states timberlands mainly by large investors. In Kansas and Nebraska, however, college scrip was probably more used by settlers than by absentees. In every land-office town in the West there were dealers who dealt in land paper, and many of them served as outlets for Lewis's purchases.[35] Lewis dealt with the ultimate market rather than with metropolitan dealers. There is no evidence that he ever sold to the Woodmans, Thompson, or Preston, Lunt, and Kean, but he probably supplied scrip to large-scale entrymen.

Lewis came into the market at a strategic moment. By the summer of 1866 most of the scrip that had been sold by states had been used for land entry and there could have been little in dealers' hands, but the prospects for the states were not at all improved.[36] They had failed to protect their interests by creating an agency for the orderly marketing of their scrip; they had discovered that they could not sell at retail effectively, and they realized that the supply of scrip hanging over the market would soon be augmented as the southern states received theirs. Worse still, the five public land states of the south would be closed to entry with college scrip, and almost 1,000,000 acres of scrip, not previously expected, would be issued to them.[37] The time was auspicious for the building of a monopoly by a man of resources and courage.

In July, 1866, Lewis made his first purchase. He took the entire Kentucky issue of 330,000 acres at 50 cents.[38] Whether in this and later purchases Lewis connived with state officials, we do not know. George Woodman claimed that he had offered to take the whole lot at 52½ cents and suspected corruption.[39]

In the next seven years Lewis was to pay over $3,500,000 for college land scrip. How far he was dependent on outside capital we do not know. In one of his many letters to Ezra Cornell he asserted that "the men behind me in this business are men of money and so far have always furnished all I asked for. I think it will continue." [40] Lewis held some valuable real estate in downtown Cleveland which he mortgaged to the firm of Fisher, Boothe, of Detroit. The same firm appears as his "associates" in buying the North Carolina scrip, and is mentioned as his backing in another project.[41] They probably supplied some capital to him, but there is evidence that he found it easier to make purchase contracts with the states than to meet the installments.[42] In many cases he dealt with the states on a hand-to-mouth basis, receiving batches of scrip COD and endlessly trying to stall off threats from the states and lobbying at state capitals to prevent auctions of scrip until he was ready to bid.[43] Whatever the source of his capital, Lewis was certainly the entrepreneur and manager who made the contacts—and the contracts. His chief capital, perhaps, was his audacity in bidding and his well-developed market for land paper.

Within a few weeks of his Kentucky purchase, Lewis took from Pennsylvania 76,800 acres at 55 cents and 76,640 at 55⅜ cents. Pennsylvania, with a total grant of 780,000 acres, had tried with little success to retail it at high prices. Down to April, 1866, they had sold but 27,000 acres, and the commissioners then invited bids with no minimum price. Under this dispensation they sold about 225,000 acres before February, 1867, with Lewis as the chief bidder.[44]

Ohio followed the same pattern. The state law of April, 1865, setting a minimum price of 80 cents was repealed a year later after disappointing sales. The state commissioners reserved 27,520 acres for retail sales and sold the remaining 575,800 acres in 1866 at 53 cents, of which Lewis took 400,000 acres. On Ohio's whole grant of 630,000 acres the state had netted, after three years' delay, an average of 55⅜ cents.[45]

In the first seven months of 1867 Lewis bought not less than 1,420,-800 acres of scrip. In January, notwithstanding the efforts of Cyrus and George Woodman to purchase inside information that would enable them to bid a shade higher, Lewis captured New Hampshire's 150,000 acres,[46] and in March he got Maryland's 210,000, both at a little over 53 cents.[47] During the same month he bought 112,000 acres at 54 cents from Massachusetts after that state abandoned its higher asking price, and probably bought another 108,000 later in the year.[48] In April Indiana offered its scrip at auction and Lewis, bidding 54 cents, took 366,080 acres of the total grant of 390,000 acres.[49] Pennsylvania had meanwhile decided to offer the 520,000 acres that had not previously been offered, and the state board set a tentative minimum price of 55 cents. Lewis took 37,760 at 55⅜ cents and later an additional 275,200 at 55 cents on which another bidder had defaulted.[50] In July Lewis, associated with David Preston and Fisher, Boothe, of Detroit, bought all of North Carolina's grant of 270,000 acres at 50 cents.[51]

Use of college scrip for land entries jumped from 651,000 acres in the fiscal year 1866 to 2,420,000 in fiscal 1867. The following year saw almost 2,000,000 acres entered with scrip. Market demand was good and

Lewis was able to liquidate his inventory rapidly. By October, 1867, he reported that his stock was reduced to 250,000 acres and that he was looking for more.[52] His optimism may have misled him, for the next month without apparent competition he contracted with the trustees of the University of Illinois to take 100,000 acres at the then high price of 90 cents.[53] In the preceding six months the state had sold 180,000 acres at 54 cents and 100,000 at 58 cents, but none of this apparently came into the hands of Lewis.[54]

With prices suddenly stiffening and much of the southern scrip still unmarketed, Lewis began negotiations with Ezra Cornell to co-operate in holding the retail price. In 1866 Cornell had bought from the state of New York a little over 900,000 acres after the state had failed to sell more than 76,000 acres at retail. Cornell agreed to donate to Cornell University any profits that he might make from his land operations. He used 500,000 acres to locate pine lands in Wisconsin and 12,000 acres for entries elsewhere, and was confident that acquisition of land was the soundest long-term disposal of the scrip. But the land was costly to locate, hold, and protect from depredation, and it produced little immediate revenue. President Andrew D. White of Cornell and some of his trustees were pressing for the liquidation of the university's capital assets. Under their pressure Cornell gave way and agreed to sell the remaining scrip. During early 1868 he negotiated with Lewis and in April sold him 100,000 acres at 90 cents and 180,000 acres at $1. In December he was to sell him the remaining 101,920 acres at 86 cents.[55]

Congress was moving meanwhile towards a partial repudiation of its contract with the states. The offer embodied in the original act of 1862 contained only the restriction that not more than 1,000,000 acres of college scrip could be entered in any one state. In 1866 Congress closed the public land states of the south to scrip entries. In 1867 Senator Alexander Ramsey of Minnesota proposed to restrict entries in any one township to an aggregate of five sections.[56] This proposal was defeated, but the following year a bill was offered that would impair the value of the scrip and change the terms on which the states had accepted the federal offer by putting a ceiling of three sections of college scrip entry in any township. Lewis lobbied against passage of the bill and attempted to organize protests among the states,[57] but his efforts were vain and the bill became law on July 27, 1868.[58] Passage of the act did not seriously depress the price of scrip, but it showed the sensitivity of Congress to pressure from squatters. Politicians had learned the advantages of standing before the people as enemies of land investors.

The trend was confirmed by the passage of a bill in 1870 that authorized the use of college scrip in payment of pre-emption entries.[59] The effect of this act was to discriminate against absentee investors by permitting only settlers under the Pre-emption Law of 1841 to enter unoffered land with college scrip and by waiving the million-acre ceiling for such entries.[60] Non-residents were still confined to the offered lands.

Lewis had contracted in May, 1868, to buy Tennessee's 300,000 acres of scrip at 90⅝ cents, after exerting what pressure he could to delay its issue so that he could clear his shelves.[61] He had contracted in July, 1867, to take the North Carolina scrip, but it had not yet been delivered, as the state had not been re-admitted.[62] Under the provisions of a joint resolution of Congress, delivery of scrip to the states of the former Confederacy was prohibited until they "shall be fully restored to their rights as States by Congress."[63] North Carolina was to be restored in July, 1868, and Lewis would then have to meet his contract. Lewis had been concerned also lest the trustees of the University of Illinois put the rest of their scrip on the market and depress the price. He always believed that the Lunt, Preston, and Kean group of Detroit and Chicago were trying to force retail prices down, presumably because they were not only dealers but land investors, and tried to get Ezra Cornell to join him in opposing such actions.[64] In December, 1869, Lewis was to buy 50,080 acres from Illinois at 89 cents, but he came to regret the contract and attempted to secure release from it.[65]

Lewis's only other direct purchase in 1869 was from Delaware, which had a grant of 90,000 acres, which he took at 88¾ cents.[66] In December he bought 101,920 acres from Ezra Cornell at 86 cents, the last of the unlocated and unsold New York scrip.[67] In 1870 Maine decided to sell 16,320 acres that had not been sold in 1866, and Lewis took it at 84 cents.[68] The only other scrip to come on the market that year was South Carolina's. State records show that it was sold to John Thompson of New York, at 72½ cents, but whether Thompson was the principal or only an agent, we do not know.[69] Lewis asserted in a private letter that he had bought it, but he never included South Carolina in his boastful advertisements, so it seems probable that he did not.[70]

After the South Carolina sale of October, 1870, Lewis was the sole buyer of scrip from the states. The northern states had disposed of all of theirs, but the remaining states of the former Confederacy were still to receive and offer 1,650,000 acres. Lewis bought all of it.

In April, 1871, Louisiana sold him 209,920 acres at 87 cents and about the same time he bought the 180,000 acres issued to Texas at the same price.[71] By June he had to pay 90 cents for the Alabama issue.[72] In July he secured at the same figure, 209,920 acres issued to Mississippi.[73]

In evaluating these prices it is helpful to examine the current retail prices at which Lewis was offering scrip. In June, 1871, he was offering quarter-section lots at $1 an acre and lots of 640 acres or more at a trifle less than 97 cents; in August he advanced prices three cents and in September another three. There prices stayed until the active land-entry season of the summer of 1872.[74] It would seem, therefore, that profits came from volume rather than from a wide spread between costs and proceeds. Lewis's overhead was probably not great, but the difference between cost and sales price was not all profit. It can hardly be overemphasized that Lewis was a dealer and not a "speculator."

In 1872 Lewis bought Georgia's scrip in January and Arkansas's in August, both at 90 cents, but he had to pay Virginia 95 cents in May for the state's grant of 300,000 acres.[75] This was the highest price ever paid a state for college scrip. After the Arkansas purchase there remained only the Florida grant of 89,920 acres, which was sold to Lewis at 90 cents on April 14, 1873.[76] At that time he was offering retail units of less than 640 acres at $1.19 and greater quantities at approximately $1.16 an acre.[77]

In summarizing the diverse experiences of the states in disposing of the college scrip, a few generalizations may be risked. Historians have marveled that the states realized so little from the seeming generosity of the land grants, and some have suggested that a ring of land specu-lators mulcted the states and deprived them of just returns.[78] A differ-ent interpretation of the facts based on a systematic investigation of the records would be that most of the states pursued a short-sighted pro-gram within the framework of a dubious federal policy. Even after Illinois had demonstrated that the scrip could be located by state colleges notwithstanding the statutory injunction against entry by the states themselves, the states continued to dump their scrip on the mar-ket. Even Illinois, Cornell, and Brown University, the assignee of Rhode Island, abandoned land entry because of pressure to liquidate their land-grant endowments, and sold a large portion of their scrip. The first simple fact is that the states were unwilling to appropriate sufficient funds to get the agricultural colleges started without using income from the investment of proceeds of scrip sales.

Assuming that the states were going to sell their scrip instead of using it to acquire public land for long-term investment, it seems questionable that the real explanation of low proceeds lies in any alleged concert of speculators. The states sold most of their scrip to land-paper dealers and not to land speculators. The only dealer who seems to have tried to hold prices down was David Preston of Detroit, and he was never a major figure in the business. The biggest dealer, Lewis, and the biggest holder of scrip, Ezra Cornell, were working desperately to keep scrip prices up, not down.

The real explanation is that the states were confronted with a depressed market. The demand for land paper was not big enough to absorb the tremendous volume poured on the market, particularly in 1866 and 1867. Demand was diminished by the operation of the Homestead Act, which reduced settlers' need for land paper. The "incongruous land system" worked both ways.[79] Even as land grants to states and railroads made more difficult the location of attractive homesteads, so did homesteading make it harder to find good land for entry with land paper. Furthermore, the failure of the federal government to offer new land at public sale after the Civil War created a scarcity of the only category of land that could be entered with college scrip before 1870.

The states advertised their auctions of scrip and usually received sealed bids. In the absence of evidence of collusion, and in view of the closeness of bids and the clear evidences of competition in bidding many times, one is forced to the conclusion that the states derived from their scrip exactly what their short-sighted policies entitled them to: the going market value.

NOTES

1 The inflationary character of this scrip and other public land paper issued by the federal government has gone unnoticed by scholars. It may be regarded as evidence of non-interest-bearing debt or as a restricted currency. Equally ignored by economists and historians is the effect on the economy of paying subsidies to transportation, education, defense, settlement, and a host of other activities in the form of land rather than cash derived from tax collections. It represented a kind of deficit finance in which the government met its obligations by drawing on its balance of physical assets.

2 12 *U.S. Stat.*, 503.

3 "Open to Private entry at $1.25 an acre" described public land that had been offered at public sale after proclamation and had gone unsold. Unoffered land was open to entry only under the Pre-emption Act of 1841. Earlier federal donations to the states were not restricted. The

internal improvements grant under the act of 1841, for example, could be selected from the unoffered lands in the beneficiary states.

4 The nominal grant was 1,770,000 acres, but, in conformity with the law, the selections had to be made in units of quarter sections. States whose entitlements were not a multiple of 160 acres were thus each deprived of 80 acres.

5 The Commissioner of the General Land Office ruled in 1875 that the statute operated prospectively to effect grants to new states upon admission to the Union. Thomas Donaldson, *The Public Domain, Its History with Statistics* (47 Congress, 2 session, House Miscellaneous Document no. 45, serial 2158, Washington, 1884), 229.

6 The act of July 1, 1870, authorized the acceptance of agricultural college scrip in payment of pre-emption claims. 16 *U.S. Stat.*, 186. Squatters were thus permitted to enter unoffered land although non-residents were still excluded.

7 Donaldson, *The Public Domain*, 229–230. Donaldson's totals are slightly excessive, as he credits several states with their legal entitlement rather than the next lower multiple of 160 acres.

8 Paul Wallace Gates, *The Wisconsin Pine Lands of Cornell University* (Ithaca, 1943), 37–39, 43–44. I am indebted to Professor Gates for a number of suggestions used in the preparation of this article.

9 Scrip due the northern states was issued in August, 1863. *Ibid.*, 38.

10 Under the ratio prescribed by Congress in 1862, 44.1 per cent of all the scrip eventually issued went to the populous states north of the Potomac and east of the Alleghenies.

11 In the fiscal years 1862–1866 land sales for cash averaged only 323,000 acres a year, as compared with an average of over 5,000,000 a year in the preceding decade.

12 Cyrus Woodman to E. Brown, July 16, 1867, in the Woodman Papers, State Historical Society of Wisconsin, Letter Books, 21:372. I am indebted to Dr. Larry Gara of Mexico City College, whose familiarity with the Woodman Papers enabled him to call my attention to a number of specific letters and thus to speed my investigation.

13 Average annual entry with cash and paper during the decade ending June 30, 1860, was 9.57 million acres. Two million acres of military bounty warrants were entered in the following year, but the average for the decade of the 1860's was only half a million.

14 Senate of the State of New York, Document 103, 97 sess. (1874), 400–401.

15 The quotation is for 160-acre warrants, comparable in size to the individual pieces of agricultural college scrip. Warrants of smaller denomination always brought better prices. George Woodman to Cyrus Woodman, April 2, 1864, in Woodman Papers, Letters Received, 20:318.

16 George Woodman to Cyrus Woodman, April 21, 1864, *ibid.*, 20:324.

17 A careful study of Thompson as a financier is long overdue. See the inadequate sketch in the *Dictionary of American Biography*, 18:462–463, and the suggestive notes in Fritz Redlich, *The Molding of American Banking* (New York, 1951), pt. 2, *passim*.

18 Benjamin F. Andrews, *The Land Grant System of 1862 and the Land Grant Colleges* (U.S. Dept. of Interior, Bureau of Education, *Bulletin*, 1918, no. 13), 14–15. (Cited hereafter as Andrews, *The Land Grant System*.)

19 Samuel D. Halliday, *History of the Agricultural College Land Grant Act of July 2, 1862* . . . (Ithaca, 1905), 21.

20 George Woodman to Cyrus Woodman, June 7, 1864, in Woodman Papers, Letters Received, 20:329.

21 New York Senate Document 103, p. 373.

22 *Ibid.*, 374–375. The 36,000 acres was sold in several lots to "parties in New Jersey."

23 The original land-grant act required acceptance of the grant within two years and the establishment of the required college within five years. The act of April 14, 1864, extended to April 14, 1866, the deadline for acceptance. The deadline to establish a college was later repeatedly extended by general statute or by joint resolutions relating to specific states, but passage of these measures could not be anticipated with certainty.

24 Thomas C. Mendenhall, ed., *History of the Ohio State University* (4 vols., Columbus, 1920), 1:9.

25 New York Senate Document 103, pp. 371–372.

26 *Ibid.*, 401–402.

27 On this firm of Chicago bankers, see Henrietta Larson, *Jay Cooke, Private Banker* (Cambridge, Mass., 1936), 339; F. Cyril James, *The Growth of Chicago Banks* (New York, 1938); and Redlich, *American Banking*, pt. 2, *passim*. Preston was also an investor in land and entered some or all of his scrip. Gates, *Wisconsin Pine Lands, passim*.

28 Cyrus Woodman proposed the corner to his brother; George promptly replied that "it would take too many dimes," as probably eight or ten million scrip-acres would be issued. Cyrus Woodman to George Woodman, April 19, 1864, in Woodman Papers, Letter Books, 16:635. George's response of April 21 will be found in the Woodman Papers, Letter Books, 20:324.

29 In 1867 George entered a bid on some of the Pennsylvania scrip but failed to secure any. Woodman Papers, Letters Received, 26:450. I find no evidence that the Woodmans dealt with Lewis. George Woodman bought 8,000 acres at 65 cents in November from an undisclosed source. George Woodman to Cyrus Woodman, November 30, 1864, *ibid.*, 20:359.

30 H. H. Kimpton, State Financial Agent, to A. J. Ransier, President of the State Senate, Columbia, S.C., February 16, 1871, Historical Commission of South Carolina, Columbia, Reconstruction Period Collection.

31 Asa E. Martin, "Pennsylvania's Land Grant under the Morrill Act of 1862," *Pennsylvania History*, 9:111 (April, 1942). Preston bid at varying prices for varying quantities of Pennsylvania scrip in April, 1867, but secured only 48,000 acres at 55⅜ cents. *Ibid.*

32 Lewis was born at East Aurora, New York, November 11, 1820, and died at Jefferson, Ohio, on December 11, 1903. His entire business ca-

reer centered in Cleveland and its suburbs. Other biographical information is scant; an obituary is found in the Cleveland *Leader*, December 12, 1903. Sketches in *Lewisiana, or the Lewis Letter*, a monthly
inter-family paper edited by Frank P. and Carroll A. Lewis (17 vols.,
Lisle, New York, 1887–1907), are unreliable.

33 Act of March 22, 1852, 10 *U.S. Stat.*, 3. I am aware that various subter-
fuges were used to evade the prohibition on assignment before that
date. In the two years ending June 30, 1856, the General Land Office
sold almost thirty-five million acres, of which 28 per cent was bought
with military warrants.

34 The only known file, irregular, is in the Western Reserve Historical
Society, Cleveland. In the same repository will be found the only known
business records of Gleason Lewis. They relate entirely to his business
in land warrants.

35 Lewis listed his field agents in the *Old Soldiers Advocate*, e.g., issue of
June, 1871.

36 By June 30, 1866, 1.3 million acres of college scrip had been used to
locate land. About the same amount had been sold by the states or used
directly by them to locate land.

37 Under the act of June 21, 1866, the public land in Alabama, Arkansas,
Florida, Louisiana, and Mississippi was closed to all forms of entry except 80-acre homesteads. 12 *U.S. Stat.*, 503. The effect of this was not
only to exclude scrip from entry in those states, but to give those states
scrip instead of land for their college grants. In a brief note dealing with
this matter, I have suggested that the latter effect was probably advantageous to the interests of the states. *Journal of Southern History*,
19:216–220 (May, 1953).

38 The date and price are given in New York Senate Document 103, p.
367. The statement that Lewis was the buyer rests on his own assertion
in the *Old Soldiers Advocate*, December, 1871. The only inaccuracy in
his statements that I have discovered are the intimations that he bought
entire issues when we know that he purchased only a large or residual
part.

39 George Woodman to Cyrus Woodman, July 10, 1866, in Woodman
Papers, Letters Received, 24:349, and same to same, July 11, 1866,
ibid., 24:351.

40 Gleason F. Lewis to Ezra Cornell, April 19, 1867, Regional History Collection, Cornell University.

41 Andrews, *The Land Grant System*, 36; *Lewisiana*, 16:191–192; Mortgage Records, Cuyahoga County, Ohio.

42 Notably in the case of the purchase of the Delaware scrip. Evans Papers, MS No. 8169, University of Delaware.

43 *Ibid.*, MS No. 38. North Carolina, Virginia, and a number of other
states made COD sales.

44 Asa E. Martin, "Pennsylvania's Land Grant," 9:85–117.

45 Mendenhall, ed., *Ohio State University*, 1:9–10; New York Senate Document 103, p. 379.

46 George Woodman to Cyrus Woodman, July 10, 1866, in Woodman

Papers, Letters Received, 24:349. Lewis is identified in a letter, same to same, January 25, 1867, 26:432.

47 Maryland, Comptroller of the Treasury Department, *Annual Report* (Fiscal year September 30, 1867, Annapolis, 1868), xi–xii.

48 Massachusetts, Archives Division, MS Council Records, Entry of March 27, 1867.

49 William M. Hepburn and Louis M. Sears, *Purdue University* (Indianapolis, 1925), 34.

50 Martin, "Pennsylvania's Land Grant," 111.

51 New York Senate Document 103, p. 375.

52 Gleason Lewis to Ezra Cornell, October 16, 1867, Regional History Collection, Cornell University.

53 "First Annual Report of the Board of Trustees of the Illinois Industrial University," in *Report Made to the General Assembly of Illinois*, 26 sess. (1869), 2:127.

54 *Ibid.*, 99.

55 The disposal of New York's scrip is treated in Gates, *Wisconsin Pine Lands*.

56 *Congressional Globe*, 40 Cong., 1 sess. (1867), 346–347.

57 Gleason F. Lewis to Ezra Cornell, June 5, 1868, Regional History Collection, Cornell University.

58 15 *U.S. Stat.*, 227. In 1870 Congress passed an act of grace affirming entries made within thirty days of July 27, 1868. 16 *U.S. Stat.*, 186.

59 Act of July 1, 1870, *ibid.*

60 Gates, *Wisconsin Pine Lands*, 33, n. 14. In asserting that "previously only speculators could use the scrip," Gates seems to be mistaken.

61 Andrews, *The Land Grant System*, 47–48; Lewis to Ezra Cornell, April 15, 1868, Regional History Collection, Cornell University.

62 *Ibid.*

63 The resolution, introduced by Congressman Julian of Indiana, passed the House on December 17, 1866, and the Senate on March 26, 1867. *Congressional Globe*, 39 Cong., 2 sess. (1866), 153; 40 Cong., 1 sess. (1867), 347.

64 Lewis to Cornell, May 25, 1868, Regional History Collection, Cornell University.

65 Illinois Industrial University, *Third Annual Report* (1870), 92. In March, 1872, the trustees abandoned the idea of locating any more land themselves and sold the remaining 24,480 acres of scrip at $1. Lewis was not the buyer, it appears. *Sixth Annual Report* (1873), 112.

66 The Delaware transaction is thoroughly documented in the Minutes of the Board of Trustees of Delaware College and in the Evans Papers at the University of Delaware. Lewis was slow in making his payments, but the officers and trustees, seeing no other alternative, went along with him in a way that suggests for him the role of an underwriter rather than purchaser. But Lewis paid interest on his unpaid balances and received the scrip only as fast as he paid for it.

67 Halliday, *History of the Agricultural College Land Grant Act*, 30.

68 New York Senate Document 103, pp. 371–372. The Maine sales were

later investigated by a legislative committee. Their report was published at Augusta in 1876 and includes, at page 27, a letter from Ezra Cornell testifying that his dealings with Lewis were "honorable and satisfactory."

69   H. H. Kimpton to A. J. Ransier, President of the State Senate, February 16, 1871, History Commission of South Carolina, Columbia, Reconstruction Period Collection.

70   Lewis to Z. K. Harmon, November 12, 1870. *Report of the evidence and conclusions of the committee to investigate the sale of the Agricultural College scrip, made to the 55th legislature* (Maine) (Portland, 1876), 27.

71   New York Senate Document 103, pp. 369–371; Andrews, *The Land Grant System,* 48. Because the scrip was improperly signed by the state's secretary of state instead of the governor, there was some delay in making it fully negotiable. *Old Soldiers Advocate,* August, 1871. The assumption that Lewis bought the Texas scrip rests on his assertion and his knowledgeability about the foregoing technical detail.

72   Alabama received 240,000 acres. New York Senate Document 103, p. 363.

73   *Ibid.,* 373.

74   *Old Soldiers Advocate,* June, August, September, 1874.

75   Georgia received 269,920 acres. The sale is recorded in the Georgia Executive Minutes for March 30, 1872, Department of Archives and History of the Office of Secretary of State, Atlanta. The Arkansas sale of the entire 150,000 acres was made to Lewis as representing the Ohio Land Company. I have seen no other mention of this company and suspect that it was an unincorporated fiction. Andrews, *The Land Grant System,* 12; Virginia, *Senate Journal,* Document 6 (1873), 1–2.

76   New York Senate Document 103, p. 365.

77   *Old Soldiers Advocate,* April, 1873.

78   This view is expressed in various writings of Paul Wallace Gates, notably his *Wisconsin Pine Lands.*

79   The quotation is from the title of an article by Paul Wallace Gates in the *American Historical Review,* 41:652–681 (July, 1936). *[Reprinted in this volume, pp. 315–348.]*

Land Policy and
Stock Raising in
the Western United States

SANFORD A. MOSK

The University of California Social Science Institute's Committee on Regional Economy of the Far West sponsored this research in 1934–1935.

Reprinted by permission from Agricultural History, Volume 17 (1943), pages 14–30.

SINCE the middle of the nineteenth century the federal government has made substantial grants of land to the western states. Some of this land has been alienated, but the larger share has remained in state ownership [1943]. Under regulation, it has been used mainly by private enterprise for grazing. The importance of its use for this purpose is partly a reflection of the large acreage involved, but it goes beyond this, for the opportunity to select lands under certain grants has put the western states in a strategic position to help stockmen solve their range "problems." Moreover, land policies in the grazing states have been flexibly adjusted to meet the apparent needs of livestock producers, even when this has involved a loss in revenues. The political weight of stockmen in the grazing states would go a long way toward accounting for this situation.

The present study, which considers in detail the relationships between state land policy and the livestock industry, grew out of an investigation of land-tenure problems in the Atlantic and Pacific Railroad grant area of New Mexico and Arizona. In making the survey, it became evident that state lands and land policies were highly important to the stock raisers of these two states. Further study showed that this was true in some degree of all the grazing states. The writer has drawn mainly on the experience of New Mexico and Arizona, but enough material on nearby states has been examined to show that the general problems of state land administration are substantially the same for the entire range area. Where pertinent, illustrations from other states have been included.

LAND GRANTS TO THE STATES

The total amount of land granted to each of the eleven western states to 1939 is as follows: Arizona, 10,543,673 acres; California, 8,516,485; Colorado, 4,433,898; Idaho, 3,639,555; Montana, 5,871,058; Nevada, 2,723,647; New Mexico, 12,789,916; Oregon, 4,375,515; Utah, 7,464,497; Washington, 3,044,471; Wyoming, 4,139,209.[1] The federal government granted these lands to the states in order to contribute to the support of various kinds of public institutions and public works, namely, public schools, universities, agricultural colleges, public buildings, and internal improvements. In discussing the use of the lands for grazing purposes it is important to recognize two general classes of grants. One of these comprises lands granted to support the public schools; the other embraces all others, generally known as "institutional grant lands."

The practice of making land grants for educational purposes originated in colonial days. The ordinance of 1785, relating to the Northwest Territory, provided that section 16 in each township should be set aside for maintenance of the public schools. This became a model for subsequent school-grant legislation, the grants being made to states upon their admission into the Union. Some variations, however, are found in the amounts awarded; these are explained mainly by differences in time and circumstances of admission.[2] States entering in the period 1802–1847 received one section (section 16) in each township; those admitted from 1848 to 1890 received two sections (sections 16 and 36); and states admitted from 1894 to 1910, with the exception of Oklahoma, received four sections (sections 2, 16, 32, and 36). Of the eleven western states, the following were given two school sections per township: California, Colorado, Idaho, Montana, Nevada, Oregon, Washington, and Wyoming. In Utah, Arizona, and New Mexico, the unappropriated public lands were arid and of little value; consequently, they received four sections.

The school land grants, in every case, comprised specified sections in each township.[3] These are known as "school sections in place." For school lands that were occupied or otherwise appropriated or reserved prior to the date of the grant, a state is allowed to make "indemnity (lieu) selections."[4] These may be chosen from unappropriated and unreserved public domain anywhere in the state. Granting particular sections has imparted a definite character to the majority of school holdings—they are isolated tracts, intermingled with lands in various classes of private and public ownership. With the exception of Nevada, the western states have been able to consolidate holdings only through the proper selection of indemnity school lands and institutional grant lands.

The problem of handling state lands has been greatly influenced by the dispersion of school sections. With lands scattered from one end of a state to another, the difficulties and costs of administration have been greatly magnified. Classification has undoubtedly been retarded by the long distances to be covered in the examination of school sections and the resulting high costs of making such surveys. Lack of classification, in turn, has hampered effective utilization. Furthermore, it has frequently been difficult to lease or sell isolated school sections. Only by consolidating them with selected state lands has this disadvantage been overcome. In such places a sufficient amount of state land could be offered to a stockman to warrant purchase or leasing. Where school lands have been unleased stockmen have commonly used them free of charge, like the public domain. This has involved a loss of revenue as well as depreciation in the grazing quality of the land.[5]

It has been pointed out that school lands were ordinarily granted upon admission to statehood. The procedure followed by Congress after 1848, with two exceptions, was to reserve school sections in the organic act creating a territory and to make the final grant in the enabling act.[6] New Mexico was one of the exceptions. In 1898, while still a territory, New Mexico was granted two sections in each township (sections 16 and 36) for the public schools, as well as lands for various institutions. The territory had been on the verge of attaining statehood for several years prior to 1898, but political matters had intervened. The land grant of 1898 was made in order to give support to public schools and other institutions, and to enable the territory to make selections before all the better lands were appropriated. New Mexico, unlike Arizona and Oklahoma, had not been permitted to lease the lands reserved in the organic act.

In allowing indemnity selections for school lands lost through prior appropriation, Congress has not followed a uniform policy. Some states have not been permitted to select lieu lands for school sections located in permanent reservations, and grants within Indian and military reservations were to become effective only when the lands were restored to the public domain.[7] Arizona and New Mexico, however, were authorized to make indemnity selections for all lands previously appropriated or reserved. In the case of school sections within national forests, title did not pass to the two states, but provision was made for them either to secure revenues from the use of these lands or to choose lieu sections.[8]

SELECTION OF STATE LANDS

The holdings designated as "institutional grant lands" were awarded to states to help support designated institutions or public improvements—state universities, agricultural colleges, mining schools, normal schools, asylums, hospitals, penal and reformatory establishments, control of water resources, etc.[9] In contrast to school lands, the states are allowed to choose their institutional lands from unappropriated public domain anywhere within their borders.

In many of the western states the selection of institutional lands, as well as indemnity school lands, has been carried out in the interests of stockmen. This is partly explained by the fact that grazing represented the most profitable immediate use for the bulk of the land, and partly by the political importance of the livestock operators.

In New Mexico, stock raisers have been able to gain control of ranges, or to "round" them out, with the aid of state selections. At the request of stockmen, the state chooses specific tracts which are then leased or sold to the applicants. In some instances, lands have been selected because of actual or potential water resources, for, on the arid ranges of the Southwest, control over the limited amount of water available ordinarily implies control over grazing. In other cases, stockmen owning large tracts of land have induced the state to make selections from adjacent public domain in order that they might purchase or lease them and thereby solidify their holdings.[10] Another method, employed where large areas of public lands existed, was to persuade the state to select rows of 40-acre tracts so as to circumscribe a considerable body of public domain. By leasing or buying these tracts, stockmen were able to dominate grazing on the encompassed public lands. Not infrequently they strengthened their control of such areas by erecting "drift fences."[11]

Several years ago, when New Mexico still had a large acreage to be selected, it was customary for the state land commissioner to hold a certain amount in abeyance, to be chosen at the instance of prospective purchasers or lessees of extensive tracts. In 1916, for example, the commissioner reported a balance of 100,000 acres held for this purpose.[12] The advantages of this arrangement were mutual, since the stockmen could obtain the lands they needed and the state could lease or sell its selections at once. It was contended, moreover, that the lands so chosen would normally be the most valuable of the remaining public domain.[13]

In Arizona, the influence of grazing interests on the selection of institutional grant lands became apparent soon after statehood was achieved. The task of choosing these lands was first placed in the hands of the three appointed members of the State Land Commission. When this board assumed office in June, 1912, it adopted a definite basic principle for selection. As stated in the first published report:

The broad principle adopted by the Commission to guide it in the selection of lands was that they should have either a present or a prospective agricultural value. This policy was based upon two grounds deemed to be of the utmost importance to the State—first, that the lands susceptible of cultivation, or of reclamation by any method, will ultimately be the most valuable; second, that the reservation to the State of the title and control of lands at present fit only for grazing, but possessing the elements of a much higher degree of economic usefulness, spells the highest type of true conservation and the insurance of steady and sane development—if not rapid development, the most rapid that can by any means be assured. In short, it spells prevention of the permanent acquisition or control by grazing interests of great bodies of land capable, under a wise State policy, of providing homes for people, or by the class of speculators who, having no anxiety for the public's welfare, are content to permit their cheaply-purchased holdings to lie idle until the unearned increments thereof may be collected by their children or their children's children, the while a rapidly growing population and the withholding of large tracts susceptible of development constantly increase the demand and the need for cultivable land.[14]

In carrying out this policy, lands of limited value in their existing state, but potentially suitable for agriculture, were chosen in preference to the best grazing lands. Selections were made only after extensive field surveys had been conducted by the commission. Up to December 1, 1914, over 636,000 acres of land were selected under the various institutional grants. Of this total, almost 619,000 were deemed fit for some form of agricultural development, over 5,000 were valuable for woodland and grazing, and about 12,000 were adapted to grazing only.[15] The last-mentioned item consisted of lands in dry-farming districts where the best form of land utilization was considered to be a combination of farming and stock raising. Naturally, much of the land selected for its potential agricultural value was fit for grazing also, although not primarily so. Of the total of 636,000 acres, only about 58,000 were considered entirely unsuited for grazing.

This policy of selection was opposed by the stock-raising interests. They wanted the state to select grazing lands, particularly the tracts that would aid them to round out or control ranges. Upon expiration of the commission's term in December, 1914, the office was replaced by a State Land Department, and a new policy, designed to appease the grazing interests, was introduced. It is generally understood in Arizona that, since that time, institutional grant and indemnity school lands have been selected primarily at the request of the livestock operators.

Other western states besides New Mexico and Arizona have made it a practice to select lands to benefit the stock-raising industry. In testifying before a Senate committee in 1925, J. H. Nash, state land commissioner of Idaho, declared that his state helped stockmen to control ranges by placing lieu land selections on watering places.[16] In Nevada, selection of lands with water facilities, at the request of stockmen, has been an important factor in enabling a few large outfits to control vast areas of public domain.[17] Wyoming experience has been identical. In reporting on the Wyoming land system in 1905, Frederick V. Coville said:

The locations are made by the State authorities, chiefly in accordance with the requests of persons who desire to lease or purchase the tracts which they ask the State to select. The lands thus selected are situated prevailingly along streams or are otherwise watered, but some of them are without water, but located in such a manner as to enable persons owning noncontiguous watered sections or alternate sections purchased from the Union Pacific Railroad land grant to consolidate their holdings by purchasing or leasing the intervening lands from the State.[18]

SALE OF STATE LANDS

Much of the land granted to the western states has been sold to private individuals or corporations. California, Nevada, Oregon, and Utah have sold the majority of their lands, while other states have kept title to most of their original holdings and leased them for grazing purposes.[19] The states were not given unlimited freedom in this matter. Congress has in several instances placed limitations on disposal in the granting acts. The grant to Colorado in 1875 established a minimum price for which school lands might be sold, and all states admitted subsequently, with the exception of Utah, have been similarly restricted.[20] The various types of restrictions and their effect upon state land disposal will be illustrated from the experience of New Mexico, Arizona, and Nevada.

State lands in New Mexico are subject to sale in accordance with the provisions of the various federal granting acts and state laws. A sale must be consummated at a public auction held in the county seat of the county in which the lands lie. Lands are not to be sold for less than their appraised value, and in no case for less than the following minimum prices: (1) for lands lying east of a line between ranges 18 and 19 east of the New Mexico principal meridian, $5 per acre; (2) for lands lying west of that line, $3 per acre; (3) for lands anywhere in the state susceptible of irrigation under federal reclamation projects, $25 per acre. At present, purchases may be made on long-term contracts, with a cash payment of 5 per cent.[21] The balance is payable within thirty years, annual interest of 4 per cent being charged on unpaid balances.[22] Practically no state lands were sold in New Mexico prior to 1910 because of restrictive clauses in the grant of 1898. Sale of university and school lands was forbidden; other institutional grant lands were open to sale, but no individual was to purchase more than 160 acres. These impediments were removed by the enabling act of 1910, and all state lands became available for purchase without limitation of amount.

Land sales were slow for some time following statehood, for the public domain still provided satisfactory free ranges for many stockmen. Moreover, as long as most of the state holdings remained unsold or unleased they could be used without payment. The minimum prices fixed in the enabling act—$3 and $5 per acre—were too high to make state lands an attractive investment for the livestock operators. Even as late as 1916, Mexican grant lands were being sold for $1.50 to $2.50 per acre.[23] As the public ranges became crowded, public lands were increasingly taken up by homesteaders, and as state lands were fenced off for individual use, sales increased. By November 30, 1911, 158 purchase contracts, comprising 11,620 acres, had been executed. Five years later, on November 30, 1916, over 700,000 acres were covered by active contracts. In 1917, legislation was enacted to liberalize the terms of sale. The cash payment required was reduced from 10 to 5 per cent of the purchase price. This modification together with the war boom stimulated sales, and in the two fiscal years 1918 and 1919 almost 1,500,000 acres were sold. By the end of 1922, the total amount of state land under purchase contract was 2,621,000 acres. However, the post-war depression in the livestock industry found many purchasers unable to make payments, and contracts involving 152,000 acres were canceled during the biennium ending December 31, 1922. In the succeeding biennial period, cancellations outweighed new purchases, so that the aggregate amount under contract on December 31, 1924 was only 2,238,000 acres. This downward trend continued. In spite of the leniency shown toward delinquencies, a number of purchase contracts were canceled in subsequent years. On June 30, 1930, the active contracts involved 1,776,000 acres, and, by June 30, 1932, the figure had declined to 1,693,000.[24] *[At this writing]*, later figures cannot be obtained.

For the earlier years, data are available on the size of tracts sold by New Mexico. Apparently, the land commissioner had been criticized for allowing "large interests" to buy up state lands, and, in his 1917 report, he attempted to refute this criticism.[25] In doing so, he pointed out that of the total number of sales made to the end of the fiscal year 1917 about 85 per cent involved tracts of 640 acres or less, while only about 3 per cent involved tracts of more than 5,000 acres. However, the figures he cited are not the most relevant ones for this question. Of much greater significance is the fact that the 86.4 per cent of the purchasers who acquired tracts of 640 acres or less bought only 20.4 per cent of the total acreage sold, while the 3.1 per cent who bought tracts in excess of 5,000 acres acquired 59.0 per cent of the total. Despite the contention of the commissioner, therefore, the evidence shows that a few purchasers were acquiring the bulk of the state lands passing into private ownership. Table 14, based upon the figures in the commissioner's report, gives the total number of tracts of state land sold by New Mexico and the total acreage by size of tracts.

For Arizona, the basic regulations on the sale of state lands were laid down in the enabling act of 1910. Lands were to be sold to the highest bidder at public auction; an appraisal was to be made before sale; and the minimum acceptable bid was the appraised value. Until recently, no land could be sold for less than $3 per acre, even when the appraised value was under that figure. In 1936, however, Congress amended the enabling act so as to remove this stipulation.

Arizona state lands may be purchased on long terms. One per cent of the purchase price, but not less than the costs of appraisal and sale, must be paid at the time of auction, and 4 per cent upon the receipt of a certificate of sale. The balance may be paid in thirty-eight annual installments, with interest at 5 per cent a year.[26] The amount of state land which may be sold to an individual or corporation is restricted by a constitutional limitation to 160 acres of agricultural land or 640 acres of grazing land.[27]

The reports of the Arizona State Land Department supply little information on sales of state lands, so that it is not possible to examine the past trends. According to the latest figures available [*at this writing*], the total amount sold through June 30, 1934, was approximately 895,000 acres; of this total, about 30 per cent had been patented to the

TABLE 14

State Lands Sold by New Mexico: Number of Tracts and Acreage
by Size of Tracts

Size of tract	Number of tracts sold	Per cent of total sales	Aggregate acreage	Per cent of total acreage
Under 40 acres	160	8.5	6,215.79	.4
40 to 80	131	6.9	10,592.56	.6
80 to 160	932	49.5	143,552.84	8.6
160 to 320	188	10.0	54,626.50	3.3
320 to 640	216	11.5	124,720.56	7.5
640 to 1,280	131	6.9	144,187.28	8.7
1,280 to 2,560	39	2.1	85,546.09	5.1
2,560 to 5,000	29	1.5	112,730.08	6.8
Over 5,000	58	3.1	982,504.43	59.0
Total	1,884	100.0	1,664,676.13	100.0

purchasers, and the remainder was held under contract to purchase.[28] These figures do not include the acreage involved in forfeited or canceled contracts.

Nevada originally received a school grant of sections 16 and 36 in each township, but, as already noted, an arrangement was made in 1880 whereby the state relinquished these sections for the right to select 2,000,000 acres from the public domain. Provision was made to sell the selected lands on easy terms; a down payment of 20 per cent was required, the balance payable in twenty-five years with interest at 6 per cent.[29] The maximum amount of land for which an individual purchaser was allowed to apply was fixed by law at 640 acres, but through "indirect" purchases many persons were able to acquire large holdings of state lands.

It was this exchange [by which Nevada obtained the right to select 2,000,-000 acres of school land] that made possible the purchase of large holdings that cover all the hay land, irrigation water, and most of the stock water found in the region, and thus dominate the use of much larger areas of contiguous and associated public range lands. The State land laws were so drawn as seemingly to prevent such a concentration of control, but the interpretation made of them allowed it, and the lands were sold.[30]

One of the major problems of state land administration arises from the failure of purchasers to complete their contracts. The minimum prices for state grazing lands, because of their low average carrying capacity, have been too high, and purchasers have often found the cost of holding them too burdensome. For various reasons, many stockmen have contracted to buy more land than they could really afford and ultimately have been forced to allow the lands to revert to the states. New Mexico provides an outstanding illustration. The Stock-Raising Homestead Act of 1916 sent a wave of settlers into New Mexico, chiefly from Texas. This broke up the public domain ranges and obliged other stockmen to turn to state lands. At that time, the state required lessees to buy a certain amount of land for each section leased, with the result that many stockmen bought more than they could pay for and subsequently defaulted on their contracts.[31] In other cases, competitive bidding for lands which are especially desirable because of location or quality has forced prices beyond the limit of economic feasibility.

Some state lands have been bought by stockmen who never intended to complete their payments. They contracted to purchase several adjoining sections of land, developed water on a few tracts, and then allowed the contracts on the undeveloped tracts to lapse. Through their control of the water they have ordinarily been able to dominate grazing on the adjacent state lands without actually owning them.

Speculative purchasing has also been a cause of reversion of state lands. Speculation in state lands will be discussed in more detail below, but it must be considered here in relation to the problem of defaulted purchase contracts. The fact that only a small down payment is required has made it possible for speculators to acquire large amounts of land with a slight investment, and to make handsome profits by reselling or leasing them. However, if it becomes unprofitable for the speculators to hold the lands, they allow them to revert to the state.

An outstanding illustration of this occurred in Nevada in recent years. The legislature passed a law that required all stockmen using Nevada ranges to own lands in Nevada. Speculators immediately made first payments on all available state lands; these they planned to sell at higher prices to stockmen from neighboring states who were using public domain in Nevada for winter range. However, the law was declared unconstitutional, and the speculation collapsed. One speculator alone lost approximately $20,000 on his venture. The land reverted to the state.[32]

An attitude of leniency has generally been adopted toward delinquent purchasers of state lands, especially in periods of economic distress in the livestock industry. Contracts have been canceled only as a last resort. In New Mexico, it was once customary not to cancel delinquent contracts until another application to purchase the same land was filed.[33] In Nevada, an act was passed in 1899 to allow the state land register to accept interest on purchase contracts overdue to the extent of one year, unless another application for the same land was received during that time.[34] In 1909, when the principal on a large number of Nevada contracts became payable, the land code was amended to extend the time of payment from twenty-five to fifty years.[35] Arizona policy, too, has borne the stamp of leniency, but delinquencies became so numerous in the depression period [*of the thirties*] that a more rigorous cancellation policy had to be adopted. This was done in 1935, when a thorough investigation was made of delinquent cases; many of these contracts were found in the hands of speculators. Cancellations on a wholesale scale followed.[36]

The small amount of New Mexico state land for which title has actually passed to private owners is revealed by figures presented to a Senate committee by the state land commissioner. By the end of the fiscal year 1930, only 155,552 acres had been sold and deeded to purchasers. This represented slightly more than 1 per cent of the 12,700,-000 acres granted to the state. At the same time, about 1,771,000 acres were under contract of sale.[37]

Attempts to prevent speculation by law—for example, restrictions on the amount of land that might be purchased by a single applicant—have not been effective. Of the western states, Arizona and Nevada have been the most plagued by speculation. According to the first published report of the Arizona State Land Commission, speculators were gaining control of large amounts of state lands in spite of the constitutional limitation on sales to a single purchaser and parceling them out on installment contracts to subpurchasers.[38] The latter usually had to pay high prices and high interest rates. Evidence secured by the commission showed that false representations were occasionally made to the purchasers regarding the titles they were getting from the speculators. Most of the subpurchasers defaulted on their contracts, and the speculators, who had already received some cash payments, got back the lands as well as any improvements that had been made on them. An identical transaction could be repeated several times with a single tract of land. Prospective farmers with a little capital were frequently victims of this type of speculation. The 1934 report of the Arizona state land commissioner showed that this situation had not substantially changed in the intervening years.

The nominal down payment has allowed land speculators to gain possession of and control large blocks of Arizona lands, at a small investment. It is not exceptional to find land which has been bid in at the rate of three dollars per acre disposed of to unfortunate men and women on the Pacific Coast at twenty-five dollars per acre. Many times these poor people have even failed to secure deeds to the land, due to the machinations of unscrupulous individuals.[39]

Leasing State Lands

State lands are more frequently leased than purchased by stockmen. In New Mexico and Arizona the total acreage rented for grazing purposes is far in excess of the amount that has been sold. The leasing policies of these two states and Wyoming serve to illustrate the principal leasing problems encountered in the grazing states.

In New Mexico, state land leases are executed under regulations specified in the federal granting acts and subsequent state legislation.[40] Rental fees are supposed to be based on a classification of state lands; the minimum rental that may be accepted is three cents per acre annually, unless the lands are advertised and leased at public auction to the highest bidder. Leases are not issued for periods exceeding five years, but a grazing lessee in good standing has certain preference rights for renewal for a second term of five years.

The act of 1898 allowed the Territory of New Mexico to lease university lands and school holdings, but not more than one section was to be rented to a single lessee; this limitation impeded leasing. Furthermore, the existence of satisfactory ranges on the public domain and the opportunity of using state lands without charge helped to minimize leasing, as well as sales.

The additional grants designated in the enabling act of 1910 allowed the state to select more lands and naturally brought about an expansion in leased acreage. All territorial leases terminated upon admission to statehood, and the enabling act permitted new leases to be executed on more liberal terms. The act removed existing restrictions on the amount of land which might be leased to an individual, and, in general, allowed the state to establish definite administrative policies for leasing.

In 1909, the total amount of New Mexico state land under lease was almost 2,000,000 acres. By 1912, the leased acreage had risen to over 2,500,000, and in the years immediately following, continued to expand rapidly. In 1914, the figure was approximately 4,900,000, and in 1916, 7,600,000.[41] This increase in leased acreage was only in part a consequence of expansion in stock-raising, for it was also an outgrowth of the heavy additions to state holdings which were reducing the available public domain. The postwar depression found the livestock industry of New Mexico in a critical condition, and many stockmen were forced to relinquish their leases in spite of the fact that most rentals in excess of the statutory minimum of three cents per acre were reduced to that figure. Expansion set in again in 1923; by December 31, 1924, almost 8,200,000 acres were under lease. During the following biennium, about 800,000 acres were added to the last figure. Improved conditions in the livestock industry brought still further increases, so that the leased area on June 30, 1930, was slightly over 10,700,000 acres. Substantially the same figure held for 1936, the last year for which data can be obtained [*at this writing*]. This represented over 85 per cent of the range land owned by the state.[42]

In Arizona, the minimum annual rental for state land is fixed by statute at three cents per acre for grazing sections, and at 2.5 per cent of the estimated value of agricultural lands.[43] In June, 1933, grazing rentals were reduced to one and one-half cents for a two-year period. Leases may be executed for periods ranging up to twenty years, but the rental specified in any lease for more than five years is subject to readjustment at the end of each five-year period. At the expiration of a contract the lessee has a preferred right of renewal, provided the commissioner believes that the lands should still be rented. Renewals may be made for five-year periods, at revised rentals.[44]

Arizona gives special privileges to homesteaders in renting state lands; they have preferred rights to lease as much land contiguous to their homesteads as they need for personal use.[45] Instances have occurred in which the homesteader of a single section, merely by exercising this preference, has interfered with longstanding ranges.

Prior to 1918, a provision of the Arizona constitution limited the amount of land that might be leased by an individual or corporation to 160 acres for farming or 640 acres for grazing. The restriction proved unsatisfactory. In those areas where the lands were suitable only for grazing, one section was too little for an adequate leasing unit. A quotation from the first published report of the State Land Commission shows early recognition of this problem.

There are a number of localities in the State, adapted only to the grazing of cattle, where hundreds of school sections are lying idle, or are being utilized without compensation, because of the limitation with respect to leasing. They are so situated that one section has no attraction for a stockman, big or little, and in some cases the same might be true of half a dozen sections, or more. Water is scarce and its development expensive. Without a considerable range appurtenant, the expenditure involved in the development of water is not justified. The small stockman who, under other and more favorable conditions, might find a single section desirable, has no use for it in a locality where there is no water. He has not the means for the development or [sic] water, and if he has its development is not justified by a range limited to six hundred and forty acres. Therefore the little stockman is not protected or benefited, in such cases, by the limit imposed by the Constitution. The consequence is that the land lies idle, without revenue to the State, or some big cattle outfit, controlling the range by virtue of the possession of scattered sections and all the available water in the neighborhood, runs its cattle over the school lands as over the public domain, and has the very potent excuse for failure to reimburse the State, that it is not allowed by law to lease more than a section.[46]

In November, 1918, the Arizona constitution was amended to remove this restriction on leasing, although the analogous limitation on purchases was retained.

Since the published reports of the Arizona State Land Department do not give complete statistics on leasing, it is not possible to trace changes in acreage leased in relation to the growth and economic condition of the state's livestock industry. The total amount of state land rented has apparently grown rapidly in recent years. In July, 1933, according to figures supplied by the department, approximately 5,957,000 acres were leased for all purposes. By 1936, the range lands under lease aggregated 7,380,000 acres, or about 90 per cent of the range land owned by the state.[47]

Wyoming is quite generally considered to have highly satisfactory leasing arrangements for state lands.[48] Its system was operating smoothly as early as 1905, according to the survey made in that year by Frederick V. Coville.[49] At that time, Wyoming state lands were handled by a board of state land commissioners. An applicant for a lease was required to present a formal application to this board, stating the rental he would be willing to pay and giving detailed information on the nature of the land. If no competitive bids were received, and if the rental offered was considered satisfactory, the application was granted. If other bids were received, a public auction had to be held in the county seat and the lease awarded to the highest bidder. The maximum term for a lease was five years, and only rarely were they issued for shorter periods. Ordinary rentals were as follows: for non-irrigable land without stock water, two and one-half cents per acre; for similar land with stock water, five cents; for irrigable land, twenty-five cents.[50] Practically all leased land was used for grazing.

Under the Wyoming enabling act of July 10, 1890, no person was allowed to lease more than 640 acres of land granted for educational purposes. No limit, however, was placed on other state lands. Lessees were required to submit bonds, in order to protect the state in case of delinquency. Leases persistently delinquent were canceled. Upon expiration of a lease the lessee was given qualified preferred rights of renewal, at the rental set by the board. This preference was limited to one section of educational land and four sections of non-educational land. A lessee might exercise his preference rights three times, which gave him presumable occupancy for twenty years. In fact, most of the leases were renewed, either by the original lessees or by assignees.

The total acreage rented by Wyoming expanded markedly in the decade preceding 1902. The number under lease was 154,000 in 1892; 888,000 in 1898; 1,513,000 in 1900; and 2,302,000 in 1902. In relation to the total acreage available for leasing, the amount rented in 1892 was 4 per cent; in 1898, 22 per cent; in 1900, 37 per cent; and in 1902, 56 per cent. The bulk of the unleased land in 1902 consisted of isolated school sections devoid of stock water and located where there was no competition for their use. Operators on adjacent ranges took advantage of them without payment. The percentage of Wyoming state lands leased has been steadily high. From figures presented in the Forest Service report on *The Western Range*, it can be ascertained that in 1936 approximately 95 per cent of the range land owned by the state was rented.[51]

It must again be emphasized that the scattering of state holdings, represented by isolated school sections, has restricted the opportunity to lease the lands. Utah provides an extreme illustration, with less than 10 per cent of its school land leased in 1934, and the rest being used without payment.[52] In lesser degree, the same condition is found in the other grazing states.

CLASSIFICATION OF STATE LANDS

The question of classifying state lands is obviously an important one. The best public policy may or may not call for maximizing the revenue obtained from these lands; other considerations of public welfare may take precedence over revenue. In any case, however, their best distribution among the various uses dictated by public policy can only be achieved if the relative values of the lands are known. This, in turn, means careful examination, appraisal, and classification.

Most of the western states have made no attempt to classify their lands other than in very general terms—for example, grazing and agricultural. So far as grazing lands are concerned, it is customary to lease them at a uniform rental, regardless of carrying capacity, presence or absence of stock water, or location. Rental fees, except where competition for a particular tract is keen, have gravitated toward the legal minimum. It is true that land classification, involving a detailed appraisal of resources, is costly; this is particularly true of the scattered school sections in the vast areas of the western states. On the other hand, appraisal could be made to pay for itself over a period of years, through higher rentals and prices for the better lands.

In Arizona, the need for classification was recognized by the first State Land Commission, and a preliminary classification of school and institutional grant lands was undertaken. However, the work was not continued by succeeding land officials, and for many years it was the practice to lease the state's grazing lands at a flat rental, regardless of quality. The disadvantages of this policy were explicitly pointed out in the 1934 report of the state land commissioner, who strongly urged that rentals be adjusted to range carrying capacity.

In January, 1936, Arizona began a comprehensive appraisal and detailed classification of its state lands. This was made possible by the organization of a WPA project to provide the staff necessary for such a large undertaking. Within six months, approximately 3,000,000 acres were classified.[53]

The primitive nature of state land classification was plainly indicated in 1931 in the report of the committee appointed by President Hoover to study the question of public domain conservation. A tabular appendix to this report summarized the land policies of the eleven western states.[54] Nevada, New Mexico, and Oregon were shown to employ no classification at all. New Mexico had provided for classification, but the expense of the task had prevented it from being done. The other eight states were credited with classified lands, but, except for Colorado, the distinctions were so rough as to be of little use in leasing and selling operations.[55] Since the publication of this report, Arizona has begun to make a systematic classification of its state lands; in the other states, the 1931 situation is apparently unchanged.

The heavy costs of appraisal, while undoubtedly significant, would not alone account for the inadequate classification of state lands. These costs could be offset by greater revenues, but this would involve higher rentals, and might adversely affect the livestock operators. Since the grazing interests have persistently been a powerful group in state politics, there is ground for suggesting that their influence has been critical in retarding the classification of state lands.

SUMMARY AND CONCLUSION

Most of the lands belonging to the western states are used for grazing, and the livestock interests have been a very strong influence in shaping state land policy. This is apparent in the selection of institutional grant and indemnity school lands. These have been chosen largely for their grazing value, and often for their grazing value to a particular stockman. They have not been selected to form economic units, except where this result was incidental to the preference of livestock operators. State ownership of isolated 40-acre tracts, of scattered sections (aside from school lands), and of strips of "forties" enclosing public domain give evidence of selections to benefit stockmen. Pointing this out does not imply that such selections were necessarily unwise. On the contrary, assurance that the state would have an immediate lessee or purchaser for a particular piece of land was an important consideration from the revenue standpoint. In selling and leasing lands, state policies have been sufficiently flexible to be responsive to livestock interests and to the condition of the stock-raising industry. Abuses of this flexibility have been evident, notably in speculative transactions.

Several factors, of unequal bearing in the various grazing states, have complicated the problem of administering state lands and have helped to shape state land policy. Outstanding among these are: (1) scattered distribution of holdings; (2) revenue needs of the state institutions that get support from land grants; (3) a prejudice in favor of alienating state lands in contrast to keeping them in state hands indefinitely; and (4) the political importance of grazing interests. It is significant that conservation of forage resources is omitted from this list.

The last point may be developed further. Range management, as it is commonly called, has been almost totally lacking in state policy.[56] In view of the general history of range exploitation in the United States it would be surprising if this were not the case. Little attempt has been made to regulate grazing on leased state lands.[57] Lessees have been allowed to graze as many head of stock as they chose. Self-interest of the lessee, fortified by a guarantee of continued usage, has been counted upon to prevent excessive forage depletion. State officials contend that state lands are no more exhausted than the bulk of privately owned range lands. Data in *The Western Range* report support this contention, but the same document stresses the fact that privately owned grazing lands have been severely depleted and that even the interest of fee-simple ownership has been insufficient to preserve range resources.[58] It is not likely, therefore, that the forage resources of state lands will be adequately conserved in the absence of a positive state policy.

The attitude of the western states toward their lands does not favor the introduction of conservation measures. These lands are viewed primarily as sources of immediate revenue. When short-run revenue considerations dominate, conservation has little weight. This has become apparent since the passage of the Taylor Act to regulate grazing on the public domain. At a meeting of land officials of the western states at Denver in February, 1935, a resolution was adopted urging the states to remove their holdings from federal grazing districts. A significant quotation from this resolution follows:

It should not be overlooked that the purposes of the original land grants to the Western States, and the purposes of the Taylor Grazing Act are far apart. The land grant measures were revenue measures; the intention was that when the lands were leased out the full rental values should be received; the lands should be sold only at public sale so that the full sales value might be obtained. The idea of obtaining the greatest legitimate revenue from the lands is basic in the Federal land grants. The Taylor Grazing Act on the other hand is a conservation measure; the obtaining of revenues for the land owners is not its main purpose.[59]

The last eight or nine years may mark an important turning point in the use of land resources in the United States. The federal government, through many agencies, has actively promoted land-use planning and land conservation. Similar policies may be adopted by the western states. Obviously, many problems would be encountered in attempting to put them into practice. It would be essential to take account of the complicated tenure situation, the "vested interests" of livestock operators, and the financial needs of the state institutions which have been partly supported by state land revenues. These are all historical products. Furthermore, it is doubtful that the individual western states can formulate sound land programs except by incorporating them into broader regional and national patterns.[60] These problems, while complex, are by no means unsurmountable, provided the objectives of land planning are clearly defined.

NOTES

1 These figures are from the U.S. General Land Office, *School Lands: Land Grants to States and Territories for Educational and other Purposes* (Information Bulletin, 1939 series, no. 1), 3.

2 For a digest of the legislation involved in state land grants, see Matthias Nordberg Orfield, *Federal Land Grants to the States with Special Reference to Minnesota* (*University of Minnesota Studies in the Social Sciences*, no. 2, Minneapolis, 1915), 7–144.

3 The grant to Nevada, made by the enabling act of March 21, 1864, conveyed sections 16 and 36 of every township. However, by act of June 16, 1880 (21 *U.S. Stat.*, 287), Nevada relinquished these sections in favor of a grant of 2,000,000 acres, to be selected from unappropriated, non-mineral public lands in the state. Congress made this exchange at Nevada's request; it was contended that, because of the arid character of the region, the state had been able to sell only a small amount of isolated school sections and that the public schools were deriving little benefit from the land grant. *Congressional Record*, 46 Congress, 2 session (1880), 10(4):3597.

4 Illustrations of prior appropriation: homestead entry, Indian allotment, mineral classification, Indian reservation.

5 *The Western Range* (74 Cong., 2 sess., Senate Doc. no. 199, Washington, 1936), 478.

6 Benjamin Horace Hibbard, *A History of the Public Land Policies* (New York, 1924), 312.

7 Orfield, *Federal Land Grants to the States*, 46.

8 See sections 6 and 24 of the enabling act for New Mexico and Arizona, June 20, 1910, in 36 *U.S. Stat.*, 1:561, 572 (1911).

9 Both Arizona and New Mexico have an unusual type of "institutional" grant, namely lands granted to pay off county railroad bonds. The Arizona case, an unsavory episode in frontier financial history, is described in Howard A. Hubbard, *A Chapter in Early Arizona Transportation*

History; The Arizona Narrow Gauge Railroad Company (*University of Arizona Social Science Bulletin* no. 6, Tucson, 1934).

10 This practice has been followed in the Atlantic and Pacific Railroad grant area, a strip of land about 100 miles wide stretching across northwestern New Mexico and northern Arizona. The railroad grant (to which the major successor is the Santa Fe Pacific Railroad) consisted of alternate sections. Some of the larger livestock operators purchased railroad lands and subsequently induced the states to select intermingled public domain sections. By purchasing or leasing these, together with the school sections, they have been able to consolidate their ranges.

11 Fences enclosing public domain were a violation of federal law, for they were forbidden by an act of February 25, 1885. 23 *U.S. Stat.*, 321. This law, however, was not generally enforced. During World War I, the federal government gave special permission to stockmen in New Mexico and Arizona to erect fences enclosing public domain, most of which were not taken down after the war.

12 New Mexico Commissioner of Public Lands, *Annual Report*, Nov. 30, 1914—Nov. 30, 1916, 16–17: 27.

13 *Ibid.*, Nov. 30, 1917, 18:39.

14 Arizona State Land Commission, *Report*, June 6, 1912—Dec. 1, 1914, pp. 22–23.

15 *Ibid.*, 27.

16 U.S. Senate Subcommittee of the Committee on Public Lands and Surveys (69 Cong., 1 sess., 1925), *Hearings . . . Relating to National Forests and the Public Domain and their Administration . . .* , pt. 10, p. 2932.

17 Romanzo Adams, "Public Range Lands—A New Policy Needed," in *American Journal of Sociology*, 22:332 (November, 1916); E. O. Wooton, *The Public Domain of Nevada and Factors Affecting its Use* (U.S. Department of Agriculture, Technical Bulletin 301, Washington, 1932), 33.

18 U.S. Forest Service, *Bulletin 62* (Washington, 1905), 55.

19 William Peterson, "Land Utilization in the Western Range Country," in National Conference on Land Utilization, Chicago, Ill., Nov. 19–21, 1931, *Proceedings* (Washington, 1932), 45.

20 Hibbard, *History of the Public Land Policies*, 317.

21 For some lands the cash payment must be 10 per cent.

22 *New Mexico Statutes Annotated, 1929 Compilation*, ch. 132, sec. 158 (Denver, 1929).

23 New Mexico Commissioner of Public Lands, *Annual Report*, Nov. 30, 1917, 18:43.

24 New Mexico Commissioner of Public Lands, *Biennial Report*, June 30, 1932, p. 4.

25 New Mexico Commissioner of Public Lands, *Annual Report*, Nov. 30, 1917, 18:5–8.

26 *Arizona Code, Revised 1928*, sec. 2989 (Phoenix, 1930).

27 *Arizona State Constitution*, art. 10, sec. 11.

28 Arizona State Land Commissioner, *Annual Report*, July 1, 1933— June 30, 1934, 22:17.

29 Nevada Surveyor-General and State Land Register, *Report*, 1885–1886, p. 20.

30 Wooton, *The Public Domain of Nevada*, 33.

31 Testimony of William R. Morley in U.S. Senate Subcommittee of the Committee on Public Lands and Surveys (69 Cong., 1 sess., 1925), *Hearings . . . Relating to National Forests and the Public Domain*, pt. 13, p. 3561.

32 Wooton, *The Public Domain of Nevada*, 35.

33 New Mexico Commissioner of Public Lands, *Biennial Report*, 1924–1926, p. 3.

34 Nevada Surveyor-General and State Land Register, *Biennial Report*, 1899–1900, p. 22.

35 *Ibid.*, 1911–1912, p. 20.

36 Arizona State Land Commissioner, *Annual Report*, July 1, 1935— June 30, 1936, p. [12].

37 U.S. Senate Committee on Public Lands and Surveys (72 Cong., 1 sess., 1932), *Hearings . . . on . . . Bills Proposing to Grant Vacant Unreserved Unappropriated Lands to Accepting States . . .* , 54.

38 Arizona State Land Commissioner, *Report*, June 6, 1912—Dec. 1, 1914, pp. 54–56.

39 Arizona State Land Commissioner, *Annual Report*, July 1, 1933— June 30, 1934, p. 13.

40 New Mexico *Statutes*, ch. 132, secs. 113, 114, 122; and *1938 Supplement*, ch. 132, sec. 115a.

41 New Mexico Commissioner of Public Lands, *Annual Report*, Nov. 30, 1914—Nov. 30, 1916, 16–17:45. The reports for the World War I years do not contain figures on the total acreage leased.

42 *The Western Range*, 232.

43 *Arizona Code*, sec. 2967.

44 *Ibid.*, secs. 2964, 2972.

45 *Ibid.*, sec. 2965.

46 Arizona State Land Commission, *Report*, June 6, 1912—Dec. 1, 1914, pp. 140–141.

47 *The Western Range*, 232.

48 The Wyoming system has been often recommended as a model for leasing the federal domain. George Stewart, *This Public Domain of Ours* (Utah Agricultural Experiment Station, Circular 49, Logan, 1924), 48.

49 U.S. Forest Service, *Bulletin 62*, 54–60.

50 The business depression of recent years induced the state to make temporary reductions in the rentals. See the testimony of Governor Leslie A. Miller in U.S. House Committee on the Public Lands (74 Cong., 1 sess., 1935), *Hearings . . . to Provide for the Orderly Use, Improvement, and Development of the Public Range*, 47.

51 *The Western Range*, 232.

52 See testimony of George A. Fisher, executive secretary of the Utah State Land Board, in U.S. Senate Committee on Public Lands and Surveys (73 Cong., 2 sess., 1934), *Hearings . . . on H.R. 6462*, 211.

53 Arizona State Land Commissioner, *Annual Report*, July 1, 1935—June 30, 1936, 24:[1].

54 U.S. Committee on the Conservation and Administration of the Public Domain, *Report . . .* January 1931, p. 38.

55 Colorado state lands are valued and classified mainly in terms of stock-watering possibilities. See Will C. Barnes, *The Story of the Range* (Washington, 1926), 42.

56 This fact is bluntly stressed in *The Western Range*, 232–234, 477–478.

57 In 1928, Idaho took moderate steps to prevent overgrazing on leased state lands. See Idaho State Land Department, *Biennial Report*, Dec. 1, 1928—Oct. 1, 1930, 20:13.

58 *The Western Range*, 6–7.

59 U.S. House Committee on Public Lands (74 Cong., 1 sess.), *Hearings . . . on H.R. 3019*, 38.

60 The need for regional considerations is emphasized in the following statement: "The boundaries of the 11 Western States are nearly all straight lines. The States are not separated by natural geographic divisions. Rivers flow from one State into another. Watersheds must be protected in one State for the benefit of another. Often water is reservoired in one State for use on lands in another. Flocks and herds must continue to make seasonal migration from one State to another, because in many of the States the winter and summer grazing are not in balance."—Peterson, "Land Utilization in the Western Range Country," 46. The same page has a table showing the approximate amount of interstate stock movement in Idaho, Nevada, and Utah.

IV

PROBLEMS OF
PROTECTION AND
MANAGEMENT OF PUBLIC DOMAIN

Introduction

MARION CLAWSON

MANAGEMENT of the public domain hardly existed in any real sense during the decades when the disposal philosophy was dominant; indeed, if one assumed that the land would shortly pass into private ownership and the forests be cleared for farming, there was no reason for management. Efforts were made to control trespass on public lands, but largely as a means of forcing the trespassers to buy the lands. Such efforts were in very large part ineffective, because dominant frontier philosophy regarded the trespasser or developer as a benefactor, not as a despoiler. A few feeble attempts were made to control forest fires on public domain. But in general fires were looked upon as beneficial in freeing land of the forests which would have to be cleared otherwise if the land was to be farmed; and techniques for forest fire control were almost unknown.

Such was the situation when the first Forest Reserves were created in 1891, and, indeed, for a decade or so later. No provision had been made in the original act for use of these new reserves or for selling products from them, and charges of "locking up" vital resources were soon heard. The act of 1897 provided a broad basis for management of these lands; several later acts have broadened that authority and extended similar authority to other lands—the Taylor Grazing Act applying similar authority to the remaining public domain. Under the legislation, often rather general in terms, specific administrative rules

435

for timber sales, grazing, recreation, mineral leasing, and other uses have been adopted. Gradually, a complex system of regulations has come into being.

In the early decades of the twentieth century, demand for the products and uses of the federal lands was comparatively low. Most applicants could be granted what they wanted without serious protest from other applicants, although the administrators often rejected applications they thought improper or inadvisable. Gradually, however, the volume of applications and the demand for resources rose. Today, much of the federal land is in heavy demand, often for more than one use, often by more than one user-group or applicant within each group. Administrators today are frequently required to choose among uses and users. Some choices are made by competitive market practices, as when timber is sold on a bid basis; in most cases, however, the decisions rest upon other and less specific grounds. "Multiple use" and "greatest good for the greatest number in the long run" are slogans which must be translated into specific administrative decisions.

Early management was often rule-of-thumb and common sense. Over the years, research and accumulated experience have led to the development of a large body of expertise. Numerous management techniques, some quite advanced and sophisticated, have been adopted. It should be added that private landowners, both forestry and grazing, have also adopted many of the same techniques. Paralleling the development of scientific and resource-management techniques has been the development of governmental procedures and of a professional bureaucracy. The latter consists, for the most part, of dedicated permanent civil servants, motivated for public service as they conceive it. One might criticize such administrators on many grounds, but one must admire their dedication and over-all skill. Generally speaking, the administrative procedures developed by the executive branch have been more satisfactory than the budgetary and appropriation processes developed by the executive and legislative branches to deal with the complex resource-management problems of the federal lands.

In the last decade or so, management of the federal lands has entered a new era, that of intensive management. With annual budgets and annual revenues each of the general order of $300,000,000 the administration of this estate has become big business, even in the modern American sense. A complex set of relationships has grown up within and between the federal agencies, and with the user public.

This phase of federal land management has had little attention from any scholars and almost none as yet from the historians. Perhaps a longer time-perspective is needed for its appraisal. The fact that this period of land history differs largely in degree or intensity, compared with the immediately preceding period, may make it harder to distinguish or dramatize than some of the earlier changes, such as the first permanent land reservations in an era of wholesale disposal.

Federal Protection of
Public Timber in the
Upper Great Lakes States

LUCILE KANE

This article was presented at the joint session of the Agricultural History Society, the Economic History Association, and the Mississippi Valley Historical Association at Rock Island, Illinois, on April 23, 1948. It is a summary of a research project of the Forest Products History Foundation at the Minnesota Historical Society.

Reprinted by permission from Agricultural History, *Volume 23 (1949), pages 135–139.*

W HEN the United States government acquired the public domain and thus became one of the largest owners of timberland in the world, it was confronted with responsibilities of property that it was not prepared to meet. A dynamic industry was moving from the East into the public land states of the West, where laws for land acquisition were fashioned for the settler rather than for an industry utilizing trees as its raw material. Like the cattleman and the miner, the lumberman conducted his business in the face of a legal system that did not recognize the needs of his industry. This article is an examination of the efforts of the federal government in the nineteenth century to enforce laws that ran counter to the interests of a powerful industry on the frontier of Wisconsin, Michigan, and Minnesota.

Although earlier laws had been passed to safeguard live oak and cedar forests for the navy, it was not until 1831 that Congress made it a felony to cut and remove timber from the public lands without permission.[1] Sometime after the passage of this law, a system of enforcement was worked out through the establishment of timber agencies under the jurisdiction of the Solicitor of the Treasury Department.[2] Since the records of this service prior to the creation of the Department of the Interior are fragmentary, no accurate estimates can be made of the activities of these early agents. The records do show that by 1838 the Solicitor was working with the district attorney in Wisconsin to suppress timber depredation, and that by 1851 agents were at work in northern Michigan and Wisconsin, and in Minnesota.[3] However, few lines of policy had been drawn, for in response to an inquiry about depredations, the Acting Secretary of the Interior stated that no instructions had been issued by his office to punish trespassers on the public domain and that when instructions did emanate from the Solicitor of the Treasury, they varied according to the section of the country and the enormity of the offense.[4]

In 1852, the Solicitor of the Treasury turned over his function as protector of the public timber to the Department of the Interior, created in 1849. When the President called for a report on what had been done to prevent depredations, the Secretary forwarded the request to the Solicitor. The latter replied by transferring the mass of documents relating to that division of his office to the Secretary of the Interior and by suggesting that all of the business which did not properly belong to his office should be assumed by the Department of the Interior.[5] The Secretary accepted the charge, sent out a notice to the timber agents, and enlisted the counsel of the Commissioner of the General Land Office in administering the small force of agents working on the forest frontiers.[6]

During these early years, the agents in the field were progressing no better than their superiors. Special agents were received with little warmth when they traveled into communities where timber had been for years a free good among farmers, loggers, and choppers. Armed with instructions to order the seizure of stolen timber wherever it could be found and to act with the United States district attorney in the prosecution of trespassers, the timber agents stepped squarely against the stronger law of custom and public opinion.[7]

Letters of complaint charging timber agents with malice, violence, and blackmail streamed into the Department of the Interior. Of agent Isaac W. Willard, a lumberman from Michigan wrote: ". . . the timber agent Openly declares He will settle with no man on the Manistee River on . . . [any] other Condition . . . [but] to Strip them of their All . . . and Says He will not leave a man there worth ten cents when he gets through with them. . . ." [8] One old shingle weaver protested against the seemingly arbitrary seizure of property in these words: "When . . . [the agent] came to seize my lumber, I told him that I had lived under 3 Kings reigns and a part of a Queens reign and I never [did] see property sized [sic] and taken away from poor people as they did from us." When the old man asked if there were a higher authority to which he could appeal, the agent answered that there was no one higher than he except God Almighty.[9]

To these charges the agent answered by reciting stories of the indignities which had been heaped upon officers trying to enforce the law in the wilds of Michigan; of loggers banded together in associations to defy law and intimidate informers; of men who untied government boats and put them to the torch; of attempts to burn down an inn where the timber agents were sleeping; of masqueraders who tried to re-enact a Boston Tea Party at Bar Lake, Michigan.[10]

Warned by the rumblings from Congress that were sounded in the letters of inquiry and protest coming from the members of that body, and spurred on by reports of serious financial mismanagement on the part of the agents, the Secretary of the Interior in 1855 decided to abolish the timber agencies in favor of a more "economical and less objectionable" system.[11] But since there was no appropriation for the suppression of depredations, the possibilities of a better policing of the public domain were seriously limited.

On December 24, 1855, after a lengthy exchange of opinions between the Secretary and the Commissioner, the General Land Office issued a circular that was to govern the administration of the timber agency for more than twenty years. By assigning to the Commissioner direct responsibility for the suppression of timber trespass, the Secretary did little more than acknowledge a situation that had existed for many months.[12] The old agents were dismissed, and the work in the field fell to the registers and receivers in the local land offices. Since their instructions limited them to investigations of cases already known to them, the local officers hardly constituted the force necessary to change the bent of the pioneers. They might appoint a deputy to gather evidence in case of emergency, but the emphasis was on a sparing use of funds and a cautious exercise of the powers delegated to them.[13]

Unfortunately for the American people, the registers and receivers accomplished few of the things that a rather optimistic Commissioner hoped they would. Pushed by the routine business of their office, restricted by a lack of money for investigation, blocked on all sides by the stubborn frontier population, the local land officers did at best a haphazard job of law enforcement. Many of the more conscientious, aware of their ineffectiveness, expressed their opinions in letters to the Commissioner. A receiver at LaCrosse who was trying to restrain the farmers around Tomah from slashing out all the young timber in the neighborhood to make hop poles voiced his irritation with the system in these words: "How it is possible for us to prevent . . . [trespass] I am unable to see, unless a sufficient number of special agents can be appointed and paid. This whole matter is a troublesome one. It is very unpleasant for any person to feel that a duty is imposed upon him that he cannot perform." [14]

To such complaints from his officers and to those who protested by letter and editorial the growing prevalence of timber trespass, the Commissioner had no happy answer. Since no funds were appropriated for such a disposition and no office was created for such a function, better protection for the public timber would have to wait on legislation.[15] And this admission of impotence came in the decade of the sixties when timber cruisers were ranging far and wide in the white-pine stands of the Lake states, when the damp dark logs floated endlessly down the streams into the booms of Saginaw, Muskegon, Stillwater, and Eau Claire.

An attempt had been made in the circular of 1855 to explain to the local officers the rules by which they were to be guided in the performance of their timber duties. Although the legal procedure was briefly outlined and the policy of the Department of the Interior was at least suggested, many of the details were left to the discretion of the register and receiver. A few energetically elicited opinions from the Commissioner as cases arose; some ignored the directions and mislaid the circular; many were confused about the specific application of orders that the men in Washington had thought so clear.

Seizure and sale of timber illegally cut on public land were the most onerous parts of the assignment given to the local officers. In a country where officers had to travel great distances through areas inhabited only by loggers and Indians, identifying logs as government property was in itself a hardship. Then after the logs were seized and offered for sale, a game of wits was played between officer and lumberman. Combinations to set prices, intimidation of possible competitive bidders, and non-attendance of sales were resorted to by the men who wished to see the effects of the seizures nullified. Many a lot of logs rotted where they lay for want of a bidder. In at least one instance, the register and receiver were sued as private persons for seizing logs, and the case was carried to the Supreme Court of Michigan.[16] The Commissioner, perhaps realizing the carelessness with which the trespass business was being conducted, urged on his officers great caution in making seizures, and thus encouraged their natural disposition to do nothing.[17]

If seizure and sale were not a restraining influence upon the wood-using population, the system of compromise that operated concurrently with it not only failed to restrain but in some measure encouraged disregard for the law. In spite of the complaints of the lumbermen that the excessive rates of stumpage demanded of innocent trespassers were ruining the lumber business, the student can read in the record a willingness on the part of wood users to pay the various rates imposed by the federal government as the cost of the raw material. The distinctions between guilty and innocent trespassers were too fine for the men in the land offices who made the immediate decisions, and compromise became through this twenty-year period a license to trespass.

In 1877 there came to the Department of the Interior Carl Schurz, a Secretary who was perhaps more concerned than his predecessors with the failure of the federal government to prevent timber depredations.[18] The General Land Office issued in May a circular notifying the registers and receivers that the orders given in 1855 were revoked. Clerks detailed from the General Land Office were assigned to investigate cases of trespass and instructed to report to the Commissioner, who would then pass his recommendations on to the Secretary of the Interior. By working with the district attorneys in the areas to which they were assigned, the clerks were to act directly in gathering evidence that could be used to prosecute trespassers in court.[19]

A pamphlet from the General Land Office published in 1883 gave to these clerks detailed for timber duty the title of "special timber agents." By outlining the laws governing the public lands, discussing the policy of the department toward timber trespass, and enumerating the duties of special agents, this circular made more explicit the directions given in 1877.[20] Since both the agents operating under the Solicitor and the local land officers had been confused about the scope of their activities, these two circulars did much to bring the new agents into closer understanding with the administrative officials in Washington.

The close supervision exercised over the special agents did not eliminate charges of fraud that had been made against the agents since the first representatives of the department had visited the pineries of the Lake states. Although petty cases of malfeasance were overshadowed during this period by the sorry revelation of how the surveyors general of Minnesota had executed the special trust confided in them, the timber agents were accused of a variety of sins—using their office for personal gain, allowing themselves to be influenced by community pressure, selling out to the lumbermen.[21] Action was taken in some of the cases, but it was difficult for the Commissioner to unravel the web of intrigue that surrounded most of the reports.

During the decades in which the special agents traveled across the snows and through the rains of the north country to enforce the law of the federal government, the emphasis in timber depredations shifted from ignoring the law to consciously evading it. In the early years when the agents rarely visited the timbered areas, the greatest depredations were made on unoccupied lands. After the government increased its vigilance, and particularly after the passage of the Homestead Act, lumbermen made use of the settlement laws to acquire a show of title to the land on which they cut.

The recitation of the ruses of the pre-emption broker, the guilt of the local land officer, the collusion of lumbermen, is now a familiar one. One timber agent estimated that in Minnesota 99 per cent of the homestead and pre-emption entries were made for the timber alone.[22] Another wrote from Duluth that in spite of the activities of seventeen special agents, evasion of the settlement laws continued. ". . . a land law," he concluded, "which was good for Cook Co., Illinois is not a good one for Cook Co., Minnesota." [23] Most of the agents who ventured a solution recommended that the land be sold to the highest bidder before fire and theft destroyed its value, but one lone agent did suggest that in areas like northern Minnesota it might be wise to create forest reserves.[24]

As the reports of the agents on illegal cutting piled up in the General Land Office, the Commissioners began to question the distinction between innocent and guilty trespassers that had formed the basis for compromise since 1860. How could an agent determine the true intent of a trespasser? Was the lumber company which encouraged the entry or the homesteader who perjured himself to make it ultimately responsible? Should the man who cut the logs or the man who received them for manufacture pay the greater penalty? And should any weight be given to the arguments of those who said that the government through past decisions had established the principle that anyone might trespass on government land and settle the obligation by paying stumpage? [25]

While the General Land Office was in the hands of men eager for reform, it became evident that the government intended to do more than recover the nominal value of the land. Secretary Schurz, in one of his first letters on the subject, declared that it was the intention of the department to put an end to timber trespass by depriving the depredators of all the profit from their transactions and by criminally prosecuting those who organized and directed the illegal activities. "As long as . . . [the trespassers] are permitted to hope," said Schurz, "that even after the seizure by government officers . . . they may, by way of compromise, acquire rightful possession of the logs . . . the temptation to continue the depredations will not cease. . . ." [26]

In practice few criminal suits were instituted against persons who did not actually do the cutting, and still fewer criminal convictions were secured against trespassers. But from the companies that received the logs, thousands of dollars were collected by court action and voluntary compromise for the Treasury of the United States. Again and again, Commissioners repeated that it was the responsibility of the lumber manufacturer to inquire into the right of homesteaders, preemptors, contractors, and railroads to sell the logs. By accepting logs cut from lands whose title was still in the government, a company made itself liable to civil action.

By the end of the nineteenth century, cases of petty trespass predominated in the reports of the timber agents. Some of the Indian reservations still held promise of a harvest, but most of the timberlands of the Lake states had been cut over or had passed from government ownership. From the lands of these states went the men of enterprise to cut out new stands in the West and in the South. For good or for ill, the age was over; the story was told.

From the beginning of settlement through more than two centuries of expansion, the American people formed certain attitudes toward the forests that stretched to the boundless west. Limitless in number, trees had value only when men cut them down, drove them down a stream, sawed them into boards at a mill, and sold the lumber in a market. When there was a choice between taking timber from unoccupied land and entering the land, many lumbermen carried out the frontier tradition of helping themselves to what they needed. The Department of the Interior tried with varying degrees of success to stop up the biggest holes in the dike. But against the force exerted by a highly competitive industry, these sporadic efforts to protect the timber and to enforce the settlement laws were all but lost. When the last forests were reached, the lumber industry began to consider a new type of forest-land management which would enable them to conduct their business on a permanent basis.

NOTES

1 4 *U.S. Stat.*, 472. The earlier laws referred to are those of March 1, 1817, and February 23, 1822.

2 J. A. Williamson, Commissioner of the General Land Office, to Zachariah Chandler, Secretary of the Interior, Jan. 24, 1877, in General Land Office Records, Letters Sent, National Archives.

3 Moses M. Strong, U.S. Attorney for Wisconsin Territory, Madison, to H. D. Gilpin, Solicitor of the Treasury, Nov. 20, 1838, in the Strong Lumber Papers, State Historical Society of Wisconsin; and A. H. H. Stuart, Secretary of the Interior, to the Solicitor of the Treasury, Apr. 23, 1851, Nov. 18, 1851, in Files of the Secretary of the Interior, Letters Sent, National Archives. By 1854, there were four agents in the field, two in Michigan, one in Wisconsin, and one in Iowa. J. A. Williamson, Commissioner of the General Land Office, to Zachariah Chandler, Secretary of the Interior, Jan. 24, 1877, in General Land Office Records, Letters Sent, National Archives. See also Paul Wallace Gates, *The Wisconsin Pine Lands of Cornell University* (Ithaca, 1943), 70–73.

4 D. C. Goddard, Acting Secretary of the Interior, to W. K. Sebastian, U.S. Senate, Aug. 28, 1850, in Files of the Secretary of the Interior, Letters Sent, National Archives.

5 A. H. H. Stuart, Secretary of the Interior, to Solicitor of the Treasury, March 4, 1852; and A. H. H. Stuart to the President of the United States, June 4, 1852, *ibid.*

6 *Ibid.;* A. H. H. Stuart, Secretary of the Interior, to Timber Agents, June 4, 1852, *ibid.*

7 R. C. McClelland, Secretary of the Interior, to Isaac W. Willard, Paw Paw, Mich., March 14, 1853, *ibid.*

8 Roswell Canfield, n.p., to John Wentworth, n.p., Dec. 24, 1853, in General Land Office Records, Letters Received, National Archives.

9 Sworn Statement of Thomas Phillips, Clay Banks, Oceana County, Mich., March 18 [1854], *ibid.* In *The Great Forest* (New York, 1947), 167–168, Richard G. Lillard relates other incidents in the career of "Ike" Willard as timber agent in Michigan.

10 Sworn Affidavit of Otis C. Fall, Wayne County, Mich., May 30, 1854, in General Land Office Records, Letters Received, National Archives.

11 R. C. McClelland, Secretary of the Interior, to Commissioner of the

General Land Office, Nov. 24, 1855, in Files of the Secretary of the Interior, Letters Sent, National Archives.

12 J. A. Williamson, Commissioner of the General Land Office, to Zachariah Chandler, Secretary of the Interior, Jan. 24, 1877, in General Land Office Records, Letters Sent, National Archives.

13 General Land Office Circular, Dec. 24, 1855.

14 S. S. Burton, Receiver, Land Office, LaCrosse, Wis., to Jos. Wilson, Commissioner of the General Land Office, Jan. 10, 1868, in General Land Office Records, Letters Received, National Archives.

15 J. M. Edmunds, Commissioner of the General Land Office, to Hon. T. O. Howe, Green Bay, Wis., June 9, 1865, in General Land Office Records, Timber, Letters Sent, National Archives.

16 J. M. Edmunds, Commissioner of the General Land Office, to Wm. L. Webber, Attorney, East Saginaw, Mich., Jan. 2, 1863, *ibid.*

17 J. M. Edmunds, Commissioner of the General Land Office to Osmond Tower, Grand Rapids, Mich., Oct. 7, 1863, *ibid.*

18 For an analysis of events in the General Land Office from 1875 to 1890, see Harold H. Dunham, "Some Crucial Years in the General Land Office," *Agricultural History*, 11:117–141 (1937) *[reprinted in this volume, pp. 181–201].*

19 General Land Office Circular, May 2, 1877.

20 Instructions to Special Agents of the General Land Office, 1883.

21 Isaac Wood, Custer, Mason Co., Mich., to the General Land Office, July 29, 1883; S. M. Stockslager, Acting Commissioner of the General Land Office, to F. W. Worden, Special Agent, Reed City, Mich., Jan. 28, 1888; Jos. E. Squire, Garden, Mich., to Geo. Carmichael, n.p., Jan. 7, 1898; and H. M. Lewis, U.S. Attorney, Western District of Wisconsin, Madison, to J. A. Williamson, Commissioner of the General Land Office, Dec. 8, 1879, in General Land Office Records, Letters Received and Letters Sent, National Archives.

22 S. M. Stockslager, Assistant Commissioner of the General Land Office, to D. LeGore, Special Agent, Duluth, Minn., Apr. 15, 1886, in General Land Office Records, Timber, National Archives.

23 Fred W. LeSueur, Special Agent, Duluth, Minn., to the Commissioner of the General Land Office, Sept. 24, 1894, in General Land Office Records, Letters Received, National Archives. Protests against the illegal use of the settlement laws came from the organs of the lumber industry as well as from the government. See the views expressed in *Mississippi Valley Lumberman*, Sept. 2, 1887, p. 4; July 6, 1888, p. 1; Feb. 21, 1890, p. 1.

24 Fred W. LeSueur, Special Agent, Duluth, Minn., to the Commissioner of the General Land Office, Sept. 24, 1894, in General Land Office Records, Letters Received, National Archives.

25 Thos. Lowry, Minneapolis, Minn., to Carl Schurz, Secretary of the Interior, Apr. 18, 1879, in General Land Office Records, Timber Trespass Reports, National Archives.

26 Carl Schurz, Secretary of the Interior, to Charles Devens, Attorney General, Aug. 29, 1877, *ibid.*

Reminiscences of the Bureau of Land Management, 1947–1948

MARION CLAWSON

From March 4, 1948, until April 30, 1953, the author of this article was Director of the Bureau of Land Management, Department of the Interior . . .

Reprinted by permission from Agricultural History, *Volume 33* (*1959*), *pages 22–28.*

NOW that the Bureau of Land Management is firmly established as a competent federal-resource–managing agency, some account of its early days may serve to provide a datum plane from which its progress can be measured. An account of how it rose from the condition shortly to be described to its present position in about eleven years, would be a more important but more difficult story to tell. Possibly no one can properly do the latter yet; aside from differences of opinion as to the relative importance of different aspects of the story, no reasonably complete account could fail to deal with personalities, some of whom are still active or at least alive. The rejuvenation of a heavily decadent or at least markedly incompetent organization has not been treated as a general problem in the literature of public administration and business, to my knowledge, although a few case histories have been written; yet it is, on the whole, more difficult than to build a new organization.

This matter of rejuvenation of old vs. creation of new organizations is not academic for the federal resource management field. As early as 1897 or 1898, on the basis of brief employment in it, Gifford Pinchot concluded that the General Land Office was so hopelessly incompetent, graft-ridden, and politically motivated that its reform for the great task of management of the Forest Reserves was impossible. A comment which carries his flavor is: "In practice, thanks to lax, stupid, and wrongheaded administration by the Interior Department, the land laws were easily twisted to the advantage of the big fellows, and Western opinion was satisfied to have it so." [1] He turned instead to the little Bureau of Forestry in the Department of Agriculture, first to build it up and then to take over to it the Forest Reserves. A typical comment made apropos the situation in 1898 was the following: "Obviously to bring Uncle Sam's forests and foresters together was nothing more than common sense. Brought together they were going to be, if I had any luck, and when they were I proposed to be the forester in charge. But until then the Government Forest Reserves seemed to be out of my reach." [2]

The rest is federal land management history. Had Pinchot chosen instead to direct his great energies and ability to reform of the Land Office, and had he been successful—two great "ifs"!—the whole course of federal land management would have been very different.

Pinchot cites several examples to illustrate his conclusion: a saloon keeper whose nearest approach to the Forest Reserve he was paid to administer was to look at it, miles away, from the porch of his saloon; nepotism, extreme and frequent; "men in charge of forestry in the Washington office who had never been West; field men who were too aged or in too poor health ever to visit the lands under their charge; and smothering red-tape over all." [3] He doubtless chose striking but true examples to make his point.

But S. A. D. Puter, in *Looters of the Public Domain*, a few years later was to cite in detail instances of fraud, bribery, and theft on a large scale. [4] One common trick was to bribe surveyors to certify to non-existent homesteads on comparatively barren areas within newly created Forest Reserves, which could then be used to trade for "in lieu" lands of excellent timber elsewhere. One priceless incident he relates concerns how two inspectors went to inspect an area, each bribed by the same man for the same purpose, but each ignorant of the other's status, and each seeking to turn in a report which the other could not refute. Old employees of the General Land Office have assured me that bribery was indeed common in those days. It is also true that much unselfish devotion to duty existed among its employees, then and earlier. Jenks Cameron graphically relates some of it. [5]

Bribery and dishonesty had disappeared from the General Land Office long before it was merged with the Grazing Service in 1946 to form the Bureau of Land Management—just how long before, I do not know, and perhaps no single date could be picked. But the major controversies over the public domain since 1908 have turned around the Secretaries of the Interior—Ballinger, Fall, and McKay—and not around the General Land Office or BLM. How many readers can give, offhand, the names of the Commissioners of the General Land Office under Ballinger and Fall? I cannot.

Some employees of the General Land Office were politically chosen to the end of its existence—its Commissioner, the Assistant Commissioner(s), and the heads of each local land office. This had been true from the beginning, in 1812, of course. Perhaps the offices were always sinecures and those filling them largely figure-heads. I do not know, and as far as I know no serious study has ever been made of the matter. But for a great many years prior to 1946 this was certainly true. As one with some experience in federal government, I would say that choice of key personnel on political grounds rather than from a career service does not necessarily lead to inferior personnel, and indeed may have the opposite result. The essential consideration is the criterion for the political choice: is it to get the best possible man to direct a program essential to the party's total program, or is it merely to reward the faithful? In the General Land Office it was most emphatically the latter. For some decades it had been a haven for political has-beens whom it was desired to pension harmlessly. One General Land Office employee who joined it in 1905 has told me that in all the remaining years of the agency, only one Commissioner (or bureau chief) either knew or cared what the work of the agency was all about. Other old employees have confirmed this judgment. (The competent one they had in mind was not my predecessor.) In the local land offices, the political head performed only routine duties, including signing all official documents and correspondence, and career employees drawing half his salary did all the work. As a result, the amount of smoldering resentment per employee was very high.

In the summer of 1948, when we closed one local land office and terminated the appointment of one of these politically chosen heads, question was raised about paying all the accumulated vacation allegedly due this person. It was a matter of common knowledge that the person in question, a woman, played the organ at one of the local funeral parlors whenever there was a funeral, and could be seen on the street at almost any hour, with no apparent need to be in her office more than an hour or so each working day. Her first defense to us was that her brother was the Democratic committeeman from that state, but since that state was then believed (it has since proved otherwise) to be safely Republican, this was neither rational nor adequate. Her telling argument was that she had done all the work she had been assigned, that she had been paid regularly and without question over a period of years, and that at no time had any deficiency in her work been called to her attention. Since these statements were true, the time of her dismissal was hardly the time to start reform, and she was paid off in full.

With the exception of these comparatively few nominal heads of the organization or of its local offices, the employees of the General Land Office by 1946 were all under the classified civil service, except for certain lawyers, and they had been chosen for merit, not for politics. But the results for resource management were scarcely happier than in Pinchot's day, though for very different reasons. At least as early as 1900, under the assumption that the agency's life would end when all the public domain had been given away, at an indefinite but comparatively early date, the permanent personnel had sought to make the work as complicated, slow, and cumbersome as possible. The great fear was "working yourself out of a job," and the answer was to spin the job out as long as possible. There were other forces that operated to the same end. In a drive for higher salaries—greatly deserved, for the Land Office was always a low-pay outfit—the work was made to appear to be as difficult as possible, so that the person who did it would appear as competent as possible. For instance, nearly every notification to an applicant for public domain was labeled a "decision" so that the writer could be given a legal position, not merely a clerical one. Decisions were often typed individually for each applicant, rather than printed forms being used, even though they customarily contained mostly paragraphs with standard phrasing. Even a notification that rent was due on a lease was a "decision."

Employees in the Land Office were aided in these objectives by others. Certain lawyers in Washington were happy over this situation, because it drove the serious applicant for public domain and his local lawyer to employ them. Many such Washington lawyers were former employees of the Land Office or Department of the Interior. Some members of Congress either liked or at least tolerated the situation, for it gave them a chance to do favors for constituents. At various times, when land activity was comparatively high, nothing moved out of the Land Office except "Congressional specials." There were many and interesting alliances and working relationships between Land Office employees, Washington lawyers, and members of Congress in those days.

There were still other forces at work to the same end. Because of the land scandals under Ballinger and Fall, and because the possibility of fraud always existed, a philosophy grew up of check and double check—of write decision and review and review, at different levels. This not only resulted in delay, but also in poor work at lower levels; if one's work were to be reviewed by someone who would feel it necessary to change some of it to show his usefulness in the agency, why bother to be careful!

At least partly as an outgrowth of the "make work" philosophy, plus also a desire for check and double check, the work of the General Land Office was highly centralized in Washington. A citizen who sought to buy a few fence posts from the public domain, or to lease a small tract for a cabin site, or to buy or homestead the land, or to lease it for wildcat oil and gas development, filed his application in the local land office. The application was forwarded to Washington. In due time, most such applications were returned to the field, but to another office, with a request for field investigation. If the applicant had filed four applications for as many nearby tracts of land, the applications were rarely returned in a group to the field, but dribbled out, thus preventing one field investigation for all of them. In due time again, the report went back to Washington, where the decision was made on what to do, by men who had never seen the land or the applicant, and often by men who had never been west of Ohio; the man who was head of the Homestead Division for many years saw his first homestead only the year before he retired, for instance. In still later due time, the applicant was notified of action, through the local land office. In the case of oil and gas leases, he was then in effect given a chance to change his mind, if it appeared that the land was not as promising as he had originally thought. After the applicant had taken whatever action he was called upon to take, all the papers went back to Washington again, and in still later due time a lease, permit, or patent issued, and forwarded to the applicant through the local land office.

Thus, at the least, "if all be regular," even the humblest requests made three round trips from the western states where the land was, to Washington, before the applicant finally got what he wanted. And often all was not regular, especially to workers alert for irregularities, fearful of moving when movement might bring censure and inaction would not, and without a chance to learn anything except by long-distance correspondence. It was rare that final action in any type of land case was completed in less than two years, unless congressional influence was brought to bear, and many land exchanges dragged out for more than five years.

When the Taylor Grazing Act was passed in 1934, its administration was not entrusted to the Land Office, but instead put in a new agency, first called the Division of Grazing, later called the Grazing Service. The trials and tribulations of that agency have been recounted in various places, but as yet—in my opinion—not completely. But that story is beside our present interest, except to note that the agency's operations were highly decentralized, at least away from Washington to state offices, and to a large extent to local district offices. Thus, when the two agencies were combined in 1946, one was highly centralized in Washington, the other largely decentralized to the field.

The work of the Washington office of the new bureau was highly centralized in the Director's office—at least the routine work was, although some of the important fiscal controls were scattered at first. All mail (except really important letters) was signed by the Director, a sincere gentleman whose health by then would not have permitted much more activity. The outgoing "decisions" and letters, each with relevant file attached, would be brought to his office, messenger's cartful after messenger's cartful. Being a methodical person, he kept a tally sheet of his signatures on his calendar pad; rarely did they run less than 180 in a day, sometimes as high as 400, but mostly around 250 to 300. After I came to Washington in March, 1948, we moved promptly to delegate the routine signing to subordinate officials. But it took a few weeks to get the new orders signed and the personnel instructed in the new routine; and the pipeline was full on the old routine, and it took a good many weeks to clear it out. At first the Assistant Director "signed," but he shortly retired; his replacement signed when he was in town, but he traveled a good deal and I was stuck with a lot of signing. I was too busy during the day for such nonsense, but would go back nearly every evening, to sign.

"Signing" was quite a process. The table in my office, about 3 by 6 feet in size, would be neatly stacked with files, to a depth of 2 feet or more. Some files would be thin, with only a few sheets of paper, while others were a few inches thick. On top of each file was fastened a little slip of white paper, on which was written by hand "1 Sig," "3 Sigs," etc., to advise me how many times I must sign for that file. I was always fascinated by assignments of oil and gas leases—I had to sign a number equal to multiples of three, plus one—4, 7, 10, etc. The highest number I ever recall for a single file was 28. Neat tabs would be placed on the side of each file that I could lift up and there would be just the spot for my name, with a neatly dotted line to be sure I knew where the signature should go. I understand someone had had an efficiency award for the suggestion that the tab to show where the signature was to go be placed on the left side of the file, so that it could be lifted with the left hand, avoiding the necessity for a right-hander to lay down his pen while turning to the next signature. Anyway, the tabs were on the left side. I would lift a tab with my left hand, sign as rapidly as I could without impairment of legibility—I preserved my pride in legibility to the end—turn with my left hand swiftly to the next spot, sign rapidly, and so on. By the fastest and most concentrated work, I could sign about 100 times per hour, but of course by reading nothing. Once in a while, when my hand threatened to cramp, I would hastily read a few lines. I have a tolerably quick eye, and sometimes I could catch a typographical error—once I caught one in arithmetic—without really slowing up. These cases I bounced back, with an indignant note, hoping in this way to fool someone that I had read the files, and thus subtly warning them not to try to put anything over on me. I found also that by simply tumbling the signed files over into a loose pile, at first on a chair, and then onto the space vacated on the table, I could speed up the signing process.

Within six months, the signing in the Director's office had been cut to fifty or fewer daily. Considerably more than half of the work, the simpler and more routine kinds, had been transferred to local offices in the West and in Alaska; most of the rest had been delegated to responsible officials in the Washington office.

A few anecdotes may catch the flavor of that office as it then was. These are, to the best of my knowledge and recollection, true and not overstated in the telling. They are unusual, because it is the unusual that makes a good story, but others at least as dramatic could be recalled.

The first concerns use of appropriations, and all took place before I arrived in Washington. As late as the 1947 fiscal year, the Washington appropriation for the bureau was divided into several legally separate items, and within the bureau these were accounted for and controlled separately by the units to which they applied, with no central fiscal control. One unit, protesting it was short of money all year, suddenly woke up about June 1 to the fact it had more money than it could spend, and let revert unspent about $50,000 out of a total appropriation of about $300,000. This unit was indeed understaffed and its work in arrears, and with that extra money could have made a dent in its backlog. To a bureaucrat, there can be no worse sin than unintentionally letting revert a substantial sum at the same time the work is suffering from inadequate manpower. In fiscal 1948, before I arrived in Washington, that was changed.

But in the spring of 1948 a different but equally serious situation faced me on arrival. The appropriation for that year had been some $15,000 short of providing enough money to pay all the salaries of local land office personnel. As soon as this was known after July 1, some reduction in personnel should have been made, even though all the competent personnel were badly needed and the politically appointed ones were "hot." Instead, the situation was allowed to drift, and in March there were no plans for meeting it, except a suggestion that all personnel should be given a two-week furlough without pay in June, but asked to report for work just the same! I could see how popular a new Director who did that would be! By promising absolutely never to get in such a mess again, we prevailed upon the Bureau of the Budget and the Congress to give us authority to transfer money from other accounts, where there was enough, and thus avoid the furloughs.

Knowing that the incoming mail, all addressed to the Director, ran to about 3,000 pieces a week, and that I could never hope to look at all of it (even if it had been wise administratively to try), I asked to see all letters the mailroom deemed were important enough to be brought to my attention, all congressional letters no matter how trivial their requests (many were for a map that schools in their districts wanted), and all letters of complaint. For the first several days my efficient secretary would bring in two large handfuls of mail: "Here is the general mail, here is the St. Christopher's mail." The latter was as big as the former. When I began to read the St. Christopher's mail, it was obviously all complaint about some crime we were about to commit, and so I asked for the file and someone to tell me what it was all about. And an interesting story it was, too.

Down on the north bank of the San Juan River in southern Utah, just across the river from the Navajo Indian Reservation, a church missionary group had bought a small tract of land, to grow some food and run a school for the needy Navajos. The only trouble was, the man who sold them the land did not own it, and never had, although he had lived on and farmed it for many years. He might have homesteaded it, with our permission, but a group could not homestead; and, in fact, there was no law by which they could secure title to it. One of our field men had pointed out their trespass situation to them, to which the missionary's reply was that he was doing good for the Indians, which the federal government should have been doing (and it should have), and why disturb him? So, we served a trespass notice on him, giving him thirty days to get off the land. Now, what the Land Office really meant was for him to come in with a proposition for legalizing his occupancy. The missionary did not understand such language (you might not have, either) and what was more, he possessed a mimeograph and a very large and distinguished mailing list. He flung them into action, and I was catching the result. In the end, I expect we heard from at least one-third of all members of the Congress and from a large number and wide variety of other citizens, mostly distinguished. There was a lot of publicity, ranging from mildly critical to outspokenly so.

As soon as I got the story, I had our attorney draft a simple bill, allowing the church to buy the land for $2.50 per acre—to give it to them free was considered an undesirable precedent. Senator Elbert Thomas, then senior senator from Utah, and Congressman Richard Welsh of California, then chairman of the House Committee to which such bills went, each gladly introduced it; it was quickly passed, and the church group got their land. But not until we had had another fling of unfavorable publicity. To answer all the accumulated congressional mail on the matter, a form letter was prepared; but the over-zealous attorney handling the matter sent it to *all* congressmen, whether they had written us or not, and immediately several wrote or called us, to inquire why we should be illegally lobbying for a bill!

Just a few days later another incident occurred. The Bureau of Reclamation had brought water to a tract of public land in southern Idaho. Homesteads were available to veterans. With a characteristic fanfare of trumpets, that bureau had had a public drawing of lucky winners of these farm tracts, all of whom had submitted proof of their veteran's status. Unfortunately, that proof had been submitted to the Bureau of Reclamation, while it was the Bureau of Land Management which "allowed" the homestead entry. Between a BLM man who followed precedent and a Reclamation man who refused to yield his files to another agency, notices were sent by BLM to all the winners of the drawing, advising them that their applications were rejected for lack of proof of military service! Again, the Land Office meant to have them send in the necessary papers. But the winners got in touch with their veterans' organizations, and with their congressmen, and we had another flood of publicity, about as bad as one could ask for. That time, after some fast footwork by my new Assistant Director, the local Bureau of Reclamation man was directed by long-distance telephone by a responsible Washington official of his agency to put the files in his car and drive at once to the BLM office some 50 miles away. The man in charge at the latter office was told by us to prepare telegrams to each applicant, to be ready and to be sent the instant the files arrived, calling the whole affair off. The retiring Assistant Director merely said, "Why should we be always on the defensive? We were clearly within our rights in calling for that proof."

Just one more incident. Senator McCarran of Nevada sent down a letter, one of those classics: written in pencil, on cheap ruled tablet paper, misspelled and ungrammatical. It started off: "Dear Pat—there is something crooked going on here." He went on to say that he had applied for a homestead in Nevada, been rejected, and now someone else (probably a friend of some official) was getting the land he had wanted. The story I unearthed was that he had applied for the land under the Homestead Law, which requires among other things that the land be cultivated. Under the classification authority of the Taylor Grazing Act, this application had been properly rejected, for the land was desert, incapable of being farmed. A "decision" starting off "Application rejected" had been prepared and sent him; it listed all the reasons that the land could not be homesteaded, and then wound up by saying, "This action is without prejudice if the applicant shall file a small tract application." Now what it meant was that, if he applied under the suitable act, he could get up to 5 acres for a homesite, without cultivation requirement. This was all he wanted, but I doubt if he ever read beyond the "application rejected." Later, when someone else did file for the land under an applicable law, and was granted it, he was sure it was favoritism that give the second party the land after he had been rejected.

In 1948 the Bureau of Land Management had an appropriation of $5,000,000 and collected in revenues the then unheard-of sum of $15,000,000; its budget request for fiscal 1958 is over $29,000,000, and it anticipates revenues in that year of $237,000,000. Impressive as this growth in size is, the growth in competence and quality of work has probably been greater—admitting that it is most difficult to define competence and quality, to say nothing of measuring it. The humble origin is often part of the American success story.

NOTES

1 Gifford Pinchot, *Breaking New Ground* (New York, 1947), xvii, 522; quote from *ibid.*, 161.
2 *Ibid.*, 137.
3 *Ibid.*, 161–172.
4 This book, written by Puter while in jail for land frauds, was published by the author in Portland, Oregon, in 1907 and has long since been out of print. It is available in relatively few libraries, of which the Library of Congress is one.
5 Jenks Cameron, *The Development of Governmental Forest Control in the United States* (Baltimore, 1928), 471.

Administration of Grazing Districts

J. RUSSELL PENNY
MARION CLAWSON

The authors of this article were Range Conservationist and Director, respectively, Bureau of Land Management, Department of the Interior.

Reprinted by permission from Land Economics, *Volume 29* (*1953*), *pages 23–34.*

THE grazing district is the largest type of land administration unit in the United States. More than 160,000,000 acres, including federal and private lands administered under agreement, are covered by grazing districts.[1] These lands make up an integral part of the total resources and economy of the ten western states. In spite of the national importance of grazing districts, little has been written of their formation, organization, and functions. A brief historical summary will help to bring the subject into proper focus.

HISTORY OF GRAZING DISTRICTS

Grazing by domestic livestock on the western range lands, other than the Spanish settlements, began with the famous Texas trail herds that brought hundreds of thousands of cattle into the Great Plains area between 1865 and 1890. Around 1870 the large cattle ranches were established. By 1890 most of the open range was in full use by domestic livestock. The coming of the railroads in the early 1880's brought an influx of settlers that continued until the First World War. The open range was homesteaded rapidly and cattlemen were crowded to the point of resisting encroachment by force. With the homesteader came fencing and the wide open spaces were gone forever.

The cattlemen sought to control the range by acquiring the limited areas of meadow land and the better watering places. Competition was intensified with the coming of the sheepman who also acquired strategic footholds by "corraling" the water, and in some areas by acquiring portions of railroad land grants made up of alternate sections of land. The notorious sheep and cattle wars resulted.

Control of the range by ownership or control of strategic lands was successful only to a relatively minor degree. The philosophy became "first come, first served." This cut-throat competitive type of grazing had a decidedly detrimental effect on the forage and land. Forage plants, under extreme heavy use, became weakened and the better plants, destroyed. In some areas vegetation became so sparse that serious erosion problems arose. Many of the stockmen knew the folly of this system of grazing but were helpless to correct it.

The need for control was recognized early. The Public Land Commission in 1880 suggested that land valuable chiefly for grazing be disposed of in blocks large enough to support ranches of 2,560 acres. In 1905 the commission suggested the creation of federal grazing districts. When this failed, many important range areas were set up as national forests, the primary administrative function of which was to control grazing. In an attempt to place grazing lands under private ownership, several special homestead acts were passed between 1904 and 1916, bringing approximately 100,000,000 acres under private ownership.

Stockmen were much divided as to whether there should be state or federal control or whether the public domain should go into private ownership. Some even wanted the status quo. They were generally unified in one basic respect; that was to obtain stability in the livestock industry. They wanted forage to be protected from trespass. By the late 1920's agitation for federal control became stronger and many bills were introduced through the early 1930's. A special act of Congress in 1928 provided for the creation of the co-operative Mizpah–Pumpkin Creek Grazing District in Montana. Rivalry sprang up between the Department of the Interior and the Department of Agriculture as to which should have jurisdiction over the public lands. The question was settled June 28, 1934, by passage of the Taylor Grazing Act, providing for administrative control of the public domain under the Department of the Interior and the creation of grazing districts.[2]

TAYLOR ACT OPENS NEW ERA

To quote the President's statement on approval of the Taylor Grazing Act:

It confers broad powers on the Secretary of the Interior to do all things necessary for the preservation of these ranges, including, amongst other powers, the right to specify from time to time the number of livestock which may graze within such districts and the seasons when they shall be permitted to do so. The authority to exercise these powers is carefully safeguarded against impairment by state or local action. Creation of a grazing district by the Secretary of the Interior and promulgation of rules and regulations respecting it will supersede State regulations of grazing on that part of the public domain included within such districts.[3]

For the first time in American land history, comprehensive and general authority was given for classification of land according to its highest and best use and for rejection of applications for other uses. Homesteading was still allowed for entries up to 320 acres of land considered most valuable or suitable for agricultural crops. Authority to make land exchanges with states and private individuals was provided, the primary purpose being to consolidate federal lands into more compact blocks. The act also provided for transfer of lands from grazing districts to national forests, and vice versa, when more effective administrative boundaries would result and for sale of isolated or disconnected tracts up to 1,520 acres and unisolated tracts, mountainous or too rough for cultivation, up to 760 acres. Conservation and propagation of wildlife with the right to hunt and fish legally within the grazing districts was preserved. Provisions were made also for programs on erosion and flood control, water development, and general improvement of the lands. The Taylor Grazing Act was in fact a multiple-use act.[4]

Regarding grazing, the act provided for the establishment of grazing districts and for issuance of leases in areas not suitable for district administration. This article is concerned chiefly with the administration of the federal range within districts where permits can be granted for periods up to a maximum of ten years.[5]

Provision was made for local hearings on appeals from the decisions of the administrative officer in charge of grazing districts. The charging of reasonable grazing fees was authorized. Fifty per cent of such fees were to be returned to the state in which they were earned, to be used as prescribed by the state legislature; 25 per cent of the fees were to be used for range improvement purposes, and 25 per cent were to remain in the United States Treasury. This distribution of fees was changed somewhat in 1947, when separate grazing fees and range improvement fees were provided, with 12.5 per cent of the grazing fees to be returned to the states, and 87.5 per cent to remain in the United States Treasury. All of the range improvement fee is made available by appropriation for construction and maintenance of range improvements.[6]

To provide for placing the remaining public lands into their best use and prevent a rush of land settlement entries before provisions of the act could be made effective, all lands were withdrawn from entry (Executive Orders 6910, November 26, 1934, and 6964, February 5, 1935). Amendments to the general orders were made from May, 1935, through May, 1936, permitting, among other uses, entries for land sales, land exchanges, and leasing for grazing use of lands outside of grazing districts.[7]

General meetings were held throughout the West by representatives of the Department of the Interior to explain the provisions of the Taylor Grazing Act to the stockmen. Shortly thereafter, as provided by the act, and before grazing districts were formed, a public hearing was announced in the state to consider establishment of grazing districts. Publication of such notice had the effect of withdrawing all public lands within the exterior boundaries of such proposed grazing districts from all forms of entry or settlement.

Farrington R. Carpenter was appointed by the Secretary of the Interior to administer the law. A separate division in the Office of the Secretary, the Division of Grazing Control (later to become the Grazing Service and then the Division of Range Management in the Bureau of Land Management), was formed. The new organization was originally staffed with seventeen men drawn from the Geological Survey, General Land Office, and Forest Service. In January, 1936, the organization was expanded through selection of persons from civil service rolls. An early fear among the livestock men that the organization might be composed of men lacking practical understanding of the range industry was offset by an amendment to the act, in 1936, requiring that prior to appointment, the administrative personnel must have at least one year's residence in the state or states in which they were to serve and that consideration be given to practical range experience.[8]

Statewide hearings were held and committees were designated by the stockmen to recommend areas in that state which should be included within grazing districts and where the district boundaries should be. The areas recommended by these state committees, far exceeding the original 80,000,000-acre limitation, indicated the strong sentiment in favor of grazing control and led to the increase to 142,000,000 acres by amendment to the Taylor Grazing Act in 1936. What districts should be established under the limitation was then determined, followed by the preparation and issuance of Executive Orders establishing thirty-seven grazing districts.[9]

ADVISORY BOARDS: A "GRASS ROOTS COUNCIL"

Immediately after the grazing districts were formed, one of the most significant aspects of the administration was put into effect—the election of advisory boards. The department, recognizing the advantage of local knowledge and experience, had proposed advisory boards elected by the stockmen themselves. These boards proved to be such an asset to the functioning of grazing districts that the act was amended in 1939, giving advisory boards legal recognition and permanent status. The act specifically provided that advisory boards include five to twelve members to be elected by the stockmen with an additional member to be appointed by the Secretary of the Interior to represent wildlife interests in the district. These boards were granted advisory powers only and could be, and sometimes were, and are overruled by administrative officials.[10]

Advisory board members in 1940 were organized into a National Advisory Board Council to consider and make recommendations on grazing administration and problems of a national scope. Shortly thereafter state advisory boards were formed in several of the states. An amendment to the Federal Range Code for Grazing Districts in 1949 officially provided for state advisory boards and the National Advisory Board Council.[11]

DEVELOPMENT OF A RANGE CODE

The consideration of applications for grazing privileges was the first act of grazing district administration. Throughout all districts the demand generally far exceeded the forage supply. To apportion the available range so that each user would get his proportionate share of forage and could use it in keeping with principles of good range management was a primary goal. Temporary rules were replaced in 1938, with the Federal Range Code approved by the Secretary of the Interior, which set forth in detail regulations governing the administration.

Possession of sufficient privately owned or controlled base property, land or water, to insure a year-round operation for the permitted livestock, was required of all users. In areas where private land is the backbone of ranching operations, land was considered as the base property. In such areas the permitted livestock was required to spend a specified amount of time on the private land being offered as a basis for securing grazing privileges. However, in the arid southwestern United States water is considered the principal basis for receiving grazing privileges. Applicants there were required to have privately owned or controlled water suitable for consumption by livestock and available, accessible, and adequate during those months for which the range was classified as suitable for use.

Preference for grazing privileges was given operators who made substantial grazing use of the public lands in connection with their private properties for two consecutive years or any three years in the five years preceding the Taylor Grazing Act (known as the "priority period," June 28, 1929, to June 28, 1934). For districts established or for additions to districts after June 28, 1938, the priority period for land base property is the five years immediately preceding the date of the order establishing them. This provision was extended to water base property on March 16, 1942. Thus grazing privileges were attached to the land rather than to the individual or the livestock.[12] By later amendment provision was made for the transfer of grazing privileges from one property to another.

The amount of available forage to be apportioned was at first estimated very largely upon the knowledge and advice of advisory boards. These estimates, although often too liberal, in a surprising number of cases were in accord with detailed range surveys and studies made later. They were altered or supported according to those findings.

Advisory board meetings are held at least annually with the grazing district officers, to recommend action on grazing applications. Applications of advisory board members are acted upon by the administrative officer (formerly grazier, now range manager). Base properties are classified according to provisions of the Federal Range Code.

Grazing permittees are afforded an opportunity to protest adverse action on their grazing applications at a protest meeting before the advisory board and the range manager. If the action on the protest is adverse they may file an appeal requesting a hearing before an examiner. They have right of appeal from the examiner's decision to the Director of the Bureau of Land Management and from the Director to the Secretary of the Interior.[13]

Temporary one-year grazing privileges only were authorized at first. Few reductions in livestock using the federal range were made during the first grazing season. The policy was to advise the operators of future reductions and allow an interval of time for them to make necessary adjustments. As information regarding the grazing capacity of the federal range and the character and amount of base property became substantiated and livestock operations became stabilized through the institution of proper range management practices, term permits for periods up to ten years were issued. These term permits were in conformity with the Taylor Grazing Act and the rules and regulations in the Federal Range Code.

Permits are subject to cancellation at any time because of: (1) noncompliance of the permittee with rules and regulations; (2) loss of control by the permittee of all or a part of the property on which a permit is based; (3) failure of the permittee to demonstrate that actual commensurate rating of the base property upon which it is based is equal to the estimated rating at the time of the issuance of the permit; (4) permittee's failure to make substantial use of the base property; or (5) diminution of forage because of withdrawal of classification of the land for a higher use.

Applications are taken each year during the term of the permit for the annual use that will be made of the federal range.[14] Free-use permits are issued to applicants for livestock kept for domestic purposes.

General rules of the range are prescribed in the Federal Range Code prohibiting the unauthorized (1) use of the federal range or stockdriveways; (2) construction or maintenance of range improvements; (3) cutting, burning or removal of vegetation, or the abuse of federal property in any way. Range-users must also comply with prescribed rules to bring about better range practices, including those pertaining to branding, trailing, salting, establishment of bed grounds, and the breed, grade, number, and time of turn-out for bulls. Provisions of the state law apply to the latter in the absence of expressed requirements by the bureau.[15]

Alleged violators of provisions of the act or the code are served with written notice. If the violation consists of unlawful grazing of livestock the notice orders the alleged violator to remove the livestock by a specified time. If the terms of the notice are not followed, legal action may be taken or the livestock may be impounded. Usually the alleged violator complies with the notice and makes an offer of settlement for the damages to the federal range or other property. If the offer of settlement is accepted it constitutes satisfaction of civil liability. Where grazing permittees are involved in cases of clearly established flagrant or repeated violations, disciplinary action may be taken by reducing, revoking, or denying the renewal of a license or permit. Before such action is taken, however, the violator is cited before an examiner of the Bureau of Land Management. As in other forms of appeal, the accused may appeal from the decision of the examiner to the Director and finally to the Secretary of the Interior. Violations by non-permittees are handled through direct action in the federal court.[16]

Grazing privileges within grazing districts have the distinction of being tied to dependent base property.[17] The transferring of these privileges under Bureau of Land Management administration is unique. Operators owning properties without privileges benefit by acquiring privileges through transfer from other properties. Livestock operations may be stabilized by transferring privileges from leased to owned lands or from relatively unproductive to highly productive lands.[18]

RANGE IMPROVEMENTS

When the Taylor Grazing Act was passed, and the situation is by no means corrected yet, vast areas of the federal range were inaccessible to livestock because of the lack of water. Considerable overgrazing occurred due to congestion of livestock around existing water holes. To alleviate these conditions, stockwater reservoirs, wells, and springs were and are being developed, fences and stock trails constructed, and salt grounds established.

"Last of the Herd," that famous early-day painting by C. M. Russell, eloquently portrays the hazards of winter grazing. Truck-trail construction made extensive areas of these winter ranges more accessible for range supervision and handling of supplementary feeds. To assist in healing old erosion scars, prevent new ones, and to increase and improve the forage supply, a program of reseeding was inaugurated on areas of denuded or reduced vegetative cover where conditions of soil and moisture were favorable.

The construction of the range improvements follows a District

Range Improvement Plan developed by the range manager in consultation with the advisory board and permittees. Work is done for the most part by contract.

Licensees and permittees now pay a grazing fee of ten cents and a range improvement fee of two cents per animal-unit month.[19] (An animal-unit month is the grazing equivalent per month of one cow or horse, or five sheep or goats.) Exceptions are made in some instances where higher fees are charged on lands administered by agreement.

The range improvement fees are used to construct and maintain the various types of developments required to rehabilitate the federal range and promote its proper use by livestock. These range improvement fees have been augmented to a very considerable extent by contributions from the licensees and permittees in the form of money, materials, and labor. This co-operative policy has proved beneficial for at least three reasons: (1) with a financial investment in the improvement project, the range-user takes a more active interest and makes more careful use of the improvements; (2) financial participation by range-users further assures the desirability of the project; and (3) with added funds the improvement program may be carried forth more rapidly. Title to the co-operative improvements goes to the United States Government. Should the co-operator's use of the project be taken over by another range-user, the co-operator may be reimbursed by the new user to the extent of his invested share in the project. Should the project be abandoned, the salvaged materials revert to the parties of interest in proportion to their invested shares.

Another substantial share of range rehabilitation has resulted from range improvement projects constructed entirely by the licensees and permittees under Section 4 of the act. Such permits are not granted if the project does not further the bureau's plans for range rehabilitation or range management. Title to such range improvements goes to the permittee.

Fire Control

To cope with the menace of fire, the range manager each year prepares a comprehensive district fire plan. The plan lays out the locations and availability of personnel and equipment and the general system of operation. The core of the plan is a system of per diem guards, most of whom are stockmen-users of the range. Fire-fighting tools are stored in strategically located caches and the per diem guard is authorized to recruit and hire fire fighters. In the event of large fires, district personnel supervise, calling on the co-operative services of other agencies, private individuals, and equipment contractors.

For those grazing districts embracing exceedingly high fire-hazard areas, such as the cheat grass ranges of South Idaho, the per diem guard system is augmented by a full-time fire-fighting organization maintained during the fire season. This organization generally includes a district fire supervisor with an emergency fire crew of temporary wage employees. A continuously manned short-wave radio system is the principal means of communication. Scouting and patrolling of fires is done largely by contracted plane service.

MULTIPLE USE OF PUBLIC LANDS

Rarely, if ever, is any part of the public lands within grazing districts used solely for grazing by livestock. These lands, in addition to supplying forage for domestic livestock, graze big game animals, furnish nesting places and general habitat for upland game birds and ducks, and provide fishing, hunting and other forms of recreation. The growing of timber and watershed protection are other important uses. The range manager attempts to balance uses to secure the most desirable combination. Generally, multiple uses do not conflict appreciably; however, where uses are not compatible, the most beneficial use or uses, e.g., watershed protection, are determined and the land managed accordingly.[20]

These many uses of public lands are accompanied with a diversity of associated programs, including soil and moisture conservation, land classification, and forestry, each a highly specialized field of its own. Local administrative responsibility for these activities within grazing districts is delegated to the district range manager. In reality he is an area manager. He is the official agent of the federal government for all activities associated with the public lands within the grazing district and on surrounding scattered public lands under his jurisdiction.

ASSOCIATED PROGRAMS OF GRAZING DISTRICTS

The program of soil and moisture conservation in grazing districts and other bureau-administered lands in the United States is a continuing activity authorized by the National Soil Conservation Act of 1935 (49 Stat. 163). Until 1940, all soil conservation activities under this act, regardless of landownership, were administered by the Soil Conservation Service of the Department of Agriculture. On April 11, 1940, the President's Reorganization Plan No. 4 provided that all such activities pertaining to public domain lands under the jurisdiction of the Department of the Interior should be transferred to that department. Where such activities are essential to rehabilitation of the public lands, soil and moisture conservation work may also be carried on by the bureau on private lands with the consent of the owners.

Conservation planning and operations of the Soil and Moisture Conservation program are organized on the basis of project areas. These are areas on which rehabilitation and conservation treatment is necessary for the reduction and prevention of critical erosion and the wastage of water resources. Management and operational plans for each area must be prepared and approved before project work may be initiated.

Major techniques used in the soil and moisture program to control erosion consist of range revegetation; construction of diversion and silt-detention dams; developing flood irrigation of otherwise dry lands; development of stock-watering places providing for better livestock distribution; and the construction of fences also for better livestock distribution and to protect newly reseeded areas.[21]

Effective co-operation from the range-users is also an important aspect of the soil and moisture program, since these conservation practices are as much in the interest of the user as of the government. This interest is evidenced by extensive financial contributions by the range-users.

Public lands within grazing districts which have more valuable uses than for grazing may be opened for disposition, settlement, or occupation. First, however, the lands must be examined and classified according to their proper use. If so classified, the lands may then be opened for agricultural homestead entries, exchanges by state or private individuals, sale of isolated tracts under 1,520 acres or unisolated rough or mountainous tracts under 760 acres, lease or sale of tracts not exceeding 5 acres for special uses, permits for rights of way and oil and gas leases, etc.[22]

Examination and classification may be done by either the area-classification method or the case method. By the area-classification method large blocks of land are examined and classified in one operation. Detailed physical and economic information is assembled to determine the suitability of these public lands for their various uses. From this survey detailed plans are formed and an action program inaugurated. The public land to be disposed of to private individuals is opened for appropriate land entry. Lands that should be more logically included under state administration or that of another federal agency are so transferred. When an individual applies for a land entry in an area not covered by the area-classification method, an examination and classification report is made for that individual tract.

Forestry is a significant part of the resource management program. Tree growth in generally sparsely timbered areas is highly valued, especially as a source of forest products for local use, for watershed protection, as scenery, and as an adjunct to recreation. Some of the grazing districts possess sizable stands of merchantable timber. Responsibility for sustained-yield management of the timber stands rests with range managers.

Prior to 1947, except for an emergency wartime act, there was no statutory authority for the sale of green timber on unreserved, vacant, public lands. Free-use permits were allowed under the act of June 3, 1878, and various other free-use laws for house logs, poles, posts or fire wood for domestic use. The Materials Act of July 31, 1947 (61 Stat. 681; 43 USC 1185 to 1187), authorized the sale of timber or other forest products, as well as other materials, from these lands.

Timber to be sold is cruised, marked, and removed in accordance with approved silvicultural practices for sustained-yield and sold at not less than the appraised value. When the appraised value of the timber or other material to be sold is $1,000 or less, it may be sold without competitive bidding. Sales involving more than an appraised value or $1,000 may be made only to the highest qualified bidder at public auction or under sealed bid.[23]

Free-use permits for poles, posts, and firewood are still authorized for domestic use. Green trees of sawtimber size may be disposed of under free-use permits only when such disposal is in the interest of the government. Free-use permits may be issued to federal or state agencies, including municipalities, without limitation as to number of permits or value, provided such materials will be used for public projects.

CO-ORDINATION WITH OTHER FEDERAL, STATE, AND LOCAL AGENCIES

Administration of Bureau of Land Management grazing districts by virtue of the multiplicity of uses of the public lands has a close relationship to numerous other federal, state, and local programs. Many grazing districts adjoin National Forests, Indian Reservations, Military Reservations, and Land Utilization Projects. Users of the Bureau of Land Management grazing districts frequently also have grazing privileges on one or more of these administratively different areas as well as on intermingled state and private lands. Problems of interagency co-ordination arise as to when the livestock may be allowed on and off these various areas so as to eliminate duplication of time of grazing use by the same animals or to fill gaps in the grazing season. Trailing schedules and routes of trailing must be considered with livestock crossing the lands of one agency to that of another.

Grazing district plans for soil and moisture rehabilitation and conservation must be co-ordinated with those of other land management and resource development agencies operating in the areas affected. This need for co-ordination is especially significant, since the problem of rehabilitation and conservation is most effectively attacked on a watershed basis. These watersheds frequently contain many different types of administrative areas upon any one of which may depend the success of the project. Furthermore, these plans must be co-ordinated with other land and water resource development plans, taking into consideration off-site or down-stream benefits.

Within many grazing districts state soil conservation districts have been formed. Co-operative agreements between the Bureau of Land Management and many of these districts have brought joint action on common problems.

The work of the Bureau of Land Management and the Bureau of Reclamation is closely related in many aspects. The watershed significance of public lands, and particularly the siltation problem as related to reclamation development, is a common one. In some areas crop land now serving as base property for grazing privileges on the federal range has been or may be flooded by reclamation storage reservoirs. When this is the case it is necessary to determine what adjustments should be made. When public domain lands are withdrawn for reclamation purposes the Bureau of Land Management may, with agreement of the Bureau of Reclamation, continue administration of the grazing resources until the lands are required for the development of the reclamation program.

Wildlife-management plans within grazing districts are concerned chiefly with the amount of suitable forage to be reserved for game animals during proper seasons of year in the right habitat. Since these game animals roam at will, they in a sense come under the administrative jurisdiction of many persons. Various federal and state land-management agencies and private individuals supply them with forage which must be properly managed; on the other hand, the states regulate harvesting of the animals. These two interests must be co-ordinated. Proper balance between the uses of wildlife and domestic livestock and other uses must also be solved.

Protection of forage and timber resources from fire is another program closely related to those of other agencies. Co-operative agreements are made with other federal and state agencies, counties, municipalities, and private concerns having fire organizations operating on adjacent lands. These agreements usually provide for the mutual use of equipment and personnel.

The impact of grazing district administration on the local and national economy is best shown by a summary of grazing district accomplishments.

SUMMARY OF ACCOMPLISHMENTS

Within grazing districts, approximately 20,000 livestock operators graze annually approximately 8,500,000 head of livestock securing 14,500,000 animal-unit months of forage from grazing district lands.[24] This forage is now being obtained without the "cut-throat" competition of pre-Taylor Act days. Responsibility for this favorable change is due to adjustments in the amount of use and the establishment of individual and group allotments for which grazing periods and numbers and class of livestock have been specified. These improved range management practices have spurred the remarkable recovery of weakened and depleted forage resources. Long-term permits have been issued to over 50 per cent of the range-users.

A more dependable forage supply on public lands together with a required adequate base of operations has assisted greatly in creating stability of livestock operations dependent upon the federal range.

Range Improvement and Soil and Moisture Conservation programs have been particularly successful in developing the public lands so that livestock are now making more efficient and conservative use of them; scars of past abuses have been and are being healed and new ones prevented. These programs have also been successful in providing additional forage by opening grazing areas which heretofore were inaccessible to livestock, and by increasing the quantity and quality of forage plants by water spreading, reseeding, etc. As a result, the necessity for a severe reduction in grazing has been eliminated or materially lessened. In some local areas an increase in livestock has been possible. Following is a tabulation of the principal type of development projects the Bureau of Land Management placed on the federal range *[between 1935 and 1951]*:

TABLE 15

Principal Range Rehabilitation and Improvement Projects
1935 through 1951

(Fiscal Years)

Livestock watering places	9,273 each
Dams, soil and moisture conservation	1,088 each
Fencing	10,214 miles
Reseeding	1,125,872 acres
Brush and weed control	951,819 acres
Pest control (rodent & insect)	14,773,846 acres
Tree planting	201,902 each
Corrals	521 each
Water spreaders, canals, and ditches	781,786 lin. feet
Truck trails	12,122 miles

Grazing district lands also supply approximately 1,172,000 animal-unit months of forage which has been reserved by the Bureau of Land Management for the exclusive use of an estimated 723,700 big game animals, including antelope, deer, elk, moose, and mountain sheep.[25] In addition, these lands serve as the habitat for large numbers of upland game birds and water fowl. Development of watering places on the federal range has provided for better distribution of big game animals and nesting places for birds. The many reservoirs also serve as resting places for migrating water fowl.

Fire control within grazing districts has made a creditable showing in reducing the number of fires reported annually by an estimated 30 per cent and the number of acres burned over by approximately 60 per cent since 1941. A major accomplishment is the reduction in the number of large fires and also the number of man-caused fires. Much forage, timber, and soil are represented in this saving.

There are still *[1953]* approximately 225,000 acres burned over annually, representing a loss of resources the nation can ill afford. The improving vegetative cover resulting from management and improvement programs creates an increasingly serious fire hazard. A more intensive pre-suppression program, more and better equipment, and increased manpower are required to cope with this problem and to reduce the acreage burned over annually. Annual appropriations to cover costs of fire control have averaged approximately two mills per acre,

During fiscal years 1942–1951, nearly 5,000,000 acres of vacant, unreserved public lands were included in over 13,000 applications for entry under the Taylor Grazing Act. Of these lands, over 65 per cent were classified as being suitable for disposition. Applications for these lands were primarily for homestead, public sale, exchange, and desert land entries. In addition to the above classification of lands by the case method, over 7,900,000 acres in the Missouri River Basin have been classified by the area-classification method. Of these areas, approximately 4.5 per cent were classified as suitable for disposition. The lands so disposed of have generally been placed to a higher use and in most instances the land pattern of the public lands has been improved, providing for better administration.[26]

The advisory board system of the Bureau of Land Management deserves real credit for these accomplishments within grazing districts. The combined membership of these boards made up a vast wealth of knowledge of the range, much of which could not have been obtained elsewhere regardless of time or money.[27]

When the regulations were being formed, their application was reviewed by the board members and changes suggested to make them more workable. With benefit of such advice the administrators were better able to weigh the pros and cons of different administrative actions and select those which would obtain the desired results with least disturbance to the program. With such advice from the National Advisory Council on matters of a national scope, from the various state advisory boards on matters of statewide concern, and on districtwide matters from the district advisory boards, better policies, regulations and administrative decisions undoubtedly resulted.

The wide variability in the character of the public ranges requires detailed knowledge of innumerable localized areas. Advisory boards with their widespread representation were able to supply this in accurate detail. Thus they were able to make wise recommendations on best locations of proposed range improvement and soil and moisture projects at considerable time and financial savings to the government.

They supplied substantially accurate estimates of the federal range's carrying capacity, which were utilized until technical range surveys could be made. They advised who had made grazing use of the public lands, when, and to what extent. This information, otherwise un-available, was essential in determining the qualifications of base prop-erties and the equitable distributions of grazing privileges.

Through their functions as Advisory Board members, the stock-men became better informed of the purposes and administration of the program. Because of this, criticism and misunderstandings due to misinformation were largely eliminated.

Advisory Board members have become familiar with the operation of this segment of government and are outstanding examples of citizen participation in government—a great source of our nation's strength.

NOTES

1   *Report of the Director of the Bureau of Land Management, Statistical Appendix* (United States Department of the Interior, 1951), Tables 4, 10, pp. 6, 12.
2   Marion Clawson, *Uncle Sam's Acres* (New York, 1951), 111–117.
3   *Taylor Grazing Act Statement of the President on Approval of the Act,* 1934, preface.
4   J. A. Krug and Marion Clawson, *The Federal Range Code for Grazing Districts, Revised to October 1, 1949* (U.S. Dept. of Interior, Bureau of Land Management, 1949), 8, 9.
5   Reference for regulations regarding grazing leases: *Title 43, Code of Federal Regulations,* 1949, part 160, pp. 240–245.
6   J. A. Krug and Marion Clawson, *The Taylor Grazing Act of June 28, 1934, with Amendments to October 1, 1949* (U.S. Dept. of Interior, Bureau of Land Management, 1949), section 10, p. 7.
7   *Title 43, Code of Federal Regulations,* 1949, sec. 297.11–18, pp. 660–662.
8   Krug and Clawson, *The Taylor Grazing Act, 1949,* sec. 17, p. 10.
9   *Title 43, Code of Federal Regulations,* 1940, sec. 502.1, pp. 19–22.
10 Krug and Clawson, *The Federal Range Code,* sec. 161.12 (a)–(i), pp. 27–31.
11 *Ibid.,* sec. 161.12 (J)–(L), p. 31.
12 *The Federal Range Code, Approved; August 31, 1938, With Amend-ments Approved, September 18, 1939, December 5, 1940, February 26, 1941* (U.S. Dept. of Interior, Grazing Service, 1941), sec. 2(9) (L), pp. 2–4.
13 Krug and Clawson, *The Federal Range Code, 1949,* sec. 161.9, pp. 16–22.
14 *Ibid.,* sec. 161.6(c), pp. 8–10.
15 *Ibid.,* sec. 161.10, pp. 23, 24.
16 *Ibid.,* sec. 161.11, pp. 24–27.
17 *Ibid.,* sec. 161.4, p. 6.
18 *Ibid.,* sec. 161.7, pp. 12, 13.

19   *Ibid.*, sec. 161.8, pp. 13–15.
20   Clawson, *Uncle Sam's Acres*, 4, 230.
21   Pamphlet: *Soil and Moisture Operations* (U.S. Dept. of Interior, Bureau of Land Management).
22   Krug and Clawson, *The Taylor Grazing Act, 1949*, sections 7, 8, 15, pp. 4–6, and 9.
23   *Title 43, Code of Federal Regulations, 1949*, part 259, as revised in Circular 1758 and published in Federal Register, vol. 15, no. 122, of June 24, 1950.
24   *Report of the Director of the Bureau of Land Management*, 1951, Tables 75, 76, pp. 96, 97.
25   *Ibid.*, Tables 77A, 77B, p. 98.
26   *Ibid.*, Tables 57, 58, pp. 74, 75, and corresponding tables from this same report for the years 1942–1950.
27   Clawson, *Uncle Sam's Acres*, 248, 249, and 368–376.

V

Appendix

Original Land Entries
1800–1934

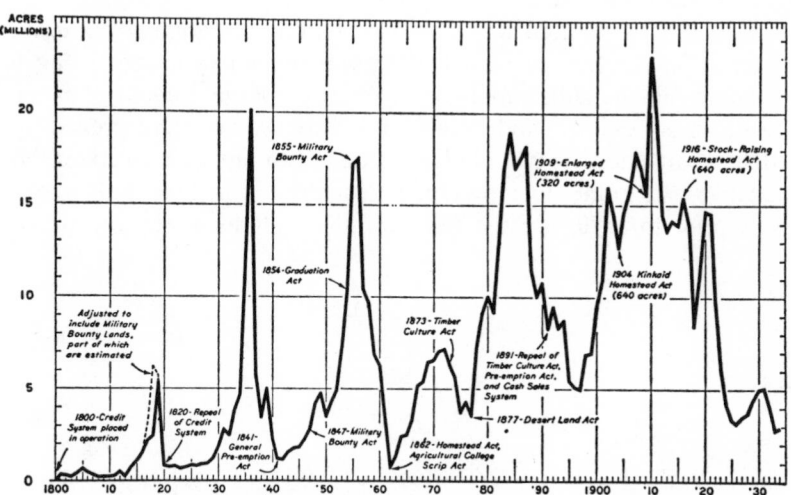

Prepared by United States Department of Agriculture, Bureau of Agricultural Economics.

From the United States National Resources Board, Land Planning Committee, Report on Land Planning, Part 7: Certain Aspects of Land Problems and Government Land Policies, *Washington, 1935, page 61.*

In the preparation of this chart, all of the original land entries under the various laws were compiled, insofar as this was possible. This chart includes the following types of cash entries: Private cash entries, public auction sales, pre-emption entries, Indian land sales, timber and stone entries under the act of 1877, mineral land entries (small), coal land entries (small), abandoned military reservations, and miscellaneous sales. It also includes entries made with military warrants and various kinds of scrip. Original entries under the Homestead, Timber Culture, and Desert Land acts are included.

It was not possible to secure data concerning all the land entered with scrip and military warrants, the amount not included in the chart being less than 3,000,000 acres, the absence of which does not materially affect the picture here presented.

It should be pointed out that this chart is for original entries. A chart of final entries or one showing the amount of entries going to patent would be substantially different, as a large amount of homestead, timber culture, and desert land entries never were proved up.

The chart does not include lands granted to railroads or states, nor certain small grants to individuals. Nor does it include Indian land sales prior to 1879, nor the sale of Indian allotments at any time.

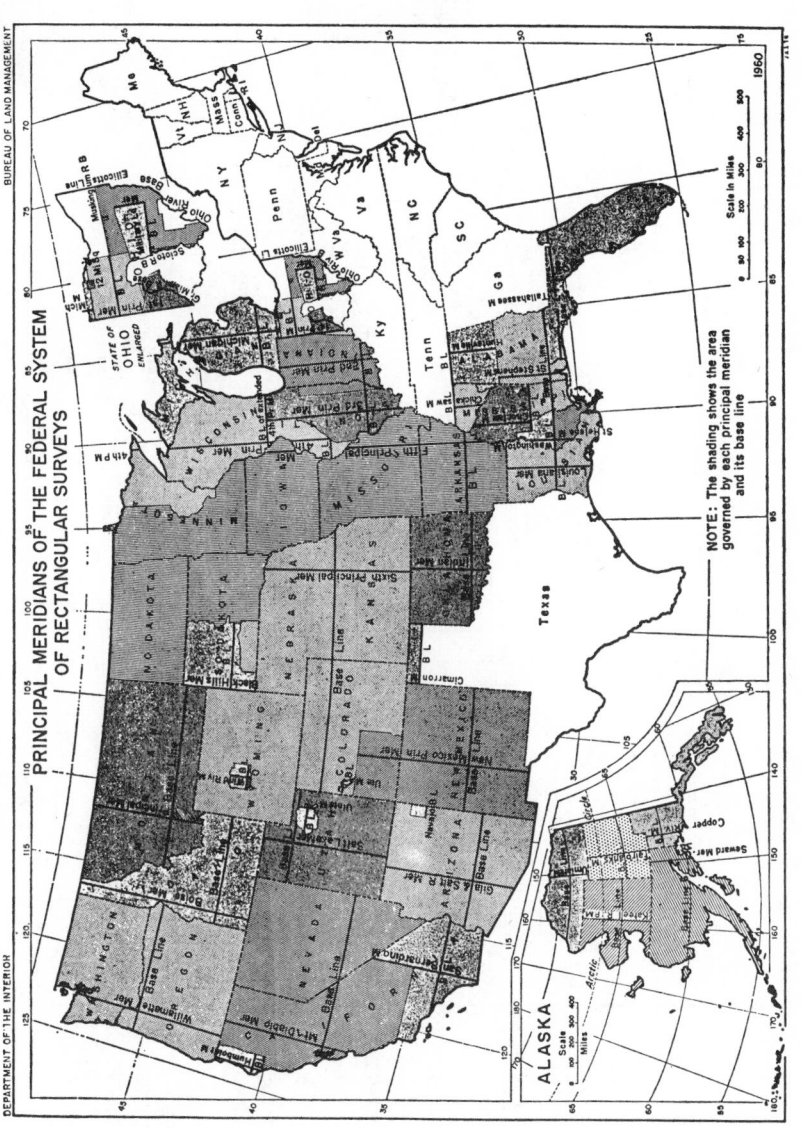

PRINCIPAL MERIDIANS OF THE FEDERAL SYSTEM OF RECTANGULAR SURVEYS

NOTE: The shading shows the area governed by each principal meridian and its base line

DEPARTMENT OF THE INTERIOR

BUREAU OF LAND MANAGEMENT

1960

483

HIGHLIGHTS IN THE HISTORY OF THE PUBLIC DOMAIN

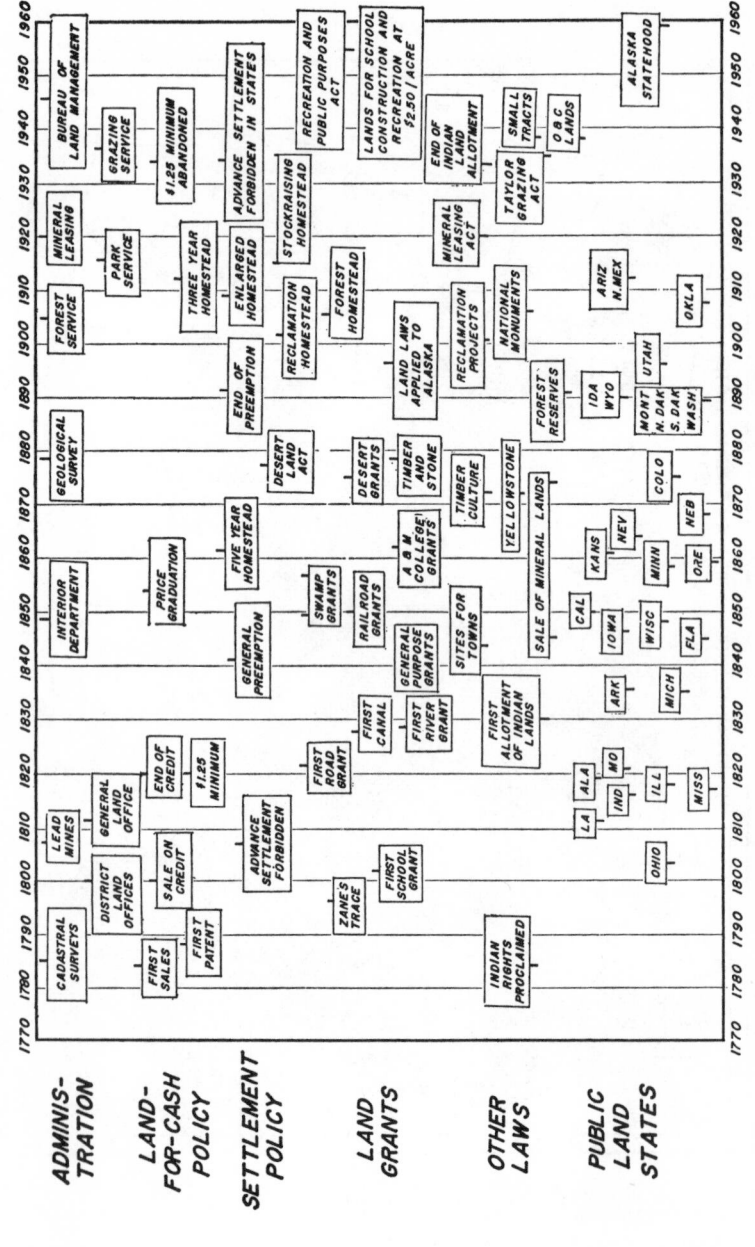

Source: Bureau of Land Management, Department of the Interior

484

Source Materials for the History of the Law of the Public Lands

THOMAS LeDUC

As an expression of public policy and as a definition of enforceable private rights, the law relating to the public lands has always been extensive, inconsistent, and filled with uncertainties. The documentary materials for the study of the history of the law of the public lands are correspondingly varied, voluminous, and vexing. They must be used with caution and perseverance.

It is estimated that several thousand federal statutes relate to the public lands. State and territorial legislatures also created or regulated property rights in and on the public lands. Additional primary material is found in treaties with Indian tribes and with foreign nations, as well as in Presidential orders and proclamations.

Mainly because of bad draftsmanship, many of these assertions of law have required endless interpretation. From an early date the General Land Office served not only as an operating office, but as a quasi-judicial body, issuing detailed orders and instructions, and as a quasi-judicial tribunal that in effect defined the meaning of the statutes as they applied to specific sets of facts. The decisions of the Land Office constitute an important body of material; until 1881 they were not published by the government but were to some extent reported by commercial services. A similar type of material will be found in the printed opinions of the Attorney General of the United States and of the attorneys general of the states.

The ambiguities of treaty, statute, and executive order generated not only administrative perplexity but endless litigation. It is perhaps not too much to say that the real meaning of the law is to be found in the judicial constructions of statute which are embodied in the decisions of the courts, federal, territorial, and state. Early precedents were not always reported, but there survives a vast body of published decisions. Anyone who explores the voluminous materials will be struck with the historical truth that only a partial understanding of the public land system can be gained from reading the few statutes that have become familiar as landmarks.

Public Land Records
of the Federal Government

ROBERT W. HARRISON

Reprinted by permission from the Mississippi Valley Historical Review, *Volume 41* (*1954*), *pages 277–288.*

ALL advanced societies keep public records, and, in most of the world, the records of landownership are among their most important documents. Special institutions are often created to assist in the preservation of land titles. In the United States, for example, one of the chief functions of the county government is to preserve the record of landed property transfer.[1] The duties of the county clerk as custodian of the local land records are generally well understood. The role of the state governments and of the federal government in land affairs is not so widely appreciated, although the land records held by the states and the United States are essential links in the titles to land throughout the greater part of the nation. Whether maintained by the local, the state, or the federal branch of government, these records are not only fundamental as title records but their value for historical purposes has long been recognized.

Of this group, however, the public land records of the federal government have received far less use by historians than their content warrants. Their volume is tremendous and partly for this reason only the more stout-hearted researchers have made extensive use of them. But the obstacles to research are not so formidable as may be thought, and the records contain significant information, not only on land development programs in the United States, but also on frontier and institutional history. They furnish information to those interested in the course of settlement, internal improvements, railroads and other forms of transportation history, agriculture and mining, and some phases of the relations between the federal and the state and local governments. This survey of the nature and uses of these records is intended as a preliminary guide, which may serve to stimulate further use of them for research purposes.

In the twenty-nine "public land states"[2] and Alaska, land titles are based upon records preserved in federal depositories. Those records which are in active use are available in the Bureau of Land Management, Department of the Interior; and the inactive records may be consulted by qualified students at the National Archives.[3]

Some idea of the magnitude of these two collections can be gained from a recent estimate of their holdings. There are 6,000 volumes of cadastral survey notes and 100,000 survey plats, covering an area of about 1,300,000,000 acres. In its vast land-disposal program, the United States has issued over 6,500,000 patents to settlers on federal land and to others. Record copies of these patents are kept in 11,550 volumes. Over 4,000 tract books are maintained, showing 25,000,000 entries relating to the status of all public lands, those which have been patented (deeded to individuals) as well as those still owned by the government. In summary, these records contain the original title evidence to approximately 1,000,000,000 acres of public domain now in private hands, as well as title and status evidence on 400,000,000 acres of land remaining in the public domain. Also covered are 50,000,000 acres of patented land on which the United States retains the mineral rights.

It has long been the policy of the United States to encourage private acquisition and development of the public domain. This policy continues, and each year substantial acreages of the public domain pass into private hands for agriculture and other surface uses, or for mineral development. In addition to outright disposal of public land, large areas of the public domain are leased to surface-users, or for oil and gas and other mineral resources. Land assigned to various public programs is held by the United States and managed in the public interest. Thus the federal land records are not dead archives, but are part of a public land system which is actively operating as an important part of our national economy and which is constantly growing. Yet [in 1954] the title to over 50 per cent of the land area of the eleven western states is still held by the federal government. About 100,000,-000 acres of public land remain to be surveyed in the western United States. Of the 365,000,000 acres in Alaska, less than 1 per cent has been surveyed. At each stage in the development of these lands, public records will accumulate, taking their place in a system which was begun more than one hundred and fifty years ago.

The several classes of public land records may be treated under the following heads: (1) survey plats and field notes, (2) tract books, (3) register's returns, (4) case files (land-entry papers), and (5) patent records. Tables 16 and 17 show in summary form the nature of these records (not including the survey plats) and the types of information they contain.[4] In many instances individual items which the researcher may wish to use appear in several distinct classes of records. As the usability of the several classes varies greatly, it is necessary for efficient use of the land archives to have an over-all knowledge of the physical nature of the several classes of records and of the information each class contains.

The whole federal system of making survey plats, the first class of these records, dates back to May 20, 1785, when Congress approved the system of rectangular surveys for location and measurement of the public domain.[5] In this measure, it was decided that the unit of land measure would be a township 6 miles square, containing 36 sections of 1 square mile each. The cadastral survey plats and the survey notes contain general descriptions of the physical characteristics of the land. In the management of the public domain, the first step includes the surveying and preparation of such plats and notes in usable form. It is the responsibility of the cadastral engineers to establish suitable markers indicating corners of townships and sections. This work is now conducted by the Division of Cadastral Engineering of the Bureau of Land Management, and great care is given to obtaining accurate surveys. Until 1910, surveys of the public domain were done under contract. This, together with the lack of modern instruments and techniques, sometimes resulted in poorly done work, and much resurveying has been required.

The descriptions of the physical features of the land surface found in the public land survey notes and plats have many uses.[6] During the peak years of homesteading, these records were frequently copied (and sometimes published) as the best guide available to the character of land open for settlement. There is, naturally, a great range in the detail and quality of the various series of plats and field notes. Students of land settlement and population movement have found some of the field plats of interest because they show houses, towns, and other cultural features in relation to vegetation. The federal surveys of

TABLE 16

Nature of the Principal Public Land Records

	Tract books	Patents	Case records	Register's returns
Standardization of final documents	Good	Good	Good	Good
Writing	Script	Part script	Script	Script
Land descriptions	Abbreviated	Not abbreviated	Abbreviated	Abbreviated
Arrangement of data:				
Geographical arrangement	By township	Prior to 1908: by land district with exceptions. After 1908, and certain other series: none	Prior to 1908: by land district with exceptions. After 1908, and certain other series: none	To 1908: by land districts. After 1908: detailed record ceased
Time arrangement	None	Prior to 1908: separate date series for each type in each land district. After 1908, and certain other series: by date	Prior to 1908: separate date series for each type in each land district. After 1908: by date for patented entries and separate date series by land district for others	Separate date series for each type in each land district
Entry arrangement	None	Prior to 1908: complete segregation. After 1908: none	Prior to 1908: complete segregation. After 1908: none	Complete segregation
Abbreviations needing interpretation	Extensive	None	Minor	Minor
Variety of records	Small	Moderate	Moderate	None
Bulk of individual case record	None	None	In part: large	None
Number of records	4,000 volumes covering 65,000 townships	6,500,000 patents	8,000,000 case records	At least 10,000 returns

lands formerly held by the French and Spanish are especially interesting because they show the patterns of settlement before the transfer was made. These surveys offer unique opportunities to study settlement patterns in general in relation to cultural and physiographic factors. Likewise, students of stream patterns and stream movements, and other topographic features, will find the public land survey an invaluable source.

Survey plats and field notes of the public land survey are kept in the Bureau of Land Management of the Department of the Interior. Constantly in demand, these materials have been made easily available for public use by the development of a convenient filing system.

TABLE 17

Information Available from Principal Public Land Records

	Tract books	Patents	Case records	Register's returns
Type of entry	X	Incomplete	X	X
Legal description	X	X	X	X
Acreage	X	X	X	X
Name of entryman	X	X	X	X
Date of application	X	Not shown	X	Not in same document
Date of final certificate	X	Not shown	X	Not in same document
Date of patent	Incomplete	X	X	Not shown
Date of settlement	Incomplete	Not shown	X	Not shown
Patent reservations	Incomplete	X	X	Not shown
Commutations	X	Not shown	X	Not in same document
Cancellations	X	Not shown	X	Not in same document
Surveys *a*	X	Not shown	Not shown	Not shown
Offerings	X	Not shown	Not shown	Not shown
Withdrawals	X	Not shown	Not shown	Not shown
Price of lands	Incomplete	Not shown	X	X
Private land claims *b*	Incomplete	Incomplete	Incomplete	Not shown
Patented mineral entries	Incomplete	X	X	Not shown
Residence of entryman	Not shown	Incomplete	X	X

X Available or complete.
a Available from separate records.
b Various records available but may not be complete.

The surveying and careful marking of public land is but the first step in the process of carrying out the land laws of the United States. Congress has found many uses for the public land, and vast areas have been made available for private use. It is in the course of this disposal of the public land that a second class of land records, the tract books, have been employed. The conditions under which citizens have been, and are, permitted to acquire public land are numerous. The methods of disposal are set forth in detail in acts of the Congress and regulations of administrative agencies. Public land is also used by many government agencies and has been frequently granted to the states for varied purposes. The use of public land in the development of school systems is well known. Canal companies, wagon roads, and railroads have received large grants of public lands. The internal improvement program, so conspicuous a part of nine-teenth-century America, rested to a large degree upon the liberal land policy developed by the Congress, particularly so after 1850 when un-der the Swamp Land Acts vast acreages were granted to the states. Later the Homestead Act provided "free" land to citizens who would put it under cultivation.

It is thus clear that the land was, and is, removed from the public domain for a variety of purposes, and under many specific acts and regulations. Some method of keeping up with the status of each sec-tion of the public domain was needed. To meet this requirement, tract books were established and have been kept up to date, providing an invaluable record of the initial use of the public domain as au-thorized by the acts of Congress and the regulations of the executive.

The tract books are ledgers arranged by townships, in which space (usually 16 lines) is provided for recording the decisions and actions affecting each section. The type of information furnished by them is shown in Table 17. These records are kept in the Bureau of Land Man-agement, but each land office also keeps the local office tract books covering the area under its jurisdiction.[7] With the closing of the land offices in those areas where the public domain was exhausted, the local office tract books were often given to the states. Some of these records were kept by agencies of the state governments, but there was no systematic attempt to preserve them. In any event, the complete settlement record is available in the full set of tract books kept in Washington. Tract books or their equivalent for Alaska are also avail-able.

No attempt has been made to put in map, or other summary form, the great quantity of data found in the tract books, which cover about two-thirds of the United States. An atlas has been prepared showing the withdrawals of lands in Alaska for public use. The value of the tract books and related land records as source material for economic and social studies cannot be overemphasized, and is the topic of a separate report now [1954] in preparation.

Another class of land records is known as "register's returns." Prior to 1908, these contained a great deal of information, as shown in Table 17. After that date, the information has limited value except as a reference to other records. Register's returns are frequently valuable in locating case records where data as to the exact geographic location is lacking but where the appropriate date of the original action is known.

In the several land offices, it has been customary since 1908 to keep a daily record or serial register of the applications received, and a summary of the actions taken on each application. These registers thus contain a synopsis of the actions taken on each case, up to and including the issuance of the lease, permit, final certificate, or patent. If the application is withdrawn or rejected, this is also shown.

In processing the applications for use of public land and related resources, numerous papers accumulate relating to each individual case. These papers form a fourth major class of public land records, and are known as case files, or, to use a more limited term, land-entry papers. In many instances, case files are very simple, containing, for example, an application to purchase specified land and a receipt for payment. There are, however, case files which contain a great list of documents accumulated over many years. It is difficult to generalize on the character of the case files. In order to facilitate the handling of case records, it has long been the practice to attach a summary sheet to each case file, showing every action that has taken place in connection with the processing of the case. When patents are issued, the volume and page number of the official copy of the patent are noted on the summary sheet. A card index is maintained to assist in locating case records when only the name of the applicant is known. This index does not cover case records closed before July 1, 1908.

The patent file represents the end product of much of the public land program. Titles throughout the public land states are derived from this huge collection of deeds. Before 1908, copies of patents were filed in many separate series, corresponding to the land-entry papers: there were patent series records for each class of warrant and scrip entry, for each district land office, and for each class of entry made at every land office. This system made it difficult to locate individual patents when duplicates had to be issued or corrections made. After July 1, 1908, all patents, regardless of type or class, were placed in one numerical series; and an index by name of patentee is maintained covering this series.

While there is no general or over-all index to land entrymen prior to 1908, several partial indexes are available. These cover the following series:

(1) warrants under the act of 1788 (incomplete), (2) Virginia military warrants, (3) private land claims, (4) coal cash entries, and (5) mineral entries. There are also name indexes for those land entries that are arranged by district land office in the States of Alabama, Arizona, Florida, Louisiana, Nevada, Utah, and the Territory of Alaska; and among the records of the Veterans' Administration in the National Archives, there is an alphabetical index to applications for military-bounty-land warrants issued under the acts of 1847, 1850, 1852, and 1855.[8]

Users of the public land records soon learn to appreciate the close relationship between the tract book, the case file (land-entry papers), and the patent record. Briefly stated, the tract books serve as an index to the case files, which in turn are an index to the record copies of patents. For the patent records prior to 1908, it is essential to consult the case file in order to locate the volume and page number of the official copy of the patent. The cross references which exist between the principal land records make it possible to trace land cases successfully when only a few facts are known. When the legal description (township, range, etc.) of the land is known, the desired case file and patent can usually be found by reference to the tract books maintained in the Bureau of Land Management. If the approximate date of entry is known and the name of the land office through which it was made, it is often possible to use the register's monthly abstract (kept in the National Archives) to locate the desired information.

In addition to these major classes of land records, a great quantity of supplemental records may also be found in the Bureau of Land Management and in the National Archives. It would be impossible in this brief report to list the many types of records which have been accumulated in carrying out the public land program of the United States. Archivists have listed the following as an illustration of the great variety of data available in this field, now on file in the National Archives:

. . . case files on contests arising over mineral lands and over land granted to railroads; case files on town sites, military reservations, canal and reservoir grants, surveys, and investigations by special agents of the General Land Office; correspondence, including all extant letters sent, 1796–1939; and all extant letters received, 1796–1908; records of "private land claims" boards and town-site boards forwarded to the General Land Office on the completion of their work; monthly abstracts of entries submitted by Registers and Receivers; financial and accounting records; map files; including canal and reservoir maps, railroad right-of-way maps and miscellaneous maps of the Division of Surveys; railroad and wagon road land grants "selection" lists and "adjustment" lists; records of the Superintendent of Logging on Chippewa ceded lands in Minnesota, 1898–1936; records of officers in charge of the leasing of lead and copper lands in Illinois, Wisconsin and Michigan, about 1824–47; local office records of closed district land offices from some states, consisting chiefly of tract books and plats, correspondence of the former Surveyor-General of the Northwest, 1796–1856, and many other small special files.[9]

Each series of records listed here relates to an important phase of the public land program as it has evolved in the United States. Preliminary studies will be required in each field to determine the value of the specific records as source material for studies in public land policy and administration.

A final group of special records should be mentioned: those which relate to the specific requirements for entry upon the public domain. A formidable series of circulars was published by the General Land Office. In these, and in the acts of Congress and reports of the related congressional committees, are found the details of the American public land problem. The decisions made by officers of the Department of the Interior are also worthy of careful study, because they cover the many complex situations which arise in administering the public land laws of the United States. In discussion of land records, these administrative records are frequently neglected. Many misconceptions concerning specific land laws and their administration would be corrected by a careful analysis of the administrative regulations set forth in the official releases mentioned above.

Like most of the source materials which economic and social historians must use, the public land records were designed for specific purposes with little, if any, thought to their value as economic and sociological data. In order to make the most efficient use of the land records, considerable study must be given each specific research problem. A broad research project in public records, even when a sampling approach is used, is so laborious and costly a task that special effort should be made to predetermine the best method of collecting and summarizing the data. There are often several ways in which particular information may be obtained from these records. Decision on the best procedure will often involve many detailed considerations. Each type of land record has certain advantages when an individual task is being considered. In deciding on the best procedures, it will be helpful to prepare an outline similar to the following, which uses public land disposals as an illustration of the varied character and usefulness of the records.

1. Disposals, by type of entry (homesteads, desert land, etc.) prior to 1908.[10]
   a. All disposals during a specified period in specified land districts.
   b. All disposals of a specified type in a specified period.
   Source: Register's schedules
   Data available: Type of entry, date, name of entryman, residence of entryman, description of land, acreage, price of land.
2. Disposals, by geographical subdivisions, full for all dates.
   Source: Tract books
   Data available: Type of entry, date, name of entryman, description of land, acreage, surveys, offerings, withdrawals.
3. Disposals, by type of entry (homesteads, desert land, etc.) prior to 1908.
   a. Similar to 1-a with the exception that some types of papers are not segregated by land districts.
   b. Same as 1-b.
   Source: Case records
   Data available: Same as Register's schedules but additional data as to date of settlement and other matters.

In general, it may be said that the tract book records offer many advantages as source material for researchers, compared with the patent records, the register's returns, and the case files. The tract books contain a relatively large amount of data, which can easily be transcribed directly to a land-description tabulation. This greatly facilitates the summation of data, particularly if it is to be presented in map form. For several types of studies, where mechanical methods of tabulation are to be used, the patent record offers distinct advantages. It is, for the most part, a printed, standard form, making standardization of the tabulation operation relatively easy.

In using the public land records, particularly the tract books, it is necessary to allow for a substantial training period before efficient use of the records can be achieved. It is sometimes possible to employ trained personnel familiar with the public land records. Where this is not possible, considerable assistance from the custodial staff is usually required, as some of the manuscript record is difficult to read and some of the notations upon the record are not completely standardized. In some instances, the interpretation of notations may become a real problem because the tract books have been kept by many different persons with opportunity for frequent discrepancy. It has been estimated that four to eight hours per township would be required to transcribe tract-book records to tabulation sheets or township diagrams, depending on the condition of the reports being used and the training of the transcriber.

Comprehensive studies of the disposal of the public domain and the advance of the American frontier must be left to those agencies (public or private) with sufficient means to sustain long-term research projects. This does not mean that highly useful work in the public land records cannot be done by individuals and research groups with limited means. Pilot studies are needed before comprehensive summaries can be properly planned and executed. Studies of limited geographic areas may frequently be undertaken with profit, as may specific aspects of the land-disposal program, such as the Desert Land Entries or the Swamp Land Grants. Excellent thesis topics can be found in almost any segment of the public land files. This is a field in which thesis work should be encouraged, because it would be cumulative in usefulness and would form an invaluable background for comprehensive studies which may be undertaken as circumstances permit.

NOTES

1 A good illustration of the many problems created by the loss of land records can be gained from recent experience in the Philippine Islands, where many land title records were destroyed during World War II.

2 These "public land states" are: Alabama, Arizona, Arkansas, California, Colorado, Florida, Idaho, Illinois, Indiana, Iowa, Kansas, Louisiana, Michigan, Minnesota, Mississippi, Missouri, Montana, Nebraska, Nevada, New Mexico, North Dakota, Ohio, Oklahoma, Oregon, South Dakota, Washington, Wisconsin, and Wyoming. In the thirteen original states and Maine, Vermont, Tennessee, Kentucky, and West Virginia, land titles are based on royal land grants. Texas retained ownership of its public lands at the time of annexation, and land titles in that state rest upon state records set up when it was an independent republic.

3 See Harry P. Yoshpe and Philip P. Brower (comps.), *Preliminary Inventory of the Land-Entry Papers of the General Land Office* (Washington, 1949). This guide covers an important segment of the General Land Office records now in the National Archives, but it by no means covers all the land records now housed there. A general inventory of land records in the Archives is now under way.

4 These tables were prepared by Irving Senzel, Bureau of Land Manage-

ment, who has also made many helpful suggestions during the preparation of this paper.

5   For a brief history of the system used in surveying public land, see S. V. Proudfit, *Public Land System of the United States* (Washington, 1924).

6   Mineral survey plats are made for mineral entries which are to be patented.

7   In some land offices, township diagrams are used to show the location of land on which applications have been received for oil and gas leases and also to show areas where leases are in force. These township diagrams are usually filed with the survey plats and are available for public use.

8   Yoshpe and Brower (comps.), *Preliminary Inventory of the Land-Entry Papers*, 4. The military bounty land warrants and the various series of land scrip are arranged in series.

9   *Ibid.*, 6.

10 After 1908, land-office records are catalogued on a serial basis and not segregated by type of entry. Accordingly, it is necessary to use intermediate records to obtain the serial numbers necessary for locating entry papers of a specific class.

Statutory Opening Dates of District Land Offices in Various States

Compiled by the Bureau of Land Management, Department of the Interior.

ALABAMA

St. Stephens	1803
Nashville (Tenn.)	1807
Huntsville	1807
Milledgeville (Ga.)	1815
Cahaba	1815
Tuscaloosa	1820
Sparta	1820
Mardisville	1832
Montgomery	1832
Demopolis	1833
Lebanon	1842
Elba	1854
Centre	1856
Greenville	1856
Mobile	1867

ALASKA

Sitka	1884
Juneau	1902
Nome	1907
Fairbanks	1907
Anchorage	1923

ARIZONA

Prescott	1868
Florence	1873

ARIZONA—Continued

Gila	1873
Tucson	1881
Phoenix	1905

ARKANSAS

Little Rock	1818
Batesville	1818
Washington	1832
Fayetteville	1832
Helena	1834
Clarksville	1838
Champagnolle	1845
Huntsville	1860
Little Rock (reopened)	1866
Washington (reopened)	1867
Clarksville (reopened)	1867
Dardanelle	1870
Harrison	1870
Camden	1871

CALIFORNIA

Los Angeles	1853
Benicia	1853
Marysville	1853
San Francisco	1857

CALIFORNIA—Continued		IDAHO	
Humboldt	1858	Boise	1866
Stockton	1858	Lewiston	1866
Visalia	1858	Oxford	1879
Sacramento	1866	Hailey	1883
Aurora (Nev.)	1868	Coeur d'Alene	1884
Susanville	1871	Blackfoot	1886
Shasta	1871		
Independence	1873	ILLINOIS	
Bodie	1878	Kaskaskia	1804
Redding	1890	Shawneetown	1812
Eureka	1899	Edwardsville	1816
Oakland	1906	Palestine	1820
		Vandalia	1820
COLORADO		Springfield	1822
Golden City	1863	Danville	1831
Denver	1864	Quincy	1831
Fair Play	1867	Chicago	1834
Central City	1867	Galena	1834
Pueblo	1870	Dixon	1840
Del Norte	1874		
Lake City	1877	INDIANA	
Leadville	1879	Vincennes	1804
Durango	1882	Jeffersonville	1810
Gunnison	1882	Terre Haute	1819
Glenwood Springs	1884	Brookville	1819
Lamar	1886	Crawfordsville	1819
Montrose	1888	Indianapolis	1820
Akron	1890	Fort Wayne	1822
Sterling	1890	La Porte	1833
Hugo	1890	Winanac	1840
		IOWA	
FLORIDA		Dubuque	1838
Tallahassee	1823	Burlington	1838
St. Augustine	1823	Fairfield	1842
Newnansville	1842	Marion	1843
Tampa	1854	Iowa City	1846
Tallahassee (reopened)	1866	Chariton	1852
Gainesville	1872	Des Moines	1852

IOWA—Continued		LOUISIANA—Continued	
Council Bluffs	1855	Greensburg	1837
Fort Dodge	1855	Natchitoches	1838
Sioux City	1855	Baton Rouge	1844
Decorah	1855		
Osage	1855	MICHIGAN	
		Detroit	1804
KANSAS		Old Monroe	1829
Lecompton	1854	White Pigeon Prairie	1831
Doniphan	1857	New Monroe	1834
Kickapoo	1857	Kalamazoo	1834
Ogden	1857	Genesee	1836
Ft. Scott	1857	Ionia	1836
Junction City	1859	Sault Ste Marie	1847
Atchison	1861	Duncan	1854
Topeka	1861	Marquette	1857
Mapleton	1861	East Saginaw	1857
Humboldt	1861	Mackinac	1858
Augusta	1870	Traverse City	1858
Salina	1870	Reed City	1878
Concordia	1870	Grayling	1888
Neodesha	1871		
Independence	1871	MINNESOTA	
Cawker City	1872	Stillwater	1847
Wichita	1872	Sauk Rapids	1852
Kirwin	1874	Brownsville	1854
Larned	1874	Winona	1854
Hays City	1874	Minneapolis	1854
Wakeeny	1879	Red Wing	1854
Oberlin	1880	Chatfield	1856
Garden City	1881	Buchanan	1856
Dodge City	1893	Henderson	1856
Colby	1893	Faribault	1857
		St. Cloud	1858
LOUISIANA		Forest City	1858
New Orleans	1811	Cambridge	1858
Opelousas	1811	St. Peter	1858
Ouachita	1811	Otter Tail City	1859
St. Helena	1819	Duluth	1859
Monroe	1821	Sunrise City	1860

MINNESOTA—Continued		MISSOURI—Continued	
Taylor's Falls	1861	Clinton	1843
Winnebago City	1861	Milan	1849
Greenleaf	1866	Warsaw	1855
Alexandria	1868	Boonville	1857
Jackson	1869	Ironton	1861
New Ulm	1870	Springfield (reopened)	1866
Litchfield	1870		
Redwood Falls	1872	MONTANA	
Oak Lake	1872	Helena	1867
Detroit	1872	Bozeman	1874
Worthington	1874	Miles City	1880
Benson	1876	Lewistown	1890
Fergus Falls	1876	Missoula	1890
Crooksten	1878	Kalispell	1897
Tracy	1880	Great Falls	1902
Marshall	1889	Billings	1906
Cass Lake	1903	Glasgow	1907

MISSISSIPPI		NEBRASKA	
Washington	1803	Omaha City	1854
Augusta	1819	Brownsville	1857
Jackson	1819	Nebraska City	1857
Mt. Salus	1827	Dakota City	1857
Columbus	1833	Beatrice	1868
Chocochuma	1833	Lincoln	1868
Pontotoc	1836	Grand Island	1868
Grenada	1840	West Point	1869
Paulding	1860	Lowell	1872
		North Platte	1872
MISSOURI		Norfolk	1873
Franklin	1818	Bloomington	1874
St. Louis	1818	Niobrara	1875
Jackson	1818	Neligh	1881
Lexington	1823	Valentine	1882
Palmyra	1824	McCook	1882
Fayette	1832	Sidney	1886
Springfield	1834	Chadron	1886
Plattsburg	1842	O'Neill	1888
		Alliance	1890

NEBRASKA—Continued		OHIO—Continued	
Broken Bow	1890	Piqua	1819
		Tiffin	1819
NEVADA		Bucyrus	1819
Carson City	1862	Wapakoneta	1819
Austin	1867	Lima	1835
Aurora	1868	Marion	1836
Belmont	1868	Upper Sandusky	1843
Elko	1872	Defiance	1848
Eureka	1873		
Pioche	1874	**OKLAHOMA**	
Reno	1911	Guthrie	1889
		Kingfisher	1889
NEW MEXICO		Oklahoma City	1890
Santa Fe	1858	Beaver	1891
La Mesilla	1874	Alva	1893
Las Cruces	1883	Enid	1893
Folsom	1888	Perry	1893
Roswell	1889	Woodward	1893
Clayton	1892	Mangum	1897
		El Reno	1901
NORTH DAKOTA		Lawton	1901
Pembina	1870		
Fargo	1874	**OREGON**	
Bismarck	1874	Oregon City	1854
Grand Forks	1880	Winchester	1855
Devils Lake	1884	Roseburg	1855
Minot	1890	La Grande	1866
Dickinson	1904	Linkville	1872
Williston	1906	The Dalles	1875
		Lakeview	1877
OHIO		Burns	1888
Steubenville	1800	Drewsey	1888
Marietta	1800	Portland	1905
Chillicothe	1800	Vale	1910
Cincinnati	1800		
Zanesville	1803	**SOUTH DAKOTA**	
Canton	1807	Vermillion	1861
Wooster	1809	Springfield	1870
Delaware	1819	Yankton	1872

SOUTH DAKOTA—Continued		WASHINGTON—Continued	
Sioux Falls	1873	Olympia (new)	1890
Deadwood	1877	Waterville	1890
Watertown	1879		
Mitchell	1880	WISCONSIN	
Aberdeen	1882	Mineral Point	1834
Huron	1882	Green Bay	1834
Rapid City	1888	Milwaukee	1836
Pierre	1890	Muscoda	1841
Chamberlain	1890	St. Croix River Falls	1848
		Hudson	1849
TENNESSEE		Menasha	1852
Nashville	1809	La Crosse	1852
		Stevens Point	1852
UTAH		Superior	1855
Salt Lake City	1868	Eau Claire	1857
Beaver City	1876	Bayfield	1860
Vernal	1905	St. Croix Falls	1860
		Wausau	1872
WASHINGTON		Ashland	1886
Olympia	1854		
Vancouver	1860–61	WYOMING	
Walla Walla	1871	Cheyenne	1870
Colfax	1876	Evanston	1876
Yakima	1880	Buffalo	1887
Spokane Falls	1883	Douglas	1890
North Yakima	1885	Lander	1890
Seattle	1887	Sundance	1890

Commissioners of the General Land Office and Directors of the Bureau of Land Management

Compiled by the Bureau of Land Management, Department of the Interior.

EDWARD TIFFIN: Born in Carlisle, England, June 19, 1766. Methodist Minister; Speaker of Territorial Legislature of Ohio; President, Ohio Constitutional Convention; United States Senator (Ohio); Surveyor General of the United States. Commissioner of General Land Office, 1812–1814.

JOSIAH MEIGS: Born in Connecticut, 1757. City Clerk, New Haven, Conn.; Professor at Yale University, New Haven, Conn.; President, University of Georgia; Surveyor General of the United States; Commissioner of General Land Office, 1814–1822.

JOHN MCLEAN: Born in Morris County, New Jersey, March 11, 1785. Member of the United States Congress; Judge of Ohio Supreme Court; Postmaster General of the United States; Justice, United States Supreme Court; Commissioner of General Land Office, 1822–1823.

GEORGE GRAHAM: Born in Virginia, 1772. Assistant Secretary of War; President, Washington Branch of the United States Bank; Professor; Soldier; Commissioner of General Land Office, 1823–1830.

ELIJAH HAYWARD: Born in Massachusetts, 1786. Librarian, Ohio Supreme Court, State of Ohio; Commissioner-Examiner, Ohio Life Insurance Co.; Commissioner of General Land Office, 1830–1835.

505

ETHAN ALLEN BROWN: Born in Darien, Connecticut, July 4, 1776. Studied Law under Alexander Hamilton; Judge, Supreme Court of Ohio; Governor of Ohio; United States Senator; United States Chargé d'Affaires to Brazil; Commissioner of General Land Office, 1835–1836.

JAMES WHITCOMB: Born near Windsor, Vermont, December 1, 1795. Practicing Attorney; State Senator; United States Senator; Commissioner of General Land Office, 1836–1841.

ELISHA HUNTINGTON: Born in New York. Lawyer; Circuit Court Judge, Indiana; Member of the State Legislature of Indiana; Commissioner of General Land Office, 1841–1842.

THOMAS H. BLAKE: Born in Calvert County, Maryland, June 14, 1792. Practicing Attorney; Served in War of 1812; Indiana Judge; Member of State Legislature; Member of the United States Congress (20th); President of the Erie and Wabash Canal Company; Commissioner of General Land Office, 1842–1846.

JAMES SHIELDS: Born in Altmore, Ireland, May 10, 1810. Immigrated to United States in 1823; Representative, State Legislature of Indiana; Indiana State Auditor; Judge, Supreme Court of Illinois; Brig. General, United States Army; Governor, Oregon Territory; United States Senator (Illinois); United States Senator (Missouri); United States Senator (Minnesota); Commissioner of General Land Office, 1846–1847.

RICHARD YOUNG: Born in Fayette County, Kentucky, February 20, 1798. Lawyer; Member of the State Legislature of Illinois; United States Senator; Commissioner of General Land Office, 1847–1849.

JUSTIN BUTTERFIELD: Born in New Hampshire. Lawyer; District Attorney for Illinois; Commissioner of General Land Office, 1849–1852.

JOHN WILSON: Born in Ireland. Clerk in the Post Office Department; Clerk in the General Land Office; Claim Agent and Attorney in the District of Columbia; Commissioner of General Land Office, 1852–1855.

THOMAS A. HENDRICKS: Born near Zanesville, Ohio, September 7, 1819.

Governor of Indiana; Member of the State Legislature of Indiana; Member of Congress; Vice-President of the United States; Commissioner of General Land Office, 1855–1859.

SAMUEL A. SMITH: Born in Monroe County, Tennessee, on June 26, 1822. Lawyer; Tennessee State Attorney; Member of the United States Congress; Confederate Army; Commissioner of General Land Office, 1859–1860.

JOSEPH S. WILSON: Born in Ireland. Chief Clerk of the General Land Office, both before and after having served as Commissioner of General Land Office; Commissioner of General Land Office, 1860–1861; 1866–1871.

JAMES M. EDMUNDS: Born in New York. Inspector of Schools in Michigan; Michigan State Senator; Member of the United States Congress; Candidate for Governor of Michigan; Comptroller of City of Detroit; Postmaster, City of Washington, D.C.; Commissioner of General Land Office, 1861–1866.

WILLIS DRUMMOND: Born in Missouri. Received appointment from Iowa for position of Commissioner of General Land Office, 1871–1874.

SAMUEL BURDETT: Born at Sutton-in-the-Elms, England, February 21, 1836. Immigrated to the United States in 1848. United States Army; Circuit Judge, Missouri; Delegate, Presidential Convention of 1868; Member of the United States Congress (41st–42d); Commissioner of General Land Office, 1874–1876.

JAMES WILLIAMSON: Born in Kentucky. Brig. and Major General in the United States Army; Commissioner of General Land Office, 1876–1881.

NOAH C. McFARLAND: Born in Pennsylvania, 1822. State Treasurer of Ohio; State Treasurer of Kansas; Regent of the State University of Kansas; Commissioner of General Land Office, 1881–1885.

WILLIAM A. J. SPARKS: Born near New Albany, Indiana, November 19, 1828. Lawyer; Land Receiver, State of Illinois; State Senator, Illinois; Member of the United States Congress (44th–47th); Commissioner of General Land Office, 1885–1887.

STROTHER M. STOCKSLAGER: Born in Manckport, Indiana, May 7, 1842. Lt. in Union Army; Lawyer; Member of the United States Congress (47th–48th); Law Practice, District of Columbia; Assistant Commissioner, General Land Office; Commissioner of General Land Office, 1888–1889.

LEWIS GROFF: Born in Ohio, March 27, 1841. Police Judge, Lincoln, Nebraska; Nebraska Land Commissioner; District Judge, Omaha, Nebraska; Postmaster of Los Angeles, California; Commissioner of General Land Office, 1889–1891.

THOMAS CARTER: Born in Portsmouth, Ohio, October 30, 1854. Lawyer; Delegate, 51st Congress, from Montana; Chairman, Republican National Committee; United States Senator; Commissioner of General Land Office, 1891–1892.

WILLIAM STONE: Born in New York, 1827. Member of First Republican National Convention; Private, Captain, Major, Colonel, United States Army; Governor of Iowa; Assistant Commissioner, General Land Office; Commissioner of General Land Office, 1892–1893.

SILAS LAMORAUX: Born in New York, 1843. Captain, United States Army; Wisconsin State Senator; Circuit Judge; Bank President; Law Practice; Commissioner of General Land Office, 1893–1897.

BINGER HERMANN: Born in Lonaconing, Maryland, February 19, 1843. Lawyer; Member of Oregon State Legislature; State Senator; Receiver, General Land Office; Member of United States Congress, (49th, 51st, 54th, and 58th); Commissioner of General Land Office, 1897–1903.

WILLIAM A. RICHARDS: Born in Hazel Green, Wisconsin, March 9, 1849. Surveyor General, Wyoming; Governor of Wyoming; Assistant Commissioner, General Land Office; Commissioner of Taxes, Wyoming; Commissioner of General Land Office, 1903–1907.

RICHARD BALLINGER: Born in Boonesboro, Iowa, July 9, 1858. Lawyer; Judge, Superior Court of Washington; Mayor of Seattle; Delegate, Republican National Convention, 1908; Secretary of the Interior; Commissioner of General Land Office, 1907–1908.

FRED DENNETT: Born in 1865. Farmer; Member of North Dakota House of Representatives; Secretary, United States Committee on Public Lands; Assistant Commissioner of General Land Office, 1908–1913.

CLAY TALLMAN: Born May 7, 1874, in Belding, Michigan. Lawyer; Nevada State Senator; Engaged in practice of mining law for many years; Commissioner of General Land Office, 1913–1921.

WILLIAM SPRY: Born in Windsor, England, January 11, 1864. Stockman; United States Marshal for Utah; Governor of Utah; Commissioner of General Land Office, 1921–1929.

CHARLES MOORE: Born February 26, 1866, in Holt County, Missouri. Postmaster in Idaho; Worked for many years in the reclamation field; Governor of Idaho; Commissioner of General Land Office, 1929–1933.

FRED W. JOHNSON: Born in Green River, Wyoming, March 11, 1881. Lawyer; Commissioner of General Land Office, 1933–1946; Director of Bureau of Land Management, 1946–1948.

MARION CLAWSON: Born in Elko, Nevada, August 10, 1905. Ph.D. in Economics from Harvard University; Economist, Bureau of Agriculture Economics; Regional Director, Bureau of Land Management, California-Nevada Region; Director of Bureau of Land Management, 1948–1953.

EDWARD WOOZLEY: Born June 16, 1902, in Malad, Idaho. State Land Commissioner; Rancher; Secretary-Treasurer for Oneida Farm Loan Association, Malad, Idaho; Director of Bureau of Land Management, 1953–1961.

KARL S. LANDSTROM: Born Lebanon, Oregon, February 12, 1909. Economist with the Department of Agriculture; Regional Chief, Bureau of Land Management Lands and Minerals Office, Portland, Oregon; Staff Member, House of Representatives Interior and Insular Affairs Committee; Director of Bureau of Land Management, 1961—.

INDEX

INDEX